W. H. AUDEN AND
CHRISTOPHER ISHERWOOD
PLAYS

THE COMPLETE
WORKS OF

W. H. AUDEN

POEMS

PLAYS (WITH CHRISTOPHER ISHERWOOD)

LIBRETTI (WITH CHESTER KALLMAN)

ESSAYS AND REVIEWS

W. H. AUDEN AND
CHRISTOPHER ISHERWOOD

PLAYS

AND OTHER DRAMATIC
WRITINGS BY
W. H. AUDEN

□

1928–1938

EDITED BY
Edward Mendelson

ff
faber and faber

First Published in Great Britain in 1989
by Faber and Faber Limited
3 Queen Square, London WC1N 3AU

Copyright 1930, 1933, 1935, 1936, 1938, by W. H. Auden. Copyright 1935, 1936, 1938 by Christopher Isherwood. Copyright 1989 by the Estate of W. H. Auden. Quotations from music manuscripts in the Britten-Pears Library are copyright 1989 by The Britten Estate. "Auden and the Group Theatre" copyright 1989 by M. J. Sidnell. Introduction and notes copyright 1989 by Edward Mendelson.

ALL RIGHTS RESERVED

British Library Cataloguing in Publication Data
Auden, W. H. (Wystan Hugh), 1907-1973
Plays and Other Dramatic Writings by W. H. Auden, 1928-1938.
I. Title II. Isherwood, Christopher III. Mendelson, Edward
822'.912

ISBN 0-571-15115-9

This book has been composed in Linotron Baskerville

Printed in the United States of America on acid-free paper

CONTENTS

Preface	ix
Acknowledgements	xi
Introduction	xiii
The Text of This Edition	xxxi

PLAYS

Paid on Both Sides [first version] (*1928*), by Auden	3
Paid on Both Sides [second version] (*1928*), by Auden	14
The Enemies of a Bishop (*1929*), by Auden and Isherwood	35
The Dance of Death (*1933*), by Auden	81
The Chase (*1934*), by Auden	109
The Dog Beneath the Skin (*1935*), by Auden and Isherwood	189
The Ascent of F 6 (*1936*), by Auden and Isherwood	293
On the Frontier (*1937-38*), by Auden and Isherwood	357

DOCUMENTARY FILMS

Coal Face (*1935*)	421
Night Mail (*1935*)	422
Negroes (*1935*)	424
Beside the Seaside (*1935*)	429
The Way to the Sea (*1936*)	430
The Londoners (*1938?*)	433

CABARET AND WIRELESS

Alfred (*1936*)	437
Hadrian's Wall (*1937*)	441

APPENDICES

I Auden and Isherwood's "Preliminary Statement" (*1929*)	459
1. The "Preliminary Statement"	459
2. Auden's "Suggestions for the Play"	462

II The Fronny: Fragments of a Lost Play (*1930*)	464
III Auden and the Group Theatre, by M. J. Sidnell	490
IV Auden and Theatre at the Downs School	503
V Two Reported Lectures	510
Poetry and Film (*1936*)	511
The Future of English Poetic Drama (*1938*)	513

TEXTUAL NOTES

Paid on Both Sides	525
The Enemies of a Bishop	530
The Dance of Death	534
1. History, Editions, and Text	534
2. Auden's Synopsis	542
The Chase	543
The Dog Beneath the Skin	553
1. History, Authorship, Texts, and Editions	553
2. Isherwood's Scenario for a New Version of *The Chase*	557
3. The Published Text and the Text Prepared for Production	566
4. The First (Published) Version of the Concluding Scene	572
5. Isherwood's Suggestions for a New Concluding Scene	586
6. The Production Version of the Concluding Scene	588
The Ascent of F 6	598
1. History, Authorship, Texts, and Editions	598
2. The First English Edition	602
3. The Lord Chamberlain's Copy and the American Edition	625
4. The Second English Edition, with Notes on the Text of the Present Edition	629
5. The Versions Produced by the Group Theatre in 1937	631
6. The Revised Endings Written in 1939	638
7. Auden's Revised Ending Written in 1945	650
On the Frontier	653
1. History, Authorship, Texts, and Editions	653
2. The Lost First Version	654
3. The Published Text and the Production Text	660
Documentary Films	665
Coal Face	665
Night Mail	666
Negroes	669

Beside the Seaside	670
The Way to the Sea	671
The Londoners	671
Other Films	672

Cabaret and Wireless — 674

Alfred	674
Hadrian's Wall	674

Index of Titles and First Lines — 677

PREFACE

THIS volume, the first to be published in a complete edition of Auden's works, includes his plays and other dramatic writings from the start of his career until his departure from England to America in 1939. The most important of these plays were written in collaboration with Christopher Isherwood. The next volume will include Auden's libretti and other dramatic works from 1939 until his death in 1973. Later volumes will present his complete essays and reviews and his complete poems. The texts of this edition are newly edited from Auden's manuscripts, and the notes report variant readings from all published versions.

ACKNOWLEDGEMENTS

To Christopher Isherwood, who died while this book was in preparation, I am indebted most of all. He made this edition possible by giving free access to his collection of manuscripts and providing vivid recollections of his work with Auden. To Michael Sidnell I am grateful not only for the pages in this edition that he wrote, but also for the care with which he improved most of the others. To Nicholas Jenkins I am grateful for the critical and scholarly strictness with which he challenged, corrected, or confirmed every word in the text and notes. To Dr John Bicknell Auden I am again indebted for his advice and encouragement.

I could not have begun work on this volume without the help and scholarship of B. C. Bloomfield. I could not have finished it without the learning and energy of John Fuller. The introduction profited from the care given it by Natasha Staller. I gathered the historical information included in the notes largely through the help of Robert Medley and Sir Stephen Spender. For important details of the Group Theatre and its productions I am grateful to John Johnson. For information about Auden's collaborations with Benjamin Britten I am indebted to the late Sir Peter Pears, Professor Donald Mitchell, Rosamund Strode, Jill Burrows, and Philip Reed. For the texts of Auden's dramatic writings at the Downs School, and for reports of his work there, I am grateful to Maurice and Alexandra Feild, Patrick Mulholland, Sir Christopher Pinsent, Bart., Professor James Iliff, and Michael Yates.

For assistance with the texts and notes, and for the trouble they endured to help locate previously unpublished material, I am grateful to Marcus Bishop, MVO, and to Alan Ansen, Kathleen Bell, Eric Birley, Alan Clodd, Louis Criss, Liz Duthie, Valerie Eliot, Brian Finney, John Haffenden, Samuel Hynes, Hilton Kelliher, Burgess Meredith, P. G. Phillips, Seyril Schochen Rubin, R. D. Smith, Alexis Solomos, and Mardi Valgemae. An unpublished ending of *The Ascent of F 6* appears in this volume through the kindness of Glenn Horowitz. I salute Professor Stuart Piggott for his learned and ingenious solution to the most difficult crux in the text.

All the resources of the library and archive of the British Film Institute seemed at times to be devoted to this edition. Equally generous help came from Dr Lola Szladits, Brian McInerney, and Patrick Lawlor at the Henry W. and Albert A. Berg Collection of The New York Public Library; from Cathy Henderson at the Harry F. Ransom Humanities Research Center at the University of Texas at Austin; and from Caroline Swinson at the University of Tulsa. The BBC Written Archives Centre at Caversham Park offered its customary resourcefulness and care. I am indebted also to the librarians and staff at the Theater Collection of the New York Public Library, the library of the Museum of Modern Art, the Poetry Collection at the State University of New York at Buffalo, the libraries of Columbia University, Harvard University, and Swarthmore College, the Bodleian Library, the Cambridge University Library, and the libraries of King's College, Cambridge, and Christ Church and Exeter College, Oxford. I am grateful also to the archivists of the Central Office of Information and the Dartington Trust.

Throughout the preparation of this book I have relied on Katherine Bucknell for biographical and critical advice, and the edition has profited from help given by Lincoln Kirstein and Martin Meisel. I am grateful also to David Bromwich, Nathaniel Bucknell, Brigitte Peucker, Michele Salzman, and Michael Seidel.

At the Princeton University Press, Andrew Mytelka edited the manuscript with a learned and exacting eye, and I am indebted to him for many important emendations. Readers of this book will share my gratitude to Jan Lilly for her lucid and elegant design of a complex and intractable text.

To the anonymous typists who worked to decipher Auden's handwriting during the 1930s I offer sympathetic tribute.

INTRODUCTION

WHEN Auden left Oxford in 1928 he had already perfected a laconic and fragmented poetry concerned mostly with his own isolation. At twenty-one, he was ready to attempt something more public and expansive. During the summer he wrote *Paid on Both Sides*, a one-act tragedy in verse and prose that portrayed an episode in a feud between two houses in the north of England. A few months later he enlarged it to twice its original length and inserted an expressionist dream play at its center. During the next ten years, until he left England for America, he continued to write increasingly ambitious works for stage, film, and broadcast; he wrote the most important of them in collaboration with Christopher Isherwood. Auden's dramatic works ranged in style from rude comedy to prophetic admonition. Their settings ranged from English villages to imperial outposts and from pre-Roman times to an apocalyptic future. They combined the energy of popular entertainment with the urgency of sacramental ritual. Some were acknowledged and abandoned failures. Others, although flawed, were both profound and exhilarating.

As a lyric poet Auden learned his craft by studying his great predecessors Hardy, Yeats, and Eliot. As a dramatic poet he learned his craft by inventing it. The verse plays of the recent past, most of them unperformable, provided embarrassingly inadequate models. He dismissed them all the first time he mentioned them in print, in a 1934 book review that began:

> This book [*Modern Poetic Drama*, by Priscilla Thouless] is like an exhibition of perpetual motion models. Here they all are, labelled Phillips, Davidson, Yeats, some on the largest scale, some on the tiniest, some ingenious in design, some beautifully made, all suffering from only one defect—they won't go.*

Auden was calculatedly mischievous when he included Yeats among this company. Stephen Phillips had enjoyed a vogue at the turn of the century among critics who were now trying to forget him. John Davidson had turned from the direct speech of his early poems to the unperformable bombast of his later plays. Yeats, for all the greatness of his poetry, had chosen a static manner and precious style for his plays, and had deliberately written them for the smallest possible audience. Auden's review

---

* Sources for quotations are listed on p. xxix.

continued with a literary polemic that had more justice than its tone suggested:

> modern English poetic drama has been of three kinds: the romantic sham-Tudor which has occasionally succeeded for a short time on the strength of the spectacle; the cosmic-philosophical which theatrically has always been a complete flop; and the high-brow chamber-music drama, artistically much the best, but a somewhat etiolated blossom. Drama is so essentially a social art that it is difficult to believe that the poets are really satisfied with this solution.

English poetic drama had forgotten the social world of its audience and the social nature of drama itself. Auden chose to remember both.

In his review Auden implied that the only plays of the period that succeeded both as poetry and as drama had been written outside England. He mentioned Jean Cocteau, André Obey, and Bertolt Brecht. Yet in his own work he had made some unacknowledged use of his English predecessors. For *Paid on Both Sides* he had adapted the northern settings and compressed revenge plots of the verse plays written by two poets of the Georgian school, Gordon Bottomley and Wilfrid Gibson. Bottomley's *The Riding to Lithend* (1909, republished 1920), set in Iceland, and Gibson's *Kestrel Edge* (1924), set in northern England, are tragedies of revenge between rival houses, with violence partly motivated—as in Auden's play—to protect or avenge a mother.* But the poetic plays of the Georgian movement tended to offer extreme solemnity in monotonous verse; few of them reached the stage. The poetic plays that found an audience in the 1920s, like the ballad operas of Clifford Bax, offered agreeable frivolity in lighthearted verse.

Auden remade English poetic drama by uniting the extremes of symbolic intensity and extravagant burlesque. This was an innovation older than Shakespeare, and at least as old as the mystery plays, but it shattered the rules of decorum that prevailed in English verse drama when Auden began writing. The mood and action of *Paid on Both Sides* veer from legendary battlefields to school playing fields, while ancient archetypes find expression in the props and diction of the present. The title is a splinter from *Beowulf* ("That was no good exchange, that they should pay on both sides with the lives of friends"), and the murders in the play are reported in the alliterative verse of Anglo-Saxon poetry. Yet the play's language also includes the Public School slang specific to Auden's social class and

---

* Auden could have heard about, and perhaps attended, the first production of Bottomley's play at Cambridge in May 1928, two months before he began writing *Paid on Both Sides*. For the parallels between Auden and these earlier dramatists, and for much else, I am grateful to Michael J. Sidnell's *Dances of Death: The Group Theatre of London in the Thirties* (1984).

the modern vocabulary of industry. The plot of the play also connects past and present; it portrays the transmission of hatred from the older generation to the new like an incurable inherited disease. Auden designated some of the characters in the first version of the play with genetic symbols instead of names.

Drama is "essentially a social art", Auden wrote later in his review of *Modern Poetic Drama*. He made *Paid on Both Sides* so essentially social that its audience and actors were the same. He conceived the play as a "charade" to be performed by the guests and hosts at a house party given by the family of one of his Oxford friends, William McElwee.* As he wrote in a manifesto on drama in 1934:

> Drama began as an act of the whole community. Ideally there would be no spectators. In practice every member of the audience should feel like an understudy.

Paid on Both Sides, an act of its whole community, portrays in schematic and symbolic form the lives of those who perform it. The players divide into two groups, as in conventional charades, but both appear in the same action, as the feuding families whose enmities thwart the young in their desire for love. "A parable of English Middle Class (professional) family life 1907-1929" was the subtitle Auden wrote in a friend's copy some years later. (The dates are those of his birth and of his last substantial revisions to the play.) In the court masques of the seventeenth century, the audience helped portray their own harmony and order by joining in the dance; in the more subversive charade of *Paid on Both Sides* the actors portray their own disorder and isolation.

When Auden rewrote the play in 1928, during a year in Berlin, he added to the social drama of the feud the psychological drama of the feud's most recent victim, John Nower. Nower has a dream—a play within the play—that takes the form of a pantomime of death and resurrection. It is presented by Father Christmas and attended by a comic doctor whose lines were lifted verbatim from the traditional (but largely forgotten) mummers' play. Nower wakes from his dream reconciled to himself, cured of his angers, and free to love the daughter of his enemies. He rejects the dead past for the love he feels *now*. But he is destroyed by the undiminished wrath of the feud that continues around him, its origins lost in a past too distant to be probed by dreams. Auden had briefly been psychoanalyzed earlier in 1928, and, not unlike Nower, found the experience stimulating but unproductive. He told his friend

---

* This was Auden's intent, but when McElwee's family read the play in advance they refused to let it be acted.

Naomi Mitchison that a critic would need no psychoanalytic knowledge to understand *Paid on Both Sides* (as she had suggested in a review), but "literary knowledge of the Mummers' play with its Old-New year symbolism is necessary". In its elliptical style, the play makes the same criticism of Freud that Auden wrote in his journal a few months later: "Freud's error is the limitation of the neurosis to the individual. The neurosis involves all society". The New Year that Nower hopes to inaugurate with his love is born in celebration and triumph, only to be destroyed by the hatreds that persist in his society, unaltered by his cure.

Auden sent the typescript of *Paid on Both Sides* to T. S. Eliot, who recognized it as "quite a brilliant piece of work" and published it in *The Criterion* in 1930. This was Auden's first appearance in print outside school and university publications. Within a few months William Empson wrote an analysis of the work that concluded by stating its immediate importance:

> One reason the scheme is so impressive is that it puts psycho-analysis and surrealism and all that, all the irrationalist tendencies which are so essential a part of the machinery of present-day thought, into their proper place; they are made part of the normal and rational tragic form, and indeed what constitutes the tragic situation. One feels as if at the crisis of many, perhaps better, tragedies, it is just this machinery which has been covertly employed. Within its scale (twenty-seven pages) there is the gamut of all the ways we have of thinking about the matter; it has the sort of completeness that makes a work seem to define the attitude of a generation.

Twenty years later Eliot looked back on Auden's charade as "the forerunner of contemporary poetic drama"—including Eliot's own.

Auden began to plan a second play, *The Reformatory*, in the spring of 1929. Around the same time he wrote his earliest surviving notes on drama. In his journal he asked himself:

> Do I want poetry in a play or is Cocteau right: "There is a poetry of the theatre but not in it"? I shall use poetry in "The Reformatory" as interlude. . . . I don't want any characters, any ideas in my play but stage-life, something which is no imitation but a new thing.

This stage-life that imitates nothing sounds like a late flower of literary symbolism. In fact Auden had in mind something far less elevated. He wrote a few days later:

> A Play is poetry of action. The dialogue should be corresponding[ly]

a simplification. E.g. Hrotswitha.* The Prep School atmosphere. That is what I want.

At some point during the next few months, Isherwood, who had been advising Auden on his poetry for almost three years, began to collaborate with him on the play. They drafted a "Preliminary Statement" on the nature of drama:

> Dramatic action is ritual. . . . Ritual is directed towards the stimulation of the spectator who passes thereby from a state of indifference to a state of acute awareness. . . .
>
> Dramatic "characters" are always abstractions.†

Later in the year, they completed *The Reformatory* under a new title: *The Enemies of a Bishop, or Die When I Say When: A Morality in Four Acts.* The finished work was written less for the stage than as a shared private joke; two of its most self-deluded characters are named Bicknell, the family name of Auden's mother. Everyone in the play, except the Bishop of the title, manifests a distortion or perversion of Eros. Robert Bicknell, the manager (and later the owner) of a lead mine that fails, is obsessed with his under-manager's wife, but his desire is a projection of his own self-love. His brother Augustus Bicknell, the governor of a reformatory, is obsessed with an escaped boy disguised as a young woman. In a nearby hotel, two white slavers, deceived by this disguise, plot to kidnap the boy for their next catalogue, while a pederastic colonel tries to persuade another escaped boy to thrash him. A psychiatrically minded police spy, Ethel Wright, becomes the unwitting ally of the white slavers in their plot against Bishop Law, the play's moral hero and its only married man.

Isherwood described the Bishop as an idealized portrait of the American psychologist Homer Lane and the Bishop's enemies as "the pseudo-healers, the wilfully ill and the mad". Auden had first heard about Lane from Lane's patient and disciple John Layard in 1928, and Auden soon began to speak of him as a heroic healer and prophet. (In the second version of *Paid on Both Sides*, John Nower's father is killed while riding to

---

* The didactic plays of Hrotswitha, a tenth-century nun from Saxony who wrote in rhymed Latin prose, were published in English translation in 1923.

† The direct stimulus for these statements may have been Eliot's essay "Dramatis Personae" in *The Criterion*, April 1923. Eliot wrote: "We know now that the gesture of daily existence is inadequate for the stage; instead of pretending that the stage gesture is a copy of reality, let us adopt a literal untruth, a thorough-going convention, a ritual. For the stage—not only in its remote origins, but always—is a ritual, and the failure of the contemporary stage to satisfy the craving for ritual is one of the reasons why it is not a living art".

"speak with Layard", perhaps in hope of learning the solution to the feud that Lane might have offered. Homer Lane, who died in 1925, had been the governor of a reformatory in Dorset whose "citizens" practiced self-government; he believed that psychological disorders could be cured by giving free expression to instinctual desires that repression or coercion had blocked from their proper channels. Lane was obliged to leave England amidst legal difficulties, including charges of sexual improprieties with his women patients; Bishop Law, before his fourth-act triumph, is arrested at Ethel Wright's instigation on a charge of trafficking in women. But the Bishop is less a portrait of Lane than an allegorical personification of Lane's teachings. Lane had characterized the child's experience of benevolent social and parental authority as "Mother Law". In *The Enemies of a Bishop* this benevolent Law is right—while the pseudo-healer, Wright, is wrong.

In a separate plot of the play, Robert Bicknell contends with his demonic double, the Spectre, a figure he alone can see. By reciting some of Auden's more obscure poems, the Spectre gives voice to the hidden and unspeakable elements in Bicknell's mind, whose extreme inner division is manifested in the separation of the secret Spectre from Bicknell's public self. The Spectre's actions fulfill Bicknell's unconscious desires while frustrating his conscious ones. Auden and Isherwood took the idea for the Spectre from *Der Student von Prag*, a film made by Henrik Galeen in 1926. Like the student of Prague, Robert Bicknell angrily destroys his Spectre at the end of the play and, in doing so, destroys himself. Auden's private doubts about the teachings of Homer Lane may be reflected in this plot. The Spectre stands outside the Bishop's knowledge, beyond his power to correct and cure.

Isherwood called the play "no more than a charade, very loosely put together and full of private jokes". Its atmosphere derived from the private fictional world of Mortmere that Isherwood and his friend Edward Upward (later a novelist) had invented while at Cambridge. Mortmere was an English town that looked entirely normal but was the setting for grotesque perversities and violent disasters. Isherwood and Upward made no attempt to publish their Mortmere stories, and Auden and Isherwood seem to have made no attempt to publish *The Enemies of a Bishop*. But they thought well enough of the play to have it typed professionally, and they returned to it two years later to work on a revised version that they never finished.

In 1930 Auden began working as a schoolmaster at Larchfield Academy, near Glasgow. During that summer he wrote his third play, *The Fronny*. It survives only as fragments from Auden's early drafts. Much of the dialogue seems to have been rhymed doggerel, with the more solemn poetry spoken by an observing chorus. This was the first of Auden's quest plays, and its characters and plot eventually developed into the characters and plot of *The Dog Beneath the Skin*. The plot of *The Fronny* apparently involved the search by Alan Norman for Francis Crewe, the missing heir of the squire of Alan's village. After Francis's death, Alan marries Francis's sister Iris. The wanderings of Alan and Francis seem to have given Auden an opportunity to portray miscellaneous scenes of corrupt English and European society. The tone of the play sounded the note of apocalyptic warning that Auden had begun to use in his poetry a few months before.

The model for Francis Crewe was an aristocratic amateur archaeologist named Francis Turville-Petre. In Berlin, where Auden and Isherwood first met him, he was nicknamed "Der Franni", which Auden and Isherwood anglicized as The Fronny. Near the end of the play the Fronny makes a rhymed Last Will and Testament. Auden, in an overly aggressive attempt to connect the audience to the stage, wrote the first version of the Will as a series of indiscreet revelations about his friends' private lives. He told Isherwood that his real intention was to make the Will "vary at every performance to implicate an incredulous and slightly scared audience". On Isherwood's advice, he wrote a second and more tactful version. T. S. Eliot had by this time accepted a book of Auden's poems for publication by Faber & Faber in 1930. Auden made a half-hearted attempt to have *The Fronny* published also, but he abandoned the play when Eliot showed little interest in it.*

Auden had now written a new play every summer from 1928 through 1930, but he had been refused a performance of the first and had no hope of seeing the second or third on stage. During the spring and summer of 1931, he made a virtue of necessity by deliberately writing a drama that was impossible to perform. This was "The Initiates", a sequence of prose monologues, interrupted by an ironic litany, which he published as the opening section of his long work in verse and prose, *The Orators*. He described it in a letter to Naomi Mitchison:

> Formally I am trying to write abstract drama—all the action implied.
> ... The four parts ... are stages in the development of the influence of the Hero (who never appears at all). ... The litany is the chorus to the play.

A few months after writing this private and abstract drama Auden was

---

* The fate of *The Fronny* suggests the extent to which publishers can influence literature. Had Faber published the play, Auden could not (for example) have lifted its nightclub scene into *The Dance of Death*, and *The Dog Beneath the Skin*, which reuses its central plot, could not have been written at all.

invited to write a play for the public and practical use of a theatre company. Auden's friend Robert Medley, a painter, was living with Rupert Doone, a young dancer and actor who had recently been instrumental in organizing the Group Theatre.* (When they were at school together in 1922, Medley first gave Auden the idea of writing poetry by asking him if he had ever done so.) In June 1932 Doone asked Auden to write a play for the Group based on the medieval allegory of the *danse macabre* and to write a ballet scenario on the Orpheus theme that Doone could perform separately. Auden worked on the two projects during the summer, but by the autumn he had shelved the first and abandoned the second. Instead of writing a drama that year, he began work on his first long poem, a modern echo of Dante and Langland that he referred to as "my epic". By this time Auden had begun to perceive the stress and disorder of his society in political as well as psychological terms, and for a few months he believed he might become a communist. The feud in *Paid on Both Sides* had been essentially timeless and unalterable: it had a past but no history. In contrast, the crisis in his epic poem was the last phase of a historical cycle that had begun in the Renaissance and was now approaching its revolutionary end. Auden abandoned the poem early in 1933, before he wrote the lines that would portray the decisive social battle anticipated in the completed sections. That summer, he returned to Doone's commission for a *danse macabre* play and wrote *The Dance of Death*.

This brash irreverent allegory of the latter days of the middle class was unlike anything written for the English stage. It combined German cabaret and English pantomime, presented Marxist analysis in rhymed verse, and offered an active and decisive role to its audience. Auden alluded to the play's implication of its audience when he referred to it as "my Masque". The silent dancer (a part written for Doone) personifies the impending death of the middle-class chorus, a death they both fear and desire. To hide them from knowledge of their doom, the dancer leads them through a round of fads and crazes, from gymnastics to nationalism to nature-worship to mysticism. As each of these distractions proves futile, the dancer declines in strength and the audience (through the voices of actors scattered among the ticket-holders) proclaims more loudly its revolutionary impatience. Finally, in a scene adapted from *The Fronny*, the dancer in his Will leaves his wealth and powers to the working class. In *Paid on Both Sides* the Old Year refuses to give way to the New, and the ritual of resurrection fails. In *The Dance of Death* the ritual succeeds. As he dies, the dancer wishes the rising workers a Happy New

---

* This had no connection with the Group Theatre that had recently begun work in New York. A full history of Doone and the Group appears in Michael J. Sidnell's *Dances of Death*; a brief account by Sidnell of Auden's work with the Group appears as an appendix in the present edition.

Year. Karl Marx, heralded by Mendelssohn's wedding march, enters and declares the dancer "liquidated". This lethal euphemism is the last word in the play, and puts a twist in its political sympathies. About ten years later Auden wrote in a friend's copy, "The communists never spotted that this was a nihilistic leg-pull."

The Dance of Death caused a small but notable sensation when the Group Theatre produced it, first for subscribing members of the theatre in 1934, then for the public in the following year. Some reviewers dismissed it as offensive or crude, while others welcomed the production as a momentous event. Harold Hobson, already coming to prominence as a theatre critic, expressed a common opinion when he wrote that Auden's "brilliant, and in my opinion, entirely successful, attempt to work out for the theater a new, significant art-form, may, in the strictest sense of the term, prove epoch-making". But Hobson warned that the importance of the play "depends far less upon its intrinsic merits than on what is to be done in the same line in the future by Mr Auden and his followers".

But Auden and his followers did not work in quite the same line afterward, and their plays gradually accepted some of the canons of more conventional drama. In the plays he produced as a schoolmaster, however, Auden made further use of the innovations of *The Dance of Death*. In 1932 he left Larchfield Academy for the brighter pupils and more congenial setting of the Downs School, in the Malvern Hills. There he experimented with communal drama, some of it written by his pupils, and his work culminated in a revue whose cast included everyone at the school.

Auden also began to expound in print the theory that he planned to put into practice in his later plays. In May 1934, in his review of Priscilla Thouless's *Modern Poetic Drama*, he proposed to adopt all the received conventions of the popular stage:

> The truth is that those who would write poetic drama, refuse to start from the only place where they can start, from the dramatic forms actually in use. These are the variety-show, the pantomime, the musical comedy and revue ..., the thriller, the drama of ideas, the comedy of manners, and, standing somewhat eccentrically to these, the ballet. Only one of these is definitely antipathetic to poetry, the comedy of manners or characters. The drama of ideas is very dangerous to touch, but not impossible.

As in all his theories on drama, he renounced any attempt to imitate unique personalities in the manner of the realistic theatre of the time:

> Poetry, the learned commentators on Shakespeare's characters notwithstanding, has very little to do with character. All characters who

speak verse are as flat as playing-cards. So are they also in the popular dramatic forms today. Poetic drama should start with the stock musical comedy characters—the rich uncle, the vamp, the mother-in-law, the sheik, and so forth—and make them, as only poetry can, memorable. Acrobatics of all kinds are popular and are poetry's natural allies. It is the pure West-end drama that is talk without action.

But in avoiding the conventions of the West End, poetic drama must also beware the pretensions of high art:

> If the would-be poetic dramatist demands extremely high-brow music and unfamiliar traditions of dancing, he will, of course, fail; but if he is willing to be humble and sympathetic, to accept what he finds to his hand and develop its latent possibilities, he may be agreeably surprised to find that after all the public will stand, nay even enjoy, a good deal of poetry.*

He presented further elements of his theory in aphoristic form in a programme note for the Group Theatre's public production of *The Dance of Death* in 1935:

> The development of the film has deprived drama of any excuse for being documentary. It is not in its nature to provide an ignorant and passive spectator with exciting news.
>
> The subject of Drama, on the other hand, is the Commonly Known, the universally familiar stories of the society or generation in which it is written. The audience, like the child listening to the fairy tale, ought to know what is going to happen next. . . .
>
> Dramatic speech should have the same compressed, significant, and undocumentary character, as dramatic movement.

The first production of *The Dance of Death* had proved the force of these precepts in a play written on a small scale and in cabaret style. Auden now began work on a second play for the Group Theatre, this one suitable for a large auditorium with a proscenium stage. *The Chase*, written in the summer of 1934, presents three separate plots, each with a

---

* This last phrase rebuked Eliot, who had written that Elizabethan drama "was aimed at a public which wanted *entertainment* of a crude sort, but would *stand* a good deal of poetry" ("The Possibility of a Poetic Drama," in *The Sacred Wood* [1920]). Eliot made what he called the "dangerous suggestion" that the music-hall comedian might be a good starting point for modern poetic drama, but he was unable to write more than two short fragments of the ironic entertainment *Sweeney Agonistes*. When Eliot began writing plays again in the 1930s, he borrowed much of his dramatic method from Auden. (See Sidnell, *Dances of Death*, chapter 4.)

different style of dialogue and motivation, and frames them within a choral commentary spoken in part by two supernatural Witnesses. Much of the play adapts material Auden had tried to use earlier. His 1933 "epic" broke off at the point where the guests arrive at a country house to attend "the chase". Now, as Auden told Naomi Mitchison, "The epic has turned in[to] a dramma [sic]", and much of the choral narration in *The Chase* comes directly from the poem. From *The Fronny* Auden took Alan Norman's pursuit of the missing heir Sir Francis Crewe. From *The Enemies of a Bishop* he took the plot of an escape from a reformatory and the theme of troubles at a lead mine. But in *The Chase* the mine's troubles are political, as they were not in the earlier play. They begin with the miners' protests against new machinery and end with the violent reaction of the army and police. The entire political plot is narrated by the chorus, and none of the miners appears on stage.

Auden did, however, include the conductor, the prompter, and members of the audience among the dramatis personae. He wrote a dialogue for Alan Norman's left and right feet, and gave a monologue to the dog's skin worn by the escaped reformatory boy. In the final scene he called for a machine gun to be brought on stage and aimed at the audience. A different and more important innovation was the new style of dramatic verse that he devised for the choruses. These were written in a clear and expansive line that deliberately echoed the rhythm and phrasing of the English psalms.

Auden felt dissatisfied with *The Chase* as soon as he finished it. When he sent a copy to Stephen Spender in the autumn of 1934, he had already decided to rewrite the ending. He asked Spender to forward the script to Isherwood, who was then living in Copenhagen. Isherwood read it and proposed a complete revision. He sent Auden a scenario in which the search for the missing heir became the central action and the reformatory and lead-mine plots disappeared entirely. Auden accepted Isherwood's plan, and they began collaborating at a distance, each filling in different parts of Isherwood's outline. By the time they met in Copenhagen for a few days in January 1935, they had rewritten most of the dialogue and added songs, dances, slapstick, and spectacle. They retitled the play *Where Is Francis?* Rupert Doone or Robert Medley later suggested the title used when the play was printed and produced, *The Dog Beneath the Skin* (a spoof on "the skull beneath the skin" in Eliot's "Whispers of Immortality"). Everyone concerned abbreviated this to *Dogskin*.

In the new version Alan takes a companion on his search, a friendly and talented dog named Francis. The dog is in fact Sir Francis Crewe, who has concealed himself in a dog's skin in order to learn the hidden truths of his English village. Francis and Alan's travels (like Isherwood's) extend from England across Europe, first to ceremonial, monarchic Ostnia, where the King himself executes revolutionaries, then to lunatic, fascist Westland, where the Leader has a loudspeaker for a face. (These two misgoverned states, loosely modeled on Austria before 1914 and Germany after 1933, figure again in Auden and Isherwood's later plays.) When Alan and Francis return to England, Alan recognizes his village as the oppressive sham that Francis has always known it to be. Francis emerges from his disguise, denounces the villagers in a long speech, and leaves the stage to become "a unit in the army of the other side". Alan and some of the villagers volunteer to join him. But, as in *The Chase*, the revolutionary action occurs only offstage. Stephen Spender described this final scene as "a picture of a society defeated by an enemy whom the writers have not put into the picture because they do not know what he looks like although they thoroughly support him".

This final scene, which was largely Isherwood's work, appeared in print when the play was published in the spring of 1935. The authors rewrote the ending when the Group Theatre began rehearsals later in the year. In a version that returned in part to the ending of *The Chase*, they killed off Sir Francis before he could join the revolution, and Isherwood made a special point of dropping Francis's call for volunteers. Auden, who wrote the new dialogue according to a scenario supplied by Isherwood, transformed the tone of Francis's long speech to the villagers. He replaced the direct, dismissive attack that Isherwood had used in the earlier version with a characteristically Audenesque appeal to the villagers and to the audience to make their own choices. With this new ending, the play opened in January 1936 to critical approval which was less intense but more widely shared than that given to *The Dance of Death*. Doone's staging was bare to the point of severity, although, as Auden told a friend, the play had been "written with a view to an elaborate production along the lines of an Edwardian musical comedy".

Auden's changing idea of the political appeal that *The Dog Beneath the Skin* should make to its audience reflected his growing sense that politically responsible drama was more difficult to write than he had hoped. When he made his revisions to the play, he was working full time on documentary films, a position he considered contradictory: he received an official government salary for making films that expressed subversive, proletarian sentiments.

Auden had first turned to films as an alternative to schoolteaching. In the spring of 1935, he asked his friend Basil Wright if a job could be found for him in the General Post Office Film Unit, where Wright worked as a director. The official task of the Film Unit was to make advertising films for the Post Office, but the head of the Unit, John Grierson, was more interested in artistic experiment and social commentary. Grierson had an eye for talent. He had already hired the painter William Coldstream and a twenty-one-year-old composer named Benjamin Britten. He now commissioned Auden to write verses for *Coal Face*, a brief film about miners, and *Night Mail*, a more elaborate production about the mail train from London to Glasgow. Then, in September 1935, Auden started work as an "apprentice" at the Film Unit offices in Soho Square. At first he carried cables and film cans when he was not writing verse, but he later directed a few scenes on his own.

Grierson, who had founded, inspired, and shepherded the documentary movement in Britain, regarded film as an art form that could be put in the service of the working class. (Sir William Coldstream recalls Grierson's anger when Coldstream and Auden advised him to cut from the narration of one of his films the line, "Ever on the alert, this worker lubricates his tool with soap".) Auden quickly came to distrust the social pieties of the documentary movement, although he gave it some of his finest verse.* After five months with the Film Unit, he went on leave for two months to pursue his own writing. About the same time, in February 1936, he wrote a review of Paul Rotha's book *Documentary Film*. He had less to say about the book than about the practical and political obstacles faced by the documentary movement:

> The first and most important of these is the time factor. . . . Inanimate objects, like machines, or facts of organisation, can be understood in a few weeks, but not human beings, and if documentary films have hitherto concentrated on the former, it is not entirely the fault of the directors, but is also due to the compulsion on them to turn out a film in a ridiculously short period. It is a misfortune that the art which is the slowest to create, should at the same time be the most expensive. The second obstacle is class. It is doubtful whether an artist can ever deal more than superficially (and cinema is not a superficial art) with characters outside his own class, and most British documentary directors are upper middle.
>
> Lastly, there is the question of financial support. A documentary film is a film that tells the truth, and truth rarely has advertisement value. One remains extremely sceptical about the disinterestedness of large-scale industry and government departments, or about the possibility that they will ever willingly pay for an exact picture of the human life within their enormous buildings.

He resigned from the Film Unit a few weeks later, but he continued to

---

* He wrote the poem "Look, stranger" for *Beside the Seaside*, a documentary made by Grierson's sister Marion, but only a few phrases were used in the sound track.

do free-lance film work. Later in 1936, he, Britten, and Wright collaborated on *The Way to the Sea*, a commercial documentary celebrating the electrification of a rail line. They made the film portentous enough to parody the solemn productions of the documentary movement but not so much so that the railway officials who commissioned it noticed anything wrong. Auden stayed on friendly terms with Grierson, and, two years later, he wrote some poetic prose for Grierson's *The Londoners* that was dignified and vigorous.

When Auden left the Film Unit, he and Isherwood had almost finished their new play *The Ascent of F6*. Its hero, the climber Michael Ransom, is a partial portrait of T. E. Lawrence and the one sustained study of personal psychology in all of Auden's plays. Two years before, Auden had written in praise of Lawrence's solitary triumphs, but now he shared Isherwood's view that Lawrence's character was uncomfortably amoral and ambitious. After his experience of work in film, with its promise of an unlimited audience, Auden used his portrayal of Lawrence in the new play as a private warning to himself: Ransom's story is the parable of an artist who yields to the flattery of public acclaim and official sponsorship and in consequence destroys both his art and his life. The speeches in which Ransom approaches a state of hysterical monomania include passages from abandoned poems that Auden had written in his own voice a few years before.

Ransom is destroyed by his messianic fantasies. He dreams of a weak and helpless humanity turning to him for salvation after he triumphs over the unconquered mountain. But his wish for homage is a neurotic compensation for his failure to win his mother's love. When the government (in the person of Ransom's brother, the head of the Colonial Office) offers to sponsor him in an expedition to F6, Ransom refuses: the government's interest is imperial and propagandistic, and he will not corrupt what he believes is his disinterested love of mountaineering. But when Ransom's mother asks him to accept the offer, his resistance breaks.*
Driven by secret and private motives, Ransom accepts a contradictory public role: while Fleet Street and the Colonial Office pay his expenses, the public acclaims him as a symbol of romantic freedom. Ransom's crisis is an extreme version of Auden's double role as spokesman for both the forces of order and the forces of revolt—salaried by the British government, celebrated as a revolutionary bard by the British left, and privately disenchanted with both. Auden said later that he recognized while writing *The Ascent of F6* that he must eventually leave England and that, if he stayed, he would inevitably become part of the British establishment.

---

* The play is dedicated to Auden's brother John Bicknell Auden, who at the time was climbing the Himalayas while working as a geologist in India.

In the summer of 1936, after finishing the manuscript of *F6*, Auden wrote a cabaret sketch, *Alfred*, a satire on "certain prominent European figures" then in power in Germany and Italy. He and Isherwood then made plans to revise *F6*; they had read the proofs without making changes, but now said they were annoyed that their first version had appeared in print. They altered Ransom's speeches to refute the suggestion that he is driven more by his followers than by his ambition and to emphasize that he and his followers die as victims of his pride. They also rewrote the endings of both acts to focus attention less on the lies of officialdom and more on Ransom's psychological disorder. Yet even as they emphasized the personal aspects of the play, the recent outbreak of the Spanish Civil War made them feel a political urgency to speak out against fascism. So Auden added to the final chorus a new stanza that placed the blame for Ransom's fate not on himself but on those whom the forces of history had already doomed and deserted. These conflicting revisions appeared in the second published edition. Early in 1937, while Auden was observing the war in Spain (his offer to serve as an ambulance driver had been refused by the Republicans), the Group Theatre began rehearsals for its production of *F6*. Isherwood and Doone tried out further versions of the ending without finding one that satisfied them. Even after the play opened to warm reviews and packed houses (Britten's music added to the excitement), they tried out different endings every night for a week. And when Auden returned to England, he and Isherwood wrote yet another ending. In all these versions, the emphasis shifted constantly between tragedy and farce, between psychology and politics.*

The success of *F6* led Auden and Isherwood to write their next play, *On the Frontier*, for a large commercial audience. Taking their theme from the political tragedies of contemporary Europe, they outlined the story in the spring of 1937 and wrote the dialogue in the autumn. The play is a warning prophecy with a double plot. One is a Shavian satire: the Westland munitions magnate tries to keep his nation's Leader calm enough to prevent a war but angry enough to maintain a profitable arms race with Ostnia. The other is a poetic melodrama set in the "Ostnia-Westland Room", a room divided between the homes of two familes—one in each nation, neither aware of the other's existence. When this room darkens, the conventional action stops, and the son of one family and daughter of the other family meet in dream visions of each other. As Westland and Ostnia move inevitably from saber rattling to total war, both plots move toward their separate tragic endings.

* In 1942 Auden wrote in Albert and Angelyn Stevens's copy of the published text: "The end of this play is all wrong, because, as I now see, it required, and I refused it, a Christian solution."

As soon as *On the Frontier* was finished, the Group Theatre made plans to stage it under the sponsorship of John Maynard Keynes, who had founded and maintained the Arts Theatre in Cambridge. But when Auden and Isherwood told Keynes they had been commissioned by their publishers to report on the Sino-Japanese War, Keynes postponed the production until their return. Late in 1937, before leaving for China, Auden wrote *Hadrian's Wall*, "an historical survey" for broadcast by the BBC. In it he returned to the northern landscape of *Paid on Both Sides* and again portrayed its archaic enmities. But where the subject of *Paid on Both Sides* was the lethal psychology of the family, the subject of *Hadrian's Wall* was the lethal politics of empire. The mood of the work was light, but its historical portrait of England was not flattering. The closing speech was a reminder that "our venerable ancestors . . . the Saxons, Danes, and Normans . . . came over in swarms, butchered, robbed and possessed; although they had no more right than I have to your coat."

In 1938, during their return voyage from China, Auden and Isherwood rewrote much of *On the Frontier*. They apparently discarded a chorus that reported the final triumph of the workers after the collapse of the two warring governments, and the play ended with plague and disaster on all sides. But by the time the Group Theatre production opened in Cambridge in November 1938, Hitler had capped his *Anschluss* with Austria by annexing the Sudetenland and humiliating his enemies at Munich, and the play's evenhanded apportionment of blame between its combatants seemed irrelevant and embarrassing.*

The play was also the victim of its authors' misunderstanding of their own purpose. Auden and Isherwood thought they were writing a topical drama suitable for a West End stage, but the play transformed the local material of politics and history into timeless lamentation and prayer. Against the conscious intent of its authors, *On the Frontier* aspired to the condition of opera. (Britten was rightly annoyed when Auden insisted that one of the lyrics be sung, not to a serious setting by Britten, but to the jaunty American folk tune "Sweet Betsy from Pike".) Auden discovered his fascination for opera later, in America, when he wrote *Paul Bunyan* for Britten and collaborated with Chester Kallman on *The Rake's Progress* for Stravinsky and *Elegy for Young Lovers* and *The Bassarids* for Hans Werner Henze.

In January 1939 Auden and Isherwood left England for America. That spring they wrote yet another ending for *The Ascent of F6*. They

---

* In a lecture in December, Auden said that for a poetic dramatist "to choose as a subject a [contemporary] political subject is a mistake, because history is always now more terrible and more moving than anything you can possibly invent and more extravagant than anything you can imagine". (See p. 522.)

now transformed Ransom's death into his triumph. In his dying vision after he attains the summit, Ransom sheds his pride, overcomes his fear of love, and acknowledges at last his common humanity. His political ambitions and personal longings fade. The division in himself between the public and the private worlds dissolves in his final lines.

REFERENCES

Page xiii
This book is like   Unsigned review, *The Listener*, 9 May 1934, p. 808.

Page xv
Drama began as an act   From Auden's statement for the programme of *The Dance of Death*, 1 October 1935; see p. 497.

A parable of English   Written in 1942 in Albert and Angelyn Stevens's copy of *Poems* (American edition, 1934).

Page xvi
literary knowledge of   Letter to Naomi Mitchison, 28 October 1930 (Berg Collection, New York Public Library).

Freud's error   From Auden's 1929 journal (Berg Collection).

quite a brilliant   Letter from Eliot to E. McKnight Kauffer, 6 January 1930 (Pierpont Morgan Library, New York).

One reason the scheme   Empson, "A Note on Auden's 'Paid on Both Sides' ", *Experiment*, Spring 1931, p. 61.

the forerunner of   Unsigned note, almost certainly by Eliot, on the jacket of Auden's *Collected Shorter Poems 1930-1944* (1950).

Do I want poetry   From Auden's 1929 journal (Berg Collection).

Page xvii
Dramatic action is   For the "Preliminary Statement" see p. 459.

the pseudo-healers   Isherwood, "Some Notes on Auden's Early Poetry", *New Verse*, November 1937, p. 7.

Page xviii
Mother Law   Reported in W. David Wills, *Homer Lane: A Biography* (1964), p. 204.

no more than a charade   Isherwood, "Some Notes", pp. 7-8.

Page xix
vary at every performance   Letter to Isherwood, [?October 1930].

Formally I am trying   Letter to Naomi Mitchison, 12 August 1931 (Berg Collection).

Page xx

my epic   Letter to Naomi Mitchison, 18 October 1932 (Berg Collection).

my Masque   Letter to Nevill Coghill, 24 April 1933 (Berg Collection).

Page xxi

The communists never   Written in 1942 in the Stevens's copy of *Poems*.

brilliant, and in my   Harold Hobson, *Christian Science Monitor*, 22 October 1935, p. 12. Another reviewer used almost the same terms: "This production for all its faults may prove epoch-making" (E. L., *Drama*, November 1935, p. 23).

The truth is that   Unsigned review, *The Listener*, 9 May 1934, p. 808.

Page xxii

The development of   From Auden's statement for the programme of *The Dance of Death*, 1 October 1935; emended from the manuscript (Berg Collection).

Page xxiii

The epic has turned   Letter to Naomi Mitchison, [?July 1934] (Berg Collection).

Page xxiv

a picture of a society   Spender, "The Poetic Dramas of W. H. Auden and Christopher Isherwood", *New Writing*, Autumn 1938, p. 105.

written with a view   Reported by John Hayward, "London Letter", *New York Sun*, 12 October 1935, p. 13.

Page xxv

The first and most   Unsigned review, *The Listener*, 19 February 1936, p. 369. Auden made no secret of his authorship of this review.

Page xxvi

the British establishment   Unpublished interview with Timothy Foote, 1963.

THE TEXT OF THIS EDITION

AUDEN's works are presented in this collected edition in the versions that he prepared and revised around the time of their publication. Works that appeared in his books appear in the versions that he prepared for those books or that he revised shortly thereafter; revisions that he made many years later for his retrospective collected editions appear in the notes.* Works that Auden abandoned before book publication or that he never considered for inclusion in a book appear in their last revised versions. For works with more complex or unusual publishing histories, these same general principles have determined the choice of text. An essay, for example, that Auden first published in book form thirty years after he printed it in a magazine appears in this edition in the earlier version, and the later revisions are listed in the notes.

All the plays in this volume present slightly different editorial problems and require slightly different editorial solutions. In general, the texts printed in the body of the book incorporate revisions made by Auden or Isherwood at about the time each play was written; revisions made when the authors went back to a play after a few years are printed in the notes. These notes also include a history of the composition, publication, and production of each play; a detailed description of the sources for the text and the variants in all earlier editions; and the texts of letters and other material that figured in the composition of the plays.

For the plays that were produced by the Group Theatre under Auden's supervision—*The Dance of Death*, *The Dog Beneath the Skin*, *The Ascent of F 6*, and *On the Frontier*—the texts printed here incorporate the additions and substitutions made by the authors before each play was handed over to the director. (Cuts made later by the director or censor, with or without the authors' approval, are described in the notes but are not reflected in the text.) The text of *The Dance of Death*, therefore, includes some passages that have not previously appeared in print. The text of *The Dog Beneath the Skin* also includes verse that Auden wrote after hand-

---

* This volume of plays notes the revisions Auden made in different versions of each of the plays as a whole and in different versions of individual scenes. When he excerpted some of the lyrics from these plays for inclusion in his later volumes of collected and selected poems, he sometimes made minor revisions in the texts. These later printings are mentioned in the notes to this volume, but the details of any revisions belong more properly to the forthcoming edition of Auden's complete poems. The minor revisions to the punctuation of *Paid on Both Sides* that Auden made when he reprinted the play as one of his longer poems will also be listed in the edition of the complete poems.

ing the play to the publisher; it substitutes Auden's revised version of the final scene for the published version, which had been put into shape by Isherwood. (Like all other altered passages in these plays, the original ending appears in full in the notes.) The text of *The Ascent of F 6*, the only play for which the authors had an opportunity to publish a revised version, is that of the second English edition, which incorporates all the changes they wished to preserve. The text of *On the Frontier* includes a verse interlude that, shortly before the first night, Auden substituted for the prose interlude in the printed text. All the plays have been newly transcribed, wherever possible, from early manuscripts and typescripts to remove errors introduced earlier by typists, printers, and publishers.

For the dramatic works that Auden published but did not see produced, such as *Paid on Both Sides* and *Alfred*, the texts have been taken from manuscripts or typescripts, but they incorporate revisions made in the course of publication. Previously unpublished works, such as *The Enemies of a Bishop* and *The Chase*, are here printed with minimal editorial interference. The published and unpublished plays appear in chronological sequence in this book because the distinction between them is largely accidental: Auden submitted two of his three unpublished plays, *The Fronny* and *The Chase*, to Faber & Faber. Although there is no evidence that he submitted the third, *The Enemies of a Bishop*, he hired a professional typist to prepare it in the same format that he used for the published plays.

I have made no attempt to impose a rigorous consistency on Auden's spelling and punctuation or to bring his usage into conformity with Isherwood's. Isherwood, who was far more careful than Auden about such matters, evidently prepared for the typist or printer the manuscripts of his collaborations with Auden, so these works appear more polished on the page than do the works Auden wrote alone. An instructive contrast may be observed between the punctuation of the speech used as the text of the General's "special record" in Auden's *The Chase* and the punctuation of the same speech used as the Vicar's sermon in a scene prepared by Isherwood for *The Dog Beneath the Skin*. Isherwood seems not to have interfered with some punctuation that readers have found puzzling in Auden's choruses for *Dogskin*. Here, as elsewhere in his poetry, Auden used heavy punctuation to indicate a pause or a caesura where conventional grammar calls for lighter pointing. Specifically, he used a semicolon to separate the parallel divisions of his choral verse and to emphasize its echoes of the parallelism of biblical poetry. A typical line in the opening chorus reads: "As at Trent Junction where the Soar comes gliding; out of green Leicestershire to swell the ampler current."

Auden was especially irregular and inconsistent in the punctuation he used to introduce quoted speech, often using a semicolon, sometimes even a full stop, where stylebooks call for a comma or colon. But his pointing indicates verbal rhythms, and a reduction to conventional consistency would remove one of the components of his style. After the early 1930s, he sometimes asked friends for help in punctuating his poems, but he made his own final decisions in these matters and was often attentive to them while reading the proofs.

Although Auden appears to have paid little or no attention to spelling, except when rendering the dialect of a social class, there seems to be no compelling reason to regularize his inconsistencies. In works by Auden alone, I have restored some spellings that earlier printers or publishers treated as errors but that were not inconsistent with common practice. In this edition Auden's customary *alright* and *aint* coexist with Isherwood's *all right* and *ain't*. But I have not hesitated to change the *do'nt* and *dont* and *dont'* of Auden's manuscripts to *don't*, and I have substituted *its* for *it's*, or the reverse, when necessary.

I have followed Auden by using "Wireless" rather than "Radio" in the headings provided for this edition.

The typographic style of this edition (not the typeface itself) is based on the design used by Faber & Faber for the original editions of the Auden-Isherwood plays. Speech headings, stage directions, and other design elements in previously unpublished works have been set in conformity with this style. Faber used some slightly different conventions in the original editions of *Paid on Both Sides* and *The Dance of Death*, and these have been preserved despite a slight sacrifice of consistency in the volume as a whole. One convention has been added: where an open square (□) appears at the foot of a page it indicates a break between stanzas or verse paragraphs that might not otherwise be evident.

PLAYS

Paid on Both Sides

A Charade

BY W. H. AUDEN

[*1928*]

TO
CECIL DAY-LEWIS

[*First Version*]

CHARACTERS.

Lintzgarth.   *Nattrass.*

JOHN NOWER.   AARON SHAW.
WILLIAM NOWER.   ANNE SHAW.
F′ GUNMEN.   FF′ GUNMEN.
F″   FF″
                                  SETH.
                                  SETH'S MOTHER.

THE MIDWIFE.
THE ANNOUNCER.
THE GUEST.
THE BUTLER.
PEOPLE.

THE CHORUS.

DRESSES.

JOHN NOWER.	Tails.
ANNE SHAW.	Evening frock.
AARON SHAW.	Plus-fours and a cap, preferably tweeds.
WILLIAM AND GUNMEN.	Dinner jackets for the last scene. For the first they wear trench coats. William and FF′ wear homburgs, the others bowlers. F″ and FF′ have field glasses. All carry sportsman's guns.
SETH.	A straw panama with an elastic under the chin. Clothes tight and too small. A large revolver.
SETH'S MOTHER.	An iron on one leg as for rickets. A stick.
MIDWIFE.	Untidy. A blue apron. Soiled lavatory towels on arm.
ANNOUNCER.	The uniform of a cinema commissionaire. A megaphone.
GUEST.	Dress suit with a yellow waistcoat. A paper cap out of a cracker.
CHORUS.	Rugger things. The leader wears a scrum cap.

The Lintzgarth party will wear its handkerchiefs round their left arms.

Both sides are to be seated on chairs on the R and L of the stage until their disappearance in the last scene. *Exeunt* means going back to their chairs.

The stage is a plain one with a raised recess which has drawing curtains in front and a back-cloth behind.

CHORUS. Often the man, alone shut, shall consider
    The killings in old winters, death of friends;
    Sitting with stranger shall expect no good.

    There was no food in the assaulted city;
    Men spoke at corners asking for news, saw
    Outside the watchfires of a stronger army.

    Spring came urging to ships, a casting off,
    But one would stay, vengeance not done: it seemed
    Doubtful to them that they should meet again.

    Fording in the cool of the day they rode
    To meet at crossroads when the year was over:
    Dead is Brody; such a man was Morl.

    I will say this not falsely; I have seen
    The just and the unjust die in the day
    All, willing or not; and some were willing.

[*Enter* MIDWIFE.]

MIDWIFE. Sometimes we read a sign; cloud in the sky,
    The wet tracks of a hare, quicken the step,
    Promise the best day. But here no remedy
    Is to be thought of; no news but the new death,
    A Nower dragged out in the night, a Shaw
    Ambushed behind the wall. Blood on the ground
    Would welcome fighters: last night at Hammergill
    A boy was born fanged like a weasel. I am old
    Will die this winter, but more than once shall hear
    The cry for help, the shooting round the house.

[*Exit C* MIDWIFE. *During her speech* F″ *enters R and squats in the centre of the stage looking L through field glasses. Enter* WILLIAM *and* F′ *R.*]

WILLIAM. Are you hurt?
F′. Nothing much sir; only a slight flesh wound. Did you get him sir?
WILLIAM. On ledge above the gulley, aimed at, seen moving, fell; looked
    down on, sprawls in the stream.
F′. Good. He sniped poor Dick last Easter, riding to Flash.
WILLIAM. I have some lint and bandages in my haversack, and there's a
    spring here. I'll dress your arm.

[*Enter L* FF′ *and* FF″.]

FF′. Did you find Tom's body?
FF″. Yes, sir. It's lying in the Hangs.
FF′. Which way did they go?
FF″. Down there sir.

[*F″ observes them and runs R.*]

F″. There are twenty men from Nattrass sir, over the gap, coming at once.
WILLIAM. Have they seen us?
F″. Not yet.
WILLIAM. We must get out. You go round by the copse and make for the Barbon road. We'll follow the old tramway. Keep low and run like hell.

[*Exeunt R. FF′ watches through field glasses.*]

FF′. Yes. No. No. Yes I can see them. They are making for the Barbon road. Go down and cut them off. There is good cover by the bridge. We've got them now.

[*A whistle. The back curtain draws showing* JOHN, ANNE, *and* AARON *and the* ANNOUNCER *grouped. Both sides enter L and R.*]

AARON. There is a time for peace; too often we
    Have gone on cold marches, have taken life,
    Till wrongs are bred like flies; the dreamer wakes
    Beating a smooth door, footsteps behind, on the left
    The pointed finger, the unendurable drum,
    To hear of horses stolen or a house burned.
    Now this shall end with marriage as it ought:
    Love turns the wind, brings up the salt smell,
    Shadow of gulls on the road to the sea.

THE ANNOUNCER. The engagement is announced of John Nower, eldest son of the late Mr and Mrs George Nower of Lintzgarth Rookhope, and Anne Shaw, only daughter of the late Mr and Mrs Joseph Shaw of Nattrass Garrigill.
ALL. Hurrah.

[*Someone does a cartwheel across the stage. Exeunt L and R. Back curtains close.*]

CHORUS. The four sat on in the bare room
    Together and the fire unlighted:
    One said; "We played duets, she turned the page,
    More quavers on the other side."

"We parted in the waiting-room
  Scraping back chairs for the wrong train."
Said Two; and Three. "All kinds of love
  Are obsolete or extremely rare."

"Yesterday", Four said, "falling on me
  Through the glass pavement overhead
  The shadow of returning girls
  Proclaimed an insolent new spring."

They said, the four distinguished men
Who sat waiting the enemy,
Saw closing upon the bare room
The weight of a whole winter night,
Beyond the reef high-breaking surf.

[*Back curtains draw.* JOHN *and* ANNE *alone.* JOHN *blows on a grass held between the thumbs and listens.*]

JOHN. On Cautley where a peregrine has nested, iced heather hurt the knuckles. Fell on the ball near time, the rushing of forwards stopped. Good-bye now, he said, would open the swing doors. These I remember but not love till now. We cannot tell where we shall find it though we all look for it till we do, and what others tell us is no use to us.

Some say that handsome raider, still at large,
A terror to the Marches, in truth is love;
And we must listen for such messengers
To tell us daily. "To-day a saint came blessing
The huts." "Seen lately in the provinces
Reading behind a tree and people passing."
But love returns:
At once all heads are turned this way, and love
Calls order—silenced the angry sons—
Steps forward, greets, repeats what he has heard
And seen, feature for feature, word for word.

ANNE. Yes, love does not begin with meeting, nor end in parting. We are always in love though we know love only by moments, and perhaps it is only ourselves that we love. Mouth to mouth is no nearer. Now I see you, but if I shut my eyes I forget. Words fail us and truth eludes us and we cannot be satisfied. But I am glad this evening that we are together.

>   Look. The flushed waterfall
>   Spouts from the hanging valley; but for us
>   The silence is unused, and life and death
>   Seem no more than the echo of an axe.

[*One of the chorus sings:*]

>   The summer quickens all
>   Scatters its promises
>   To you and me no less,
>   Though neither can compel
>
>   The wish to last the year,
>   The longest look to live,
>   The urgent word survive
>   The movement of the air.
>
>   But loving now let none
>   Think of divided days
>   When we shall choose from ways,
>   All of them evil, one:
>
>   Look on with stricter brows
>   The sacked and burning town,
>   The ice-sheet moving down,
>   The fall of an old house.

ANNE. John, I have a car waiting. Let's get away from here. We sleep in beds where men have died howling.

JOHN. You may be right, but we shall stay. No one can avoid to-morrow.

ANNE. To-morrow may change us.

JOHN. We only love what changes.

ANNE. To-night the many come to mind
>   Sent forward in the thaw with anxious marrow,
>   For such might now return with a bleak face,
>   An image pause half-lighted in the door,
>   A greater but not fortunate in all;
>   Come home deprived of an astonishing end—
>   Morgan's who took a clean death in the north
>   Shouting against the wind, or Cousin Dodds'
>   Passed out asleep in her chair, the snow falling.
>   The too-loved clays, borne over by diverse drifts,
>   Fallen upon the far side of all enjoyment,
>   Unable to move closer, shall not speak

Out of that grave stern on no capital fault:
Enough to have lightly touched the unworthy thing.

JOHN. We live still.
ANNE. But what has become of the dead? They forget.
JOHN. These. Smilers, all who stand on promontories, slinkers, whisperers; deliberate approaches, echoes, time, promises of mercy, what dreams or goes masked, embraces that fail, insufficient evidence, touches of the old wound. . . . But let us not think of things which we hope will be long in coming.

CHORUS. The Spring will come,
    Not hesitate for one employer who
    Though a fine day and every pulley running
    Would quick lie down; nor save the wanted one
    That wounded in escaping swam the lake
    Safe to the reeds, collapsed in shallow water.

    You have tasted good and what is it? For you
    Sick in the green plain, healed in the tundra, shall
    Turn westward back from your alone success
    Under a dwindling Alp to see your friends
    Cut down the wheat.

JOHN. It's getting cold, dear, let's go in.

[*Exeunt C. Back curtains close.*]

CHORUS. For where are Basley who won the Ten,
    Dickon so tarted by the House,
    Thomas who kept a sparrow-hawk?
    The clock strikes, it is time to go
    The tongue ashamed, deceived by a shake of the hand.

[*Enter bridal party from one side L, guests from the other R. The* CHIEF GUEST *comes forward and presents a bouquet to the bride.*]

PEOPLE. Ssh.
GUEST. With gift in hand we come
    From every neighbour farm
    To celebrate in wine
    The certain union of
    A woman and a man;
    And may their double love
    Be shown to the stranger's eye

In a son's symmetry.
Now hate is swallowed down,
All anger put away;
The spirit comes to its own,
The beast to its play.

[*All clap. The* GUEST *addresses the audience.*]

GUEST. Will any lady be so kind as to oblige us with a dance? Thank you very much. This way, miss. What tune would you like?

[*Gramophone. Dance. Enter* BUTLER.]

BUTLER. Dinner is served.

[AARON *goes to the dancer.*]

AARON. You'll dine with us of course.
PEOPLE. It will be a good year for them I think.
   You don't mean that he—well you know what.
   Rather off his form lately.
   The vein is showing well in the Quarry Hazel.
   One of Edward's friends.
   Well it does seem to show.
   Etc.

[*Exeunt except* SETH *and his* MOTHER. *This time they go right off.*]

MOTHER. Seth.
SETH. Yes, mother.
MOTHER. William Nower is here.
SETH. I know that. What do you want me to do?
MOTHER. Kill him.
SETH. I can't do that. There is peace now, besides he is our guest.
MOTHER. Have you forgotten your brother's death at the Hangs? It is a nice thing for me to hear people saying that I have a coward for a son. I am thankful your Father is not alive to see it.
SETH. I'm not afraid of anybody or anything; but I don't want to.
MOTHER. I shall have to take steps.
SETH. It shall be as you like. But I think that much will come of this, chiefly harm.
MOTHER. I have thought of that.

[*Exeunt. A shot. More shots. Shouting.*]

PEOPLE OUTSIDE. A trap. I might have known.
   Take that damn you.

Open the window.
You swine.
Jimmy. O my God.
Etc.

[*Two of the Shaw party enter L and R.*]

FF'. The Master's killed. Some of them got away: fetching help will attack in an hour.

FF". See that all the doors are bolted.

[*Exeunt R and L. Back curtains draw.* ANNE *with the dead.*]

ANNE. Now we have seen the story to its end.
    The hands that were to help will not be lifted,
    And bad followed by worse leaves to us tears,
    An empty bed, hope from less noble men.
    I had seen joy
    Received and given upon both sides for years,
    Now not.

CHORUS. Light strives with darkness, right with wrong:
    Man thinks to be called the fortunate,
    To bring home a wife, to live long.

    But he is defeated; let the son
    Sell the farm lest the mountain fall:
    His mother and her mother won.

    His fields are used up where the moles visit,
    The contours worn flat; if there show
    Passage for water he will miss it:

    Give up his breath, his woman, his team;
    No life to touch, though later there be
    Big fruit, eagles above the stream.

CURTAIN

[*Second Version*]

CHARACTERS

Lintzgarth   *Nattrass*

JOHN NOWER   AARON SHAW*****
DICK   SETH SHAW
GEORGE****   THE SPY—SETH'S BROTHER
WALTER   BERNARD
KURT   SETH'S MOTHER***
CULLEY   ANNE SHAW
STEPHEN**
ZEPPEL—JOHN NOWER'S SERVANT
NO. 6
STURTON
JOAN—MOTHER OF JOHN NOWER
TRUDY***

         FATHER XMAS*
         THE DOCTOR
         BO****
         PO*****
         THE MAN-WOMAN
         THE DOCTOR'S BOY**
         THE PHOTOGRAPHER
         THE ANNOUNCER*
         THE CHIEF GUEST*
         THE BUTLER*

         THE CHORUS

The starred parts should be doubled

No scenery is required. The stage should have a curtained-off recess. The distinction between the two hostile parties should be marked by different coloured arm-bands. The chorus, which should not consist of more than three persons, wear similar and distinctive clothing.

[*Enter* TRUDY *and* WALTER.]

T. You've only just heard?
W. Yes. A breakdown at the Mill needed attention, kept me all morning. I guessed no harm. But lately, riding at leisure, Dick met me, panted disaster. I came here at once. How did they get him?
T. In Kettledale above Colefangs road passes where high banks overhang dangerous from ambush. To Colefangs had to go, would speak with Layard, Jerry and Hunter with him only. They must have stolen news, for Red Shaw waited with ten, so Jerry said, till for last time unconscious. Hunter was killed at first shot. They fought, exhausted ammunition, a brave defence but fight no more.
W. Has Joan been told yet?
T. Yes. It couldn't be helped. Shock, starting birth pangs, caused a premature delivery.
W. How is she?
T. Bad, I believe. But here's the doctor.

[*Enter* DOCTOR.]

Well, Doctor, how are things going?
D. Better, thanks. We've had a hard fight, but it's going to be all right. She'll pull through and have a fine infant as well. My God, I'm thirsty after all that. Where can I get a drink?
W. Here in the next room, Doctor.

[*Exeunt. Back curtains draw.* JOAN *with child and corpse.*]

J. Not from this life, not from this life is any
To keep; sleep, day and play would not help there
Dangerous to new ghost; new ghost learns from many
Learns from old termers what death is, where.

Who's jealous of his latest company
From one day to the next final to us,
A changed one; would use sorrow to deny
Sorrow, to replace death; sorrow is sleeping thus.

Unforgetting is not to-day's forgetting
For yesterday, not bedrid scorning,
But a new begetting
An unforgiving morning.

[*Baby squeals.*]

O see, he is impatient

To pass beyond this pretty lisping time:
There'll be some crying out when he's come there.

[*Back curtains close.*]

CHORUS. Can speak of trouble, pressure on men
    Born all the time, brought forward into light
    For warm dark moan.
    Though heart fears all heart cries for, rebuffs with mortal beat
    Skyfall, the legs sucked under, adder's bite.
    That prize held out of reach
    Guides the unwilling tread,
    The asking breath,
    Till on attended bed
    Or in untracked dishonour comes to each
    His natural death.

    We pass our days
    Speak, man to men, easy, learning to point
    To jump before ladies, to show our scars:
    But no
    We were mistaken, these faces are not ours.
    They smile no more when we smile back:
    Eyes, ears, tongue, nostrils bring
    News of revolt, inadequate counsel to
    An infirm king.

    O watcher in the dark, you wake
    Our dream of waking, we feel
    Your finger on the flesh that has been skinned,
    By your bright day
    See clear what we were doing, that we were vile.
    Your sudden hand
    Shall humble great
    Pride, break it, wear down to stumps old systems which await
    The last transgression of the sea.

[*Enter* JOHN NOWER *and* DICK.]

J.   If you have really made up your mind, Dick, I won't try and persuade you to stop. But I shall be sorry to lose you.

D.   I have thought it all over and I think it is the best thing to do. My cousin writes that the ranch is a thoroughly good proposition. I don't know how I shall like the Colonies but I feel I must get away from

here. There is not room enough ... but the actual moving is unpleasant.
J. I understand. When are you thinking of sailing?
D. My cousin is sailing to-morrow. If I am going I am to join him at the Docks.
J. Right. Tell one of the men to go down to the post-office and send a wire for you. If you want anything else, let me know.
D. Thank you.

[*Exit* DICK. *Enter* ZEPPEL.]

Z. Number Six wishes to see you, sir.
J. Alright, show him in.

[*Enter* NUMBER SIX.]

    Well, what is it?
6. My area is Rookhope. Last night at Horse and Farrier, drank alone, one of Shaw's men. I sat down friendly next, till muzzed with drink and lateness he was blabbing. Red Shaw goes to Brandon Walls to-day, visits a woman.
J. Alone?
6. No, sir. He takes a few. I got no numbers.
J. This is good news. Here is a pound for you.
6. Thank you very much, sir.

[*Exit* NUMBER SIX.]

J. Zeppel.
Z. Sir.
J. Ask George to come here at once.
Z. Very good sir.

[JOHN *gets a map out. Enter* GEORGE.]

J. Red Shaw is spending the day at Brandon Walls. We must get him. You know the ground well, don't you, George?
G. Pretty well. Let me see the map. There's a barn about a hundred yards from the house. Yes, here it is. If we can occupy that without attracting attention it will form a good base for operations, commands both house and road. If I remember rightly, on the other side of the stream is a steep bank. Yes, you can see from the contours. They couldn't get out that way, but lower down is marshy ground and possible. You want to post some men there to catch those who try.

J. Good. Who do you suggest to lead that party?
G. Send Sturton. He knows the whole district blindfold. He and I as boys fished all those streams together.
J. I shall come with you. Let's see: it's dark now about five. Fortunately there's no moon and it's cloudy. We'll start then about half-past. Pick your men and get some sandwiches made up in the kitchen. I'll see about the ammunition if you will remember to bring a compass. We meet outside at a quarter past.

[*Exeunt. Enter* KURT *and* CULLEY.]

K. There's time for a quick one before changing. What's yours?
C. I'll have a sidecar, thanks.
K. Zeppel, one sidecar and one C.P.S. I hear Chapman did the lake in eight.
C. Yes, he is developing a very pretty style. I am not sure though that Pepys won't beat him next year if he can get out of that double kick. Thanks. Prosit.
K. Cheerio.

[*Enter* WALTER *and* TRUDY.]

W. Two half pints, Zeppel, please. [*To* KURT.] Can you let me have a match? How is the Rugger going?
K. Alright, thank you. We have not got a bad team this season.
W. Where do you play yourself?
K. Wing 3Q.
W. Did you ever see Warner? No, he'd be before your time. You remember him don't you, Trudy?
T. He was killed in the fight at Colefangs, wasn't he?
W. You are muddling him up with Hunter. He was the best three-quarter I have ever seen. His sprinting was marvellous to watch.
Z. [*producing Christmas turkey*]. Not bad eh?
T. [*feeling it*]. Oh a fine one. For to-morrow's dinner?
Z. Yes. Here, puss . . . gobble, gobble . . .
T. [*to* W]. What have you got Ingo for Christmas?
W. A model crane. Do you think he will like it?
T. He loves anything mechanical. He's so excited he can't sleep.
K. Come on, Culley, finish your drink. We must be getting along. [*To* W.] You must come down to the field on Monday and see us.
W. I will if I can.

[*Exit* KURT *and* CULLEY.]

T. Is there any news yet?

W. Nothing has come through. If things are going right they may be back any time now.
T. I suppose they will get him?
W. It's almost certain. Nower has waited long enough.
T. I am sick of this feud. What do we want to go killing each other for? We are all the same. He's trash, yet if I cut my finger it bleeds like his. But he's swell, keeps double shifts working all night by flares. His mother squealed like a pig when he came crouching out.

    Sometimes we read a sign, cloud in the sky,
    The wet tracks of a hare, quicken the step
    Promise the best day. But here no remedy
    Is to be thought of, no news but the new death;
    A Nower dragged out in the night, a Shaw
    Ambushed behind the wall. Blood on the ground
    Would welcome fighters. Last night at Hammergill
    A boy was born fanged like a weasel. I am old,
    Shall die before next winter, but more than once shall hear
    The cry for help, the shooting round the house.

W. The best are gone.

    Often the man, alone shut, shall consider
    The killings in old winters, death of friends.
    Sitting with stranger shall expect no good.

    Spring came, urging to ships, a casting off,
    But one would stay, vengeance not done; it seemed
    Doubtful to them that they would meet again.

    Fording in the cool of the day they rode
    To meet at crossroads when the year was over:
    Dead is Brody, such a man was Maul.

    I will say this not falsely; I have seen
    The just and the unjust die in the day,
    All, willing or not, and some were willing.

    Here they are.

[*Enter* NOWER, GEORGE, STURTON *and others. The three speak alternately.*]

    Day was gone Night covered sky
    Black over earth When we came there
    To Brandon Walls Where Red Shaw lay
    Hateful and sleeping Unfriendly visit.

I wished to revenge Quit fully
Who my father At Colefangs valley
Lying in ambush Cruelly shot
With life for life.

Then watchers saw They were attacked
Shouted in fear A night alarm
To men asleep Doomed men awoke
Felt for their guns Ran to the doors
Would wake their master Who lay with woman
Upstairs together Tired after love.
He saw then There would be shooting
Hard fight.

Shot answered shot Bullets screamed
Guns shook Hot in the hand
Fighters lay Groaning on ground
Gave up life Edward fell
Shot through the chest First of our lot
By no means refused fight Stephen was good
His first encounter Showed no fear
Wounded many.

Then Shaw knew We were too strong
Would get away Over the moor
Return alive But found at the ford
Sturton waiting Greatest gun anger
There he died Nor any came
Fighters home Nor wives shall go
Smiling to bed They boast no more.

[STEPHEN *suddenly gets up.*]

S. A forward forward can never be a backward backward.
G. Help me put Stephen to bed, somebody. He got tight on the way back. Hullo, they've caught a spy.
VOICES OUTSIDE. Look out. There he is. Catch him. Got you.

[*Enter* KURT *and others with prisoner.*]

K. We found this chap hiding in an outhouse.
J. Bring him here. Who are you?
S. I know him. I saw him once at Eickhamp. He's Seth Shaw's brother.
J. He is, is he. What do you come here for? You know what we do to spies. I'll destroy the whole lot of you. Take him out.

Spy. You may look big, but we'll get you one day, Nower.

[*Exeunt all but* John, Stephen *following.*]

S. Don't go, darling.

[John *sits. A shot outside followed by cheers.*]
[*Enter* Zeppel.]

Z. Will you be wanting anything more to-night, sir?
J. No, that will be all thank you.
Z. Good night, sir.

J. Always the following wind of history
Of others' wisdom makes a buoyant air
Till we come suddenly on pockets where
Is nothing loud but us; where voices seem
Abrupt, untrained, competing with no lie
Our fathers shouted once. They taught us war,
To scamper after darlings, to climb hills,
To emigrate from weakness, find ourselves
The easy conquerors of empty bays:
But never told us this, left each to learn,
Hear something of that soon-arriving day
When to gaze longer and delighted on
A face or idea be impossible.
Could I have been some simpleton that lived
Before disaster sent his runners here;
Younger than worms, worms have too much to bear.
Yes, mineral were best: could I but see
These woods, these fields of green, this lively world
Sterile as moon.

Chorus. The Spring unsettles sleeping partnerships,
Foundries improve their casting process, shops
Open a further wing on credit till
The winter. In summer boys grow tall
With running races on the froth-wet sand,
War is declared there, here a treaty signed;
Here a scrum breaks up like a bomb, there troops
Deploy like birds. But proudest into traps
Have fallen. These gears which ran in oil for week
By week, needing no look, now will not work;
Those manors mortgaged twice to pay for love
Go to another.

O how shall man live
Whose thought is born, child of one farcical night,
To find him old? The body warm but not
By choice, he dreams of folk in dancing bunches,
Of tart wine spilt on home-made benches,
Where learns, one drawn apart, a secret will
Restore the dead; but comes thence to a wall.
Outside on frozen soil lie armies killed
Who seem familiar but they are cold.
Now the most solid wish he tries to keep
His hands show through; he never will look up,
Say "I am good". On him misfortune falls
More than enough. Better where no one feels,
The out-of-sight, buried too deep for shafts.

[*Enter* FATHER CHRISTMAS. *He speaks to the audience.*]

X. Ladies and Gentlemen: I should like to thank you all very much for coming here to-night. Now we have a little surprise for you. When you go home, I hope you will tell your friends to come and bring the kiddies, but you will remember to keep this a secret, won't you? Thank you. Now I will not keep you waiting any longer.

[*Lights. A trial.* JOHN *as the accuser. The* SPY *as accused.* JOAN *as his warder with a gigantic feeding bottle.* XMAS *as president, the rest as Jury, wearing school caps.*]

X. Is there any more evidence?
J. Yes. I know we have and are making terrific sacrifices, but we cannot give in. We cannot betray the dead. As we pass their graves can we be deaf to the simple eloquence of their inscriptions, those who in the glory of their early manhood gave up their lives for us? No, we must fight to the finish.
X. Very well. Call the witness.

[*Enter* BO.]

B. In these days during the migrations, days
Freshening with rain reported from the mountains,
By loss of memory we are reborn,
For memory is death; by taking leave,
Parting in anger and glad to go
Where we are still unwelcome, and if we count
What dead the tides wash in, only to make
Notches for enemies. On northern ridges

Where flags fly, seen and lost, denying rumour
We baffle proof, speakers of a strange tongue.

[*The* SPY *groans. His cries are produced by jazz instruments at the back of the stage.* JOAN *brandishes her bottle.*]

JOAN. Be quiet, or I'll give you a taste of this.
X. Next, please.

[*Enter* PO.]

P. Past victory is honour, to accept
An island governorship, back to estates
Explored as child; coming at last to love
Lost publicly, found secretly again
In private flats, admitted to a sign.
An understanding sorrow knows no more,
Sits waiting for the lamp, far from those hills
Where rifts open unfenced, mark of a fall,
And flakes fall softly softly burying
Deeper and deeper down her loving son.

[*The* SPY *groans.* JOHN *produces a revolver.*]

J. Better to get it over.
JOAN. This way for the Angel of Peace.
X. Leave him alone. This fellow is very very ill. But he will get well.

[*The* MAN-WOMAN *appears as a prisoner of war behind barbed wire, in the snow.*]

MW. Because I'm come it does not mean to hold
An anniversary, think illness healed,
As to renew the lease, consider costs
Of derelict ironworks on deserted coasts.
Love was not love for you but episodes,
Traffic in memoirs, views from different sides;
You thought oaths of comparison a bond,
And though you had your orders to disband,
Refused to listen, but remained in woods
Poorly concealed your profits under wads.
Nothing was any use; therefore I went
Hearing you call for what you did not want.
I lay with you; you made that an excuse
For playing with yourself, but homesick because
Your mother told you that's what flowers did,

And thought you lived since you were bored, not dead,
And could not stop. So I was cold to make
No difference, but you were quickly meek
Altered for safety. I tried then to demand
Proud habits, protestations called your mind
To show you it was extra, but instead
You overworked yourself, misunderstood,
Adored me for the chance. Lastly I tried
To teach you acting, but always you had nerves
To fear performances as some fear knives.
Now I shall go. No, you, if you come,
Will not enjoy yourself, for where I am
All talking is forbidden . . .

[*The* SPY *groans*.]

J.   I can't bear it.

[*Shoots him. Lights out.*]

VOICES. Quick, fetch a doctor.
   Ten pounds for a doctor.
   Ten pounds to keep him away.
   Coming, coming.

[*Lights.* XMAS, JOHN *and the* SPY *remain. The Jury has gone, but there is a* PHOTOGRAPHER.]

X.   Stand back there. Here comes the doctor.

[*Enter* DOCTOR *and his* BOY.]

B.   Tickle your arse with a feather, sir.
D.   What's that?
B.   Particularly nasty weather, sir.
D.   Yes, it is. Tell me, is my hair tidy? One must always be careful with a new client.
B.   It's full of lice, sir.
D.   What's that?
B.   It's looking nice, sir. [*For the rest of the scene the* BOY *fools about.*]
X.   Are you the doctor?
D.   I am.
X.   What can you cure?
D.   Tennis elbow, Graves' Disease, Derbyshire neck and Housemaids' knees.

X. Is that all you can cure?
D. No, I have discovered the origin of life. Fourteen months I hesitated before I concluded this diagnosis. I received the morning star for this. My head will be left at death for clever medical analysis. The laugh will be gone and the microbe in command.
X. Well, let's see what you can do.

[DOCTOR *takes circular saws, bicycle pumps, etc., from his bag. He farts as he does so.*]

B. You need a pill, sir.
D. What's that.
B. You'll need your skill, sir. O sir you're hurting.

[BOY *is kicked out.*]
[JOHN *tries to get a look.*]

D. Go away. Your presence will be necessary at Scotland Yard when the criminals of the war are tried, but your evidence will not be needed. It is valueless. Cages will be provided for some of the more interesting specimens. [*Examines the body.*] Um, yes. Very interesting. The conscious brain appears normal except under emotion. Fancy it. The Devil couldn't do that. This advances and retreats under control and poisons everything round it. My diagnosis is; Adamant will, cool brain and laughing spirit. Hullo, what's this? [*Produces a large pair of pliers and extracts an enormous tooth from the body.*] Come along, that's better. Ladies and Gentlemen, you see I have nothing up my sleeve. This tooth was growing ninety-nine years before his great grandmother was born. If it hadn't been taken out to-day he would have died yesterday. You may get up now.

[*The* SPY *gets up. The* PHOTOGRAPHER *gets ready.*]

P. Just one minute, please. A little brighter, a little brighter. No, moisten the lips and start afresh. Hold it.

[PHOTOGRAPHER *lets off his flash. Lights out.* XMAS *blows a whistle.*]

X. All change.

[*Lights.* SPY *behind a gate guarded by* XMAS. *Enter* JOHN *running.*]

J. I'm late, I'm late. Which way is it? I must hurry.
X. You can't come in here without a pass.

[JOHN *turns back his coat lapel.*]

X. O I beg your pardon, sir. This way, sir.

[*Exit* XMAS. *The Accuser and Accused plant a tree.*]

JOHN. Sametime sharers of the same house
　　　We know not the builder nor the name of his son.
　　　Now cannot mean to them; boy's voice among dishonoured portraits
　　　To dockside barmaid speaking
　　　Sorry through wires, pretended speech.
SPY. Escaped
　　　Armies pursuit, rebellion and eclipse
　　　Together in a cart
　　　After all journeys
　　　We stay and are not known.

[*Lights out.*]

　　　Sharers of the same house
　　　Attendants on the same machine
　　　Rarely a word, in silence understood.

[*Lights.* JOHN *alone in his chair. Enter* DICK.]

D. Hullo. I've come to say good-bye.
　　　Yesterday we sat at table together
　　　Fought side by side at enemies' face to face meeting
　　　To-day we take our leave, time of departure.
　　　I'm sorry.
J. Here, give me your knife and take mine. By these
　　　We may remember each other.
　　　There are two chances, but more of one
　　　Parting for ever, not hearing the other
　　　Though he need help.
　　　Have you got everything you want?
D. Yes, thanks. Good-bye, John.
J. Good-bye.

[*Exit* DICK.]

　　　There is the city,
　　　Lighted and clean once, pleasure for builders
　　　And I
　　　Letting to cheaper tenants, have made a slum
　　　Houses at which the passer shakes his fist
　　　Remembering evil.
　　　Pride and Indifference have shared with me, and I

Have kissed them in the dark, for mind has dark,
Shaded commemorations, midnight accidents
In streets where heirs may dine.

But love, sent east for peace
From tunnels under those
Bursts now to pass
On trestles over meaner quarters
A noise and flashing glass.

Feels morning streaming down
Wind from the snows
Nowise withdrawn by doubting flinch
Nor joined to any by belief's firm flange
Refreshed sees all
The tugged-at teat
The hopper's steady feed, the frothing leat.

Zeppel.

[*Enter* ZEPPEL.]

Z. Sir.
J. Get my horse ready at once, please.

[*Exeunt.*]

CHORUS. To throw away the key and walk away
    Not abrupt exile, the neighbours asking why,
    But following a line with left and right
    An altered gradient at another rate
    Learns more than maps upon the whitewashed wall
    The hand put up to ask; and makes us well
    Without confession of the ill. All pasts
    Are single old past now, although some posts
    Are forwarded, held looking on a new view;
    The future shall fulfil a surer vow
    Not smiling at queen over the glass rim
    Nor making gunpowder in the top room,
    Not swooping at the surface still like gulls
    But with prolonged drowning shall develop gills.

    But there are still to tempt; areas not seen
    Because of blizzards or an erring sign
    Whose guessed-at wonders would be worth alleging,
    And lies about the cost of a night's lodging.

Travellers may meet at inns but not attach,
They sleep one night together, not asked to touch;
Receive no normal welcome, not the pressed lip,
Children to lift, not the assuaging lap.
Crossing the pass descend the growing stream
Too tired to hear except the pulse's strum,
Reach villages to ask for a bed in
Rock shutting out the sky, the old life done.

[CULLEY *enters right and squats in the centre of the stage, looking left through field glasses. Several shots are heard off. Enter* GEORGE *and* KURT.]

G. Are you much hurt?
K. Nothing much, sir. Only a slight flesh wound. Did you get him, sir?
G. On ledge above the gulley, aimed at, seen moving, fell; looked down on, sprawls in the stream.
K. Good. He sniped poor Billy last Easter, riding to Flash.
G. I have some lint and bandages in my haversack, and there is a spring here. I'll dress your arm.

[*Enter* SETH *and* BERNARD, *left.*]

S. Did you find Tom's body?
B. Yes, sir. It's lying in the Hangs.
S. Which way did they go?
B. Down there, sir.

[CULLEY *observes them and runs right.*]

C. There are twenty men from Nattrass, sir, over the gap, coming at once.
G. Have they seen us?
C. Not yet.
G. We must get out. You go down to the copse and make for the Barbon road. We'll follow the old tramway. Keep low and run like hell.

[*Exeunt right.* SETH *watches through field glasses.*]

S. Yes. No. No. Yes, I can see them. They are making for the Barbon road. Go down and cut them off. There is good cover by the bridge. We've got them now.

[*A whistle. The back curtains draw, showing* JOHN, ANNE *and* AARON *and the* ANNOUNCER *grouped. Both sides enter left and right.*]

Aa. There is a time for peace; too often we
   Have gone on cold marches, have taken life,
   Till wrongs are bred like flies; the dreamer wakes
   Who beats a smooth door, behind footsteps, on the left
   The pointed finger, the unendurable drum,
   To hear of horses stolen or a house burned.
   Now this shall end with marriage as it ought:
   Love turns the wind, brings up the salt smell,
   Shadow of gulls on the road to the sea.
Announcer. The engagement is announced of John Nower, eldest son of the late Mr and Mrs George Nower of Lintzgarth, Rookhope, and Anne Shaw, only daughter of the late Mr and Mrs Joseph Shaw of Nattrass, Garrigill.
All. Hurrah.

[George and Seth *advance to the centre, shake hands and cross over the stage to their opposite sides. Back curtains close. Exeunt in different directions, talking as they go.*]

G. It was a close shave that time. We had a lucky escape. How are you feeling?
K. The arm is rather painful. I owe Bernard one for that.
B. It's a shame. Just when we had them fixed.
S. Don't you worry. You'll get your chance.
B. But what about this peace?
S. That remains to be seen. Only wait.

[*Exeunt. Back curtains draw.* John *and* Anne *alone.* John *blows on a grass held between the thumbs and listens.*]

J. On Cautley where a peregrine has nested, iced heather hurt the knuckles. Fell on the ball near time, the forwards stopped. Good-bye now, he said, would open the swing doors. . . . These I remember, but not love till now. We cannot tell where we shall find it, though we all look for it till we do, and what others tell us is no use to us.

   Some say that handsome raider still at large,
   A terror to the Marches, in truth is love;
   And we must listen for such messengers
   To tell us daily "To-day a saint came blessing
   The huts." "Seen lately in the provinces
   Reading behind a tree and people passing."
   But love returns;

At once all heads are turned this way, and love
Calls order—silenced the angry sons—
Steps forward, greets, repeats what he has heard
And seen, feature for feature, word for word.

ANNE. Yes, I am glad this evening that we are together. The silence is unused, death seems
An axe's echo.

The summer quickens all,
Scatters its promises
To you and me no less
Though neither can compel

J. The wish to last the year,
The longest look to live,
The urgent word survive
The movement of the air.

A. But loving now let none
Think of divided days
When we shall choose from ways,
All of them evil, one.

J. Look on with stricter brows
The sacked and burning town,
The ice-sheet moving down,
The fall of an old house.

A. John, I have a car waiting. There is time to join Dick before the boat sails. We sleep in beds where men have died howling.

J. You may be right, but we shall stay.

A. To-night the many come to mind
Sent forward in the thaw with anxious marrow,
For such might now return with a bleak face,
An image pause half-lighted in the door,
A greater but not fortunate in all;
Come home deprived of an astonishing end . . .
Morgan's who took a clean death in the north
Shouting against the wind, or Cousin Dodds',
Passed out in her chair, the snow falling.
The too-loved clays, borne over by diverse drifts,
Fallen upon the far side of all enjoyment,
Unable to move closer, shall not speak

J. We live still.
A. But what has become of the dead? They forget.
J. These. Smilers, all who stand on promontories, slinkers, whisperers, deliberate approaches, echoes, time, promises of mercy, what dreams or goes masked, embraces that fail, insufficient evidence, touches of the old wound.
But let us not think of things which we hope will be long in coming.

CHORUS. The Spring will come,
   Not hesitate for one employer who
   Though a fine day and every pulley running
   Would quick lie down; nor save the wanted one
   That, wounded in escaping, swam the lake
   Safe to the reeds, collapsed in shallow water.

   You have tasted good and what is it? For you,
   Sick in the green plain, healed in the tundra, shall
   Turn westward back from your alone success,
   Under a dwindling Alp to see your friends
   Cut down the wheat.

J. It's getting cold, dear, let's go in.

[*Exeunt. Back curtains close.*]

CHORUS. For where are Basley who won the Ten,
   Dickon so tarted by the House,
   Thomas who kept a sparrow-hawk?

   The clock strikes, it is time to go,
   The tongue ashamed, deceived by a shake of the hand.

[*Enter Bridal Party left, guests right.*]

GUESTS. Ssh.

[*The* CHIEF GUEST *comes forward and presents a bouquet to the bride.*]

C.G. With gift in hand we come
   From every neighbour farm
   To celebrate in wine
   The certain union of
   A woman and a man;
   And may their double love

Be shown to the stranger's eye
   In a son's symmetry.
   Now hate is swallowed down,
   All anger put away;
   The spirit comes to its own,
   The beast to its play.

[*All clap. The* CHIEF GUEST *addresses the Audience.*]

   Will any lady be so kind as to oblige us with a dance? . . . Thank you very much . . . This way, miss . . . What tune would you like?

[*Gramophone. A dance. As the dance ends, the back curtains draw and the* BUTLER *enters centre.*]

BUTLER. Dinner is served.

[AARON *goes to the Dancer.*]

AA. You'll dine with us, of course?

[*Exeunt all except* SETH *and his* MOTHER.]

GUESTS [*as they go out*]. It will be a good year for them, I think.
   You don't mean that he . . . well, you know what.
   Rather off his form lately.
   The vein is showing good in the Quarry Hazel.
   One of Edward's friends.
   You must come and have a look at the Kennels some day.
   Well it does seem to show.
      [*Etc., etc.*]

[*Back curtains close.*]

MOTHER. Seth.
S. Yes, Mother.
M. John Nower is here.
S. I know that. What do you want me to do?
M. Kill him.
S. I can't do that. There is peace now; besides he is a guest in our house.
M. Have you forgotten your brother's death . . . taken out and shot like a dog? It is a nice thing for me to hear people saying that I have a coward for a son. I am thankful your father is not here to see it.
S. I'm not afraid of anything or anybody, but I don't want to.
M. I shall have to take steps.

S. It shall be as you like. Though I think that much will come of this, chiefly harm.
M. I have thought of that. [*Exit.*]
S. The little funk. Sunlight on sparkling water, its shades dissolved, reforming, unreal activity where others laughed but he blubbed clinging, homesick, an undeveloped form. I'll do it. Men point in after days. He always was. But wrongly. He fought and overcame, a stern self-ruler. You didn't hear. Hearing they look ashamed too late for shaking hands. Of course I'll do it. [*Exit.*]

[*A shot. More shots. Shouting.*]

VOICES OUTSIDE. A trap. I might have known.
    Take that, damn you.
    Open the window.
    You swine.
    Jimmy, O my God.

[*Enter* SETH *and* BERNARD.]

B. The Master's killed. So is John Nower, but some of them got away, fetching help, will attack in an hour.
S. See that all the doors are bolted.

[*Exeunt right and left. The back curtains draw.* ANNE *with the dead.*]

ANNE. Now we have seen the story to its end.
    The hands that were to help will not be lifted,
    And bad followed by worse leaves to us tears,
    An empty bed, hope from less noble men.
    I had seen joy
    Received and given, upon both sides, for years.
    Now not.

CHORUS. Though he believe it, no man is strong.
    He thinks to be called the fortunate,
    To bring home a wife, to live long.

    But he is defeated; let the son
    Sell the farm lest the mountain fall:
    His mother and her mother won.

    His fields are used up where the moles visit,
    The contours worn flat; if there show
    Passage for water he will miss it:

Give up his breath, his woman, his team;
No life to touch, though later there be
Big fruit, eagles above the stream.

CURTAIN

The Enemies of a Bishop

or

Die When I Say When

A Morality in Four Acts

BY W. H. AUDEN AND
CHRISTOPHER ISHERWOOD

[*1929*]

TO
OTTO KÜSEL AND BERTHOLD SZCZESNY

CHARACTERS

The Spectre
Robert Bicknell
Augustus Bicknell *
George *
Jimmy
Maximilian Luder
Ceslaus Luder **
Bishop Law **
Katherine Law

Miss Ethel Wright
Colonel Tearer
Warder Bunyan
Porter of the Nineveh
  Hotel
{ The Flying Squad
{ Two Local Policemen
Boys at Templin
  Reformatory

* and ** *These parts may be doubled.*

PROLOGUE

[To be spoken by the Bishop]

Will you turn a deaf ear
To what they said on the shore,
Interrogate their poises
In their rich houses?

Of stork-legged heaven-reachers,
Of the compulsory touchers,
The sensitive amusers
And masked amazers.

Yet wear no ruffian badge
Nor lie behind the hedge,
Waiting with bombs of conspiracy
In arm-pit secrecy.

Carry no talisman
For germ or the abrupt pain,
Needing no concrete shelter
Nor porcelain filter.

Will you wheel death anywhere
In his invalid chair
With no affectionate instant
But his attendant?

For to be held as a friend
By an undeveloped mind,
To be joke for children is
Death's happiness.

Whose anecdotes betray
His favourite colour as blue,
Colour of distant bells
And boys' overalls.

His tales of the bad lands
Disturb the sewing hands;
Hard to be superior
On parting nausea.

To accept the cushions from
Women against martyrdom,

Yet applauding the circuits
Of racing cyclists.

Never to make signs,
Fear neither maelstrom nor zones,
Salute with soldiers' wives
When the flag waves.

Remembering there is
No recognized gift for this,
No income, no bounty,
No promised country.

But to see brave sent home
Hermetically sealed with shame
And cold's victorious wrestle
With molten metal.

A neutralising peace
And an average disgrace
Are honour to discover
For later other.

Act I Scene 1

[ROBERT BICKNELL's *flat in Town.* THE SPECTRE *is sitting in an armchair with his feet on the mantelpiece. He puffs a large cigar and reads a letter. He is in full evening dress, with an opera hat on the back of his head. He wears a black silk half-mask. There is a wireless loud speaker on the table.*]

WIRELESS. Hullo kiddies. Just back from the City, are you? Isn't home lovesome? Hmpsch! Hmpsch! That's Tootie and Babs sending you a kiss.
TOOTIE. I say, Babs, what shall we play?
BABS. Let's have the servants up and play families.
TOOTIE. I think that's perfectly scrumptious, don't you?
BABS. Well, ring the bell, Tootie.
JAMES. You rang, sir.
TOOTIE. Fetch Maud and come and play with us.
JAMES. Very good, sir.
TOOTIE. I'll take off my collar.
BABS. You'll find your sailor suit in the drawer.
TOOTIE. Mm! Num! Num!

JAMES AND MAUD. You wanted us, sir.
BABS. Hullo, Daddy. Give Babs a kiss.
JAMES. Really, madam . . .
BABS. James, you're not playing pwoperly.
TOOTIE. I'se hungry. Mummie give Tootie suck-suck.
MAUD. Really, sir . . .
TOOTIE. Maud not playing pwoperly. Tootie give Maud the sack.
BABS. Babs want to play Doctors with Tootie.
TOOTIE. All right, James. You and Maud can go.
JAMES. Thank you, sir.
TOOTIE. Tootie play too. Tootie bwing Babs a dear ickle . . .
SPECTRE. Now then. That's enough. [*The wireless immediately stops.* THE SPECTRE *goes on reading.*]

[*Enter* ROBERT BICKNELL.]

ROBERT. Well!
SPECTRE. Well.
ROBERT. Well? How's everything?
SPECTRE. Exactly as you left it.
ROBERT. Splendid!
SPECTRE. I see you've been enjoying yourself.
ROBERT. Enjoying myself! That's a funny way of putting it. Why, man, after all those weeks, I've succeeded at last! I can scarcely believe it.
SPECTRE. Well, come on. Tell me the whole story. We shall have to have it sooner or later, I suppose.
ROBERT. You'd really like to hear?
SPECTRE [*yawning*]. Yes, yes, of course.
ROBERT. I told you about my enquiries, didn't I? How I discovered that they had a house in the marshes, with only one approach, along the causeway with two drawbridges. The father is a homicidal maniac, who spends the day at the sitting-room window with a machine gun. And the whole place is surrounded with electrified barbed wire. I told you all that?
SPECTRE. Often.
ROBERT. Well, yesterday night seemed ideal for me. The servants were all away at a dance in the village, except the negro eunuch. I reckoned I'd a clear three hours. It was black as pitch. I've got everything ready in the car, my rubber overalls, an electric torch fixed to my cap, for swimming, and the climbing irons and burglar's tools. I had a fairly decent aerial photograph, too; but I wasn't taking any chances, so I'd brought a bag of gelatine and an exploder, in case the wall was thicker than it looked.

SPECTRE. Always thoughtful.
ROBERT. However, as it happened, everything went like clockwork. The inner wall was rather a problem. I as near as anything bust my neck. There was a light in her room. I knew from enquiries that her brother would be downstairs in the cellar kissing his wife's coffin. So the coast was clear. I did a standing jump from the roof on to her balcony, forced the catch of the window, and there she was. I got away quite easily, too. Just made a dash for it. The motor boat was waiting. They put a bullet through my cuff. Look!
SPECTRE. And what did you say to her when you saw her?
ROBERT. Say? Oh—I forget exactly. I couldn't stay long.
SPECTRE. You were too busy kissing?
ROBERT. Kissing? Good God, no! There was no time for that.
SPECTRE. By the way, what's she like? What coloured hair and eyes?
ROBERT. Do you know, it's funny you should ask, because I haven't the least idea.

SPECTRE.   Love by ambition
    Of definition
    Suffers partition,
    And cannot go
    From yes to no,
    For no is not love, no is no.
    The shutting of a door,
    The tightening jaw,
    A conscious sorrow
    And saying yes
    Turns love into success
    Views from the rail
    Of land and happiness.
    Assured of all
    The sofa's creak,
    And were this all, love were
    But cheek to cheek
    And dear to dear.

    Voices explain
    Love's pleasure and love's pain
    Still tap the knee
    And cannot disagree.
    Hushed for aggression
    Of full confession

Likeness to likeness
Of each old weakness.
Love is not there,
Love has moved to another chair,
Aware already
Of what stands next
And is not vexed
And is not giddy
Leaves the North in place
With a good grace,
And would not gather
Another to another,
Designs his own unhappiness,
Foretells his own death and is faithless.

ROBERT. Well, I'm afraid all that's a bit above my head. But let me tell you, it's very easy to sneer at what you aren't capable of feeling for yourself.

SPECTRE. Quite. Too true. [*Showing letter.*] By the way, I suppose this will hardly interest you. It came while you were away.

ROBERT. Let's hear.

SPECTRE. The Old Mountain Lead Company want you to go as Manager to their mine at Stunhead. You can name your own salary. The last man died of the horrors.

ROBERT [*taking letter*]. Let me look. [*He begins pacing the room.*] By Jove, you know, I've a good mind to accept this. Yes, by God, I will. It's just what I've been wanting. One gets soft in this town. And, after all, a man's work does come first. If one isn't careful, love becomes a destroyer. You said that yourself.

SPECTRE. Liar!

ROBERT. By Jove, yes. The Old Mountain Lead Company. I heard something about them only last week, at the Club. They're nearly on their last legs. But I'll pull them round. By George, it's just the sort of job I like. An uphill fight.

SPECTRE. If that's what you want, you shall have it.

ROBERT. Stunhead. That's right up in the Sheared Flysch Range. God's own country. We shall be up against things in the winter. One feels free on those fells. And clean. Not like this dirty town life.

SPECTRE. About a mile away from the mine is one of the biggest hotels in the British Isles.

ROBERT. And that reminds me of something else. Isn't Templin Reformatory somewhere in those parts? God, yes. I must look up old Gus.

SPECTRE. Your brother?
ROBERT. Yes. Why, I haven't seen him for nearly fifteen years. And now he's head of Templin. I hear he treats the boys like dirt. Never mind, I should like to see the old buffer again. Damned if I don't wire to him now. He might come over for a week-end to see me. And of course I must let the Company know.
SPECTRE. You needn't. I've done that.
ROBERT. Do you mean you accepted? In my name?
SPECTRE. Yes. Wasn't I right?
ROBERT. You've got a nerve, haven't you? Well, as it happens, you were. But I won't stand much more of this sort of thing, see? Anyone'd think I hadn't a mind of my own.
SPECTRE. Shall I send the telegram to your brother while you pack?
ROBERT. No. I don't trust you.
SPECTRE. You're not such a fool as I took you for.
ROBERT. For heaven's sake, behave yourself until I come back. [*Exit.*]

SPECTRE.   Watch any day his nonchalant pauses, see
           His dexterous handling of a wrap as he
           Steps after into cars—the beggars' envy.

   "There is a free one", many say, but err:
   He is not that returning conqueror,
   Nor ever the Pole's circumnavigator.

   But, poised between shocking falls on razor edge
   Has taught himself this balancing subterfuge
   Of the accosting profile, the erect carriage.

   The song, the varied movement of the blood
   Would drown the warning from the iron wood,
   Would cancel the inertia of the buried.

   Travelling by daylight on from house to house
   The longest way to the intrinsic peace
   With love's fidelity and with love's weakness.

CURTAIN

Act I Scene 2

[*Templin Reformatory. A bare room with a barred window and a table and benches. Doors left and right. A door at the back opens into a yard. Enter* WARDER BUNYAN *from the yard, with* GEORGE *and* JIMMY, *boys of about sixteen, wearing flash East End suits and check caps.*]

GEORGE. Nah, then, cheese it Guv'nor—who in hell d'yer think yer pushin'?

BUNYAN. That's all right, sonny. I'm not pushing nothing I don't know of.

GEORGE. Thinks yer bleedin' funny, don't yer?

BUNYAN. Don't think. I knows.

GEORGE. Jest yer wyte till I hinforms me pal the Prince o' Wyles wot yer bin an' done ter us.

JIMMY. Aw, cheese it, George. Wot's the bleedin' use? We copped it this time.

GEORGE. Copped it my arse. Yer wyte till I tells me pal the Prince o' Wyles—

BUNYAN. That's all right, sonny. 'E's been a pal to 'undreds 'ere, but I never see 'im 'elp any on 'em out.

[*A steamer siren blows, off. Enter a crowd of boys in broad-arrow suits, from the yard, with tin mugs. They sit down at the table and begin banging and shouting.*]

BOYS. Soup! We wants our soup! We wants our bleedin' soup!

BUNYAN. All right, yer lordships. All right. All right. [*Exit.*]

A BOY [*to* GEORGE]. Wot's yer nyme?

GEORGE. The Right Honorrible Stanley Baldwin. M.P. A.R.S.E.

ANOTHER BOY. Coo, Christ! Aint they toffs?

ANOTHER BOY [*snatching off* GEORGE's *cap and putting it on rakishly*]. Ow, chyse me!

[GEORGE *snatches it back and knocks the boy down.*]

Yer wyte, yer bleedin' barstard!

ANOTHER BOY. Wot sy, boys? Let's give 'im wot the curate gyve the choir-boy.

SEVERAL. Not 'arf. Git the poker, one of yer. [*They hold* GEORGE *and* JIMMY.]

A BOY. Stow it. 'Ere's Uncle.

[*Enter* BUNYAN *with a bucket.*]

BOYS. We wants our soup! [*They scramble for the soup.*] 'Ere, this ain't soup. 'O's misbehyved hisself? Shyme!
BUNYAN. It's all you'll git. Pore little bleeders. [*Exit.*]
A BOY [*smelling his soup*]. Cor, don't it whistle?
ANOTHER BOY [*jumping on to the table and holding up a bootlace*]. Dees ces zoo mooch. Gomrades, 'ow long shall we deese oppressions endure? Are we to be treated like the hoonds?
ALL. Nah!!
A BOY. We've 'ad enough.
ANOTHER BOY. Joostice!
THE BOY ON THE TABLE. We demand der free air. Der zunlicht.
ANOTHER BOY. Good ole Fritz!
ANOTHER BOY. Three cheers fer Fritz!
ALL. Ip, ip, Oory! Oory! Oory!
A BOY AT THE DOOR. 'Ere comes 'is nibs.

> [*General stampede for the door to the yard.* JIMMY *is knocked down by the rush and finds himself alone in the room, as* AUGUSTUS BICKNELL *and* BUNYAN *enter.*]

AUGUSTUS. It's risky my going away just now, with the Inspector coming tomorrow.
BUNYAN. Don't you worry, sir. 'E'll never notice nothing. 'E's near stone blind, pore old gentleman.
AUGUSTUS. Well, mind you put the wax fruit on the table at lunch. Have you got your lessons ready?
BUNYAN. They been doing that there sum every day a month come Tuesday. They should know it.
AUGUSTUS. Good. [*Seeing* JIMMY.] Who's that?
BUNYAN. Come in this evening, sir. With another.
AUGUSTUS. Hm! What's he here for?
BUNYAN. Cigarette machines and loitering with intent, sir.
AUGUSTUS. And the usual, I suppose?
BUNYAN. Yes, sir.
AUGUSTUS. Oh, by the way, you might fetch me those testimonials. You'll find them on my desk.
BUNYAN. Yessir. [*Exit.*]
AUGUSTUS. Come here. [JIMMY *comes forward.*] What's your name?
JIMMY. Jymes Halbert 'Enery Platt.
AUGUSTUS. Say Sir when you're speaking to me.
JIMMY. Sir.

AUGUSTUS. And take off your cap. [JIMMY *does so.*] Now listen to me, Platt. I say this to every boy who comes to Templin. This is not a prison. It's a Home. You understand?

JIMMY. Yes.

AUGUSTUS. Yes, sir.

JIMMY. Sir.

AUGUSTUS. I've been governor of this place now for ten years. And all the time I've been drilling into you boys' heads that this is a Home. Boys come here determined to regard this place as a Prison. I'm determined that they shall regard it as a Home. Very well. It's my will against theirs. And you'll find that I invariably win.

JIMMY. Yes, sir.

AUGUSTUS. I divide the boys who come here into two sorts, the rotters and the slackers. The rotters I break and the slackers I put the fear of God into. Now which sort are you?

JIMMY. Dunno, sir.

AUGUSTUS. Well, we'll soon find out. And when we've found out, we can start work. I wish you could see yourself as you'll be in a month from now. Your own mother wouldn't recognise you. But get this clear right at the start. This is a Home. Whatever you make of yourself here, you'll make by self-discipline and self-control. The Templin code will help you build up both. If you need a hiding for the good of your soul, we'll give it you. If you need to put a curb on your beastly physical appetites—all you boys are as greedy as hogs—we'll keep you on dog biscuit for a month. Now do you quite understand?

JIMMY. Yes, sir.

[*Enter* BUNYAN *with papers.*]

BUNYAN. 'Ere they are, sir.

AUGUSTUS. Good. [*To* JIMMY.] You can go. [*Exit* JIMMY.] Yes, these are right. "Tommy was apprenticed to a gang of diamond thieves and drove his own car. Now he's earning ten shillings a week crossing-sweeping. How can we ever thank you?" Show the Inspector that one.

BUNYAN. Yessir.

AUGUSTUS. Shoot any boy you find in the cook's bedroom. I'm determined to put a stop to that sort of thing.

BUNYAN. Yessir.

AUGUSTUS. Then that's everything. Good. Well, I'm only staying the week-end. I shall be back without fail on Tuesday. You've got the keys?

BUNYAN. Yes, sir. [*Exit* AUGUSTUS.] Three into four thousand, eight 'undred and sixty-nine goes—blessed if I haven't forgotten already. 'Ere, let's 'ave a look. Where's my pencil?

> [*The siren blows, off. All the boys, including* GEORGE *and* JIMMY, *enter from the yard and crowd across stage, going out, right.*]

BUNYAN [*to* GEORGE *and* JIMMY]. 'Ere, you two. You'll 'ave to sleep in the office tonight. There isn't room in there. I'll go and get some blankets. [*Exit.*]
GEORGE. See 'ere, Jimmy. This is our chance. Ter-night we'll 'op it. Yer gyme?
JIMMY. Bet yer life.
GEORGE. We'll 'ave ter git a disguise, like, when we're aht. I reckon we can pinch some duds at the stytion. [*As* BUNYAN *returns with blankets.*] Luvverly night, ain't it? I don't think.
BUNYAN. Now then, sonny. You cut along. Know the way, don't you?
GEORGE. 'Appy dreams. An' I 'opes they're dry.

> [*Exeunt, left.*]

BUNYAN. Three into four thousand, eight 'undred—
VOICE [*off, right*]. Uncle, ain't yer comin' ter kiss us good-night?
ANOTHER VOICE. Hi, Uncle, want a spot o' brown?
BUNYAN. Lights out in five minutes. And then we'll 'ave complete silence. [*Exit.*]

> [*Various noises off. Then the boys begin to sing. Enter* GEORGE *and* JIMMY, *left, stealthily. They cross the stage and exit by the door into the yard.*]

THE BOYS [*singing off*].

> Do yer want ter see me agyne?
> Then come ter the stytion before the tryne.
> In the gen'ral waitin' 'all
> We'll see each other fer the last time of all.

CURTAIN

Act I Scene 3

[*The lounge of the Nineveh Hotel, Stunhead. The atmosphere is Mediterranean. At back of the stage is a gilded staircase. A large window reveals the heads of palms and the brilliant blue water of a lake.* COLONEL TEARER *and* MAXIMILIAN *and* CESLAUS LUDER *are sitting smoking.* TEARER *wears an eyeglass and white spats.* MAXIMILIAN *is dressed like a Bank Manager and* CESLAUS *as a parson.*]

TEARER. Oh, it's such a delightful place, don't you know. I found it so extraordinarily amusin'. My gweat fwend, Lady Starkey— [*Glancing out through a doorway, left.*] Excuse me a moment, won't you?

MAX. Certainly. [*Exit* TEARER.] He's seen that lift-boy again.

CESLAUS. How sordid! Max, I'm afraid this place is going to be just like all the others. No poise.

MAX. We shall have to make the best of it now we're here. We can't afford to move again till we've done some business.

CESLAUS [*sighing*]. No, I suppose not. Certainly, this is the worst year we've had since 1911.

MAX. I got a cable from Rio this morning. The last consignment was beginning to go bad when it arrived. That's the second in six months. We shall have to dismiss our Cardiff agent.

CESLAUS. I expect he was responsible for that wooden leg being overlooked in the Buenos Aires cargo. I can't imagine how anyone could be so careless.

MAX. It makes any customer lose confidence in the firm. That's why it's essential we should select the next lot personally.

CESLAUS. Are you sure you've remembered everything? The chloroform?

MAX. Yes.

CESLAUS. And the sacks?

MAX. Yes.

CESLAUS. And the hypodermic syringe?

MAX. Yes. It's sewed inside my cuff. Here.

CESLAUS [*fingering his collar*]. I wish to God I hadn't dressed up like this. If I'd known your friend the Bishop was staying here, I shouldn't have been such a fool. I know I shall get caught out—

MAX. Well, you ought to have all that stuff by heart by this time. You've done it often enough.

CESLAUS. I must sweat up this new prayer-book. I bought a copy on the bookstall at Euston.

MAX. By the way, I forgot to tell you. There's one possible I saw yesterday. Mrs Stagg—the wife of the under-manager at Windyacre Mine.

We might do worse. [*The* PORTER *crosses the stage.*] Vegery gegoegod begust.

CESLAUS. Tegight cegunt?

MAX. I should think so. Her mouth's small enough, anyhow.

CESLAUS. Well, let's go out for a drive now and see what we can see. You've got the field-glasses, I hope?

MAX. Yes, they're in the car.

CESLAUS. Here's that awful woman.

[*On their way out, they meet* MISS ETHEL WRIGHT *and* MRS LAW. ETHEL *wears a blouse and tie.* KATHERINE LAW *is feminine and water-coloured.*]

MAX. Good morning, Mrs Law. Good morning, Miss Wright.

ETHEL. Good morning, Mr Luder. Are you going fishing?

MAX. Yes.

[*They go out.*]

KATHERINE. My dear, how lucky we are to have this wonderful hot weather, especially while there've been such fearful storms in the mountains. It's doing the Bishop such a lot of good. He's beginning to look quite brown already.

ETHEL. I can't help it. I take sun-baths every day after lunch, but it makes absolutely no impression. Of course, I know it's some impurity of heart, but I can't find it out. I went through all Mother's letters to Father during her pregnancy, looking for expressions of a death-wish. But she must have been too repressed to put them down. By the by, you ought to stop your husband smoking. You know what that means?

KATHERINE. I think so—

ETHEL. Now, Kath, you're not telling the truth. You know you've forgotten. What does it? Be frank.

KATHERINE. Well, isn't it—?

ETHEL. You *have* forgotten! But it's no good telling you now, as I see you have a resistance about it. Shall we go out on the lake?

KATHERINE. I should love to. [*As they are walking across the lounge, she trips slightly.*]

ETHEL [*taking off her hat and coat*]. That's very interesting. All right, my dear. I don't mind in the least.

KATHERINE. What is it, Ethel? Aren't you coming?

ETHEL. You don't want to.

KATHERINE. But I do. I was so looking forward to it.

ETHEL. I'm not in the least offended. You tripped over that mat. You wouldn't have done that if your unconscious mind had wanted to go out. It would be very unsafe to go now.

KATHERINE. But Ethel—

[*Enter* BISHOP LAW.]

ETHEL. Here's your husband. You run along with him for a bit. You would quarrel with me if we stayed together this morning. Good morning, Bishop. Katherine's been looking for you.

LAW. Good morning, Miss Wright. Still talking over old schooldays? I thought, my dear, we might go on the lake this morning. I hear the fishing is excellent. Are you coming, Miss Wright?

ETHEL. No. I've got my notes to write up. Au revoir. I hope you'll have a nice time.

[*Exeunt* BISHOP *and* KATHERINE.]

ETHEL. Porter.

[*The* PORTER *enters.*]

What day did the Bishop arrive?

PORTER. Tuesday, Miss.

ETHEL. Has he a car?

PORTER. Yes, Miss.

ETHEL. What make is it?

PORTER. Really, Miss—I— [ETHEL *lifts her tie, showing a police badge.*] I beg your pardon, Miss. I didn't know you was one of them. What is it?

ETHEL. I can't tell you, but it's very serious. What's the make of the car?

PORTER. A Daimler, I think.

ETHEL. Thank you. That will be all for the present. Keep an eye on his letters, please. If any come marked with a foreign stamp, let me know. I want to communicate now with Scotland Yard. Put it through yourself. And, remember, not a word to anyone, or—

PORTER. You can trust me, Miss.

CURTAIN

Act II Scene 1

[ROBERT's *hut at Windyacre Mine, Stunhead. A Canadian movie log shack with skins, a carbine and snow shoes on the walls. A wireless loud speaker on the table and a telephone. In one corner is a huge packing-case labelled:* Flowers. With great care.]

ROBERT [*at the telephone*]. Is that you, Mr Stagg? Yes, Bicknell speaking. I've ordered two magnetic separators to be sent from Town on trial to see if they can deal with the pyrites in the blende. The dressing plant is a disgrace. No proper sizing. I'm glad you think so. No, but look at the great chunks of rock and boltheads we get fed to the rollers. One might just as well— [*A loud banging from inside the packing-case.*] Be quiet, can't you? No [*laughing*], I beg your pardon, Mr Stagg, I wasn't speaking to you. It's a stray dog I've got in here. Will keep barking. What was I saying? Our water-wheel must have been made in the year one—and we've enough power to electrify the State Railways. I don't like to think about our loss in tailings. No. As soon as we get the plant into shape I'm going to start working over the dumps at Rodderup. Yes. Good-bye. See you in an hour.

VOICE FROM THE CASE [*beginning to sing*]. ". . . be it ev-er so 'umble—"

ROBERT. Oh, all right. I suppose I can't keep you in there for ever. More's the pity.

[*He picks up a hammer and prises open the lid of the case.* THE SPECTRE *steps out, popping his opera hat.*]

SPECTRE. Thanks. I had an idea, somehow, that you'd let me out to-day.

ROBERT. Indeed? And why, may I ask?

SPECTRE. I fancy that having me in there was beginning to get on your nerves. Admit that, once or twice, when I'd kept quite quiet for two or three hours on end, you suddenly had a moment of panic that the box was really empty.

ROBERT. Panic? I like that! A moment of hope, you mean.

SPECTRE. Panic and hope, then.

ROBERT. After your behaviour on the journey, you deserve to have stayed in that case for the rest of my life. Are you aware that at Euston you broke a porter's wrist?

SPECTRE. Yes, and deliberately. You were feeling annoyed with him because he was surly and didn't say "thank you" for your tip.

ROBERT. I'm still in correspondence with the Company about compensation. They want £100. That doesn't include those crates of eggs you smashed in the van.

SPECTRE. Well, well. Don't let's keep harping on it. How are you getting along here?
ROBERT. Not too badly. By Jove, it's hard work—but I like it. I'm reorganising the whole outfit from top to bottom. Stagg, my under-manager, isn't a bad sort, but he's conservative, too cautious. I have to keep pushing him forward the whole time.
SPECTRE. And Mrs Stagg? Seen her lately?
ROBERT. Stagg's wife? No. Why? What the hell are you driving at?
SPECTRE. That time she brought you some flowers for your desk.
ROBERT. She's got a kid of six months. She nurses it nearly all day.
SPECTRE. That time you lent her your great-coat because it came on to snow.
ROBERT. She goes to chapel regularly every Sunday.
SPECTRE. That time you stood together at the window and you asked her the names of the different fells.
ROBERT. Do you think I'm an utter bounder? What about Stagg? He's a dry stick, it's true, and I'm sorry for her, but—Good God—
SPECTRE. You stood quite close, and twice your hand brushed against hers.
ROBERT. I never gave a sign. Neither did she.

SPECTRE.   Sentries against inner and outer
             At stated intervals is feature.
             And how shall enemy on these
             Make sudden raid or lasting peace?
             For bribery were vain to try
             Upon the incorruptible eye
             Too amply paid with tears; the chin
             Has hairs to hide its weakness in,
             And proud bridge and indignant nostril
             Nothing to do but look noble.
             Yet in between these lies the mouth;
             Watch that; that you may parley with;
             There strategy comes easiest
             Though it seem stern, was seen compressed,
             Over a lathe, refusing answer:
             It will release the ill-fed prisoner,
             It will do murder or betray
             For either party equally;
             Yielding at last to a close kiss
             It will admit tongue's soft advance,
             So longed for, given in abandon,
             Given long since had it but known.

ROBERT. Don't be beastly.
SPECTRE. Suppose, for instance, you were to see her now.
ROBERT. She's at home, doing the washing.
SPECTRE. Well, let's imagine that she's yielded to the impulse, put on her shawl, stepped out at the back door, taken the path which leads up to the mine.
ROBERT. Don't be a fool.
SPECTRE. It isn't far. It wouldn't take her long.
ROBERT. By Jove—if I thought she—
SPECTRE. Let's suppose that she's standing outside the door now, hesitating whether to knock—
ROBERT. But she isn't.
SPECTRE. She raises her hand, takes a step forward—then changes her mind, turns away.
ROBERT. Stop this comic stuff. It's getting on my nerves.
SPECTRE. She walks a few paces. Stops. Takes another step. Stops. Turns round suddenly, runs up to the door, and— [*He raps sharply on the table with a ruler.*]
ROBERT [*starting violently*]. Curse you, don't do that!
SPECTRE. Come in, Mrs Stagg.

> [*He goes to the door, opens it, goes out for a moment and returns pushing before him a beautiful milliner's wax figure of a woman, on a little pedestal on wheels. The dummy is dressed in a simple dove-grey frock with a white collar and cuffs. There is a girdle of barbed wire, round the dummy's hips.*]

ROBERT. Julia!
SPECTRE [*standing just behind the dummy and speaking falsetto*]. I—I don't know whatever made me come here, Mr Bicknell. I didn't know you'd be busy—
ROBERT. I'm not busy. Do stay a moment. Please.
SPECTRE [*falsetto*]. I don't know whether I ought to—
ROBERT. Ought? What does ought matter? If you care to stay— [*Taking the dummy's hand.*] Forgive me—I don't know what I'm saying. All the morning, all yesterday, I've been hoping that perhaps I might see you. Do you mind my telling you this—?
SPECTRE [*falsetto*]. Oh, Mr Bicknell—
ROBERT. Robert.
SPECTRE [*falsetto*]. Oh, Robert—
ROBERT. What, Julia?
SPECTRE [*falsetto*]. Oh, I don't know—

ROBERT. Julia, I'm a beast to say this, but if ever you should need anything, any help, anyone to—oh, I don't know how to tell you. [*Kneeling down and kissing the dummy's hand.*] You know I'd do anything on earth to save you an instant's pain—
SPECTRE [*falsetto*]. It's very kind of you, Mr Bicknell—
ROBERT. Robert.
SPECTRE [*falsetto*]. Robert, but—
ROBERT. But what?
SPECTRE [*falsetto*]. Oh, I don't know—
ROBERT. My dear. [*He kisses the dummy's foot.*] Say you care for me a little—
SPECTRE [*falsetto*]. Oh, I don't know. I'm not sure—I think I'd better be going home—
ROBERT. I shall see you again? Soon?
SPECTRE [*falsetto*]. Perhaps. Oh, I'm not sure. I don't know—
ROBERT [*kissing the dummy's wheels*]. My darling.

> [*He rises to his feet.* THE SPECTRE *wheels out the dummy and returns. The telephone bell rings.* ROBERT *collects himself and goes to answer it.*]

ROBERT [*at the telephone*]. Hullo. Yes, Bicknell speaking. Is that you, Stagg? Yes. A new vein? What! How big? Good God! Four feet from cheek to cheek—but, man, it'll be the making of the mine—yes, I'll come at once— [*To* THE SPECTRE.] A new vein! Do you realise? Our fortune's probably made! Do you hear! Send down to the hotel for some champagne. [*Taking* THE SPECTRE'*s hands.*] How can I ever thank you? This is all your doing. My dear old boy! [*He begins waltzing* THE SPECTRE *round and round.*] But for all your encouragement—I'll never forget it—Never—

CURTAIN

Act II Scene 2

[*The Nineveh Hotel.* COLONEL TEARER *sitting reading. Enter* GEORGE *and* JIMMY *with suitcases.* GEORGE *wears plus fours which are a little too big for him.* JIMMY *is dressed as a woman, in smart tweeds, with a beret.* TEARER *watches them.*]

JIMMY. Coo, Christ, George, let's 'op it. This plyce is fer toffs. Let's go back ter the Bunch o' Grypes.
GEORGE. Shut yer fyce. Leave it all ter me. [*To* TEARER.] Beg pardon,

mister. Do yer 'appen ter know if they got a couple o' rooms 'andy wot they can let us 'ave?

TEARER. You'd better ask at the office. Wait a minute, I'll wing for the porter. [*He presses the bell.*] Extwordinary how they inwariably keep one waitin'. They're most fwightfully careless here, don't you know.

GEORGE. Jest wot I sez to me sister as we come in.

TEARER. Shall you be stayin' here long? The countwy wound here is weally quite charmin'.

GEORGE. Well, we'ad thought o' goin' on ter Blackpool, reely. I ain't never bin.

TEARER. Oh, you'd far better stay here. I'm sure we can find somethin' much more amusin' for you, what? [*He pokes* GEORGE *in the ribs.*] Somethin' extwordinarily amusin'. [*Enter the* PORTER.] Porter, you've been neglectin' your duty, don't you know. This gentleman and his sister want wooms. You'll see that they're given nice ones, won't you? He's a gweat fwend of mine.

PORTER. Yessir. Certainly, sir. [*To* GEORGE.] Will you come this way, please, sir?

TEARER. I shall see you later, I hope?

GEORGE [*winking*]. You bet.

[GEORGE, JIMMY *and the* PORTER *go out, left.* TEARER *goes up the staircase. Re-enter* GEORGE *and* JIMMY *with the* PORTER.]

PORTER. Your rooms'll be ready in a few moments, sir. Would you care to wait 'ere or in the smoking room?

GEORGE. That's orl right. We'll wyte 'ere. [*Gives* PORTER *a couple of £1 notes.*]

PORTER. Thank you very much, sir. [*He retires to the doorway.*]

GEORGE. Col'nel Tearer. Thought I knew 'is fyce. 'E used to be one o' the crahd at the Cosy Corner, didn't 'e? Proper ole terror 'e is? Reckon we're in luck, Jim.

JIMMY. Curse these 'ere knickers. 'Ope ter Christ the blokes wot these duds belong to ain't stoppin' 'ere. We'd get quod next packet. 'Ow do I look, George?

GEORGE. Not so dusty. Yer want some doins, though. Wait till I pinch a couple o' saucers.

[*Enter* AUGUSTUS *and* ROBERT, *followed by* THE SPECTRE, *who strolls about the stage with his hands in his pockets.*]

JIMMY. Christ, if it isn't the ole bleeder from Templin. Lor lummy—we're for it this time. 'E'll know me, sure as Fyte.
GEORGE. Nah, 'e won't. Not 'im. Not if yer don't stand starin' there like a ruptured duck. 'Ave a fag.
AUGUSTUS. It's uphill work. I do all I can for the boys, but they're so unresponsive. Deceitful. What can you expect, with the sort of homes most of them come from? I've had to install microphones in the dormitories. Only to-day, I get a wire to say that two of them have bolted. Now that'll mean that I shall have to go back tomorrow. My staff are much too lenient. After anything of this kind the only possible course is to put the whole lot on bread and water for a month. Or the morale goes to pieces.
ROBERT. I'm sorry you can't stay, because I'd have liked to show you this new vein. I feel I want everyone to see it—
AUGUSTUS [*preoccupied, having noticed* JIMMY]. Yes, yes. I'm sorry, too. Porter.
PORTER. Yes, sir.
AUGUSTUS. Who are that lady and gentleman over there? I'm not sure—I seem to know one of them.
PORTER. A Mr and Miss Becker, sir.
AUGUSTUS. Becker? Let me see. Yes, of course. Why, by Jove, yes— [*He crosses the stage and says to* GEORGE, *who is smoking, with his back turned to the other group.*] Mr Becker, I believe? You won't remember me. But your father was a great friend of mine. Before you were born. His sudden death was a great shock to me.
GEORGE [*suspicious of a trap*]. Ho yus. It must 'ave bin.
AUGUSTUS. And this is your sister?
GEORGE. Yes, this is 'er.
AUGUSTUS. And what are you doing now?
GEORGE. Jest travellin' abaht.

> [THE SPECTRE, *who has been hanging round, suddenly hops on to a table behind* AUGUSTUS *and assumes the posture of the Eros statue.* ROBERT *sees him.*]

ROBERT [*in a whisper*]. Get down at once! [THE SPECTRE *gets down and goes and sits on the stairs.*]
AUGUSTUS [*looking at* JIMMY]. I see . . . Your mother had such a lovely Chippendale, I remember. I suppose you still have that at home, now?

GEORGE. Yes. We keeps it fer the spare-room bed.
AUGUSTUS. And the Rembrandt?
GEORGE. The how much?
AUGUSTUS. Your beautiful Rembrandt.
GEORGE. Oh, that. Yes, she wasn't 'alf a bad ole bus in 'er dy. But we ran 'er into a wall and broke 'er up.
AUGUSTUS [*who has not been listening, looking at* JIMMY]. I wonder—would you and—your sister care to have lunch with me?
GEORGE. Would we? I should sy so. I don't 'arf feel empty.
AUGUSTUS. Splendid. Then we'll go in now.

> [AUGUSTUS *leads the way with* GEORGE *and* JIMMY. ROBERT *and* THE SPECTRE *follow.*]

AUGUSTUS [*turning to* ROBERT]. By the way, Bob, I've changed my mind. I can't resist seeing this famous new vein of yours. I think I will stay on a day or two, after all. We haven't seen much of each other, yet.
ROBERT. Splendid.

> [THE SPECTRE *has come behind* AUGUSTUS *and is pinning a large red plush heart to his coat tails.* ROBERT *sees it.*]

ROBERT [*snatching away the heart and throwing it into a corner*]. Any more of this and you go home at once, see?

> [*Exeunt.*]

CURTAIN

Act II Scene 3

[ROBERT'S *hut.* ROBERT *is pacing up and down.* THE SPECTRE *lolls in a chair.*]

ROBERT. So you were right after all. I took her round the old workings. While we were looking down into the Great West Stope there was a fall of rock. Somehow, we found ourselves in each other's arms. Poor girl, her life must have been terrible. But now all that's going to end. Just think, in an hour we shall be together, in the sleeping carriage, alone—
SPECTRE. And then—?

ROBERT. Oh, I don't know. London. Paris. Naples. I want to take her away into the Sun.
SPECTRE. The mine?
ROBERT. Don't talk about it. What's all that beside Love?
SPECTRE. How will you live?
ROBERT. I'll work for her, steal for her—beg—anything.
SPECTRE. I can imagine you with a barrel organ and a monkey.
ROBERT. This is the greatest moment of my life.

SPECTRE.
Upon this line between adventure
Prolong our meeting out of good-nature
Obvious in each agreeable feature.

Calling of each other by name,
Smiling, taking a willing arm,
Has the companionship of a game.

But should the step do more than this
Out of bravado or drunkenness
Forward or back are menaces.

On neither side let foot slip over
Invading Always, exploring Never,
For this is hate, and this is fear.

On narrowness stand, for sunlight is
Brightest only on surfaces,
No anger, no traitor, but peace.

ROBERT. It's time we were going. She can't get down to the bridge before nine and the express leaves Carr Bridge junction at nine thirty. You'll have to drive like hell.
SPECTRE. I will.
ROBERT [*putting his hands on* THE SPECTRE's *shoulders*]. Old friend, you won't fail me now?
SPECTRE. I shall never fail you. [*He picks up a motoring coat and changes his opera hat for a chauffeur's cap.*]
ROBERT. I'll go and get the car out. Will you bring my suitcase? [*Exit.*]

[*The telephone bell rings.*]

SPECTRE [*at the telephone*]. Hullo. Yes. Is that Mr Stagg? Yes, Bicknell speaking. Your boy's ill? I'm sorry to hear that. Very sorry. No, I haven't seen Mrs Stagg. Yes, of course, I'll tell her if I do. Perhaps she's down at the hotel. I'd try there if I were you. Good-bye.

ROBERT [*looking in*]. Did I hear the telephone?
SPECTRE. No.

> [*Exeunt. The sound of a car starting, gathering speed, dying away.*]

CURTAIN

INTERVAL
For discussion & refreshments.

Act III Scene 1

[ROBERT's *hut*. ROBERT *busy with papers*. THE SPECTRE *lounging. Through the* WIRELESS, *an American recitative with jazz accompaniment.*]

WIRELESS. It's no use raising a shout.
No, Honey, you can cut that right out.
I don't want any more hugs,
Make me some fresh tea, fetch me some rugs—
Here am I, here are you,
But what does it mean? What are we going to do?

A long time ago I told my mother
I was leaving home to find another.
I never answered her letter
But I never found a better—
Here am I, *etc.*

It wasn't always like this—
Perhaps it wasn't, but it is.
Put the car away; when life fails
What's the good of going to Wales?
Here am I, *etc.*

In my spine there was a base
And I know the general's face;
But they've severed all the wires
And I can't tell what the general desires—
Here am I, *etc.*

In my veins there is a wish
And a memory of fish,

When I lie crying on the floor,
It says: "You've often done this before."—
Here am I, *etc.*

A bird used to visit this shore.
It isn't going to come any more.
I've come a very long way to prove
No land, no water and no love—
Here am I, *etc.*

[*The telephone bell rings.* ROBERT *switches off the* WIRELESS *and answers it.*]

ROBERT [*at the telephone*]. Hullo, Mr Stagg. Yes, it's Bicknell. You've got those separators installed? Good. Satisfactory? I'm glad. You must bag samples of the takings for comparison with the old buddles. Can you come up on Thursday evening? You can't? Mrs Stagg's going to this dance, is she? It'll be a great do, I hear. Yes, sit and mind the baby, eh? I'll come down this afternoon. Good-bye. [*To* THE SPECTRE.] Stagg always seems so genial. I don't think Julia can have said anything. You know, I can't make it out. The morning after the accident I got a note from her saying that she realised she'd been very foolish and wrong, that she could never forgive me for lying about the child and she never wanted to see me again. I tried to see her once or twice, but she was always out or busy. How she should imagine I knew the kid was ill I don't know.

SPECTRE. Extraordinary, isn't it?

ROBERT. Well, if she's fool enough to like that sort of life, she can stew in it. I've got better things to think of. The mine's doing jolly well. The ore from the new vein is so clean that it hardly needs any dressing, except for taking the pyrites out. The Mill can treat ten tons of crude ore an hour now. The Directors wrote me a letter the other day congratulating me and saying that the Company wouldn't forget my services. They mentioned that their shares had already risen six points.

SPECTRE.   Again in conversations
Speaking of fear and throwing off reserve
The voice is nearer
But no clearer
Than first love
Than peace-time occupations.

□

> For every news
> Means pairing off in twos and twos
> Another I, another You,
> Each knowing what to do
> But of no use.
>
> Never stronger
> But younger and younger
> Saying good-bye, but coming back, for fear
> Is over there,
> And the centre of anger
> Is out of danger.

ROBERT. You know, I see now that it was really quite providential that we should have run into that hay-cart. It was a most extraordinary accident. We were going dead slow when it happened, weren't we? And you're an expert driver. Of course, I could have wrung your neck at the time. But now it all seems to have happened for the best. The mine's a success, and I'm body and soul in the work. I believe I'm fonder of that vein than I ever was of Julia. Do you know, I sometimes go down after the men have stopped work and stand staring at it for ages? I like to be near it. I love it.

[The telephone rings.]

[*At the telephone.*] Yes, Bicknell speaking. Oh, it's you, Gus. No, I'm afraid I shan't be able to come to the dance. Sorry, but I'm up to the roof in work. I'll come and see you when I can. So long. [*To* THE SPECTRE.] Now there's a case. That's the sort of thing a woman can do to you. My brother's got himself hopelessly entangled with this Becker girl, who's nothing but a common little whore. She's sucking him dry. And he gets absolutely nothing in return.

SPECTRE.
> Before this loved one
> Was that one and that one
> A family
> And history
> And ghost's adversity
> Whose pleasing name
> Was neighbourly shame.
> Before this last one
> Was much to be done
> Frontiers to cross
> As clothes grew worse

And coins to pass
In a cheaper house
Before this last one
Before this loved one.

Face that the Sun
Is supple on
May stir but here
Is no New Year
The gratitude for gifts is less
Than the old loss
Touching is shaking hands
On mortgaged lands
And smiling of
This gracious greeting
"Good Day. Good luck"
Is no real meeting
But instinctive look
A backward love.

ROBERT. Yes, I've been through all that kind of madness, God knows. I can sympathise. But thank God I've got beyond it now. I've put all those feelings into my work. I love that mine. I'd give my life for it. I want to have a hand in everything connected with it. To help the men. Yes, I want to be a father to them. It sounds absurd, I know.

SPECTRE. And why not?

ROBERT. Stagg and all the rest of them are scared by this success. They think it can't last. I'll show them it can. Take that question of the ropeway to the Rodderup dumps. It's only ten miles. Stagg's against it.

SPECTRE. Never mind, you're manager.

ROBERT. I know I am.

SPECTRE. Well, order it to be made.

ROBERT. You think I should?

SPECTRE. Undoubtedly.

ROBERT. By God, I will.

SPECTRE. The other day you noticed that some of the miners have to come nine or ten miles to work.

ROBERT. I know, poor devils.

SPECTRE. Well, why not build a garden city for them, here?

ROBERT. But, God, it would cost thousands.

SPECTRE. The mine's going to bring you thousands.

ROBERT. It'd be a terrific job.

SPECTRE. Of course it would. It'd be worthy of you.
ROBERT. Mind you, if I did it, it wouldn't be a shoddy affair, either. I'd employ the best architects. And we'd have electric light laid on.
SPECTRE. A bath in each cottage.
ROBERT. Playing-fields.
SPECTRE. A free cinema.
ROBERT. Swimming baths.
SPECTRE. A church.
ROBERT. A lending library.
SPECTRE. An Art Gallery and Museum.
ROBERT. One day, perhaps—
SPECTRE. Why not now?
ROBERT. We haven't a tenth of the capital we'd need.
SPECTRE. That will come. Make a start.
ROBERT. It's madness.
SPECTRE. Who cares?
ROBERT. One can't take the responsibility.
SPECTRE. Think of Caesar, Napoleon, Henry Ford.
ROBERT. Of course, one might lead up to the subject with the Directors. But they'd sack me at once.
SPECTRE. Then buy the mine.
ROBERT. Buy the mine!
SPECTRE. Yes, buy the mine. I'll arrange everything. I'll get a call through to the London Office now.
ROBERT. Stop! You must be crazy! [*He jumps up.*]
SPECTRE [*putting on a crown*]. Sit down.

[ROBERT *collapses weakly into a chair.*]

This is my hour. I'm King. [*He picks up the telephone.*]

CURTAIN

Act III Scene 2

[*The Nineveh Hotel. Enter* COLONEL TEARER *and* GEORGE.]

GEORGE. Geoff, when yer goin' ter git me that swell kyse for fags yer was tellin' me abaht? All gold, an' that?
TEARER. I've written for it to town, my dear. They're so stoopid. It's sure to be here tomowow . . . But cigawette cases are for good little boys, don't you know. When are you goin' to do what I want?

GEORGE. Wot's that?
TEARER. My dear, don't pwetend you don't know.
GEORGE. Honest, I don't.
TEARER. Somethin' fwightfully amusin'.
GEORGE. Well, coff it aht.
TEARER. I like to be thwashed. Perfectly delicious.
GEORGE. Well, you ought to be ashymed o' yerself. Stryte, yer ought. Ain't yer goin' ter tyke Olive an me aht in the car this evenin'?
TEARER. Olive as well?
GEORGE. If she can't come, I don't. See?
TEARER. All wight, my dear. Don't be angwy. It's only that your sister doesn't dwive very well. She makes me a little nervous, don't you know.
GEORGE. I won't let her drive, see? I'll drive orl the wy meself. [*Enter* JIMMY.] Wot, oh, Olive. Comin' drivin' with me this evenin'? I'm tyking Geoff aht in me Rolls.
JIMMY. Reckon I will. I was 'avin dinner with Gus. But it ain't arf dry with 'im. Though 'e does yer well. I will sy that for 'im.
GEORGE. See yer in ten minutes, then. We got some pertiklar himportant bisness ter atten' ter. Aint we, Geoff? [*Winks at* TEARER.]

[*They go up the staircase arm in arm. Enter* AUGUSTUS.]

AUGUSTUS. Ah, there you are, Olive. My darling, you look wonderful this evening.
JIMMY. Give us a fag, Gus.
AUGUSTUS. Yes, yes. Of course. [*Producing cigarettes.*] Tell me how you like these? I ordered them specially for you from Angora. Let me. [*He tries to light* JIMMY's *cigarette.*]
JIMMY. Yer aint 'alf clumsy, Gus. Look at yer. Yer 'ands are shykin'. Wot's up?
AUGUSTUS. Oh, Olive, my darling—you don't, you can't realise what you mean to me. I worship you. You've changed my whole life. Oh, I know I'm just an old fool. I'm not worth your wasting your time with. And you've been very patient with me. You've been wonderful, these weeks we've spent here together. You're different from everybody else in the world. I never dreamed there could be a girl like you. I'm the luckiest man on earth. [*He bursts into tears and kneels down in front of* JIMMY.]
JIMMY. 'Ere, cheese it, Gus. Yer'd best go an' lie dahn. Wot if anyone was ter come in? They'd think yer was balmy.
AUGUSTUS. You've made me see what a fool I've been. How blind. How conceited. How selfish. My whole life was wasted until I met you.

JIMMY. Git yerself up, Gus, Chris' syke.
AUGUSTUS [*rising*]. I'll do anything you ask me, my dearest. You see? I'll be good. I'll be quite calm . . . Oh, Olive, come away with me now, to-night.
JIMMY. If I've told yer once, I've told yer an 'undred times, Gus. I can't.
AUGUSTUS. God knows, I wouldn't ask you to marry me—or—anything else that you didn't wish, but let me adopt you. Anything. As long as I can be near you, speak to you sometimes. And if you fall in love, I'll pay for everything. I'll support your husband. Let me be your servant, I can't live without you.
JIMMY. It aint any use, Gus. I'm sorry. It can't be did. Now, jest yer go an' lie dahn.
AUGUSTUS. Very well, my darling, if you wish it. You'll dine with me this evening?
JIMMY. That's jest wot I was goin' ter tell yer, Gus. I can't. I 'ave ter go aht with me brother. 'E wants me ter.
AUGUSTUS. Would he care to dine too, do you think? Tell him, we'd have that champagne he likes.
JIMMY. Very sorry, Gus. It's imposs.
AUGUSTUS. Very well, my dear, I understand.
JIMMY. Yer not mad with me, Gus?
AUGUSTUS. How could I be? Whatever you do is right.
JIMMY. Yer not a bad sort, yer know, Gus.
AUGUSTUS. Oh, my darling—
JIMMY. Orl right. If yer like. [AUGUSTUS *kisses him.*] Look aht, 'ere's someone.

> [GEORGE *and* TEARER *appear at the top of the staircase.* TEARER *is in a condition of extreme exhaustion,* GEORGE *supports him.*]

GEORGE. 'Ere buck up, Geoff. 'Ave a brandy. I didn't mean ter 'urt yer, yer know. Yer'll be O.K. in 'alf a tick. Yer ready, Olive? 'ere, gimme an 'and with 'im. 'E'll be all right in the open air.
TEARER [*faintly*]. Perfectly—delicious—
JIMMY. So long, Gus. See yer termorrer mornin'.

> [AUGUSTUS *tries to smile, bursts into tears and goes out.*]

GEORGE [*as they help* TEARER *out*]. Yer aint drivin' this evenin', see?
JIMMY. Gawd's strewth, I bleedin' well am.
GEORGE. You aint.

JIMMY. We'll bleedin' well see abaht that.

[*Exeunt. Enter* ETHEL WRIGHT.]

ETHEL. Porter.

[*Enter* PORTER.]

PORTER. Yes, miss?
ETHEL. Any news?
PORTER. Yes, miss. There was a letter from South America for the Bishop this morning, miss.
ETHEL. You're a sensible man, Porter. [*Tips him.*]
PORTER. Thank you very much, miss. I suppose you couldn't tell me anything more?
ETHEL. Not yet, but you will all know very soon.

[*Enter* KATHERINE LAW. *The* PORTER *retires.*]

KATHERINE. Oh, Ethel. I'm so worried. I can't make out what's happened. We seem to have offended the Hotel people somehow. They were so charming before, and now they've suddenly become quite different. So rude and careless. The Bishop's shaving-water was forgotten this morning, and he had to ring for nearly ten minutes before anyone came. And when I asked for some chicken for Googlums, he's our Peke, you know; the maid said that they couldn't spare it and that if I wanted some I should have to buy it myself. I can't understand it. The Bishop's always so popular wherever he goes. I believe that Mr Luder has something to do with it. Ethel, I don't like that man. He's not straight.
ETHEL. Now my dear, you must guard against subconscious jealousy of your husband's men friends. I know it's hard—the hardest thing a woman has to face. But you must try. As for Mr Luder, I've had several long talks with him myself, and I can assure you he's a most delightful and interesting man, with an extraordinary knowledge of people. He's given me several ideas for my work.

[*Enter* BISHOP LAW *talking to* MAXIMILIAN LUDER.]

LAW. The vicar has just rung me up to say that he's in bed with a chill and did I know of anyone who could take duty for him. I wondered if your brother would be so kind?
MAX. I'm sure he'd be delighted.
LAW. That's excellent. I'll introduce them after dinner. He's an old Blue, and doing such splendid work. My dear, we ought to go and dress.

KATHERINE. Very well, Travers.

[They go upstairs.]

MAX. Ah, Miss Wright, I've been looking forward for a long time to having another talk with you. It's so seldom that one's lucky enough to meet a woman with brains and—may I say?—charm.
ETHEL. I'm afraid you're flattering, Mr Luder. But I agree that it's very sad how few women ever develop. Men seem to think it bad form in women to have interests, so they never acquire any. Take Katherine for instance—By-the-by, you were at school with the Bishop, weren't you?
MAX. Yes.
ETHEL. What was he like?
MAX. Oh—er—all right. I didn't know him very well.
ETHEL. Now, Mr Luder, you're not being frank. It's no good trying to conceal your thoughts from me. You know something.
MAX. You're too clever for me, Miss Wright. As a matter of fact, I do. But one hates saying anything against an old school-fellow. Besides, I expect he's given all that up long ago . . . Though I *have* looked at his wife and wondered—
ETHEL. Tell me—
MAX. One hardly likes to speak of these things to a lady.
ETHEL. I'm a woman of Science. It's our duty to know everything, to understand everything.
MAX. It's wonderful to find a woman whom one can talk freely to . . . Well, it's—
ETHEL. Yes? Goats?
MAX. Worse than that. Gramophone discs.
ETHEL. How dreadful. Wait a moment. Yes, I see it all now. Poor, poor Katherine!
MAX. Of course, Miss Wright, I can trust you to be absolutely discreet?
ETHEL. Naturally, Mr Luder.

[Enter CESLAUS LUDER.*]*

MAX. Hullo, Ceslaus, how were the fish rising after the rain?
CESLAUS. Nothing to be seen, I'm afraid.
ETHEL. I think, if you'll excuse me, I'll go and dress.

[She goes upstairs.]

MAX. I'm quite certain of it now. That woman's a tec. We shall have to be careful. But she's barking up the wrong tree, at present.

CESLAUS. Let's clear out of this place, Max. I'm afraid we shall find nothing more here. The hotel's full of old cats. It's a waste of time.
MAX. I believe you're right. We'll make certain of Mrs Stagg. And what about the Becker girl?
CESLAUS. She's dreadfully common.
MAX. I know. And her figure's all wrong for the South American market. But she's tolerable, and probably her technique's quite fair.
CESLAUS. Yes, I suppose we shall have to have her. It seems a come-down, doesn't it, from the days when we sent off regular fortnightly consignments, and nothing below a gentleman's daughter? Why, many of them could play the piano and speak three languages.
MAX. Never mind. Times will change. Don't let's be downhearted. By-the-way, Ceslaus, I've got a little surprise for you. The Bishop wants you to do duty for the vicar here tomorrow. I said you would.
CESLAUS. Oh, Max, how could you? I know I shall put my foot in it.
MAX. Oh no, you won't. You'll be as right as rain . . . Look here, if you've got your buttonhole camera you might get a few snaps of the Becker girl this evening. We'd better have them put in the new catalogue, and the printers'll be wanting the stuff next week.
CESLAUS. Very well, I will.

CURTAIN

Act III Scene 3

[*The Nineveh Hotel.* AUGUSTUS *is telephoning.*]

AUGUSTUS. Yes. That's Templin Reformatory. Yes, Mr Bicknell speaking. Oh, it's you Bunyan . . . I'm afraid I can't. I've been in bed ever since I last telephoned. The influenza was followed by a slight attack of pleurisy. The doctor says I must stay here at least three more weeks. The boys are getting out of hand, are they? Then get some girls in. Can't you hear me? GET SOME GIRLS IN. They want love. What's that? No, no. LOVE. L for lighthouse, O for orange, V for vision. Yes. The girls' parents may object, you think? Well, you'll find the machine guns in the attic. They were put there after the last rebellion. Let me have any news.

[*Enter the* PORTER.]

AUGUSTUS. Have you seen Miss Becker anywhere?
PORTER. No, sir.

[*Exit* AUGUSTUS. *Enter* ETHEL WRIGHT.]

ETHEL. Oh, Porter, I want you to keep out there in the passage for the next quarter of an hour. Don't go away on any account. I may need your help.
PORTER. Very good, miss. [*Exit.*]

[*Enter* MAXIMILIAN LUDER.]

MAX. Good morning, Miss Wright. I wanted to see you to say good-bye. I have to go away to-day—rather unexpectedly.
ETHEL. Oh—I'm so sorry.
MAX. Yes, I shall often think of this place, and the talks we used to have ... I should like, before I go, to give you this little picture of myself as a memento of our acquaintance.
ETHEL. Thank you so much. But you must sign it.
MAX. Let's see. "For Ethel from Max. In homage to a woman of understanding." How will that do?
ETHEL. That's lovely. I shall always keep it by me. Where are you going? Perhaps we might meet each other sometimes?
MAX. I'm going abroad, I'm afraid. It may be a long time before I come back. But we needn't take our final farewells quite yet. I'm not going till this evening. [*He kisses her hand.*]
ETHEL. I shall see you at lunch.

[*She goes out, much moved. Enter* CESLAUS LUDER.]

MAX. Well, everything's fixed. We leave this evening, during the dance. Mrs Stagg will be down here for it. You'd better deal with her. I'll settle the Becker girl. We'll make a clear getaway. Probably they won't be missed for hours in the crowd. The yacht's waiting off Ravenglass. We'll be at sea before dawn ... By the way, how did your clerical duties go off?
CESLAUS. I made one rather unfortunate mistake. I was in the vestry at about eight o'clock and a lady came in all muffled up. So I took her and churched her. When I'd finished, I discovered that she'd come to arrange about a bazaar for the Zenana Mission. I hear she's the worst ingrown virgin in the village.

[*Enter* JIMMY.]

MAX. Well, Miss Becker. Looking forward to the dance?
JIMMY. Oh, I dunno. Jazzin' aint much in my line.
MAX. Perhaps sitting out is, eh? Ha ha! You won't forget me when you're making up your programme, I hope? What about numbers 7 and 8?

JIMMY. Right y'are. S'long as yer doesn't expec' me to do them Yile Blues. They get me fair tied up.
MAX. You shan't do anything you don't like, Miss Becker. I shall see you later, then.

[*Exit* MAX *and* CESLAUS. *Enter* GEORGE.]

JIMMY. Let me borrer some o' your duds agyne, George. I got a dyte with that tart down village. Coo, she aint 'alf 'ot stuff, neither.
GEORGE. Why can't yer get some duds o' yer own? Always cadgin', you are. 'Ow much did yer git for that fur cloak Gus gyve yer?
JIMMY. The bloody ole Jew wouldn't let me 'ave no more'n twenty-five quid for it. I reckon it wuz worth an 'undred.
GEORGE. Give us a fiver, then.
JIMMY. A fiver? Strewth, I likez that! An' you gettin' Gawd knows 'ow much from yer ole mug.
GEORGE. 'Ere, oo's show wuz this, anyway? 'F if weren't for me, yer'd be in Templin now, sittin' on yer arse and cryin' fer Muvver.
JIMMY. You? If it weren't for you—? Wot the bleedin' Christ d'yer think you are, when yer at 'ome? Many's the night I stood you a cup o' tea, when yer 'adn't the price of a bed at Levy's. And glad yer was of it; an' glad enuff yer was if yer cud git away with some pore 'alf blind ole mug wot couldn't see yer ugly fyce.
GEORGE. Jest you be careful, yer little barstard, or I'll myke yer so as yer won't be yble ter give darlin' Gussy wot 'e likes fer a munf.
JIMMY. Garn then. Garn. 'It me. Jest you 'it me. Yer dirty little 'arf-crahn poof.
GEORGE. Yer bleedin' little—

[*Enter* BISHOP LAW.]

LAW. Dear me! Quarrelling? You mustn't speak to your sister like that, Mr Becker. What's it all about? Well, nothing very serious, I'm sure? Come, come. You young people must learn to give and take. Have some coffee with me now, and make it up?

[*Enter* ETHEL, *the* PORTER *and two* POLICEMEN.]

ETHEL. There he is, sergeant, do your duty.
POLICEMAN. Which is Bishop Law?
LAW. I am.
POLICEMAN. I 'ave a warrant for your arrest on a charge of illicit traffic in women.

CURTAIN

Act III Scene 4

[ROBERT's *hut.* THE SPECTRE *reading. Enter* ROBERT.]

ROBERT. I'm done. The vein has faulted—thrown down a hundred feet, and when we put down borings we found it had pinched out completely. This is the end. The mine's doomed. I've lost every farthing.
SPECTRE. And more.
ROBERT. All I've done, all I'd hoped—has come to nothing. It isn't fair.

[*He sits down and buries his face in his arms.*]

SPECTRE. Head asleep
Falling forward
Must stop and go backward
Must keep, hard to keep
Its old importance, its chief position

ROBERT. Oh, do be quiet. I'm so tired.

SPECTRE. But trusted here
Choosing to tell
A chosen listener
Slapstick adventures, views from holidays
Receive due praise
Praise giving and taking
Before waking
And reproachful morning.
All's well
Each act has place
Each word has number
And praise takes breath
Before death
For death is a case
With no examples to remember.

CURTAIN

Act IV Scene 1

[ROBERT's *hut.* ROBERT *at the window.* THE SPECTRE *smoking.*]

ROBERT. She'll be down there now, dancing.

SPECTRE. The strings' excitement, the applauding drum
Are but the initiating ceremony
That out of cloud the ancestral face may come

And never hear their subaltern mockery
Graffiti-writers, moss-grown with whimsies,
Loquacious when the water course is dry.

It is your face I see and morning's praise
Of you is ghost's approval of the choice
Filtered through roots of the effacing grass.

Fear taking me aside would give advice:
"To conquer her, the visible enemy
It is enough to turn away the eyes".

Yet there's no peace in this assaulted city
But speeches at the corners, hope for news
Outside the watch-fires of a stronger army.

And all emotions to expressions come
Recovering the archaic imagery.
This longing for assurance takes the form

Of a hawk's vertical stooping from the sky;
These tears, salt for a disobedient dream,
The lunatic agitation of the sea.

While this despair, with hardened eyeballs cries:
"A golden age, a silver . . ." rather this,
Massive and taciturn years, the age of ice.

ROBERT. I can't bear this. I must see her once again. It's all I've got left, now. [*Exit.*]

SPECTRE [*taking up the telephone*]. Hullo, Is that the Nineveh Hotel? Can I speak to Mrs Stagg, please? Yes . . . Julia, is that you? It's Jim. Baby's bad again. He's feverish, I think. Can you come home at once? Yes, I've sent for the doctor. But come now, won't you? No, I won't leave him. Good-bye.

CURTAIN

Act IV Scene 2

[*The Nineveh Hotel. Dance music, off. Enter* ETHEL, MAXIMILIAN, CESLAUS *and* PORTER.]

ETHEL. But we must still be careful. He generally works with an accomplice. We must keep our eyes open.

PORTER. 'E's a disgrece to 'is country, 'is sex and 'is cless. Them parsons are mostly preaching 'ypocrites. Begging your pardon, Mr Luder. I knows there are some that are real good 'uns, but there's some a decent man wouldn't clean 'is teeth into a basin after. They ought to give the likes of 'im the cat. It's what 'e deserves—a good 'iding, and I'm itching to give it 'im myself.

MAX. I wouldn't have believed it of a member of my old school. A man I've kept wicket for.

CESLAUS. Well, thank God and Miss Wright that he was frustrated in time. If it hadn't been for her courage and cleverness—but we needn't think of such ugly things. I only hope, Miss Wright, that everyone in the hotel will show their appreciation of your plucky victory over the fiend—every mother who has a daughter ought to go down on her knees to you—and that your chief will give you the promotion you deserve.

MAX AND PORTER. Hear, hear.

ETHEL. You're making me blush, Mr Luder. I've tried to do my duty, as anyone would; but I should never have been so successful if it hadn't been for the loyal help of my friend here. I'm going to speak to the Manager about you.

PORTER. It's very kind of you to put it like that, Miss. I did nothing. You were the boss and I was the willing 'and, as you might say.

MAX. Is all my baggage down yet?

PORTER. I'll go and see, sir. [*Exit.*]

MAX. We needn't start for another half hour. I'm hoping to have a dance or two before I leave. I suppose you wouldn't do me the honour, Miss Wright?

ETHEL. I'm afraid dancing isn't much in my line, Mr Luder. Besides, I must be about keeping watch. We've scored the first point, but one never knows. It doesn't do to rest on one's laurels.

MAX. I shall see you again, before we start?

ETHEL. Of course. I shall be down there in the passage. [*Exit.*]

MAX. That Stagg woman's gone home. She had a telephone call. Everything seems to be against us, to-night. However, we can't very well stop on, now. We'll get the Becker girl and be off. She's better than nothing. You go out and have the car ready. Here she is.

[*Enter* JIMMY, *dressed for the dance.*]

Megind yegoegu degont fegorgeget thege chlegoregofegorm. Well, Miss Becker, I hope I may claim my dance?

[*Exit* CESLAUS.]

JIMMY. Right y'are. Only let's look slippy, 'cos ole Bicknell keeps followin' me abaht.
MAX. Shall we go outside for a few minutes, to avoid him?
JIMMY. Yus, that's the ticket.

[*Enter* AUGUSTUS.]

AUGUSTUS. Ah, there you are, Olive. Can I have the next dance?
JIMMY. Sorry, Gus. I'm booked with Mr Luder.
AUGUSTUS. Well, which can you put me down for?
JIMMY. I'm booked for the evenin'.
AUGUSTUS. What's the matter with you to-day, Olive? Why are you angry with me? Where's that fur cloak?
JIMMY. I've told yer. I've put it awy.
AUGUSTUS. I happen to know that you've sold it.
JIMMY. It's a bleedin' lie.
MAX. Mr Bicknell, I'm afraid I really cannot permit you to address a lady in such tones in my presence.
AUGUSTUS. Mind your own business, sir. Forgive me, Olive. I don't know what's the matter with me this evening. When you're unkind to me, I can't bear it.
JIMMY. That's all right, Gus.
MAX. Come along, Miss Becker. [*Exeunt.*]

[*Enter* ROBERT.]

ROBERT. Hullo, Gus. Enjoying the dance?
AUGUSTUS. No. [*He goes out after* MAX *and* JIMMY.]
ROBERT. Porter?
PORTER [*appearing*]. Yes sir?
ROBERT. I suppose Mrs Stagg is at the dance?
PORTER. She was, sir. Then she got a telephone message to go 'ome, because the baby was ill. The funny thing was, 'er 'usband rang up from 'ome five minutes later and didn't seem to know nothing about it. A mistake, I expect.
ROBERT. A mistake! By God— [*Exit.*]

[*A shout and a scream from outside.* AUGUSTUS *rushes in.*]

AUGUSTUS. Quick, porter. The police! The fiends have got her. I saw it all. I followed. Just too late. The telephone—

> [BISHOP LAW, *wearing a police hat and medals, appears at the top of the staircase, followed by* THE FLYING SQUAD. *These are dressed in gym-shoes, shorts and zephyrs marked with a scarlet* F.]

LAW. Put that down.
PORTER. Gawd! It's 'is Reverence.
LAW. Flying Squad. 'Shun! Number! [*They do so.*] Private Loring.
LORING. Adsum!
LAW. Private Foot.
FOOT. Adsum!
LAW. Private Cockshoot.
COCKSHOOT. Adsum.
LAW. Private Jesser-Coop.
J-COOP. Adsum!
LAW. On the line.

> [*They bend down, one foot forward, as if in a race.*]

LORING. Come on, chaps, we'll debag them.
FOOT. Won't we jolly well scrag them?
COCKSHOOT. We'll gorse-bush them.
J-COOP. We'll squirt water on them. We'll milk them.
LAW. Are you ready? Steady? Go!

> [THE FLYING SQUAD *rush out*.]

PORTER. Please, sir, may I go with them? I'd like to do something to show I'm sorry.
LAW. You may.

> [*Enter* ETHEL *and* KATHERINE.]

PORTER. Thank you, sir. [*Exit.*]
LAW. Miss Wright, you've failed. You know the penalty?
ETHEL. Yes, sir.
LAW. You know what to do?
ETHEL. Yes, sir. Please lend me your revolver. My automatic is too small. [LAW *gives it.*] Thank you, sir. Good-bye, Katherine, I'm sorry.
KATHERINE. Oh, Ethel . . . [*Exit* ETHEL.]

> [*A scuffle. The* LUDERS *are brought in with* JIMMY *by* THE FLYING SQUAD *and the* PORTER.]

PORTER. Got you, you beasts. My roller-skating's not what it was, but I caught 'em up.

LAW. Stand over there.

> [*A shot, off.* THE BISHOP *and* THE FLYING SQUAD *salute.*]

LAW. Private Loring. Fetch my revolver back from Miss Wright. [*Exit* LORING.] Private Foot, bring Colonel Tearer here. [*Exit* FOOT.]

LORING [*returning*]. Your revolver, sir.

LAW. Dead?

LORING. Through both temples, sir.

> [COLONEL TEARER *is brought in by* FOOT. GEORGE *follows them.*]

LAW. Katherine, will you please take Miss Becker into the next room and search her?

GEORGE [*roaring with laughter*]. Oh, coo, Christ—!

JIMMY. Shut yer bleedin' fyce. 'Ere, I protes'!

LAW. Do as you're told.

> [*Exeunt* KATHERINE *and* JIMMY.]

LAW. Mr Augustus Bicknell.

> [AUGUSTUS *is led forward by* COCKSHOOT.]

KATHERINE [*entering with a scream*]. Oh, Travers, it's a man!

LAW. There, there, my dear. Calm yourself. Private Jesser-Coop, just go and verify this.

> [*Exit* JESSER-COOP. *He returns immediately with* JIMMY.]

J-COOP. The party is male, sir.

MAX. To think, after all these years, we should be caught for a bloody little boy.

AUGUSTUS. I'm free. I'm pure.

LAW. Mr Bicknell. You are head of Templin Reformatory?

AUGUSTUS. Yes.

LAW. A few weeks ago, I should have been inclined to deal severely with you. But I think you have suffered a good deal. I hope it will be a lesson to you. I shall exile you to Brighton for a year. If, at the end of that time, you wish to return to Templin, you may do so.

AUGUSTUS. Never, never again.

Law. I'm glad you take it in the right spirit, Mr Bicknell. Next please. Colonel Geoffrey Tearer.

[TEARER *is brought forward by* FOOT.]

TEARER. Yes, sir.
Law. Colonel Tearer, my department has had trouble with you before. Your face has become too familiar in Algiers. I'm afraid I shall have to be severe.
TEARER. Quite weady to take my punishment, Bishop. Must gwin and bear it. Old soldier, don't you know. Honour of the wegiment, what?
Law. Very proper sentiments. You will do the Cautley Spout run every afternoon for two months. You will be timed, and my men will be posted at various points to see that you make no short cuts. Also, every Saturday morning, before lunch, you will bring me five thousand lines. The motto for this week will be "Mummy's been dead quite a long time now". That will do.

[TEARER *salutes and retires.*]

Law. The Luders.

[MAXIMILIAN *and* CESLAUS *are brought forward by* JESSER-COOP *and* LORING.]

Law. Maximilian and Ceslaus Luder, it is unnecessary for me to dwell at length upon your record. For a very long time, now, you have persistently worked against me and the powers which I represent. You are well aware of the penalty which your conduct has incurred. Have you anything to say?
MAX. No.
CESLAUS. No.
Law. Very well. Katherine, please leave the room. [*Exit* KATHERINE.] Private Loring, my cane. [LORING *gives the cane and places a chair in the centre of the stage.*] Maximilian Luder.

[MAXIMILIAN *comes forward and kneels on the chair.*]

CURTAIN

Act IV Scene 3

[ROBERT's *hut*. THE SPECTRE *at the telephone.*]

SPECTRE. Is that the Stunhead police-station? Oh, good evening, Sergeant. It's Mr Robert Bicknell, of Windyacre Mine speaking. Will you please come up here at once? I've just committed a murder and I want to give myself up.

[*Enter* ROBERT.]

SPECTRE. You're back early.
ROBERT. Yes, I've come for you.
SPECTRE. Honoured, I'm sure.
ROBERT. You've cheated me all my life.
SPECTRE. Really? I've done what you wanted me to.
ROBERT. It's a lie!
SPECTRE. That makes no difference.
ROBERT. It's the shame of it— But I know you now, you devil. [*He draws a revolver and fires.* THE SPECTRE *falls.*] You'll never trick me again. [*He comes forward and addresses the audience:*]

> Men pass through doors and travel to the sea
> Stand grouped in attitudes of play or labour,
> Bending to children, raise equals' glass,
> Are many times together, man with woman.
> We are in this, this wonderful life,
> On lawns in flannels, in garages, in golf-clubs
> Talking, starting slightly at the shooting,
> The small disaster on the limitless plains,
> We see the unit fall apart
> On bridges in all lands its fragments leaning
> Outworn like processes, in each the past,
> Gradual accumulations of its own production
> Sitting in corners till it die, and see
> On the sky-line of life death's tall destructors
> Consuming rubbish. This is our view
> Of fidgeting, preening, comforting and cadging,
> Where love returns to epoch of the poisoner,
> Willing transforms itself to influenza
> And guilty rashes, speeding descent
> Of noble mind, the brakes burnt out.
>
> We know who have done this; are several here,

There you sit who smooth sick pillows
Devoted as lice and have no day-dream,
Wince at no curse, are never ill,
Put kindness, words, and sleekness in.
You're going to have friends, to bring up children,
You're going to be like this for ever, all the time,
More terrible than the bursting of the bolted door,
Or the exhausting adverse wind of dreams.

[*Enter two* POLICEMEN.]

POLICEMAN [*looking at body*]. 'E's dead. 'Oo is 'e?
ROBERT. My spectre. I had one.
POLICEMAN. That's unusual. I 'ope you're coming quietly, Mr Bicknell? I should take your coat, it's snowing.
ROBERT. Thank you.

[ROBERT *turns at the door.*]

You who have come to watch us play and go
Openly to face the outer sky, you may
As guests or as possessor enter in
To the mysterious joy of a lighted house.
But never think our thoughts are strange to yours;
We, too, have watched life's circular career
How seed woken by touches in the dark
Out of this inarticulate recognition
And changing every moment come at last
By fortunate prejudice to delighting form
And the indifference of profuse production.
We saw all this, but what have we to do
With the felicities of natural growth?
What reference theirs to ours, where shame
Invasive daily into deeper tissues
Has all convicted? Remain we here
Sitting too late among the lights and music,
Without hope waiting for a soothing hush;
Never to day-break can we say "at last"
And eyes from vistas have brought nothing back;
The pane of glass is always there, looked through,
Bewilders with left-handed images.
If when the curtain falls, if you should speak,
Turning together, as of neighbours lately gone,

Although our anguish seem but summer lightning,
Sudden, soon over, in another place,
Although immune then, do not say of us
"It was nothing, their loss." It was all.

CURTAIN

The Dance of Death

BY W. H. AUDEN

[*1933*]

TO
ROBERT MEDLEY AND RUPERT DOONE

Announcer. We present to you this evening a picture of the decline of a class.
Chorus [*behind curtain*]. Middle class.
Announcer. Of how its members dream of a new life.
Chorus. We dream of a new life.
Announcer. But secretly desire the old, for there is death inside them. We show you that death as a dancer.
Chorus. Death for us.
Announcer. Do you care for Musical Comedy, Worm's eye view, red lips?

[*The italic letters indicate performers on the stage, the Greek letters performers in the auditorium.*]

STAGING NOTE:

[*The stage is bare with a simple backcloth, in front of which are the steps on which the* Announcer *sits, like the umpire at a tennis tournament. Down stage is a small jazz orchestra. In front of the conductor a microphone. When* Box *and* Cox *are to speak the conductor sits down and they take his place.*]

SCENE:

[Chorus *in silk dressing gowns. Their clothes on the ground. As they sing they take off their dressing gowns revealing handsome two-piece bathing suits. They dance and lie on the stage in various patterns. A Medicine Ball.*]

Gents from Norway
Ladies from Sweden
Don't stand in the doorway
Come, this is what you've been needing.
Boys from France
Join in our dance;
Italian belles, valiant belles
And anyone else
With profs. from Germany
All sing in harmony
Come out into the sun.

Strip off your shirt
Kick off your shoes
It won't hurt
To leave behind those office blues
Here on the beach
You're out of reach

Of sad news, bad news
You can refuse
The invitation
To self-examination
Come out into the sun.

Are you too fat
And getting bigger
He'll see to that
He'll give you a grecian figure
Exercises
As the sun rises
Shall strengthen you, lengthen you
Build you anew.
When day is ended
You shall feel splendid;
Come out into the sun.

Lie down on the sand
Feel the sun on your flesh;
It's so grand;
O Boy, you'll soon want to get fresh.
Living with nature
Is the life of the future
The new life, the true life
The life for you.
Europe's in a hole
Millions on the dole
But come out into the sun.

We shall build to-morrow
A new clean town
With no more sorrow
Where lovely people walk up and down.
We shall all be strong
We shall all be young
No more tearful days, fearful days
Or unhappy affairs
We shall all pull our weight
In the ship of state
Come out into the sun.

A. Can you turn a cartwheel yet?

B. I've often been taught but I always forget.
A. I can. Shall I show you?
B.   Please. [*Business.*]
    How wonderful. You do it with such ease.
C. Heavens I've left my oil behind.
D. Madam, use mine.
C.   You're very kind.
ANNOUNCER. Get ready, your instructor comes
    Stand up at ease, and beat the drums.

[*A human arch is formed.* DANCER *enters through audience.*]

A. He's marvellous
    He's Greek.
    When I see him
    My legs go weak.
B. Lend me your comb
    To do my hair
    I must look my best
    When he is here.
C. He walks with such grace
    Just like a cat
    Where's my kodak
    I must snap him like that.
α. 'E's a bit of orlright, ain't 'e Bill?

[CHORUS *form up with dumb-bells for exercises.* DANCER *has a drum for these.*]

CHORUS. Vital young man
    Do what you can
    For our dust
    We who are weak
    Want a splendid physique
    You must, you must.
    Do not forsake us, make us, give us your word
    As strong as a horse as quick as a bird.
    You're our ideal
    Make it come real
    For us.
    Vital young man
    Do what you can
    You must. [*Business.*]
ANNOUNCER. Well done, well done. Let new desire

Come to those whose muscles tire.
After exercise comes leisure,
The arms of love, the dance of pleasure.
Among the crowd when you would rest
One seems especially the best.
Ladies and gentlemen, the sea
Waits for you, tall upon the shore
So fill your lungs and take a plunge
Choose your partners and delay no more.

[*Select partners for old-time Waltz.*]

CHORUS. You were a great Cunarder, I
  Was only a fishing smack
  Once you passed across my bows
  And of course you did not look back
  It was only a single moment yet
  I watch the sea and sigh
  Because my heart can never forget
  The day you passed me by.

Hand stretched out to lie in hand
And eye looked into eye,
Two hearts sang a simple tune
In an old-world harmony.
Oh the moon is shining; come back to me
And make my dreams come true
For ever salter grows the sea
And ever sweeter you. [*Exeunt* CHORUS.]

[*Dance. Solo dance as* SUN GOD, *creator and destroyer. At the end of the dance he picks up the clothes of the* CHORUS, *puts them in a clothes basket and shoves the basket into the wings.*]

ANNOUNCER. Though they forget him, for Romance makes them dizzy,
  Death will not forget them; as you see, he is busy
  Hiding away their clothes, their social defences
  That the cold wind of the future may freeze their senses.

  Do not be mistaken for a moment about this stranger,
  The lives of many here are already in danger.
  He looks on the just and the unjust as he has always done.
  Some of you think he loves you. He is leading you on.

  He dances, and of course the barley and the trees grow tall,
  His help is powerful but does not apply to you all:

The bones of the beggared listen from underground;
To them his dancing has long been a familiar sound.

For he has an evil eye as well as a good.
He's certainly able to bewitch with it those whom he would.
He's fond of flowers, and doves will fly to his hand.
Yes, but what is he doing here to-day in our land?

The young people turn to him now in their green desire
Perhaps they imagine he'll set their hearts on fire.
Will touch them alive as he touches the barley seed—
Perhaps they'll find they've been very mistaken indeed.

[*Re-enter* BATHERS—*stiff and mechanical from cold.*]

- A. I feel so cold.
- B. I'm getting old.
- C. I don't really hold
  With this lying about
  In the sun without
  A stitch or a clout.
- D. I've got a pain.
- E. The sun's gone in.
- F. It's going to rain.
- G. I've got a hunch
  I want my lunch.
- α. You ought to be ashamed of yourself, Maudie, appearing in public like that. Where do you think you are? The Garden of Eden? If father were to see you, e'd give you a good 'iding.
- A. Come on, let's dress.
- B. Why, where's our clothing?
- C. They're gone—there's nothing!
- D. Stolen, I guess.
- E. We're in a mess.
- α [*excitedly*]. 'E took 'em—I saw 'im.

[DANCER *bangs his drum to drown her.*]

[*Still louder.*] No, Mr Noisy, you can't stop me. You took 'em—you know it, and put 'em in that basket. Didn't 'e, 'Arry, own up?
- β. What did you say, ma?
- α. 'E took 'em.
- β. Took what, ma?

α. The clothes.
β. What clothes, ma?
α. Why, their clothes.
β. Did 'e really, coo. [*Laughs.*]
CHORUS [*excitedly*]. If this is true
    It's mean of you.
    Is this a game?
    We think it's a shame.
    Is it a stunt?
    Give them back at once.
    Please don't be silly.
    We're getting chilly.
ANNOUNCER. Calm, please, calm. Now as you accuse him
    He will call the manager, excuse him.

[*Exit and enter with* MANAGER.]

MANAGER. Vy make so a trobble in my theatre
    Explain yourself quick. Vot is de matter?
CHORUS. This lady declares, he has put our clothes in a basket.
    Let us see for ourselves. Bring it, we ask it.
α. That's right, 'e did.

[DANCER *makes a nose at* α.]

    Harry, did you see what 'e did? Are you going to let your mother be insulted? Go and 'it 'im.
MANAGER. Please, lady, please
    Not so loud, please
    I fetch dis basket, we see
    Vot in it dere be
    Ullo, ullo.

[*Two* STAGE HANDS *enter.*]

    Is there a basket there?
STAGE HANDS. Yes, sir.
MANAGER. Bring it here.
α. Now we'll see oo's right.

[*Basket is brought in. It contains miscellaneous uniforms.*]

CHORUS. But these aren't ours. We've never seen them before.
    Why, they're uniforms. This isn't the war.
MANAGER. Vot does this mean?
    I am astounded.

STAGE HANDS. In 1916
    A musical revue, sir,
    The Lady of the Guard
    Was put on by you, sir
    In aid of the wounded.
    There was a scene
    In the palace yard;
    This was worn, I believe, sir
    By Miss Annabelle Eve, sir.
MANAGER. Oh, yes, I remember
    It began in November.
    What was the number
    That made such a hit?
STAGE HANDS. "Soldiers of the King of Kings".
MANAGER. Yes, that was it
    Conductor, can you play it?
CONDUCTOR. I must ask my strings—
    Yes, sir, we can.
MANAGER.   I'll say it.

    They are ever stepping onward
    They are eager with the hope of youth.
    They never fear the foe
    But strike a gallant blow
    For God and the cause of truth.
    They are ever stepping homeward
    They are looking unto higher ways
    Free as the flag that waves overhead
    Soldiers of the King of Kings.

CHORUS. We are getting so cold,
    These uniforms are old.
    But ours or not
    We'll wear the lot.
MANAGER. Gut, then every thing ends
    Happily, my friends.
    Now, come along
    And sing this song.
    Are you ready
    Are you steady?
γ.   What about Abyssinia?
δ.   One moment, sir, the Kellogg pact
    Has outlawed war as a national act.

ε. Scholarships—not battleships.
   Red front, red front,
   Red united, fighting front.
   Red front, red front,
   Red united, fighting front.
α. This is an attack on the working-class.
ζ. Workers unite before it's too late.
ε. Down with the bosses' class,
   Up with the workers' class.
   Red front, red front,
   Red united, fighting front.
   Red front, red front,
   Red united, fighting front.
AUDIENCE. One, two, three, four
   The last war was a bosses' war.
   Five, six, seven, eight
   Rise and make a workers' state.
   Nine, ten, eleven, twelve
   Seize the factories and run them yourself.
β. It's 'is fault. I told you so.
AUDIENCE [*pointing at* DANCER]. Put him out. Put him out.
CHORUS. You are responsible,
   You are impossible,
   Out you go.
   We will liquidate,
   The capitalist state
   Overthrow.
AUDIENCE. Atta boys.
MANAGER. Do something, man,
   As quick as you can.
   Prevent such behaviour
   And be our saviour.
   Get us out of this trouble
   As I guarantee
   My theatre will double
   Your salary.

[DANCER *dances as the demagogue. The* CHORUS *lose their menacing attitude and become fascinated. Crowd as* ♂. *Demagogue as* ♀.]

ANNOUNCER. Comrades, I absolutely agree with you. We must have a revolution. But wait a moment. All this talk about class war won't get us anywhere. The circumstances here are quite different from Russia. Russia has no middle class, no tradition of official administrative service. We must have an English revolution suited to English conditions, a revolution not to put one class on top but to abolish class, to ensure not less for some but more for all, a revolution of Englishmen for Englishmen. After all, are we not all of one blood, the blood of King Arthur, and Wayland the Smith? We have Lancelot's courage, Merlin's wisdom. Our first duty is to keep the race pure, and not let these dirty foreigners come in and take our jobs. Down with the dictatorship of international capital. Away with their filthy books which corrupt our innocent sons and daughters. English justice, English morals, England for the English.

CHORUS. Perhaps you are right, perhaps you are right.
You put things in another light.

ANNOUNCER. The Anglo-Saxon race is in danger. Who will follow him to save it?

A. I was a farmer during the war,
I sold my bacon at two and four,
If you keep out Denmark, I can do it once more—
    I'll follow thee.

B. I was a girl that had nice young men,
But they've all been going abroad since then
If you can bring them back again,
    I'll follow thee.

C. In the good old days, I was a Black and Tan
I was always there when the tortures began
If you give us a whip I'll do what I can,
    I'll follow thee.

D. For five years now I've been out of a job,
I don't care whether you're a Jew or a nob,
If you will promise to give me a bob,
    I'll follow thee.

CHORUS. The English revolution
Is the only solution
We take a resolution
    To follow thee.

ANNOUNCER [*pointing to* MANAGER]. We'll begin here
Look at him there
A dirty Jew
You know what to do. [*They assault and beat him, etc.*]

[*Ship formation.*]

> Take your place, take your place,
> To save the Anglo-Saxon race,
> Follow our gallant captain for ever
> Our dandy, our dancer, our deep sea diver.

CHORUS. We are all of one blood, we are thoroughbred,
    We'll not lose our courage, we'd sooner be dead.
    Like one big family we're all united
    In our hearts burns a fire that has been long lighted.

> Hurrah for me and hurrah for you
> Line up in file
> In a regimental style
> With the shovel, the pick, and the rake and the plough
> The beautiful old plough
>   Salute, Salute,
> Toot a toot toot,
> We'll make old England new.

The ship of England crosses the ocean
Her sails are spread, she is beautiful in motion.
We love her and obey her captain's orders
We know our mind, no enemy shall board us.

> Then hurrah for me and hurrah for you
> Though the decks may heel
> We'll be true as steel
> The captain, the bo'sun, the mate and the boy
> The pretty cabin boy
>   Salute, Salute,
> Toot a toot toot,
> Hurrah for the English crew.

Let the whirlpools boil as the billows rise higher,
We'll steer through them all to what we require
Over monsters deadly in the deep sea sand
Our keel rides on to the Promised Land.
    Then hurrah, *etc.*

God bless the wind that blows us over
God bless the will that binds us like a lover.
God bless our ship that carries us so rightly

God bless our captain day and nightly.
　　Then hurrah, *etc.*

[AUDIENCE *makes a noise like waves.*]

A. I'm pretty tough,
　　But these waves are rough,
　　I'm beginning to feel
　　A little ill,
　　Let's ask the lookout
　　What it's all about
　　Hullo, up there—
　　Have you anything to declare?
ANNOUNCER. Storm ahead.
AUDIENCE. We are the storm. [*Noises.*]
CHORUS. What shall we do
　　To pull us through?
A. Furl the sails.
B. Jettison the cargo.
C. Cast anchor.
A. This way.
B. This way.
C. This way.
A. Hold it like this.
B. Hold it like this.
C. Hold it like this.
ANNOUNCER. Lightning and thunder.
AUDIENCE. We are the lightning. Crash. Fizz.
　　We are the thunder. Boom.
A. I've got a weak heart
　　Oh, why did I ever start?
B. I shall see no more
　　The roses round the door.
C. I am an only son.
　　O what's to be done?
ANNOUNCER. Rocks ahead.
AUDIENCE. We are the rocks. [*Noises.*]
A. We shall soon run aground,
　　We shall all be drowned.
B. George, hold me tight,
　　I'm in such a fright.
C. Full steam ahead.

B. Reverse, man, reverse.
C. Stop, stop.
A. Our Father which art in—
C.   Mother!
A. Hallowed be thy—
C.   Mother!
A. Thy kingdom come.
C. Mother. Mother.

[*Crash.*]

[*During the storm the formation gets more and more disintegrated.* DANCER *gradually works into a whirling movement which culminates in a falling fit.*]

CHORUS. He's sick,
 A doctor quick.
ANNOUNCER. The condition of these people is so drastic
 Any prophet can make them enthusiastic.
 It is pleasant to march about and all shout "glory"
 But the after results are another story.
A. Hold his legs,
 Put a gag in his mouth.
CHORUS. A doctor, please.
DOCTOR [*comes up from the Audience*]. I'm a doctor,
 Let me examine him.

[*Pause.*]

CHORUS. What is it, doctor?
DOCTOR. An epileptic fit. He'll be better soon, but we must get him into bed. I am afraid this will have to be the end of his performance tonight, and for many nights to come.
CHORUS. Oh, but, doctor, the play—the play. We can't get on without him. What about us? We can't lose our job suddenly like this.
DOCTOR. I'm sorry, but it can't be helped.

[*Enter* SIR EDWARD.]

SIR E. One moment, doctor.
DOCTOR. Oh, good evening, Sir Edward. I didn't know you were here.
SIR E. Can't you really do something for the poor chap? He'll be so disappointed if he can't go on. Incidentally, there's the audience, you know. After all, they've paid for their seats.
DOCTOR. Honestly, Sir Edward, I couldn't. He's in a most critical condition. Any exertion now might be fatal.

Sir E. Couldn't you give him an injection or something? I've a friend with me who would be most annoyed if the performance were to come to an end now. I don't know what I shall say to him. You must do something. I know that he'd see that your position was secure if anything unfortunate happens.
Doctor. Who is he?
Sir E. 'Sh not so loud. [*Whispers in* Doctor's *ear.*] As a matter of fact he is very anxious to meet you. Come and have supper with us when the show's over.
Doctor. Very well, but I don't like it. I'll give him an injection. [*Turning to actors.*] Listen. I've decided to let him go on.
Chorus. O thank you, doctor.
Doctor. But mind. There's to be no excitement of any kind—no politics, for instance, something quite peaceful, something, shall we say, about the country or home life?
Chorus. We understand.
Sir E. Is he alright?
Doctor. Oh, he'll pull through, I think, if they're careful of him. He's very run down.
Sir E. You gave him an injection?
Doctor. Well, Sir Edward, what would you do with a business that was in low water?
Sir E. Why, pump in fresh capital.
Doctor. Exactly. After you, Sir Edward.
Sir E. After *you* doctor.

[*Exeunt to audience.*]

Announcer. The conscience of that poor Doctor is ill at ease
    But money is a master he is forced to please.
    The field of knowledge is so extensive
    The exploration has become expensive
    Those who seek truth discover soon
    Who pays the piper calls the tune.
A. Very well, fellows, what shall we do?
α. Oh, go and drown yourselves.

[*Exit* α *from the theatre with a great deal of noise.*]

Announcer. Notice how these are driven in desperation
    From sport to war, from action to sensation.
    Turning this way, that way, doubling on their track
    Death standing always before them, driving them back.
    In empire outposts, or flats in the South of France,

On still walking tour or enjoying the dance,
The fear is the same. We show you phases
Of its expression in their different places.
B.   Be true
To the inner self. Retire to a wood
The will of the blood is the only good
We must learn to know it.
A.   I see what you mean
We must keep our primal integrity clean.
B. Exactly.
C.   That's clear.
What a good idea.
A. Be perfectly calm.
B. Live on a farm.
C. Well out of harm.
CHORUS. Knowing no sin.
A. Only obeying.
B. Without delaying.
C. The slightest saying.
CHORUS. Of the voice within.
A [*to* AUDIENCE]. Listen, friends we
    Are a colony
    Equal and free
    Of boys and girls.

[DANCER *shakes his head.*]

β. There's something the matter with your dancing friend.
    He's getting excited.
A. He doesn't agree
    With something which we
    Have said. What can it be?
ANNOUNCER. It's about the girls. Man must be the leader whom women must obey. He must go forward into the unknown at dawn, while she waits at home trusting and believing in him, till at night he returns tired, and as such becomes as a little child again. This is her hour. She shall care for and refresh him that he may set out once more in search of the Ideal.
CHORUS. That leaves no doubt
    We must leave the girls out
    Come on, let's start.
GIRLS IN CHORUS. This is a shame
    We want a part.

MEN. You do what we say
    And run away.
β. Don't be so tame. You stay where you are.
    Don't you let 'em put that stuff on you.
GIRLS. We're going to play in this show
    Whether you like it or no.
    We won't go.
A [*to* ANNOUNCER]. They refuse to go flat
    What do you say about that?
ANNOUNCER. Make them into scenery.
A. Brilliant. My word
    That never occurred
    To me. [*To* GIRLS.] You be a bird,
    You be a tree
    So, crook your knee.
    You be a cow
    So we'll begin now.

CHORUS [*folk dance*]. Are you living in the city
    Where the traffic won't stop;
    Haggard and anxious
    For life's a flop
        Why not stop?

    Are you tired of parties
    All that clever talk?
    O boy, have you ever
    Seen a sparrowhawk?
        Learn to walk.

    Sailor, that assurance
    You lost at birth
    You can have it, recover
    A sense of worth
        Come back to earth.

    Gay girl to whom petting
    Matters so much
    Poor kid, the reason's
    You're out of touch
        With flowers and such.

    Revolutionary worker
    I get what you mean.

But what you're needing
'S a revolution within
      So let's begin.

Banker, boxer, burglar
Hostess and girl gone wrong
We've got you beat to a frazzle
This is where you belong
      Hear our song.

How happy are we
In our country colony
We play games
We call each other by our christian names
Sitting by streams
We have sweet dreams
You can take it as true
That Voltaire knew
We cultivate our gardens when we're feeling blue
Lying close to the soil
Our hearts strike oil
We live day and night
In the inner light
We contemplate our navels till we've second sight
Gosh, it's all right
In our country colony.

[*Towards the end of the dance* A *gets out of time.*]

    Clumsy, can't you count one, two, three, four. You're spoiling the dance.
β.   And I don't blame him. 'E wants his girl friend. Did you see 'im making eyes at that little bit over there on the right?
A [*breaking off and coming forward*].
    I won't dance any more
    You are mistaken
    About the path you have taken
    What you desire
    Is no earthly fire
    You won't find the truth
    In a beautiful youth
    Nor will it be found
    In tilling the ground

For the Eternal Word
Has no habitation
In beast or bird
In sea or stone
Nor in the circumstances
Of country dances
It abideth alone.
He who would prove
The Primal love
Must leave behind
All love of his kind
And fly alone
To the Alone.

CHORUS. We don't understand.
WOMEN [*ceasing to be scenery*].
We do, and he's right
You were fooled all right
You thought you were escaping from sin
By leaving us out but you left yourselves in.

CHORUS. This is something new
We don't know what to do
This doctrine is at variance
With all our past experience.

ANNOUNCER. For those who found life evil
Fearing the devices of the devil
In the middle ages
There were stone cages
Cells were built
Where they could expiate their guilt
Where they could retire
And seek their heart's desire,
Conquering temptation
Through self-abnegation.
But at the present day
There is a more modern way
Explore dry deserts, go
Across the Arctic snow,
Or any dangerous region
Or join the Foreign Legion
Race death and all his power
At three hundred miles an hour
Or fly above the clouds

        And the ease-loving crowds
        Through the astringent air
        And face death lonely there.
CHORUS. You may perhaps be right
        About this mystic flight
        Again it may be fiction
        To tell the truth we lack conviction
        It would be best we feel
        If someone would appeal
        To our imagination
        And give a demonstration
        And shew us the technique
        This is what we seek.
        Now, who will be our master? Who will be the one
        To teach us how to fly from the alone to the Alone?

[*Pause.*]

[DANCER *comes forward. While the* ANNOUNCER *is speaking, he should be rubbed down by masseurs and generally got ready.*]

ANNOUNCER. Hullo, everybody. As you all know, the greatest feat, the most stupendous risk in human history is being undertaken this evening by a gentleman who prefers to remain known simply as the Pilot. His ambition is no less than to reach the very heart of Reality.
γ.   I'll bet my boots he can't do it.
δ.   I'll bet my opera hat he can.
γ.   Bet you my car.
δ.   Bet you my wife.
γ.   Bet you my house.
δ.   Bet you my Scotch grouse moor.
ANNOUNCER. The Pilot desires me—one moment please. The news has just come through that two listeners are betting a pair of boots, a car and a house to an opera hat, a wife and a Scotch grouse moor on the result. As I was saying, the Pilot desires me to thank all those who have been kind enough to send him messages of good luck, knitted scarves, crystallised fruits, killing-bottles, copies of the Outline of Modern Knowledge for Boys and Girls, pamphlets relating to the pyramids, birth-control, a universal language, etc. He regrets that owing to pressure he is unable to answer each correspondent individually, but trusts that they will accept this public acknowledgment. The time is now (*whatever it is*) so we are going over to the ground itself where Mr Box and Mr Cox will carry on and give you an eye-witness's account of this unique event.

[*While* Box *and* Cox *are speaking, the* Audience *should render the appropriate noises they describe.*]

Box. I should say it's freezing. What do you think, Cox?

Cox. There *is* a nip in the air, Box.

Box. The crowd are stamping their feet and swinging their arms to keep warm. I hear some of the women have been here since the day before yesterday. There must be fifty thousand people here.

Cox. Fifty, Box.

Box. Mr Cox thinks there are fifty thousand. I'm going to toss him for it. You call, Cox.

Cox. Tails.

Box. Tails it is. Very well, then, there are fifty thousand here. It's a beautifully clear starlight night, and they're as happy as sandboys. Away to the right a member of the Green Cheese Society is making a spirited speech. David Johnstone, the six year old marvel, is thrilling a portion of the monster audience by the instantaneous conversion of logarithms into improper fractions. There are a lot of distinguished people here. [*Mentions any there may be in the audience.*] I say, Cox, can you make out with your glasses what's going on on the left?

Cox. It looks as though they had caught a pickpocket. Yes ugh, don't look, they're breaking his back against the railings.

Box. Very regrettable. [*Cheers.*] Ah, can you hear that? What is it, Cox? Wait a moment. Yes, it is. Here he comes. Splendid fellow. I think he's looking a bit pale. You carry on, Cox; you've got field glasses and see more detail.

Cox. He's coming into the enclosure. The crowd are frantic. The police are holding them. They're giving way. Hold them. Well done. The police are marvellous. Now he's acknowledging the cheers of the crowd. Someone at back mentioned Jules Verne. No one answered him.

Box. How would you like to be going with them, Cox?

Cox. I think I'd rather stay where I am.

Box. Perhaps you're right. But still it does make one feel young again. Do you remember how we cheered you when you did that run through in the Ampleforth match and scored as the whistle went?

Cox. A fluke, Box. He's getting ready. One, two, three. He's off.

[*Dance begins.*]

Cox. The crowd are holding their breath. Marvellous. Did you see that turn? He's doing it. I'm afraid that listener will lose his boots. He's well away now. What did I say, Box?

Box. Yes, I admit you read him right. Hullo, look, what's the matter?

Cox. What is it? He's waving. Something's up. He's righting himself. No, he isn't. O God, he's fallen.

[DANCER *falls and staggers up being paralysed from the feet up.*]

CHORUS. Get him into a chair
    And give him some air
    If we only knew
    What we could do
    Does anyone know
    Where we can go?

[*Enter* MANAGER.]

MANAGER. Gut evening friends. The last time we met
    Ve had a leetle quarrel. But let's forget
    No? Now leesen, I have given op
    My theatre beesness and opened a clob
    A cosy little night-club just like home.
ANNOUNCER. In the face of death however violent their self-assertion
    There comes at last an end to every exertion.
    Nothing they desire now but to return to earth
    To live for ever in the peace that preceded their birth.

[*As he is talking the* STAGE HANDS *bring in a dumb-waiter with drinks and set the stage.* MANAGER *produces a card with* Alma Mater *written on it and hangs it up.*]

MANAGER. I hev called it the Alma Mater just to remind you
    Of the beautiful English homes you leave behind you
    Beautiful food, lovely wines. Now won't you come?
ANNOUNCER. Who is ugly
    Who is sick
    Who is lonely
    Come on quick
           Hither.

[*The* AUDIENCE *begin to come up on to the stage.*]

γ. Hopeless at games, despising self in room not knocked at black hat well down, I come for secret triumph, cause for smiling when others turn away. I come for you.

δ. Hating a village spire, my simple people's answer, prospect of everlasting rain on half-ploughed fields. I come for expensive shoes to take applause from tables. I come for you.

γ. How goes it then?

THE DANCE OF DEATH

δ. It goes me well.
γ. Comest thou with?
δ. Self-understandingly I come.
ε. Needing its food and warmth, my body, unfeeling instrument of my will, shall serve the other hunger. Once I knew desire and its sorrow. May no embraces ever again make me taste that pleasure, lest, tasting, I place myself once more within the circle of Another, and there, enchanted, perish.
ζ. Blessed be my father who, toiling for a lifetime, left me such a gift. These coins have power to transform her whom I shall choose into a mother. Through them and her I shall recover the primal sleep, freely receive that love which does not have to be deserved.
η. To-day my dog died. No sound greeted my footstep on the stair. I could not stay at home. Had overheard last Autumn in the office, Crowder speaking of his, forgotten until now. My name is Alfred Jones. Please speak to me.
θ. Little they guess, the rats. Confidante of great ladies, the pride of salons, bowed to at private views, I could blast them with a word, for I am greater than them all. Common, they would not dare to come here, but I dare. On these, who do not ask them, I bestow my honours. To these, because the basest, it is my pleasure to be humble.

[*The* DANCER *is wheeled forward.*]

ANNOUNCER. Make way. Make way. He's living still,
   But remember he is very ill,
   But wheel him further away from the wall,
   So he can see better. It is his last time at all.
A [*his attendant*]. Oh, don't say that, sir.
   He'll soon be about.
ANNOUNCER. He thanks you for your words, but there's no doubt
   Fetch him a half—
A. Do you think he better?
ANNOUNCER. Very well then, he'll have a whole litre.
B. Day, my sir.
C. Day, my sir. How goes it thee?
D. Thou seest dreadful out—
   Thou hast thyself too well amused, not true?
   No, swindle not.
B. Hast a cigarette for me?
A [*distributing cigarettes for* DANCER *by throwing them from a box*]. Catch.
B. I thank.
A. Thee also.

C. I thank.

D. Forget me not, my sire, I thank.

ANNOUNCER. Fetch him some pen and paper and write
    He is going to make his will to-night.
    And tell the story of his life to you
    As dying men are apt to do.

[*Tune, Casey Jones.*]

    He leaves his body, he leaves his wife
    He leaves the years, he leaves the life
    For the power and the glory of his kingdom they must pass
    To work their will among the working class.

CHORUS. The Greeks were balanced, their art was great
    They thought out in detail the city state
    But a gap to the interior was found at Carcassonne
    So trade moved westward and they were gone.

ANNOUNCER. He leaves you his horses the light and the dark
    He leaves the oaks in the long deer park
    He leaves you his meadows, his harvests and his heath
    With the coal and the minerals that lie underneath.

CHORUS. The Romans as every schoolboy knows
    United an empire with their roman nose
    But they caught malaria and they couldn't keep accounts
    And barbarians conquered them who couldn't pronounce.

ANNOUNCER. He leaves you his engines and his machines
    The sum of all his productive means.
    He leaves you his railways, his liners and his banks
    And he leaves you his money to spend with thanks.

CHORUS. The feudal barons they did their part
    Their virtues were not of the head but the heart.
    Their ways were suited to an agricultural land
    But lending on interest they did not understand.

ANNOUNCER. To the medical student who came in tight
    That chandelier there to sleep with to-night.
    And then to that lady who ought never to have come
    A tip for the attendant and a taxi home.

CHORUS. Luther and Calvin put in a word
    The god of your priests, they said, is absurd.

His laws are inscrutable and depend upon grace
So laissez-faire please for the chosen race.

The bourgeois thought this splendid advice
They cut off the head of their king in a trice
They enclosed the common lands and laid them for sheep
And the peasants were told they could play bo-peep.

ANNOUNCER. And last he would like to congratulate
    The actors, orchestra and authors to-night
    Upon this performance and as soon as it is done
    May engagements be offered them by everyone.

CHORUS. They invited them into a squalid town
    They put them in factories and did them down
    Then they ruined each other for they didn't know how
    They were making the conditions that are killing them now.

ANNOUNCER. He asks for free drinks for the company here.
    To make their lives not so hard to bear
    So drink to his funeral in claret and beer
    For he wishes you all a very happy new year.

[*Clocks strikes 12.*]

CHORUS. New Year. New Year. We have thirst.
ANNOUNCER. Send round the boot, waiter.
WAITER. So direct, my sir.
B.   He's sending me the boot.
A.   He's not mean. He's goot.
D.   Pass it.
C.   Pass it.
B.   New Year. Now, altogether.

CHORUS. Hail the strange electric writing
    Alma Mater on the door
    Like a secret sign inviting
    All the rich to meet the poor
    Alma Mater, ave salve
    Floreas in secula.

GIRLS. You sent us men with lots of money,
    You sent us men you knew were clean,
    You sent us men as sweet as honey,
    With whom we could be really keen.

> Always even though we marry
> Though we wear ancestral pearls
> One memory we'll always carry
> We were Alma Mater girls.

CHORUS. Alma Mater, ave salve, *etc.*

THIEVES. Let Americans with purses
> Go for short strolls after dark,
> Let the absent-minded nurses
> Leave an heiress in the park,
> Though the bullers sooner or later
> Clap us handcuffed into jail,
> We will remember Alma Mater,
> We will remember without fail.

CHORUS. Alma Mater, ave salve, *etc.*

BOYS. The French are mean and Germans lazy,
> Dutchmen will leave you in the end.
> Only the Englishman though he's crazy,
> He will keep you for a friend.
> Always though a king in cotton
> Waft us all to foreign parts
> Alma Mater shall not be forgotten,
> She is written on our hearts.

CHORUS. Alma Mater, ave salve, *etc.*

BLACKMAILERS. We must thank our mugs' relations
> For our income and man's laws.
> But the first congratulations
> Alma Mater they are yours.

COINERS. When the fool believes our story
> When he thinks our coins are true
> To Alma Mater be the glory
> For she taught us what to do.

CHORUS. Alma Mater, ave salve, *etc.*

OLD HACKS AND TROTS. We cannot dance upon the table
> Now we're old as souvenirs
> Yet as long as we are able
> We will remember bygone years
> Still as when we were the attraction
> Come the people from abroad,

Spending though we're out of action,
More than they can well afford.

CHORUS. Alma Mater, ave salve, *etc.*

GRAND CHORUS. Navies rust and nations perish
Currency is never sure
But Alma Mater she shall flourish
While the sexes shall endure.
Alma Mater, ave salve
Floreas in secula.

A. Some brandy quick
He's sick.
ANNOUNCER. He's dead.

[*Pause.*]
[*Noise without.*]

A. Quick under the table, it's the 'tecs and their narks,
O no, salute—it's Mr Karl Marx.

CHORUS [*singing to Mendelssohn's "Wedding March"*].
O Mr Marx, you've gathered
All the material facts
You know the economic
Reasons for our acts.

[*Enter* KARL MARX *with two young communists.*]

KARL MARX. The instruments of production have been too much for him. He is liquidated.

[*Exeunt to a Dead March.*]

THE END

The Chase

A Play in Three Acts

BY W. H. AUDEN

[1934]

TO
TYRONE GUTHRIE

My relations are but three
And they live in a tree
   They are beautiful birds
But sometimes they are cruel.

JOHN BOWES

PRINCIPAL CHARACTERS

The Vicar of Pressan Ambo
General Hotham of Puffin Conyers
Augustus Bicknell, Head of Tudro Reformatory
Alan Norman
Sergeant Bunyan, assistant at Tudro
Mr Hayboy, research chemist
Jimmy
George
Derek
Hector
The Surgeon

1st ⎫
2nd ⎬ Pressmen
3rd ⎭
1st ⎫
2nd ⎬ Policemen
3rd ⎭

The Manager of the Nineveh Hotel
Mrs Hotham
Mildred Luce, the Vicar's sister
Jean
Miss Iris Crewe of Honeypot Hall
Miss Lou Vipond

The Witnesses
Chorus

Villagers, Boys, Waiters, Pages, Soldiers, Medical Students, etc.

Chorus

The summer holds: upon its glittering lake
Lie Europe and the islands, many rivers
Wrinkling her surface like a ploughman's palm
Under the bellies of the grazing horses
On the far side of posts and bridges
The vigorous shadows dwindle; nothing wavers.
Between the cathedrals and the wide feminine valleys
Where dragonflies race above the still and treacherous reaches
Between the big farms and the arterial roads
We show you a hedgeless country, the source of streams,
Deadstones above Redam, Thackmoss, Halfpenny Scar,
Two-top and Muska, Pity Mea, Bullpot Brow.
Land of the stone chat: a bird stone-haunting, an unquiet bird.
Before the Romans built their rational roads
Man mined for lead here, honoured the hammer.
In a mound near The Viols; was found a lead pig, dating from Hadrian
A stone lamp at Midge Pits; a bronze axe head at Softly Side.
A charter records the murder of a German miner; and copper at Skeers.
Here generations farmed at the week-ends only
They loved their lamps; and were obedient to their fathers.
Marshalls were appointed: to supervise the buying and selling of ore; to detect false measure.
New veins were discovered; special laws awarded the ownership to the discoverer.
No one remembers the first mine at Hardshins; nor the day when Hubberdale Pipe was struck.
Susannah was rich in the water-sill; and the Hospital down to the Jew bottom limestone.
A trial was made at Elphytorey: Triddle pinched out in the Whinsill
Stafford's Dream was good while it lasted; a fortune came out of Surrender
But alas this is not a historical comedy: full of quaint and beautiful dresses
Dancing at the wedding; a background of English glory and humour.
We speak of the numbing uncertainty of the present; near in the North
Hiker with sunburn blisters on your office pallor
Cross-country champion with corks in your hands
When you have eaten your sandwich, your salt and your apple
When you have begged your glass of milk from ill-kept farm
What is it you see?

□

The shafts are filled with water; the mosses grope over the washing
  floors.
I look through the rigid arms of broken waterwheels: I see lambs
  feeding.
Trucks lie overturned; an old rail patches a gap in the wall
Rain falls through the gaping roofs of sheds; it falls on the obsolete
  inventions and structures.
Those who sang in the inns at evening have departed; they saw their
  hope in another country.
"What is going to happen to us" they said: "Lead is ten pounds a ton"
Their sons also; their daughters entered service in the suburban areas;
  they became typists, mannequins and factory operatives; they
  desired a different rhythm of life.

That was an ill bargain that was struck; a bargain with nasal-voiced
  Australia
They were to build us cruisers: Nelson was not forgotten
Destroyers to sweep the seas; flotillas against fear.
We were to take their lead; to import at their price our whole supply
There is no smoke from Fleming's chimney; the cupolas are cold in
  Washtub Wood
Daddry and Noonstones weep: At Broken Hill you were defeated.

But one mine is working: At Windyacre the wheels turn
Yes at Windyacre; in the parish of Pressan Ambo
Mr Fordham has made it pay; he has installed the latest machinery
A power house at Sally Grain; a power house with a pelton wheel.
He has replaced the buddles by magnetic separators, separating blende
  from galena.
One man can tend five machines: He needs less labour.
He has turned off hands: the men are angry.
He has dismissed Corder; Forge-Hammond, Ormerod and Rylands
  have received their notice
They gather at the corners of the village street; they argue in the
  evening
They are holding a meeting of protest to-morrow; They threaten a
  strike; Their wives are with them.
Fordham is firm. He loves his creation.
He argues with them; either that or nothing.
We must work efficiently: or not at all.
Without the machines we should have to close down; the last mine in
  the district; you can take it or leave it.
He is a liar they say: The company is rich

Or why do the directors go about in Daimlers; why do their wives drink
    tea in the yew avenues, talking of art.
Their sons read the classics at Oxford; and their daughters play tennis
    on the Riviera.

Man is changed by his living; but not fast enough
His concern to-day; is for that which yesterday did not occur.
In the hour of the Blue Bird and the Bristol Bomber; his thoughts are
    suitable to the years of the Penny-Farthing.
He tosses at night who at noonday found no truth.

But stand aside; the play is beginning.
It appears to concern itself with quite other matters; with private
    salvation
The scene is Pressan, the speaker the Vicar
Listen.

Act I Scene 1

VICAR. Good evening, gentlemen, you wished to see me.
3 PRESSMEN. Yes, if you please.

> [*Taking out notebooks and writing aside.*]

> Tall, scholarly, and dreamy.

1ST PRESSMAN. The papers which we represent,
    The Post, The Telegraph, The Mail, have sent
    Us here about the great event
    To-morrow. We must gather news
    Get local colour, interviews.
    But firstly let me introduce
    Myself and friends. This man is What
    He's Why, he's Where. And that's the lot.
2ND PRESSMAN. The Morning Post
    Is England's ghost. [*Makes the secret sign of his paper.*]
1ST PRESSMAN. The Daily Telegraph
    Raises no foolish laugh. [*Ditto.*]
3RD PRESSMAN. But look at the sale
    Of the Daily Mail. [*Ditto.*]
TOGETHER. We're pleased to meet you, sir
    And so says each reporter
    And if you don't feel flattered
    You're a B-F, cause you oughter.

1st Pressman. And now, explain, sir, if you please
　　About to-morrow's ceremonies.
Vicar. The ancient family of Crewe
　　　It may perhaps be known to you
2nd Pressman. It is; it fought at Waterloo
3rd Pressman. And many other places too.
Vicar. For generations has owned the land
　　　The mines, the fells on which we stand.
　　　Sir Vauncey Crewe who was the last
　—God rest his soul for he has passed—

　　　　　　　　[*Crosses himself. The* Pressmen *take off their bowler hats.*]

　　　We touched our hats to, had a son
　　　A handsome lad, his only one,
　　　Called Francis who was to succeed him
　—Would he were here, we badly need him.
　　　They quarrelled I am sad to say
　　　And twenty years ago to-day
　　　Young Francis packed and ran away
　　　Leaving behind him no address.
3rd Pressman. Why did they quarrel?
1st Pressman.　　　　　　　　I can guess.

　　　　　　　　　　　　　　　[*Whisper together.*]

2nd Pressman. Mem.; question the servants at the hall.
Vicar. And since that day no news at all
　　　Has ever come. We do not know
　　　If he be living still or no.

　　　　　　　　　　　　　　　[*Clears his throat.*]

　　　Sir Vauncey died ten years ago
　　　Francis, his heir being missing still
　　　And left these clauses in his will
　　　Each year his villages in turn
　　　Should choose by lottery a man
　　　To find Sir Francis if he can
　　　Further he promised half his land
　　　And Iris his daughter adds her hand
　　　In marriage to the lucky one
　　　Who comes home with his only son

This year is Pressan's turn to choose
But now, I hope you will excuse
Me but I still have preparations
For to-morrow's celebrations.
1ST PRESSMAN. Before you go sir, we have one request
Please face this way and look your best
The Mail, The Post, and The Telegraph
Will be honoured with your photograph.

[*Cameras. Flashlight.*]

ALL. We hope to-morrow will be bright.
We thank you sir, and wish good night.
1ST PRESSMAN. Well boys that's all to-day, I think
It's opening time and time to drink.
O Damn, we've a visit still to pay
To Bicknell, Major and B.A.
3RD PRESSMAN. Who's he?
1ST PRESSMAN. You are an ignoramus
He is the principal of the most famous
Reformatory in England, built at Pressan
To teach town-lads a nature lesson.
To quote from the prospectus. Tudro is
The most select of reformatories
Classes are small; the beds are aired
The diet is scientifically prepared
And what we value highest here
Is just a Christian character
Our pupils find fit preparation
In thoughts to suit their humble station
Was it Kipling who said. No it must have been some other fella:

In the boiler rooms of liners from Vancouver to Penang
    In bars and factories up and down the land
You will know a Tudro product 'cause he never uses slang
    And always has a wash before he shakes your hand.

You will know him on the quayside by the way he takes your bag
    And the way he says "Ay Ay sir" in an obedient sort of tone
If you quote, when you have tipped him, an apt Vergilian tag
    He will cap it, if he's Tudro to the bone.

2ND PRESSMAN. It's getting much too late
So let Tudro wait

Until the morning
My stomach gives me warning
The Press must feed
If the Press is to succeed.

[*Song and dance.*]

> Rhythm of life
> That's what we're after
> Tragedy, laughter
>   Death.
> Birth, marriage and love
> The breath
> Of life in the modern and odd
> At binges and on the fringes
> Of Civilisation.
> What film stars wish, the lives of certain fish,
> Thoughts on, reports on
> God in his heaven above
> The Modern Press
>   Depends for its success
> On you and you
> What you desire and what you do
>   On your imagination.
> We watch your faces
> We hear when your blood races
> We capture your rapture, your
>   Rhythm of life.

[*Exeunt.*]

Act I Scene 2

[*Tudro Reformatory. A bare room with a barred window and a table and benches. Doors left and right. A door at the back opens into a yard. Enter* WARDER BUNYAN *from the yard, with* GEORGE *and* JIMMY, *boys of about sixteen, wearing flash East End suits and check caps.*]

GEORGE. Nah then, cheese it Guv'nor—who in hell d'yer think yer pushin'?

BUNYAN. That's all right, sonny. I'm not pushing nothing I don't know of.

GEORGE. Thinks yer bleedin' funny, don't yer?

BUNYAN. Don't think. I knows.
GEORGE. Jest yer wyte till I hinforms me pal the Prince o' Wyles wot yer bin an' done ter us.
JIMMY. Aw, cheese it, George. Wot's the bleedin' use? We copped it this time.
GEORGE. Copped it my foot. Yer wyte till I tells me pal the Prince o' Wyles—
BUNYAN. That's all right, sonny. 'E's been a pal to 'undreds 'ere, but I never see 'im 'elp any on 'em out.

> [*A steam siren blows, off. Enter a crowd of boys in broad-arrow suits, from the yard, with tin mugs. They sit down at the table and begin banging and shouting.*]

BOYS. Soup! We wants our soup! We wants our bleedin' soup!
BUNYAN. All right, yer lordships. All right. All right. [*Exit.*]
A BOY [*to* GEORGE]. Wot's yer nyme?
GEORGE. The Right Honorrible Stanley Baldwin. M.P.
ANOTHER BOY. Coo, Christ. Aint they toffs?
ANOTHER BOY [*snatching off* GEORGE's *cap and putting it on rakishly*]. Ow, chyse me! [GEORGE *snatches it back and knocks the boy down.*]
THE BOY. Yer wyte, yer bleedin' barstard!

> [*Uproar.*]
> [*Enter* VICAR.]

A BOY. Look, 'ere's Uncle.

> [*Uproar. They crowd round him, banging and shouting.*]

ALL. Ullo Uncle.
1ST BOY. Got a fag fer me, Uncle?
2ND BOY. Ere, smell this soup.
3RD BOY. Stop shuvving, can't yer. I wornt to show 'im ma boät. Ooncle, luke whart arve maäde.
4TH BOY. Got annuver book fer me, Uncle? Oive finished this wan. Aint it thrilling when Dick gets shut up wiv the gerilla.
VICAR. Please. Please. One at a time.

> [*Cries of Shut up. Noise subsides.* BOYS *form a rough ring round him.*]

Here you are, Henry, catch. You'll never grow if you smoke like that, I'm afraid. Now Albert, what is it? O yes the soup. Hm. It does smell a bit strong I admit. I'll speak to Mr Bicknell about it. Well, Henry,

I must congratulate you. That's a beautiful piece of work. You haven't got the rudder quite right yet, have you? Glad you liked the book, Arthur. I haven't read this one but I believe it's quite good. [*Noticing* GEORGE *and* JIMMY.] Hullo. I don't remember seeing your faces before. Are you new arrivals? [*They nod.*] What's your name?

JIMMY. Jimmy.

VICAR. And yours?

GEORGE. George.

VICAR. Well, Jimmy and George, I'm very sorry to see you here but least said soonest mended. Have a bull's eye. Where do you two come from?

GEORGE. Colestreet.

VICAR. You ought to find plenty of friends here, then. Most of them come from there.

BOY. Read us some more of yer istory abaht the Great War.

VOICES. Yes. Go on Uncle.

VICAR [*fishes envelopes from his pocket*]. Where did I get to last time?

BOY. Gordon was aving a chat with a German prisoner.

ANOTHER BOY. Naaw, we're much further on than that. 'E was waiting for the attack larst tyme.

VOICES. Yus, that's right.

VICAR [*reading*]. He could feel his heart pounding against his ribs. "That's good. That's good" it seemed to say. He looked at his wrist-watch, trying to seem calm. Ten more seconds, nine, eight, seven, six, five, four, three, two.

BOY. Look out, here comes his nibs.

[*Enter* SERGEANT BUNYAN *and* BICKNELL.]

SERGEANT. Atten. . . . shun.

BICKNELL. Hullo, Vicar; spoiling the boys as usual. You don't know them. Give them an inch and they'll take a mile.

VICAR. Good-evening, Bicknell. I've just dropped in to see you about the arrangements for to-morrow afternoon. I'm delighted you've decided.

BICKNELL. Ssh. [*Aside to* VICAR.] I haven't told them yet. [*Aloud.*] Come along and have some coffee in the study.

[*Exeunt* BICKNELL *and* VICAR.]

SERGEANT. Now boys. Steady now steady. Not a movement. Class. Dis . . . miss. As you were. We'll have O'Grady. Smartly now. Head turning quickly by numbers beginning with the right. One. Two. Harry and Arthur I saw you. Off you go and fetch the soup. O'Grady says Two.

Arms bend. O'Grady says Arms bend. Hands down. Quick. You four lay the table. O'Grady says Hands down. Hips firm. O'Grady says Hips firm. O'Grady says Heels raise. Knees bend. Got you. Go and Fetch the cups. O'Grady says Knees stretch. O'Grady says Heels lower. Hands down. O'Grady says Hands down. As you were. Alright that'll do. Class. Dismiss.

BOYS [*scrambling for places and soup*]. 'Ere this aint soup. Shyme!
SERGEANT. It's all you'll get. Pore little bleeders.
1ST BOY [*smelling it*]. Cor, don't it whistle?
2ND BOY [*jumping onto table and holding up bootlace*]. Dees is zoo mooch Gomrades; ow long shall we deese oppressions endure? Are we to be treated like the hoonds?
ALL. Nah.
3RD BOY. We've ad enough.
4TH BOY. Joostice.
2ND BOY. We demand der free air. Der zunlicht.
4TH BOY. Good ole Fritz.
5TH BOY. Three cheers for Fritz.
ALL. Ip, ip, Oory! Oory! Oory!
A BOY AT THE DOOR. Look aht. Ere comes 'is nibs.

[*Enter* SERGEANT *and* BICKNELL.]

SERGEANT. Atten.... shun. [*Goes to piano.*]
BICKNELL. The Vicar has very kindly invited you to the ceremony tomorrow afternoon. At two o'clock a bell will be rung. You will go upstairs and you will put on your blue stockings and your blue suits. Every boy will see that he has a clean handkerchief. At two-fifteen a second bell will be rung and you will assemble in the quad for call-over. When call-over is finished you will line up in age order and will then march down to the village in double file and in silence—IN SILENCE. Remember please there is to be no ragging of any kind. Any boy who is seen ragging will be very severely dealt with indeed. I have one other announcement. The mine at Windyacre is Out of Bounds until further notice. I want to see those who sleep in Durham and Carlisle in five minutes' time in the study. New boys stay behind for a moment *now* please. [*Rings a bell.*]
BOYS [*sing grace, accompanied at piano by* SERGEANT].
        For health and strength and daily food
        We praise thy name, O God.

[*Exeunt* BOYS *in silence, followed by* SERGEANT.]

BICKNELL. Come here. [JIMMY *comes forward.*] What's your name?

JIMMY. Jymes Halbert 'Enery Platt.
BICKNELL. Say Sir when you're speaking to me.
JIMMY. Sir.
BICKNELL. And take off your cap. [JIMMY *does so*.] Now listen to me, Platt. I say this to every boy who comes to Tudro. This is not a prison. It's a Home. You understand?
JIMMY. Yes.
BICKNELL. Yes, sir.
JIMMY. Sir.
BICKNELL. I've been governor of this place now for ten years. And all the time I've been drilling into you boys' heads that this is a Home. Boys come here determined to regard this place as a Prison. I'm determined that they shall regard it as a Home. Very well. It's my will against theirs. And you'll find that I invariably win.
JIMMY. Yes, sir.
BICKNELL. I divide the boys who come here into two sorts, the rotters and the slackers. The rotters I break and the slackers I put the fear of God into. Now which sort are you?
JIMMY. Dunno, sir.
BICKNELL. Well, we'll soon find out. And when we've found out, we can start work. I wish you could see yourself as you'll be in a month from now. Your own mother wouldn't recognize you. But get this clear right at the start. This is a Home. Whatever you make of yourself here, you'll make by self-discipline and self-control. The Tudro code will help you to build up both. If you need a damn good hiding, we'll give it you. If you need to put a curb on your beastly physical appetites—all you boys are greedy as hogs—we'll keep you on dog biscuit for a month. Now do you quite understand?
JIMMY. Yes, sir.
BICKNELL. Good, that is all. Good night. [*Exit* BICKNELL.]

> [*The siren blows, off. All the* BOYS *enter chasing one of the maids across the stage, singing. (Tune: The Great American Railway.)*]

BOYS.
    In nineteen hundred and thirty-three
    The Bishop started to rescue me
    He started just above the knee
       When I was a parson's daughter.

[*Exeunt.*]
[*Enter* SERGEANT.]

SERGEANT. Ere you two. You'll ave to sleep in the office to-night. There isn't room in there. I'll go and get some blankets. [*Exit.*]
GEORGE. See 'ere Jimmy. This is our chance. Ter-night, we'll 'op it. Yer gyme?
JIMMY. Bet yur life.
GEORGE. We'll ave to get a disguise like, when we're aht. I reckon we can pinch some duds in the village. [*As* SERGEANT *returns with blankets.*] Luvverly night, aint it. I don't think.
SERGEANT. Now then, sonny. You cut along. Know the way don't you?
GEORGE. 'Appy dreams. An I opes they're dry.

                    [*Exeunt* GEORGE *and* JIMMY.]

VOICE OFF. Sergeant, aint yer comin to kiss us goodnight.
SERGEANT. Lights out in five minutes. And then we'll have silence please. [*Exit.*]

         [*Various noises off. The* BOYS *begin to sing. Enter* GEORGE *and* JIMMY, *left. Stealthily they cross the stage and exit left into the yard.*]

BOYS [*singing off*]. Do yer want to see me agyne
              Then come to the stytion before the tryne
              In the gen'ral waitin' 'all
              We'll see each other for the last time of all.

                    BLACK OUT

Act I Scene 3

[*Curtains open at the top of the Cyclorama, disclosing the* WITNESSES, *old men identical in nightshirts and night caps.*]

1ST WITNESS.   The young men in Pressan to-night
                    Toss on their beds
             Their pillows do not comfort
                    Their uneasy heads
             The lot that decides their fate
                    Is cast to-morrow
             One must depart and face
                    Danger and sorrow.

VOICES. Is it me? Is it me? Is it—me?

2ND WITNESS. Look in your heart and see
  There lies the answer
Though the heart like a clever
  Conjuror or dancer
Deceives you often into many
  A curious sleight
And motives like stowaways
  Are found too late.

VOICES. What shall he do whose heart
Chooses to depart?

1ST WITNESS. He shall against his peace
  Feel his heart harden
Envy the heavy birds
  At home in a garden.
For walk he must the empty
  Selfish journey
Between the needless risk
  And the endless safety.

VOICES. Will he safe and sound
Return to his own ground?

2ND WITNESS. Clouds and lions stand
  Before him dangerous.
And the hostility of dreams
  O let him honour us.
Lest he should be ashamed
  In the hour of crisis
In the valleys of corrosion
  Tarnish his brightness.

VOICES. Who are you whose speech
Sounds far out of reach?

WITNESSES [*song*]. You are the town and we are the clock
 We are the guardians of the gate in the rock
  The Two
 On your left and on your right
 In the day and in the night
  We are watching you.

THE CHASE

Wiser not to ask just what has occurred
To them who disobeyed our word
    To those
We were the whirlpool, we were the reef,
We were the formal nightmare, grief
    And the unlucky rose.

Climb up the crane, learn the sailor's words
When the ships from the islands laden with birds
    Come in
Tell your stories of fishing and other men's wives
The expansive moments of constricted lives
    In the lighted inn.

But do not imagine we do not know
Nor that what you hide with such care won't show
    At a glance.
Nothing is done, nothing is said
But don't make the mistake of believing us dead
    I shouldn't dance.

We're afraid in that case you'll have a fall
We've been watching you over the garden wall
    For hours
The sky is darkening like a stain
Something is going to fall like rain
    And it won't be flowers.

When the green field comes off like a lid
Revealing what was much better hid
    Unpleasant
And look behind you without a sound
The woods have come up and are standing round
    In deadly crescent.

The bolt is sliding in its groove
Outside the window is the black remov-
    -ers van
And now with sudden swift emergence
Come the woman in dark glasses and the humpbacked surgeons
    And the scissor man.

This might happen any day
So be careful what you say
    Or do

Be clean, be tidy, oil the lock
Trim the garden, wind the clock
   Remember the Two.

[*Both pick up telephone receivers.*]

BLACK OUT

Act I Scene 4

[*The Vicarage garden. It is just getting light.* GEORGE *and* JIMMY *discovered sheltering by a bush.*]

GEORGE. It's perishin' cold. This ere dew fair makes you damp. My plates are cold. Where the 'ell are we?

JIMMY. It's gettin a bit lighter now. Arf-a-mo. Yus, look George, there's a church or somethink. Wonder oose garden we've got into. Shouldn't wonder if it's that there parson's. A decent kind of bloke he seemed larst night but wouldn't he arf jump if he found us ere among his vegetables. I wish we was safe back in Colestreet. Do yer think we'll get there orlright, George?

GEORGE. Corse we shall. Gimme a fag.

JIMMY. Why can't yer git some of yer own. Always cadgin, you are. Besides, I aint got none.

GEORGE [*snatching a case out of* JIMMY's *pocket*]. O aint yer.

JIMMY [*furious*]. You jest give those back, yer dirty thief. And you wiv a notecase you found at the stytion with Gawd knows ow many notes in it.

GEORGE. 'Ere, oose show wuz this anyway? If it wasn't for me you'd be in Tudro, sittin on yer be'ind and cryin for Muvver.

JIMMY. You. If it wasn't for you. And oo the ell do yer think you are when you're at ome? Many's the time I've stood you a cup of tea when you adn't the price of a bed at Levy's. An' glad you was of it, an' glad enuff yer was if yer cud git awy wiv some pore arf-blind ole mug wot cudn't see yer ugly fyce.

GEORGE. Jest you take care, yer bleedin little barstard. Der yer see this?

JIMMY. Garn then. Garn. Jest you it me, yer dirty little arf-crahn pouf.

GEORGE [*suddenly subsiding as* VICAR *and his* COOK *emerge from the house*]. Sh. Someone's coming.

VICAR. But Mrs Burke what shall I do?
   I can't get dinner by myself.

Mrs Burke. You'll find the cold meat on the shelf.
Vicar. But I've got guests. It must be hot.
Mrs Burke. I'll make a stew and leave it in the pot.
　　You'll only have to put it on at six.
　　I'm sorry to leave you in a fix
　　But I promised Maggie I'd go to the meeting
　　And lend her a hand with arranging the seating
　　And a promise is a promise. It's only to-day
　　And her boy is one that they've turned away.
　　Mr Fordham and the company can say what they like
　　If they don't take them back, there's going to be a strike.
Vicar. Very well. Dear me. I suppose it's alright
　　But what shall I do for dinner to-night?

> [*Extracts envelopes from his pockets.*]

Now where does this passage come from?
I think it must be the battle of the Somme.

> [*Picks up a rake and stabs at the bushes with it.*]

Burs. Burs. Burs. They're falling back on the left.

> [*Putting his hand to his ear.*]

Is that Brigade? We're being overwhelmed by superior numbers. Send reinforcements. Yes quick. Burs. Burs. Ow. Platoon get ready to attack. Are you all there? One. Two. Three. Charge. Burs. Burs. Grrr. Grrr. Grrr. Burs. I'm killed.

> [*Falls over the rockery into the arms of* Jimmy *and* George.]

Excuse me. Who are you? I'm sure
I've seen you two somewhere before.
Was it on the Embankment last September?
No wait a bit. Now I remember.
Last night at Tudro. But I thought as a rule
At this hour you were doing early school.
O I see. [*Pause.*]
　　　　You're running away. [*Pause.*]

> [*Aside, looks at the audience, not at the ceiling.*]

What were you sent here for? [*Pause.*]
　　　　　　　　For? [*Gesture. They nod.*]

And now already you want to go. [*Pause.*]
You haven't tried it yet you know.

GEORGE [*bursting out*]. No, but I ad a pal wot was inside. E thought isself smart enuff afore he went in, but he found he was only a pore innocent kid arter all. E told me things as goes on up there wot I never eard tell of before. Ask any of the boys down our way. They'll tell yer. There's more crooks comes out of that plyce than ever goes in.

JIMMY. Yus, and they treats yer like dirt. 'Arry Bartlett told me.

GEORGE. Give us jest anuvver charnce, Mister, can't yer? We'll go stryte, after this, we promise yer, don't we Jimmy?

JIMMY. Yus, George, when I think of Muvver and all the shyme and disgryce I've bin to er. [*Starts to howl. So does* GEORGE.]

VICAR [*bursting into a terrible tenor*].
    Don't know my father's name
    I am my mother's shame
    I mayn't die all the same
     I'm still too young.

            [*That stops them.*]

 For the Lord's sake don't make such a fuss.
 Now George. You are George aren't you?

GEORGE   Yus.

VICAR. If you have no hanky, the hand will do.
 A cigarette? How old are you?
 Sit down.

GEORGE.   Sixteen.

VICAR.   Sixteen. That's splendid.
 And what will you do when your youth is ended?

GEORGE. I'm going to be a gryte explorer
 And go to Africa and hunt for lions
 And ave my photer in the picture papers
 And shyke ands wiv the Prince of Wyles.

VICAR. Now Jimmy it's your turn.

JIMMY. I'm fifteen. Shall I tell you what I'm going to be?
 I'm going to be a tec and in disguise
 Find out oo pinched the Duchess's pearls,
 Rescue my young pal from the Master Crook
 And tyke is ole gang single 'anded.

VICAR. And what do you propose to do
 To find the cash? I think we know.

    [*Gets up, lights pipe and walks about the stage.*]

George. Honest.
Vicar.   Be quiet. [*Pause.*]
          It isn't easy I confess.
 I wonder, dare I, dare I.

       [*Curtains draw back revealing* Witnesses.]

Witness.   Yes.
Vicar. You see that toolshed. Get in there you two.
 I'll tell you what I want you both to do. [*Exeunt.*]

Witness. Their lives are on the wrong side of the mirror
 Death lies in wait there and with all his terror
 And life's entire performance comes to nothing
 But broken china, laughter, and self-loathing
 O comfort them, assist them now to pass
 Where they may feed upon the living grass.

      [*Curtains draw to again. Enter* Sergeant *on a bicycle.*]

Sergeant. Vicar. Vicar.

        [Vicar *peeps out of toolshed.*]

Vicar.   Who is it? O it's you.
 Hullo Bunyan. What can I do?
Sergeant. Have you seen them here?
Vicar.   Seen who?
Sergeant. Haven't you heard? You know those two who came in yesterday. You spoke to them.
Vicar. Yes, I remember. I thought them charming.
 The younger one's smile was so disarming.
Sergeant. Charming I don't think. They've gorn. Opped it in the middle of the night. The guvnor's in a proper fury, I can tell yer. Said it was my fault, but ow was I to know he'd left that blasted—begging your pardon Vicar,—that garden door unbolted. Says I've got ter find em and I needn't come back till I've found em both. Threatened me wiv the sack. Me. After all these years I've elped im. You aint seen em anywhere abouts then.
Vicar. I'm afraid I haven't. Have you tried Curly?
 The Milkman. He's up early.
Sergeant. I adn't thought of im. Thanks for the tip. I'll be pushing off then at once if you don't mind.
Vicar. I say your tyre looks pretty dicky.

[*While* SERGEANT *is talking,* GEORGE *wrapped in a dog-skin and* JIMMY *half-dressed as a woman tiptoe out.* JIMMY *has a nail and sticks it out in the path. They tiptoe back into the shed and watch through the door.*]

SERGEANT. Vicar, if I've asked the guvnor once for a new bicycle I've asked im a hundred times. One day, I says, this bicycle will be the death of me, and you'll be ter blame. It'll haunt yer. But do he listen? No. You might as well ask at the Miners Arms for a glass of water. Look at the old fossil. As I said to cook last Sunday; cook, I says, Adam might have leant it against the fatal tree when 'e was courtin Eve. She didn't laughed. She eaved. It was like tickling a blancmange. Well, I must be gettin along or there won't be no boys left to look for. Wait till I catch the little bleeders.

[*Exit, watched by all three. After a moment there is a loud bang off as the tyre bursts.*]

[*Enter* PROMPTER *in front of the curtain.*]

PROMPTER. Ladies and gentlemen, the vicar is awfully sorry but there is a slight delay in starting the next scene. He's not quite ready for this ceremony of his, I mean the choosing of someone to go and hunt for the missing heir. Naturally there's always a great deal to get ready and this year he's got those two boys to look after. As a matter of fact I've left him dressing them up.

VOICE FROM THE ORCHESTRA. Damn silly idea, if you ask me.

PROMPTER. Yes, he's let me into the secret, but no one else, so you won't give them away, will you, especially to those reporters. While you're waiting, the vicar thought you might like to know the names of some of the people who are coming to the ceremony. They've already started arriving [*peeping through curtain*] and the vicarage lawn's getting quite black. He's given me a list which I'm going to ask the conductor to read to you. Do you mind, Edgar? I've got to lend a hand. [*Exit.*]

CONDUCTOR. From Honeypot Hall, haunt of doves
Driving dangerously in a blue Daimler
Iris Crewe, an orphan beauty
Mourning her father, and missing her brother.
From Puffin Conyers, place for peacocks

General Hotham in white moustaches
Beside him Betty his obedient wife
Geoffrey their son with the great glasses
And a dun face like a drop of water
And Antonelli, their Italian chauffeur,
Sweep past the sycamores of their sumptuous drive
A family in fortune, rich in Rolls.
Augustus Bicknell from Tudro, his mouth
Padlocked for fear of property and person
A dried boy on a back-pedalling bicycle
As peevish as if he had pissed on a nettle
With one-eyed Bunyan, warm, in shirtsleeves,
His old school sergeant puffing beside him.
From deep-walled Larchwood and its weedy garden
In cotton black and bird-cage hat
Jerkily hurrying, hating the Germans
Mildred Luce, the Vicar's sister.
Gilbert. Gilbert.

[*Enter* PROMPTER.]

I say, I can't read this word.
PROMPTER. Akers, silly. [*Exit.*]
CONDUCTOR. Akers the poet in an open shirt
And khaki shorts, smoking a pipe.
Young Dr Stag in a standard coupé
Wearing a club tie, come from Cambridge.
Mrs Aster Lynch in an Aero Morgan
With spat-coloured tyres, scatters the gravel
Billy her Sealyham on the seat beside her.
In a second-hand Riley from a small bungalow
Their faultless flannels, factory-fresh
Very attractive, the solicitor's sons,
Derek and Hector. In a dinky straw hat
Her make-up matching the morning, Miss Jean McKay
Deliberately fails to turn in drive
Till Hector has to help. And heaps more.

[*Enter* PROMPTER.]

PROMPTER. Hurry up, we're waiting.
CONDUCTOR. Girls on foot, farmers in gigs.

[*The church bell begins to ring.*]

Act I Scene 5

[*Curtain rises. The scene should be as much a musical comedy or pantomime village garden as possible. Crowds, the middle, lower-middle, and working, keeping themselves to themselves but not completely so. Some tennis rackets. Some bags of tools. Brass band in distance.*]

BOY. They're waving from the marquee. Come on. Surely there will be ices now.

1ST GIRL. Ursula you said he did.

2ND GIRL. I didn't say he didn't, Mary.

1ST WOMAN. Have you heard about those boys at Tudro? Only just come and they've run away already. Disgraceful carelessness, I call it. Did you lock up all the windows before you came out? It makes you so nervous. I shan't be able to sleep to-night.

2ND WOMAN. Poor little things. It's a shame the way they treat them. I don't like Mr Bicknell. Got a nasty look in his eye, don't you think? He's like a bottle with the label missing.

1ST WOMAN. I don't know. People are too soft about children these days, if you ask me. If a few of those boys got a good whipping now and then it would do them a world of good.

POET [*reading out of a notebook*].
    Words disappear here
    Sinking heavily through stagnant minds
    But these are depth charges, disturbing sleep
    Warning we know
    From spiritual enclosure, but are in vain.

MRS HOTHAM. Thursday then. That will be fine
    We hope to make a start at nine
    Derek and Hector have promised and I
    Will ask the Vicar by and by
    We'll see to lunch, but bring your car
    Ours has trouble in the clutch
    We shan't be going very far.

JEAN. I shall look forward to Thursday so much
    O I do hope it isn't going to rain
    This is my best frock and it will stain
    Last night the wireless said local showers
    But it looked so fine in the early hours.
    I thought I'd risk it. Good afternoon
    How are you, General?

GENERAL. Ugh. This thundery weather doesn't suit me. Who's this?

Mrs Hotham. O darling this is Mr Hayboy who's doing some chemical tests for Mr Fordham at the mine. Mr Hayboy, this is my husband, General Hotham.
General. Ugh.
Man. Neither did I.
Woman. I wish we knew.
Man. We must be very careful.
2nd Pressman [*tight*]. Where's Toby?
1st Pressman.   Gone to the strike meeting.
Many more speeches and much less eating.
Now Frank you come and lie down for a bit.
2nd Pressman [*breaking loose and running up to the* General]. Sir, I just want to tell you, I think you're a . . .

[1st Pressman *pulls him away.*]

Augustus [*to* General]. It's uphill work. I do all I can for the boys but they're so unresponsive. Deceitful. What can you expect with the sort of homes most of them come from. I've had to install microphones in the dormitories. Only to-day two of them have bolted. My staff are much too lenient. After anything of this kind the only possible course is to put the whole lot on bread and water for a month. Or the morale goes to pieces. [*Noticing* Jimmy *with* Vicar.] Hullo, who has the Vicar got staying with him this time?
Vicar. O Bicknell, I was sorry to hear your news.
It must be tiresome but I daresay
You'll see them here again to-day.
And now I'd like to introduce
Miss James, my secretary-chauffeur.
No car I touch will ever stir.
I hope she'll cook too. Mrs Burke
Is not devoted to her work.
Mr Bicknell. Miss Olive James.

[Policeman *comes up.*]

Policeman. The names have all come in.
We're ready to begin.
Vicar. Right.

[*Rings a small hand bell. Silence. Groups. Choir boys.*
Master *produces a tuning fork and sings.*]

Choirmaster. Bass. Tenor. Alto. Treble. One two three four.

CHORUS.   Ten years ago
                We lost our master
                In Pressan Ambo
                O that was a disaster
            He went away one Sunday morning
            Without a word of warning left us mourning.
                We wish we knew then
                What we could do then
                To bring our master back
                O he is what we lack
                    So who
            (It may be me, it may be you)
            Will find the heir Sir Francis Crewe?

                Were we to tell
                You all his virtue
                The contrast—well,
                Of you and him would hurt you.
            Though noble he was never haughty.
            He was a beauty but he had a sense of duty.
                Who shall we send now
                To find our friend now
                Our heir and our sun
                Without him we're undone.
                    O who
            (It may be me, it may be you)
            Will find the heir Sir Francis Crewe?

                This summer day
                One must be chosen
                To send away
                For hope is almost frozen.
            This year perhaps our choice may find him.
            Good luck be kind to us, good luck not blind to us.
                Could we see Sir Francis
                How light our dances
                Whoever we may choose
                Will go and not refuse
                    O who
            (It may be me, it may be you)
            Will find the heir, Sir Francis Crewe?

VICAR [*stands up. A top hat is passed him by the* POLICE SERGEANT].

          Do you swear
    That all the names are written here
    Of every man in this village alive
    Unmarried and under twenty-five?
SERGEANT. I swear it.
VICAR. Miss Iris Crewe.

                                      [*She comes forward.*]

    Iris Crewe, are you willing now
    In the presence of these people to make your vow?
IRIS. I am.
VICAR AND IRIS [*she repeats each phrase after him*].
    I, Iris Crewe, do solemnly swear
    In the presence of these people here
    That I will be the wedded wife
    To love and cherish all my life
    Of him whoever he may be
    Who brings my brother back to me
    Or if that cannot be, instead
    Certain proof that he is dead.
VICAR. Read the names of those we sent
    Who failed to do the thing they meant.
SERGEANT [*reading*]. Nobby Sollers.
    Sorbo Lamb.
    Kid Barnet.
    Battling Walter.
    Frenchie Joe.
    Chimp Eagle.
    The Midget.
    Muffin Todd.
    Nicky Peterson.

                    [*The* VICAR'S *eyes are bound with a handkerchief.*
                    He stirs the hat and draws, saying:]

VICAR. Divvy Divvy Divvy Divvy Divvy Divvy Di
    Divvy Divvy Divvy Divvy Divvy Divvy Di
        Swans in the air, swans in the air
        Let the chosen one appear,
           —Alan Norman.

                                      [*Short burst of cheering.*]

VOICE. Norman. Fancy that. 'E don't know who 'is own father was. That's a nice thing. They might have chosen someone respectable.
VICAR. Alan Norman.

[*He comes forward and kneels.*]

    Alan Norman, will you go
    Cross any border in sand or snow
    Will you do whatever may be needful
    Though people and customs both be hateful
    When mind and members go opposite way
    Watching wake folding long on sea
    Will you remain a passenger still
    Nor desperate plunge for home?
ALAN.   I will.
VICAR [*with a bag*]. Here is what the trustees give
    That as you journey you may live
    Five hundred pounds, no more no less
    May it help you to success.

    Angels of air and darkness from this hour
    Put and keep our friend in power
    Let not the reckless heavenly riders
    Treat him or me as rank outsiders.
ALL. We ask it.
VICAR. From the fascinating sickness and
    Love's accosting biassed hand
    The lovely grievance and the false address
    From gunman and coiner protect and bless.
ALL. We ask it.
VICAR. We stand a moment in silent prayer.

[*Curtains draw back showing the* WITNESSES *as dispatch riders. Motor bicycles. Crash helmets.*]

1ST WITNESS. Enter with him
    These legends love
    For him assume
    Each diverse form
    As legend simple
    As legend queer
    That he may do
    What these require
    Be, love, like him
    To legend true.

2ND WITNESS. When he to ease
    His heart's disease
    Must cross in sorrow
    Corrosive seas
    As Dolphin go
    As cunning fox
    Guide through the rocks
    Tell in his ear
    The common phrase
    Required to please
    The guardians there.
    And when across
    The livid marsh
    Big birds pursue
    Again be true
    Between his thighs
    As pony rise
    As swift as wind
    Bear him away
    Till cries and they
    Are left behind.

1ST WITNESS. But when at last
    These dangers past
    His grown desire
    Of legends tire
    O then, love standing
    At legends' ending
    Claim your reward
    Submit your neck
    To the ungrateful stroke
    Of his reluctant sword
    That starting back
    His eyes may look
    Amazed on you
    Find what he wanted
    Is faithful too
    But disenchanted
    Your simplest love.

            [*Gesture of Benediction. Curtains close. A buzz of excitement.*]

VICAR. Well Alan let me congratulate

You first and then ourselves and fate.
She could not have chosen a better man.
If you can't succeed, then no one can.
One moment. I've a small surprise
A little present. Close your eyes.

> [*Whistles. Enter* GEORGE *as a dog.*]

There. This is Alan. This is George.
A hand. A paw. Alan, take him
And feed him. George, do not forsake him.

AUGUSTUS [*to* JIMMY]. I've been trying to remember why your face seemed familiar to me. Of course, you're one of the Leicestershire James.

JIMMY. You bet.

AUGUSTUS. Then you must be the daughter of my old friend Sir Arthur. He was a great friend of mine. Before you were born. His sudden death was a great shock to me.

JIMMY. Ho. Yus. It must ave bin.

AUGUSTUS. Your mother had some lovely Chippendale I remember. I suppose you still have that at home, now.

JIMMY. Yus. We keeps it for the spare room bed.

AUGUSTUS. And the Rembrandt.

JIMMY. The how much?

AUGUSTUS. Your beautiful Rembrandt.

JIMMY. O that. She wasn't alf a bad ol bus in er dy. Till we ran er into a wall and broke er up.

AUGUSTUS. I wonder—er—would you care for an ice with me now? I should love to have a chat about old times.

JIMMY. An ice? I should sy so. I don't arf feel empty.

AUGUSTUS. Splendid. Come along.

> [GEORGE *who has been watching has crept up and pinned a large red heart to the tails of* AUGUSTUS's *coat.*]

2ND PRESSMAN. All the hills are covered in . . .

1ST PRESSMAN. Do be quiet.

2ND PRESSMAN.   . . . Old Ireland.

1ST PRESSMAN. Pull yourself together Frank.
You'd better stick your head in the tank.

2ND PRESSMAN [*seeing* GEORGE]. Look at that dog. I love dogs
Bogey Bogey. Naughty
Ow. He's haughty.

    Hogs and dogs: dogs and hogs
    Never need to use the bogs.

                [*Toot on horn. Enter* BUS CONDUCTOR.]

BUS CONDUCTOR. The village bus is about to start
    Those who are coming prepare to depart.
FRIEND. I've packed your suitcase and your jacket
    You'll find inside addressed a packet
    Of postcards ready stamped to send
    News of your journey to your friend.
MIDDLE-AGED LADY. And here's some fruit fresh from our garden. Take
    It and eat it for my sake.
IRIS. Alan dearest, take this ring
    Upon your finger ever to wear
    Whatever you may have to bear
    My heart goes with you in everything.
ALAN. Iris, give me a parting kiss
    In promise of our future bliss.
IRIS. Gladly, Alan, I give you this.
VOICES. 1. O dear, it's beginning to rain.
2.   You ought to weed it.
3.   The farmers need it.
4.   Mummy, I've got a pain.
ALAN. Is there anything that I can do
    Ladies and Gentlemen for you . . .

                [MISS MILDRED LUCE *suddenly appears.*]

2ND PRESSMAN. O my God what a face
    Teddy. Take me away from this place.
MILDRED LUCE.   Yes
    Set off for Germany and shoot them all
    Poison the wells till her people drink the sea
    And perish howling. Strew all her fields
    With arsenic, leave a land whose crop
    Would starve the unparticular hyena.
    But you are young and it is useless
    To look to youth. In the November silence
    I have heard more shuffling every year
    Seen more of the up-to-date young men there waiting
    Impatient in the crowd to catch a train
    And shake a German gently by the hand
    I had two sons as tall as you

A German sniper shot them both.
They crawled to me across the floor
I put their earliest prattle in a book
A German sniper shot them both.
I saw them win prizes at their prep-school sports
I had their friends at half term out to tea
A German sniper shot them both
I heard their voices alter as they grew
Shyer of me and more like men.

[Taking out a large watch.]

O Ticker, ticker, they are dead
As the Grimaldi infants
Justice has gone a summer cruise and let
Her mansion to a madman. Say something,
Ticker. Nothing. Nothing. I protest.
VICAR. Mildred dear, go home and rest
And calm yourself. That will be best.

[More toots.]

BUS CONDUCTOR. The bus is leaving in a minute
Those who are coming must step in it.
CHORUS AND SOLO [*descant*].
 Now ${\text{I} \atop \text{we}}$ must part
 It's time for ${\text{me} \atop \text{you}}$ to start
 With tears in ${\text{my} \atop \text{our}}$ eyes ${\text{I} \atop \text{we}}$ say good-byes
  [*Chorus.*] Success and satisfaction
  We wish to you in every action.
  [*Solo.*] I thank you for your sympathies.
  In June and December
  ${\text{I} \atop \text{We}}$ will remember you.

CURTAIN

Act II

Chorus

Norman
Call him the hero: if it helps your attention
Pressan is now behind him; but not forgotten
Do not forget it either; do not forget Iris nor the Headmaster
Do not forget the strike; of miners at Windyacre.
He is entering the city; he is approaching a centre of culture
First the suburban dormitories; spreading over fields
Villas on vegetation; like saxifrage on stone.
Isolated from each other; like cases of fever
And uniform in design; uniform as nurses.
To each a lean-to shed; containing a well-oiled engine of escape
Section these dwellings: expose the life of a people
Living by law; and the length of a reference.
See love in its disguises; and the losses of the heart
Cats and old silver; inspire heroic virtues
And psychic fields accidentally generated, have destroyed whole families
Extraordinary tasks are set: a ploughman's hand acquires the most
    exquisite calligraphy
A scheme is prepared for draining the North Sea; with the aid of books
    from the local library
One has a vision in the bathroom after a family quarrel: he kneels on
    the cork mat.
A naturalist leaves in a cab: in time for the breaking of the meres
A youth with boils lies face down on bed; his mother over him
Tenderly she squeezes from his trembling body; the last dregs of his
    childhood
Writers be glib: please them with scenes of theatrical bliss and horror
Whose own slight gestures tell their doom; with a subtlety quite foreign
    to the stage
For who dare patiently tell; tell of their sorrow
Without let or variation of season; streaming up in parallel from the
    little houses
And unabsorbed by their ironic treasures
Exerts on the rigid dome of the unpierced sky; its enormous pressures.

But look
While we were talking; he has not stood still
He has passed up the parade; the site of shops
Goods are displayed: behind plate glass

One satin slipper: austerely arranged
On an inky background: of blackest velvet
A waxen sandboy: in ski-ing kit
Dumb and violet: among vapour lamps
High in the air: in empty space
Five times a minute: a mug is filled
And in ten-foot letters: time after time
Words are spelt out: and wiped away.
He moves amazed: among the well-fed multitudes
They glance at the stranger: with the gaze of those
Who have paid their allowance: to be left alone.

And now he reaches: The Nineveh Hotel
He stands at the entrance: His dog George with him
Consider this hotel; its appointments and fittings.
500 bedrooms: with h and c
300 bathrooms: 375 WC's.
Inspect the dining hall: seating 2000.
The waiters scuttling from side to side
Like gold-fish feeding the valuable people.
Admire the shining silver and cutlery
Stamped with the mark of that sombre town
Which fouls the Don still fresh from the moor
And the beautiful glassware blown on the Danube.
And stand in the vestibule spacious and gilded
As our hero enters to sign his name.
Old men afraid of reflections in glass
Are ushering ladies out to their cars
Veiled and valued through revolving doors
Paid to be pretty, pumped into cloth
Ranked by pillars pages wait
At signals like gulls from a nesting stack
To rise on their toes and tear away.
Enter.

Act II Scene 1

ALAN. Feeling shy George
    So am I George
    Look at those palms
    This is different from the Miners Arms.

PORTER. I'm glad you've come, sir
     You want a room, sir?
ALAN. Please.
PORTER. I'm sorry to be a trouble, sir
     A single or a double, sir?
ALAN. A single please.
PORTER. I'm still in doubt, sir
     With bathroom or without, sir?
ALAN. With bathroom please.
PORTER. Just sign your name, sir
     And date the same, sir.
     Here quickly page boy
     Or you'll put me in a rage, boy.
     Show this gentleman up to
     Room 132.
PAGE. Let me take your bag, sir
     It'll save you fag, sir
     Please follow me, sir
     I've got the key, sir.
CHORUS. Make way, make way
     This gentleman has come to stay
     He wants a room where he may rest
     But not the best, but not the best
     He's only a provincial guest.
PORTER [*seeing* GEORGE]. I'm sorry dogs are not allowed, sir,
     I didn't see in the crowd, sir.
ALAN. But that's absurd, my dog and I
     Are never parted; tell me why
     If not; well here are my keys
     I'll leave this moment if you please.
CHORUS. He wants his dog like all the rest
     He's only a provincial guest.

                                                  [*Trumpet.*]

     Silence. Here comes Miss Lou Vipond
     The star of whom the world is fond.

               [MISS VIPOND *descends the marble stairs. As she
               does so, top curtains draw back revealing the* WIT-
               NESSES *with a small statue of Cupid. She speaks with
               a foreign accent and is husky.*]

Miss Vipond. What is this noise you make
    It is keeping me awake
    It makes the head ache.
Chorus. He wants his dog like all the rest
    He's only a provincial guest.
Miss Vipond. Dog, what dog? Explain please
    I don't understand. Whose dog is thees?
Alan. I'm sorry, Madam; he is mine
    They say they will not let him in
    But he and I are never parted.
Miss Vipond. I understand, my friend; don't be downhearted

[George *starts limping.*]

    I like him. What is his name?
Alan. George.
Miss Vipond. That is charming. But he's lame
    Poor George. Come here. Let me see your foot
    I've something upstairs that will make it goot.
    Porter.
Porter. Bless Madam
    Yes Madam.
Miss Vipond. Please tell the manager I say
    This dog is going to stay.
Porter. Very good, Madam
    I've quite understood, Madam.
Alan. How can I thank you Miss . . .
Voice. I'm glad we came in time for this.
Miss Vipond. Vipond. You have not heard my name before.
Alan. I do not think so.
Voice.   That will make her sore.
Miss Vipond. You do not go to the pictures much.
Alan. Only once in my life have I been to such.
Miss Vipond. What did you see?
Voice.   He's in her clutch.
Alan. I saw a film called Flame of Desire
    About a youth who played with fire
    An artist who to ruin came
    For the sake of a harlot with eyes of flame.
Miss Vipond. I was the harlot. No I do not mind
    You were quite right. She was unkind.
    But now my friend since you know my name
    Will you not do for me the same?

ALAN. My name's Norman, Alan Norman.
MISS VIPOND. And where is your home?
ALAN. O you won't ever have heard it. I come
   From a little village up in the hills
   Called Pressan Ambo.

[MISS VIPOND *faints*.]

   What's the matter? You're ill.
   Help someone.
MISS VIPOND. It is nothing. That was foolish of me
   I do not sleep very well you see
   Pressan Ambo you said. But that is strange.
ALAN. You know it? Up in the Sheared Flysch Range.
MISS VIPOND. May be. O I'm so tired.
1ST VOICE. Well was I wrong.
2ND VOICE.   She's inspired.
ALAN. Let me help you to your room.
MISS VIPOND. If you like. Thank you. You're strong
   Mr Alan Norman.
VOICE. He goes to his doom.
CHORUS. Inform the Press, Inform the Press
   Miss Vipond scores one more success
   It's in the air, it's in the air
   She's going to have a new affair.

   Make way, make way
   This gentleman has come to say
   He wants the best, he wants the best
   He's more than a provincial guest.

   He quickly fell, he quickly fell
   He lost his heart in a hotel
   He's going to start, he's going to start
   He's starting now to break his heart.

CURTAIN

Chorus

Return to Pressan; to the deserted mine by the Hodder
They are having a picnic there: the general and his friends
But while we have been absent; conditions have shown no improvement

The men have called a strike. Fordham has answered with a lockout
The men are divided in opinion: they agree like London clocks
Some are for arbitration; others call them traitors
Not a penny off, they say; not a minute on.
Their wives are anxious; the children puling and constipated; there is a shortage of milk and fresh vegetables
There are rumours at nightfall: rumours of the importation of blacklegs.
Plans for picketting are being prepared; Scales Tarn waits for the intruders, black under basalt.

The well-off are uneasy; they cannot fully attend to their books and their pleasures
Those with a university education; are sympathetic but deplore violence
They talk of moderation in large rooms.
Those who decorate the church for festivals; have engaged in relief work.
Those who own land and those who keep shops are in agreement; they demand order
The intervention of the military: they want their money.

Act II Scene 2a

[*The deserted mine. A picnic.* GENERAL, MRS *and* GEOFFREY HOTHAM. *The* VICAR. HAYBOY. AUGUSTUS BICKNELL. MISS JAMES (JIMMY). MISS JEAN MCKAY. DEREK. HECTOR.]

JEAN. Derek, put on the Haunted Mill
    It's near the bottom.
DEREK.   Right. I will.

                          [*Searching through the records.*]

    It is not good to be alone.
    I loved no one but my mother.
    Do you get what I mean.
    She gave herself away in the Sahara.
    Shakespeare knew a thing or two.
    The Haunt...
             Here it is. You hold. I'll wind.
HECTOR. After you with the bottle. Mind.
JEAN. I bet you sixpence that you can't finish it
    In a single breath.

HECTOR. You do? I'll diminish it
    Here's mud in your eye.
JEAN. O look. Hector is going to try
    To finish the bottle without taking a breath
    Make him laugh, someone.
VARIOUS. He's choking to death
    His Adam's apple's working
    Like a piston
    Or the ballcock of a cistern
    Start him gurking
    Tickle his nose with a piece of bracken
    He's beginning to slacken
    I can see the island. Hurry.
HECTOR. Sixpence, please, Jean. [*Gurks.*] Sorry.
DEREK. Jean, he led you to the slaughter
    Hector always does you down
    Once I bet him half a crown
    He wouldn't kiss the Greystoke porter
    I lost.
MRS HOTHAM. O by the way
    Is there any news of Alan to-day?
VICAR. There's been no news for a week I believe
    Iris, poor girl, is beginning to grieve.
DEREK. Who's coming to get cool
    I know a perfect pool.
HECTOR [*getting up*]. It will be Jean's fault
    If my stomach calls a halt.
DEREK. Coming Jean?
JEAN. Do you think I'm safe without
    A chaperone when you're about?
HECTOR. What about you, Miss James?
JIMMY. Wot, me? I aint got a fish frightener.
HECTOR. If you'll wait till Jean comes out
    She'll lend you hers.
JIMMY. Nothin doin. I can't swim.
AUGUSTUS. O but Miss James, I thought you told me the other day you won all the swimming cups at school.
JIMMY. That was before I 'it me ead on the bottom of the bath and lorst my memory. When I came rahnd I couldn't remember one of them fancy strokes.
AUGUSTUS. Anyway I'm sure Miss James wants to be quiet. She's looking tired.

JIMMY. Yus. Them lobster patties we ad last night, Gus, didn't arf give
  me dreams.
DEREK. That's the lot then so let's drive.
  Jean, I want to see you dive.
JEAN. Vicar, if you hear me scream
    Run till you are out of breath
    Save little Jeanie from worse than death.

> [*Exeunt.*]
> [*Pause.*]

AUGUSTUS. I know a rock from which you get a marvellous view. I
  should like to show it to you. Would you care to see it?
JIMMY. Don't mind if I do; but I opes it isn't too slippy. My eels are too
  igh. They give me corns.

> [*Exeunt* AUGUSTUS *and* JIMMY.]

MRS HOTHAM. Well now the young people have all gone away
    I shall be able to get on with my knitting.
    Ernest darling, hold your arms this way
    I want to see how this pullover is fitting.
    Isn't the strike too terrible. Yesterday
    I heard one of the village girls say
    She couldn't get milk for her baby at all.
    I tell you when I got home to the Hall
    I simply couldn't drink my tea
    It all seems so unjust to me.
GENERAL HOTHAM. Nonsense, my dear. It's all their fault.
    "It is unjust. Had things been different"—
    That is the whimper of the underdog
    Who dare not own up to his weakness.
    Unjust. The greatest injury we did them
    Was teaching them to read and write
    To imagine that a smattering of knowledge
    Put reverence and duty in the shade
    Books have debauched them as the trader's gin
    Degrades the savage.
    Now every typist with a two-line reference,
    Each Sunday lad in his purple suiting
    Spots spreading on his features like a chain of stores
    His head as empty as a school in August
              The sweaty crowds
    That make the beaches stink in summer—

Each thinks himself the flower of the earth
Sees a Napoleon or a Shakespeare in the mirror
And holds the latest notions of the café
Born of a gasper and a greasy stew
Has made the wisdom of the ages stale.
                    I am a soldier
And I know why private soldiers are admired.
It is obedience makes them beautiful
Take that away as in a panic
And in the instant squalor rushes back.
Each to his duty. That is justice.
A few whom birth and breeding fits
Must order and the rest obey that all
Be happy and at peace. As for those
Who flattering their ignorant conceit
Would start a cancer in the commonwealth
They need the short sharp treatment of the surgeon.
HAYBOY. Yes I agree.
   You notice the same kind of thing in my job
   Of chemical research. How often am I asked
   When I show visitors my lab, the question
  "What is the use of what you do
   Are people better fed for it or richer
   What practical results have you to show?"
   Even my lab boy when my back is turned
   Sneers at my labours as a waste of time.
   Comfort acquired without an effort
   Has stuck them up and they will ruin
   Themselves and us. Already I can see
   The deserts racing on towards us
   Where the fauna of experimental man
   A stranger creature than the unicorn
   Is finally extinct, and with him, all.
   Now Vicar, you've said nothing.
   You're a historian. What's your opinion?
VICAR. Does my opinion matter? As you will.
   I think that both what you complain of
   And your complaints are symptoms of a sickness
   Inclusive of us all. You, General, fancy
   A couple of machine guns and a barked command
   Can frighten death away. You, Hayboy,
   That you and a few colleagues, helped of course

By General Hotham, will raise us from the dead.
If I may say so, you too are patients
Prone in the general epidemic like the rest
And these the personal mouthings of delirium
That has not reached its crisis; signs
Significant as are the twitchings which precede
An epileptic seizure, of fever
To which we had been made susceptible
Before our bodies cast a shadow.
That wave which already was washing the heart
When the cruel Turk took Constantine's city
And the apples of knowledge were hawked from barrows
To the cunning and greedy by Greek refugees,
To-day all spent is withdrawing itself.
Unhappy he who after it is sucked.
Then the mind cried out I'm king of the earth
And the body became its beautiful pet
Dangerous no longer but a dog for show
To roast in the kitchen or run the house
While the mind in its study spoke with its god.
And for the sordid commerce of the soul was minted
The counterfeit coin still current amongst us.
The nickel with love thy neighbour as thyself
On the one side for superscription stamped
And on the back imprinted "My purse and I."
The self was away now
Harried and haunted by the hounds of fear.
The troupe of explorers by that terror fired
From Columbus and Magellan to Mallory and Scott
Still honoured in our schools on Sunday evenings,
Diverted with markets but made no cure.
Play was an insult to prayer. Wesley
Spent all his life in the saddle preaching
To the gentiles in Britain the gospel of work
And to get and to keep was to be as good as gold.
Machines created by clergymen and boys
Lured them like magnets from mountain and meadow
Into towns on to the coal measures, crowded and dark
Where the careful with the careless drove a bitter bargain
But sowed in the act the seed of a hatred
Which germinating in tenement and gas-lit cellar
Is now bursting the floors of the beautiful mansions,

Where their sons sit certain of their safety still
And will shake the world in a war to which
The last was only a manoeuvre.
Who cheats, must cheat himself. The disinherited
They are the agents of our common guilt
To execute our judgement on ourselves
And still with murder. Through fissures in our nature,
Fear builds intrusive like a sill
Tremendous ranges, casting shadows
Heavy, bird-silencing upon the outer world,
Peaks that our grief sighs over like a Shelley
Because impassible, dividing
That which we feel from that we perceive
Desire from data, the watershed between
The lonely unstable mad executives
We recognize in banks and restaurants as our friends
And the unprogressive blind society
Knowing no argument but the absolute veto.
Blind, private, arbitrary and base
We parch for water and grow cruel
The timely warnings of the tender to the tough
Grow more insistent. Pierce them we must
Or in a scandalous explosion of the stolid perish.

[Fadeout during end of speech.]

Act II Scene 2b

[A box lights up. IRIS *alone.]*

IRIS. Day brings no news
   And nights no clues
   When shall I learn
   Of Alan's return.

> *[The* WITNESSES *disclosed, as explorers with maps and compasses.]*

WITNESS.   Be patient, trust us, though
                The images beckon
             His footsteps along a route
                You cannot reckon

>   For Man must learn by choice
>   Desire can lead him
>   Only by indirection
>   To those who need him.

[Curtains hide them.]

IRIS [*song*].   Seen when night was silent
                  The bean shaped island

                  And our ugly comic servant
                  Who is observant

                  O the verandah and the fruit
                  The tiny steamer in the bay
                  Startling summer with its hoot

                  You have gone away.

[Light goes out.]

Act II Scene 2c

[*Light up opposite box.* AUGUSTUS *and* JIMMY.]

JIMMY. Give us a fag, Gus.

AUGUSTUS. Yes, yes. Of course. [*Producing cigarettes.*] Tell me how you like these? I ordered them specially for you from Angora. Let me. [*He tries to light* JIMMY's *cigarette.*]

JIMMY. Yer aint 'alf clumsy, Gus. Look at yer. Yer 'ands are shykin'. Wot's up?

AUGUSTUS. O Olive, my darling—you don't, you can't realise what you mean to me. I worship you. You've changed my whole life. Oh, I know I'm just an old fool. I'm not worth your wasting your time with. And you've been very patient with me. You've been wonderful, these weeks we've spent here together. You're different from everybody else in the world. I never dreamed there could be a girl like you. I'm the luckiest man on earth. [*He bursts into tears and kneels down in front of* JIMMY.]

JIMMY. 'Ere, cheese it, Gus. Yer'd best go an' lie dahn. Wot if anyone was ter come in? They'd think yer was balmy.

AUGUSTUS. You've made me see what a fool I've been. How blind. How conceited. How selfish. My whole life was wasted until I met you.

JIMMY. Git yerself up, Gus, Chris' syke.

AUGUSTUS [*rising*]. I'll do anything you ask me, my dearest. You see? I'll be good. I'll be quite calm . . . Oh, Olive, come away with me now, to-night.

JIMMY. If I've told yer once, I've told yer an 'undred times, Gus. I can't.

AUGUSTUS. God knows, I wouldn't ask you to marry me—or—anything else that you didn't wish. Let me adopt you. Anything. As long as I can be near you, speak to you sometimes. And if you fall in love, I'll pay for everything. I'll support your husband. Let me be your servant. I can't live without you.

JIMMY. It aint any use, Gus. I'm sorry. It can't be did. Now, jest yer go an' lie dahn.

AUGUSTUS. Very well, my darling, if you wish it. You'll dine with me this evening?

JIMMY. That's jest wot I was goin' ter tell yer, Gus. I can't. I 'ave ter go aht with Hector. 'E wants me ter.

AUGUSTUS. Would he care to dine too, do you think? Tell him, we'd have that champagne he likes.

JIMMY. Very sorry, Gus. It's imposs.

AUGUSTUS. Very well, my dear. I understand.

JIMMY. Yer not mad with me, Gus?

AUGUSTUS. How could I be? Whatever you do is right.

JIMMY. Yer not a bad sort, yer know, Gus.

AUGUSTUS. Oh, my darling—

JIMMY. Orl right. If yer like. [AUGUSTUS *kisses him*.]

[*Light up on stage.* SERGEANT *with bicycle.*]

BUNYAN. Mr Bicknell, Mr Bicknell.

JIMMY. Look aht. 'Ere's someone.

AUGUSTUS. Hullo. Who's that.

BUNYAN. It's Bunyan sir. Where are you.

AUGUSTUS. At the top of the cliff. You can't get up this side. What is it?

BUNYAN. It's the boys, sir. They're getting out of hand. I don't know what to do. Last night they threw all the soup out of the window and now they say they're going to this strike meeting this afternoon. I can't hold them, sir.

AUGUSTUS. Get some girls in and have a dance.

BUNYAN. —What.

AUGUSTUS. Can't you hear me? GET SOME GIRLS IN. They want love.

BUNYAN. Heavens above.

AUGUSTUS. No. No. Love. L for Lighthouse. O for Orange. V for Vision. Love.

[*Crowd of* BOYS *rush on.*]

BOYS. Come on or we'll be late. Why if it isn't Sergeant. You coming to the meetin? Corse you are. Eave him up. [*They hoist him on to the bicycle.*] My, 'e's heavy. Give Enery a ride on your carrier, Sergeant. 'E's only a little un.

[*Exeunt singing:*]

> The bluebells bloomed on the Baltic shore
> When Kit was Schneider Creusot's love.

Act II Scene 3

[*Nineveh Hotel. The staircase up to* MISS VIPOND's *bedroom. A grandfather clock in the corner.*]

MANAGER.
> When he gets his bill to-morrow
> What will Mr Norman say?
> Will he shoot himself for sorrow
> All on a summer's day?

CHORUS OF WAITERS, PAGES AND CHAMBERMAIDS.
> Perhaps he'll only lose his mind
> Go wild and feed among the lilies
> Tell us if you'd be so kind
> Tell us what the bill is?

MANAGER. 20 cases of champagne
A finest pedigree Great Dane
½ doz Paris frocks
A sable fur, a silver fox
Bottles of scent and beauty salves
An MG Midget with overhead valves
1 doz pairs of shoes and boots
6 lounge, 1 tails, and 3 dress suits
A handsome two-piece bathing dress
An electric razor, a trouser press
A cutter for cigars, two lighters
10 autographs of famous writers
Berths and tickets in advance
For a trip round southern France
Add to this his bed and board.

CHORUS. It's more than one man can afford.

MANAGER. This we'll keep until the morning
　　Remember, do not give him warning.

　　　　　　　　　　　　　　　　　　[*Exit* MANAGER.]

[*Song and step dance.*]

WAITERS.　　　　　If we're late
　　　　　　　　　Or break a plate
　　　　　　　　　He won't be rude.
　　　　　　　　　If we served him nude
　　　　　　　　　Would he know
　　　　　　　　　No No No
　　　　　　　　　He's in love.

PAGES.　　　　　　If we lose
　　　　　　　　　All his shoes
　　　　　　　　　Say go to hell
　　　　　　　　　When he rings the bell
　　　　　　　　　He won't know
　　　　　　　　　No No No
　　　　　　　　　He's in love.

CHAMBERMAID.　　If I stops
　　　　　　　　　Emptying the slops
　　　　　　　　　Leaves a dead
　　　　　　　　　Mouse in the bed
　　　　　　　　　He won't know
　　　　　　　　　No No No
　　　　　　　　　He's in love.

　　　　　　　　　[*A bell rings.* CHORUS *arrange themselves under the*
　　　　　　　　　HEAD WAITER.]

CHORUS. You who return to-night to a narrow bed
　　With one name running sorrowfully through your sorrowful head
　　You who have never been touched and you pale lover
　　Who left the house this morning kissed all over
　　You little boys also of quite fourteen
　　Beginning to realise just what we mean
　　Fill up glasses with champagne and drink again.

　　It's not a new school or factory to which we summon.
　　We're rejoicing to-day because of a man and a woman
　　　O Chef employ your continental arts

    To celebrate the union of two loving hearts
    Waiters be deft and skip you pages by
    To honour the god to name whom is to lie
    Fill up glasses with champagne and drink again.

    Already he has brought the swallows past the Scillies
    To chase each other shining under English bridges
    Has loosed the urgent pollen on the glittering country
    To find the pistil, force its burglar's entry
    He moves us also and up the marble stair
    He leads the figures matched in beauty and desire
    Fill up glasses with champagne and drink again.

> [*Enter* MISS VIPOND *and* ALAN. *Spotlighted. Evening feathers.* GEORGE *following.*]

ALAN. My swan so beautiful to my five senses
    When I look on you, in a moment I lose my defences
    My clumsy heart forgets herself and dances.

MISS VIPOND. O lion, O sun, encompass me with power
    Feed lion, shine sun, for in your glory I flower
    Create the huge and gorgeous summer in an hour.

CHORUS. What would you give that she might live?

ALAN. I would give the Netherlands with all their canals
    The earth of the Ukraine, the Niagara falls
    The Eiffel Tower also, and the Dome of St Paul's.

CHORUS. What would you do to keep her true?

ALAN. I would hunt the enormous whale in the Arctic lowlands
    I would count all the starlings in the British Islands
    I would run through fighting Europe in absolute silence.

MISS VIPOND. Our sails are set. O launch upon love's ocean
    Fear has no means there of locomotion
    And death cannot exhaust us with his endless devotion.

> [*They pass into the bedroom. Above the* WITNESSES *appear wearing paper hats and carrying balloons and scatter confetti.*]

CHORUS [*receding*]. It's not only this we praise; it's the general love
    Let cat's mew rise to a scream on the tool-shed roof
    Let son come home to-night to his anxious mother

Let the vicar lead the choir boy into a dark corner
The orchid shall flower to-night that flowers every hundred years
The boots and the slavey be found Dutch-kissing on the stairs.
Fill up glasses with champagne and drink again.

Let this be kept as a generous hour by all
This once let the uncle settle his nephew's bill
Let the nervous lady's table gaucheness be forgiven
Let the thief's explanation of the theft be taken
The boy caught smoking shall escape the usual whipping
To-night the expensive whore shall give herself for nothing.
Fill up glasses with champagne and drink again.

The landlocked state shall get its port to-day
The midnight worker in the laboratory by the sea
Shall discover under the cross wire that which he looks for
To-night the asthmatic clerk shall dream he's a boxer
Let the cold heart's wish be granted, the desire for a desire,
O give to the coward now his hour of power.
Fill up glasses with champagne and drink again.

[*Scene darkens leaving* GEORGE *outside the door.*]

GEORGE. Being a dawg aint much fun. It's alright for 'im 'e got 'is tart, and I ave to run rahnd after the two of em while they does their shoppin, and oos goin to py for it, I should like ter know. If I does catch the eye of a skirt, she only pats me. Wonder ow they're gettin' on in there. [*Peeps through keyhole.*] Now isn't that a shyme. If she asn't blocked up the keyole with pyper. [*To* CONDUCTOR.] Got a pin, mister? [CONDUCTOR *gives him one.*] Thanks. Now then. Come on. 'Ere wot's this. A letter. [*Whistles into the wings on his fingers.*] Oi give us a spot of light to read by can't yer.

[*Light comes on.*]

    St James Infirmary Tuesday. That's to-day.
Darling,
  I was hit by a police bullet during the street fighting down
at the Power House last night. I'm dying. Come and see me,
before I peg out. Please. I forgive you everything. Francis.

Francis. Oos 'e. Arf a mo. Aint that the nyme of the bloke wot 'e's lookin fer? I'll fetch im aht. [*Scratches at the door and barks.*] Nothin' doin'. E's busy and I don't blyme im. Well it'll keep till mornin' I suppose. There yer are, yer see. Just like a dawg to ave no pockets.

I'll stick it down by the clock so I sees it first thing. Gawd I'm sleepy. [*Lies down. Short pause.*] Oi. Put that bloody light aht.

[*Light out.*]
[*The* Dog's Skin *speaks.*]

Dog's Skin. Ticker. Ticker. Are you awake? [*Clock strikes one.*] It's only me, the dog's skin that hides this vulgar little boy. I hope you admire my accent. I've lived so long with them, I have all the emigré's pride at having forgotten my own. I'm quite déraciné as they say in Bloomsbury. When I first paid them a visit, before I gave up my nationality, when I was still an Irish Wolfhound, I was very romantic. The odour of a particular arm-chair, the touch of certain fingers, excited me to rash generalisations which I believed to be profound. I composed poems that I imagined highly idiomatic; on the words "walk" and "dinner". And it was in this romantic mood that I decided to sever all ties with my past, and throw in my lot with theirs. My dearest ambition was to be accepted naturally as one of them. I was soon disillusioned. To them I was only a skin, valued for its associations with that very life I had hoped to abandon. Small children misunderstood by their parents rubbed tearful cheeks against me and whispered secrets to their doggie. I ask you—Doggie. Young men wore me at charades to arouse in others undisguised human amusement and desire. Talking about charades, Ticker, are you interested in literature at all? [*Clock strikes two.*] You are? So am I.

In the old days, before I became a skin, I used to be the pet of a very famous author. He used to talk all day to yours truly. He suffered terribly from indigestion, poor fellow, and used to write what was called "virile" poetry. He was knighted for it during the war. Well I'll tell you a story about him. One night, it was nearly one o'clock in the morning as a matter of fact, and he was pretty tight on whisky, we had a real heart-to-heart. George, he says, funnily enough I was called George even in those days—George, he says, come here. I came, rather crossly, to tell you the truth, I was sleepy and wishing he'd go to bed. George, look at me. Do I make you sick? (By the way, I forgot to tell you it was during the war, at the time of the big German offensive in March of '18.) Less than a hundred miles from here men, young men, are being blown to pieces. Listen, you can hear the guns doing it. (It was quite true you could. We lived on the South Downs and it was a still night.) Every time I hear that, I say to myself, you fired that shell. It isn't the cold general on his white horse, nor the owner of the huge factory, nor the luckless poor, but you. Yes I and those like me. Invalid poets with a fountain pen, undersized professors in a classroom, we the sedentary and learned whose schooling cost the most, the least conspicuous of them all are the assassins. (I'm giving you his own words. Whiskey always made him a bit rhetorical.) We have conjured up all vigours and all splendours, skillfully transformed our envy into an image of the universal mother, for which the lad of seventeen whom we have always sent and will again against our terrors, gladly immolates himself. Men are falling through the air in flames and choking slowly in the dark recesses of the sea to assuage our pride. Our pride who cannot work without incessant cups of tea, spend whole days weeping in our rooms, immoderately desire little girls on beaches and buy them sweets, cannot pass a mirror without staring, whom a slight cold is enough to make daydream of our death bed with appropriate organ music. Now wasn't that queer? It was the last talk I ever had with him. He couldn't bear the sight of me after that evening and sold me as soon as he could.

Just like a man. You know, Ticker, I think the important thing to remember about man is that pictures mean more to him than people. Take sex, for instance. I remember how it used to be with me. It was like a thunderstorm. You felt a bit queer for a day or two. Suddenly something happened to you, and then it was gone till the next time. With them it's different—well, you've seen what it's like this evening—sometimes it's funny, and sometimes it's sad, but it's always hanging about like a smell of drains. Too many ideas in their heads. To them I'm an idea, you're an idea, everything's an idea. That's why we're here. Funny thing, Ticker, we should both be in the same play. They can't do without us. If it wasn't for me this boy here would never be able to get a good night's rest; and if it wasn't for you he'd never wake up. And look what we do to the audience. When I come on they start sighing, thinking of nuns, spring, meadows and goodness knows what else. You on the other hand make them demand a tragic ending, with you they associate an immensely complicated system of awards and punishments.

Heavens, it's getting light and you've forgotten to strike. Hurry up. [*Clock strikes six.*] Hush, someone's coming. So long. Abyssinia.

> [MANAGER, WAITERS, *etc. come up the stairs singing. (Tune: John Peel.)*]

MANAGER. The sun has risen and it shines through the blind
        This lover must awaken and recall to mind
        Though the pillow be soft and the lady kind
        Yet the man has to pay in the morning

CHORUS.   For in Nineveh Hotel the most humble guest
              Be he old, be he young, he may take a good rest
              He may smoke cigars, he may order the best
              But we hand him the bill in the morning.

MANAGER [*seeing* GEORGE]. There's that ugly brute
    I've an itch in my boot.

[*Kicks him out of the way. Knocks loudly. Door opens.* ALAN *appears in pyjamas.*]

ALAN. What's all this row?
    I can't see you now.
CHORUS. I'm sorry, sir
    To be a worry, sir
    But we're in a hurry, sir
    We want our money, sir
    Here is our bill, sir.

[*Gives him the bill. Pause.*]

    O don't be ill, sir.
ALAN. 1500. It's absurd
    This will have to be deferred
    I'm sorry gentlemen to say
    Just at this moment I cannot pay
    You shall have your money another day.
CHORUS. Till we have our due we stay.
ALAN. Here's a to-do
    I must borrow from Lou.

[*Speaks into bedroom.*]

    Darling, I'm sorry to be such a bother
    But some stupid tradesmen are making a pother
    —It's nothing really—about my account
    So will you lend it me, darling Lou
    1500 pounds will do.
VOICE OF LOU [*off*]. My friend
    I do not lend
    I spend.
ALAN. Darling, please
    Don't be a tease
    They're waiting here
    They will fetch the police
    Please, be a dear.

VOICE OF LOU. My friend, you're foolish, you must learn
 Your troubles are not my concern.
ALAN. But I am your lover.
VOICE OF LOU. That is over.
ALAN. What do you mean?
VOICE OF LOU. O don't make a scene
 I've said what I mean.
 Now go.
ALAN. Lou.
VOICE OF LOU. Don't do that
 Leave me flat.
ALAN. I can't believe it.
VOICE OF LOU. Must I ring the bell?
ALAN. Alright. I'll leave it
 Oh I'm in Hell.

[*Comes out of bedroom.*]

[*To* MANAGER.] Gentlemen, what can I say?
 I cannot pay.
MANAGER. This is a most regrettable occasion
 You must come with me to the police station.
 Alphonse, fetch his trunks and cases
 And store them in the usual places.
 Giuseppi, take that diamond ring
 Off his little finger.
ALAN.   O anything
 Rather than that. Please leave me that.
MANAGER. O and Alphonse, remember his opera hat.
WAITER. The dog, sar.
MANAGER.   Pah. He scatters his hairs
 All over my sofas and best arm-chairs
 Kick him downstairs.

[GEORGE *is kicked out.*]

ALAN. George.
VOICE OF GEORGE [*from below, forgetting he is a dog*]. Dontcher worry sir.
 I'll get yer aht of this fix. The password is Letter.
MANAGER. What was that noise?
WAITERS.
 { I don't know sah
 { Must be one of the boys, sah
 { On the floor below sah.

MANAGER. Disgraceful. I'm always telling the porter
  To keep these pages in better order
  Are we ready?
  Let's go.
  [*To* ALAN.] Now steady.

> [*Exeunt.*]
> [ALPHONSE *comes along with bags, etc., and opera hat on the back of his head. He catches sight of the letter. Picks it up, reads it, glances at the door and downstairs, shrugs his shoulders, puts it in his pocket, winks at the audience, picks up bags and follows down the stairs.*]
> [*A bell rings. French maid enters and goes into bedroom.*]

VOICE OF LOU. Delice. Delice.
MAID. Modom desired?
VOICE OF LOU. O I'm so tired
  These men are such a bother
  They're all the same, they want their mother.

> [*Curtains draw back. The* WITNESSES *holding a model toll gate.*]

WITNESS. Do not imagine that he distracted to-day
  By hopelessness and terror has lost his way
  The way be careful to remember is never lost
  But to our tolls for upkeep you must pay the cost.

CURTAIN

Chorus

The strike continues. At Windyacre it is worse
Blacklegs have arrived in lorries: they came over Yadmoss
Through Daddry at dawn: protected by policemen.
Already there have been clashes: free-fights at Ipetones.
Heads were broken at Leadgate; there was blood in the beck.
A shot was fired at Sedling; from an old revolver.
Really serious trouble; is quite on the cards.
Hayboy the chemist has gone back quick to his laboratory; to the
  pursuit of pure knowledge.

The General is in communication with the War Office: he has wired
   "Am ready".
The Vicar is very unhappy: his history of the war is interrupted
Iris also grieves. Alan is not with her.
So does Augustus but for another reason: he weeps in his study.
But Jimmy, alias Miss James, is contented; he has associated
Himself with the strikers; he has found his place.
Here is our scene: the reformatory of Tudro
They have cleared away supper; they are having a concert.

Act II Scene 4

[MILDRED *comes through the curtains.*]

MILDRED. It's an outrage. [*Exit.*]

> [*Curtain. The gymnasium. An improvised stage.* FRITZ *dressed up as a German admiral is singing a song.*]

VOICES. Encore. Encore.
FRITZ.   Liebling, ein abschieds Kuss: Lebwohl die Mutter
      Das Insel wo Du bist liegt hell und klein
   Ich bin genannt an der unsicher Flotte
      Das Vaterland muss ja gerettet sein.

> [*Deafening applause.*]

WOMAN [*to* VICAR]. Isn't he sweet.
2ND VISITOR. Is that my mac
   Under your seat?
VICAR. Yes, he's fine.
   It takes me back
   To a walking tour I took on the Rhine
   In that scorching summer of 1911.
3RD VISITOR. I've left my hanky in the porch.
BOY. I'll swop this penknife for your torch.

> [AUGUSTUS *rings a bell.*]

AUGUSTUS. Item no. 7.

> [*Any available member or members of the cast who have a suitable non-musical turn, a conjuring feat, a gymnastic act, etc., should perform it here.*]
> [*Applause. The stage is got ready for prize giving.*]

1st Boy. Wots the matter wiv is nibs? E's been actin very queer lytely. E copped me yesterdy smokin behind the woodshed. I thought I was in for a proper 'idin. But do yer know wot 'e did? Erbert, he says, you'll find this better than the trash you're smokin. Try one. An he brings out is cyse and gives me one of them fancy fags tipped with vilets. It tysted like 'y but I didn't like to disappoint 'im.

2nd Boy. Yers an Soonday a was göin oop t'stair an a passed im like. Ow's foonds lad, a says. A'rve nowt boot thruppence, a says. 'Ere's some brass, lad, a says and gives me a shillin. A was bate.

3rd Boy. Garn. Don't yer know wy? Cos e's balmy abaht Miss Jymes, that's wy. 'Ot stuff she looks, too.

[Augustus *rings his bell.*]

Augustus. Well boys, I need hardly say how delighted we all are to have Miss James with us to-night. As you know, since she came here a little while ago she has taken a keen interest in us, and now in spite of the many calls upon her very valuable time—she is a very busy woman—she has consented, with her usual generosity, to give away our few prizes, or perhaps I should say, tokens.

Miss James. O come orf it, Gus.

Augustus. The Vicarage prize for woodwork has been won by Moreland One.

[*Clapping. Boy comes up to receive prize.*]

Miss James. Av yer got the key of the gunroom?

Boy. Oo ah.

Augustus. The Hotham shield for snob cricket—and may I say how sorry we are not to see General and Mrs Hotham here this evening, but they have been unavoidably detained—the shield goes this year to The Badgers with a grand total of 146 points. Runners-up, The Owls with 127 points.

[*Business.*]

Miss James. Are the bombs ready?

Boy. Yus, Miss. We couldn't finish the last one cos we run out of nitric acid. They're upstairs in the boxroom.

Augustus. Now the garden prize. The standard of the gardens has been very high and we have found it a hard task to adjudicate the prize. But I think, and Miss James agrees with me, that it ought to be awarded to Bowden and Spedding equally, and we are giving a special prize to Kemp.

[*Business.*]

MISS JAMES. Have you seen to the barbed wire?
BOY. Yus, Miss. The rolls are behind the laurels near the scullery winder.
AUGUSTUS. Some of you are familiar with Sergeant Bunyan's bicycle. [*Laughter.*] Sergeant Bunyan has been with us for many years now but I'm sorry to say he is not likely to be here much longer if he goes on riding that bicycle. Some of the senior boys have had a collection and they are and I am delighted to be able to present him with a new one. Sergeant Bunyan.

[*Great applause.*]

AUGUSTUS. And now let's all join hands in a circle and sing the Tudro song.

[*They do so.*]

BOYS [*song*].
Omne bene
Sine poenae
Tempus est ludendi
Venit hora
Absque mora
Neque deponendi

Quomodo vadis
Mi sodalis
Visne edere pomum
Qui non vis
Mirabile est
Dulc' adire domum

Domum, Domum
Dulce Domum
Domum domum divo
Hic haec hoc
Perry werry way
Hip Hip Hurrah.

[*Enter a* DETECTIVE *and a* WOMAN POLICEMAN *and an ordinary bobby who guards the door. The first two come up to* AUGUSTUS.]

DETECTIVE. I'm sorry to disturb your party sir. Is Miss James here?
AUGUSTUS. Yes. There she is. What is it?
DETECTIVE. I think you'd better send everybody away, sir.
AUGUSTUS. I don't understand.
DETECTIVE. You'd better, sir, really. We don't want a scene.

AUGUSTUS. Well. Alright. [*Raising his voice.*] Now Juniors off to bed. If the visitors will go to the drawing-room, they will find some refreshments.

[*Exeunt all but* POLICE, MISS JAMES *and* AUGUSTUS.]

Now then. What's all this?
DETECTIVE. Information has been received that Miss James is a dangerous agitator. I have a warrant for her arrest.
AUGUSTUS. But this is ridiculous. Miss James . . .
DETECTIVE [*to* WOMAN POLICEMAN]. Take her up there and search her.

[WOMAN POLICEMAN *takes* MISS JAMES *on to the stage and draws the curtains.*]

MISS JAMES. 'Ere, I protest.
AUGUSTUS. I shall complain to headquarters.
DETECTIVE. I'm sorry sir. Orders is orders.

[WOMAN POLICEMAN *comes out with* MISS JAMES.]

WOMAN POLICEMAN. The party is male, sergeant.
DETECTIVE. You see, sir. I told you. [*Pause.*] Bring him along.

[*Exeunt* POLICE. AUGUSTUS *wanders about, sits down at the piano, strikes a few odd notes and begins to sing.*]

AUGUSTUS [*song*]. A beastly devil came last night
    He said he was going to kill you quite
    I was going to faint
    The virgin came down and made me a saint
    Olive I am renowned
    For the devil I have drowned
    A saint am I and a saint are you
    It's perfectly perfectly perfectly true.

    Olive will you be my wife
    I have saved your life
    Just say you'll be mine
    You shall have kisses like wine
    When the wine gets into your head
    I will see that you're not misled
    A saint am I and a saint are you
    It's perfectly perfectly perfectly true.

    Olive when we are wed
    We shall have a lovely clean bed

You know how little babies are made
Now don't be afraid
You understand
They are made with God's hand
A saint am I and a saint are you
It's perfectly perfectly perfectly true.

Olive I love your hair
I love your clothes, I love you bare
A cathedral we will build
For the devil I have killed
We'll go up to the skies
And eat sweet mince pies
A saint am I and a saint are you
It's perfectly, perfectly, perfectly true.

CURTAIN

Act III

Chorus

You with shooting sticks and cases for field glasses, your limousines parked in a circle: who visit the public games, observing in burberries the feats of the body,
You who stand before the west fronts of cathedrals: appraising the curious carving
The virgin creeping like a cat to the desert: the trumpetting angels, the usurers boiling
And you also who look for truth; alone in tower
Follow our hero and his escort on his latest journey: from the square surrounded by Georgian houses, take the lurching tram eastward
South of the ship cranes, of the Slythe canal: stopping at Fruby and Drulger street
Past boys, ball using: shrill in alleys
Passing the cinemas blazing with bulbs: bowers of bliss
Where thousands are holding hands: they gape at the tropical vegetation, at the Ionic pillars and the organ solo
Look left: the moon shows locked sheds, wharves by water
On your right is the Power House; its chimneys fume gently above us like rifles recently fired.

Look through the grating at the vast machinery: at the dynamos and turbines
Grave, giving no sign: of the hurricane of steam within their huge steel bottles.
At the Diesel engines like howdahed elephants; at the dials with their flickering pointers
Power to the city; whose loyalties are not those of the family.

And now: enter.
O human pity gripped by the crying of a captured bird: wincing at sight of surgeon's lance
Shudder indeed; that life on its narrow littoral so lucky
Can match against eternity a time so cruel.
The street we enter with setts is paved: cracked and uneven as an Alpine glacier
Garbage chucked in the gutters; has collected in the hollows in loathsome pools
Back to back houses on both sides stretch: a dead straight line of dung-coloured brick
Wretched and dirty as a run for chickens.
Full as a theatre is this foul thoroughfare: some sitting like sacks, some slackly standing
Their faces grey in the glimmering gaslight: their eyeballs drugged like a dead rabbit's.
From a window a child is looking, by want so fretted; his face has assumed the features of a tortoise.
A human forest; all by one infection cancelled.
Despair so far invading every tissue has destroyed in these: the hidden seat of the desire and the intelligence.

Act III Scene 1

[*Before the drop. A slum street. Enter* GEORGE.]

GEORGE. Good evening lydies and gentlemen. Betcha don't know oo I am. Give yer three guesses an 'ere's a box of chocolates for the lucky one.

VERY JEWELLED LADY. Albert!

GEORGE. Sorry, lydy. I'm not yer ol man come back from America. That's one.

UNDERGRADUATE. My deah felleah.

GEORGE. Now then, Mister, speak up. I can't ear yer.

UNDERGRADUATE. My deah felleah, that's easy.

GEORGE. I'm afryde I'm not the college Portah. Would yer mind sayin that agyne.

UNDERGRADUATE. I ss-aid, th-tha-at's easy.

GEORGE. Oh, that's easy. Come on then, Montmorency, spit it aht.

UNDERGRADUATE. You're a s-s-s-ymbol of M-m-m-m-arx and Lenin.

GEORGE. M-m-m-m-arx and Lenin. N-n-n-n-ever eard of em. That's two. Only one more.

DREADFULLY CLEVER LITTLE GIRL. I know who he is, mummy.

MOTHER. Ssh, darling.

GEORGE. Let the little girl speak, Madam. Well, girlie, and oo do yer think I am?

GIRL. You're the dog.

GEORGE. Bravo. Got it in one. What's your name, little girl?

GIRL. Betty.

GEORGE. Well done, Betty, 'ere's a box of chocolates for yer. [*To* MOTHER.] Don't let the attendant see it, Madam, cos I pinched it off the Buffet.

Yus, the little girl is right. I'm George and glad ter be my own shype agyne. It appened like this. When the wyter kicked me downstairs, the stitches broke and the skin fell off. Coo, you should ave seen 'is fyce. E was as white as a fresh 'addock. And now ere we are. There's no plyce like 'ome is there. I tell yer I could ave cried when I saw ol Fishy, the copper wot pinched me, standin ahtside the Kings 'Ead. Talkin of coppers, they've tyken poor Mister Norman to the stytion. Wonder if 'e's got the letter. But jest yer wyte. We'll ave 'im aht in no time.

[*Enter a* SLUM BOY.]

BOY. Blymey. George.

GEORGE. 'Arry.

HARRY. 'Ow do you come ere? I thought you was doin' a stretch.

GEORGE. I'll tell yer abaht that lyter. 'Ow's 'evrythin?

HARRY. Rotten. You won't know the plyce.
   Cautious Cutie
   As lost er beauty
   Arelip Hetty
   As jumped off a jetty
   Lousy Lill
   Is very ill
   And the Fruly Fox

GEORGE. Oo taught me ter box?

HARRY. Yus. 'E's on the rocks
   'E's got the pox.
GEORGE. Ow's Sammy the Sap?
HARRY. 'E's off the map.
GEORGE. And ow's the Mask?
HARRY. Yer must never ask. Come on, let's go dahn to Levy's. Ma will be glad ter see yer.
GEORGE. Nothin doin. Got some partiklar bisiness to attend ter. Ain't I? [*Winks at audience.*] Look ere, 'Arry. Got a jemmy and a blowlamp yer could lend me?
HARRY. O so that's it. Got a job, ave yer. Sorry I can't oblyge myself, but I'll tyke yer to see Paddy. E'll be yble to fix yer up. O, I saw Fanny yesterday and she said . . .

[*Exeunt.*]

Act III Scene 2

[*The Police Station. Enter* SERGEANT *and three* RECRUITS.]

SERGEANT. Left right. Left right. Class. Halt. Left turn. Stand at ease. No. 1. Atten-shun. Your lesson, please.
No. 1. The author of a criminal act
   Is shown by motive, class, and fact
   As motives we must recognize
   Women and their jealousies
   Money, love of power, and drink
   Is now and then the cause we think.
   Criminal are butchers, bakers,
   Locksmiths, dyers, carpet makers
   But little crime we see in Quakers
   And least of all is found to be
   'Mongst those engaged in carpentry.
SERGEANT. Very good. Stand at ease. No. 2. Atten-shun. Your lesson please.
No. 2 [*he sticks often*]. As indecent we define
   Books and papers that incline
   Average members of the Force
   To certain feelings which are coarse
   That is, sensations which are felt
   Below the regulation belt.
   Shameful and indecent are

The Bible in particular
The plays of Massinger and Ford
The bits in Shakespeare about a bawd
Herrick's verse and Mr Pope's.

[*Sticks.*]

Sorry, sir. I just can't get these names into my head.
SERGEANT. Come on man. Think of the rhyme. What rhymes with Pope's. The works of Dr Marie Stopes. *You'll* never get into the Staff College. Alright that'll do for you. Stand at ease. Now then No. 3. Atten-shun. Your lesson please.
NO. 3. The English law concerning libel
To define we are unyble.

[*Enter* POLICEMAN.]

POLICEMAN. There's a party outside has been sent to this station
By the Nineveh Hotel for interrogation.
SERGEANT. Bring him in. Class atten-shun. Dis-miss.

[*Enter* POLICEMAN *with* ALAN.]

Name.
ALAN. Norman.
SERGEANT. Look 'ere young feller, don't you try and be funny with us, see. What's your name?
ALAN. Norman. Alan Norman.
SERGEANT. O so you're going to be saucy, are you. Where's your papers?
ALAN. I haven't got any.
SERGEANT. So that's it. No address either I suppose.
ALAN. No.
SERGEANT. No name, no papers, no address. You might as well be dead. [*Telephone rings.*] Ullo. The police station. Yes, sir, speaking. Yes. Yes. No. Yes. Right, sir, we'll be down in five minutes. [*He blows his whistle. The* POLICE *all fall in.*] They're holding a demonstration at the Power House. Have you all got your truncheons?
ALL. Yes, sir.
SERGEANT. No. 2 fall out and guard the prisoner. (O and get him something to wear. I can't have people sitting about my station in pyjamas.) Company. Shun. Right turn. Left wheel. Quick march.

[*Exeunt to the tune of the Policeman's Holiday.*]
[NO. 2 *goes out and comes back with some workman's clothes.*]

No. 2. Ere. They aint exactly West End but they'll be warmer than them beach pyjamas.

Of all the ungryteful, you might sy thank yer. Wot's the trouble mate? Women I should think, judging by the 'airs on yer coller. Well, if yer don't want to be civil, don't.

ALAN. I'm sorry. Thank you but please leave me alone. I want to be quiet.

No. 2. No offence. As yer like. Live and let live, that's wot I sy. Where's my book? [*Pause.*] Was you any good at learnin by eart when you was at school? I wish I was. [*Spells out slowly.*]

Offences under Schedule B
Restraint of Princes, Ba, Ba.

Wot's this word? B-A-R-R-A-T-R-Y. Ba, Ba, Ba. Give it up. What is it anyway? Something improper, most likely. These long words makes me air curl. Where's the paper? [*Picks it up.*] Bishop bites Dog. Well did you ever. Triplets born in Iran. Glad I'm not the father. If it 'ad been me I'd ave said they belonged to the lydy opposite. Pickets at Pressan. Tense situation at Windyacre Mine. Hm. Russian Gold.

ALAN. Give me that paper.

No. 2. 'Ere, steady, steady. Wot yer snatchin at? Yer can ave it but yer needn't be in such an urry abaht it. Don't want the crossword pyge as well I suppose.

[*Both read. Stage darkens.*]

ALAN'S RIGHT FOOT. What are you pushing for, Left?
LEFT FOOT. You're taking up all the room.
R.F. Well you needn't push so. You're always pushing.
L.F. It's damned cold. Scratch my back for me, will you, Right. No, a bit higher.
R.F. There?
L.F. Yes. That's good. O Hell, I'm tired.
R.F. It's been a tiring day.
L.F. I always feel tired now. Don't want to get up in the morning. I'm getting old. The cramp keeps getting me. It gets me bad sometimes.
R.F. You ought to see a doctor.
L.F. I know, but the master won't let me. Mean I call it. Well, if I let him come a stinker one of these days it won't be my fault.
R.F. I'll mention it to him next time he wants to go for a walk, and if he won't listen, I'll slip. After all, we feet must stick together.
L.F. You're dead right. [*Pause.*] Seen anything of the Monk lately?
R.F. Ssh. He may be listening. You know what a one he is for coming round the corner suddenly when you're not expecting him. Come

closer. It's my opinion, Left, he's had some sort of unpleasant shock. Something's happened. You know how high and mighty he's been all this last week, ordering us about like dirt, and giving the Master sauce, till one wanted to slap him. Well, I saw him this morning and honest I wouldn't have known him he was so changed. Hanging his head down as meek as you please. Someone must have told him where he got off, and I can't say I'm sorry.

L.F. Nor I either. Who is he anyway? He's kept like you or me.

R.F. Ssh.

> [*Enter* GEORGE *with a pocket torch.* ALAN *and* POLICEMAN *are sound asleep.*]

GEORGE. Mister Norman. [*Flashes torch in his face.*]

ALAN. Who's that?

GEORGE. It's George.

ALAN. O I'm going mad. I thought George was a dog.

GEORGE. Ssh, or yer'll wyke up yer fat friend. It's George. I'm the dawg or rather I was. I can't explyne now cos we must urry. Did yer find the letter?

ALAN. What letter?

GEORGE. Didn't yer ear me shout up the stairs? I found a letter in Miss Vipond's keyole from a bloke called Francis. It 'ad a coat of arms on it so I thought it might be from the gentleman you was lookin for. That's wy we must urry cos if it is im, e's dyin.

ALAN. Dying. Where is he now?

GEORGE. In St Jymes' Infirmary. I know the plyce.

ALAN. How did you get in?

GEORGE. Broke in at the winder at the back. That's our wy out. Come on.

ALAN. Is it too late
   Be merciful Fate.

> [*Exeunt.*]

NO. 2 [*talking in his sleep.*] The plays of Massinger and Ford
   The bits in Shakespeare about a bawd
   Herrick's verse . . .

CURTAIN

Act III Scene 3

[*The door of the Infirmary.*]

PRESSMAN. Why must I go to the demonstration
    It's a long long way to the Power Station
    I shall never get so far
    I shall find the nearest bar.
    Let the Daily Mail
    Lose its sale
    On a night of rain and mist
    Who would be a journalist?

      [*Song.*]

On a wet Sunday evening
  I met my love
She wore an old ulster
  And one black glove
She opened a suitcase
  And brought out in her hand
10 semi-detached villas with
  lean-to garage
  9 double beds with Kumfy-
  sleep mattresses
  8 Telescopic hat-stands
  7 rolls of cheque linoleum
  6 Dinky tea cloths
  5 garden mowers
  4 Gents pyjama suiting
  3 shaving mirrors
  2 Dr Wellingdon's pink pills
  for gout, rheumatism,
  varicose veins, acidosis,
  chilblains, body odour,
  baldness and nervous debility
And
One small packet of Woodbines
  THE ONLY BRAND.

      [*Alternative song.*]

[*Tune: Jesu the very thought of thee.*]
Alice has gone and I'm alone
  Nobody understands
How lovely were her fire alarms
  How fair her German bands.

O how I cried when Alice died
  The day we were to have wed
We never had our roasted duck
  And now she's a loaf of bread.

[*Enter* ALAN *and* GEORGE.]

  Good-evening. Are you looking for me?
ALAN. Is this the entrance to the Infirmary?

2ND PRESSMAN. Over there is the door.
    I'll show you. Yes I'm tight
    But I won't fight.

[Rings bell for them.]

    I've seen your face before
    But where I'm not sure.

[PORTER comes out.]

ALAN. Can I see Mr Crewe?
PORTER. You cannot do
    They're taking him now into the theatre
    I'm afraid you will have to come back later
    And you'll be lucky if you see him alive
    He's not expected to survive.

[Exit PORTER.]

ALAN. Too late.
GEORGE. That's gorn and bent it.
2ND PRESSMAN. Here, Misery, wait
    There's a back door that I know
    To the theatre we will go.
GEORGE. It seems ter me I've done all I can, so if you'll excuse me I'll be getting back to my pals. Good-bye Mr Norman, and I 'opes yer finds im breathin.
ALAN. Good-bye George, I shall never forget
    All that you did when you were my pet
    And I'm glad that in person we have met.
GEORGE. Syme ter you. So long.

[Exit GEORGE.]

PRESSMAN [*as they exit by a small door*].
        There's a back door in Soho
        Only commercial travellers know.

[Exeunt.]

Act III Scene 4

[*An operating theatre in the Infirmary. Benches of* STUDENTS.]

MEDICAL STUDENT. Do you know the story of the curate and the B.B.A.?

[*Enter* PROMPTER *very quickly.*]

PROMPTER. I'm sorry gentlemen. The Censor does not allow that one.
MEDICAL STUDENT. O very well. Do you know the story—
PROMPTER. Nor that one either.
MEDICAL STUDENT. But you don't know yet what the story is going to be.
PROMPTER. You're a medical student, sir, and that's enough for him. All your stories are tabu in this theatre.
ALL. But what are we to do while you're waiting?
PROMPTER [*scratching his head*]. Well, if you were to whisper them I don't suppose there'd be any harm in it.
ALL [*whisper*].

| ... And so you see | ... He said there's a stigma |
| It was D and C. | About the letter Sigma. |

[*A harmonium begins to play a voluntary. Procession of* NURSES, DRESSERS, PATIENT, *and* SURGEON. *He takes up a position at the end of the table with his back to the audience. The note is given. ff subito. Flavour of Bach in his dramatic mood.*]

ALL STUDENTS [*heavy 4-part harmony*].
   We see death every day
   But do not understand him.
SURGEON. I believe
ALL. in the physical causation of all phenomena material or mental, and in the germ theory of disease. And in Hippocrates, the father of Medicine, Galen, Ambrose Paré, Liston of the enormous hands, Syme, Lister who discovered the use of antiseptics, Hunter and Sir Frederick Treves.

   And I believe in surgical treatment for duodenal ulcer, cerebral abscess, pyloric stenosis, aneurism, and all forms of endocrine disturbance.
SURGEON. Let not the patient react unfavourably to the anaesthetic.
ALL. But let it save him from pain.
SURGEON. Let there be no unforeseen complications.
ALL. Neither let sepsis have the advantage.
SURGEON. May my skill not desert me.
ALL. But guide your hands.

SURGEON. Gentlemen, we have before us a case of abdominal injury, caused by a bullet piercing the bowel. I intend therefore to make a 5-inch median incision, dividing the rectus abdominus, bring the bowel forward, resect it, wash out the peritoneum with warm saline, and insert a tube for drainage. Is it clear?

ALL. It is.

> [SURGEON *turns to wash his hands. During this process the* STUDENTS *sing the following to a C of E chant. The* PRESSMEN *and* ALAN *enter during the singing.*]

DECANI. The surgeon is great: let his name appear in the birthday honours.

CANTORIS. I was in danger of death; and he delivered me.

DEC. I was in fever and I could not sleep; the pain assailed me all the day long.

CAN. I groaned in the darkness; I was in terror for my life: I took no pleasure in women, neither in the innocent pastimes of children, my food had lost its flavour.

DEC. The Physicians shook their heads: they consulted together in the next room and they were perplexed.

CAN. They prescribed diets, cathartics, drugs and all manner of salves and ointments; but no one of them relieved me.

2ND HALF. But the surgeon, he relieved me; he removed the emphasis of my trouble and I was healed.

PRESSMAN. You see Mr. Norman
    I told you I never forget a face
    Fancy meeting you in this place
    Fancy the patient being Sir Francis
    You will see how my editor dances
        I'm cock o whoop
        Boy what a scoop.

STUDENTS. Ssh.

SURGEON [*adjusting his gloves and picking up a scalpel*]. It's a terrible thing, nurse, to keep wicket for a man's life.

ALAN. Who's the surgeon?

PRESSMAN. Sir William Spurgeon
    The famour amateur cricketer
    He captained the Hospital's team last year.

STUDENTS. Ssh.

> [*Rolls of drums like a tight rope act.* SURGEON *be-*

gins. Back curtains draw showing WITNESSES *dressed as boxing seconds. They throw up their right hands and the lights go out.*]

SURGEON. Lights, Nurse, dresser, you dresser next to that damned dresser. For God's sake get a torch. Light, give me a bloody light. Christ is there no one in this bloody theatre who understands plain English? Fetch the manager, the scene shifter and find out what the devil it's all about.

[*There is a flash of magnesium light.*]

PRESSMAN. Here you are, sir.
The Mail but not the Telegraph
Will be honoured with your photograph.

SURGEON. You bloody fool. You've blinded me. Scalpel, Nurse. Not that one, idiot. Artery forceps. More forceps. More. More. More.

[*Enter* SCENE SHIFTER.]

SCENE SHIFTER. The Power House has cut us off. The police are storming it now.

SURGEON. I have cut the mesenteric
Death has declared. [*Throws instruments about.*]

STUDENTS. The papers said there was going to be trouble.

ANAESTHETIST. He's sinking sir. I'd better give him an injection of adrenalin.

SURGEON. God, man, don't chatter. Do something. [*To* DRESSER.] How the Hell do you think I can see if you stand a mile away. Hold the torch nearer. Get out of my way.

THEATRE SISTER. Something's the matter. The patient's coming to. Holy Mary, mother of all the saints have mercy.

ANAESTHETIST. What was in the bottle, sister?

SISTER. Adrenalin, sir.

ANAESTHETIST. Give it here. Can't you read? It's hydrochloric acid.

SURGEON. It isn't cricket. [*Gives up.*]

[*The music of the ensuing duet between* FRANCIS *and* ALAN *should be in the style of Wagnerian opera. If the actors cannot sing, the singing might either be done by the singers concealed in the chorus, or by using a panatrope concealed under the operating table.*]

FRANCIS. O Pressan Fells
How beautiful you are

I hear your bells
Alas I cannot come
To Pressan home
I have wandered too far.
CHORUS. (Pain makes him wander in his mind
There's nothing audible of any kind.)
ALAN. O Francis.
FRANCIS. I hear a voice
That makes me rejoice
Who is it standing there
I cannot see you clear.
ALAN. Francis, it is I
Alan Norman standing by
And I have come
To take you home.
FRANCIS. I cannot see.
Twixt you and me
Death's great tired face
Hangs in space.
CHORUS. (Death makes him wander in his mind
There's nothing visible of any kind.)
ALAN. I am near
Do not fear.
FRANCIS. I hear her say
That she has come
To take me to-day.
ALAN. O Francis stay.
FRANCIS. Nay
She beckons me away
Beasts and flowers are in her keeping
In her arms I would be sleeping.
ALAN. O Francis give
Your blessing first that I may live
Give me your hand to kiss.
FRANCIS. Gladly, Alan, I give you this.
ALAN. O what shall I do?
FRANCIS. Be true, be true
To Pressan. She
Will teach you what to be
More I cannot tell
Darkness assails me and I fail
Farewell.

[*One of the* WITNESSES *counts like a referee. At Ten, he raises the right arm of the other* WITNESS.]

[*Shouts of* NEWSBOYS.]

NEWSBOYS. Evening special. Martial law in Pressan. Evening special. Riots at Windyacre. Evening special.

A SHOUT OUTSIDE. Here come the Mounted Police. They're going to charge the crowd.

[*Sounds of mounted police charging crowd. Cries of* Bloody Murderers, *etc., etc.*]

ONE OF THE STUDENTS [*looking out the window*]. They went through them like a dose of salts.

ALAN. I hear and obey.

CURTAIN

Chorus

Finally and under the local images our blood has conjured
We show you man caught in the trap of his terror, destroying himself.
From his favourite pool between the yewhedge and the roses; it is no
    fairy tale his line catches
But grey white and horrid, the monster of his childhood raises; its huge
    domed forehead
As death moves in to take; his inner luck.
Lands on the beaches of his love; like Coghlan's coffin.
Do not speak only of a change of heart; meaning 500 a year and a room
    of one's own:
As if that were all that is necessary; in these islands alone there are
    some forty-seven million hearts, each of four chambers
You cannot avoid the issue; by becoming simply a community digger
Neither blame only the system; it is your collective production
The secretion of your several greeds and envies; and no less of your
    courages and your loves.
O you who prattle about the wonderful middle ages; you who expect
    the millennium after a few trifling adjustments, remember.
Wonderful slogans are adopted; down in its depths the soul does not
    adapt.

Visit from house to house, from country to country: consider the
    populations

Beneath the communions and the coiffures: discover your image
Man divided always and restless always: afraid and unable to forgive
Unable to forgive his parents: or his first voluptuous rectal sins
Afraid of the clock, afraid of catching his neighbour's cold; afraid of his own body
Desperately anxious about his health and his position: calling upon the universe to justify his existence
Slovenly in posture and thinking: the greater part of the will devoted
To warding off pain from the waterlogged areas
An isolated bundle of nerve and desire: suffering alone
Seeing others only in reference to himself; as a long-lost mother or his ideal self at sixteen.

Watch him asleep and waking
Dreaming of continuous sexual enjoyment: or perpetual applause
Reading of accidents over the breakfast-table, thinking: "This could never happen to me"
Reading the reports of trials: flushed at the downfall of a fellow creature
Examine his satisfactions
Some turn to the time-honoured solutions of sickness and crime: some to the latest model of aeroplane or the sport of the moment
Some take to good works: to a mechanical ritual of giving
Some adopt an irrefragable system of beliefs or a political programme: others have escaped to the ascetic mountains
Or taken refuge in the family circle, among the boys on the bar-stools: on the small uncritical islands.

Men will profess devotion to almost anything, to God, to Humanity, to Truth, to Beauty; but their first thought on meeting is "Beware"
They put their trust in Reason or in the Feelings of the Blood: but they will not trust a stranger with half-a-crown.
So beware then of those with no obvious vices: of the chaste, the non-smoker and drinker, the vegetarian
Beware of those who show no inclination towards making money: there are even less innocent forms of power.

Beware of yourself.
Have you not heard your own heart whisper: "I am the nicest person in this room"
Asking to be introduced to someone "real": someone unlike all those people over there?

Repent

You have wonderful hospitals and a few good schools
Repent
The precision of your instruments and the skill of your designers is
    unparalleled
Repent
Your knowledge and your power are capable of infinite extension
Repent
One theory may be truer or falser than another: but that is not enough
A belief may be foolish or sensible: that is not enough either
A way of living may give opportunity to good or to evil: but it is not
    self-supporting
Refuse no such assistance: explore every avenue of enlightenment
For there is nothing that is not unimportant: but the final issue is always
Between the loving and the unloving; the unforgiving and the
    forgiving: the trust and the fear.

Act III Scene 5

[*Curtain rises. Pressan. The* VICAR *and* IRIS.]

IRIS. Any news of Jimmy?
VICAR.   Dead
    Shot while trying to escape
    The official bulletin said
    But you know what that means
    O Jimmy, I shall hear your screams
    For ever in my dreams.
IRIS. I saw Major Bicknell to-day
    He refuses to go away
    He refuses to speak
    Or even eat
    But he sits in his room
    And waits for his doom.
    Will Alan never come?
VICAR. Dear Lord and Master
    Who hung on tree
    In this disaster
    Strengthen me
    To bear the scorn
    Of all men born
    Christ crucified
    Confirm my mind

That I be kind
To those who assert and hurt
On either side.

> [*Enter* GENERAL *in full uniform.* HECTOR *in attendance.*]

GENERAL. Good morning, Padre, you're the man I want
    I've got the traitors by the short hairs now
    We've driven 'em into the reformatory
    Where we can round them up. Somehow or other
    They've got some arms, however, and I want
    Some reinforcements. That's where you come in
    Just preach a sermon to the audience, will you,
    You know the kind of thing to call 'em round.
VICAR. I won't.
GENERAL. O come. Perhaps I put it a bit crudely.
    But that's a soldier's way.
    There's no offence intended, my dear Padre.
    Come on. Render to Caesar, Caesar's things you know.

> [VICAR *says nothing.*]

    What? Pacifist? That's something new for you
    What's happened to your history of the war?
    There is some hanky-panky somewhere. Speak, man. [*Pause.*]
    My God, we'll see how deep it goes. Take that. [*Hits his paunch.*]
    I do believe the senile idiot has gone Socialist
    Well. I'll soon show you what they think of you.
    Hey. Corporal. Bring a prisoner here.
    Allow me to introduce you two. The Vicar.

> [PRISONER, *beaten up, dragged in.*]

VICAR. Freddy.
PRISONER. Leave me alone. I don't want you and your bloody prayers.

> [PRISONER *taken away.*]

GENERAL. You see. [*Whistles. Enter several* SOLDIERS.] This man is under
    my arrest
    Leave him alone but keep an eye on him.
    Fetch me the gramophone and special record
    Train a machine gun on the audience
    In case there's [*gramophone brought in*] any trouble. Put it here.
    [*To* VICAR.] And now, you cissy, listen to a man.

GRAMOPHONE. What was the weather on Eternity's worst day? And where was the Son of God during that fatal second—pausing before a mirror in an anteroom, or near to the Supreme Presence itself in the middle of an awful crescendo of praise, or again withdrawn apart, regarding pensively the unspeakable beauties of the heavenly landscape?

The divinest of books says nothing. Of the primary crises of the soul no history is ever written. Yon citizen crossing the street while the policeman holds up the traffic like the Red Sea. He leaves one curb an honest man. But O, quickly constable, handcuffs out! Roll on you heavy lorries. He is Pharaoh. Mercifully exterminate this pest. Too late. The warning cannot be given. It's done: the poison administered, the soul infected. The other curb is reached and our John Bull, honest-seeming, undistinguished, unsuspected, is free to walk away, within a few years to involve widows in financial ruin or a party of schoolchildren in some frightful accident.

So on this inconceivably more catastrophic occasion, no door banged, no dog barked. There was no alarm of any kind. But consider its importance. No judge's sentence had ever yet been passed. Basedow's disease had not occurred. Love. Joy. Peace. God. No words but these. No population but angels. And after—the whole lexicon of sin, the sullen proletariat of hell.

Then what of the central figure in the tragedy? First among the Sons of God. Power. No Caliph or Mikado had one grain of it. Beauty. Alcibiades beside him were extraordinarily plain. Wits. Einstein were a stammerer. But for him it was not enough. For him nothing was enough but the unique majority of God. That or—Ah had he reckoned with the dread alternative—unqualified ruin. Alas for us, he raised the question. The answer was to lie with Another.

O even then, when the thought first tempted, was all irrevocably lost? Was there not still time, wonderful creature, to cast it from you with a phew of disgust? It doesn't matter now. Altered for ever, and for the worse, he went out to corrupt others, to form his notorious and infamous societies. Gone for ever were the frank handshake, the obvious look, the direct and simple speech. The Golden Age was definitely over. Language had become symbolic, gesture a code of signals. The arrangement of books on a table conveyed a shamefaced message: flowers in a vase expressed some unsavoury double-entendre. Personalities acquired a new and sinister significance, lost all but that. For or against; on this side of the ledger or on that. Gabriel and Michael—out of the question. What glorious praise. Demogorgon—safe. What a shameful comment. Abdiel and Azazael—

Possible. Beware, you unsuspecting couple. This is a terrible examination, decisive of your everlasting career. Here are but two colours from which to choose, the whitest white or the blackest black. Salvation or damnation at 100%. Azazael chooses. What! the black? Miserable, unlucky he. He's failed. Now Abdiel. You hesitate? Quick man, the white. Bravissimo, he passes. Baffled, they slink away, to make their preparations. Too late for diplomacy or apologetic telegrams. It is war.

On the details of that appalling combat, history is mercifully silent. To the vanquished, unable to consider such reminiscences without a shudder, the subject is tabu: and the victors, to whom all boasting is by nature abhorrent, have been content to leave the matter in a decent obscurity. But remember, they were divine, and therefore omniscient, omnipotent. No new-fangled auxiliary arm, the value of which is realised only by a few enthusiastic subalterns, no depth charges or detectors, no tricks of camouflage, no poison gas which in times of peace even generals do not see how they could bring themselves to use, no technique of deployment or barrage, can have been unknown to them. It was conflict on an astronomical scale and with the gloves off. There were no Quakers or strikers, no international Red Cross, no question of colonies or reparations. Where all were committed absolutely there could be no ironic misgivings.

Every schoolboy knows the result. To the rebels it was destruction. The reservoirs of the divine wrath were inexhaustible. Nothing was signed. There was no one left to discharge so unnecessary an office. Into the fosse of hell they fell like water. Hurrah. Hurrah. Hurrah.

Yet, my friends, you know and I know, don't we, that the events I have just narrated were not the last. Would God they had been. The scene of operations was transferred to another front, to us. Impotent to attack him directly, the defeated sought to strike at God through his creatures, to wound where it be most tender, his artist's love. And to our shame, they succeeded. The world became an everlasting invalid. Of course God could have dismissed us with a snap of the fingers. One little stellar collision and . . . no more bother for him. Why not? All reason was for it. It would have been quite cricket. But God is no eugenist. There was no talk of sterilisation or euthanasia. Only the treatment of a very merciful and loving physician. He set over us a kindly strictness, appointed his authorities, severe but just, a kind of martial law. He gave them power to govern in his name, and access to his presence in their prayers, to make their reports, and ask for help and guidance, that through them the people might learn his primary will.

And so, to-day we are here for a very good reason. His enemies have launched another offensive on the grandest scale perhaps that this poor planet of ours has witnessed. As on the first awful occasion in Eden, so now, under the same deluding banner of freedom.

For their technique of propaganda has never varied: It has been far too successful for them to need to change it. In silk-clad China or the naked Archipelagoes, in the Bermudas or Brighton, in the stone hamlet among the beechwoods or the steel flats of the Metropolis, that three-syllabled whisper—"You are God" has been, is, and alas, will be sufficient to convert in a moment the chapped-handed but loyal ploughboy, the patient sufferer from incurable disease, the tired economical student, or the beautiful juvenile mama into a very spiteful maniac indeed, into whose hands modern science has placed an all too efficient axe.

I should like you just to try and imagine for a moment what the world would be like if they succeeded; if this lunacy of theirs with its grim fanatic theories were to spread over the civilised globe. I tell you there would exist a tyranny compared with which a termite colony would seem dangerously lax. No family love. Sons would inform against fathers, mothers cheerfully send daughters to the execution cellars. No romance. Even the peasant must beget the standard child under laboratory conditions; motherhood would be by licence. Truth and beauty would be proscribed as dangerously obstructive. To be beautiful would be treason against the State, thought a sabotage deadly to the thinker. No books. No art. No music. A year of this and, I say, even the grass would cease to grow, flowers would not risk appearing, heifers would not dare to calve.

So you see our job. To those whom danger in God's cause makes them exclaim, like a schoolboy confronted with an ice "How Lush" this is a lucky day. God has given them extraordinary privileges. But if there be any doubters, cowards wavering like the cowl on an oast house, I say "Go out of that door before it is too late". Only those whose decisions are swift as the Sirocco, senses keen as the finest mirror galvanometer, will constant as the standard inch, and of a chemical purity need apply.

And to these last I say. Remember. God is behind you, and Nelson, Henry V, Shakespeare, Shackleton, Julius Caesar. But as for our enemies, those rats, they shall skedaddle like a brook. Nature herself is on our side. Their boasts are vain. You cannot threaten a thunderstorm with a revolver. They shall be trapped by the stalks of flowers. Sheep shall chase them away. Useless for them to imitate natural objects such as a boulder or a tree. Even the spade-handed moles shall declare their folly.

But mind, God first. To God the glory, and let him reward. For God is no summer tourist. We're more than scenery to him. He has a farmer's eye for ergot and tares. But O delight higher than Everest and deeper than the Challenger Gulf. His commodores come into his council and his lieutenants know his love. Lord, I confess, I confess. All too weak and utterly unworthy I am. But I am thine. All actions and diversions of the people, their greyhound races, their football competitions, their clumsy acts of love, what are they but the pitiful maimed expression of that entire passion, the positive tropism of the soul to God.

O Father, I have always praised Thee, I praise Thee now, I shall always praise Thee. Listen to the sabots of thy eager child, running to thy arms. Admit him to the fairs of that blessed country where the saints move happily about their neat clean houses under the blue sky. O windmills. O cocks. O clouds and ponds. Mother is waving to me from the tiny door. The quilt is turned down in my beautiful blue and gold room. Father, I thank Thee in advance. Everything has been grand. I am coming home.

> [*Just before the last paragraph "O Father . . ." the doors at the back of the auditorium open and* RECRUITS *pour in. As they come on to the stage, they are handed arms.*]

GENERAL. Are all the doorways guarded?
VOICES. Yes sir.
GENERAL. And the gangways patrolled.
VOICES. Yes sir.
GENERAL. Company. Fall in.
VOICE 1. Halt. Who goes there?
VOICE 2. Don't be ridiculous. I've got to catch a train.
VOICE 1. Stand or I fire.
VOICE 2. You're an awfully good actor but really I've got to go.

[*Shot.*]

GENERAL. Company. Shun. The attack on the reformatory will begin at once. Company left turn. Quick march.

[*Exeunt.*]

VICAR. Let me go away
    I will go and pray
    To one who is greater.
SOLDIER. Greater than who?
VICAR. Greater than you. [*Exit.*]

[*A clatter. Enter running from back of Auditorium,*
ALAN NORMAN. *The machine gun fires. As he
reaches the steps onto the stage he collapses.*]

IRIS. Alan.
ALAN.   Too late.
    Once more I'm cheated by my Fate
    I cannot fight
    With the miners to-night
    Iris, I saw
    Francis once more
    To him I swore
    I would be true
    To Pressan and to you.
    Now he is dead and I . . .
IRIS. You shall not die.
ALAN. No, Iris, no.
    A surgeon now
    Is ignorant as a dove,
    Farewell my love. [*Dies.*]

[*Curtains draw back disclosing* WITNESSES *as
Everyman.*]

WITNESS. In all their strivings men must err
    He lies in death at last, immune
    From mute frustration's false alarm
    Now he through errors of his own
    Has also made man's weakness known.

[*A red glow in the background.*]
[*Enter* MILDRED.]

MILDRED. They have fired the reformatory; they are burning alive
    Flesh fusing for fuel, bodies burning.
    I had two sons; the sniper shot them
    It is the general protest of the earth
    Against the Germans and my desolation.
    [*Sings.*] Break their teeth O God in their mouths; smite the jaw bones of the lions, O Lord: let them fall away like water that runneth apace; and when they shoot their arrows let them be rooted out.
    Let them consume away like a snail, and be like the untimely fruit of a woman; and them not see the sun.
    The righteous shall rejoice when he seeth the vengeance; he shall wash his footsteps in the blood of the ungodly.

So that a man shall say: verily there is a reward for the righteous;
doubtless there is a God that judgeth the earth.

CHORUS. If we end to-night with the apparent triumph of reaction and
    folly: there is an alternative ending.
  And the choice is your own.

WITNESS. Love loath to enter
  The suffering winter
  Still willing to rejoice
  With the unbroken voice
  At the precocious charm
  Enter and suffer,
  Within the quarrel
  Be most at home
  Among the sterile prove
  Your vigours, Love.

CHORUS. Mourn not for these: these are ghosts who chose their pain
  Mourn rather for yourselves; for your inability to make up your
    minds.
  Whose hours of self-hatred and contempt, are all your majesty and
    crisis
  Between your fear for your little survival, and your fear of the
    future and its infinite duties
  Choose that you may recover: both your charity and your place
  Determining not this that you have lately witnessed; but another
    country
  Where grace may grow outward and be given praise
  Beauty and virtue be vivid there.

WITNESS. Where time flies on as chalk stream clear
  And lovers by themselves forgiven
  The whole dream genuine, the charm mature
  Walk in the great and general light
  In their delight a part of heaven
  Its furniture and choir.

CHORUS. To each his need; from each his power.

                CURTAIN

The Dog Beneath the Skin
or
Where Is Francis?
A Play in Three Acts

BY W. H. AUDEN AND
CHRISTOPHER ISHERWOOD

[*1935*]

TO
ROBERT MOODY

Boy with lancet, speech or gun
 Among the dangerous ruins, learn
From each devastated organ
 The power of the genteel dragon.

DRAMATIS PERSONAE

Principal Characters

THE VICAR of Pressan Ambo
GENERAL HOTHAM
MRS HOTHAM, his wife
MISS IRIS CREWE, of Honeypot Hall
SIR FRANCIS CREWE, Bart., her brother
ALAN NORMAN
FIRST JOURNALIST (*The Evening Moon*)
SECOND JOURNALIST (*The Thunderbolt*)

Minor Characters

CURATE	SORBO LAMB
MILDRED LUCE	CHIMP EAGLE
H.M. THE KING OF OSTNIA	SIR WILLIAM SPURGEON,
H.M. THE QUEEN OF OSTNIA	the Surgeon
GRABSTEIN, a Financier	MADAME BUBBI

DESTRUCTIVE DESMOND

Others

Bus Conductor. Hotel Porter. Village Chemist. Scoutmaster. Master of Ceremonies. Poet. Cabaret Announcer. Head Waiter. Art Expert. Hotel Manager. Barman.

Chorus Girls. Courtiers. Diners. Doctors. Dressers. Invalids. Lunatics. Nurses. Police. Priests. Procurers. Prostitutes. Students. Waiters. Villagers.

Two Lovers
Two Touts

Chorus

The Summer holds: upon its glittering lake
Lie Europe and the islands; many rivers
Wrinkling its surface like a ploughman's palm.
Under the bellies of the grazing horses
On the far side of posts and bridges
The vigorous shadows dwindle; nothing wavers,
Calm at this moment the Dutch sea so shallow
That sunk St Paul's would ever show its golden cross
And still the deep water that divides us still from Norway.
We would show you at first an English village: You shall choose its
    location
Wherever your heart directs you most longingly to look; you are loving
    towards it:
Whether north to Scot's Gap and Bellingham where the black rams defy
    the panting engine:
Or west to the Welsh Marches; to the lilting speech and the magicians'
    faces:
Wherever you were a child or had your first affair
There it stands amidst your darling scenery:
A parish bounded by the wreckers' cliff; or meadows where browse the
    Shorthorn and the maplike Frisian
As at Trent Junction where the Soar comes gliding; out of green
    Leicestershire to swell the ampler current.

Hiker with sunburn blisters on your office pallor,
Cross-country champion with corks in your hands,
When you have eaten your sandwich, your salt and your apple,
When you have begged your glass of milk from the ill-kept farm,
What is it you see?

I see barns falling, fences broken,
Pasture not ploughland, weeds not wheat.
The great houses remain but only half are inhabited,
Dusty the gunrooms and the stable clocks stationary.
Some have been turned into prep-schools where the diet is in the hands
    of an experienced matron,
Others into club-houses for the golf-bore and the top-hole.
Those who sang in the inns at evening have departed; they saw their
    hope in another country,
Their children have entered the service of the suburban areas; they
    have become typists, mannequins and factory operatives; they
    desired a different rhythm of life.

But their places are taken by another population, with views about
    nature,
Brought in charabanc and saloon along arterial roads;
Tourists to whom the Tudor cafés
Offer Bovril and buns upon Breton ware
With leather work as a sideline: Filling stations
Supplying petrol from rustic pumps.
Those who fancy themselves as foxes or desire a special setting for
    spooning
Erect their villas at the right places,
Airtight, lighted, elaborately warmed;
And nervous people who will never marry
Live upon dividends in the old-world cottages
With an animal for friend or a volume of memoirs.

Man is changed by his living; but not fast enough.
His concern to-day is for that which yesterday did not occur.
In the hour of the Blue Bird and the Bristol Bomber, his thoughts are
    appropriate to the years of the Penny Farthing:
He tosses at night who at noonday found no truth.

Stand aside now: The play is beginning
In the village of which we have spoken; called Pressan Ambo:
Here too corruption spreads its peculiar and emphatic odours
And Life lurks, evil, out of its epoch.

LEADER OF SEMI-CHORUS I.
    The young men in Pressan to-night
     Toss on their beds
    Their pillows do not comfort
     Their uneasy heads,
    The lot that decides their fate
     Is cast to-morrow,
    One must depart and face
     Danger and sorrow.

VOICES.   Is it me? Is it me? Is it . . . me?

LEADER OF SEMI-CHORUS II.
    Look in your heart and see:
     There lies the answer.
    Though the heart like a clever
     Conjuror or dancer
    Deceive you often into many
     A curious sleight

                    And motives like stowaways
                        Are found too late.

VOICES.   What shall he do, whose heart
                        Chooses to depart?

LEADER OF SEMI-CHORUS I.
                    He shall against his peace
                        Feel his heart harden,
                    Envy the heavy birds
                        At home in a garden.
                    For walk he must the empty
                        Selfish journey
                    Between the needless risk
                        And the endless safety.

VOICES.   Will he safe and sound
                        Return to his own ground?

LEADER OF SEMI-CHORUS II.
                    Clouds and lions stand
                        Before him dangerous
                    And the hostility of dreams.
                        Oh let him honour us
                    Lest he should be ashamed
                        In the hour of crisis,
                    In the valleys of corrosion
                        Tarnish his brightness.

VOICES.   Who are you, whose speech
                        Sounds far out of reach?

BOTH LEADERS [*singing*].
    You are the town and we are the clock.
    We are the guardians of the gate in the rock.
        The Two.
    On your left and on your right
    In the day and in the night,
        We are watching you.

    Wiser not to ask just what has occurred
    To them who disobeyed our word;
        To those
    We were the whirlpool, we were the reef,
    We were the formal nightmare, grief
        And the unlucky rose.

Climb up the crane, learn the sailor's words
When the ships from the islands laden with birds
   Come in.
Tell your stories of fishing and other men's wives:
The expansive moments of constricted lives
   In the lighted inn.

But do not imagine we do not know
Nor that what you hide with such care won't show
   At a glance.
Nothing is done, nothing is said,
But don't make the mistake of believing us dead:
   I shouldn't dance.

We're afraid in that case you'll have a fall.
We've been watching you over the garden wall
   For hours.
The sky is darkening like a stain,
Something is going to fall like rain
   And it won't be flowers.

When the green field comes off like a lid
Revealing what was much better hid:
   Unpleasant.
And look, behind you without a sound
The woods have come up and are standing round
   In deadly crescent.

The bolt is sliding in its groove,
Outside the window is the black remov-
   ers van.
And now with sudden swift emergence
Come the woman in dark glasses and the humpbacked surgeons
   And the scissor man.

This might happen any day
So be careful what you say
   Or do.
Be clean, be tidy, oil the lock,
Trim the garden, wind the clock,
   Remember the Two.

Act I Scene 1

[*The garden of the Vicarage at Pressan Ambo. The scene suggests the setting of a pre-war musical comedy. The stage is crowded with villagers of all classes, who promenade to the strains of a distant band. The characters, as they pass in turn along the footlights, address the audience.*]

VICAR. Here come I, the Vicar good
    Of Pressan Ambo, it's understood;
      Within this parish border
    I labour to expound the truth
    To train the tender plant of Youth
      And guard the moral order.

CHORUS. With troups of scouts for village louts
    And preaching zest he does his best
      To guard the moral order.

GENERAL. General Hotham is my name.
    At Tatra Lakes I won my fame,
      I took the Spanish Lion.
    In Pressan now my home I've made
    And rule my house like a brigade
      With discipline of iron.

CHORUS. Side by side his peacocks stride:
    He rules them all at Conyers Hall
      With discipline of iron.

GENERAL'S WIFE. Woman, though weak, must do her part
    And I who keep the General's heart
      Know well our island story
    And do my utmost to advance
    In India, Russia, Finland, France,
      The just and English glory.

CHORUS. With subtle wile and female smile,
    With speech and vote she will promote
      The just and English glory.

IRIS. And here am I, Miss Iris Crewe,
    I live in Pressan Ambo too,
      The prize at village dances.
    From Honeypot Hall, the haunt of doves,
    In my blue Daimler and white gloves
      I come to take your glances.

CHORUS.   With nose and ear and mouth and hair
          With fur and hat and things like that
            She takes our loving glances.
VICAR [*to* CHOIRBOYS]. Well, Ernie, how's your mother? Good.
          I hope you're behaving as you should?
          Jerry, you've got a dirty face;
          Go and wash. Then we'll have a race.
1ST VILLAGER. Brazen! I should think she is!
          She doesn't care who sees them kiss,
          Can't even trouble to draw the blind.
          She's a trollop to my mind.
2ND V.   The brooder's really excellent.
          I rear now 98 per cent.
          I have a new batch out to-day:
          Leghorns, for I find they pay.
3RD V.   I shan't mind if they choose me.
          There's lots of places I want to see:
          Paris, Vienna, Berlin, Rome.
          I shouldn't be sorry to leave the home.
4TH V.   Roll the pieces then in flour
          And stew them for at least an hour,
          Put some nutmeg in the pot
          Garnish with parsley and serve hot.
3RD V.   Perhaps they will, you never know;
          What will you do if you have to do?
2ND V.   There's money to be made in sheep;
          Only you mustn't go to sleep.
4TH V.   A glass of stout before the meal
          Is always a good thing, I feel.
VICAR [*starting the race*]. Are we ready? Now Chubb, don't cheat!
          Behind the line and touch your feet.
1ST V.   No wonder they have had a quarrel,
          The Continent is so immoral.
4TH V.   Be very careful how you add the salt.
1ST V.   Well, anyway, it's not his fault.
3RD V.   After eight years, it seems absurd.
VICAR.   Ernie first, Chubb second, Pring third.
1ST V.   That dance at least should have opened his eyes.
2ND V.   Roger's heifer won first prize.
1ST V.   She's carrying on with Fred.
VICAR.   Run up!
          You'll beat him yet!

4TH V.	This cider-cup
	Is good.
2ND V.	Ten shillings profit on the porks.
3RD V.	Chimp Eagle.
4TH V.	Recipe from wireless talks.
1ST V.	Someone ought to.
2ND V.	Well, we can't complain.
VICAR.	Caught you, my lad!
3RD V.	He'll be lost again.
1ST V.	You saw her.
VICAR.	Clever boy!
2ND V.	It's sold.
4TH V.	Taste it.
3RD V.	Choose someone.
1ST V.	He's too old.
2ND V.	Barley.
3RD V.	The Choice.
VICAR.	Your legs.
1ST V.	Her name.
VICAR.	Jolly!
4TH V.	Roasted.
3RD V.	The Hall.
1ST V.	The shame.
4TH V.	Ursula.
3RD V.	Saxifrage.
2ND V.	Wyandottes.
VICAR.	Game!
2ND V.	He didn't!
1ST V.	She did!
VICAR.	We must.
3RD V.	Yes.
4TH V.	No.

VOICES [*in crescendo*].
    Good.
        Bad.
            Poor.
                Rich.
                    White.
                        Black.
                            High.
                                Low.

Touch.
 Find.
  Pay.
   Eat.
    Weep.
     Hurt.
      Come.
       Go.
Boy.
 Tea.
  Lamb.
   Crewe.
    Shame.
     Price.
      O!

[*The hubbub is interrupted by the* VICAR, *who mounts on to a chair and begins ringing a Stationmaster's bell. Everybody is silent.*]

VICAR. Ladies and Gentlemen. I think that there
Are several strangers to Pressan here.
On your behalf I give them greeting
And will explain the purpose of our meeting:

The ancient family of Crewe
(It may perhaps be known to you)
For generations owned the land,
The farms, the fields on which we stand.
Sir Bingham Crewe, who was the last
(God rest his soul, for he has passed)
We touched our hats to, had a son,
A handsome lad, his only one,
Called Francis, who was to succeed him.
Would he were here! We badly need him.
They quarrelled, I am sad to say,
And so, ten years ago to-day,
Young Francis packed and ran away
Leaving behind him no address.
Where he has gone, we cannot guess;
For since that day no news at all
Of where he is has reached the Hall.
In fact, we do not even know
If he be living still or no.

□

Sir Bingham died eight years ago,
Francis his heir being missing still,
And left these clauses in his will:
Each year, his villages in turn
Should choose by lottery a man
To find Sir Francis if he can:
Further, he promised half his land,
And Iris his daughter adds her hand
In marriage to the lucky one
Who comes home with his only son.

This year is Pressan's turn to choose.
Oh may this year bring the good news!

A Villager [*sings*]. It seems such ages since the Master's son
>   Went away.
> He left his books, his clothes, his boots, his car, his gun
>   On that dreadful summer's day.
> He vanished suddenly without a single word of warning:
>   Left us alone to make our moan;
>   He left us mourning.

Chorus. Why has Fate been blind to our tears?
Why has she been so unkind to our fears?
Who shall we send this time who shall look for him,
Search every corner and cranny and nook for him?
>   It may be you the lot will fall upon,
>   It may be me the lot will call upon
>   To guide back
>   With pride back
> Our young heir Sir Francis Crewe!

Villager. Without his face we don't know what to do,
>   We're undone.
> He was a beauty with a sense of duty too,
>   He was our brother and our son.
> His wit, his charm, his strength, his manners, his
>   modesty and his virtue
>   Were we to tell, your contrast, well,
>   With him would hurt you.

Chorus. Why has Fate ... *etc.*

Curate [*to the* Vicar]. The names have all come in.
   We're ready to begin.

VICAR. Excellent. Excellent.

[*A top hat is passed to him by the* POLICE SERGEANT.]

    Do you swear
That all the names are written here
Of every man in this village alive,
Unmarried and over twenty-five?
SERGEANT. I swear it.
VICAR. Miss Iris Crewe.

[IRIS *comes forward.*]

Iris Crewe, are you willing now
In the presence of these people to make your vow?
IRIS. I am.
VICAR [IRIS *repeats each phrase after him*].
I, Iris Crewe, do solemnly swear
In the presence of these people here,
That I will be the wedded wife
To love and cherish all my life
Of him, whoever he may be,
Who brings my brother back to me.
VICAR. Read the names of these we sent
Who failed to do the thing they meant.
SERGEANT. Nobby Sollers.
Sorbo Lamb.
Frenchie Joe.
Chimp Eagle.
The Midget.
Muffin Todd.
Nicky Peterson.

[*The* VICAR's *eyes are bound with a handkerchief. He stirs the hat and draws, saying:*]

Divvy Divvy Divvy Divvy Divvy Divvy Di
Divvy Divvy Divvy Divvy Divvy Divvy Di.
  Swans in the air. Swans in the air.
  Let the chosen one appear!
CURATE [*taking paper from him and reading.*] Alan Norman.

[*A short burst of cheering.*]

VICAR [*removing the bandage*]. Alan Norman.

[ALAN *comes forward and kneels.*]

Alan Norman, will you go
Cross any border in sand or snow,
Will you do whatever may be needful
Though people and customs both be hateful,
When mind and members go opposite way,
Watching wake folding long on sea;
Will you remain a passenger still
Nor desperate plunge for home?

ALAN. I will.

VICAR [*producing a bag*]. Here is what the trustees give
That as you journey you may live:
Five hundred pounds; no more, no less.
May it help you to success.

[ALAN *accepts the bag and bows.*]

Let us stand a moment in silent prayer.

[*All the men present remove their hats. The* DOG *enters and begins sniffing about. People surreptitiously kick it or pat it, but it refuses to stay quiet.*]

SEMI-CHORUS I. Enter with him
These legends, love,
For him assume
Each diverse form
As legend simple
As legend queer
That he may do
What these require
Be, love, like him
To legend true.

SEMI-CHORUS II. When he to ease
His heart's disease
Must cross in sorrow
Corrosive seas
As dolphin go,
As cunning fox
Guide through the rocks,
Tell in his ear
The common phrase
Required to please
The guardians there.
And when across

>   The livid marsh
>   Big birds pursue
>   Again be true
>   Between his thighs
>   As pony rise
>   As swift as wind
>   Bear him away
>   Till cries and they
>   Are left behind.
>
> CHORUS. But when at last
>   These dangers past
>   His grown desire
>   Of legends tire
>   O then, love, standing
>   At legends' ending,
>   Claim your reward
>   Submit your neck
>   To the ungrateful stroke
>   Of his reluctant sword
>   That starting back
>   His eyes may look
>   Amazed on you
>   Find what he wanted
>   Is faithful too
>   But disenchanted
>   Your simplest love.
>
> VICAR. Well, Alan, let me congratulate
>   You first and then ourselves and Fate.
>   We couldn't have chosen a better man.
>   If you can't succeed, then no one can. [*Sees* DOG.]
>   There's that dog again! I'm blest!
>   I thought I'd lost him like the rest.
>   George, George! Good dog! Come here!
>   Walk George, walk.

[*He whistles. The* DOG *runs away.*]

>   That's queer!

[*Everyone looks at the* DOG, *who walks round, snuffling and refusing advances.*]

GENERAL. If you ask me, I shouldn't wonder if that dog wasn't sickening for the rabies. Most extraordinary animal I ever came across. Turns up on your doorstep one morning with his tongue hanging out, like the prodigal son; lets you feed him, slobber over him, pet him, makes himself quite at home. In an hour or two he's one of the family. And then, after a week or a fortnight, he'll be off again, cool as you please. Doesn't know you if you meet him in the street. And he's played the same trick on all of us. Confounded ungrateful brute! It's his mongrel blood, of course. No loyalty; no proper feeling. Though I'm bound to say, while he was with me he was the best gun-dog I ever had. [*To* DOG.] Come here, sir. Heel, sir. Heel!!

> [*The* DOG *regards the* GENERAL *for a moment with an almost human contempt. Then it continues its snuffling.*]

VILLAGERS. Isn't he sweet?
    Here is some meat.
    If he were to choose
    Me, I couldn't refuse.
    If he'd come to me
    I'd give him cake for tea.

> [*The* DOG *reaches* ALAN *and begins to fawn upon him and wag its tail.*]

VILLAGERS. Oh look! He's chosen you!
    What are you going to do?
ALAN. I'll take him too.
ALL. You must name him anew.
ALAN. For luck I'll call him Francis.
ALL. Oh, look how he prances!
BUS CONDUCTOR. The village bus is about to start
    Those who are coming prepare to depart.
VICAR [*giving a small parcel to* ALAN].
    Here is a tin of Church of England Mixture
    Just to show you that our friendship is a fixture.
    Smoke it while you are a vagrant
    And may it keep our memory fragrant.
CURATE. I have a little present here,
    It's just some trustworthy underwear.
    May its high-grade Botany wool
    Keep you warm and keep you cool.

VILLAGE CHEMIST. Here is some Victo for the nerves, in case
    The Man Next Door should take your place.
A SCOUTMASTER. Here is a Kron watch; like a wife
    To keep exact time all your life,
    Generously designed to offer beauty
    And like an Englishman to do its duty.
    A nameless watch is scarcely better
    Than an anonymous letter.

[*During these speeches, the* GENERAL *has been having a whispered consultation with his* WIFE.]

GENERAL'S WIFE. Oh *no*, dear! I'm sure ten shillings would be *ample*.
GENERAL [*advancing pompously to* ALAN]. Ahem! Ahem! [*He gives money with the air of tipping a porter.*] Don't disgrace Pressan Ambo, my boy.
ALAN. Rather not, sir! Thanks awfully, sir!
IRIS. Alan dearest, we must part
    But keep this photo near your heart,
    Wherever you go, by land or sea,
    Look on this and think of me:
    For whatever you must do
    My thoughts are always with you too.
ALAN. Iris, give me a parting kiss
    In promise of our future bliss.
IRIS. Gladly, Alan, I give you this. [*Embrace.*]
VOICES. Oh dear, it's beginning to rain!
    You ought to weed it.
    The farmers need it.
    Mummy, I've got a pain.
ALL. Speech! Speech!
ALAN. You've been so ripping and kind
    It puts all words out of my mind,
    But if there's anything I can do,
    Ladies and Gentlemen, for you . . .
MILDRED LUCE [*suddenly appearing*].   Yes!
    Set off for Germany and shoot them all!
    Poison the wells, till her people drink the sea
    And perish howling. Strew all her fields
    With arsenic, leave a land whose crops
    Would starve the unparticular hyena!
    But you are young and it is useless
    To look to Youth. In the November Silence

I have heard more shuffling every year,
Seen more of the up-to-date young men there waiting
Impatient in the crowd to catch a train
And shake a German gently by the hand.
I had two sons as tall as you:
A German sniper shot them both.
They crawled to me across the floor;
I put their earliest prattle in a book.
A German sniper shot them both.
I saw them win prizes at their prep-school sports;
I had their friends at half-term out to tea.
A German sniper shot them both.
I heard their voices alter as they grew
Shyer of me and more like men. [*Taking out a large watch.*]
O Ticker, Ticker, they are dead
As the Grimaldi infants.
Justice has gone a summer cruise and let
Her mansion to a madman. Say something,
Ticker. Nothing. Nothing. I protest.

VICAR. Mildred dear, go home and rest
And calm yourself. That will be best.

[*Sounds of a motor-horn.*]

BUS CONDUCTOR. The bus is leaving in a minute:
Those who are coming must step in it.

ALAN AND CHORUS. Now $\{^{I}_{we}\}$ must part

It's time to start

With tears in $\{^{my}_{our}\}$ eyes $\{^{I}_{we}\}$ say good-byes

Success be with you and satisfaction
We wish to you in your every action.
In July and December

$\{^{I}_{We}\}$ will remember you.

[ALAN *goes out.* ALL *wave handkerchiefs and hands.*]

CURTAIN

Chorus

Salmon leaping the ladder, eel in damp grass, the mole and the tiercel:
Such images of travel do not apply.
Our impulses are unseasonable and image-ridden: our trifling
    disturbances are without crisis.
Our sex and our sorrow are ever about us, like the sultriness of a
    summer
As about our hero on his human journey,
Crossing a channel: on sea in steamer
For Ostnia and Westland, in post-war Europe.

    Creatures of air and darkness, from this hour
        Put and keep our friends in power.
    Let not the reckless heavenly riders
        Treat him and us as rank outsiders.

    From the accosting sickness and
        Love's fascinating biassed hand,
    The lovely grievance and the false address,
        From con-man and coiner protect and bless.

Act I Scene 2

[*The saloon of a Channel steamer. Behind the bar, the* BARMAN *is polishing glasses. The two* JOURNALISTS *are seated, drinking. A small piano against the wall.*]

1ST JOURNALIST. The Old Man sent for me before I left. Wants me to get the low-down on the Dripping Merger. Officially, I'm covering the Danube floods.

2ND J. I saw Timmy last night. He's just back from the Carpathians. Tight as usual. He had all the dope about the Army Contracts trial. Some kid, Timmy.

1ST J. I heard a bit about that from Gus. Blankets, wasn't it?

2ND J. Blankets nothing! Why, man, it was tarpaulin!

1ST J. You've got it wrong, old horse. Gus said five million blankets.

2ND J. Six million . . .

1ST J. Gus swears it was five.

2ND J. To Hell with Gus. As I was saying, these tarpaulins . . .

1ST J. My dear old fish, Gus had it from the War Minister himself . . . "Blankets", he said . . .

2ND J. Boy, you give me a pain. The whole *beauty* of the thing was that they were tarpaulins, don't you see . . . ?

[*Enter* ALAN *and the* DOG. *The* JOURNALISTS *stop arguing and watch him.* ALAN *crosses the stage to the bar.*]

ALAN [*diffidently*]. A double whisky, please: and a glass of milk.

BARMAN. Certainly, sir.

ALAN [*embarrassed*]. And I wonder if you'd mind putting the whisky in a bowl?

BARMAN [*puzzled*]. A bowl, sir?

ALAN. It's for my dog, you see.

[*The* BARMAN *winks at the* JOURNALISTS. 1ST JOURNALIST *taps his head significantly.* 2ND JOURNALIST *nods agreement.*]

BARMAN [*suavely*]. Ah, to be sure, sir.

ALAN [*confidentially*]. Did *you* ever hear of a dog drinking whisky before? *I* never did. I only found it out as we were coming down on the train. An old gent in our compartment had ordered a bottle, and before you could say Jack Robinson, Francis had swallowed the lot!

BARMAN. Most remarkable, sir. Water or soda, sir?

[*The* DOG *begins howling.*]

ALAN. Rather not! He always drinks it neat, don't you, Francis, old boy? [*The* DOG *wags its tail.*] Perhaps we'd better say two double whiskies. It doesn't look much when you pour it into a bowl, does it? [*The* BARMAN *adds the whiskies.* ALAN *gives the bowl to the* DOG, *who laps eagerly.*] You see? And he won't touch anything else. I've tried him with tea, coffee, cocoa, lemonade, beer, wine, everything you can think of . . . I'm afraid I'm going to find it rather expensive. [*He sighs and sips his glass of milk.*]

BARMAN. You're teetotal yourself, I see, sir?

ALAN [*blushing*]. Ha ha! You mustn't think I've given it up on moral grounds, or any rot of that sort. . . . The fact is, I only started yesterday. You see, I want to keep a clear head all the time. I've got some rather difficult business to settle.

BARMAN. Indeed, sir?

ALAN. Yes. I'm looking for someone. Perhaps you might be able to help me? Have you been working on this boat for long?

BARMAN. A matter of fifteen years, sir.

ALAN. Why, that's splendid! Then you're almost sure to have seen him. His name's Francis Crewe.

BARMAN. Can't say that I seem to recall it, sir. Can you describe him at all?

ALAN. Well, no. I'm afraid I can't do that. You see, he left home ten years ago and that was before we came to live in the village. Here's the only photograph they'd got of him. It isn't much use. It was taken when he was six months old.

BARMAN [*examining photo*]. Bless his little heart! Why, he's the spit and image of what my Jacky used to be. And now he can lift his poor old father up with one arm. In the marines, is my Jacky. Getting married next month.

ALAN. I'm getting married too, soon. At least, I hope I am. Look, here's a picture of my fiancée. What do you think of her? Isn't she a ripper?

BARMAN. I congratulate you, sir.

[*The* DOG *growls.*]

ALAN. Shut up, Francis, you old silly! [*To* BARMAN.] It's an extraordinary thing: whenever I show that photograph of Iris to anybody, he begins to growl. Just as though he were jealous. . . . Here, Francis. Shake a paw.

[*The* DOG *turns away.*]

BARMAN. You see, sir, he's offended. [*Slyly.*] If you were to offer him another whisky, he'd be ready to make it up, I'm sure.

ALAN [*reluctantly*]. All right, if you think so.

[*The* DOG *immediately turns round and begins barking and licking* ALAN's *hand.*]

BARMAN. What did I tell you, sir? Nobody can resist a good whisky. [*He looks pointedly at the bottle.*]

ALAN. I say, I'm most awfully sorry. I ought to have asked you if you'd have a drink, too.

BARMAN. Well, sir: since you're so pressing.

ALAN. By the way, have you ever been to Ostnia?

BARMAN. Can't say I have, sir. My brother was waiter at the Grand Hotel in the capital at one time.

ALAN. Do you know if it's the sort of country where people are likely to get lost?

BARMAN. I'm not sure I take your meaning, sir.

ALAN. You see, I thought of beginning my search there. I didn't know where to start, so I just shut my eyes and put my finger on the map.

BARMAN. And a very good idea too, sir. Your health, sir.

> [*They touch glasses. The* DOG *lifts up the bowl in its paws and touches* ALAN's *glass. They all drink.*]

1ST J. What do you make of him?

2ND J. Queer sort of card. Might be a munitions agent.

1ST J. Doubt it. I know most of them by sight.

2ND J. Or in the dope traffic.

1ST J. Hasn't got a scarab ring.

2ND J. A white slaver?

1ST J. They generally wear spats.

2ND J. Secret Service, maybe.

1ST J. With that tie? Not on your life!

2ND J. There's something phoney about him, anyhow. Come on, let's get acquainted. There'll be a story in it, you bet. [*Loudly, to* ALAN.] Pardon me, sir. Did I hear you saying just now that you were travelling to Ostnia?

ALAN. Why, yes. Can you tell me anything about it? I'd be ever so grateful.

1ST J. Can we? I should say so! My colleague here knows Ostnia like the inside of his hat.

2ND J. Pretty little country, Ostnia. Biggest national debt and lowest birth-rate in Europe. Half the budget goes into frontier forts, which are no more use than a headache because the contractor's a crook. The railways are so old they aren't safe, the mines are mostly flooded and the factories do nothing but catch fire. The Commander-in-Chief is no better than a bandit: he makes all the big stores pay for protection. The Archbishop spends his time copying naval plans for the Westland Intelligence Bureau. And meanwhile, the peasants die of typhus. Believe me, kid, it's God's own land.

ALAN. I say! It must be awfully dangerous there, isn't it?

1ST J. Not for tourists. They only see the mountains and the Renaissance Palace. . . . Of course, when you get behind the scenes, you're liable to be bumped off if you don't watch out.

ALAN. I shall have to be careful, then. You see, I'm looking for someone named Francis Crewe . . .

2ND J. See here, boy. You can keep that blue-eyed stuff for the others. You don't have to do it on us. We're not inquisitive.

1ST J. Don't worry. We'll show you the ropes.

2ND J. Maybe we should introduce ourselves. I'm on the *Thunderbolt*.

1ST J. And I'm the live wire of the *Evening Moon*.

ALAN [*shaking hands*]. I say! Are you really? I've always wanted to meet some proper writers. [*To* DOG.] Francis, come here and be introduced!

> [*The* DOG *leaves the bar and comes over to them. It is obviously intoxicated. It makes the* JOURNALISTS *a profound bow.*]

1ST J. That's a pretty cute hound of yours. What'll you take for him?

ALAN. Oh, I couldn't possibly sell him, thank you. Why, I wouldn't be parted from Francis for a thousand pounds. You've no idea how clever he is. It's quite uncanny, sometimes. ... Francis, show the gentlemen what you can do.

> [*The* DOG *attempts to balance a chair on his nose, but is too drunk to do so. Suddenly he rushes out of the saloon and is seen leaning over the rail of the ship.*]

2ND J. Your canine friend appears to be slightly overcome.

ALAN. Poor Francis! He'll be better soon. I hope it'll be a lesson to him. ... Do please go on with what you were telling me. It's so awfully interesting. Tell me about some other countries.

2ND J. All countries are the same. Everywhere you go, it's the same: nothing but a racket!

> [*The* 1ST JOURNALIST *goes to the piano and begins to play.*]

2ND J. [*singing*]. The General Public has no notion
    Of what's behind the scenes.
  They vote at times with some emotion
    But don't know what it means.
  Doctored information
    Is all they have to judge things by:
  The hidden situation
    Develops secretly.

CHORUS. If the Queen of Poland swears,
    If the Pope kicks his cardinals down the stairs,
  If the Brazilian Consul
    Misses his train at Crewe,
  If Irish Clergy
  Lose their en*er*gy
    And dons have too much to do:
  The reason is just simply this:
    They're in the racket, too.

1st J.   To grasp the morning dailies you must
           Read between the lines.
         The evening specials make just nonsense
           Unless you've shares in mines.
         National estrangements
           Are not what they seem to be:
         Underground arrangements
           Are the master-key.

Chorus. If Chanel gowns have a train this year,
           If Morris cars fit a self-changing gear,
         If Lord Peter Whimsey
           Misses an obvious clue,
         If Wallace Beery
         Should act a fairy
           And Chaplin the Wandering Jew;
         The reason is
                   Just simply this:
           They're in the racket, too!

         [*The* Dog *re-enters the Saloon. He holds out his arms to* Alan. *They dance. The* Barman *juggles with the cocktail-shaker.*]

2nd J.   There's lots of little things that happen
           Almost every day
         That show the way the wind is blowing
           So keep awake, we say.
         We have got the lowdown
           On all European affairs;
         To History we'll go down
           As the men with the longest ears.

Chorus. If the postman is three minutes late,
           If the grocer's boy scratches your gate,
         If you get the wrong number,
           If Cook has burnt the stew,
         If all your rock-plants
         Come up as dock-plants
           And your tennis-court turns blue;
         The reason is just simply this:
           You're in the racket, too!

CURTAIN

Chorus

                Ostnia and Westland;
Products of the peace which that old man provided,
Of the sobriquet of Tiger senilely vain.
Do not content yourself with their identification,
Saying: This is the southern country with the shape of Cornwall,
Or the Danube receives the effluence from this: Or that must shiver in
    the Carpathian shadow.
Do not comfort yourself with the reflection: "How very unEnglish".
If your follies are different, it is because you are richer;
Your clocks have completed fewer revolutions since the complacent
    years
When Corelli was the keeper of the Avon Swan
And the naughty life-forcer in the norfolk jacket
Was the rebels' only uncle.
                Remember more clearly their suaver images:
The glamour of the cadet-schools, the footman and the enormous hats.
But already, like an air-bubble under a microscope-slide, the film of
    poverty is expanding
And soon it will reach your treasure and your gentlemanly behaviour.
Observe, therefore, and be more prepared than our hero.

Act I Scene 3

[*Ostnia. Before the Palace. A* POLICEMAN *on duty. Enter* ALAN, *the* JOURNALISTS *and the* DOG.]

1ST J. The trams are stopped, the streets are still,
    Black flags hang from each window-sill
    And the whole city is in mourning.
    The King can't have died?
2ND J.   We had no warning.
1ST J. You ask the bobby on the corner there.
2ND J. Officer, what's happening here?
POLICEMAN. Twelfth of the month, sir: Execution Day
    There's been a revolt, I'm sorry to say.
2ND J. Another? But you had one when I was here before.
POLICEMAN. When was that, sir?
2ND J.   Only last May.

POLICEMAN. Since then, we've had four.
   We have them every fortnight, now;
   But they're generally over without much row.
   We round them up and then the King [*Salutes.*]
   Himself arranges everything.
   Go inside and see. Strangers are always invited.
   I know His Majesty will be delighted.
1ST J. Boy, what a scoop!
   I'm cock a whoop!
   Have you got your pencil?
   It's quite essential.

> [*The* JOURNALISTS *go into the Palace, followed by* ALAN *and the* DOG.]

CURTAIN

Act I Scene 4

[*Ostnia. A room in the Palace.* KING, QUEEN, COURTIERS, PRIESTS. *An organ voluntary is just finishing. The* MASTER OF THE CEREMONIES *approaches the* KING.]

M.C. Everything is ready, your Majesty.
KING. You've had a dress rehearsal, I hope? We don't want any hitches this time.
M.C. Yes, your Majesty. I took your part myself. With a dummy revolver, of course.
KING. And what about my little suggestion?
M.C. We've cut the Dies Irae, your Majesty.
KING. Good. I'm so glad you agree with me. I heard several complaints last time, that it was too gruesome. As you know, I am particularly anxious not to hurt anybody's feelings. It's a beautiful piece, of course, but one can't expect them to be quite educated up to it yet. One has to make allowances. . . . Oh, and by the way, you might tell the male alto to moderate his top notes a bit. Last time, he gave the Queen a headache.
M.C. I will, your Majesty.
KING. Excellent. Then I think, we can begin. Bring in the prisoners. [*To the* QUEEN.] My dear, your crown is a little crooked. Allow me.

> [*Solemn music. The* PRISONERS, *with their wives and mothers, are brought in. The* PRISONERS *are workmen, dressed neatly in their Sunday clothes. The women, like the ladies of the court, are dressed in black.*]

CHOIR. Requiem aeternam dona et lux perpetua luceat eis.
KING [*rising to address the* PRISONERS]. Gentlemen. I do not intend to keep you long; but I cannot let this opportunity slip by without saying how much I and the Queen appreciate and admire the spirit in which you have acted and how extremely sorry we both are that our little differences can only be settled in this er . . . somewhat drastic fashion.

Believe me, I sympathise with your aims from the bottom of my heart. Are we not all socialists nowadays? But as men of the world I am sure you will agree with me that order has to be maintained. In spite of everything which has happened, I do want us to keep this solemn moment free from any thought of malice. If any of you have a complaint to make about your treatment, I hope you will say so now before it is too late. You haven't? I am very glad indeed to hear it. Before going on to the next part of the ceremony, let me conclude by wishing you Bon Voyage and every happiness in the next world.

> [*Music. The* PRISONERS *are led out. A footman brings a gold revolver on a cushion and presents it to the* KING, *who follows the* PRISONERS.]

CANTOR. Kyrie eleison.
CHOIR. Mars eleison.
CANTOR. Kyrie eleison.
CANTOR. Homo natus de muliere, brevi vivens tempore, repletur multis miseriis. Qui quasi flos egreditur et conteritur et fugit velut umbra, et nunquam in eodem statu permanet.

Media via in morte sumus; quem quaerimus adjutorem nisi te, Domine, qui pro peccatis nostris juste irasceris?

Sancte Zeus, sancte fortis, sancte et misericors Salvator amaris mortis aeternae poenis ne tradas nos. Mars omnipotens. Frater Jovis, qui tollis peccata mundi.
CHOIR. Miserere nobis.
CANTOR. Qui tollis peccata mundi.
CHOIR. Miserere nobis.
CANTOR. Qui tollis peccata mundi.
CHOIR. Suscipe deprecationem nostram.
CANTOR. Qui sedet ad dextram Jovis.

CHOIR. Miserere nobis.

> [*Shots are heard, off. The Last Post is sounded.*]

CHOIR. Proficiscere Anima Ostniana, de hoc mundo.

> [*Re-enter the* KING. *A footman brings a silk handkerchief to clean the revolver. Another footman brings a basin of water and a towel. The* KING *washes his hands. The four corpses are brought in on stretchers.*]

CHOIR. Rex tremendae majestatis, qui salvandos salvas gratis salva me fons pietatis.

> [*Trumpet.*]

M.C. Her Majesty the Queen will now address the bereaved.

QUEEN [*to the wives and mothers of the* PRISONERS]. Ladies (or may I call you Sisters?). On this day of national sorrow, my woman's heart bleeds for you. I too am a mother. I too have borne the pangs of childbirth and known the unutterable comfort of seeing a little curly head asleep on my breast. I too am a wife and have lain in the strong arms of the beloved. Remember, then, in your loss, that in all you suffer, I suffer with you. And remember that Suffering is Woman's fate and Woman's glory. By suffering we are ennobled; we rise to higher things. Be comforted, therefore, and abide patiently, strong in the hope that you will meet your loved ones again in another and better world where there are no tears, no pains, no misunderstandings; where we shall all walk hand in hand from everlasting to everlasting.

M.C. The ladies of the Court will offer the bereaved some light refreshment.

> [*The* LADIES *take round champagne and cakes to the* PRISONERS' WOMEN.]

A WOMAN [*with a sudden hysterical scream*]. Murderers!!

> [*All the* WOMEN *are instantly and politely removed by footmen. The* COURTIERS *cough and look at the ceiling in pained embarrassment.*]

KING. Poor things! They don't really mean it, you know.
QUEEN. They lead such terrible lives!

> [*All the* COURTIERS *sigh deeply. The* LADIES *of the court begin to admire the corpses.*]

1st Lady. How lovely they look:
   Like pictures in a children's book!
2nd L. Look at this one. He seems so calm,
   As if he were asleep with his head in his arm.
   He's the handsomest, don't you think, of the four?
   How I wish I'd met him before!
   I'll put some blood on my hanky, a weeny spot,
   So that he never shall be forgot.
3rd L. Oh Duchess, isn't he just a duck!
   His fiancée certainly had the luck.
   He can't have been more than nineteen, I should say.
   He must have been full of Vitamin A.
2nd L. Dear Lady Emily,
   What a clever simile!
4th L. What beautiful hair; as white as wool!
   And such strong hands. Why, they're not yet cool!
   Lend me a pair of scissors, dear.
   I want a lock as a souvenir.
M.C. Three Englishmen crave an audience with your Majesty.
King. Oh, certainly, certainly. I'll see them at once.

> [*Trumpet.*]

M.C. Mr Alan Norman and friends.

> [*Enter* Alan *and two* Journalists. *They kiss the* King's *hand.*]

King. How do you do? Delighted to see anyone from England. I have very happy memories of visits there before the War. The singing in King's Chapel was marvellous, quite marvellous. And Melba, ah, delicious! Talking of which, I hope you liked our singing today? I'm always most grateful for any criticisms. . . . How's London? My dear London! Those evenings at the Crystal Palace! What a building! What fireworks! I hear Regent Street is quite unrecognizable now. Dear me, how time flies, hm, indeed, yes. . . . But I mustn't bore you with an old man's memories. What can I do for you?
Alan. I'm looking for Sir Francis Crewe:
   Is his name, Sire, known to you?
King. Sir Francis Crewe? Hm, let me think. He wasn't one of your ambassadors, by any chance? I'm so stupid about names. [*To the* Master of Ceremonies.] Ask the Court if they know anything about an Englishman called Sir Francis Crewe.

> [*Trumpet.*]

M.C. Is an Englishman, Sir Francis Crewe,
Familiar to anyone of you?

[*Silence.*]

KING. You see? I'm so sorry. . . . But I tell you what: You might try the Red Light District. It's always full of foreign visitors. [*To* M.C.] Is the Crown Prince in?

M.C. No, your Majesty.

KING. What a pity. He'd have been delighted to show you round. He's always going down there. It worries the Queen dreadfully, but I tell her not to take it to heart so: Boys will be boys. . . . Have you got a plan of the city?

M.C. Here's one, your Majesty.

KING. Thanks. [*Opening the plan, to* ALAN.] Come round on this side, you'll see better. Here's the Palace and here's the Palace Underground Station, just opposite. You take the tube to the Triangle: It's a two angel fare, I think. Then you take a number four tram to the Butter Kiln. After that, I'm afraid you'll have to walk. Keep left at the Cemetery.

M.C. Excuse me, your Majesty, but the trams aren't running and everything's shut because of the executions.

KING. Of course! How silly of me to forget! Ring up the Broadcasting Station at once and have the mourning called off.

[M.C. *bows and retires.*]

KING. Well, goodbye, and I hope you find your friend. I'm sorry we couldn't do more for you. . . . By the by, are you sure you didn't see anything in the least bit out of taste in our ceremony? I always think the English have such good taste in matters of ritual. You didn't? That's very encouraging. When you get back to England, remember me to Lord Harborne, if he's still alive. One of the real old English eccentrics. Used to breakfast at midnight on champagne and raw beef. . . . Won't you have a drink before you go?

ALAN. No, thank you, your Majesty. You see, we haven't got much time.

KING. Well, goodbye. Goodbye. [*Aside to the* M.C. *crossly.*] What on earth is the band-master thinking of? Tell him to play something suitable at once, in honour of our guests.

[As ALAN *and the* JOURNALISTS *retire backwards, bowing, the band begins to play "Rule, Britannia".*]

CURTAIN

Chorus

You with shooting-sticks and cases for field-glasses, your limousines parked in a circle; who visit the public games, observing in burberries the feats of the body:
You who stand before the west fronts of cathedrals; appraising the curious carving:
The virgin creeping like a cat to the desert, the trumpetting angels, the usurers boiling:
And you also who look for truth: alone in tower:
Follow our hero and his escort on his latest journey: from the square surrounded by Georgian houses, take the lurching tram eastward
South of the ship-cranes, of the Slythe canal: stopping at Fruby and Drulger Street,
Past boys ball-using: shrill in alleys.
Passing the cinemas blazing with bulbs: bowers of bliss
Where thousands are holding hands: they gape at the tropical vegetation, at the Ionic pillars and the organ solo.
Look left: the moon shows locked sheds, wharves by water,
On your right is the Power House: its chimneys fume gently above us like rifles recently fired.
Look through the grating at the vast machinery: at the dynamos and turbines
Grave, giving no sign of the hurricane of steam within their huge steel bottles,
At the Diesel engines like howdahed elephants: at the dials with their flickering pointers:
Power to the city: whose loyalties are not those of the family.

And now, enter:
O human pity, gripped by the crying of a captured bird: wincing at sight of surgeon's lance,
Shudder indeed: that life on its narrow littoral so lucky
Can match against eternity a time so cruel!
The street we enter with setts is paved: cracked and uneven as an Alpine glacier,
Garbage chucked in the gutters has collected in the hollows in loathsome pools,
Back to back houses on both sides stretch: a dead-straight line of dung-coloured brick
Wretched and dirty as a run for chickens.
Full as a theatre is the foul thoroughfare: some sitting like sacks, some slackly standing,

Their faces grey in the glimmering gaslight: their eyeballs drugged like
    a dead rabbit's,
From a window a child is looking, by want so fretted his face has
    assumed the features of a tortoise:
A human forest: all by one infection cancelled.
Despair so far invading every tissue has destroyed in these the hidden
    seat of the desire and the intelligence.

A little further, and now: enter the street of some of your dreams:
Here come the untidy jokers and the spruce who love military secrets
And those whose houses are dustless and full of Ming vases:
Those rebels who have freed nothing in the whole universe from the
    tyranny of the mothers, except a tiny sensitive area:
Those who are ashamed of their baldness or the size of their members,
Those suffering from self-deceptions necessary to life
And all who have compounded envy and hopelessness into desire
Perform here nightly their magical acts of identification
Among the Chinese lanterns and the champagne served in shoes.
You may kiss what you like; it has often been kissed before.
Use what words you wish; they will often be heard again.

Act I Scene 5

[*Ostnia. A street in the Red Light District. Each café has a small lighted peep-hole, resembling a theatre box-office. Above each of the four peep-holes is a signboard with the name:* TIGER JACK'S. YAMA THE PIT. COSY CORNER. MOTHER HUBBARD'S. *The heads of the four* PROPRIETORS *are visible at the peep-holes.*]

FOUR PROPRIETORS [*singing together*]. To Red Lamp Street you are all
    invited;
  Here Plato's halves are at last united.
  Whatever you dream of alone in bed,
  Come to us and we will make it real instead.

TIGER JACK. Do you feel like a bit of fun?
  At Tiger Jack's you will find it done.
  We've girls of eighty and women of four;
  Let them teach you things you never knew before.

PROPRIETRESS OF YAMA THE PIT. Or does the thought of a thorough
    whipping
  By ladies in boots set your pulse skipping.

> At Yama the Pit you must pay a call
> And soon you won't be able to sit down at all.

BOSS OF COSY CORNER. But perhaps you're a woman-scorner?
> Then step inside at the Cosy Corner.
> We've boys of every shape and size:
> Come and gaze into their great big eyes.

MOTHER HUBBARD. If you've taken a fancy to snow,
> Mother Hubbard's the place to go.
> With Cokey Minnie and Dopey Jim
> You can hold a party till the stars are dim.

ALL TOGETHER. Ladies and gentlemen, bear in mind
> Kisses in the graveyard are hard to find.
> "Tempus fugit", the poet said:
> So come to us at once for you will soon be dead.

> > [*Enter* ALAN, *the* JOURNALISTS *and the* DOG. *They are immediately accosted by two touts. The* 1ST TOUT *is very old and bleary. The* 2ND TOUT *is a boy of eight.*]

1ST T. Buy a post-card, guvnor?
2ND T. Come wiv me. Good Jig-a-Jig.
ALAN [*going up to* TIGER JACK].
> Good evening. Is Sir Francis Crewe,
> English, known perhaps to you?
TIGER JACK. Money, money
> Makes our speech as sweet as honey.

> > > [ALAN *gives money.*]

> Now ask again
> And not in vain.
ALAN. Good evening. Is Sir Francis Crewe,
> English, known perhaps to you?
TIGER JACK. Phyllis, Lou,
> All of you,
> Have you heard of Sir Francis Crewe?
VOICES [*from within*]. A Francis I knew
> (A nice boy, too)
> And I a Crewe.
> But none of us know Sir Francis Crewe.

TIGER JACK. But stay.
　　Here it is gay.
ALAN. No thank you, no.
　　I must go. [*Moves on.*]
1ST TOUT. Buy a post-card, guvnor?
2ND TOUT. Come wiv me. Good Jig-a Jig.
ALAN [*to* PROPRIETRESS OF YAMA THE PIT].
　　Good evening. Is Sir Francis Crewe,
　　English, known perhaps to you?
PROPRIETRESS OF Y.P. Money, money
　　Makes our speech as sweet as honey.

　　　　　　　　　　　　　　　　　[ALAN *gives money.*]

　　At this door
　　You must pay more.

　　　　　　　　　　　　　　　　　[ALAN *gives more.*]

　　Now speak again,
　　Not in vain.
ALAN. Good evening. Is Sir Francis Crewe,
　　English, known perhaps to you?
PROPRIETRESS OF Y.P. Sue, Sue,
　　That will do!
　　He's already black and blue.
　　Have you heard of Sir Francis Crewe?
SUE'S VOICE. I had an Englishman last year
　　Who wore a pendant in each ear,
　　Then there was one with a false nose:
　　It wasn't either of them, I suppose?
PROPRIETRESS OF Y.P. But stay,
　　Here it is gay.
ALAN. No thank you, no.
　　I must go. [*Moves away.*]
1ST T. Buy a post-card, guvnor?

　　　　　　　　　　　　　　　　　[2ND J. *buys one.*]

1ST J. [*looking at it over his shoulder, in disgust*].
　　Horrible hips and too much flesh:
　　Why can't they get hold of someone fresh?
2ND T. Come wiv me. Good Jig-a-Jig.

ALAN [*giving money to the* BOSS OF COSY CORNER].
>   Good evening. Is Sir Francis Crewe,
>   English, known perhaps to you?

BOSS OF C.C. You speak English? But I too!
>   Am I acquaint with Sir Francis Crewe?
>   Every English Lord come here.
>   Is it he in the corner there?
>   Wait a moment while I send
>   For Willy. . . . Willy,
>   How calls himself your English friend?

WILLY'S VOICE. Harold. . . . Have you a cigarette for me?

BOSS OF C.C. Is it he?
>   Well, come inside and wait and see.
>   Many come in after ten.
>   Perhaps he will be one of them.

ALAN. No thank you, no.
>   I must go. [*Moves away.*]

1ST J. Remember the sign.

2ND T. Come wiv me. Good Jig-a-Jig.

>   [1ST J. *chases him away.*]

2ND J. And say the line.

>   [ALAN *knocks three times at the door of* MOTHER
>   HUBBARD'S.]

MOTHER HUBBARD. The cupboard was bare.

ALAN. And yet the poor dog got some. [*Gives money.*]
>   Is the name of Sir Francis Crewe,
>   English, known perhaps to you?

MOTHER HUBBARD. Wait a moment, please. I'll get Dopey Jim.

>   [*She disappears.*]

1ST J. Hurry, hurry, do!
>   Our train leaves for Westland at twenty to.

2ND J. Chuck up hunting for your boy friend.
>   It's clear that he's come to a sticky end.

>   [*The face of a drug addict hopelessly dazed, appears
>   at the peep-hole.*]

ALAN. Good evening. Are you Mr Dopey Jim?

ADDICT. That's what they call me here: up there, in the world, I had

another name. For I could dance lightly and spring high like a rubber ball in the air: being champion at Flash Green of all such sports.
ALAN. You know Flash Green? Why, that's where Sorbo Lamb came from! He went away seven years ago to look for Sir Francis Crewe. Did you ever meet him?
ADDICT. My mother bore no twins.
ALAN. Sorbo!
ADDICT. Alas.
ALAN. Oh, I am so glad! Whatever are you doing here? Have you seen Francis? Come along, we'll look for him together.
ADDICT. I may not leave this place.
ALAN. Do you mean they won't let you out? We'll soon see about that! There's four of us, and my dog can fight like a tiger. Just let them try to stop you!
ADDICT. You do not understand. [*Holds up his hands, which are free.*] Don't you see these chains? My punishment and my reward. The light of your world would dazzle me and its noises offend my ears. Fools! How could you possibly appreciate my exquisite pleasures? Sometimes I lie quite still for days together, comtemplating the flame of a candle or the oscillating shadow of a lamp. What revelations, what bottomless despairs! Please leave me alone.
ALAN. Sorbo. . . . Isn't there anything I can do?
ADDICT. Yes. Tell them at Flash Green that I am dead. More I ask not. Farewell. [*He disappears.*]
ALAN. What shall I do? What shall I do?
I cannot find Sir Francis Crewe!
2ND J. Pull your socks up, kid, and don't make a fuss!
Come along to Westland now with us.
Your friend may be there: you never know:
And we'll show you all there is to show.

[*All three exeunt with* DOG, *singing.*]

>   If yer wants to see me agyne
>   Then come to the styion before the tryne.
>   In the general wytin' 'all
>   We'll see each other fer the very las' time of all!

[*The* FOUR PROPRIETORS *sing, accompanied by* FIRST TOUT *on the concertina and* SECOND TOUT *on the penny whistle.*]

ALL TOGETHER. Let us remember in a little song

Those who were with us but not for long.
Some were beautiful and some were gay
But Death's Black Maria took them all away.

TIGER JACK. Lucky Lil got a rope of pearls,
Olive had autographed letters from earls,
Grace looked lovely when she danced the Fern
But Death took them yachting and they won't return.

YAMA THE PIT. Pixie had a baron as a customer,
He brought a zeppelin, just for her.
You should have seen her with a hunting crop,
But in Death's sound-proof room she's got to stop.

COSY CORNER. Tony the Kid looked a god in shorts,
Phil was asked to Switzerland for winter sports,
Jimmy sent them crazy in his thick white socks,
But Death has shut them all up in a long black box.

MOTHER HUBBARD. Sammy and Di beat the gong around,
Wherever they walked there was snow on the ground.
Jessie and Colin had rings round their eyes
But Death put them where they can't get supplies.

ALL TOGETHER. When we are dead we shan't thank for flowers,
We shan't hear the parson preaching for hours,
We shan't be sorry to be white bare bone
At last we shan't be hungry and can sleep alone.

CURTAIN

Act II

Chorus

A land ruled by fear may be easily recognized by the behaviour of its
  frontier officials.
Those in whom private terrors breed a love of insult and interference
  are always with us. But only such a country offers them a splendid
  career in the public services.
The brutal voices and the fawning, the padlocked pleasure-hating
  mouths, the fussy assertive adam's apples, the popping horrified
  eyes, the furtive rodent noses.
Each one dingily afraid of his immediate superior.

□

Picture them now at the Frontier between Ostnia and Westland, among
 the coloured forms in the stuffy little station. The swallows
 swooping in the dawn over the simmering railway engine, in the
 background the beautiful ignorant mountains.
See them scraping to the richer passenger, but to the poor outrageous.
See them now with Alan and his friends.
Passing the Journalists at once. Foreign opinion must be cajoled.
But suspicious of Alan.
Asking insolent questions.
Sniffing in his trunks, longing to find something juicy.
Not satisfied. Why with a dog. A dog.
Not satisfied. Must be espionage.
Espionage or lunacy. Anyway dangerous.
Better say lunacy. Shut them both up.
Westland has excellent asylums, equipped for such cases.
Alan is taken but the dog slips out of their clutches.
Alan is taken away; in a closed van with two male nurses.
But the dog escapes. You shall see the sequel.

Act II Scene 1

[*Westland. A room in a lunatic asylum. At the back of the stage is a large portrait of a man in uniform: beneath which is written "Our Leader". The man has a loudspeaker instead of a face. The room is full of lunatics, male and female, who sit on their beds absorbed in various occupations or wander up and down the stage. On meeting each other, they exchange the Westland Salute: bringing the palm of the right hand smartly against the nape of the neck. Their manner is furtive and scared.*]

1st MAD LADY [*wanders across the stage, singing*].
        Seen when night was silent,
        The bean-shaped island
        And our ugly comic servant
        Who is observant.
        O the verandah and the fruit
        The tiny steamer in the bay
        Startling summer with its hoot.
        You have gone away.

1st LUNATIC [*whispering with* 2nd LUNATIC *in a corner*]. Heard any rumours?
2nd L. Heaps!

1st L. Oh, do tell me!
2nd L. Ssh! not so loud. I think they may be watching us.
1st L. I tell you what: I've got a plan. We'll say goodbye now and then meet later, as if by accident.
2nd L. All right. But do be careful.

[*They exchange the Westland Salute and separate to their respective beds.*]
[*Enter* Two Medical Officers *with* Alan *in a strait-waistcoat, in a wheeled chair.*]

1st M.O. The Ostnia Frontier wasn't it? They've sent us several beauties.
2nd M.O. Yes.
1st M.O. What do they say?
2nd M.O. Travelling with a dog.
1st M.O. Hm. Canophilia.
2nd M.O. States he is looking for someone he doesn't know.
1st M.O. Phantasy Building. Go on.
2nd M.O. Doesn't know the Westland Song.
1st M.O. Amnesia. Pretty serious. [*To* Alan.] Now you. Have you ever been to the North Pole?
Alan. No.
1st M.O. Can you speak Chinese?
Alan. No!
2nd M.O. Do you dye your hair?
Alan. No!
1st M.O. Was your mother a negress?
Alan. No!!
2nd M.O. Do you drink your bathwater?
Alan. No!!!
1st M.O. Do you like my face?
Alan [*losing his temper and yelling*]. No!!!!
1st M.O. Just as I feared. A typical case of negativism.
Alan. What are you going to do? Let me out of here.
2nd M.O. The gag, I think, don't you?
1st M.O. Yes, I think so.

[*They gag* Alan.]

2nd M.O. Quite classic. He'll be an ornament to our collection.

[*Exeunt* Medical Officers.]

2nd Mad Lady [*promenading with* 3rd M.L.]. The Leader says that next year he's going to put all us women into coops, like hens. And if we don't lay properly we shall be fattened for the Christmas Market.

3RD M.L. Oh, what a lovely idea!

2ND M.L. Yes, isn't it? And so beautiful, too. I mean, it will really make Motherhood sacred. And so away with all this horrible unwomanly nonsense about girls being independent. I'm sure *I* never wanted to be independent!

3RD M.L. I should think not, indeed! [*Shivers.*] Ugh, the idea!

[*Several* LUNATICS *surround a* LUNATIC *who is naked except for a bath-towel round his waist and has covered his body with smears of ink.*]

NAKED LUNATIC. I am the President of the newly-formed League of the Forefathers of Westland, which the Leader himself has officially approved. After careful historical investigations, I have discovered that this is the exact costume worn by the inhabitants of Westland two thousand years ago. All modern dress is effeminate and foreign. The L.F.W. will lead Westland back to the manly customs of our ancestors. Down with Machinery! Down with knives and forks! Down with bathrooms and books! Let us take to the woods and live on roots!

[*The other* LUNATICS, *in great excitement, begin tearing off their clothes and scratching on the floor, as if to dig up plants from the ground. Meanwhile, the* 1ST *and* 2ND LUNATICS *leave their beds and greet each other with much ceremony.*]

1ST L. Ah, good morning, my dear Baron!

2ND L. Your Worship, this is indeed a pleasure!

1ST L. Remarkably mild weather, is it not?

2ND L. [*in the same tone of voice, nodding his head slightly in the direction of one of the other* LUNATICS]. I hear the Admiral is going to be denounced.

1ST L. [*obviously delighted*]. Oh, I'm so sorry! Poor fellow! What for?

2ND L. The usual. Byzantinism, of course: and Disaffection and Hoarding.

1ST L. Tut, tut! I should never have believed it of him!

2ND L. Oh, he's got a bad record. They say there's more than two thousand anonymous letters been written complaining about him to the Secret Police. *And all in invisible ink!*

1ST L. Whew, that's nasty! [*Gleefully.*] What do you think they'll do with him?

2ND L. Send him to the Lead Mines, I expect.

1ST L. [*rubbing his hands together*]. Poor fellow!

[LUNATIC, *who has just fastened a flag to the end of his bed, shouts across to the* LUNATIC *sitting on the bed opposite.*]

FLAG-LUNATIC. Hi, you! Why haven't you got your flag out? Don't you know what today is?

LUNATIC WITHOUT FLAG. Of course I do! It's the Day of National Rejoicing.

FLAG-L. Then why don't you hang out your flag? If your flag isn't out, you can't be rejoicing.

L. WITHOUT F. Of course, I'm rejoicing. I was just sitting rejoicing quietly by myself when you disturbed me.

FLAG-L. I don't believe you're rejoicing a bit! You don't look as if you were rejoicing.

L. WITHOUT F. Well, neither do you, for that matter.

FLAG-L. It doesn't matter how I look. I've got my flag out. Everyone knows *I'm* rejoicing.

L. WITHOUT F. What are you rejoicing about?

FLAG-L. I shan't tell you. What are you?

L WITHOUT F. I shan't tell you either.

FLAG-L. Oh yes you will!

L WITHOUT F. No I won't!

FLAG-L. Will!

L WITHOUT F. Won't!

[*The two* LUNATICS *adopt threatening attitudes and make horrible faces at each other.*]

[*A trumpet.*]

1ST LUNATIC. Silence everybody! The Leader is going to speak to us!

[*All the* LUNATICS *stand up and give the Westland Salute.*]

THE VOICE OF THE LEADER [*through the loud-speaker in the picture*]. A short time ago, I was spending a week-end at a little village in the mountains. I sat on the verandah of the simple old Westland inn, looking out across the street to the meadows and the mountains beyond, those snow-capped peaks already flushed with the sunset glow. Westland swallows swooped in and out of the eaves overhead. In a doorway opposite, a young mother looked down at her suckling babe with ineffable Westland tenderness. In another, a Westland granny gazed out into the dusk with perfect serenity on her beautiful old face. Sturdy rosy-cheeked Westland youngsters romped in the new-mown hay a little further off. And presently down the street came the returning cattle, all their bells a-chiming in a sweet symphony, followed by the peasants, so honest, so thrifty, so frugal, wedded to the dear Westland earth in an eternal, holy marriage.

> [*The* LUNATICS *have been much affected by this part of the speech. They sigh, shed tears and embrace each other with loud smacking kisses. One of the male lunatics takes flowers from a vase and distributes them among the ladies, who put the flowers in their hair.*]

VOICE OF THE LEADER [*continuing*]. My eyes filled with tears. I could not speak just then. Perish the man, I thought, who can imagine this people capable of any base or unworthy deed! Westland! *Our* Westland! *My* Westland! All, all mine!

BUT:

A chill struck my heart. There *was* a shadow!

Not two hundred miles from where I stand, there is a Nation: trained to arms from infancy, schooled in military obedience and precision, saluting even in the cradle, splendidly equipped with every invention of modern science, able, resolute, taught to regard the individual as nothing and the State as all, scorning treaties as mere scraps of paper to be rent asunder when the interests of the State demand. My mind's eye saw the long silent grey ranks. I heard the shouting of the captains, the brazen call of the trumpet and the pawing of the chargers. And a voice said: Woe, woe to the unprepared: For their inheritance shall be taken away and their home be left desolate!

> [*The* LUNATICS *are now violently agitated. Some of them moan and shiver with fear, lie flat on the floor or crawl under the beds. Others blow trumpets, wave toy swords and strike down imaginary enemies.*]

From how slight a cause may proceed terrifying results! A piece of paper left by a picnic party which has inadvertently strayed over the frontier, a rash word in a letter about the superiority of Westland beer or a humorous sketch in a revue misunderstood: and in a moment it is too late. Destruction might come upon us like a thief in the night: while you are innocently dozing in your chair, or making an omelette or washing dishes at the kitchen sink. A secret cabinet meeting, a word whispered into the telephone and within half an hour, within twenty minutes, the black hordes of death are darkening the Westland air with their horrible shadows.

Picture the scene, Oh mothers! Your baby's face, pinched and puckered: Not by hunger, no. Sated with poison from the air it breathes, its tender little mouth agape, choking up froth and green bile.

Sons, see your aged father who has taught you to reverence truth and purity: see him caught as the house collapses, his skull smashed like an egg before your eyes by a falling beam!

Think, teachers, of the bombs falling suddenly in the playing-field! There goes that splendid young forward ... ah! he's down: collapsing even as he reaches the goal-post, his beautiful hinged limbs contracted in agony!

> [*Most of the* LUNATICS *are now staring up at the ceiling in fascinated horror, as though awaiting the aeroplanes' arrival.*]

VOICE OF THE LEADER [*continuing*]. Nor is this all. The flame once lit would spread into a universal conflagration. England, Iceland, Ecuador and Siam would flare and within a week our civilisation, all that our statesmen and thinkers, our poets and musicians, have travailed for down the ages of history, would lie a smoking ruin!

No, this must not be! Westland is the guardian of Europe. We love peace (I say it in absolute confidence) more than any other country. Let us be ready and able to enforce it. We must build an air force of such a magnitude that any enemy, however ferocious, will think twice before daring to strike. Within three weeks we must have a million planes, not one less! We must make a stupendous effort. No sacrifice is too great. I expect every man, woman and child in Westland to help. Give up that cigar after lunch, do without an extra lipstick, abstain from your favourite sweets. Is that too much to ask when the safety of the Homeland is at stake? Our responsibilities are vast: Let us be worthy of them. And God help us all.

> [*Tremendous enthusiasm. The* LUNATICS *jump up and down in their delight, cheer, embrace, pillow-fight, and box each other's ears.*]

THE LUNATIC WITH THE FLAG. Let's build a great big plane for our Leader!

LUNATICS. Oh, yes! Let's!!

> [*The* LUNATICS *begin dragging beds together and piling furniture upon them. The din is tremendous. Suddenly, at the window, appear the heads of the*

> Two Journalists *and the* Dog. *They peer cautiously into the room, looking for* Alan. *After a moment, they hastily withdraw.*]

1st Lunatic [*who evidently considers himself the most important of them all and is rather piqued that the plane-building should have been suggested by someone else, stands on a chair and begins clapping his hands to command attention; after some time, he succeeds in getting the* Lunatics *to stop working and listen to him*]. Madmen of Westland!

In this hour of supreme crisis, I feel called upon to say a few words. This is my message to you all. Let us never forget that we are Westlanders first and madmen second. As Westlanders, we have a great tradition to uphold. Westland has always produced ten percent more lunatics than any other country in Europe. And are we going to show ourselves inferior to our forefathers? Never!

> [*The* Journalists *reappear at the window, try the strength of the bars and shake their heads. The* Dog *is seen arguing with them in dumb show and indicating that they come with him. They all disappear.*]

1st Lunatic [*continuing*]. Of recent years, there have appeared in our midst, masquerading as men of science, certain Jews, obscurantists and Marxist traitors. These men have published enormous books, attempting to provide new classifications and forms of lunacy. But we are not deceived. No foreign brand of madness, however spectacular, however noisy or pleasant, will ever seduce us from the grand old Westland Mania. What was good enough for our forefathers, we declare, is good enough for us! We shall continue to go mad in the time-honoured Westland way.

A Lunatic. Three cheers for the Westland Loonies!

All. Hurrah! Hurrah! Hurrah!

Another Lunatic [*suddenly seeing* Alan]. Hullo, you! Why don't you cheer?

> [*All the* Lunatics *stop shouting and look at* Alan. *At this moment, unseen by any of them, the* Two Journalists *enter the room by a door on the right of the stage.*]

Another Lunatic. His mouth's tied up! He's got the toothache! [*Begins to giggle.*]

Another Lunatic. He's been sent here to spy on us!

Another. He's been hoarding butter!

ANOTHER. He's insulted the Leader!
ANOTHER. Rumour-monger!
ANOTHER. Non-Aryan!
ANOTHER. Separatist!
ANOTHER. Grumbler!

> [*All this time, they draw closer to him, rushing forward in turns to tug at his hair, tweak his nose or pull his ears.*]

A LUNATIC. Squirt water at him!
ANOTHER. Put a rat in his bed!
ANOTHER. Tickle his toes!
ANOTHER. Shave off his eyebrows!
ANOTHER. I say, chaps! Let's do something really exciting! Let's put lavatory paper under his chair and burn it!

> [*They seem about to make a final rush at* ALAN, *when the* 1ST JOURNALIST *speaks, in a very loud and impressive voice, like a conjurer.*]

1ST J. Ladies and Gentlemen! [*All the* LUNATICS *turn round to stare at him.*] I am about to show you a simple but extremely interesting scientific experiment. [*Holds up his hand.*] Now, watch the duck's head and please keep absolutely still while I count a hundred. One. Two. Three. . . .

> [*While the* 1ST JOURNALIST *is counting, the* 2ND JOURNALIST, *on all fours, worms his way through the crowd to* ALAN's *side and begins hastily undoing the ropes and straps.*]

2ND J. [*in a low voice, to* ALAN]. Gosh, that was a close shave!
ALAN. How on earth did you find me?
2ND J. Your Dog guided us here. That animal is better than the whole of Scotland Yard put together. He's outside now, keeping guard over the warders until we get you loose. . . . Curse these knots!

> [*Meanwhile, the* 1ST J. *continues to count. But the* LUNATICS *are becoming less attentive. Those who are standing close to* ALAN *begin to take an interest in the* 2ND J.'s *activities.*]

LUNATIC. What are you doing that for?
2ND J. Can't you see? I'm tying him up tighter. The ropes had got loose. See this one? [*He holds it up.*] It had slipped right off. [*He throws it*

away.] No good at all. [*He continues to unfasten the other ropes and straps.*]
LUNATIC. I'll help you. [*Begins to refasten the straps.*]
2ND J. Don't bother, old boy. I can manage by myself. [*Unfastens them again.*]
LUNATIC. It's no bother. I like helping people. I'm a Boy Scout.
2ND J. Well, do your day's good deed by leaving me alone, see?
LUNATIC. I don't think that would be a good deed, would it?
2ND J. You bet it would!
LUNATIC. Perhaps you're right. But I'd better just ask the others what they think. [*In a very loud voice.*] I say! [*All the* LUNATICS *turn round to look at him.*]
2ND J. Holy Moses, that's torn it!
1ST LUNATIC. What are you doing with our prisoner?
2ND L. Where's your warrant?
3RD L. Habeas Corpus!
4TH L. It's a rescue!
5TH L. Stand by the doors!
OTHERS. Fire! Murder! Treason!

> [*The* 1ST J., *now disregarded, rushes to the Leader's picture and gets behind it.*]

1ST J. [*through the loud-speaker*]. Company! Fall in!

> [*The* LUNATICS *immediately form a double rank, facing the Leader's picture.* 2ND J. *continues feverishly with the work of untying* ALAN.]

1ST J. Slooope Hyppp!

> [*The* LUNATICS *go through the motion of sloping arms.*]

1ST J. Oddah Hyppp!

> [LUNATICS *order arms.*]

1ST J. Slooope Hyppp! [*They do so.*]
  Oddah Hyppp! [*They do so.*]
2ND J. [*to* ALAN]. That's all the drill he knows! [*Undoing the last strap.*] There! Come on, this is where we scoot! [*They rush out.*]
1ST J. Company! Man the aeroplane! Fall out!

> [*The* LUNATICS *rush to the structure of beds and scramble upon it. The* 1ST J. *slips from behind the picture and runs out after the others.*]

1st Lunatic. Start her up!

> [*The* Lunatics *imitate the roaring of the engines.*]

1st L. Off we go! Faster! Faster! She's left the ground! We're rising! Higher! Higher!

> [*The* Lunatics *wave their handkerchiefs and grimace at the audience.*]

A Mad Lady. Isn't the view gorgeous!
2nd Mad Lady. Look, there's the asylum. Just a tiny little speck!
A Mad Lady. I'll spit down the chimney! [*Spits.*]
The Pilot. Hold on tight! I'm going to loop the loop!

> [*Shrieks of dismay. The* Lunatics *heave the beds up on end until the whole structure collapses. General confusion.* Alan, *the* Journalists *and the* Dog *peep in for a moment at the window and disappear laughing.*]

CURTAIN

Chorus

Paddington. King's Cross. Euston. Liverpool Street:
Each hiding behind a gothic hotel its gigantic greenhouse
And the long trains groomed before dawn departing at ten,
Picking their way through slums between the washing and the privies
To a clear run through open country,
Ignoring alike the cathedral towns in their wide feminine valleys, and the lonely junctions.
In such a train sit Norman and his dog
Moving backwards through Westland at a mile a minute
And playing hearts with their two friends on an open mackintosh:
Picture the Pullman car with its deft attendants
And the usual passengers: the spoilt child, the corridor addict,
The lady who expects you to admire her ankles: the ostentatious peruser of important papers, etc. etc.

They have been travelling all day, it is late afternoon.
Outside the windows of the warm sealed tube, as a background to their conversation,

Imagine a hedgeless country, the source of streams;
Such as the driver, changing up at last, sees stretching from Hartside
 east and south,
Deadstones above Redan, Thackmoss, Halfpenny Scar,
Two Top and Muska, Pity Mea, Bullpot Brow:
Land of the ring ousel: a bird stone-haunting, an unquiet bird.

Act II Scene 2

[*In a railway-train.* ALAN, *the* TWO JOURNALISTS *and the* DOG *are playing cards. A little distance off sits the* FINANCIER, *at present half hidden by his newspaper.*]

1ST J. Your lead, Alan.

[ALAN *plays.*]
[1ST J. *plays a card.*]

ALAN [*to* 2ND J.]. Eight to beat.
2ND J. [*looking at* DOG]. Hm . . . shall I risk it? No, I don't think so.

[*He plays a card. The* DOG *also plays a card.*]

1ST J. [*suspiciously*]. Hullo, you short-suited? Here, let's see your hand.

[*He reaches out to take the* DOG's *cards. The* DOG *growls and refuses to show them.*]

ALAN. Show them to me, Francis. Good Dog! [DOG *reluctantly hands over the cards.*] But you've got Slippery Anne here, look!
2ND J. Darned if he hasn't been cheating again.
ALAN [*indignantly*]. He wasn't cheating! He just doesn't understand the rules, do you Doggy?
1ST J. If you ask me, that Dog of yours understands a damn sight too much. He's too smart by half. [*Yawns.*] Well, gentlemen, you've cleaned me out. I'll go and stretch myself a bit. [*Standing up, he catches sight of the* FINANCIER: *sits down abruptly: to* 2ND J., *in a whisper.*] Great God, man, look!
2ND J. Where?
1ST J. There!
2ND J. Snakes! It isn't . . . ?
1ST J. Bet you a fiver it is!
2ND J. The papers say he's in Manchukuo.
1ST J. Just eyewash!

2ND J. Boy! I believe you're right!
ALAN [*loudly*]. What's all the fuss about?
1ST J. Ssh!
2ND J. Sssh!!
ALAN. You might tell a fellow!
1ST J. [*stage whisper*]. Grabstein! Sitting just behind you!
ALAN. Grabstein?
2ND J. Ssh!
ALAN. Who's he when he's at home?
1ST J. Oh boy, where were you educated? [*Wearily, to* 2ND J.] Go on, you tell him.
2ND J. President of the X.Y.Z.
1ST J. Chairman of the Pan-Asiatic.
2ND J. Practically owns South America.
1ST J. The biggest crook in Europe. Got his finger in everything. Whatever happens, he's in on the ground floor. Why, he even gets to hear of things before *we* do, sometimes!
ALAN. I say! Not really! I wonder if he knows where Francis is?
2ND J. Most likely he does. The question is: would he tell you?
1ST J. [*winking at* 2ND J.]. Go and ask him.
ALAN. Shall I really?
2ND J. [*winking at* 1ST J.]. Atta boy!
ALAN [*doubtfully*]. All right.... If you don't think he'd mind?
1ST J. Hell! Why should he?
2ND J. He'll welcome you with open arms.
1ST J. [*artfully*]. By the way, you might ask him a few other questions while you're about it. Find out what holdings he has in Sahara Electrics.
2ND J. And how much it cost him to start the war in Spitsbergen?
1ST J. And what became of the Cloaguan Prime Minister after the Platinum Scandals?
ALAN. I say, hold on a minute: I shall never remember all that! Just give me time to write it down.

> [*He takes a piece of paper from his pocket and makes notes. The* JOURNALISTS *whisper instructions into his ear.*]

ALAN. But won't he think me awfully inquisitive?
2ND J. Oh, he loves being asked questions.... Just go up to him and say: "Potts". That's the name of a very dear friend of his. It'll put him in a good temper at once.
ALAN [*doubtfully*]. Righto.

[*He approaches the* FINANCIER. *The* JOURNALISTS *shake hands with each other in ecstasies of delight.*]

1ST J. Oh boy, I wouldn't have missed this for a thousand pounds!

[*During the following scene, the* JOURNALISTS *take photographs and make notes.*]

ALAN [*rather nervously*]. Potts.

[*The* FINANCIER *looks up from his newspaper, stares at him for a moment, turns deadly pale. Then, with a shrug of his shoulders, he takes a cheque-book from his pocket and unscrews the cap of his fountain-pen.*]

FINANCIER [*with a deep sigh*]. How much do you want?

ALAN. I beg your pardon, sir. I don't quite understand.

FINANCIER [*more firmly*]. I'll give you a thousand: Not one penny more. And you understand that I'm doing it because I don't choose to be annoyed at this particular moment. I have reason for remaining incognito. I suppose you counted on that? Very well. . . . But let me warn you, if you're fool enough to imagine that you can play this game twice, you were never more mistaken. I have ways of dealing with gentry of your sort. Understand?

ALAN. I'm awfully sorry, sir. But I think you must be making some mistake. . . . I only wanted to ask you a few questions. . . . It's frightful cheek of me, I know. . . .

FINANCIER. Oh, a journalist, eh? That's bad enough. Still, as you're here, I suppose I can let you have five minutes. Ask away. . . .

ALAN [*consulting his notes*]. First of all, did you forge the report on the diamond mines on Tuesday Island?

[*The* FINANCIER *gasps.*]

ALAN [*continuing hurriedly*]. Secondly, is it true that you staged the fake attempt on the Prince of the Hellespont in order to corner the rubber market?

FINANCIER. Do you seriously expect me to answer that?

ALAN. Well, no sir. To be quite candid, I don't. Please don't be angry. . . . Thirdly, did you have the men murdered who were going to show up the Bishop of Pluvium?

FINANCIER [*laughs*]. Young man, you amuse me. Very well, since you're the first newspaper man who's ever dared to talk to me like this, I'll tell you the truth. The answer to all your three questions is: "Yes. I did." There! Now you've got a grand story, haven't you? Go and ask your editor to print it and he'll kick you out into the street. What's your paper, by the way? Ten to one, I own it.

ALAN. The Pressan Ambo Parish Magazine.

FINANCIER. Never heard of it. But I'll buy it to-morrow, lock stock and barrel. How much would your boss take, do you suppose?

ALAN. I'm afraid I couldn't tell you that, sir. You see, I only write for it occasionally. A bit of poetry now and then. Awful rot, I expect you'd think it.

FINANCIER [*groans*]. Good God! Don't say you're a poet too!

ALAN. Oh rather not, sir!

FINANCIER. Glad to hear it. Of course, mind you, I've nothing against poets, provided they make good. They say that one or two fellows at the top of the tree are earning as much as four thousand a year. I doubt it myself. . . . But the fact remains that most of them are moral degenerates or Bolsheviks, or both. The scum of the earth. My son's a poet.

ALAN. I'm sorry, sir.

FINANCIER [*sentimentally*]. It's been the greatest disappointment of my whole life. Who have I got to work for, to be proud of? Nobody. And my wife encourages him; the bitch. As long as she's got her cocaine and her gigolos, we can all go to hell as far as she's concerned. . . . I don't know why I'm telling you all this.

ALAN [*politely*]. It's rotten luck for you, sir.

FINANCIER. Look here. I've taken a fancy to you. Will you be my secretary? Starting at five thousand a year, with all extras. Yes or no?

ALAN. It's most awfully kind of you, sir: but I'm afraid I can't. . . .

FINANCIER [*emotionally*]. There, you see! I knew it! You don't like me. None of them like me. Wherever I go I see it. I can't so much as get a really friendly smile out of a railway-porter, though Heaven knows I tip them enough. . . .

[*Sings. Accompaniment by dining-car attendant with gong.*]

When I was young I showed such application,
  I worked the whole day long;
I hoped to rise above my station,
  To rise just like a song:
I did so want to be a hero
  In just a rich man's way
But I might just as well be Nero,
  And this is all I have to say:

CHORUS [*with* ATTENDANT *and* JOURNALISTS].
    Why are they so rude to { him? / me? }

    It seems so crude to { him, / me, }

    { He wants / I want } to be friendly

    But it's no good, for

    No one has love for { him, / me, }

    Only a shove for { him, / me, }

    They bait { him / me } and hate { him, he's / me, I'm }

    Misunderstood.

FINANCIER. I've founded hospitals and rest-homes,
    Subscribed to public funds,
Promoted schemes for planning Best Homes
    And built a school for nuns.
I've studied all the Italian Masters,
    I've tried to read French books,
But all my efforts seem disasters:
    I only get such nasty looks.

CHORUS.   Why are they so rude to me. . . . *etc.*

FINANCIER. Now what is it? Tell me straight out; don't be afraid. Is it my face? Is it my voice? Is it my manner? Or are you all just jealous of my damned money?

ALAN. It isn't that, sir. Really it isn't. But you see . . . I'm not free. I've got a kind of job . . . if you can call it a job. . . .

FINANCIER. Chuck it. I'll give you six thousand.

ALAN. You see, sir, it's not that kind of job: that you can chuck up, I mean. . . . I've got to look for someone. He's Sir Francis Crewe, Bart. At least, he's Bart if he's alive. . . . That's what I really came to ask you about. . . . He ran away from home ten years ago. I thought you might happen to know where he is.

FINANCIER. What do you take me for? A nursemaid?

    [*The train stops. A* PORTER *looks in at the window.*]

PORTER. All change for Malaga, Reykjavik and Omsk!

FINANCIER. I must get out here. Will you take ten thousand? Yes or no? It's my last word.

ALAN. I'm truly most terribly sorry, but. . . .
FINANCIER. You're more of a fool than I took you for. [*Sentimentally.*] Write to me sometimes and tell me how you're getting on. It would be so lovely to get a letter which had nothing to do with business!
ALAN. Rather, sir!
FINANCIER. Oh, by the way, a good place to look for that Baronet of yours would be Paradise Park. This train'll take you there. It's where most wasters and cranks land up sooner or later, if they've still got some cash to be swindled out of. You'll meet my dear Son, among others. Perhaps you'll be able to knock some sense into him. Tell him I offer him a hundred thousand if he'll stop writing his drivel and clean a sewer. Goodbye.
ALAN. Goodbye, sir. Thanks awfully.

[*The* FINANCIER, *with the help of* ALAN *and the* PORTER, *descends from the train.*]

1ST J. [*to* 2ND J.]. Quick, we mustn't lose sight of him! If we follow him now, maybe we'll get the dope on that Dripping Merger, after all!

[*They leave the train.*]

2ND J. [*to* ALAN]. You coming, Kid?
ALAN. I can't, I'm afraid. I've just got a new clue.
1ST J. Well, good luck.
2ND J. Ta ta.
ALAN. Goodbye, and thanks most awfully for all you've done.

[*The train moves on.* ALAN *waves from the window. Then he turns to the* DOG.]

ALAN. Well, Doggy. We're all alone, now. Just you and me. [*He puts his arm round the* DOG's *neck.*] I wonder what Iris is doing? Oh dear, I wish we weren't such a long way from home. . . .

[*He gazes sadly out of the window.*]

CURTAIN

Chorus

Happy the hare at morning, for she cannot read
The Hunter's waking thoughts. Lucky the leaf
Unable to predict the fall. Lucky indeed

The rampant suffering suffocating jelly
Burgeoning in pools, lapping the grits of the desert,
The elementary sensual cures,
The hibernations and the growth of hair assuage:
Or best of all the mineral stars disintegrating quietly into light.
But what shall man do, who can whistle tunes by heart,
Knows to the bar when death shall cut him short, like the cry of the shearwater?
We will show you what he has done.

How comely are his places of refuge and the tabernacles of his peace,
The new books upon the morning table, the lawns and the afternoon terraces!
Here are the playing-fields where he may forget his ignorance
To operate within a gentleman's agreement: twenty-two sins have here a certain licence.
Here are the thickets where accosted lovers combattant
May warm each other with their wicked hands,
Here are the avenues for incantation and workshops for the cunning engravers.
The galleries are full of music, the pianist is storming the keys, the great cellist is crucified over his instrument,
That none may hear the ejaculations of the sentinels
Nor the sigh of the most numerous and the most poor; the thud of their falling bodies
Who with their lives have banished hence the serpent and the faceless insect.

Act II Scene 3

[The gardens of Paradise Park. A beautifully-kept lawn. Numbers of people are walking about the stage in sports clothes of various kinds or propelling themselves hither and thither in invalid chairs. Some lie on the grass absorbed in books. In the background are two large trees. In one of the trees sits the POET, *smoking cigarettes: In the other are two* LOVERS *dressed in nursery-teapot-Dutch costumes. In the distance, the band plays a waltz.]*

CHORUS.   When you're in trouble,
               When you get the air,
           When everything returns your ring
               Do not despair, because although

Friends may forsake you
   And all skies are dark
You can be gay if you just step this way
   Into Paradise Park.

Was it a tiring day
   On your office stool?
Has your wife all your life
   Made you feel a fool? Don't cry, for though
Landlords perplex you
   And all bosses frown,
In Paradise Park you can feel a young spark
   And do them down!

        [*Enter* ALAN *and the* DOG. *They approach the* POET's *tree.*]

ALAN [*to* POET]. Excuse me, sir. Is this Paradise Park?
POET. ἔστιν θάλασσα, τίς δέ νιν κατασβέσει.
ALAN. I beg your pardon?
POET. Nil nimium studeo, Caesar, tibi velle placere nec scire utrum sis albus an ater homo.
ALAN. I'm awfully sorry, but I don't understand. Do you speak English?
POET. Nessun maggior dolore che ricordarsi del tempo felice.
ALAN. I know a little German, if that will do. . . . Entschuldigen Sie, bitte. Koennen Sie mir sagen, ob dies ist der Garten von Paradies?
POET. Dans l'an trentième de mon age . . . [ALAN *begins to move off.*] Oh well, if you insist on talking our filthy native language, I suppose I must. . . . Give me a cigarette. I've finished mine.
ALAN. I'm so sorry. . . . Of course. . . .
   Is the name Sir Francis Crewe
   Known by any chance to you?
POET. Did you like it?
ALAN. Er . . . ?
POET. I'm so glad you did! I wrote it!
ALAN. Wrote what?
POET. "Advances New", of course. Now tell me, which section did you like the best? *Mandrake* is the best technically, of course. But *Cinders* is more the real me, I think.
ALAN. I'm afraid you misunderstood me. I said Sir Francis Crewe. I've been looking for him.
POET. "Your chase had a beast in view."
ALAN. You know where he is?

POET. Well of course.

ALAN. Where?

POET [*tapping his forehead*]. Here. Everything's here. You're here. He's here. This park's here. This tree's here. If I shut my eyes they all disappear.

ALAN. And what happens if I shut *my* eyes? Do you disappear, too?

POET [*crossly*]. No, of course not! I'm the only real person in the whole world.

ALAN. Well, suppose your tree was cut down? It wouldn't be there when you looked for it.

POET. Nonsense! The axe wouldn't exist unless I thought of it. The woodcutter wouldn't exist either.

ALAN. Isn't your Father the famous financier?

POET. I used to think so. But I got tired of that and forgot him. Give me another cigarette.

> [*As he leans down, the* DOG *jumps up and bites his hand.*]

POET [*nursing his hand*]. Why can't you keep your blasted dog in order? Oh, my poor hand!

ALAN. I'm most dreadfully sorry. But you see, he's never seen a real person before. When you're only an imaginary dog and have been eating imaginary biscuits all your life, a real hand must taste simply delicious. You couldn't resist it, could you, Francis old boy? [*To* POET.] Never mind. Just shut your eyes and you'll forget all about us.

POET [*with his eyes shut*]. Oh, I've forgotten *you* long ago! It's my hand I keep remembering!

> [ALAN *and* DOG *move to the* LOVERS' *tree.*]

1ST LOVER. Little white dove, it's you that I love,
Fairer than hollyhocks far!
How nice and how neat
Are your dear little feet!
You make my heart beat!
How terribly sweet, how terribly sweet,
How terribly sweet you are!

> [*They hug each other, taking no notice of* ALAN.]

ALAN. Excuse me, please, disturbing you:
But have you heard of Sir Francis Crewe?

2ND L. Have you, darling?

1ST L. Oh, pretty starling!

>   Say that again
>   And again and again!
>   I love to watch your cheek
>   Move when you speak!

2ND L. Oh dearest, you mustn't go on so!
>   There's a nice man down below
>   And there is something he wants to know.

1ST L. Good morning. Let me introduce my wife.
>   We're going to be lovers all our life:
>   Two as one and one as two.
>   Is there anything we can do?

ALAN. Have you heard of Sir Francis Crewe?

1ST L. Sir Francis Crewe? Do *you* know, sweet?
>   Was that the funny old man on the seat
>   Who looked so cross when I gave you a kiss?

2ND L. You were so naughty! Oh!

1ST L. [*embracing her*].   Just like this!

ALAN. No, he's not very old.

1ST L. Darling, you're cold.
>   Put my coat on. What dear little shoulders!

[ALAN *begins to move off.*]

>   Don't go, old man. You mustn't scold us.
>   We'd ask you up, but there isn't room.
>   But when we've a large tree you must come.

[ALAN *moves off.*]

2ND L. Wonderful boy, you're all my joy!
1ST L. I'd like to eat you for tea!
2ND L. You're so tender and strong!
1ST L. You're just like a song!
2ND L. To you I belong!
BOTH. You cannot do wrong, you cannot do wrong,
>   You cannot do wrong with me!

[*Two* FEMALE INVALIDS *in bath-chairs move to the front of the stage.*]

1ST INVALID. How many stitches have you got?
2ND I. [*proudly*]. Four.
1ST I. Oh do let me see!
2ND I. Not now, wait till the dressing.
1ST I. Oh please! Just one peep!

2ND I. Very well. [*Shows wound.*]
1ST I. Oh, what a beauty!
2ND I. Don't tell Alice. Promise! She's terribly jealous. They only put two in her. When they told her after she'd come round, she cried.
1ST I. Betty's a lucky girl. She's got tubes.
2ND I. She hasn't!
1ST I. Yes! Only it's a secret. She told me all about it at breakfast. My dear, they took out *everything*! She even thinks they may give her a real silver set!
2ND I. How too marvellous! Won't her Ted be proud?
ALAN [*approaching them*]. Excuse me.
   Is the name Sir Francis Crewe
   Known perhaps to either of you?
1ST I. What's he got?
ALAN. Got?
1ST I. What illness has he got?
ALAN. What? Is he ill?
1ST I. Of course he is, silly: if he's here. Aren't you?
ALAN. No. I don't think so.
BOTH INVALIDS [*turning their chairs away*]. How *disgusting*!

> [*Enter a* COLONEL *in a bath-chair, with an ear-trumpet.*]

ALAN. Excuse me, sir, but is Sir Francis Crewe
   Known by any chance to you?
COLONEL. Can't hear a word, sir. Stone deaf, thank God!

> [ALAN *wanders off asking various other people. The two* INVALIDS *return.*]

1ST I. Have you ever noticed his hands? Just like a violinist's.
2ND I. I wonder who he'll choose for the operation today?
1ST I. [*blushing*]. Well, I don't like to be presumptuous, but I think . . .
2ND I. No? Not really!
1ST I. [*complacent*]. Hm, hm. . . .
2ND I. My dear, I *do* congratulate you!
1ST I. It was only a look, mind you: but you can't mistake him when he looks at you like that. Made me feel quite goosey! Oh look, there he is coming out of the ward! Quickly, dear, lend me your powder-puff. I must look my best when I go under. . . . Ooh, the brute! He's chosen that new case! It isn't fair! [*Bursts into tears.*]
2ND I. There, there, darling! Don't take on so! It's sure to be you next time.

1st I. [*blubbering*]. I don't care! I was counting on it to-day. It's too bad! He only came in this morning.

[*The* Invalids *move away as the* Surgeon *and* Anaesthetist *enter, followed by a* Nurse *pushing* Chimp Eagle, *the patient, on a wheeled stretcher.*]

Sur. What do you think, Doctor? Intraspinal or general?
An. Oh, general in this case.
Sur. You're playing on Saturday, aren't you?
An. Yes, I hope so.
Sur. Good man! We can't do without you in the deep. Young Waters is playing too. He's no snyde at the game.

[*Exeunt* Surgeon *and* Anaesthetist.]

Chimp Eagle [*recognizing* Alan]. Hullo, Alan!
Alan. Why, it's Chimp Eagle! What's the matter with you, old man?
Chimp. A strike down at the Docks. The Police had a machine-gun. Got me in the guts. . . . I say, you aren't in with our lot too, are you?
Alan. No, I'm looking for Francis.
Chimp. Francis: The missing heir! [*Smiles.*] How long ago that seems. I'd forgotten all about him.
Alan. Chimp . . . did you ever find out anything?
Chimp. I can't remember. . . . No. . . . That is, yes. . . . I. . . . [*He is too exhausted to say more.*]
Nurse [*coming forward*]. Now then, sir: That's enough. You're tiring the patient.
Alan [*withdrawing to the other side of stage, to* Dog]. Oh Doggy, what shall I do? They're coming to take him away. And I *must* speak to him again somehow. . . . Oh dear . . . !

[*The* Dog *gives* Alan *a glance, as much as to say: Watch me! Then it runs across the stage and begins fawning on the* Nurse.]

Nurse. What a lovely doggie! May I pat him? [*The* Dog *jumps at her and begins tearing off her uniform.*] Oh! Oh! Help!
Alan. What on earth are you doing! Naughty dog! Stop it this minute! [*Suddenly understanding.*] No, don't stop! Splendid! Good dog! I'll help.

[*They strip the* Nurse *of her uniform and tie her up. The* Dog *is dressed by* Alan *in the* Nurse's *uni-*

form. They dump the NURSE *in a disused bath-chair and cover her with a rug. Scarcely are they ready when the* SURGEON *returns.*]

SUR. Nurse, what the Dickens are you waiting for? Bring the patient at once, please.

[*The* DOG *wheels* CHIMP EAGLE *out.* ALAN *follows at a discreet distance.*]

CHORUS.   There's consolations here to suit
    Every mood and means:
Skating-rinks, booths for drinks,
    Gambling-machines and switchbacks and
Art for the Highbrow
    And Sport for the Low-:
Life is a lark at Paradise Park;
    For the fast and the slow.

CURTAIN

Chorus

Seeding and harvest, the mating of lions, the divergent migrations
Are themes for another occasion than this:
In this white world of order and professional attentions
Of airy wards, the smell of iodoform,
The squeak of rubber-tyred stretchers: solar time is unreal.
Against these walls the waves of action and charity must wash in vain.

1600 beds
10 theatres magnificently equipped
A special wing for infectious cases
A chapel, a mortuary, labs for research, and really adequate nursing accommodation
And, opened last year, a solarium for the convalescent.

1600 beds: in each one patient, apparently alone;
One who has forsaken family and friends; to set up house here with his hostile shadow.
You who are amorous and active, pause here an instant.
See passion transformed into rheumatism; rebellion into paralysis; power into a tumour.

That which was hated, become hateful; that which was creative, a
   stalking destruction; that which was loving, a tormenting flame
For those who reject their gifts: choose here their punishment.

Act II Scene 4

[*Paradise Park. The operating theatre. Railed off, at the side of the stage, are benches for students. Two* STUDENTS *are already seated there. The theatre itself is empty.*]

1ST STUDENT. But surely you know that one?
2ND S. It is about the Italian and the two goats?
1ST S. No, no. This is about a man who wanted to buy a bird-cage. . . .
   [*Whispers.*]
   . . . He said: There's a stigma
   About the letter sigma. . . .
2ND S. [*laughing*]. That's damn good! Damn good, that is!

   [ALAN *enters shyly and sits down in the corner, looking round him.*]

1ST S. [*indicating* ALAN]. Who's that johnny? Don't know him.
2ND S. A sweat-pot from one of the other hospitals, probably.
1ST S. [*to* ALAN]. Hullo. Are you from St. Gag's?
ALAN [*nervously*]. Er, yes.
1ST S. What did you score this afternoon against Bullocks'?
2ND S. Who's batting?
ALAN. Er, I think . . .

   [*At this moment, a* 3RD STUDENT *comes in. He is struggling to get a white coat over his dinner-jacket.*]

3RD S. Thank God I'm not late! The old man had it in for me to-day.
2ND S. Hullo, Sandy. Were you at the Boat Club Supper?
3RD S. Was I not! Just my luck to have to leave when things were getting lively! They're just starting to wreck the hall. Fatty's smashed his collar-bone already and Roy's lost a tooth. It's going to be a ripping rag.
1ST S. Let's hope this case doesn't take long. [*Turning to* ALAN.] By the way, what did you say the score was?
2ND S. Ssh! They're coming!

   [*An harmonium begins to play a voluntary. The* STUDENTS *and* ALAN *rise to their feet. Procession of* NURSES *(including* DOG*),* DRESSERS, *the* PATIENT *on his stretcher,* ANAESTHETIST *and* SURGEON. *The* SURGEON *takes up a position at the end of the table with his back to the audience. The note is given. ff subito. Flavour of Bach in his dramatic mood.*]

ALL STUDENTS [*heavy 4-part harmony*].
>We see death every day
>But do not understand him.

SUR. I believe

ALL. in the physical causation of all phenomena, material or mental: and in the germ theory of disease. And in Hippocrates, the father of Medicine, Galen, Ambrose Paré, Liston of the enormous hands, Syme, Lister who discovered the use of antiseptics, Hunter and Sir Frederick Treves.

And I believe in surgical treatment for duodenal ulcer, cerebral abscess, pyloric stenosis, aneurism and all forms of endocrine disturbance.

SUR. Let not the patient react unfavourably to the anaesthetic.

ALL. But let it save him from pain.

SUR. Let there be no unforeseen complications.

ALL. Neither let sepsis have the advantage.

SUR. May my skill not desert me.

ALL. But guide your hands.

SUR. Gentlemen, we have before us a case of abdominal injury, caused by a bullet piercing the bowel. I intend therefore to make a five-inch median incision, dividing the Rectus Abdominus, bring the bowel forward, resect it, wash out the peritoneum with warm saline and insert a tube for drainage. Is it clear?

ALL. It is.

>[SURGEON *turns to wash his hands. During this process, the* STUDENTS *sing the following C of E chant.*]

DEC. The surgeon is great: Let his name appear in the birthday honours.

CAN. I was in danger of death: And he delivered me.

DEC. I was in fever and I could not sleep: The pain assailed me all day long.

CAN. I groaned in the darkness: I was in terror for my life: I took no pleasure in women, neither in the innocent pastimes of children, my food had lost its flavour.

DEC. The physicians shook their heads: they consulted together in the next room and were perplexed.
CAN. They prescribed diets, carthartics, drugs and all manner of salves and ointments: but no one of them relieved me.
UNISON. But the surgeon, he relieved me: he removed the emphasis of my trouble and I was healed.
SURGEON [*adjusting his gloves and picking up a scalpel*]. It's a terrible thing, nurse, to keep wicket for a man's life.
ALAN. Who's the surgeon?
1ST STUDENT. Sir William Spurgeon,
The famous amateur cricketer:
He captained the Hospital's team last year.
OTHER STUDENTS. Ssh!

[*Roll of drums, as if before a tight-rope act in the circus. The* SURGEON *begins to operate. Suddenly the lights go out.*]

SURGEON. Lights! Nurse! Dresser! You dresser next to that damned dresser! For God's sake get a torch! Light, give me a bloody light! Christ, is there no one in this bloody theatre who understands plain English? Someone go and find out what it's all about.

[*Electric torches are brought. One of the* NURSES *goes out.*]

SURGEON. Scalpel, nurse. Not that one, idiot! Forceps. More forceps! More! More! More!
I have cut the mesenteric!
Death has declared!

[*Throws instruments about the room.*]

ANAESTHETIST. He's sinking, sir. I'd better give him an injection of adrenalin.
SURGEON [*to* DRESSER]. God man, don't chatter! Do something! How the hell do you think I can see if you stand a mile away? Hold the torch nearer! Get out of my way!
SISTER [*returning*]. It was the Boat Club, Sir William. They're having a supper to-night, you know. One of the students fused the lights. He says he's very sorry. They'll be on again in a few minutes.
SURGEON. Oh, he's sorry, is he? That's good. That's very good. I'll make him sorry he was ever born. I'll break him! I'll break the Hospital Boat! I'll have rowing forbidden in this Hospital for ever! [*He utters a terrible roar and rushes out.*]

3RD STUDENT. Just our luck! If it had been his precious cricketers, he'd have been as meek as a lamb.
A NURSE. Something's the matter. The patient's coming to! Holy Mother of all the Saints, have mercy!

> [CHIMP EAGLE *sits up. The music of the ensuing duet should be in the style of Wagnerian opera.*]

CHIMP.   O Pressan Fells
    How beautiful you are!
I hear your bells
    Alas I cannot come
To Pressan home:
    I have wandered too far.

CHORUS.   (Pain makes him wander in his mind,
There's nothing audible of any kind.)

ALAN.   O my Eagle!
CHIMP.   I hear a voice
    That makes me rejoice.
Who is it standing there?
    I cannot see you clear.
ALAN.   Eagle, it is I,
    Alan Norman standing by.
CHIMP.   I cannot see.
    Twixt you and me
Death's great tired face
    Hangs in space.

CHORUS.   (Death makes him wander in his mind,
There's nothing visible of any kind.)

ALAN.   I am near.
Do not fear.
CHIMP.   She gives me loving glances.
ALAN.   Where is Francis?
CHIMP.   When the Midget died
I was by his side.
He said to me then
Out of his pain:
"Return again
    To England. I swear
That Francis is there."

ALAN.	And you forgot
	Your choice and lot?
CHIMP.	No I did not
	But for me
	Was another destiny
	Chance made it clear
	My work was here
	For me the single-handed
	Search was ended
	But for you I see
	It is still necessary
	To continue your looking
	For what is lacking.
	More I cannot tell.
	Darkness assails me and I fail:
	Farewell.
ALAN.	O Eagle stay.
	I will take you home.
CHIMP.	Nay, death has come.
	She beckons me away.
	Beasts and flowers are in her keeping,
	In her arms I would be sleeping.
ALAN.	You shall not die!
CHIMP.	No, Alan, no.
	The surgeon now
	Is ignorant as a dove.
	To Iris my love. [*Dies.*]

[*The lights go on again. The* SURGEON *comes in.*]

SURGEON. That's settled 'em, I think. . . . Well, Sister, how's the patient?

SISTER. The patient is dead, Sir William.

SURGEON. Dead! How dare you let him die? Great God, couldn't a dozen of you keep him alive for five minutes? This is the sort of thing which invariably happens whenever my back is turned. Typical. Typical. . . . What about this injection you gave the patient? Show me the bottle. [NURSE *gives it him.*] And you can look me in the face and say you thought this was Adrenalin? Why, you blind miserable cow, this is hydrochloric acid!

SISTER [*in tears*]. The new probationer gave it me, Sir William.

SURGEON. The new probationer, eh? This is becoming amusing! Bring me the new probationer.

[*The* NURSES *push the* DOG *forward.*]

SURGEON. So you're the culprit, eh? Well, let me tell you, my good girl, if I ever see you in this theatre again, I'll . . .

> [*He becomes aware that he is staring into a* DOG*'s face. There is an awful pause. The* SURGEON *makes some inarticulate sounds as if about to have a fit. The* DOG *utters a long-drawn howl. Then it turns and bolts for the door, its cap flying from its head. General dismay, confusion, screams, laughter, pursuit.* ALAN *rushes out after the others.*]

CURTAIN

Act II Scene 5

[*Night. The Highroad. In the middle of the stage stands a milestone.*]

CHORUS. Night. And crooked Europe hidden in shadow:
    The Rhine catching the moonlight for hundreds of miles, watched
        by lovers:
    Night in England: Over Lincolnshire and the great churches:
    Glimpses of the constellations between their pinnacles and flying
        buttresses:
    And here Alan and his companion, on foot on road, a forest on
        either side:
    A strong moon pitches their shadows forward:
    Sounds of their footsteps break against the woody masses
    But the tide in the tall trees is taciturn, another life:
    Alan lifting his eyes sees the Bear, the Waggoner, the Scales
    And Algol waxing and waning as his hope, no life at all.

[*Enter* ALAN *and* DOG.]

ALAN.   Night has fallen, we have lost our way.
            You are tired and so am I.
        Let us wait till it is day.
            Against this milestone let us lie
        And sleep as best we may.

[*They both lie down behind the milestone.*]

CHORUS. Dear Sleep, the secretary of that strange club
Where all are members upon one condition,
That they forget their own importance;
Where Lord and Link-Boy leave themselves with others
And night after night for nothing are refreshed:
May our names from your register never be struck off!

[*Enter, from behind the milestone,* ALAN's LEFT *and* RIGHT FOOT. *The* RIGHT FOOT *speaks in a cultured voice, the* LEFT FOOT *has a Cockney accent.*]*

RIGHT FOOT. Why are you pushing me, Left?
LEFT F. Cos yer tiking up all the room, that's why.
RIGHT F. Well, that's no reason to push. Pushing won't make things better for either of us.
LEFT F. It's bleedin' cold. Scratch me back for me, will yer, Right? Naow, a bit 'igher up.
RIGHT F. Is that better?
LEFT F. That's fine. Hell, I'm tired!
RIGHT F. So am I. It's been a tiring day.
LEFT F. I always feels tired now. Proper done in. The cramp keeps gettin' me. It gets me bad, sometimes.
RIGHT F. You ought to see a doctor.
LEFT F. Corse I ort. But the Boss won't let me. Jest let 'im wyte. One o' these dys I'll 'ave 'is guts fer garters.
RIGHT F. I don't think you should talk like that, after all he's done for us.
LEFT F. An' wot's 'e done fer us, I'd like ter know? Works us daown ter ther bone without so much as Thank You. And fer wot, I arsks yer? Fer wot? Chysin' abaht after some bloke wot's been dead fer years. A lot I care whether the Boss finds 'im. I 'aven't seen the inside of a carpet slipper fer weeks. Wot wouldn't I give fer a bath? Cor! I don't 'alf whistle!
RIGHT F. Yes, the odour *is* unpleasant, certainly. Especially to feet like us, who've always been brought up to regard cleanliness as next to godliness.... Still, I must say, I don't see that grumbling does much good. And, look here, old chap, I do wish you wouldn't speak of the Master in that way. It makes such a bad impression when other people are about. Of course, I know you and I know quite well you don't mean a word of it....

* In a performance the ensuing dialogue should probably be cut.

Left F. Don't I, jest? That's all you knows! Look 'ere, wot'd you and yer precious Boss do if I was ter tell yer I wasn't goin' a step further? You'd 'ave ter carry me! 'Ow'd yer like that, eh?

Right F. [*coldly*]. Of course, you're perfectly entitled to act as you think best. We can't stop you. I might just as well take the same attitude myself. . . . It's a matter of loyalty: either one appreciates that kind of thing, or one doesn't.

Left F. You and yer Public School edjerkytion! Ort ter 'ave bin a sky pilot, you ort!

Right F. It's very easy to sneer. But the fact remains that without some kind of standards a fellow just goes to pieces. One saw enough of that in the War. Who were the best officers? The boys who had been captains of their school fifteens. And the more one knocks about the world, the more one comes to realise. . . .

Left F. Ow, lay orf it! Yer mikes me sick! I ain't goin' ter listen ter another of yer lectures on the Team Spirit, an' that's stryte!

Right F. Sorry, old chap. I didn't mean to jaw. Let's change the subject, shall we? . . . You said just now that Sir Francis Crewe was dead. Well, I'm sure he's not. . . . And what's more, I'm on his track at last!

Left F. Go on! You're kiddin'.

Right F. Oh no, I'm not. I'll prove it to you. I've been working on the case for months, now: I didn't want to say anything till I'd got it watertight. . . . And it's all so beautifully simple, really. . . . Do you know what gave me the first clue?

Left F. Wot?

Right F. I happened to notice, one morning, that the Master's brown shoes had a little indentation on either side of the toe-cap, about half an inch long. At the time, I thought no more about it: It wasn't till the other day, fitting the facts together and trying them this way and that, that the whole thing flashed upon me. Do you know what had made those marks? [*Dramatically.*] Roller-skates!

Left F. But wot's that got ter do with Sir Francis Crewe?

Right F. I'll give you all the stages of my reasoning later: But it was really those skate-marks which led me to his hiding-place.

Left F. Yer means you've seen 'im?

Right F. Oh no. I've never seen him yet. How could I? The Master never lets us go out alone.

Left F. But yer knows where 'e is?

Right F. I do.

Left F. Go on then, spit it aht!

Right F. [*impressively*]. At this very moment, Sir Francis Crewe is . . .

[*glances round him*]. No. Better not tell you here. There may be spies about. Come behind the milestone.

[*The* FEET *disappear.*]

TWO CHORUS LEADERS.
   Now through night's caressing grip
   Earth and all her oceans slip,
   Capes of China slide away
   From her fingers into day
   And the Americas incline
   Coasts towards her shadow line.
   Now the ragged vagrants creep
   Into crooked holes to sleep:
   Just and unjust, worst and best,
   Change their places as they rest:
   Awkward lovers lie in fields
   Where disdainful beauty yields:
   While the splendid and the proud
   Naked stand before the crowd
   And the losing gambler gains
   And the beggar entertains:
   May sleep's healing power extend
   Through these hours to our friend.
   Unpursued by hostile force,
   Traction engine, bull or horse
   Or revolting succubus;
   Calmly till the morning break
   Let him lie, then gently wake.

CURTAIN

Act III

Chorus

A man and a dog are entering a city: They are approaching a centre of
   culture:
First the suburban dormitories spreading over fields,
Villas on vegetation like saxifrage on stone,
Isolated from each other like cases of fever
And uniform in design, uniform as nurses.

To each a lean-to shed, containing a well-oiled engine of escape.
Section these dwellings: expose the life of a people
Living by law and the length of a reference,
See love in its disguises and the losses of the heart,
Cats and old silver inspire heroic virtues
And psychic fields, accidentally generated, destroy whole families.
Extraordinary tasks are set: a ploughman's hand acquires the most
    exquisite calligraphy,
A scheme is prepared for draining the North Sea, with the aid of books
    from the local library:
One has a vision in the bathroom after a family quarrel: he kneels on
    the cork mat:
A naturalist leaves in a cab in time for the breaking of the meres.
A youth with boils lies face down on bed, his mother over him;
Tenderly she squeezes from his trembling body the last dregs of his
    childhood.

Writer, be glib: please them with scenes of theatrical bliss and horror,
Whose own slight gestures tell their doom with a subtlety quite foreign
    to the stage.
For who dare patiently tell, tell of their sorrow
Without let or variation of season, streaming up in parallel from the
    little houses
And unabsorbed by their ironic treasures
Exerts on the rigid dome of the unpierced sky its enormous pressures?

But look: While we were talking, they have not stood still,
They have passed up the parade, the site of shops:
Goods are displayed: behind plate glass
One satin slipper austerely arranged
On an inky background of blackest velvet:
A waxen sandboy in skiing kit
Dumb and violet among vapour lamps.
High in the air, in empty space,
Five times a minute a mug is filled
And in ten-foot letters, time after time,
Words are spelt out and wiped away.
He moves amazed among the well-fed multitudes;
They glance at the stranger with the glance of those
Who have paid their allowance to be left alone.
And now they reach the Nineveh Hotel;
Consider this hotel: its appointments and fittings:
Five hundred bedrooms, with h and c,

Three hundred bathrooms: 375 W.C.s:
Inspect the dining-hall: seating 2000:
The waiters scuttling from side to side
Like goldfish feeding the valuable people:
Admire the shining silver and cutlery
Stamped with the mark of that sombre town
Which fouls the Don still fresh from the moor
And the beautiful glassware blown on the Danube:
And stand in the vestibule spacious and gilded
As our hero enters to sign his name.
Old men afraid of reflections in glass
Are ushering ladies out to their cars,
Veiled and valued, through revolving doors.
Paid to be pretty, pumped into cloth,
Ranked by pillars pages wait,
At signals, like gulls from a nesting stack,
To rise on their toes and tear away.

Come in:

Act III Scene I

[*The vestibule of the Nineveh Hotel.* PORTER. PAGES. *Enter* ALAN *and* DOG.]

PORTER. I'm glad you've come, sir.
    You want a room, sir?
ALAN. Please.
PORTER. I'm sorry to be a trouble, sir:
    A single or a double, sir?
ALAN. A single, please.
PORTER. I'm still in doubt, sir.
    With bathroom or without, sir?
ALAN. With bathroom. please.
PORTER. Just sign your name, sir.
    And date the same, sir.
    Here, quickly, page boy,
    Or you'll put me in a rage, boy.
    Show this gentleman up to
    Room 132.
PAGE. Let me take your bag, sir.
    It'll save you fag, sir.

Please follow me, sir.
　　　I've got the key, sir.
CHORUS. Make way, make way:
　　　This gentleman has come to stay.
　　　He wants a room where he may rest,
　　　But not the best, but not the best:
　　　He's only a provincial guest.
PORTER [*sees* DOG]. I'm sorry, dogs are not allowed, sir,
　　　I didn't see him in the crowd, sir.
ALAN. But that's absurd, my dog and I
　　　Are never parted: tell me why,
　　　If not I'll give you back my keys
　　　And leave this moment, if you please!

> [*Enter the* TWO JOURNALISTS. *The* 2ND JOURNALIST *is very drunk.*]

2ND JOURNALIST [*singing*].
　　　　　　The bluebells bloomed on the Baltic shore
　　　　　　When Kit was Schneider-Creusot's love.
1ST J. Why look, there's Alan!
2ND J. 　　　　　　　　My dear old boy!
　　　To see you once more is indeed a joy!

> [2ND J. *throws his arms round* ALAN'S *neck.*]

1ST J. He means no evil
　　　But he's tight as the devil.
ALAN. I always hoped we should meet again.
1ST J. What about your search? Has it been in vain?
ALAN. He never left England at all, it appears.
2ND J. [*who has wandered off into a corner, sings*].
　　　　　　Alice is gone and I'm alone,
　　　　　　Nobody understands
　　　　　　How lovely were her Fire Alarms,
　　　　　　How fair her German Bands!
1ST J. [*to* 2ND J.]. Stop! Stop! You make
　　　My stomach ache!
　　　[*To* ALAN.] Are you staying here?
ALAN. I'd hoped to. But they won't allow the dog.
1ST J. They won't?
　　　I'll settle that: You see if I don't!
　　　Porter!

PORTER. What can I do, sir?
   To satisfy you, sir?

[1ST J. *whispers something in his ear.*]

PORTER. O O Sir,
   I didn't know, sir!
   [*To* ALAN.] I'm so sorry, sir.
   I made a mistake, sir.
   I was in a hurry, sir.
   Don't worry, sir.
   Of course we'll take, sir,
   Your dog too, sir,
   As well as you, sir.
   [*To* PAGE.] This dog you must take, boy.
   And feed on cake, boy.

[*Exeunt* PORTER, PAGE *and* DOG.]

ALAN. Whatever did you say?
1ST J. Ah, that's a secret I can't give away!
   Let's come and eat.

[*They go out.* 2ND J. *lingering behind, sings, out of tune and with great pathos:*]

2ND J. [*singing*].   O how I cried when Alice died
   The day we were to have wed!
   We never had our Roasted Duck
   And now she's a Loaf of Bread!

[*He staggers out.*]

CURTAIN

Act III Scene 2

[*The restaurant of the Nineveh Hotel. In the foreground are tables with diners: including* ALAN *and the* TWO JOURNALISTS. *In the background is a small stage for cabaret. The entire setting of this scene should convey an impression of brutal, noisy vulgarity and tasteless extravagance. Band music.*]

VOICES. And as for her hat, my dear . . .
   Le Touquet was lousy this year.
   Have you read *The Virgin Policeman*?

Yes we did. We got right to the Docks.
There's his new one.
There were lots of children without any socks.
You mean the blue one?
It was divine. We found a dive.
I'm flying next week to the Bahamas.
And danced with the sailors. I felt so *alive*.
What I say is: damn a man with holes in his pyjamas!
Darling, you look wonderful to-night!
One of those schools one has never heard of.

CABARET ANNOUNCER. Ladies and Gentlemen! The romance of foreign lands has been celebrated by every song-writer. But we feel that insufficient justice has been done to our own country. We are presenting therefore to you to-night Madame Bubbi, in a new song entitled: *Rhondda Moon*. When you have heard her, I'm sure you will be convinced, as we are, that, in the opportunities which she offers to the Tender Passion, Britain is second to none! Madame Bubbi!

[*Enter* MADAME BUBBI, *an immense woman in a sequin dress.*]

M.B. [*sings*]. I come with a message to the farmers and the cities;
　　　　I've simple slogan, it's just: Love British!
　　　　British Romance, British joys,
　　　　British chorus girls and chorus boys.

　　　　The Sahara makes hearts to pit-a-pat,
　　　　Glamorganshire can do better than that!
　　　　Wherever you go, be it east or west,
　　　　Remember British Love is quite the best.

　　　　People sing songs about Tennessee
　　　　But foreign men won't do for me.
　　　　I don't want a dago, I don't want a Greek,
　　　　I've got what I want and that's a British Sheik.

CHORUS. On the Rhondda
　　　　My time I squander
　　　　Watching for my miner boy:
　　　　He may be rough and tough
　　　　But he surely is hot stuff
　　　　And he's slender, to-me-tender,
　　　　He's my only joy:
　　　　Lovers' meeting,
　　　　Lovers' greeting,

O his arms will be around me soon!
For I am growing fonder
Out yonder as I wander
And I ponder 'neath a Rhondda moon!

VOICES OF DINERS. I bought five yards.
    I always use Corps de Femme myself.
    He's in the Guards.
    Oh, she's already on the shelf.
    I told him I couldn't do without it.
    Have you read *The Virgin Policeman?*
    The customs officer was perfectly sweet about it.

[Enter the NINEVEH GIRLS. *All that is mechanical, shallow, silly, hideous and unbearably tragic in the antics of a modern cabaret chorus should be expressed here in its most exaggerated form. Crude lighting. Rowdy music.]*

NINEVEH GIRLS [*sing*]. We are girls of different ages.
    All sorts of girls at all sorts of stages, we've
        Come to delight you,
        Come to excite you,
        Come to present our revue!
    Fair girls, dear girls,
    Dark girls, stark girls,
    Glad girls, bad girls,
    Poor girls, we've-met-before-girls, we
        All would welcome you.

    Desires, ambitions, anxieties fill us,
    We come from brick rectories and sham-Tudor villas,
        It's our profession
        To cure your depression
        And banish those melancholy blues.
    Old girls, bold girls,
    Shy girls, fly girls,
    Kiss-girls, sis-girls,
    Lean girls, do-you-get-what-I-mean-girls, you
        Only have to choose.

    We lift our legs for your masculine inspection,
    You can admire us without our correction, we
        Do this nightly,

We hope we're not unsightly
Or all our labours are vain!
Neat girls, sweet girls,
Gym girls, slim girls,
Meek girls, technique girls,
Pat girls, come-up-to-my-flat-girls, we
Hope to see you again!

> [*Applause. A solitary* DINER *with an eye-glass beckons the* WAITER.]

DINER. Waiter!
WAITER. At once, sir!
   You want, sir?
DINER. Bring me the third girl from the right.

> [*The* WAITER *blows a signal on his whistle and the chosen girl comes down from the stage. The* WAITER *catches her head under his arm as though she were a fowl and holds her so that the* DINER *can pinch her thigh. The girl does not offer the least resistance.*]

WAITER. Will she do, sir?
   Or will you choose anew, sir?
DINER. No. I'll have this one.
WAITER. Will you have her roast, sir.
   Or on Japanese Toast, sir?
   With Sauce Allemagne, sir,
   Or stewed in white wine, sir?
DINER. Stewed, I think. But I'll have the finger-nails served separately as a savoury. Oh, and don't forget to remind the Chef to stir the pot with a sprig of rosemary. It makes all the difference.

> [WAITER *bows and retires, carrying the girl over his shoulder.*]

CABARET ANNOUNCER. Our next item is Destructive Desmond!

> [*Deafening applause.* DESTRUCTIVE DESMOND *comes on to the stage, followed by attendants carrying a large oil painting.* DESMOND *is dressed as a schoolboy, with ink-stains on his cheeks, a crumpled eton collar, a striped cap, broken bootlaces, dishevelled stockings and shorts. He is a stocky, middle-aged man, with an inflamed, pugnacious face and very hairy knees.*]

ONE OF THE DINERS TO ANOTHER. Haven't you seen him before? Oh, he's marvellous! I saw him last winter in New York. He burnt an entire first folio Shakespeare, page by page. I've never laughed so much in all my life.

DESMOND. Hullo, fellows! Here we are again! Has anyone got a nice old poetry-book for me to read? I do love a bit of poetry! [*Loud laughter from the audience.*] You haven't? Never mind! This evening, I've got a real treat for you. But, first of all, is there any gentlemen in the audience who knows anything about painting? no, not painting the greenhouse. [*Laughter.*] Pictures! Comes on, don't be shy. Thank you, sir. Will you step up on the stage a moment?

> [*An* ART EXPERT, *a nice, rather ineffective man in pince-nez, comes up. He is evidently a bona-fide member of the audience and not in the conspiracy. He does not at first understand what is going to happen.*]

DESMOND [*winking at the audience*]. So you're an Art expert, sir?

ART EXPERT. Well, er, without wishing to be immodest, I think I have some claim to that title, yes. I am the curator of the gallery at Barchester.

DESMOND. Excellent! Just the man I wanted to meet! You see, sir, I wanted to ask your advice about a picture I've just bought. Would you care to look at it?

A.E. [*adjusting his pince-nez*]. Certainly, certainly. If I can be of any service ...

> [DESMOND *signs to the attendants to uncover the picture. The* ART EXPERT *bends down to examine it. After a moment, he utters an exclamation, takes a magnifying glass from his pocket and studies every inch of the canvas with great care. The audience titters with delight: everybody else in the room seems to know exactly what will happen.*]

A.E. [*standing up, evidently very much excited*]. Do you know, Mr, er Desmond ... it's a very remarkable thing, very remarkable indeed ... this picture is a Rembrandt!

DESMOND. Are you sure of that?

A.E. Quite positive. There can be no doubt whatever.

DESMOND [*playing always to the audience, and mimicking the over-cultured tones of the* ART EXPERT]. No doubt whatever? Fancy that, now! And will you be so kind as to tell these ladies and gentlemen how much this Rembrandt of mine is worth?

A.E. Oh, speaking offhand, I should say about sixty thousand pounds.
DESMOND [*as before*]. Isn't that a lot of money! Dear, Oh dear! And suppose something were to *happen* to my beautiful picture [*unseen by the* ART EXPERT, *but visible to the audience, he produces an enormous penknife: the audience are delighted*] do you think Mr Rembrandt would paint me another one like it?
A.E. [*smiling*]. No, he couldn't, I'm afraid. He's dead.
DESMOND. Oh, he's dead, is he? I *am* sorry! I must send some flowers. What did he die of?

> [*The* ART EXPERT *doesn't quite know what to make of this fooling. He has become aware of the curiously hostile mood of* DESMOND *and the audience towards himself. He stands there awkwardly, smiling but uneasy.*]

DESMOND. Well, well [*he flourishes the knife*] if Mr Rembrandt's dead, he won't be angry with me: that's one comfort. And anyhow, I suppose I can do what I like with my own picture. . . .
A.E. [*suddenly realising what* DESMOND *is going to do*]. Mr Desmond! . . . You're not going to . . . ?
DESMOND. Not going to what?
A.E. [*gasping*]. To . . . destroy this picture?
DESMOND [*now openly sneering at him*]. And why shouldn't I destroy it, may I ask? Isn't it mine?
A.E. . . . Yes, er, of course. . . . But I mean. . . . You *can't* . . . it's a masterpiece!
DESMOND. Oh, it's a masterpiece, is it? And how would you define a masterpiece, Mr Art Expert?
A.E. Something unique . . . a work of genius . . . which can't be replaced . . . priceless . . . [*He stammers, amidst the merriment of the audience, and cannot go on.*]
DESMOND [*signs to the attendants to uncover a second picture*]. Is *this* a masterpiece?
A.E. [*contemptuously*]. No, most certainly not!
DESMOND. Why isn't it?
A.E. In the first place because it's a completely tasteless piece of third-rate Victorian landscape painting of which you'll find examples in every boarding-house in England: And secondly, because it isn't even an original. You could get as many copies as you wanted from the publishers for a shilling a piece.
DESMOND. Well, all I can say is: I think it's a very nice picture. I like it much better than Mr Rembrandt's, which you say is so valuable.

[*Pointing to the Rembrandt.*] Why, this is all *brown*! More like a chest of drawers! Ugh, how I hate you! [*Raises knife to slash the Rembrandt canvas.*]

A.E. [*almost in tears*]. Stop! I protest against this disgraceful exhibition! I appeal to the ladies and gentlemen of the audience. Surely you won't allow this to go on?

DESMOND. Aha! So you appeal to the audience, do you? Very well! [*To the audience.*] Ladies and gentlemen, I leave it entirely in your hands: which picture would you rather see cut to bits, this landscape which Mr Expert so much despises, or old mahogany Rembrandt?

ALL THE DINERS. Rembrandt! Rembrandt!

DESMOND [*brutally, to* ART EXPERT]. You hear what they say? And now, get off my platform! If you don't like it, you can do the other thing!

A.E. [*putting his hands to his head*]. Either these people are mad, or I am! [*He jumps down from the stage and runs out of the restaurant.*]

> [DESMOND *waves an ironic goodbye after him. The drums begin to roll. The audience groan with delight.* DESMOND, *standing before the Rembrandt, works himself up into a state of hysterical fury. He makes faces at the canvas, shows his teeth, shakes his fist, spits.*]

DESMOND [*as the drums reach their climax*]. Grrrr! Take that, you brute! [*slashes canvas with his knife*] and that! and that!

> [*Finale of trumpets. The attendants hold up the slashed picture and* DESMOND *puts his arm through it several times. Then he strikes it from their hands and tramples on it on the floor. Terrific applause.* DESMOND *bows and exits.*]
>
> [*A trumpet.*]

A VOICE. Here comes Miss Lou Vipond,
The star of whom the world is fond!

> [*All the diners jump up and rush towards the entrance, to get a peep.* ALAN *is one of the first. As* MISS VIPOND *passes across the stage, she is completely hidden by the crowd.*]

1ST JOURNALIST. Alan, old boy, come back! come back!
Don't you cross that harpy's track!

2ND J. If you fall for that dame, it'll be your undoing:
She's brought enough good men to their ruin.

ALAN [*who is standing on a table in order to see better*].
>   You fellows talk the most utter rot!
>   All other women can go to pot!
>   I'm true to Iris. [*He catches sight of* MISS VIPOND.]
>   By Jove, she's a stunner!
>   What a face! I'm dazzled!

>>   [*He jumps down from his table into the middle of the crowd.*]

1ST J. [*covering his eyes*]. The kid's a gonner!
VOICES FROM THE CROWD ROUND ALAN.
>   She's stopped to speak to a stranger!
>   Then he's in danger!
>   Look at her eyes!
>   What a lovely surprise!
>   She pretends she feels tired!
>   O she's inspired!
>   She leans on his arm!
>   She knows her charm!
>   She's going to speak!
>   It makes his knees weak!
>   She has asked him to visit her room!
>   He goes to his doom!

>>   [ALAN, *his face transformed by joy, breaks through the crowd and rushes forward.*]

ALAN [*to* JOURNALISTS].
>   Where can I get some flowers
>   So long after hours?

>>   [*Without waiting for an answer, he runs out.*]

CHORUS. Inform the Press, inform the Press,
>   Miss Vipond's had one more success!
>   It's in the air, it's in the air,
>   She's going to have a new affair!

>   Make way, make way,
>   This gentleman has come to stay!
>   He wants the best, he wants the best,
>   He's more than a provincial guest!

>   He quickly fell, he quickly fell,
>   He lost his heart in our hotel!

He's going to start, he's going to start,
He's starting now to break his heart!

CURTAIN

Act III Scene 3

[*Before the curtain. Enter simultaneously* ALAN *(left) and the* DOG *(right). They meet in the middle of the stage.* ALAN *is in tails. He carries an immense bouquet of flowers.*]

ALAN [*in a great hurry*]. Hullo, Doggy! How's life? [*The* DOG *fawns on him.*] Not now, there's a good dog! I'm in an awful hurry. Just think, in another minute I shall be with her! I believe, if I didn't see her again, I should go crazy! But you can't understand that, can you, Doggy? As long as you get your food and a nice warm mat to lie on, you're perfectly happy. I wish I were a dog! No, I'm damn glad I'm not! [*He pats the* DOG's *head absent-mindedly.*] Well, I must be off. [*The* DOG *puts its paws on* ALAN's *shoulders.*] Here, I say! That's enough! Let me alone, can't you? What's the matter with you this evening? Down, sir! [*He pushes the* DOG *roughly aside.*] Now you've made my coat dirty. I shall have to get it brushed. Silly fool! [*He takes a step forward. Immediately, the* DOG *jumps up and drags the flowers from his hand, scattering them in all directions.*] Francis, how dare you! You clumsy brute! [ALAN *gives the* DOG *a kick.*] Get out! [*The* DOG *does not move. There is a pause.*] I say, Francis, old boy, I didn't mean to do that! Honestly I didn't! I've never kicked you before, have I? You just made me angry with you for the moment. I'm sorry. . . . Why do you look at me like that? You can't pretend I really hurt you: Now, can you? Let me see. . . . [*He moves his hand towards the* DOG. *The* DOG *retreats a little.*] Oh, very well, if you'd rather not. Here: Shake a paw! [*The* DOG *does not move.*] All right, then: sulk if you want to. I've said I'm sorry. I can't do any more, can I? And anyhow, it was all your fault. [*Pointing to the flowers.*] Just look at them: all ruined! Now I shall have to get some more, and they cost five shillings each. What made you do it, Francis? Ha ha ha! I believe you're jealous again! Was that why? Well, you are a queer dog! But you wait till you see her, Francis. She's the most marvellous creature in the world! Goodness knows what she can see in a chap like me! Her eyes, why, you've no idea. . . . [*But the* DOG *has turned and, with great dignity, slowly walked off the stage.*] He's gone! Funny! I expect he'll be all right tomorrow. . . .

And now! [ALAN *straightens his coat and smooths his hair.*] I must get those flowers. [*Looks at his watch.*] Good God! I'm five seconds late already!

[*He rushes out.*]

Act III Scene 4

[*The Nineveh Hotel. The stage is divided in half. The right-hand scene represents* MISS VIPOND's *bedroom. The left-hand scene is the corridor outside it. When the curtain rises, the bedroom is in darkness. The corridor is illuminated. The* DOG *is sitting on a chest outside the bedroom door. A grandfather clock stands in the corner. Enter the* MANAGER, *with a chorus of* WAITERS, PAGES *and* CHAMBERMAIDS.]

MANAGER. When he gets his bill to-morrow
    What will Mr Norman say?
Will he shoot himself for sorrow
    All on a summer's day?

CHORUS. Perhaps he'll only lose his mind,
    Go wild and feed among the lilies:
Tell us, if you'd be so kind,
    Tell us what the bill is.

MANAGER. 20 cases of champagne,
A finest pedigree Great Dane,
Half a dozen Paris frocks,
A sable fur, a silver fox,
Bottles of scent and beauty salves,
An MG Midget with overhead valves,
1 doz pairs of shoes and boots,
6 lounge, 1 tails and 3 dress suits,
A handsome two-piece bathing-dress,
An electric razor, a trouser-press,
A cutter for cigars, two lighters,
10 autographs of famous writers,
Berths and tickets in advance
For a trip round Southern France:
Add to this his bed and board.

CHORUS. It's more than one man can afford.

MANAGER. This we'll keep until the morning.
Remember, do not give him warning. [*Exit.*]

[*Song and Step Dance.*]

WAITERS.
    If we're late
    Or break a plate
    He won't be rude.
    If we served him nude
    Would he know?
    No No No!
    He's in love!

PAGES.
    If we lose
    All his shoes,
    Say Go to Hell
    When he rings the bell,
    He won't know:
    No No No!
    He's in love!

CHAMBERMAID.
    If I stops
    Emptying the slops,
    Leaves a dead
    Mouse in the bed,
    He won't know:
    No No No,
    He's in love!

[*A bell rings. The* CHORUS *arrange themselves under the* HEAD WAITER.]

HEAD WAITER. The Nineveh Hotel holds the copyright
    Of the Epithalamium we are going to recite.

CHORUS [*reciting, with a background of eighteenth-century music*].
    You who return to-night to a narrow bed
    With one name running sorrowfully through your sorrowful head,
    You who have never been touched, and you, pale lover,
    Who left the house this morning kissed all over,
    You little boys also of quite fourteen
    Beginning to realise just what we mean,
    Fill up glasses with champagne and drink again.

    It's not a new school or factory to which we summon,
    We're here to-day because of a man and a woman.
    Oh Chef, employ your continental arts
    To celebrate the union of two loving hearts!

Waiters, be deft, and slip, you pages, by
To honour the god to name whom is to lie:
Fill up glasses with champagne and drink again.

[*The corridor begins to darken.*]

Already he has brought the swallows past the Scillies
To chase each other skimming under English bridges,
Has loosed the urgent pollen on the glittering country
To find the pistil, force its burglar's entry,
He moves us also and up the marble stair
He leads the figures matched in beauty and desire:
Fill up glasses with champagne and drink again.

[*The corridor is now completely dark.* MISS VIPOND'S *bedroom is illuminated.* ALAN *stands embracing* MISS VIPOND, *who is a shopwindow dummy, very beautifully dressed. When the dummy is to speak,* ALAN *runs behind it and speaks in falsetto.*]

ALAN. My swan, so beautiful to my five senses,
  When I look on you, in a moment I lose my defences,
  My clumsy heart forgets herself and dances.

DUMMY. O lion, O sun, encompass me with power,
  Feed lion, shine sun, for in your glory I flower,
  Create the huge and gorgeous summer in an hour.

VOICES OF WAITERS' CHORUS [*outside in the corridor*].
  What would you give that she might live?

ALAN. I would give the Netherlands with all their canals,
  The earth of the Ukraine, the Niagara Falls,
  The Eiffel Tower also and the Dome of St Paul's.

CHORUS OUTSIDE. What would you do to keep her true?

ALAN. I would hunt the enormous whale in the Arctic lowlands,
  I would count all the starlings in the British Islands,
  I would run through fighting Europe in absolute silence.

DUMMY. But men are treacherous, I know, as the North-East wind,
  They speak of loving but another is in their mind,
  And you will leave me to-morrow morning for another find.

ALAN. True, there was one I thought I loved beyond measure.
  Here is her picture, I destroy it to give you pleasure.
  For, love, in your arms I find the only treasure.

> [*He tears up the photograph of* IRIS *and scatters the pieces at the dummy's feet.*]

DUMMY. Our sails are set. O launch upon love's ocean,
    Fear has no means there of locomotion
    And death cannot exhaust us with his endless devotion.

> [ALAN *begins to embrace and undress the dummy. The bedroom slowly darkens. From the complete darkness of the corridor, the voices of the* WAITERS' CHORUS *are heard, gradually receding.*]

CHORUS. It's not only this we praise, it's the general love:
    Let cat's mew rise to a scream on the tool-shed roof,
    Let son come home to-night to his anxious mother,
    Let the vicar lead the choirboy into a dark corner.
    The orchid shall flower to-night that flowers every hundred years,
    The boots and the slavey be found dutch-kissing on the stairs:
    Fill up glasses with champagne and drink again.

    Let this be kept as a generous hour by all,
    This once let the uncle settle his nephew's bill,
    Let the nervous lady's table gaucheness be forgiven,
    Let the thief's explanation of the theft be taken,
    The boy caught smoking shall escape the usual whipping,
    To-night the expensive whore shall give herself for nothing:
    Fill up glasses with champagne and drink again.

    The landlocked state shall get its port to-day,
    The midnight worker in the laboratory by the sea
    Shall discover under the cross-wires that which he looks for,
    To-night the asthmatic clerk shall dream he's a boxer,
    Let the cold heart's wish be granted, the desire for a desire,
    O give to the coward now his hour of power:
    Fill up glasses with champagne and drink again.

> [*The bedroom is now completely dark. In the corridor, spotlights suddenly illuminate the chest and the grandfather clock. Beside the chest the* DOG *is lying with its paws crossed.*]

DOG'S SKIN. Ticker! Ticker! Are you awake? [*The Clock strikes one.*] It's only me, the dog's skin that hides that eccentric young man. I hope you admire my accent? I've lived so long with them, I have all the émigré's pride at having forgotten my own. I'm quite déraciné, as they say in Bloomsbury. When I first paid them a visit, before I gave up my nationality and was still an Irish Wolfhound, I was very romantic. The odour of a particular arm-chair, the touch of certain fingers, excited me to rash generalisations which I believed to be profound. I composed poems that I imagined highly idiomatic, on the words "walk" and "dinner". And it was in this romantic mood that I decided to throw in my lot with theirs and sever all ties with my past. My dearest ambition was to be accepted naturally as one of them. I was soon disillusioned! To them I was only a skin, valued for its associations with that very life I had hoped to abandon. Small children misunderstood by their parents rubbed tearful cheeks against me and whispered secrets to their doggie. I ask you . . . Doggie! Young men wore me at charades to arouse in others undisguised human amusement and desire. Talking about charades, Ticker, are you interested in literature at all? [*The Clock strikes two.*] You are? So am I.

In the old days, before I became a skin, I used to be the pet of a very famous author. He talked all day to yours truly. He suffered terribly from indigestion, poor fellow, and wrote what was called "virile" poetry. He was knighted for it during the war. Well, I'll tell you a story about him. One night (it was nearly one o'clock in the morning, as a matter of fact) he was pretty tight on whisky and we had a real heart-to-heart. George, he says (I was called George in those days), George, he says, come here. I came, rather crossly, to tell you the truth, I was sleepy and wishing he'd go to bed. George, look at me. Do I make you sick? (By the way, I forgot to tell you that it was during the war, at the time of the big German offensive in March of '18). Less than a hundred miles from here, young men are being blown to pieces. Listen, you can hear the guns doing it. (It was quite true, you could. We lived on the South Downs and it was a still night.) Every time I hear that, I say to myself: You fired that shell. It isn't the cold general on his white horse, nor the owner of the huge factory, nor the luckless poor, but you. Yes, I and those like me. Invalid poets with a fountain pen, undersized professors in a classroom, we, the sedentary and learned, whose schooling cost the most, the least conspicuous of them all, are the assassins. (I'm giving you his own words. Whisky always made him a bit rhetorical.) We have conjured up all the vigours and all the splendors, skilfully transformed our envy into an image of the universal mother, for which the lad of seventeen whom we have always sent and will send again against our terrors, gladly immolates himself. Men are falling through the air in flames and choking slowly in the dark recesses of the sea to assuage our pride. Our pride! Who cannot work without incessant cups of tea, spend whole days weeping in our rooms, immoderately desire little girls on beaches and buy them sweets, cannot pass a mirror without staring, for whom a slight cold is enough to create a day-dream of our deathbed with appropriate organ-music. ... Now wasn't that queer? It was the last talk I ever had with him. He couldn't bear the sight of me after that evening and sold me as soon as he could.

Just like a man! You know, Ticker, I think the important thing to remember about Man is that pictures mean more to him than people. Take sex, for instance. Well, you've seen what it was like this evening. Sometimes it's funny and sometimes it's sad, but it's always hanging about like a smell of drains. Too many ideas in their heads! To them I'm an idea, you're an idea, everything's an idea. That's why we're here. Funny thing, Ticker, that we should both be in the same play. They can't do without us. If it wasn't for me, this young man of mine would never be able to get a good night's rest: and if it wasn't for you he'd never wake up. And look what we do to the audience! When I come on, they start sighing, thinking of spring, meadows and goodness knows what else: While you make them demand a tragic ending, with you they associate an immensely complicated system of awards and punishments.

[*During this speech, the corridor has been gradually illuminated.*]

Heavens, it's getting light and you've forgotten to strike! Hurry up! [*The Clock strikes six.*] I think someone's coming and my lodger is waking up. So long! Abyssinia.

[*The* DOG *stretches.* FRANCIS CREWE *gets out of the skin, lays it on the chest, looks cautiously round and tip-toes out.*]
[MANAGER, WAITERS, PAGES, *etc. enter singing* (Air: *John Peel*).]

MANAGER. The sun has risen and it shines through the blind,
    This lover must awaken and recall to mind
    Though the pillow be soft and the lady be kind,
    Yet the man has to pay in the morning.

CHORUS. For in Nineveh Hotel the most humble guest,
    Be he old, be he young, he may take a good rest,

He may smoke cigars, he may order the best,
But we hand him the bill in the morning.

> [*The* MANAGER *knocks loudly at the bedroom door.*
> ALAN *appears in pyjamas.*]

ALAN. What's all this row?
  I can't see you now.
CHORUS. We're sorry, sir,
  To be a worry, sir,
  But we're in a hurry, sir.
  We want our money, sir.
  Here is our bill, sir.

> [*They give him the bill. Pause.*]

  Oh, don't be ill, sir!
ALAN. Fifteen hundred! It's absurd!
  This will have to be deferred.
  I'm sorry, gentlemen, to say
  Just at this moment I cannot pay.
  You shall have your money another day.
CHORUS. Till we have our due, we stay.
ALAN. Here's a to-do!
  I must borrow from Lou.

> [*He speaks into the bedroom, which is in darkness.*]

Darling, I'm sorry to be such a bother
But some stupid tradesman is making a pother
(It's nothing really) about my account:
So will you lend it me, darling Lou?
Fifteen hundred pounds will do.

> [*No answer.*]

Darling, please,
Don't be a tease,
They're waiting here,
They will fetch the Police.
Please be a dear!

> [*No answer.*]

Say something do!
I want help, Lou!

> [*No answer.*]

Why don't you answer?
I tell you, I'm in danger!

[*No answer.*]

Last night you spoke.
This is no joke!

[*No answer.*]

What is the matter, what have I done?
Last night you called me your lion and your sun.
Speak to me, please, just one little word,
I don't understand you! Oh, this is absurd!

[*A pause.*]

I am your lover!
Don't say that's over!
That can't be what you mean!

[*A pause.*]

I won't believe it!

[*A pause.*]

All right, I'll leave it.
Oh, I'm in hell!

[*He turns to the* MANAGER *and others outside in the corridor.*]

MANAGER. Well?
ALAN. Gentlemen, what can I say?
　　I cannot pay!
MANAGER. This is a most regrettable occasion.
　　I must go at once to the police station.
　　Alphonse.
ALPHONSE. Yes sah?
MANAGER. Tell the Porter he's not to let
　　This man go out: and don't forget!

[*Exeunt* MANAGER *and others.*]

ALAN. Lou! Lou!
　　There is only one thing left to do.
　　Something that the Romans knew,
　　In a bath I'll open a vein

And end my life with little pain.
I'll go at once and turn
The water on and then return
For the razor to relieve
Me for ever of my grief.

> [*He enters the darkened bedroom and disappears.* FRANCIS CREWE *comes into the corridor, takes the skin from the chest and hastily begins getting into it. While he is doing so,* ALAN *reappears at the bedroom door.*]

ALAN. What are you doing to my dog? You've killed him! Oh, this is the end of everything!

FRANCIS. Alan!

ALAN. You know my name? Who are you? What do you want?

FRANCIS. I ought to know your name by this time. I've been with you long enough.

ALAN. My Goodness! You don't mean . . . ?

FRANCIS. Yes, I'm your faithful doggy. This is how I look in mufti. But you can go on calling me Francis. It's my real name.

ALAN. My God, who are you? You're not . . . ?

FRANCIS [*mimicking* ALAN's *voice*].
"Is the name Sir Francis Crewe,
English, known perhaps to you?"

ALAN. Francis! At last! [*They embrace.*] Oh, this is the happiest moment of my life! Everything's all right now!

FRANCIS. I'm glad you think so.

ALAN. Well, isn't it?

FRANCIS [*nodding towards the bedroom door*]. What about Miss Vipond?

ALAN. Oh, that's all over. I was mad, I think. She's the most utter bitch.

FRANCIS. I could have told you that.

ALAN [*laughing*]. You did try to, didn't you? I say, Francis, I'm most awfully sorry I kicked you.

FRANCIS. That's all right. It was my fault, really. My attempts at dissuasion were somewhat crude. You've no idea what self-control it took not to answer you back, though. You'd have got a shock if the dog had spoken!

ALAN. Yes, shouldn't I? . . . I say, Francis, there's so much I want to ask you, I don't know where to begin! Whatever made you dress up as a dog, at all?

FRANCIS. I'll tell you all about that, but not now. The first question is, what are we going to do?

ALAN. Well . . . go back to Pressan Ambo, of course.
FRANCIS. You really want to?
ALAN. Of course I want to.
FRANCIS. And marry my charming sister?
ALAN. Yes . . . rather!
FRANCIS. You don't sound quite so enthusiastic as you were. Still, a promise is a promise, isn't it? Let's hope it won't be broken. . . . You're longing to be back in Pressan again, I suppose? You know, you may find it rather changed.
ALAN. Rot! Dear old Pressan will never change.
FRANCIS. Places sometimes look different when one comes back to them. . . . However, we'll go there together and you shall judge for yourself.
ALAN. That's ripping! My word, won't they be delighted to see you!
FRANCIS. Yes, I can just picture Hotham's face; streaming with tears of joy. And the dear Vicar.
ALAN. You sound as if you didn't like them much.
FRANCIS. Perhaps I don't.
ALAN. What a queer sort of chap you are, Francis! I can't make you out at all. You're not a bit like I imagined you would be. . . . You must have led a funny sort of life, all these years. Did you often go out by yourself, like last night?
FRANCIS. Not often, no. I had to be very careful. The last few weeks I've been more reckless, because I knew you'd catch me sooner or later. In fact, I was considering whether I oughtn't to reveal myself. It was selfish of me not to, I know; but I've enjoyed our trip so much I didn't want it to end. . . . That reminds me, here are your shoes. I always had to borrow them. You can't wear shoes in this skin, you see.
VOICES OF THE WAITERS *are heard singing, off.*
   For in Nineveh Hotel the most humble guest . . . *etc.*
ALAN. Great God! I quite forgot! Francis, I'm in the most awful fix! They're coming to arrest me for not paying my bill. Whatever shall I do?
FRANCIS. Don't worry. I'd thought of that. Here, get into the dog's skin. I'll manage the rest.

> [*He helps* ALAN *to put on the dog's skin. Enter the* MANAGER, *with* POLICEMEN, WAITERS, *etc.*]

FRANCIS. Waiter, I've lost my way. How do I get to the Roof Garden?
WAITER. Take the lift on the right, sir.
   At the Fifth you alight, sir. [*Bows.*]

MANAGER [*seeing* DOG]. That ugly brute!
  I've an itch in my foot! [*Kicks it.*]
  This is the door, officer.
ALAN [*rubbing himself with his paw, in a low voice to* FRANCIS]. The swine!
FRANCIS. Ha ha! Now you know how it feels!
POLICE SERGEANT [*at bedroom door*]. Open this door
  In the name of the Law! [*Knocks.*]
FRANCIS [*in a low voice to* ALAN]. We'll try and find your two Journalist friends and take them with us to Pressan. They may as well see how this business ends.

> [*Exeunt* FRANCIS *and* ALAN.]
> [*The* MANAGER, WAITERS, POLICEMEN *all stand round the door. The* POLICEMAN *knocks for the second time.*]

CURTAIN

Chorus

So, under the local images your blood has conjured,
We show you man caught in the trap of his terror, destroying himself.
From his favourite pool between the yew-hedge and the roses, it is no fairy-tale his line catches
But grey-white and horrid, the monster of his childhood raises its huge domed forehead
And death moves in to take his inner luck,
Lands on the beaches of his love, like Coghlan's coffin.

Do not speak of a change of heart, meaning five hundred a year and a room of one's own,
As if that were all that is necessary. In these islands alone there are some forty-seven million hearts, each of four chambers:
You cannot avoid the issue by becoming simply a community digger,
O you who prattle about the wonderful Middle Ages: you who expect the millennium after a few trifling adjustments.

Visit from house to house, from country to country: consider the populations
Beneath the communions and the coiffures: discover your image.
Man divided always and restless always: afraid and unable to forgive:
Unable to forgive his parents, or his first voluptuous rectal sins,

Afraid of the clock, afraid of catching his neighbour's cold, afraid of his
    own body,
Desperately anxious about his health and his position: calling upon the
    Universe to justify his existence,
Slovenly in posture and thinking: the greater part of the will devoted
To warding off pain from the water-logged areas,
An isolated bundle of nerve and desire, suffering alone,
Seeing others only in reference to himself: as a long-lost mother or as
    his ideal self at sixteen.

Watch him asleep and waking:
Dreaming of continuous sexual enjoyment or perpetual applause;
Reading of accidents over the breakfast-table, thinking: "This could
    never happen to me."
Reading the reports of trials, flushed at the downfall of a fellow
    creature.
Examine his satisfactions:
Some turn to the time-honoured solutions of sickness and crime: some
    to the latest model of aeroplane or the sport of the moment.
Some to good works, to a mechanical ritual of giving.
Some have adopted an irrefragable system of beliefs or a political
    programme, others have escaped to the ascetic mountains
Or taken refuge in the family circle, among the boys on the bar-stools,
    on the small uncritical islands.

Men will profess devotion to almost anything; to God, to Humanity, to
    Truth, to Beauty: but their first thought on meeting is: "Beware!"
They put their trust in Reason or the Feelings of the Blood, but they
    will not trust a stranger with half-a-crown.
Beware of those with no obvious vices; of the chaste, the non-smoker
    and drinker, the vegetarian:
Beware of those who show no inclination towards making money: there
    are even less innocent forms of power.

Beware of yourself:
Have you not heard your own heart whisper: "I am the nicest person in
    this room"?
Asking to be introduced to someone "real": someone unlike all those
    people over there?

You have wonderful hospitals and a few good schools:
Repent.

The precision of your instruments and the skill of your designers is
    unparalleled:

Unite.

Your knowledge and your power are capable of infinite extension:
Act.

Act III Scene 5

[*The Garden of the Vicarage at Pressan Ambo. The stage decorated, as for a wedding, with streamers, etc. Enter* ALAN, FRANCIS *and the* TWO JOURNALISTS.]

ALAN. Whatever can have happened? There are decorations all down the street.

1ST JOURNALIST. Looks like a wedding to me.

ALAN. Do you think old Mrs Luce has married again? She couldn't have. Won't they get a surprise when we appear.

FRANCIS. Yes, they will.

ALAN. Here are some people coming. Let's see if they guess who you are.

FRANCIS. Not yet. Better wait a bit. Look here. We'll hide behind these bushes. [*To the* JOURNALISTS.] You two can ask a few questions and find out what's happening. Come along, Alan.

> [ALAN *and* FRANCIS *hide. The* TWO JOURNALISTS *retire to the side of the stage. Enter* VILLAGERS.]

A VILLAGER [*putting up decorations*]. You can say what you like. He may be clever but I don't like him. He's got eyes like bootbuttons and flat feet and what's more I don't think she likes him either. Effie says she heard her last night crying her eyes out.

ANOTHER. Still thinking of her beautiful blue-eyed boy I suppose. Well, you can't have everything. He may be common but he knows where to get it.

ANOTHER. Yes, and I shouldn't be surprised if the General's mortgage hadn't something to do with his enthusiasm. As old Horseface says, "Of course he's not quite quite, you know, but my dear, so able and generous, and in these days one is more broadminded, isn't one?"

ANOTHER. The Vicar's delighted too. He's telling everyone that he's promised him a new parish hall. By the way, there hasn't been any news of Alan, has there?

ANOTHER. Of course not. He's found something nice and cosy abroad, you can be sure. And I don't blame him. I wouldn't come back to this dead-alive hole if I were in his shoes.

ALAN [*hidden*]. Well, you're wrong.

FRANCIS [*to* ALAN]. Shut up.
VILLAGERS. What was that? I'm sure I heard voices.
 Where?
 Over there. Perhaps it was tramps.

> [*They start to look. Enter* VILLAGE ORGANIST *before they can find them.*]

VILLAGE ORGANIST [*to* VILLAGERS]. Ah, here you are. I'm so sorry to have kept you waiting. One of the pedals on the organ was sticking and I had to put it right. Here are your copies [*handing out music*]. We'll just run through the words, speaking them first, to make sure you know them before we try the music. Remember: every syllable as distinctly as you can. All together with me.

ALL.   O Day of Joy in happiness abounding
 Streams in the hills with laughter are resounding
 For Pressan is delighted
 To see you thus united.
 Handsome he.
   Lovely she.
 Riches, children, every blessing
 Be to you for your possessing
 Love be round you everywhere
 Happy, Happy, Happy Pair.

V.O. Good. Now we'll try it with the music.
1ST JOURNALIST. Excuse me, sir. We're from *The Thunderbolt* and *The Evening Moon*. Perhaps you'd care to tell us something about your interesting celebrations?
V.O. Certainly. Miss Iris Crewe is being married this afternoon to Mr Rudolph Trunnion-James. I've written a little madrigal for the occasion. Perhaps you would like to hear it?
1ST J. O not just now, thank you. I'm not the music critic, you know.
V.O. Well, in that case if you'll excuse me, we'll be getting along to the church, as time's getting short. The Vicar will be charmed to give you any further details you want, I'm sure.

> [*Exeunt* VILLAGERS *and* ORGANIST. ALAN *and* FRANCIS *come out.*]

ALAN. I don't believe it. Iris wouldn't do a thing like that.
FRANCIS. I'm sorry, Alan, about this.
1ST JOURNALIST. Trunnion-James. Now where have I heard that name before?

2ND J. Sure. He's in with the Shetland Building Society crowd.
1ST J. Not our little National Independent member for Lundy East. Well, well. [*To* ALAN.] Your girl friend's got her head screwed on. Boy, that kid will go a long, long way.
2ND J. And here comes the bride.
ALAN. I'll stop this now.
FRANCIS. Better not, Alan. Wait a little. Come back.

[*They all hide again.*]

2ND J. Well, she doesn't look as if she was going to a school treat.

[*Enter* IRIS *in tears, with* GENERAL *and* GENERAL'S WIFE.]

MRS HOTHAM. Now dear, pull yourself together. It's nearly time for church.
IRIS. I don't want to go. I wish I was dead.
MRS HOTHAM. You mustn't say such naughty things. It will soon be over. [*To* GENERAL.] Ernest, give her a drop from your flask.
GENERAL. Can't understand it. All this fuss. Nerves, I suppose.
MRS HOTHAM [*to* IRIS]. There, there. I understand exactly how you feel. I was just the same before I married the General. Here, use my hanky. And now just a spot of powder on the nose. You look lovely.

[*Enter* VICAR.]

VICAR. Well, I think everything's ready now. I'll go off to the vestry and robe.
IRIS. Alan—why hasn't he come back?
MRS HOTHAM. Now dear, we don't want to go over all that again, do we? You know he won't come back. Besides, you agreed yourself that it would be much better if he didn't, and promised to forget him, didn't you? Rudolph's twice the man he is.
ALAN [*hidden*]. Is he?
IRIS. What's that?
MRS HOTHAM. What's what?
IRIS. I thought I heard something.
MRS HOTHAM. Nonsense, dear. You're overwrought.
VICAR. Well, we'd better be moving.

[*Enter* MILDRED LUCE.]

MILDRED LUCE. Stop!
   O think one moment what you do
   Have you no eyes
   Or have caresses so debauched your judgement

> That life seems splendid as a skivvy's dream?
> Are you so numbed or naughty you dare think
> To order chaos with the common kiss? O look
> Show me one virtue that's not lethal, one vice
> That's not contagious as the itch. Look, look, look,
> Look at your flowers; the sweaty crowds
> That make the beaches stink in the summer
> Or crawl out daily to their dingy labours.
> Look at your great men
> That before their mirrors falsify their faces.
> Well, will you marry and multiply for these
> Blandly give girls and boys an introduction
> To madmen, footpads, murderers and whores,
> The forced commanders of this fraudulent star
> Deliberately create their rosy beauty
> And then watch sorrow like an awful cold
> Making it hideous? Because I know
> My sons were lovely and they died of it
> O that the sun would splutter and go out
> And all bone crumble in the universal frost
> Or that a reef would suddenly rise up
> Out of the cold and infinite abyss
> Our aimless cruising to arrest at last
> And our ship crammed with all its bestial cargo
> Plunge roaring into nothing.

VICAR. Mildred dear, go home and rest. [*To* IRIS.] My dear, I'm so sorry—

ALAN [*emerging*]. Here! I say!

VICAR. I'm so sorry—

ALAN. Stop! You've got to listen to me!

GENERAL. Confound it, sir! Can't you hear the Vicar is speaking? Who the devil are you?

ALAN. Alan Norman. Iris, what does this mean?

IRIS. O Alan—

MRS HOTHAM. Remember your promise, dear.

ALAN. Iris, why didn't you wait?

IRIS. O go away. I hate you all. I hate you!

GENERAL [*to* ALAN]. And why the blazes have you come back?

ALAN. Because I've found Francis. Francis! Come here!

[*Huge sensation.* FRANCIS *emerges from hiding.*]

VICAR AND GENERAL [*together: equally dismayed*]. Sir Francis! Upon my soul!
FRANCIS. Hullo, General. Fight back those unmanly tears. Vicar, you needn't kiss me if you don't want to. [*Looking round.*] Well, isn't anybody pleased to see me?
GENERAL. And where do you come from?
FRANCIS. Look. [*Shows his skin.*]
ALL. What! The Dog! You were the Dog!
FRANCIS. Yes, I am, or rather was, the Dog, and here you all are, looking extremely uncomfortable—as well you may, considering that you know I've had a dog's-eye view of you for the last ten years.

At first I only intended to keep my new shape for a week or two but after the first six months I didn't really want to come back. You see, I had begun to regard you in a new light. I was fascinated and horrified by you all. I thought such obscene, cruel, hypocritical, mean, vulgar creatures had never existed before in the history of the planet and that it was my peculiar duty to record what you were like. I began to keep a diary. As a dog I learnt for the first time with what a mixture of fear, bullying and condescending kindness you treat those you consider your inferiors, but whom you depend on for your pleasures. It's an awful shock to start seeing people from underneath.

The diary became my greatest friend. I worked away at it like a scientist, polishing, punctuating, searching for the exact epithet, devoting months and even years to each one of you, noting every gesture, every intonation. I even managed to take photographs to illustrate my records, and very remarkable some of them are.

And then slowly, the horror and the pseudo-scientific interest began to wear off. I began to feel that I had been foolishly wasting my time. Wasn't it life itself I was afraid of, hiding in my dogskin? I think that soon I should have gone away anyhow. But as it happened, Alan Norman was chosen. I'd always liked him, and so I took the opportunity of leaving you when I did.

And now since I've been away from you, I've come to understand you better. I don't hate you any more. You are significant but not in the way I used to imagine.

You are not the extraordinary monsters I thought. You are not individually important. You are just units in an immense army; and most of you would probably die without knowing either what your leaders are really fighting for or even that you are fighting at all. That is why I have come back. That ignorance at least I can do something to remove. I can't dictate to you what to do and I don't want to either. I can only try to show you what you are doing and so force you to choose. For choice is what you are all afraid of. Every technical invention, every advance of knowledge, has slowly eaten away your old dependence on nature. The life of the peasant whose behaviour was largely regulated by the seasons and the soil is over for ever. You can grow wheat in winter and make the fields barren in June. Whether you visit New York next week or speak with a friend in Hammerfest before dinner is cooked depends now on nothing but your own wish. That is what terrifies you. "Anything", you cry, "anything for the old feeling of security and harmony; if nature won't give it, give us a dictator, an authority who will take the responsibility of thinking and planning off our shoulders." Well, it is too late. You were already separated from nature before civilisation began and you can no more retrace history than the perturbed adolescent can re-enter his mother's womb. If as a whole you are unpleasant, you are unpleasant like an invalid. You are fighting your own nature, which is to learn and to choose. Fear of growth is making you ill.

VICAR. Don't listen to him. He is trying to destroy religion. Satan will destroy us all.

FRANCIS. You, Vicar, for example, speaking Sunday after Sunday about the good life, telling us to love God and each other and all our troubles will be solved. Why is it you will not lift a finger to destroy a social system in which one man can only succeed at the expense of injury to another? Sorrows, poverties, temptations are sent to try us, you say. Perhaps. Is that any excuse for refusing to reduce them. To send a liner into an iceberg-infested sea, equipped with only one lifeboat, may afford a splendid test of self-sacrifice but we should accuse the owners of criminal negligence. Your preaching voice betrays you. You do not speak with the only authority there is, the authority of experience. Your faith in a loving God is not real to you, like your feeling that man is evil. Goodness and happiness are not real to you, or you would know that when people are happy they are good, and that self-interest as a motive is the refuge of the miserable. They are not real to you as your sense of guilt is real. Only that is as real to you as the early gothic work in your church and this beautiful ivy-covered vicarage. Happiness is not real to you, only comforts. That is why you are afraid of losing them, for no one gives up what is real to them for what is not.

GENERAL. Insolent young puppy. He wants a good hiding. You've got to have law and order. It's common sense.

FRANCIS. And you, General, what are you fighting for? Once wealth was real. The world did not produce enough to go round and there was necessarily a struggle over the sharing of it. But now it is possible for everyone to have all they can require. What are you afraid of, then? This. You've lost belief in yourself. There will always be clever and stupid people, successes and failures in the world, you say. You can't change human nature. Men are not equal. Precisely. You are terrified that perhaps after all you are not a superior person. Take away the visible signs of superiority, take away Conyers Hall and the peacocks, or let everybody else have them, and is there anything about Mrs Hotham that will still command respect? Suppose no one was to call you Sir, would you still exist as a personality? That is the question you dare not answer.

MILDRED LUCE. Traitor! I hear the infamy before you say it. That Germans should be loved. God strike you dumb!

FRANCIS. Yes, Mrs Luce. That too. Your grievance is just, but it is neither what Pressan thinks it is nor what you dare not admit to yourself. When I stayed with you as a dog (and may I take this opportunity of thanking you. You were kinder and more understanding than any of the others), when I stayed with you, I thought the photographs on your bureau seemed vaguely familiar and one day when you were away, I took them to the photographer whose name was on them. He identified them at once as two young actors who had some success in juvenile leads about thirty years ago. Later I paid a visit to the village where you lived before you came to Pressan and discovered something else. You lived at home helping your mother with the house. She was poor and could not afford a maid. Were you ever married, I asked. No, they said, but there was talk at one time of an engagement to a young German cavalry officer. But you hadn't the heart to leave your mother alone.

A doctor would say you hate the Germans because you dare not hate your mother and he would be mistaken. It is foolish and neurotic to hate anybody. What you really hate is a social system in which love is controlled by money. Won't you help us to destroy it?

MRS HOTHAM. Mildred, dear, do you hear what he's saying? Answer him.

GENERAL. He's trampling the honour of your dead boys in the mud.

VICAR. He's insulting your mother. He should be stopped.

SEVERAL VOICES. Answer him.

Make him ashamed of himself.

Tell him he's a liar.

MRS HOTHAM. You know what people will say, don't you, dear? As a matter of fact, I'd often wondered about those photographs myself. You poor thing.

MILDRED [*to* FRANCIS]. You beast! [*Stabs him with a hat-pin; suddenly appalled.*] O Ticker, what have I done? [*Starts screaming.*]

GENERAL [*taking command of the situation*]. Don't let the ladies see. [*To* VICAR.] Take Mrs Luce home and get the doctor to her and bring him on here at once.

VICAR. How is he, General?

GENERAL. Sh. [*To* MRS HOTHAM.] My dear, take the others indoors at once. [*To* JOURNALISTS.] You two guard the gate, please, and don't let anyone in. I'm going to get the police.

[JOURNALISTS *to side of stage. The others exeunt, leaving* ALAN *alone with* FRANCIS.]

ALAN. Francis, are you badly hurt?

FRANCIS. Alan, my friend
    My life is now at end
    Grieve not for me at all
    My life is nothing especial
    Only remember when I am gone
    All we have seen done
    All we have heard said
    Remember when I am dead
    The plain and the extraordinary
    On our devious journey
    Remember. No longer in ignorance
    Of its significance
    But through knowledge of each fact
    Able more clearly to act
    Man's history to fulfill
    And since it is impossible
    In Pressan to stay
    Slip quickly away
    Without their knowing
    That you are going
    And wherever circumstance
    May permit you residence
    Long may you live
    Your powers to give
    In every season
    For justice and for reason.

ALAN. Wait till the police come. I'll tell them everything.
FRANCIS. No, do as I say
    And go away
    For here is nothing you
    Can usefully do
    Go now and do not wait
    Go before it is too late. [*Dies.*]
ALAN. Francis! Francis!

SEMI-CHORUS I. Love, loath to enter
    The suffering winter
    Still willing to rejoice
    With the unbroken voice
    At the precocious charm
    Blithe in the dream
    Afraid to wake, afraid
    To doubt one term
    Of summer's perfect fraud,
    Enter and suffer
    Within the quarrel
    Be most at home,
    Among the sterile prove
    Your vigours, love.

SEMI-CHORUS II. Mourn not for these; these are ghosts who chose their pain,
    Mourn rather for yourselves; and your inability to make up your minds
    Whose hours of self-hatred and contempt were all your majesty and crisis,
    Choose therefore that you may recover: both your charity and your place
    Determining not this that we have lately witnessed: but another country
    Where grace may grow outward and be given praise
    Beauty and virtue be vivid there.

SEMI-CHORUS I. Where time flows on as chalk stream clear
    And lovers by themselves forgiven
    The whole dream genuine, the charm mature
    Walk in the great and general light
    In their delight a part of heaven
    Its furniture and choir.

CHORUS. To each his need: from each his power.

[ALAN *gets up and goes down through the audience.*]

1ST JOURNALIST. Here, where are you off to?
ALAN. Tell them I'm gone and won't be back.
2ND JOURNALIST. O.K. Come up and see us sometime.

[*Exit* ALAN.]
[*Enter* VICAR *and* GENERAL.]

GENERAL. The sergeant's just coming. Where's the doctor?
VICAR. He's seeing Mildred. He'll be along in a moment.
GENERAL [*looking at* FRANCIS]. Well, there's not much for him to do.
VICAR. Dead? Poor poor Mildred. What'll happen to her?
GENERAL. She'll have to be certified after this, of course. You realise that.
VICAR. Yes. But what are we going to say to the police?
GENERAL. Oh, they'll understand. Mildred, you know. Overwrought.
VICAR. But what will Alan say? Where is he?
JOURNALISTS. Mr Norman asked us to say that he's gone and won't be back.
[*Singing*.]   He won't be back
                 He won't be back
     He's chasing Hannah down the railroad track.
                 They're starting soon
                 Their honeymoon
     In an enormous yellow gas balloon.
GENERAL. Damned good job too. Confound his impudence, coming back like that.

[*Enter* GENERAL'S WIFE.]

MRS HOTHAM. I've left Cook with Iris. What's happened?
VICAR. Dear, O dear. In Pressan of all places. It's like a nightmare. It can't have happened.
JOURNALISTS [*coming forward; as they talk they sew* FRANCIS *up again into his dogskin*]. You're quite right, sir. It hasn't happened.
VICAR. Hasn't happened? But—
2ND JOURNALIST. I entirely agree with my colleague. Dozens of things occur every day, curious, embarrassing, shocking incidents: but how few of them happen! The Press disregards them: therefore they cannot have taken place! The Press is an Artist: It has a certain picture to paint. Whatever fails to harmonise with that picture, it discards; regretfully perhaps, but firmly.

1st Journalist. The Press has no use for the incident you believe yourselves to have just witnessed. It has no place in our scale of values. Long-lost Baronets do not disguise themselves as dogs; or at any rate, only for erotic reasons. The behaviour of Sir Francis Crewe falls into no artistic category which we recognize: therefore it cannot be represented in our picture of the day's events.

2nd Journalist. And since all events are recorded by the Press, what the Press does not record cannot be an event.

[*As they work, it dawns on the others what they are doing.*]
[*Enter* Police Sergeant.]

Sergeant. Now what's all this?

Vicar. I'm so sorry to have bothered you, Sergeant, but I thought you ought to know. Something very disagreeable has happened. This dog was wandering about the garden and savagely attacked Mrs Luce. She defended herself with a hat-pin and killed it.

Sergeant. Hm. I'd like a word with Mrs Luce.

Vicar. I'm afraid that's impossible. She can't see anyone just now. She's in a state of complete nervous prostration.

Sergeant. Well. Does anyone know who this animal belongs to? No collar or anything. It strikes me I've seen it before somewhere. I've got it. It's uncommonly like the one Mr Norman took with him. He hasn't come back, has he?

Vicar. Of course not, Sergeant. But there must be a lot of dogs like that one. It's a common breed you know.

Alan's Voice [*from the back of the auditorium*]. Liar!

Sergeant. Hi. Who was that?

General. I heard nothing. Did you, Vicar?

Vicar. No, no. Must have been a bird.

[*Enter* Doctor.]

Doctor. Now what's all this about a body and Francis. I've just seen Luce. The old girl's raving. Always was.

Vicar. She must have been too upset to know what she was saying. She was attacked by this dog.

Doctor. Well, that settles it. I won't have it. The woman's a public menace. I'll get her certified. She ought to have been long ago.

Vicar. Poor Mildred. She had such a terrible time in the war. Her sons, you know. You will find her a really good nursing home, where they treat them properly, won't you?

Doctor. Who's going to pay for it? She hasn't got a bean.

VICAR. I'm sure the General and I—
GENERAL. Of course. Delighted. Do anything I can. Anything you think proper, Doctor.
DOCTOR. Well then, I'll arrange it.
VICAR [*looking at watch*]. Good gracious. We're ten minutes late for the wedding already. The bridegroom will be in a fever.

> [*Enter* IRIS, *appearing dazed. The others rush to support her.*]

IRIS. Where's Alan?
MRS HOTHAM. Alan? What do you mean, dear? He's been away a long time and that's all over.
IRIS. But he found Francis.
MRS HOTTAM. Oh, no dear. What can have put that idea into your silly little head? [*Aside to* GENERAL.] Don't let her see it. [*To* IRIS.] You must have had a bad dream. But you're awake now. Everything's going to be alright. You're among friends.
JOURNALISTS [*producing camera*]. Allow me. Thank you. If you will be so kind . . .
MRS HOTHAM. Look, dear. The photographers.
JOURNALISTS [*to* IRIS]. A little brighter, please.
MRS HOTHAM. Smile, darling.
VICAR. Let the villagers in. Better have the fireworks now on the way to church. Music, quickly.

> [*The* VILLAGERS *rush in. Fireworks go off. Balloons rise. Bells toll.* IRIS *is borne off to church.*]

ALL [*singing*]. O Day of Joy in happiness abounding
    Streams through the hills with laughter are resounding
    For Pressan is delighted
    To see you thus united.
    Handsome he.
        Lovely she.
    Riches, children, every blessing
    Be to you for your possessing
    Love be round you everywhere
    Happy, Happy, Happy Pair.

CURTAIN

The Ascent of F 6

A Tragedy in Two Acts

BY W. H. AUDEN AND
CHRISTOPHER ISHERWOOD

[1936]

TO
JOHN BICKNELL AUDEN

Ghosts whom Honour never paid,
In the foolish battle made,
Wandering through the stricken grove
Pluck the bitter herb of Love.

CHARACTERS
in the order of their appearance

Michael Forsyth Ransom

Sir James Ransom
his twin brother

Lady Isabel Welwyn

General Dellaby-Couch

Lord Stagmantle

David Gunn

Ian Shawcross

Edward Lamp

Doctor Thomas Williams

Mrs Ransom
mother of Michael and James

The Abbot

Mr A.	Announcer
Mrs A.	Monks

Act I Scene 1

[*The Summit of the Pillar Rock, above Wastdale. Late afternoon.*]

[MICHAEL RANSOM *is seated, reading a pocket volume of Dante.*]

RANSOM [*reads*]. " 'O brothers!' I said, 'who through a hundred thousand dangers have reached the West, deny not, to this brief vigil of your senses that remains, experience of the unpeopled world behind the Sun. Consider your origin: ye were not formed to live like brutes, but to follow virtue and knowledge.' " [*Putting down the book.*] Virtue and Knowledge! One can picture Ulysses' audience: a crook speaking to crooks. Seedy adventurers, of whose expensive education nothing remained but a few grammatical tags and certain gestures of the head; refugees from the consequences of vice or eccentric and conceited opinions; natural murderers whom a peaceful winter had reduced to palsied wrecks; the ugly and cowardly who foresaw in a virgin land an era of unlimited and effortless indulgence; teachers without pupils, tormentors without victims, parasites without hosts, lunatic missionaries, orphans.

And glad they must have been to believe it, during the long uneventful voyage westward: yes, even up to the very end, when the last deceptions were choked from each in turn by the strangling Atlantic. Who was Dante—to whom the Universe was peopled only by his aristocratic Italian acquaintances and a few classical literary characters, the fruit of an exile's reading—who was Dante, to speak of Virtue and Knowledge? It was not Virtue those lips, which involuntary privation had made so bitter, could pray for; it was not Knowledge; it was Power. Power to exact for every snub, every headache, every unfallen beauty, an absolute revenge; with a stroke of the pen to make a neighbour's vineyard a lake of fire and to create in his private desert the austere music of the angels or the happy extravagance of a fair. Friends whom the world honours shall lament their eternal losses in the profoundest of crevasses, while he on the green mountains converses gently with his unapproachable love.

Virtue. Knowledge. We have heard these words before; and we shall hear them again—during the nursery luncheon, on the prize-giving afternoon, in the quack advertisement, at the conference of generals or industrial captains: justifying every baseness and excusing every failure, comforting the stilted schoolboy lives, charming the wax-like and baroque, inflaming the obstinate and the odd and all those hungry and cheerful persons whom the holiday now discharges into these lake-filled valleys radiating from the rocky hub on which I sit.

Beyond the Isle of Man, behind the towers of Peel Castle, the sun slides now towards the creasing sea; and it is into a Wastwater utterly in shadow that the screes now make their unhalting plunge. Along the lake shores lovers pace, each wrapped in a disturbing and estranging vision. In the white house among the pines coffee will be drunk, there will be talk of art at the week-end. Under I cannot tell how many of these green slate roofs, the stupid peasants are making their stupid children.

Nevertheless, let me receive such vigour as the impassive embraces of this sullen rock afford, from which no mastery can elicit a gratifying response, nor defeat sighs capable of despairing misinterpretation. Here is no knowledge, no communication, no possession; nothing that a bishop could justify, a stockbroker purchase or an elderly scientist devote years to explaining—only the voluntary homage paid by the living to the unqualified and dangerous dead. Let me pay it, then; pay it now, before I descend to the valley and all its varieties of desperation: the calculations of shopkeepers under the gas-flares and the destructive idleness of the soldier; the governess in the dead of night giving the Universe nought for behaviour and the abandonment of the prophet to the merciless curiosity of a demon; the plotting of diseases to establish an epoch of international justice and the struggle of beauty to master and transform the most recalcitrant features; the web of guilt that prisons every upright person and all those thousands of thoughtless jailers from whom Life pants to be delivered—myself not least; all swept and driven by the possessive incompetent fury and the disbelief. O, happy the foetus that miscarries and the frozen idiot that cannot cry "Mama"! Happy those run over in the street to-day or drowned at sea, or sure of death to-morrow from incurable diseases! They cannot be made a party to the general fiasco. For of that growth which in maturity had seemed eternal it is now no tint of thought or feeling that has tarnished, but the great ordered flower itself is withering; its life-blood dwindled to an unimportant trickle, stands under heaven now a fright and ruin, only to crows and larvae a gracious refuge. . . .

VOICE OF SHAWCROSS [*from below*]. Where are you, M.F.?

VOICE OF GUNN. When you've finished saying your prayers, we should like to go down!

VOICE OF SHAWCROSS. It'll be dark soon, if we don't make a start.

RANSOM [*shouting back*]. All right! I'm coming!

[*He begins to descend as the* CURTAIN *falls.*]

[*The* STAGE-BOX, *right, is illuminated.* MRS A. *is discovered cooking.*]

MRS A. Evening. A slick and unctuous Time
    Has sold us yet another shop-soiled day,
    Patently rusty, not even in a gaudy box.
    I have dusted the six small rooms:
    The parlour, once the magnificent image of my freedom,
    And the bedroom, which once held for me
    The mysterious languors of Egypt and the terrifying Indias.
    The delivery-vans have paid their brief impersonal visits.
    I have eaten a scrappy lunch from a plate on my knee.
    I have spoken with acquaintances in the Stores;
    Under our treble gossip heard the menacing throb of our hearts
    As I hear them now, as all of us hear them,
    Standing at our stoves in these villas, expecting our husbands:
    The drums of an enormous and routed army,
    Throbbing raggedly, fitfully, scatteredly, madly.
    We are lost. We are lost.

[*Enter* MR A. *from work.*]

MR A. Has anything happened?
MRS A.   What should happen?
    The cat has died at Ivy Dene,
    The Crowthers' pimply son has passed Matric,
    St Neots has put up light blue curtains,
    Frankie is walking out with Winnie
    And Georgie loves himself. What should happen?
    Nothing that matters will ever happen.
MR A. No, nothing that matters will ever happen;
    Nothing you'd want to put in a book;
    Nothing to tell to impress your friends—
    The old old story that never ends:
    The eight o'clock train, the customary place,
    Holding the paper in front of your face,
    The public stairs, the glass swing-door,
    The peg for your hat, the linoleum floor,
    The office stool and the office jokes
    And the fear in your ribs that slyly pokes:
    Are they satisfied with you?
    Nothing interesting to do,
    Nothing interesting to say,
    Nothing remarkable in any way;
    Then the journey home again

> In the hot suburban train
> To the tawdry new estate,
> Crumpled, grubby, dazed and late:
> Home to supper and to bed.
> Shall we be like this when we are dead?

Mrs A. It's time for the news, John. Turn on the wireless.

Mr A. I'm sick of the news. All you can hear
> Is politics, politics everywhere:
> Talk in Westminster, talk at Geneva, talk in the lobbies and talk on the throne;
> Talk about treaties, talk about honour, mad dogs quarrelling over a bone.
> What have they ever done, I ask you? What are they ever likely to do
> To make life easier, make life happier? What have they done for me or for you?

Mrs A. Smiling at all the photographers, smoking, walking in top hats down by the lake,
> Treating the people as if they were pigeons, giving the crumbs and keeping the cake.
> When will they notice us? When will they flatter us? When will they help us? When there's a war!
> Then they will ask for our children and kill them; sympathise deeply and ask for some more.

Mr A. Night after night we have listened to the ignoble news.

Mrs A. We have heard
> The glib justification of the sorry act.

Mr A. The frantic washing of the grimy fact.

Mrs A. But nothing to bring a smile to the face.

Mr A. Nothing to make us proud of our race.

Mrs A. Nothing we should have been glad to have done
> In a dream, or would wish for an only son.

Mr A. Nothing to take us out of ourselves,
> Out of the oppression of this city,
> This abstract civic space imposed upon the fields,
> Destroying that tie with the nearest which in Nature rules.

Mrs A. Where we are unable to lose sight of the fruits of our extraordinary industry.

Mr A. And everything is emphatically provided:
> The Dial Exchange and the voice of the lift.
> We must accept them all and there is no one to thank.

Mrs A. Give us something to be thankful for.

Mr A. Give it quickly.
   I have read "Too Late" in the hands of the office clock.
Mrs A. I have received singular warnings:
   In the eyes of the beggar I have experienced the earthquake and the simoom.
Mr A. Sitting in the crowded restaurant, I have overheard the confabulations of weasels.
Mrs A. Give us something to live for. We have waited too long.

[*The* STAGE-BOX *is darkened.*]

Act I Scene 2

[Sir James Ransom's *room at the Colonial Office. On the wall at the back of the stage, hangs a large boldly-printed map showing British Sudoland and Ostnian Sudoland, coloured respectively pink and blue. The frontier between the two colonies is formed by a chain of mountains: one peak, prominently marked* F 6, *is ringed with a red circle to emphasise its importance.*]

[*At a table covered with papers, maps and books of reference are seated, from L. to R.,* Lord Stagmantle, Sir James Ransom, General Dellaby-Couch *and* Lady Isabel Welwyn.]

[*As the curtain rises,* James *lays down a document from which he has been reading aloud to the others.*]

James. That, briefly, is the position. I think you'll all agree with me that it is deplorable.
Isabel. But surely, surely the report exaggerates? My poor darling Sudoland—it's still like home to me, you know! No, I simply can't believe it!
James. We all appreciate your feelings, Lady Isabel. They are most natural. Unfortunately I have reason to believe that this report, so far from exaggerating, may even underestimate the gravity of the situation.... From other sources—not official, it is true, but as a rule absolutely reliable—we hear that the whole southern province is in a state of uproar. Government stores have been burnt, British officers have been attacked. In a few hill stations, the women of the European settlements have been grossly insulted—
Isabel. The cowardly fiends! How they can *dare*! In my Father's time—
General. In your Father's time, Lady Isabel, a British Governor was required to rule, not to coddle a native population according to the

sentimental notions of a gang of home-bred politicians. The Sudoese hillman has not changed since your Father's day: take him for what he is, he's a fine fellow. He's a man and he expects to be ruled by men. He understands strength and he respects it. He despises weakness and he takes advantage of it. Show him the business end of a machine-gun and he'll—

JAMES [*acidly*]. I think, General, you can hardly complain that the Government of which I am a member shows any lack of respect for your great practical experience in administration. Otherwise you would not have been invited to attend this conference to-day. But I should like to suggest that, in your wholesale condemnation of politicians, you are apt to forget that we are only the servants of the Public. Public opinion has changed greatly, during the last twenty years, with regard to the native populations of the Empire. There have been unfortunate incidents which unscrupulous party agitators have not hesitated to misrepresent. . . . To take your own case, that most regrettable *contretemps* at Bolo-Bolo. . . .

ISABEL. Really, Sir James, is it necessary, at a time like this, to stoop to personalities?

JAMES [*smoothly*]. My dear Lady Isabel, I'm sure I had no intention of hurting the General's feelings. General, please accept my apologies. I only wished to remind you—not, alas, that any of us need reminding—how grossly a valued public servant can be maligned in the performance of a painful duty by the venom of the popular press—

STAGMANTLE [*beginning to laugh wheezily*]. *British General Butchers Unarmed Mob! Children Massacred In Mothers' Arms! Murder Stains The Jack!*

JAMES [*hastily*]. Yes, yes. . . . The nauseating clichés of gutter socialism—

STAGMANTLE. Socialism my foot! Why, that's out of the *Evening Moon*! Splashed it all over the front page—nearly doubled our sales, that week! No offence, General. We were out to smash the Labour Government, you know: and, by God, we did! Your little stunt came in handy: any stick's good enough to beat a dog with, you know! Ha, ha, ha!

ISABEL. Of all the utterly low and contemptible things I ever heard . . .

JAMES [*hastily intervening*]. As Lord Stagmantle quite rightly observes, the tactical problems raised by a great democratic electorate are exceedingly complex. One must try to see things in perspective. . . . I'm sure nobody doubts Lord Stagmantle's loyalty in this present crisis. Had it not been for his assistance in presenting the events of the last month to the public in their true proportions—

STAGMANTLE. Look here, Ransom; that's just what I came to tell you to-day. We can't keep this up for ever, you know. *The Thunderbolt* has been featuring the Sudoland revolts now for a week or more. How much longer do you expect us to play hush-hush? It's beginning to affect our circulation already. You've got to do something, quick.

ISABEL. But surely, Lord Stagmantle, all this suppression and misrepresentation of facts is a very mistaken policy? Why can't you have more courage? Why not let the Public judge for itself? I should have thought that the truth—

STAGMANTLE. The truth, Lady Isabel, is that the natives of British Sudoland would like us to go to hell—pardon my language—and stay there. The truth is that we've got fifty millions invested in the country and we don't intend to budge—not if we have to shoot every nigger from one end of the land to the other. The truth is that we're under-garrisoned and under-policed and that we're in a blue funk that the Ostnians will come over the frontier and drive us into the sea. Already, they've spent thousands on propaganda among our natives, promising reforms which neither they nor we nor any other colonial power could ever carry out. This revolt is the result. . . . There's the truth for you: and you want me to tell that to the Public! What do you take me for—a bolshevik?

JAMES. Lord Stagmantle is perfectly right: though, with his characteristic flair for essentials, he over-simplifies the situation, perhaps, a little. . . . He asks me to do something. I shall not disappoint him. I did not call this meeting merely in order to alarm you. His Majesty's Government has a plan. [*He rises and points dramatically to the map on the wall, indicating* F 6.] The key to the problem lies there!

ISABEL. Why, but that's the Haunted Mountain! I used to be able to see it from my bedroom window at the Residency, when the weather was clear. . . . Let me think, now, what did the natives call it?

JAMES. The mountain has, I understand, many local names; most of them unpronounceable. The survey refers to it simply as F 6.

STAGMANTLE. A haunted mountain, eh? What's the story in it?

JAMES. Merely that the mountain is said to be haunted by a guardian demon. For this reason, no native will set foot upon it. As you will notice, it stands exactly on the frontier line. Both Ostnia and ourselves claim it; but, up to the present, no European has ever visited the district at all.

ISABEL. I remember, when I was a little girl, being afraid that the demon would come and carry me away with him to the top! Aren't children absurd?

GENERAL. May I ask if we came here this morning to discuss fairy-tales?

JAMES. A fairy-tale, General, is significant according to the number of people who believe in it. This one is credited by several millions of natives on both sides of the frontier. . . . Also, the legend has lately developed a sequel which may appeal more strongly to your imagination: The natives have begun telling each other that the white man who first reaches the summit of F 6, will be lord over *both* the Sudolands, with his descendants, for a thousand years.

STAGMANTLE. Aha, so that's their little game! The Ostnians started this yarn, of course?

JAMES. You are very quick to follow me, Lord Stagmantle. And perfectly correct. Yes, the Ostnian agents have been propagating this story for the past six months. We've traced it right down into the plains.

GENERAL. But, Ransom, you don't seriously suggest that the Ostnians expect to gain anything by spreading this absurd nonsense? The hillmen may believe them, I admit—the Sudoese are credulous beggars—but, hang it all, what good can it do Ostnia? None whatever. If you ask me, this is just another Ostnian bluff. Bluffing's their strong suit.

JAMES. I wish I could agree with you, General. But this morning this telegram reached us, through the Intelligence. [*Reads.*] Expedition under Blavek left Ostnia for Ostnian Sudoland yesterday great secrecy intending attempt ascent of F 6.

ISABEL. Monstrous!

GENERAL. The beggars are mad as coots!

STAGMANTLE. Not so mad as you may think, General. I ought to know something about propaganda stunts: this is one of the best I ever struck. If the Ostnians get to the top of F 6, your natives are going to make big trouble. Whether you like it or not, you'll have to start shooting. And Ostnia will intervene, in the name of the poor oppressed subject races. They'll have world opinion on their side, into the bargain. . . . You're in a cleft stick.

ISABEL. Can't we send a cruiser to stop this expedition?

STAGMANTLE. Certainly. If you care to start a European war.

GENERAL. At any rate, these chaps will never reach the summit.

JAMES. We can't be too sure of that, I'm afraid There's a great deal at stake.

ISABEL. You sit here calmly and say so! Oh, if only I were a man! What are you going to *do*?

JAMES. His Majesty's Government proposes to send an expedition to Sudoland without delay.

ISABEL. Oh, good! Good!

STAGMANTLE. Now you're talking!

GENERAL. Never heard such damned tomfoolery in all my life!

STAGMANTLE. I must congratulate you, Ransom. You're on to a big thing—a big thing for all of us! *The Evening Moon* will subscribe two thousand to the funds of the expedition ...

JAMES [*shaking hands with him*]. I knew we could rely on your public spirit, Lord Stagmantle!

STAGMANTLE. ... provided, of course, that we get the exclusive rights—pictures, film, lecture-tours, story. We can discuss details later. ...

JAMES [*rather taken aback*]. Er, yes, quite so, of course—

ISABEL. And now, there's not a moment to be lost! We must think quickly: who are you going to send? How will you find the right man to lead them?

JAMES. I am happy to say that I have found him already.

ISABEL. You've found him! Oh, Sir James, I think you're wonderful! Who is he?

JAMES. My brother.

ISABEL. You have a brother! And we never even knew!

JAMES. My brother Michael is considered, by competent experts, to be one of the best climbers in this country.

ISABEL. How I should adore to meet him—the man who can save Sudoland!

JAMES. We'll go to him at once. My car is waiting. [*To* GENERAL *and* STAGMANTLE.] You'll come with us, I hope?

GENERAL. I refuse to be a party to this wild goose chase. When you have ceased to occupy yourselves with demons and need some serious advice, you will find me at my club. Good morning.

ISABEL. Oh, General!

[*The* GENERAL, *taking no notice, goes out.*]

STAGMANTLE. Never mind him, Lady Isabel. ... A remarkable old gentleman, but conservative: no vision. He'll come round to the idea in time. ... [*Rubbing his hands gleefully.*] Well, Ransom, let's see this brother of yours! I'll write the interview myself! By George, what a day for the *Evening Moon*!

ISABEL [*reprovingly*]. What a day for *England*, Lord Stagmantle!

STAGMANTLE. Oh, England—yes, quite so, of course. ... [*Looking up at map.*] The Ascent of F 6!

[ALL *three of them stand regarding the map in reverent silence as the—*]

CURTAIN FALLS

[*The* STAGE-BOXES, *left and right, are illuminated. In the right* BOX, MR A. *sits listening to the radio* ANNOUNCER, *who speaks from the* BOX *on the left.*]

ANNOUNCER. If you drink coffee for breakfast, you will be familiar with Sudoland as the name of one of the most delicious brands in the world, said by connoisseurs to be equal even to Blue Mountain and only half the price. But, unless you have a brother or a nephew there, I don't expect you know much more about this beautiful and exciting country. It is about as big as Ireland and embraces a wide variety of scenery and climate, from the moist hot river-plains in the north to the magnificent escarpment of mountains on the southern border. The natives are delightful people, of wonderful physique and very humorous and artistic. Their villages consist of mud huts and they live very simply, chiefly on boiled bamboo shoots, which they call KHA. Most of them are employed on the coffee estates, where they make excellent workmen. You may have read recently, in some of the papers, of riots in Sudoland, but from personal experience I can tell you that these stories have been grossly exaggerated. They were confined to a very small section of irresponsibles egged on by foreign agitators. Hospitals, clinics and schools have done much to raise the standard of personal hygiene and education among the Sudoese and the vast majority are happy and contented.

[*At this point*, MRS A. *enters the* STAGE-BOX, *right, bringing coffee.*]

If ever I make enough money to retire from journalism, it is to a small hill-station in Sudoland called Fort George that I should like to go, to spend the evening of my days. I have knocked about the world a good deal and seen most of the famous views, but never have I seen anything to compare with the one you get from the English Cemetery there. From this point you see the whole mountain range which culminates in that terrifying fang of rock and ice called so prosaically on our maps "F 6", but in the native tongue "Chormopuloda"—that is, the Haunted Mountain. There are many legends about this mountain and the troll who lives on the summit and devours all human beings who dare approach it. No Europeans have, so far, ventured into this region, which is barren to a degree and inhabited only by monks who resent foreigners. These monks practise a mysterious cult which is believed to be descended from the religion of Ancient Egypt; and there are wonderful tales current of their mystical and psychic powers. Be that as it may, I do not think it likely that it will be long before our young climbers will discover a new ground for their sport, offering more magnificent opportunities for their skill and their love of nature, than even those afforded by the Alps or the Himalayas. . . . [*Exit.*]

Mrs A. It's all very well for him, he can travel.

Mr A. Cousin Bertie's boy was there;
Poor lad, he had to come home last year:
They've reduced the staff on his coffee estate.
He said that the people and country were great.

Mrs A. Why do you never take me abroad?

Mr A. Darling, you know that we can't afford . . .

Mrs A. Afford! It's always the same excuse—
Money, money!

Mr A.   Dear, what's the use
Of talking like this?

Mrs A.   You don't really care;
If you did, we shouldn't be here.
Why don't you do something, something that pays;
Not be a clerk to the end of your days?
A dreary little clerk on a dreary little screw—
Can't you find something proper to do?
But you don't care, it's the same to you
Whether I live or whether I die.
I wish I were dead!

Mr A.   Mary, don't cry!
You never know, perhaps one day
Better luck will come our way:
It might be to-morrow. You wait and see.
But, whenever it happens, we'll go on the spree!
From the first-class gilt saloon of channel-steamer we shall peer,
While the cliffs of Dover vanish and the Calais flats appear,
Land there, take the fastest train, have dinner in the dining-car,
Through the evening rush to Paris, where the ladies' dresses are.
Nothing your most daring whisper prayed for in the night alone—
Evening frocks and shoes and jewels; you shall have them for your own.
Rome and Munich for the opera; Mürren for the winter sports;
See the relics of crusaders in the grey Dalmatian ports;
Climb the pyramids in Egypt; walk in Versailles' ordered parks;
Sail in gondolas at Venice; feed the pigeons at St Mark's. . . .

Mrs A. O, what's the use of your pretending?
As if life had a chance of mending!
There will be nothing to remember

But the fortnight in August or early September,
The boarding-house food, the boarding-house faces,
The rain-spoilt picnics in the windswept places,
The camera lost and the suspicion,
The failure in the putting-competition,
The silly performance on the pier—
And it's going to happen again next year!

M<small>R</small> A. Mary!

M<small>RS</small> A.   Don't touch me! Go away! Do you hear?

       [*She bursts into tears; he shrugs his shoulders and goes out, slamming the door. The* BOX *is darkened.*]

Act I Scene 3

[*Parlour of a public house in the Lake District. Shabby late Victorian furniture. A window at the back gives a view towards the fells. By the door, L., is a telephone. On the right, a cottage piano. After supper.*]

       [*At a large table, in the centre of the stage,* M<small>ICHAEL</small> R<small>ANSOM</small> *and the* D<small>OCTOR</small> *are playing chess. At a smaller table, L.,* L<small>AMP</small> *is bending over a microscope. In an armchair, R.,* S<small>HAWCROSS</small> *is writing in a notebook.* G<small>UNN</small> *is at the piano, strumming and singing. As he writes,* S<small>HAWCROSS</small> *frowns with suppressed annoyance.*]

G<small>UNN</small> [*singing*].
   The chimney sweepers
     Wash their faces and forget to wash the neck;
   The lighthouse keepers
     Let the lamps go out and leave the ships to wreck;
   The prosperous baker
     Leaves the rolls in hundreds in the oven to burn;
   The undertaker
     Pins a small note on the coffin saying "Wait till I return,
   I've got a date with Love!"

   And deep-sea divers
     Cut their boots off and come bubbling to the top,
   And engine-drivers
     Bring expresses in the tunnel to a stop;

The village rector
>   Dashes down the side-aisle half-way through a psalm;

The sanitary inspector
>   Runs off with the cover of the cesspool on his arm—

To keep his date with Love!

> [*Jumps up from the piano and goes over to* SHAWCROSS.]

Still sweating at that old diary?
SHAWCROSS. I was doing my best to, in spite of your filthy row.
GUNN. So glad you enjoyed it, dearie. I'll play you something else. [*Goes back to piano.*]
RANSOM. Shut up, David. [*To* DOCTOR.] Check.
GUNN [*leaving piano and looking over* SHAWCROSS' *shoulder*]. Hullo, what's all this? [*Reads.*] ". . . followed up a splendid short pitch to the north summit. Gunn, as usual . . ."
SHAWCROSS [*snatching book*]. Leave that alone, damn you!
GUNN [*grabs book back and reading*]. ". . . Gunn, as usual, fooling about, completely irresponsible. I can never understand M.F.'s patience with him. . . ."

> [SHAWCROSS *tries to snatch book*. GUNN *dodges round the chair.*]

SHAWCROSS. Give it here, blast your eyes!
GUNN. Ha, ha! Wouldn't you like it! Why can't you be patient with me, like M.F.?
SHAWCROSS. You little fool! Do you want me to hurt you?
RANSOM. Give it back, David. [*To* DOCTOR.] Check.
GUNN. Sorry, Ian. You're not cross with me, are you? Come and have a drink?
SHAWCROSS. Surely you ought to know by this time that I never drink the day before a climb.
GUNN. To hear you talk, one'd think we were a lot of monks.
SHAWCROSS. It just happens that I take climbing seriously. You don't.
GUNN. All right. Keep your hair on. No offence. [*Strolls over to* LAMP.] Let's have a squint, Teddy. [*Looks into microscope.*] What's this stuff that looks like mouldy cheese?
LAMP. If I were to tell you, you wouldn't be any the wiser.
GUNN. No, I expect I shouldn't. [*He wanders over to watch the chess players.*]
SHAWCROSS. M.F., may I take your climbing boots? I'd like to oil them for you.

RANSOM. It's very kind of you, Ian; but I gave them to the maid.
SHAWCROSS. I wish you wouldn't, M.F. How can you expect a girl to oil boots? I'll just do them over again, myself.
RANSOM [*smiling*]. You spoil me, Ian. One day, you'll regret it. I shall become as helpless as a baby without its nurse.
SHAWCROSS [*blushing*]. It's no trouble at all. I like to keep things decent.
GUNN [*yawning and stretching himself*]. Gosh, I'm bored! If I had a thousand pounds, I'd buy an aeroplane and try to fly across the Atlantic: if I had five hundred pounds, I'd go to Africa and shoot lions. As it is, I've got seven and elevenpence, so I suppose I'd better get drunk.

[*As he moves towards the door, the telephone rings.*]

SHAWCROSS. I expect that'll be the man about the new ropes. [*Goes to telephone.*] Hullo.... No, it's a call from London. [*To* GUNN.] For you.
GUNN. Ask who it is. Wait a minute.... Don't, for Heaven's sake, say I'm here!
RANSOM [*to* DOCTOR]. Look out for that castle, Tom.
SHAWCROSS. Who's speaking? [*To* GUNN.] It's a lady. A Mrs da Silva.
GUNN. Gosh, that's torn it! Tell her I've gone away! Tell her I'm dead!
SHAWCROSS [*listening*]. She says she knows you're here and that it's no good saying you aren't. [*Holding out receiver to* GUNN.] Here, take it! I'm not going to do your dirty work for you.
GUNN [*after making frantic signals, advances gingerly to the telephone*]. Oh, hullo, darling—how lovely to hear your voice! No, of *course* not! How *could* you think so! Well, you know, I'm terribly busy just now. I *could* get up to town this week-end, if it's really absolutely necessary.... No, darling, I *swear* there isn't! Listen, here comes a kiss! Good-bye! [*Hanging up receiver and mopping his forehead.*] And now *she's* on the track again! Says her husband's going to divorce her! Oh, whatever shall I do?
SHAWCROSS. I hardly see what else you can expect, when you've got about as much self-control as a tom-cat.... What we do object to is the way you involve us all in your nasty little intrigues.
GUNN. Everybody seems to be finding out my address. This morning, I had five more bills.... Oh, if only I could get right out of England for six months, they might forget about me.
RANSOM. Check.
DOCTOR [*making a move*]. Aha, M.F., that's got you!... No, it hasn't.... Oh, dear!
RANSOM. Mate. Thank you, Tom.
DOCTOR. Why do I always do something silly when I play with you? It's no good. You get me every time. [*Rising.*] Oh, I'm so fat, I'm so fat!
GUNN. Doc, I believe you forgot your exercises this morning!

DOCTOR. As if I ever forgot them! As if I ever could forget them! [*Sighs.*] Perhaps it would be better if I stopped them altogether. But I haven't the nerve.

GUNN. Poor old Doc! Come and have a drink. Whisky shrivels up your flesh.

DOCTOR. Do you really think so? I've got to a stage where I can believe almost anything.

[*A knock at the door.*]

ISABEL'S VOICE. May we come in?

GUNN. Another woman! Don't open it, for the Lord's sake! Let me hide! [*Dives under the larger table.*]

[SHAWCROSS *opens the door. Enter* LADY ISABEL, *followed by* STAGMANTLE *and* SIR JAMES RANSOM.]

ISABEL [*to* JAMES]. I told you they'd be in here!

RANSOM [*unpleasantly surprised*]. James!

JAMES. Ah, Michael, there you are! Very glad to find you at home. I thought I'd pay you a surprise visit. I've brought some friends who were anxious to meet you. . . . May I introduce my brother—Lady Isabel Welwyn, Lord Stagmantle.

RANSOM [*with a rather stiff bow*]. How do you do? These are my friends—Doctor Williams, Mr Shawcross, Mr Lamp. . . . David, come out. . . .

[GUNN *scrambles out from under the table.*]

Mr Gunn.

GUNN [*politely*]. How do you do?

JAMES [*to* RANSOM]. I've been telling Lady Isabel and Lord Stagmantle about your climbing exploits. They were greatly interested.

ISABEL. You know, Mr Ransom, you're not a bit like Sir James! I should never have taken you for brothers, at all!

STAGMANTLE. It's a great pleasure to meet you, Mr Ransom. I'm always glad to make contacts with prominent personalities, in any walk of life. Sir James tells me that you have many sidelines. You're a scholar, I believe? Well, now, that intrigues me. Scholar and man of action: an unusual mixture, eh?

JAMES. As I never fail to observe, my brother has all the brains of our family. In all humility I say it—my brother is a great man.

RANSOM [*who has listened to the above remarks with growing uneasiness, now turns on* JAMES *and blurts out*]. Why have you come here? What do you want?

JAMES [*smiling awkwardly*]. Hardly very friendly, are you, Michael? How do you know that I want anything—beyond the pleasure of seeing you again after so long?

RANSOM. How often, when we were boys, you used to come to me as you come to-day, with that peculiar smile on your face, half impudent, half timid! What do you want this time—my toy engine, my cricket bat, my rare West Indian stamps? Or shall I do you a favour—run that errand to the butcher's, correct your Latin verses, clean the motor-bicycle? Let's hear what it is, James: we're grown men now.

JAMES [*with a change of manner*]. You are quite right, Michael. I shall not waste words. There is no time to lose. [*Lowering his voice.*] Isn't it possible for me to speak to you alone?

RANSOM. If you have no secrets from your friends, I have none from mine.

JAMES. Very well, since you wish it. . . . [*Clearing his throat.*] In the name of His Majesty's Government, I have come to make you a most important proposition—

RANSOM. Which I unconditionally refuse.

JAMES [*taken aback*]. But—Michael—I haven't even told you what it is!

RANSOM. You have told me quite enough. I know your propositions, James: they are all alike. They are exceedingly convincing. They contain certain reservations. They are concerned with prestige, tactics, money and the privately pre-arranged meanings of familiar words. I will have nothing to do with any of them. Keep to your world. I will keep to mine.

JAMES. You are not being fair to me, Michael. You have never been fair to me. What I am offering you is an opportunity—the greatest of your whole life—to do something after your own heart. We want you to lead an expedition which will attempt the ascent of F 6.

RANSOM [*startled*]. F 6! What have you and your world to do with F 6?

JAMES. Ah, you see, Michael; I told you you would be interested!

RANSOM. Since boyhood, in dreams, I have seen the huge north face. On nights when I could not sleep I worked up those couloirs, crawled along the eastern arête, planning every movement, foreseeing every hold. Through how many thousand years have those virgin buttresses been awaiting me! F 6 is my fate. . . . But not now. Not like this! No, no, no! I refuse!

JAMES. But, Michael, this is sheer caprice! I must explain: the future of England, of the Empire, may be at stake. Weighty political considerations, the Government—

RANSOM. And your own career? Be honest, James, and add the heaviest weight to the scales. . . . No, I am sorry, but F 6 is more important to me even than that. I will not go.

ISABEL. Mr Ransom, if you lead this expedition—no matter whether you succeed or fail: and of course you *will* succeed—there is not a woman in England who will not feel proud of you—*more* than proud! I appeal to you, as an Englishwoman, in the name of all Englishwomen. You refused your brother. Can you refuse *me*?

RANSOM. I can refuse you, Lady Isabel.

ISABEL. You disappoint me, Mr Ransom. Sir James made me hope great things of you. He was too generous. I had never expected this. I see it in your eyes. You are afraid.

RANSOM. I am afraid of a great many things, Lady Isabel. But of nothing which you in your worst nightmares could ever imagine; and of that word least of all.

STAGMANTLE. Look here, Ransom; let's understand each other. I'm not going to talk a lot of blarney to you about England and Idealism. I'm a practical man. You're a practical man—of course you are! Only failures are idealists. My dear fellow, think what this climb will mean to you! Cash, and lots of it! You need cash to pursue your hobby? Of course you do! Look at it in a sensible light. [*Lowers his voice.*] Between ourselves, this expedition's nothing more or less than a political racket. You know that. So do I. Well, who cares! Leave the dirty work to your brother and me: we're used to it. Forget about us. Go out to F 6 and enjoy yourself. Make climbing history. By God, I envy you! If I were twenty years younger, I swear I'd ask you to take me along!

RANSOM. I like your reasons best, Lord Stagmantle. And I respect you. You talk like a man. I'd rather have you in front of me on a rope than behind me with a loud-speaker. . . . I am sorry. I know you won't understand my refusal. But I do refuse.

STAGMANTLE. Is that your last word?

RANSOM. It is.

[*There is a knock at the door.*]

STAGMANTLE. Too bad. . . . Well, Ransom, it seems we shall have to look elsewhere.

JAMES [*triumphantly*]. Not yet! [*He goes to the door, opens it and speaks to someone outside.*] Ah, splendid! So you got my telegram? Yes, he's here!

[*Enter* MRS RANSOM.]

Here is somebody who may be able to persuade you, Michael!

RANSOM [*with a cry of dismay*]. Mother!

MOTHER [*advancing to* RANSOM]. Michael, I am so proud—

RANSOM [*recoiling*]. You too! No, it is impossible!
    You come so late, it is an accident
    Your shadow adds to theirs, a trick of the light.
    If this was purposed—

> [*In the course of the following dialogue, the light becomes entirely concentrated upon* RANSOM *and his* MOTHER. *The rest of the stage is darkened: the other figures being seen only as indistinct shapes in the background.*]

MOTHER. I have no purpose but to see you happy,
    And do you find that so remarkable?
    What mother could deny it and be honest?
    I know my son the greatest climber in the world;
    I know F 6 the greatest mountain in the world.
    May not a mother come at once to bring
    Her only gift, her love? When the news came,
    I was in bed, for lately
    I've not been very well. But what's a headache
    When I can stand beside my son and see him
    In the hour of his triumph?
RANSOM. If I have triumphed
    It is not as you think. I have refused it.
MOTHER. Refused it? Why? But no—I must not question
    My grown-up son. You have your reasons, and I
    Shall try to trust them always.
    James, I remember—
RANSOM. James! Was there no other name you could remember,
    No niece or cousin? Ever since we were born
    I have heard the note of preference in your voice:
    And must I hear it now? When we could barely walk,
    I watched him romping through the children's party;
    When we were boys at school,
    I saw him charm his way to every heart
    And idly win the prizes.
    That would not matter; we are older now
    And I have found myself. But James who has
    The gaping world to ogle with his speeches
    Must fill the last gap in his great collection
    And pot-hunt for his brother. Years ago
    He stole my share of you; and must he now
    Estrange me even from myself?

MOTHER.   Michael,
    There is a secret I have kept so long
    My tongue is rusty. What you have said
    I knew and I have always known. Why do you start?
    You are my Michael and I know my own:
    A mother has no heaven but to look.
    That was your secret; there is also mine:
    From the good day when both of you were born,
    And I first held you both in my two arms,
    James, bigger, prettier, the doctor's pride,
    Responding promptly to the nurse's cluck,
    And you, the tiny, serious and reserved,
    I knew your natures. You never knew your father:
    But I can never see James toss his head
    Or laugh, or take a lady's arm, but I
    Must see your father in his popular pulpit.
    Everyone thought your father wonderful
    And so did I, until I married him
    And knew him for a shell: James is like him.
    He cannot live an hour without applause.
    No one can say that I have stinted it.
    But you, you were to be the truly strong
    Who must be kept from all that could infect
    Or weaken; it was for you I steeled my love
    Deliberately and hid it. Do you think that it was easy
    To shut you out? I who yearned to make
    My heart the cosiest nook in all the world
    And warm you there for ever, so to leave you
    Stark to the indifferent blizzard and the lightning?
    How many nights have I not bit my pillow
    As the temptation fought to pick you out of bed
    And cover you with kisses? But I won.
    You were to be unlike your father and your brother
    You were to have the power to stand alone;
    And to withhold from loving must be all my love.
    I won, I said—but was the victory real?
    There was a mother crucified herself
    To save her favourite son from weakness,
    Unlike his twin, his brother who depended
    Upon the constant praises of the little.
    She saved him nothing: he must have them too
    Because his brother had them. She had died

    To make him free; but when the moment came
    To choose the greatest action of his life
    He could not do it, for his brother asked him
    And he was padlocked to a brother's hatred—
RANSOM. Mother, stop!
MOTHER.   Michael! You mean—
RANSOM. Yes. Go to James and tell him that you won.
    And may it give him pleasure.
MOTHER. My boy!

> [*She attempts to embrace him. He turns away.*]

    BLACK OUT

> [*Music. The darkness is filled with* VOICES *of* NEWS-BOYS, *screaming like cats.*]

  Evening Special! Evening Special!
  Ransom to lead Expedition!
  Famous Climber's Decision!
  Evening Moon: Late Night Final!
  Young English Climber's Daredevil Attempt!
  The Haunted Mountain: Full Story and Pictures!
  Monasteries in Sudoland: Amazing Revelations!

> [*The* STAGE-BOX *on the right is illuminated.* MRS A. *is reading a morning paper.*]

MRS A. I read the papers; there is nothing there
  But news of failure and despair:
  The savage train-wreck in the dead of night,
  The fire in the school, the children caught alight,
  The starving actor in the oven lying,
  The cashier shot in the grab-raid and left dying,
  The young girl slain upon the surgeon's table,
  The poison-bottle with the harmless label,
  The workman fallen in the scalding vat,
  The father's strained heart stopping as he sat,
  The student driven crazy by his reading,
  The roadside accident hopelessly bleeding,
  The bankrupt quaking at the postman's knock,
  The moaning murderer baited in the dock—

> [*Enter* MR A. *with evening paper.*]

MR A. Look, Mary! Read this!

> [*As they read,* VOICES *are heard from the darkness of the stage.*]

VOICES. Michael Forsyth Ransom.
  Eight stone six. Aged twenty-eight years.
  Short and blue-eyed.
  His first experiences the rectory elms and the garden quarry.
  Kept a tame rook. Was privately educated,
  By a Hungarian tutor.
  Climbed the west buttress of Clogwyn Du'r Arddu
  While still in his teens. The late Colonel Bow said:
"That boy will go far."
  Visited Switzerland; in a single season
  Made a new traverse on the Grandes Jorasses,
  Did the Furggen Shoulder and the Green Needle of Chamonix.
  Studied physiology in Vienna under Niedermeyer.
  Went to the Julian Alps,
  Conquered Triglav, mastered the Scarlet Crag.
  Disappeared into Asia Minor, appeared in the Caucasus
  On two-headed Ushba, returned to England,
  In an old windmill near the mouth of the Nen
  Translated Confucius during a summer.
  Is unmarried. Hates dogs. Plays the viola da gamba.
  Is said to be an authority on Goya.
  Drinks and eats little but is fond of crystallised apricots. . . .

> [*The* STAGE-BOX *on the left is illuminated.* LORD STAGMANTLE *is seen at the microphone.*]

STAGMANTLE. It goes without saying that the other members of the Expedition are the finest flower of English Mountaineering; and, in hands as capable and brilliant as these, the honour and prestige of Britain, may, I am sure, be safely left. In this machine-ridden age, some people are tempted to suppose that Adventure is dead; but the spirit of Man has never refused to respond to the challenge of the unknown and men will always be found ready to take up the gauntlet, mindless of worldly profit, undaunted by hardship and risk, unheeding the dull spirit which can only sneer: Cui bono? From such pioneers, the man in the street may learn to play his part in the great game of life, small though it may be, with a keener zest and daring—
[*Exit.*]

[*Meanwhile, the* A.'s *have been cutting photographs and articles out of the paper and pinning them to the walls of the* BOX.]

MR A. Cut out the photos and pin them to the wall,
Cut out the map and follow the details of it all,
Follow the progress of this mountain mission,
Day by day let it inspire our lowly condition.
MRS A. Many have come to us often with their conscious charms,
They stood upon platforms and madly waved their arms,
At the top of their voices they promised all we lack,
They offered us glory but they wanted it back.
MR A. But these are prepared to risk their lives in action
In which the peril is their only satisfaction.
They have not asked us to alter our lives
Or to eat less meat or to be more kind to our wives.

[LADY ISABEL *appears at the microphone in the* STAGE-BOX, *L.*]

ISABEL. The Englishman is reserved. He does not wear his heart on his sleeve nor put his best goods in his shop-window. He smokes his pipe and answers in words of one syllable. So that those who do not know him think that he is stupid and cold. But every now and then, now in this part of the world, now in that, something generous, something brave or beautiful, just happens. And when we start to investigate it we shall generally find that, at the bottom of it all, is an Englishman. I have had the privilege of meeting Mr Ransom and his companions on this expedition personally; and I can say with absolute sincerity that never in my life have I come away feeling so exalted, so proud that I belonged to the same country and the same race as these gallant men. . . . [*Exit.*]
MRS A. They make no promise to improve our station,
At our weakness they make no show of indignation,
They do not offer contemptuously to lend a hand
But their courage is something the least can understand.
MR A. The corner tobacconist and the booking-clerk,
The naked miner hewing in the dark,
The forge-hand sweating at the huge steam-hammer,
The girl imprisoned in the tower of a stammer—
MRS A. The invalid, sheep-counting all the night,
The small, the tall, the black-haired and the white
See something each can estimate,
They can read of these actions and know them great.

[G‍UNN *appears at the microphone in the* STAGE-BOX, *left.*]

GUNN. I don't really know exactly what to say. We none of us know what F 6 is going to be like. If you ask me, I think she's probably an ugly old maid. I'm scared stiff, but Ransom will hold our hands, I expect. . . . We shall be a jolly party; at least, I hope so. I've been on one or two of these expeditions and no one's murdered me yet. They say that there's a ghost at the top; but I've made Doctor Williams promise that if we see anything he'll let me hide behind him. Well, I don't think I've got anything else to say, so I'll tell you a limerick I've just made up:
> There was an old man of F 6
> Who had some extraordinary tricks:
> He took off—

[*An* ANNOUNCER *comes hastily into the* BOX, *pushes* GUNN *aside and speaks into the microphone.*]

ANNOUNCER. We are all most grateful to Mr Gunn for his very interesting talk. Listeners will no doubt join us in wishing the party every success. There will now be a short interval in the programme.

[*Exit* BOTH. STAGE-BOX, *left, is darkened.*]

MRS A. John, I'm so happy! Can't we do something to celebrate?
MR A. Let's go away for the week-end. Let's go now!
MRS A. But it's seven o'clock and supper's nearly ready!
MR A. O, bother the supper! Let it burn!
MRS A. Let's go away and never return;
  Catch the last train to—
MR A. Where to?
MRS A. What does it matter?
  Anywhere out of this rush and this clatter!
  Get your toothbrush, get your pyjamas,
  Fetch your razor and let us be gone,
  Hurry and pack, may we never come back;
  For Youth goes quickly and Age comes on!

[T‍HEY *begin to put on their outdoor clothes, pack, etc.*]

MR A. Dover would like us, Margate would welcome us,
  Hastings and Folkestone would give us a part,
  Hove be excited and Brighton delighted,
  Southend would take us warm to her heart.
BOTH. Moments of happiness do not come often,

Opportunity's easy to miss.
O, let us seize them, of all their joy squeeze them,
For Monday returns when none may kiss!

[*Exeunt.*]
[*After the* A.'s *have departed for Hove, the* STAGE-BOXES *are darkened. A sudden penumbra of light on the stage shows* MRS RANSOM *seated in a high-backed chair facing the audience.*]

MRS RANSOM [*talking to herself in a hoarse and penetrating whisper*]. Michael ... Michael darling ... can you hear me? There, there. ... It's all right. ... There's nothing to be frightened about. Mother's with you. Of course she won't leave you alone, Michael, never. Wherever you are, whatever you're doing, whether you know it or not, she's near you with her love; for you belong to her always. She's with you now, at sea, on board the ship with your foolish companions, and she'll be with you on the mountain, too. ... Of course you'll get to the top, darling. Mother will help you. She'll always help you. Wasn't she with you from the very beginning, when you were a tiny baby? Of course she was! And she'll be with you at the very end. ...

RANSOM [*voice heard, very far off, frightened*]. It's the Demon, Mother!
MRS RANSOM [*sings*].

>   Michael, you shall be renowned,
>   When the Demon you have drowned,
>   A cathedral we will build
>   When the Demon you have killed.
>   When the Demon is dead,
>   You shall have a lovely clean bed.
>
>   You shall be mine, all mine,
>   You shall have kisses like wine,
>   When the wine gets into your head
>   Mother will see that you're not misled;
>   A saint am I and a saint are you
>   It's perfectly, perfectly, perfectly true.

BLACK OUT

Act II Scene 1

[F 6. *Room in a Monastery on the Great Glacier. A high, gloomy, vaulted chamber, with doors L. into the courtyard and R. into the interior of the building. In the back wall, arches open into a cloister, beyond which the greenish, faintly glowing ice of the glacier is visible.*]

[MICHAEL RANSOM *and* SHAWCROSS *are seated at a table in the foreground, on which stand three silver candlesticks with church candles of coloured wax.* RANSOM *and* SHAWCROSS *both have notebooks and pencils; they are checking stores.*]

RANSOM. How many tins of malted milk?

SHAWCROSS. Fifty.

RANSOM. How are we off for pemmican?

SHAWCROSS. Three two-pound tins.

RANSOM. We must remember to ask the monks for yak butter. . . . How about the petrol for the primus?

SHAWCROSS. God, that reminds me! [*He jumps up and goes to the door L. Looks out into the courtyard.*] The porters haven't finished unloading it yet! [*Shouts.*] Hi! Sing ko, pan no ah! Teng fang! Naga! Naga! [*Returns to table.*] Lazy devils! And it'll be dark in a few minutes. . . . That's what comes of leaving things to Gunn. He treats this whole business like a picnic. [*He glances quickly at* RANSOM, *who does not, however, respond.*]

RANSOM. Have we got enough soup cubes?

SHAWCROSS. Three large packets. [*Hesitates.*] Look here, M.F., I've been wanting to talk to you about Gunn for a long time now. . . . You know, I hate to bother you with this sort of thing. . . . I've tried to keep you from noticing . . .

RANSOM [*smiles*]. Have you?

SHAWCROSS. You mean, you *did* see something? Well, in a way, I'm glad. Because, if you hadn't, you mightn't have believed me—

RANSOM. I saw that Gunn teased the yaks and scared the porters and played tricks on Tom and Teddy—and on you, too, Ian. I agree that he's often an intolerable nuisance; and I think that without him this expedition would be much more businesslike and very gloomy indeed.

SHAWCROSS [*exasperated*]. The thing I admire most about you, M.F., is your wonderful broadmindedness. It's an example to me. I'm not very tolerant, I'm afraid. If Gunn amuses you and the others, I'm glad. I hope I can see a joke as well as anyone. . . . But that wasn't quite what I meant, just now. This is something quite different. I hardly like to tell you—

RANSOM. If you hadn't meant to tell me, Ian, you wouldn't have started this conversation at all.

SHAWCROSS [*blurting it out*]. Well then—Gunn steals!

RANSOM [*laughs*]. Oh, that!

SHAWCROSS. So you *did* know!

RANSOM. I'm surprised that you've only just noticed it. He steals like a magpie; bits of indiarubber, chiefly, but also watches, pencils, and, occasionally, money. . . . That reminds me, I expect he's taken my camera. I was imagining I'd lost it down in the gorge, while we were fording the river.

SHAWCROSS. But, M.F., you can't tolerate this kind of thing! What are you going to do?

RANSOM. Ask him if he's got it.

SHAWCROSS. But surely there's more to it than that? How can you take a man with you who's just a common thief? One has to have some standards of decency, I suppose?

RANSOM [*smiles*]. You haven't changed much, have you, Ian, since you were captain of your school?

SHAWCROSS [*bitterly*]. You're always laughing at me. I suppose you think I'm just a priggish fool?

RANSOM. I certainly don't think you're a fool. You know that I rely on your help more than anybody's to make this expedition a success.

SHAWCROSS. Thank you, M.F. You make me feel ashamed. As long as you trust me, then I don't give a damn what anybody else says or thinks. You know I'd follow you anywhere. We all would. . . . The wonderful thing about a man like you is that you can use all kinds of people and get the best out of each. I think I understand better, now, what it is you get out of Gunn. I don't want to run him down—just because his brand of humour's a bit too subtle for me. [*With increasing bitterness.*] He's not a bad sort in his way; he's all right to have about the place, I suppose, as long as there's no special difficulty or danger. He's a damn good climber, too, I admit—only he simply hasn't got the temperament. I'm wondering what he'll be like up there, on the north face. You remember how he screamed, that day in the Coolins, and wouldn't budge for an hour? It was pitiful.

RANSOM. David's always frightened when he climbs. Otherwise, he wouldn't climb. Being frightened is his chief pleasure in life. He's frightened when he drives a racing-car or seduces somebody's wife. At present he prefers mountaineering because it frightens him most of all.

SHAWCROSS. How well you understand him, M.F.! Now, that's just the point I wanted to make: wouldn't it be better, when we get to Camp A, to leave Gunn behind?

RANSOM [*smiles*]. To damage all the instruments and eat up all the stores?

SHAWCROSS. Well, but, I mean, he'll have to be dropped somewhere, won't he? [*Pause.*] Do you really think it's wise to take him as far as Camp B?

RANSOM. I shall decide when the time comes.

SHAWCROSS. I mean, it's quite settled, isn't it, that only two of us shall try to reach the summit?

RANSOM. Yes. There'll be only two of us.

SHAWCROSS. And you can't, for a moment, be thinking of taking Gunn? [*Pause.*] My God, it'd be madness! M.F.—you couldn't!

RANSOM. Have I said I shall?

SHAWCROSS [*with growing excitement*]. If I thought such a thing was possible, I'd—I don't know what I'd do! Gunn, that miserable little rotter! Why, he's not a climber at all! He's just a neurotic! He poses. He does everything for effect! Just a beastly little posing coward! [*Pause.*] Oh, I know you think I'm simply jealous!

[*Enter* LAMP *and the* DOCTOR, *L.*]

LAMP [*excited*]. The flora here is amazing, simply amazing! I've had one of the most wonderful afternoons of my life! I tell you what, Doctor— [*Sees the others.*] Oh, here you are, M.F.! Didn't see you in the dark.

[SHAWCROSS *silently lights the candles.*]

I was just telling the Doctor, I've had a field-day! Extraordinarily interesting! M.F., I'm convinced that Hawkins is wrong when he denies the possibility of a five-leaved Polus Naufrangia! And what's more, I don't mind betting you I shall find one here, on F 6.

RANSOM. Let's see what you got this afternoon.

LAMP [*opens his vasculum*]. Here's Stagnium Menengitis and Frustrax Abominum.... Isn't it a beauty! And look here, here's something to surprise you: you told me there wasn't a Rossus Monstrens with blue petals! Well, what do you say to this?

RANSOM [*examines flower*]. This is interesting.

[*Enter* GUNN, *L.*]

GUNN. Ah, here you all are! Thank goodness! I've been hunting for you everywhere! I began to think something had happened to you.... [*Sits down and mops his forehead.*]

DOCTOR. What's the matter with you, David? You look rattled.
GUNN. You'd be rattled if you'd been hanging round this place all the afternoon. Ugh! It gives me the creeps!
DOCTOR. Why, what's wrong with it?
GUNN. Those beastly monks. . . . Don't they make you feel damned queer, with those cowls over their faces? I've been watching them for hours, out there: they never seem to speak or make any signs; they just stand facing each other, like this—and yet you have a nasty sort of feeling that they're talking, somehow. . . . I shouldn't wonder if they do it by telepathy or something.
DOCTOR. They seemed quite friendly and harmless when we arrived.
GUNN. Don't you believe it. . . . They're plotting to do us in while we're asleep, I bet you they are. . . . This afternoon, when I was sitting watching the porters unload, I kept imagining there was somebody standing just behind me. Several times I turned round quickly to try and catch him, but there was nothing there. . . . And then I saw a monk and I thought I'd ask him which room we could use for the stores. So I went over to him and made signs and he seemed to understand all right. He turned round and went to one of the doors and opened it and went inside. Naturally, I followed him. But when I got into the room, there was nobody there. And there wasn't even a window he could have got out of. . . . No, I don't like this place!
DOCTOR. I tell you what, David, you've had a touch of the sun. I'll give you something to make you sleep well to-night.
RANSOM. Oh, by the way, David, where's my camera? You've got it, haven't you?
GUNN [*with a charming smile*]. Yes. It's in my room. I thought I'd look after it for you for a bit.
SHAWCROSS. Well, of all the blasted—!
RANSOM. That was very kind of you. Would you bring it here now, please?
GUNN. Very well—if you'd rather—

[*As he moves towards the door, L., a low chanting begins from the courtyard outside. This chant continues throughout the following scene. Its words are:*]

Go Ga, morum tonga tara
Mi no tang hum valka vara
So so so kum mooni lara

Korkra ha Chormopuloda
Antifora lampisoda
Kang ku gar, bari baroda

Ming ting ishta sokloskaya
No rum ga ga, no rum gaya
Nong Chormopuloda saya.

GUNN. My God! What's that? [*Retreats hastily behind* RANSOM's *chair.*]
SHAWCROSS [*goes to door, L., and looks out*]. They're all gathered out there in the courtyard. They're starting a procession. Now they're beginning to go round in circles. They've got torches and banners. . . .
GUNN. Lock that door, for Heaven's sake! Suppose they come in here!
SHAWCROSS. Do you ever think of anything except your own beastly little skin?

[*Meanwhile the others have joined him at the door.* GUNN *comes last, unwillingly, curious in spite of himself.*]

DOCTOR. From the way they walk it might be a funeral.
LAMP. I believe it *is* a funeral. Look what they're carrying.
GUNN. A coffin! Gosh, did you see?
DOCTOR. Cheer up, David; there's only one! Perhaps they won't choose you.
GUNN. It's most likely some wretched traveller they've murdered.
DOCTOR. Very curious, those masks. A pity it's too dark for a photograph.
SHAWCROSS. Now they're going. I wonder where that door leads to? Probably into the temple precincts.

[*The chanting dies away.*]

LAMP [*as they close the door and return downstage to the table*]. What did you make of it, M.F.?
RANSOM. I've read about these rites, somewhere. They're supposed to propitiate the spirits which guard the house of the dead.
GUNN. Anyhow, I hope there won't be any more! Phew! This place is about as cheerful as Woking Cemetery!

[*As he speaks, the door on the R. opens noiselessly and a cowled* MONK *enters, carrying in his hands a crystal which glows faintly with a bluish light.*]

You chaps didn't really think I was scared, did you? I was only ragging. It takes more than a few old monks to frighten *me*! [*Turns and suddenly sees the* MONK. *Screams.*] Oh, God!

[*As the* MONK *advances towards the front of the stage,* GUNN *retreats backwards before him.*]

What does he want? Help! Do something, somebody! M.F., you speak to him!

RANSOM. Om no hum, no na num se? [*Pause.*] No num seng ka, gang se gang? [*Pause.*] King t'sang po, ka no ah? [*Pause.*] Either he doesn't understand any of the three hill-dialects, or he isn't allowed to answer.

DOCTOR. Funny kind of a lamp he's got there. [*Approaches.*]

GUNN. I say! Do be careful! He may have a knife up his sleeve!

DOCTOR. Extraordinary thing—it doesn't seem to be a lamp at all. It just shines. [*Bends over the crystal.*] Why, it's a kind of mirror—I can see myself in it! Am I really as fat as that? Gracious, I'm quite bald! Hullo, what's this? I'm sitting in an arm-chair. I seem to know that room. . . . Yes, it's the Reform Club! I say, I think I must have got a touch of the sun like David. Am I just seeing things? Here, Teddy, you come and look!

LAMP [*looks*]. Polus Naufrangia! As plain as anything: all five leaves. By Jove, what a beauty! [*Rubs his eyes.*] I must be going mad!

GUNN. He's hypnotising you, that's what it is! When we're all in a trance, we shall probably be murdered. . . . I say, I must have a look!

LAMP [*excited*]. I saw it as plain as that candle! Five distinct leaves!

GUNN [*looks*]. Why, there's my old Alfa Romeo! And someone's sitting in it—it's a woman, dressed all in black! She seems to be at a crossroads. I see the sign-post, but I can't read what's written on it. . . . Now she's turning her head. My God, it's Toni—Mrs da Silva! [*Comes away.*] Do you think that means her husband's died and now she'll follow me out here? Come on, Ian. Your turn!

SHAWCROSS [*takes a pace towards the crystal, stops, bursts out violently*]. I'm not going to have anything to do with this damned business! You others please yourselves. It isn't right. We aren't meant to know these things. [*Calmer.*] It's probably some kind of trick, anyhow. . . . M.F., I'm going to get the wireless ready. It's nearly time to pick up the weather report from Fort George. [*Takes up one of the candles and exits, L.*]

GUNN. You'll have a look, won't you, M.F.?

RANSOM [*hesitates a moment*]. Very well. [*Looks into crystal.*]

[*As he does so,* VOICES *are heard from the darkened* STAGE-BOXES.]

VOICES. Give me bread

                    Restore my dead

I am sick

                    Help me quick

Give me a car	
	Make me a star
Make me neat	
	Guide my feet
Make me strong	
	Teach me where I belong
Strengthen my will	
	Make me still
Make me admired	
	Make me desired
Make me just	
	Cool my lust.
[*Together.*]	Make us kind
	Make us of one mind
	Make us brave
	Save
	Save
	Save
	Save.

DOCTOR. Well, what is it this time? Motors or flowers or London clubs?

GUNN. Try and see something useful. Ask it to tell you the best route up F 6.

RANSOM [*after a long pause*]. I can see nothing.

GUNN. Nothing at all? Oh, M.F.!

DOCTOR. That all goes to support your hypnotism theory. M.F. was a bit too strong for him.

[*The* MONK *turns silently and goes out by the door, R.*]

GUNN. Ought we to have tipped him, or anything? Gosh, you know, that crystal has given me quite a headache! I can't understand your not seeing anything, M.F. Or was it so awful that you won't tell us?

DOCTOR. I feel I could do with a change of air. Let's go and see if Ian's got Fort George.

GUNN. Right you are. Coming, M.F.?

RANSOM. No. I'll stay here. The Abbot may wish to speak to me.

[GUNN *and* DOCTOR *go out, L.*]

RANSOM. Bring back the crystal. Let me look again and prove my vision a poor fake. Was it to me they turned their rodent faces, those ragged denizens of the waterfronts, and squealed so piteously: "Restore us! Restore us to our uniqueness and our human condition." Was it for me the prayer of the sad artist on the crowded beaches was indeed intended? "Assassinate my horrible detachment. My love for these bathers is hopeless and excessive. Make me also a servant." I thought I saw the raddled sick cheeks of the world light up at my approach as at the home-coming of an only son.... How could I tell them that?

[*Enter the* ABBOT *and* TWO ACOLYTES, *R.*]

ABBOT [*makes sign of benediction*]. Only God is great.
RANSOM [*kneels and kisses his hand*]. But His power is for mercy.
ABBOT. I hope everything has been arranged to your satisfaction?
RANSOM. It is perfect.
ABBOT. I am glad. Please be seated, Mr Ransom. Will you do me the honour of taking a glass of wine with me? In these mountains, I fear we can offer but poor hospitality, but I think you will not find this wine totally unworthy of your palate. Your health, Mr Ransom.

[*Toast.*]
[*The* ACOLYTES *exeunt R.*]

Now tell me. You wish to start soon on your ascension of our mountain?
RANSOM. To-morrow. If He permit it, Whose will must be done.
ABBOT. You know the legend?
RANSOM. I have read the Book of the Dead.
ABBOT. Such interest, Mr Ransom, is uncommon in one of your race. In that case, you will have comprehended the meaning of the ceremony that was performed this evening out in the courtyard: the office for the souls of the dead and the placation of the Demon. I am afraid that you, with your western civilisation, must consider us here excessively superstitious.... No, you need not contradict me out of politeness. I understand. You see the painted mask and the horns and the eyes of fire and you think: "This Demon is only a bogey that nurses use to frighten their children: I have outgrown such nonsense. It is fit only for ignorant Monks and peasants. With our factory chimneys and our furnaces and our locomotives we have banished these fairy-tales. I shall climb the mountain and I shall see nothing." But you would be wrong.

The peasants, as you surmise rightly, are simple and uneducated; so their vision is simple and uneducated. They see the truth as a crude and coloured picture. Perhaps, for that reason, they see it more clearly than you or I. For it is a picture of truth. The Demon is real. Only his ministry and his visitation are unique for every nature. To the complicated and sensitive like yourself, Mr Ransom, his disguises are more subtle. He is—what shall I say?—the formless terror in the dream, the stooping shadow that withdraws itself as you wake in the half-dawn. You have heard his gnashing accusations in the high fever at a very great distance. You have felt his presence in the sinister contours of a valley or the sudden hostility of a copse or the choking apprehension that fills you unaccountably in the middle of the most intimate dinner-party. I did you an injustice just now when I said that you expected to see nothing on the mountain. You do expect to see something. That is why you are intending to climb it. You do not make that foolish, that terrible mistake so common among your fellow-countrymen of imagining that it is fortunate to be alive. No. You know, as I do, that Life is evil. You have conquered the first temptation of the Demon, which is to blind Man to his existence. But that victory exposes you to a second and infinitely more dangerous temptation; the temptation of pity; the temptation to overcome the Demon by will. Mr Ransom, I think I understand your temptation. You wish to conquer the Demon and then to save Mankind. Am I right?

RANSOM. So you know of my vision in the crystal?

ABBOT. Ah, you saw it there, too? That is not strange. For all men see reflected there some fragment of their nature and glimpse a knowledge of those forces by whose free operation the future is forecast and limited. That is not supernatural. Nothing is revealed but what we have hidden from ourselves; the treasure we have buried and accursed. Your temptation, Mr Ransom, is written in your face. You know your powers and your intelligence. You could ask the world to follow you and it would serve you with blind obedience; for most men long to be delivered from the terror of thinking and feeling for themselves. And yours is the nature to which those are always attracted in whom the desire for devotion and self-immolation is strongest. And you would do them much good. Because men desire evil, they must be governed by those who understand the corruption of their hearts, and can set bounds to it. As long as the world endures, there must be order, there must be government: but woe to the governors, for, by the very operation of their duty, however excellent, they themselves are destroyed. For you can only rule men by appealing to their fear and their lust; government requires the exercise of the human will: and the human will is from the Demon.

RANSOM. Supposing you are right. Supposing I abandon the mountain. What shall I do? Return to England and become a farm labourer or a factory hand?

ABBOT. You have gone too far for that.

RANSOM. Well then—

ABBOT. There is an alternative, Mr Ransom; and I offer it you.

RANSOM. What?

ABBOT. To remain here and make the complete abnegation of the will.

RANSOM. And that means—?

ABBOT. You saw the corpse in the procession?

RANSOM. Yes.

ABBOT. In the course of your studies you have become acquainted, no doubt, with the mysteries of the rites of Chöd? The celebrant withdraws to a wild and lonely spot and there the corpse is divided and its limbs scattered. The celebrant, sounding on his bone trumpet, summons the gluttonous demons of the air to their appointed feast. At this moment there issues from the crown of his head a terrible goddess. This goddess is his Will, and she is armed with a sword. And as the ghouls of the mountain and of the sky and of the waters under the glacier assemble to partake of the banquet, the goddess with her sword cuts off the limbs of the celebrant's esoteric body, scatters them and apportions his entrails among the demon guests. And the celebrant must wish them good appetite, urging them to devour every morsel. These rites, Mr Ransom, are so terrible that frequently the novices who witness them foam at the mouth, or become unconscious or fall dead where they stand. And yet, so tedious is the path that leads us to perfection that, when all these rites have been accomplished, the process of self surrender can hardly be said to have begun. . . . Well, Mr Ransom, I must leave you now. Do not make up your mind at once. Think my proposal over.

RANSOM. Before you go, may I ask you a question? As Abbot, you rule this monastery?

ABBOT. That is a wise observation. Mr Ransom, I am going to tell you a secret which I have never told a living soul. We have spoken of your temptation. I am now going to tell you of mine. Sometimes, when I am tired or ill, I am subject to very strange attacks. They come without warning, in the middle of the night, in the noon siesta, even during the observance of the most sacred religious rites. Sometimes they come frequently, sometimes they do not occur for months or even years at a time. When they come I am filled with an intoxicating excitement, so that my hand trembles and all the hairs on my body bristle, and there comes suddenly into my mind strange words, snatches of song and even whole poems. These poems sing always of the same world. A strange world. The world of the common people. The world of blood and violent death, of peasant soldiers and murderers, of graves and disappointed lust. And when I come to myself again and see these monastery walls around me, I am filled with horror and despair. For I know that it is a visitation of the Demon. I know that, for me, nothing matters any more: it is too late. I am already among the lost. Good night, Mr Ransom. [*Exit R.*]

RANSOM. Is it too late for me? I recognize my purpose. There was a choice once, in the Lakeland Inn. I made it wrong; and if I choose again now, I must choose for myself alone, not for these others. Oh, You who are the history and the creator of all these forms in which we are condemned to suffer, to whom the necessary is also the just, show me, show each of us upon this mortal star the danger that under his hand is softly palpitating. Save us, save us from the destructive element of our will, for all we do is evil.

[*Enter* GUNN, *L.*]

GUNN. You alone? Good. I was afraid I might be butting in; but Ian and the others threw me out. And I didn't much like the idea of sitting by myself in the dark, with all those Monks around. [*Pause.*] Are you busy, M.F.? Would you rather I didn't talk?

> [RANSOM *is deep in his thoughts. He doesn't answer.* GUNN, *after regarding him for a moment in silence, begins again.*]

The wireless is coming through beautifully. No atmospherics at all. I heard the weather report; first class. We'll be able to start to-morrow for a cert.

RANSOM. You sound pleased.

GUNN. Of course I'm pleased! Who wouldn't be—after all these weeks of messing about? To-morrow we shall be on the ice!

RANSOM. Tell me, David; what is it that makes you so keen to climb this mountain?

GUNN [*laughs*]. What is it that makes one keen to climb any mountain?

RANSOM. F 6 is not like any mountain you have ever climbed.

GUNN. Why not? It's got a top, hasn't it? And we want to get to it, don't we? I don't see anything very unusual in that.

RANSOM. You've thought enough about the ascent of F 6 no doubt; about the couloirs and the north buttress and the arête.... Have you thought about the descent, too: the descent that goes down and down into the place where Stagmantle and my Brother and all their gang are waiting? Have you thought about the crowds in the streets down there, and the loud-speakers and the posing and the photographing and the hack-written articles you'll be paid thousands to sign? Have you smelt the smell of their ceremonial banquets? Have you loathed them, and even as you were loathing them, begun to like it all? [*Becomes hysterically excited.*] Have you? Have you?

GUNN [*scared*]. M.F., what on earth do you mean?

RANSOM. Don't lie to me now, David. Are you corrupt, like the rest of us? I must know. [*Seizes* GUNN *by the wrists and stares into his face.*] Yes. Yes. I see it! You too. How horrible! [*Throws him violently aside.*] Get out of my sight!

> [*Enter* SHAWCROSS, DOCTOR *and* LAMP; *all far too excited to notice that anything unusual has been happening.*]

SHAWCROSS. M.F.! A message has just come through: Blavek and his party are on the mountain already!

GUNN. But it's impossible! When we last heard, he was still on the other side of the Tung Desert!

SHAWCROSS. Well, this is official. He must have been making forced marches. These fellows aren't mountaineers at all—they're soldiers! There's a whole regiment of them! Do you know, M.F., what they're doing? They're hammering the whole south face full of pitons and hauling each other up like sacks! Good God, they'll be using fire-escapes before they've finished! Well, that settles it! We haven't a moment to lose!

RANSOM. And you are all anxious to play their game: the race to the summit? This won't be mountaineering. It'll be a steeplechase. Are you so sure the prize is worth it? Ian, you're the purist: is this your idea of climbing? No time for observations; no time for reconnoitre. Teddy, hadn't you better stay out of this? We can't wait a week, you know, while you look for your flowers.

LAMP. I'll take my chance of that later. We've got to beat Blavek!

RANSOM. Blavek is only another victim of the mountain. And you, Tom?

DOCTOR. You don't expect me to stay here, do you, M.F.? Why, this makes me feel twenty years younger already!

RANSOM. You, too. . . . Stagmantle's latest convert. He should be honoured.

SHAWCROSS. What's the point of all this talk? The people in England expect us to get to the top before the Ostnians. They believe in us. Are we going to let them down?

GUNN. I think this makes it all the more exciting. Good old Blavek!

RANSOM. Very well then, since you wish it. I obey you. The summit will be reached, the Ostnians defeated, the Empire saved. And I have failed. We start at dawn. . . .

CURTAIN

[*The* STAGE-BOX *on the right is illuminated. The* A.'s *are having breakfast.*]

MRS A. Give me some money before you go
 There are a number of bills we owe
 And you can go to the bank to-day
 During the lunch-hour.
MR A.   I dare say;
 But, as it happens, I'm overdrawn.
MRS A. Overdrawn? What on earth have you done
 With all the money? Where's it gone?
MR A. How does money always go?
 Papers, lunches, tube-fares, teas,
 Tooth-paste, stamps and doctor's fees,
 Our trip to Hove cost a bit, you know.
MRS A. Can we never have fun? Can we never have any
 And not have to count every single penny?
 Why can't you find a way to earn more?
 It's so degrading and dull to be poor.
 Get another job.
MR A.   My job may be small
 But I'm damned lucky to have one at all.
 When I think of those I knew in the War,
 All the fellows about my age:
 How many are earning a decent wage?
 There was O'Shea, the middle-weight champion; slouches from bar
  to bar now in a battered hat, cadging for drinks;
 There was Morgan, famous for his stories; sells ladies' underwear
  from door to door;
 There was Polewhele, with his university education; now Dan the
  Lavatory Man at a third-rate night-club;
 And Holmes in our office, well past fifty, was dismissed last week to
  bring down expenses;
 Next week another: who shall it be?
 It may be anyone. It may be me.

  [*A newspaper is dropped through the door into the
  back of the* BOX. MR A. *goes to fetch it.*]

MRS A. It's all this foreign competition:
 Czechoslovakia, Russia, Japan,
 Ostnia and Westland do all they can
 To ruin our trade with their cheap goods,
 Dumping them on our market in floods.

It makes my blood boil! You can find
No British goods of any kind
In any of the big shops now.
The Government ought to stop it somehow—

Mr A. Listen to this. [*Reads.*] Our Special Correspondent reports that the Ostnian Expedition to F 6, headed by Blavek, has crossed the Tung Desert and is about to commence its final assault on the mountain. Blavek is confident of success and, in mountaineering circles, it is believed that the British climbers will have to make very strenuous efforts indeed if they are to beat their formidable opponents. . . .

Mrs A. You see? The foreigner everywhere,
Competing in trade, competing in sport,
Competing in science and abstract thought:
And we just sit down and let them take
The prizes! There's more than a mountain at stake.

Mr A. The travelogue showed us a Babylon buried in sand.

Mrs A. And books have spoken of a Spain that was the brilliant centre of an Empire.

Mr A. I have found a spider in the opulent boardroom.

Mrs A. I have dreamed of a threadbare barnstorming actor, and he was a national symbol.

Mr A. England's honour is covered with rust.

Mrs A. Ransom must beat them! He must! He must!

Mr A. Or England falls. She has had her hour
And now must decline to a second-class power.

> [*Puts on his bowler hat and exit, brandishing his newspaper. The* STAGE-BOX *is darkened.*]

Act II Scene 2

[*On F 6. At the foot of the West Buttress. The back of the stage rises slightly, suggesting a precipice beyond. A magnificent panorama of distant mountains. On the right of the stage, the wall of the buttress rises, with an overhang.*]

> [*Mid-day.* RANSOM, SHAWCROSS *and* LAMP *stand roped on the edge of the precipice, assisting the* DOCTOR *and* GUNN, *who are still out of sight, below. The rope is belayed round a rock.*]

RANSOM [*looking down*]. There's a hold to your left, Tom. No, a little higher up. Good. Now you're all right.

GUNN'S VOICE [*from below*]. Look out, Doc! Don't tread on my face!
RANSOM. Now then. . . .

>   [*After a moment, the* DOCTOR *hoists himself into view, panting.*]

Now you take it easy, Tom. Fifteen minutes' rest, here.
LAMP. We've made good time, this morning.
RANSOM [*looking down*]. You all right, David?
GUNN'S VOICE [*from below*]. I think so. . . . No! Ooh, er! Gosh, this rock is soft! Here we come! [*He appears.*]
DOCTOR. Well, thank goodness, that couloir's behind us, anyhow. Though how we shall ever get down it again is another matter.
RANSOM. You were splendid, Tom. Never known you in better form.
DOCTOR. I must have lost at least two stone. That's one comfort.
GUNN. While we were in the chimney, I felt his sweat dripping on to me like a shower-bath. . . . I say, isn't there anything more to eat?
RANSOM. I'm afraid we must keep to our rations, David. We're only carrying the minimum, you know.
SHAWCROSS. I should have thought you'd eaten enough to satisfy even *your* appetite—considering you had all my chocolate, as well.
GUNN. Well, you needn't make a grievance out of it. You didn't want it, did you?
DOCTOR. Still feeling sick, Ian?
SHAWCROSS [*crossly*]. I'm all right.
DOCTOR. You don't look any too good.
SHAWCROSS. Anyhow, I don't see that it helps much to keep fussing about trifles and thinking of one's comfort.

>   [*A pause.*]

LAMP. Well, if we've got another ten minutes to spare, I think I'll be taking a look round. Might spot a clump of Polus Naufrangia. You never know. It's about the right altitude, now.

>   [*He goes to the back of the stage and looks over, through his binoculars.*]

GUNN [*following him*]. See anything?

>   [LAMP *shakes his head.*]

Gosh, that's a drop! [*He balances on the edge and pretends to wobble.*] Ooh, er! Help!
RANSOM. Come away from there, David.

>   [GUNN *obeys and begins wandering about the stage.*]

DOCTOR [*pointing upwards*]. How high do you make that buttress?
RANSOM. About seventeen hundred feet. We shall be on it all this afternoon. We ought to reach the ridge easily by sunset.
GUNN [*poking about*]. Hullo, what's this? [*Picks up a skull.*] Doctor Livingstone, I presume?

> [*The others, except* LAMP, *who continues to peer through his binoculars, collect round* GUNN.]

How on earth did he get here?
DOCTOR. Goodness knows. May have fallen from above. See this crack? It's hardly likely to have been murder, up here.
SHAWCROSS. Anyhow, he must have been a pretty useful climber to have got as far as he did. I suppose there's no doubt it's a native skull?
DOCTOR. Impossible to say. It may have been some mad European who thought he'd have a shot at F6 on his own; but that's scarcely possible. Some herdsman, probably.... What do you think, M.F.? [*Hands him the skull.*]
LAMP [*shouting excitedly*]. Come here! Look!
GUNN. What's the matter, Teddy?
LAMP. Polus Naufrangia! Five-leaved! A beauty! Only just spotted it. And it was right under my nose! [*He begins lowering himself over the edge.*]
DOCTOR. Wait a moment, Teddy. Better do that on the rope.
GUNN [*looking over*]. He'll be all right. It's a broad ledge. Only about twenty feet down.
DOCTOR [*looking over*]. Careful, Teddy. Careful. Take your time.
LAMP'S VOICE [*from below*]. I'm all right.

> [*The others, except* RANSOM, *stand looking over the edge.*]

RANSOM [*to skull*]. Well, Master; the novices are here. Have your dry bones no rustle of advice to give them? Or are you done with climbing? But that's improbable. Imagination sees the ranges in the Country of the Dead, where those to whom a mountain is a mother find an eternal playground. There Antoine de Ville scales pinnacles with subtle engines; Gesner drinks water, shares his dreams with Saussure, whose passion for Mont Blanc became a kind of illness, Paccard is reconciled with Balmat, and Bourrit, the cathedral precentor, no longer falsifies their story. Marie-Coutett still keeps his nickname of The Weasel; Donkin and Fox are talking of the Caucasus; Whymper goes climbing with his friends again and Hadow, who made the slip of inexperience, has no faults. While, on the strictest buttresses, the younger shadows look for fresher routes: Toni Schmidt is there and the Bavarian cyclists; and that pair also whom Odell saw on the step of Everest before the cloud hid them for ever, in the gigantic shadow of whose achievement we pitch our miserable tent—

[*The roar of an approaching avalanche is heard.*]

DOCTOR. An avalanche! My God!

[RANSOM *runs to join the others.*]

Look out Teddy! Look out!
GUNN. Quick, man!
SHAWCROSS. Stay where you are!
GUNN. Jump for it!
DOCTOR. Oh, God! He's done for!

[*The roar of the avalanche drowns their voices; then gradually dies away.*]

SHAWCROSS. He was just stooping to pick the flower, when the first stone got him.
DOCTOR. It was all over in a moment. He was probably knocked right out.
SHAWCROSS. As he went over the edge, you could see the flower in his hand.
GUNN. Gosh, I feel beastly! [*Sits down on a rock.*]
SHAWCROSS. He was a damn good man!
DOCTOR. I'm glad he found the Naufrangia, anyway. We must tell them that in London. Perhaps the five-leaved kind will be named after him. He'd like that, I think.
SHAWCROSS. I just can't believe it. Five minutes ago, he was standing here.
DOCTOR [*looking at* LAMP's *rucksack, which is lying on a rock*]. What do you think we ought to do with this? His people might like to have it.
SHAWCROSS. We can't very well take it with us now. I think we'd better bury it here. We can pick it up on our way down.
DOCTOR. Right you are. I'll help you. [*Begins collecting stones.*]

[SHAWCROSS *picks up the rucksack.*]

GUNN. Poor old Teddy! [*To* SHAWCROSS.] Half a minute! [*Feels in the pocket of the rucksack.*] Oh, good! [*Pulls out a piece of chocolate and begins eating it.*]
SHAWCROSS [*horrified*]. My God! Haven't you any decency left in you at all?
GUNN [*with his mouth full*]. Why, what's the matter now?

SHAWCROSS. Of all the filthy callousness!
GUNN. But, honestly, I don't see anything wrong. He doesn't want it now, does he?
SHAWCROSS. If that's the line you take, I suppose there's no more to be said. . . . Get some stones!

> [*While the others are burying the rucksack,* RANSOM *stoops and picks up* LAMP's *snow-glasses, which he has left lying on the rocks at the back of the stage.*]

RANSOM. The first victim to my pride. If I had never asked him, he would not have come. The Abbot was perfectly right. My minor place in history is with the aberrant group of Caesars: the dullard murderers who hale the gentle from their beds of love and, with a quacking drum, escort them to the drowning ditch and the death in the desert. . . . [*To the others.*] You have forgotten these. [*Gives glasses.*] Hurry up. We must be getting on, Ian, will you change places with David?

> [*Music. They rope up in silence.* RANSOM *begins the traverse round the buttress, as the* CURTAIN *slowly falls.*]

[*Both* STAGE-BOXES *are illuminated. In the left-hand box,* STAGMANTLE *is at the microphone. In the right-hand box, the* A.'s *sit, listening.* MR A. *is playing Patience.* MRS A. *is darning socks.*]

STAGMANTLE. It is with the deepest regret that we have to announce the death of Mr Edward Lamp, a member of the F 6 Expedition. He was climbing along a ridge on the north face after a rare botanical specimen when he was caught by an avalanche and killed. He was twenty-four years of age.

In Edward Lamp, Science has lost one of her most brilliant recruits. At Cambridge he carried everything before him; and his career, so tragically cut short, promised to be of the highest distinction. He died as he had lived: in the service of his austere mistress. This is as he would have wished; and no man can do more. Nor could one design him a more fitting grave than among the alpine flowers he loved so passionately and with such understanding. . . . [*Exit.*]

MRS A. [*moved*]. Death like his is right and splendid;
  That is how life should be ended!
  He cannot calculate nor dread

            The mortifying in the bed,
            Powers wasting day by day
            While the courage ebbs away.
            Ever-charming, he will miss
            The insulting paralysis,
            Ruined intellect's confusion,
            Ulcer's patient persecution,
            Sciatica's intolerance
            And the cancer's sly advance;
            Never hear, among the dead,
            The rival's brilliant paper read,
            Colleague's deprecating cough
            And the praises falling off;
            Never know how in the best
            Passion loses interest;
            Beauty sliding from the bone
            Leaves the rigid skeleton.
MR A.   If you had seen a dead man, you would not
            Think it so beautiful to lie and rot;
            I've watched men writhing on the dug-out floor
            Cursing the land for which they went to war;
            The joker cut off halfway through his story,
            The coward blown involuntary to glory,
            The steel butt smashing at the eyes that beg,
            The stupid clutching at the shattered leg,
            The twitching scarecrows on the rusty wire;
            I've smelt Adonis stinking in the mire,
            The puddle stolid round his golden curls,
            Far from his precious mater and the girls;
            I've heard the gas-case gargle, green as grass,
            And, in the guns, Death's lasting animus.
            Do you think it would comfort Lamp to know
            The British Public mourns him so?
            I tell you, he'd give his rarest flower
            Merely to breathe for one more hour!
            What is this expedition? He has died
            To satisfy our smug suburban pride. . . .

                                    [*The* STAGE-BOXES *are darkened.*]

Act II Scene 3

[*On F 6. Camp B. The left of stage is occupied by a tent, which is open at the end facing the audience. Behind it, to the right, the ground rises to a platform of rock, overhanging a precipice. It is early evening: during the dialogue which follows, the stage slowly darkens. Wind-noises.*]

> [RANSOM *and the* DOCTOR *are inside the tent, preparing a meal. The* DOCTOR *is cooking on the Primus stove.*]

DOCTOR. The wind's getting up again. It's going to be a bad night. . . . I wish those two would turn up.

RANSOM. We can't expect them just yet. They're loaded, remember; and the going isn't easy.

DOCTOR. What was the psychrometer reading?

RANSOM. 6·5.

DOCTOR. We're in for a lot more snow.

RANSOM. It looks like it.

DOCTOR. And if it's bad down here, what's it going to be like up there on the arête?

RANSOM [*smiling*]. Worse.

DOCTOR. M.F.—you can't start to-morrow!

RANSOM. I must.

DOCTOR. If you try it in this weather, you haven't a chance!

RANSOM. We shall have a better chance to-morrow than the day after. Three days from now, there'd be none at all. We can't hang on here for more than four days: we haven't the stores.

DOCTOR. To try the arête in a blizzard is sheer madness!

RANSOM. Hasn't this whole climb been madness, Tom? We've done things in the last week which ought to have been planned and prepared for months. We've scrambled up here somehow, and now we must make a rush for it. . . . Whatever the weather is, I must leave for the summit to-morrow.

DOCTOR. Very well, M.F. You didn't bring me up here to argue with you. I won't. Just tell me what you want me to do.

RANSOM. To-day is Tuesday. You'll wait for us here till Friday, at dawn. If we aren't back by then, you'll descend at once to Camp A, rest there as long as necessary and then carry out the evacuation of the mountain, as we arranged. . . . You understand, Tom? At once. There is to be no delay of any kind.

DOCTOR. You mean: no search party?

RANSOM. Nothing. If you like, I'll put that in writing. I forbid all useless risks. [*Smiling.*] I order you to return to England alive.
DOCTOR [*smiling*]. You'd better repeat that order to David personally.
RANSOM. David?
DOCTOR. He'll be second in command now, I suppose?

[RANSOM *looks at him, smiles slightly and is silent.*]

Michael—you aren't thinking of taking him with you to the summit?
RANSOM. What if I am?
DOCTOR. Then you've chosen already?
RANSOM. Please don't question me now, Tom. Perhaps I have chosen. Perhaps I haven't, yet. We'll speak about it later. I can't tell you any more now.
DOCTOR. Very well, Michael. Just as you wish.

[*A pause.*]

RANSOM. I know what you're thinking. Ian is steady, reliable, a first-class climber: David is only a brilliant amateur, a novice with an extraordinary flair, unsound, uneven, liable to moments of panic, without staying power. Yes, it's all true.
DOCTOR. Ian's wanted to do this climb with you more than he's ever wanted to do anything in his whole life.
RANSOM. I know. I've felt that, often. All these weeks, he's been on edge, straining every muscle and every nerve, never relaxing, torturing himself, denying himself, watching me like a dog waiting for a sign. . . . Already he's utterly exhausted; he's a feverish invalid. Take this sickness of his: as long as I've known him, Ian's never been sick on a mountain before. . . . You see, Tom, the ascent of F 6 represents, for Ian, a kind of triumph which he not only desires but of which he's desperately afraid. He can't face it. He wants me to order him to face it. But if I do, it will destroy him.
DOCTOR [*after a pause*]. Perhaps you're right, M.F. . . . Yes, I think you are. But surely—you've admitted it yourself—David is afraid, too?
RANSOM. David is afraid of precipices, avalanches, cornices, falling stones. He is afraid of being killed; not of dying. He is not afraid of F 6, nor of himself.
DOCTOR. M.F.—The boys have their whole lives before them. Take me.
RANSOM [*after a pause*]. Yes, I'd thought of that, too. Thank you for asking me, Tom. I am very honoured.
DOCTOR. Oh, I know it's impossible, of course. I'm a fat old man. The crystal was right: I shall die in my bed.

RANSOM. You will die at the end of a long and useful life. You will have helped a great many people and comforted all whom you could not help. . . . But the Demon demands another kind of victim—

> [*Whistling from* GUNN, *off. Enter* GUNN *and* SHAWCROSS, *R. Both of them are carrying stores. They cross the stage and enter the tent.*]

GUNN. Hullo, M.F.! Hullo, Doc! Are we late for supper?
DOCTOR. No, it's just ready now.

> [GUNN *and* SHAWCROSS *put down their loads.* SHAWCROSS *is much exhausted:* GUNN *fresh and lively.* RANSOM *lights the tent lantern.*]

GUNN. Gosh, I'm hungry! The altitude doesn't seem to affect *my* appetite. What is there to eat?
DOCTOR. Cocoa and oatmeal. [*Hands round rations.*]
GUNN. Oatmeal again!
DOCTOR. Perhaps you'd prefer a mutton chop?
GUNN. Don't, Tom, you swine! You make my mouth water! The first thing I'll do when I get back, I'll stand you dinner at Boulestin's. We'll start with two dozen Royal Whitstables—
DOCTOR. Oh, but David, Danish are much better!
GUNN. Just as you like. What about soup? Minestrone, I think?
DOCTOR. You have that. I prefer a really good tomato to anything.
GUNN. And now, what would you say to Lobster Newberg?
DOCTOR. I oughtn't to, really; but I can't resist.
GUNN. Good Lord! We've forgotten the wine!
SHAWCROSS [*bitterly*]. Must you always be talking about food?
GUNN. Was I? Sorry.
SHAWCROSS. Well, for God's sake, shut up then!

> [*A pause.*]

DOCTOR. You're not eating anything, Ian.
SHAWCROSS. I don't want any, thanks.
DOCTOR. Take just a little. You must eat something, you know.
SHAWCROSS [*angrily*]. You heard me say No once. Are you going deaf?
RANSOM. Doctor's orders, Ian.
SHAWCROSS. All right, M.F. If you say so—
RANSOM [*handing him his mug of cocoa*]. Try this. It's good.

> [SHAWCROSS *sips listlessly, putting the mug down almost at once.*]

GUNN. Thank God for my good dinner! Please may I get down? [*Pretending to strum on mandolin, sings:*]
>
> Some have tennis-elbow
> And some have housemaid's knee,
> And some I know have got B.O.:
> But these are not for me.
> There's love the whole world over
> Wherever you may be;
> I had an aunt who loved a plant—
> But you're my cup of tea!

DOCTOR [*laughing and applauding*]. Bravo!

[GUNN *bows.*]

You know, M.F., this reminds me of our first climb together, on the Meije. Do you remember that hut?

RANSOM. And our Primus that wouldn't light? Shall I ever forget it?

DOCTOR. And the fleas in the straw? Extraordinary the altitudes fleas can live at! Funny things, fleas.... If a flea were as big as a man, it could jump over St. Paul's.

GUNN. When I was at school, I tried to keep a flea circus. But I could never train them to do anything at all. They're not really very intelligent.

DOCTOR. Perhaps you didn't go the right way about it. A man told me once that if—

SHAWCROSS [*passionately*]. Oh, for Christ's sake, shut up!

DOCTOR. Why, what's the matter, Ian?

SHAWCROSS. Do you expect me to sit listening to your drivel the whole night? Why do we keep pretending like this? Why don't we talk of what we're all thinking about? M.F., I've had about as much of this as I can stand! You've got to tell us now: which of us are you taking with you to-morrow?

DOCTOR. Steady, Ian! [*Puts a hand on his arm.*]

SHAWCROSS [*shaking him off*]. Let me alone, damn you! I wasn't talking to you! M.F., you've bloody well got to choose!

RANSOM. I have chosen, Ian. I'm taking David.

SHAWCROSS. Oh, my God! [*Pause.*] And I knew it all the time!

GUNN. Rotten luck, Ian.... I say, let me stay behind.... I don't mind, so very much....

SHAWCROSS [*shouting*]. My God, do you think I'm going to crawl for favours to *you*, you little swine! You were always his favourite! I don't know how I've kept my hands off you so long! [*He tries to throttle* GUNN: *the* DOCTOR *seizes him.*]

DOCTOR. Ian, that's enough!

SHAWCROSS [*struggling free*]. Oh, I know—you're on his side, too! Do you think I haven't heard you whispering behind my back?

RANSOM. Is this what all your talk of loyalty amounts to, Ian? Tom and David have nothing to do with this. I am in charge of this expedition. If you have anything to complain of, be man enough to say so to me.

SHAWCROSS. I'm sorry, M.F. Forgive me. You're quite right. I'm no damn good: I realize that now. You're all better men than I am. I had a pretty fine opinion of myself, once. I imagined I was indispensable. Even my admiration of you was only another kind of conceit. You were just an ideal of myself. But F6 has broken me; it's shown me what I am—a rotten weakling. . . . I'll never give orders to anybody again.

RANSOM. No, Ian. You're wrong. F6 hasn't broken you. It has made a man of you. You know yourself now. Go back to England with Tom. One day you will do something better worth while than this fool's errand on which David and I are going. I am giving you a harder job than mine.

SHAWCROSS [*hesitating*]. If I only could—! But you don't really believe it: I see you don't! No one will ever— [*With rising excitement.*] They'd look at me and think—No, I couldn't bear it! He failed—I can't—no, no—I'll never let them! Never! [*He turns to rush out of the tent.*]

DOCTOR. Ian! [*They struggle at the tent flap;* SHAWCROSS *breaks free and runs across to the rock above the precipice; the others following.*]

RANSOM. Stop him!

GUNN. Ian, you fool, come back!

> [SHAWCROSS, *with a loud cry, springs over the precipice. The others reach the rock and stand peering down into the darkness. Gale noises and music.*]

CURTAIN

[*Both* STAGE-BOXES *are illuminated.*]

> [*In the right-hand* BOX, *the* A.'s *are listening.* MRS A. *is adjusting the wireless:* MR A. *stands restlessly cleaning his pipe. In the left-hand* BOX, *the* AN- NOUNCER *is at the microphone.*]

ANNOUNCER. There is still no news of the British Expedition to F6. Fort

George reports that a severe blizzard is general over the whole range. The gravest anxiety is felt as to their safety—

Mr A. Turn off the wireless; we are tired of descriptions of travel;
We are bored by the exploits of amazing heroes;
We do not wish to be heroes, nor are we likely to travel.
We shall not penetrate the Arctic Circle
And see the Northern Lights flashing far beyond Iceland;
We shall not hear the prayer from the minaret echoing over Arabia
Nor the surf on the coral atoll.

Mrs A. Nor do we hope to be very distinguished;
The embossed card of invitation is not for us;
No photographers lurk at our door;
The house-party and the grouse-moor we know by hearsay only;
We know of all these from the lending library and the super cinema.

Mr A. They excite us; but not very much. It is not our life.

Mrs A. For the skidding car and the neighbours' gossip
Are more terrifying to us than the snarling leap of the tiger;
And the shop-fronts at Christmas a greater marvel than Greece.

Mr A. Let our fears and our achievements be sufficient to our day.

Mrs A. The luck at the bargain counter:

Mr A.   The giant marrow grown on the allotment.

Mrs A. Our moments of exaltation have not been extraordinary
But they have been real.

Mr A. In the sea-side hotel, we experienced genuine passion:

Mrs A. Straying from the charabanc, under tremendous beeches,
We were amazed at the profusion of bluebells and the nameless birds;
And the Ghost Train and the switchback did not always disappoint.

Mr A. Turn on the wireless. Tune in to another station;
To the tricks of variety or the rhythm of jazz.
Let us roll back the carpet from the parlour floor
And dance to the wireless through the open door.

[*They turn on the wireless and a dance band is heard. The A's leave the* BOX.]

ANNOUNCER [*sings*].
Forget the Dead, what you've read,
All the errors and the terrors of the bed;
Dance, John, dance!

Ignore the Law, it's a bore,
Don't enumer all the rumours of a war;
> Dance, John, dance!
>> Chin up!
>> Kiss me!
>> Atta Boy!
Dance till dawn among the ruins of a burning Troy!

Forget the Boss when he's cross,
All the bills and all the ills that make you toss:
> Dance, John, dance!
Some get disease, others freeze,
Some have learned the way to turn themselves to trees;
> Dance, John, *etc.*

[*The* STAGE-BOXES *are darkened.*]

Act II Scene 4

[*On* F 6. *The Arête. Hurricane. Late afternoon.* RANSOM *supporting* GUNN.]

RANSOM. Steady. Lean on me.
GUNN. No, it's no use. I can't go any further. Help me down there, out of this bloody blizzard. [*They descend to a ledge.*] [*Collapsing.*] Thanks. But hurry. Go on, now, and reach the top. F 6 is a household word already. The nursemaids in the park go into raptures. The barber's chatter's full of nothing else. You mustn't disappoint them. In London now, they are unlocking the entrances to tubes. I should be still asleep but not alone. Toni was nice but very difficult. . . . Now no policeman will summons me again for careless driving. . . . They're flagging from the pits. . . . I cannot stop. . . . The brakes are gone. . . . Ian would be feeling as sick as a cat. . . . Where is that brake? Two hundred. . . . Christ, what banking! [*Dies.*]
RANSOM. You always had good luck; it has not failed you
> Even in this, your brightest escapade,
> But extricates you now
> From the most cruel cunning trap of all,
> Sets you at large and leaves no trace behind,
> Except this dummy.
>> O senseless hurricanes,
> That waste yourselves upon the unvexed rock,
> Find some employment proper to your powers,

Press on the neck of Man your murdering thumbs
And earn real gratitude! Astrologers,
Can you not scold the fated loitering star
To run to its collision and our end?
The Church and Chapel can agree in this,
The vagrant and the widow mumble for it
And those with millions belch their heavy prayers
To take away this luggage. Let the ape buy it
Or the insipid hen. Is Death so busy
That we must fidget in a draughty world
That's stale and tasteless; must we still kick our heels
And wait for his obsequious secretaries
To page Mankind at last and lead him
To the distinguished Presence?

CURTAIN

[*The* STAGE-BOXES *remain darkened. A voice from each is heard, in duet. They are like people speaking in their sleep.*]

LEFT BOX.	RIGHT BOX.
No news	
	Useless to wait
Too late	
	Their fate
	We do not know
Snow on the pass	
	Alas
Nothing to report	
	Caught in the blizzard
Fought through the storm;	
	Warm in our beds we wonder
Thunder and hail	
	Will they fail? Will they miss their success?
Yes. They will die	
	We sigh. We cannot aid
They fade from our mind	
	They find no breath
But Death.	

Act II Scene 5

[F 6. *The stage rises steeply, in a series of rock terraces, to the small platform at the back which forms the summit of the mountain. Blizzard. Gathering darkness.*]

> [*In the front of the stage* RANSOM *is struggling upwards. After a few numbed movements, he falls exhausted. Music throughout. The light now fades into complete darkness. The voices of the* CHORUS, *dressed in the habit of the monks from the glacier monastery, are heard.*]

CHORUS. Let the eye of the traveller consider this country and weep,
    For toads croak in the cisterns; the aqueducts choke with leaves:
    The highways are out of repair and infested with thieves:
    The ragged population are crazy for lack of sleep:
    Our chimneys are smokeless; the implements rust in the field
      And our tall constructions are felled.

Over our empty playgrounds the wet winds sough;
The crab and the sandhopper possess our abandoned beaches;
Upon our gardens the dock and the darnel encroaches;
The crumbling lighthouse is circled with moss like a muff;
The weasel inhabits the courts and the sacred places;
    Despair is in our faces.

> [*The summit of the mountain is illuminated, revealing a veiled, seated* FIGURE.]

For the Dragon has wasted the forest and set fire to the farm;
He has mutilated our sons in his terrible rages
And our daughters he has stolen to be victims of his dissolute
    orgies;
He has cracked the skulls of our children in the crook of his arm;
With the blast of his nostrils he scatters death through the land;
    We are babes in his hairy hand.

O, when shall the deliverer come to destroy this dragon?
For it is stated in the prophecies that such a one shall appear,
Shall ride on a white horse and pierce his heart with a spear;
Our elders shall welcome him home with trumpet and organ,
Load him with treasure, yes, and our most beautiful maidenhead
    He shall have for his bed.

> [*The veiled* FIGURE *on the summit raises its hand.*

There is a fanfare of trumpets. The DRAGON, *in the form of* JAMES RANSOM, *appears. He wears full ceremonial dress, with orders. He is illuminated by a spot-light. The* CHORUS, *throughout the whole scene, remain in semi-darkness.*]

[*As* JAMES *appears, the* CHORUS *utter a cry of dismay.* JAMES *bows to the* FIGURE.]

JAMES. I am sorry to say that our civilising mission has been subject to grave misinterpretations. Our critics have been unhelpful and, I am constrained to add, unfair. The powers which I represent stand unequivocally for peace. We have declared our willingness to conclude pacts of non-aggression with all of you—on condition, of course, that our demands are reasonably met. During the past few years we have carried unilateral disarmament to the utmost limits of safety; others, whom I need not specify, have unfortunately failed to follow our example. We now find ourselves in a position of inferiority which is intolerable to the honour and interests of a great power; and in self-defence we are reluctantly obliged to take the necessary measures to rectify the situation. We have constantly reiterated our earnest desire for peace; but in the face of unprovoked aggression I must utter a solemn warning to you all that we are prepared to defend ourselves to the fullest extent of our forces against all comers.

[JAMES *is seated. Duet from the darkened* STAGE-BOXES.]

DUET. Him who comes to set us free
    Save whoever it may be,
    From the fountain's thirsty snare,
    From the music in the air,
    From the tempting fit of slumber,
    From the odd unlucky number,
    From the riddle's easy trap,
    From the ignorance of the map,
    From the locked forbidden room,
    From the Guardian of the Tomb,
    From the siren's wrecking call,
    Save him now and save us all.

[*Flourish on the wood-wind.* MICHAEL RANSOM *steps into the light which surrounds the Dragon* JAMES. *He still wears his climbing things but is without helmet, goggles or ice-axe.*]

JAMES. Michael! Why have you come here? What do you want?
RANSOM. Hardly very friendly, are you?
JAMES. What is it this time? We are grown men now.
RANSOM. There is no time to lose. I have come to make you a most important proposition.
JAMES. Which I accept—on my own conditions.

> [*At his signal a complete set of life-size chessmen appear. The chief pieces on* JAMES' *side are* STAGMANTLE, ISABEL *and the* GENERAL; *and on* MICHAEL'S, SHAWCROSS, GUNN *and* LAMP. *All have masks which partially disguise them.*]

Before we continue, if any of you have any questions you would like to put either to my colleagues or myself, we shall be delighted to do our best to answer them.

> [*As each character answers his question, he or she removes the mask.*]

MR A. [*from stage-box*]. Why is my work so dull?
GENERAL. That is a most insubordinate remark. Every man has his job in life, and all he has to think about is doing it as well as it can be done. What is needed is loyalty, not criticism. Think of those climbers up on F 6. No decent food. No fires. No nice warm beds. Do you think *they* grumble? You ought to be ashamed of yourself.
MRS A. Why doesn't my husband love me any more?
ISABEL. My dear, I'm terribly sorry for you. I do understand. But aren't you being just a teeny-weeny bit morbid? Now think of those young climbers up there on F 6. They're not worrying about their love affairs. [*Archly.*] And I'm sure they must have several. Of course, I know people like you and me can't do big things like that, but we can find little simple everyday things which help to take us out of ourselves. Try to learn Bridge or get a book from the lending library. Reorganise your life. I know it won't be easy at first, but I'm sure if you stick to it you'll find you won't brood so much. And you'll be ever so much happier.
MR A. Why have I so little money?
STAGMANTLE. Ah, I was expecting that one! I'm a practical man like yourself, and as it happens I'm a rich one, so I ought to know something about money. I know there are far too many people who have too little. It's a damned shame, but there it is. That's the world we live in. But speaking quite seriously as a business man, I can tell you

that money doesn't necessarily bring happiness. In fact, the more you worry about it, the unhappier you are. The finest and happiest man I ever met—he's leading the expedition up F 6 at the moment—doesn't care a brass button for money, and never has. So my advice is: Get all the cash you can and stick to it, but don't worry.

MR A. AND MRS A. Why were we born?

JAMES. That's a very interesting question, and I'm not sure I can answer it myself. But I know what my brother, the climber, thinks. When we take, he said to me once, the life of the individual, with its tiny circumscribed area in space and time, and measure it against the geological epochs, the gigantic movements of history and the immensity of the universe, we are forced, I think, to the conclusion that, taking the large view, the life of the individual has no real existence or importance apart from the great whole; that he is here indeed but to serve for his brief moment his community, his race, his planet, his universe; and then, passing on the torch of life undiminished to others, his little task accomplished, to die and be forgotten.

RANSOM. You're not being fair to me.

JAMES. Keep to your world. I will keep to mine.

> [*The chess game begins. Complete silence, accompanied only by a drum roll. At intervals* JAMES *or* MICHAEL *says:* "*Check!*"]

JAMES. Check!

RANSOM [*looking for the first time towards the summit and seeing the* FIGURE]. Look!

JAMES. Mate! I've won!

> [*The* FIGURE *shakes its head.*]

RANSOM [*his eyes still fixed upon it*]. But was the victory real?

JAMES [*half rises to his feet, totters; in a choking voice*]. It was not Virtue—it was not Knowledge—it was Power! [*Collapses.*]

CHORUS. What have you done? What have you done?
You have killed, you have murdered her favourite son!

> [*Confusion. During the following speeches,* STAGMANTLE, *the* GENERAL *and* ISABEL *jostle each other, jump on each other's shoulders to get a better hearing and behave in general like the Marx brothers.*]

STAGMANTLE. The whole of England is plunged into mourning for one of her greatest sons; but it is a sorrow tempered with pride, that once again Englishmen have been weighed in the balance and not found wanting.

ISABEL. At this hour, the thoughts of the whole nation go out to a very brave and very lonely woman in a little South country cottage; already a widow and now a bereaved mother.

GENERAL. I am no climber; but I know courage when I see it. He was a brave man and courage is the greatest quality a man can have.

STAGMANTLE. Sport transcends all national barriers, and it is some comfort to realize that this tragedy has brought two great nations closer together.

ISABEL. In the face of this terrible tragedy, one is almost tempted to believe in the grim old legend of the Demon.

> [*A figure having the shape of the* ABBOT, *wearing a monk's habit and a judge's wig and holding the crystal in his hands, is illuminated at a somewhat higher level of the stage.*]

ABBOT. I am truly sorry for this young man, but I must ask for the Court to be cleared.

> [*Exeunt* SHAWCROSS, LAMP *and* GUNN.]
> [*A Blues.* MONKS *enter with a stretcher,* JAMES' *body is carried in slow procession round the stage and away into the darkness.*]

STAGMANTLE AND ISABEL.
>Stop all the clocks, cut off the telephone,
>Prevent the dog from barking with a juicy bone,
>Silence the pianos and with muffled drum
>Bring out the coffin, let the mourners come.
>
>Let aeroplanes circle moaning overhead
>Scribbling on the sky the message: He is dead.
>Put crepe bows round the white necks of the public doves.
>Let the traffic policemen wear black cotton gloves.
>
>Hold up your umbrellas to keep off the rain
>From Doctor Williams while he opens a vein;
>Life, he pronounces, it is finally extinct.
>Sergeant, arrest that man who said he winked!
>
>Shawcross will say a few words sad and kind
>To the weeping crowds about the Master-Mind,

    While Lamp with a powerful microscope
    Searches their faces for a sign of hope.

    And Gunn, of course, will drive the motor-hearse:
    None could drive it better, most would drive it worse.
    He'll open up the throttle to its fullest power
    And drive him to the grave at ninety miles an hour.

ABBOT. Please be seated, Mr Ransom. I hope everything has been arranged here to your satisfaction?
RANSOM. I didn't do it! I swear I didn't touch him! It wasn't my fault! [*Pointing to* FIGURE.] The Demon gave the sign! The Demon is real!
ABBOT. In that case, we will call the victims of his pride. Call Ian Shawcross!
CHORUS. Ian Shawcross!

> [SHAWCROSS *appears. He is bloodstained and pale.*]

RANSOM. I've had about as much of this as I can stand. You've got to tell them! I hate to bother you with this sort of thing.
SHAWCROSS. I'm afraid you haven't succeeded very well.
RANSOM. You mean, you *did* see something? If you hadn't, you mightn't believe me.
SHAWCROSS. Oh, for Christ's sake, shut up! If what you've done amuses you, I'm glad. I'm not very tolerant, I'm afraid. [*Exit.*]
ABBOT. Call David Gunn!
CHORUS. David Gunn!

> [*Enter* DAVID GUNN, *pale and covered with snow. His face is entirely without features.*]

RANSOM. David, you saw what happened?
GUNN. Didn't I just? You did it beautifully. It was first class!
RANSOM. You sound pleased!
GUNN. Of course I'm pleased! Who wouldn't be!
RANSOM. David, there's something I *must* tell you—

> [*Exit* GUNN.]

ABBOT. Call Edward Lamp!
CHORUS. Edward Lamp! Edward Lamp! Edward Lamp!
LAMP'S VOICE [*far away, off*]. I'm all right.
RANSOM [*shouts*]. Teddy, what did *you* see?
LAMP'S VOICE. If I told you, you wouldn't be any the wiser.
RANSOM. You're on their side, too! Is this all your talk of loyalty amounts to?

Mrs A. O, what's the use of your pretending
   As if Life had a chance of mending?
   There will be nothing to remember
   But the fortnight in August or early September.
Mr A. Home to supper and to bed.
   It'll be like this till we are dead.

[DOCTOR *appears.*]

RANSOM. Tom!
DOCTOR. Just tell me what you want me to do.
RANSOM. I can't face it!
DOCTOR. Perhaps you are right. The Demon demands another kind of victim. Ask the crystal. [*Exit* DOCTOR.]
ABBOT. You wish to appeal to the crystal, Mr Ransom? Do not ask at once, but think it over.
RANSOM. We haven't a moment to lose. I appeal to the crystal.
ABBOT. Very well, since you wish it, I obey you. [*Looks into crystal.*]

[*Music. Duet from* STAGE-BOXES, *the* A.'s *sing.*]

MRS A. AND MR A. Make us kind,
   Make us of one mind,
   Make us brave,
   Save, save, save, save.
ABBOT. Mr Ransom, I did you an injustice. I thought I understood your temptation, but I was wrong. The temptation is not the Demon. If there were no Demon, there would be no temptation.
RANSOM. What have I said? I didn't mean it! Forgive me! It was all my fault. F6 has shown me what I am. I'm a coward and a prig. I withdraw the charge.
ABBOT. Such altruism, Mr Ransom, is uncommon in one of your race. But I am afraid it is too late now. The case is being brought by the Crown. [*Turning to the* FIGURE *on the summit.*] Have you anything to say in your defence? [*Pause.*] You realise the consequences of silence? [*Pause.*] As long as the world endures there must be law and order. [*To* CHORUS.] Gentlemen, consider your verdict.

CHORUS. At last the secret is out, as it always must come in the end,
   The delicious story is ripe to tell to the intimate friend;
   Over the tea-cups and in the square the tongue has its desire;
   Still waters run deep, my dear, there's never smoke without fire.

   Behind the corpse in the reservoir, behind the ghost on the links,
   Behind the lady who dances and the man who madly drinks,

Under the look of fatigue, the attack of migraine and the sigh
There is always another story, there is more than meets the eye.

For the clear voice suddenly singing, high up in the convent wall,
The scent of the elder bushes, the sporting prints in the hall,
The croquet matches in summer, the handshake, the cough, the kiss,
There is always a wicked secret, a private reason for this.

ABBOT. Have you considered your verdict?
RANSOM. Stop!

> [*He rushes up to the summit and places himself in front of the* FIGURE, *with his arms outstretched, as if to protect it.*]

RANSOM. No one shall ever—! I couldn't bear it! I'll never let them! Never!
ABBOT [*to* CHORUS]. Guilty or not guilty?
CHORUS [*all pointing to the* FIGURE]. Guilty!
GENERAL. Die for England!
ISABEL. Honour!
STAGMANTLE. Service!
GENERAL. Duty!
ISABEL. Sacrifice!
ALL. Die for England.
VOICE. Ostnia.
ALL. England. England. England.
MRS A. AND MR A. Die for us!

> [*Thunder and the roar of an avalanche are heard. All lights are extinguished below; only the* FIGURE *and* RANSOM *remain illuminated.* RANSOM *turns to the* FIGURE, *whose draperies fall away, revealing* MRS RANSOM *as a young mother.*]

RANSOM. Mother!
MOTHER [MRS RANSOM]. My boy! At last!

> [*He falls at her feet with his head in her lap. She strokes his hair.*]

CHORUS. Acts of injustice done
   Between the setting and the rising sun
   In history lie like bones, each one.

Mrs Ransom. Still the dark forest, quiet the deep,
    Softly the clock ticks, baby must sleep!
    The Pole star is shining, bright the Great Bear,
    Orion is watching, high up in the air.

Chorus. Memory sees them down there,
    Paces alive beside his fear
    That's slow to die and still here.

Mrs Ransom. Reindeer are coming to drive you away
    Over the snow on an ebony sleigh,
    Over the mountain and over the sea
    You shall go happy and handsome and free.

Chorus. The future, hard to mark,
    Of a world turning in the dark
    Where ghosts are walking and dogs bark.

Mrs Ransom. Over the green grass pastures there
    You shall go hunting the beautiful deer,
    You shall pick flowers, the white and the blue,
    Shepherds shall flute their sweetest for you.

Chorus. True, Love finally is great,
    Greater than all; but large the hate,
    Far larger than Man can ever estimate.

Mrs Ransom. And in the castle tower above,
    The princess' cheek burns red for your love,
    You shall be king and queen of the land,
    Happy for ever, hand in hand.

Chorus. But between the day and night
    The choice is free to all, and light
    Falls equally on black and white.

    [*During the first verse of the Chorale which follows, the light fades from the summit, so that the stage is completely darkened. Then, after a moment, the entire stage is gradually illuminated by the rising sun. The stage is empty, except for the body of* Ransom, *who lies dead on the summit of the mountain.*]

Hidden Chorus. Free now from indignation,
    Immune from all frustration
    He lies in death alone;

Now he with secret terror
And every minor error
Has also made Man's weakness known.

Whom History hath deserted,
These have their power exerted,
In one convulsive throe;
With sudden drowning suction
Drew him to his destruction.
[*Cresc.*] But they to dissolution go.

SLOW CURTAIN

On the Frontier
A Melodrama in Three Acts

BY W. H. AUDEN AND
CHRISTOPHER ISHERWOOD

[1937-38]

TO
BENJAMIN BRITTEN

The drums tap out sensational bulletins;
Frantic the efforts of the violins
To drown the song behind the guarded hill:
The dancers do not listen; but they will.

DRAMATIS PERSONAE

Dr Oliver Thorvald: lecturer at a Westland university
Hilda Thorvald: his wife
Eric Thorvald: their son
Martha Thorvald: Dr Thorvald's sister
Colonel Hussek: late of the Ostnian Army
Louisa Vrodny: his daughter
Anna Vrodny: her daughter
Oswald Vrodny: brother-in-law to Mrs Vrodny
Valerian: head of the Westland Steel Trust
Lessep: his secretary
Manners: his butler
Stahl: a director of the Westland Steel Trust
The Leader: of Westland
Storm-Trooper Grimm: of the Leader's Bodyguard
A Chorus of Eight: five men and three women

NOTES ON THE CHARACTERS

(*All the* Chorus *must be able to sing*)

Dr Thorvald: Middle-aged, pedantic, would have been a liberal under a democratic régime.
Hilda Thorvald: Good-natured, a bit slatternly. Has been the butterfly type. Hates rows. Wears dressing-jackets, kimonos, arty clothes.
Eric Thorvald: Untidy, angular. About twenty.
Martha Thorvald: Violently repressed, fanatical. Wears glasses. Not to be played too broadly: remember that, beneath her fanaticism, she is an educated, intelligent woman. She is conscious of having a better brain than her sister-in-law.
Col. Hussek: An old lobster.
Mrs Vrodny: Embittered by poverty and household responsibilities; but with considerable reserves of power. The Vrodny-Hussek family has aristocratic traditions.
Anna Vrodny: Must not be played as a mouse. She has character, but has hardly realised it.
Oswald Vrodny: A cheerful ne'er-do-well. Might even speak with an Irish accent.

VALERIAN: Tall, suave, courteous, sardonic. Speaks precisely, with a slight foreign accent. About forty-five.
LESSEP: About twenty-seven. Intriguing. Can be spiteful. In dress and manner slightly pansy.
MANNERS: A stage butler.
STAHL: Though, with Valerian, he plays second fiddle, he is a man of considerable presence and power. He is not quite as tall as Valerian, but broader. About fifty-five.
THE LEADER: Try to avoid resemblances to living personages. The Leader wears a beard. He is about forty-five, anxious and ill. In the first act, he plays very stiffly, like a newsreel photograph of himself. His platform voice is like a trance-voice, loud and unnatural. He wears uniform throughout.
GRIMM: About twenty-five. Pale and tense. Wears uniform throughout.

TIME: THE PRESENT

ACT ONE: EARLY SUMMER

Prologue: At the gates of the Valerian Works
Scene One: Valerian's Study
Interlude: A prison in Westland
Scene Two: The Ostnia-Westland Room

ACT TWO: A WEEK LATER

Scene One: The Ostnia-Westland Room
Interlude: A dance-hall in Westland
Scene Two: Valerian's Study

ACT THREE: NINE MONTHS LATER

Scene One: The Ostnia-Westland Room
Interlude: In the Westland Front Line
Scene Two: Valerian's Study (a fortnight later)
Interlude: The War Correspondents
Scene Three: The Ostnia-Westland Room

Act I

(Before the Curtain)

[*Slow music. Eight workers—three women and five men—are grouped as if waiting for the gates of a factory to open. They sing in turn the following couplets:*]

The clock on the wall gives an electric tick,
I'm feeling sick, brother; I'm feeling sick.

The sirens blow at eight; the sirens blow at noon;
Goodbye, sister, goodbye; we shall die soon.

Mr Valerian has a mansion on the hill;
It's a long way to the grave, brother; a long way still.

The assembly-belt is like an army on the move;
It's stronger than hate, brother; it's stronger than love.

The major came down with a pipe in his face;
Work faster, sister, faster, or you'll lose your place.

The major wears pointed shoes, and calls himself a gent;
I'm behind with the rent, brother; I'm behind with the rent.

The missus came in with her hair down, a-crying:
"Stay at home, George, stay at home, for baby's dying!"

There's grit in my lungs, there's sweat on my brow;
You were pretty once, Lisa, but oh, just look at you now!

You looked so handsome in your overalls of blue;
It was summer, Johnny, and I never knew.

My mother told me, when I was still a lad:
"Johnny, leave the girls alone." I wish I had.

The lathe on number five has got no safety-guard.
It's hard to lose your fingers, sister, mighty hard.

Went last night to the pictures; the girl was almost bare,
The boy spent a million dollars on that love-affair.

> [*The factory siren sounds. The workers begin to move across the stage and exit L. The last verses are punctuated by the sound of clocking-in.*]

When the hammer falls, the sparks fly up like stars;
If I were rich, brother, I'd have ten motor-cars.

Pass the word, sister, pass it along the line:
There's a meeting tonight at number forty-nine.

Oil that bearing, watch that dynamo;
When it's time to strike, brother, I'll let you know.

Stoke up the fires in furnace number three;
The day is coming, brother, when we shall all be free!

Act I Scene 1

[VALERIAN's *study.* VALERIAN's *house is supposed to stand on high ground, overlooking the capital city of Westland. At the back of the stage there is a deep bay-window. The furniture is chiefly modern, but there are a number of statuettes and valuable etchings. A desk with telephones. A radiogram. Doors L. and R.*]

[*When the curtain rises,* MANNERS *is arranging the chair-cushions, while* LESSEP *puts papers in order on the desk. It is a fine morning in early summer.*]

LESSEP. Oh, by the way, Manners ... your Master will be lunching on the terrace, this morning.

MANNERS. Indeed, Sir? Are those Mr Valerian's orders, Sir?

LESSEP [*sharply*]. Of course they're Mr Valerian's orders. What did you suppose?

MANNERS. I beg your pardon, Sir. I mention it only because Mr Valerian has been accustomed to leave the management of this household entirely in *my* hands. This is the first time, in twelve years, that he has thought it necessary to say where he wished to lunch.

LESSEP. Well, it won't be the last time, I can assure you!

MANNERS. No, Sir?

LESSEP. No!

[*Enter* VALERIAN, *L.*]

VALERIAN. Good morning, Lessep.

LESSEP. Good morning, Mr Valerian.

VALERIAN. Are those ready for me to sign? [*Sees* MANNERS *is waiting.*] Yes, what is it?

MANNERS. Excuse me, Sir. Am I to take it that you ordered lunch to be served on the terrace?

VALERIAN. Since when, Manners, have I given you orders about my meals? I am the master of this house, not the mistress.

MANNERS. Exactly, Sir. To-day I had thought of serving lunch in the Winter Garden. The terrace, in my humble opinion, would be too hot in this weather. The Leader, I am given to understand, dislikes the heat. But Mr Lessep said—

VALERIAN. Mr Lessep was mistaken. We bow to your judgment, Manners. The Winter Garden.

MANNERS. Thank you, Sir.

[*Bows and exit, R.*]

LESSEP. Mr Valerian . . . I hope you'll forgive me. . . .

VALERIAN. I can forgive anything, Lessep—except incompetence. Just now you behaved officiously, and tactlessly. Never mind. I am quite fairly satisfied with you, at present. As long as you continue to be competent, I shall not have to bother the Ostnians for another secretary. . . .

LESSEP [*staggered*]. I . . . I don't think I quite understand. . . .

VALERIAN. No? Then I will speak more plainly. You are in the employ of the Ostnian Steel Combine. . . . Oh, pray don't suppose that you are the first! Despite the general identity of our interests, it is a regrettable fact that the Ostnian industrialists do not trust us—and that we, I am sorry to say, do not entirely trust the Ostnians. So we both prefer to rely on inside information. . . . It is an arrangement which suits me very well. All I ask is that the employees the Ostnians send us (always by the most devious routes) shall be efficient. We also have sent them some admirable secretaries. . . . Now, do we understand each other?

LESSEP. Mr Valerian, on my word of honour—

VALERIAN [*signing papers*]. Very well. I have no time for arguments. I am not asking for a confession. . . . Oh, one more little point: yesterday, you took from my safe the plans of the new Valerian tank and photographed them. Clumsily. You are not accustomed to this kind of work, I think? It requires practice.

LESSEP. I'm ready to swear that I never touched—

VALERIAN [*still writing*]. Yes, yes. Of course. . . . But in order that you shall not commit a gaffe which might seriously prejudice your prospects with your employers, let me tell you that we have already sold this tank to the Ostnian War Office. . . . You didn't know? Too stupid, isn't it? Lack of departmental co-operation, as always. It will be the ruin of both our countries. . . .

LESSEP [*collapsing*]. I'd better leave at once. . . .

VALERIAN. Nonsense! You will learn. . . . No tears, I beg! They bore me indescribably. ... We have wasted four minutes on an exceedingly dull subject.... And now tell me, please: what are my appointments for to-day?

LESSEP [*pulling himself together with an effort*]. Mr Stahl is coming in to see you at twelve-thirty. He will remain to meet the Leader, at lunch. This afternoon you will accompany the Leader on his inspection of the Works. And you wanted, if possible, to get away in time for the Poussin auction, at four forty-five. ...

VALERIAN. Ah, to be sure—the Poussins! The one bright moment of a dreary day! I mustn't miss them on any account. And the Leader will speak for an hour, at least. ... Please arrange an interruption. At the first opportunity, our operatives are to burst spontaneously into the National Hymn. Spontaneously, mind you. ... It's the only known method of cutting short the Leader's flow of imperatives.

LESSEP. I'll see to it, Mr Valerian.

VALERIAN. You'd better go down there now, and talk to some of our foremen. They're accustomed to organise these things.

LESSEP. Is there anything else?

VALERIAN. Nothing, thank you.

LESSEP [*prepares to go, hesitates*]. Mr Valerian—I just want to say: I shall never forget your generosity. ...

VALERIAN. My dear boy, I am never generous—as you will very soon discover, to your cost. Please do not flatter yourself that your conscience and its scruples interest me in the very slightest degree. In this establishment, there is no joy over the sinner that repents. ... Very well. You may go.

[*Exit* LESSEP, *R.* VALERIAN *goes thoughtfully upstage to the window, and stands looking out over the city.*]

VALERIAN. The Valerian Works. ... How beautiful they look from here! Much nicer than the cathedral next door. ... A few people still go there to pray, I suppose—peasants who have only been in the city a generation, middle-class women who can't get husbands. ... Curious to think that it was once the centre of popular life. If I had been born in the thirteenth century, I suppose I should have wanted to be a bishop. [*Factory sirens, off, sound the lunch-hour.*] Now my sirens have supplanted his bells. But the crowd down there haven't changed much. The Dole is as terrifying as Hell-Fire—probably worse. ... Run along, little man. Lunch is ready for you in the Valerian Cafeteria. Why so anxious? You shall have every care. You may spoon in the Valerian Park, and buy the ring next day at the Valerian Store.

Then you shall settle down in a cosy Valerian Villa, which, I assure you, has been highly praised by architectural experts. The Valerian School, equipped with the very latest apparatus, will educate your dear little kiddies in Patriotism and Personal Hygiene. A smart Valerian Family Runabout will take you on Sundays to picnic by the waterfall, along with several hundred others of your kind. The Valerian Bank will look after your savings, if any; our doctors will see to your health, and our funeral parlours will bury you. . . . And then you talk about Socialism! Oh yes, I am well aware that university professors, who ought to know better, have assured you that you are the heir to all the ages, Nature's last and most daring experiment. Believe them, by all means, if it helps you to forget the whip. Indulge in all the longings that aspirin and sweet tea and stump oratory can arouse. Dream of your never-never land, where the parks are covered with naked cow-like women, quite free; where the rich are cooked over a slow fire, and pigeons coo from the cupolas. Let the band in my park convince you that Life is seriously interested in marital fidelity and the right use of leisure, in the reign of happiness and peace. Go on, go on. Think what you like, vote for whom you like. What difference does it make? Make your little protest. Get a new master if you can. You will soon be made to realise that he is as exacting as the old, and probably less intelligent. . . . The truth is, Nature is not interested in underlings—in the lazy, the inefficient, the self-indulgent, the People. Nor, for that matter, in the Aristocracy, which is now only another name for the Idle Rich. The idle are never powerful. With their gigolos and quack doctors, they are as unhappy as the working classes who can afford neither, and a great deal more bored. The world has never been governed by the People or by the merely Rich, and it never will be. It is governed by men like myself—though, in practice, we are usually rich and often come from the People.

> [*He moves away from the window to the desk and picks up a signed photograph of the Leader.*]

No, not by you, dear Leader. You're one of the People, really, which is why they love you, you poor muddle-headed bundle of nerves, so over-worked and so hypnotised by the sound of your own voice that you will never know what's happening nor who pulls the strings. Do you think, my modern Caesar, that the Roman emperors were important? They weren't. It was the Greek freedmen, who kept the accounts, who mattered. The cardinals mattered in the Middle Ages, not those dreary feudal barons.

[*He picks up a statuette.*]

No, perhaps that's wrong, too. Real political power is only made possible by electricity, double entry and high explosives. Perhaps, after all, the hermits and the artists were wiser. Nothing is worth while except complete mastery, and, in those days, that could only be achieved over the Self. I wonder what it felt like to be St Francis Stylites or Poussin. Well, times have changed. The arts haven't been important since the eighteenth century. To-day, a creative man becomes an engineer or a scientist, not an artist. He leaves that career to neurotics and humbugs who can't succeed at anything else. [*Back at the window.*] This is probably the last period of human history. The political régimes of the future may have many fancy names, but never again will the common man be allowed to rule his own life or judge for himself. To be an artist or a saint has ceased to be modern. . . . Yes, for the man of power, there can now be but one aim—absolute control of mankind.

[*Enter* MANNERS, *R.*]

MANNERS. Mr Stahl, Sir.

[*Enter* STAHL, *R.*]

VALERIAN. Ah, my dear Stahl, welcome home!

[*Exit* MANNERS, *R.*]

STAHL. How are you, Valerian? You're looking well. [*Looks round the room.*] It seems strange to be in this room again. . . . You've bought a new etching, I see?

VALERIAN. Oh, I have a great deal to show you. But that can wait. You had a pleasant journey, I hope?

STAHL. Thanks, yes. Excellent.

VALERIAN. You only got back yesterday morning?

STAHL. And I've been run off my feet ever since!

VALERIAN. Your wife is well, I trust?

STAHL. Not as well as I should like. She's been suffering a lot with her migraine, lately. Extraordinary thing, migraine. Nobody really understands it. She stayed on in Paris to see that new Swedish man; he's discovered a special injection. I hope it'll do her some good.

VALERIAN. I am truly sorry to hear this. . . . And your boy? I hope his studies are progressing favourably?

STAHL. Well . . . yes and no. Igor works hard enough, but he's so undecided. He wants to give up engineering and read Icelandic. . . . I suppose it's just a phase. . . .

VALERIAN. My dear Stahl, you are indeed the model family man! Your worries never cease!

STAHL. Upon my word, Valerian, I sometimes envy you. When one sees you in this charming house, surrounded by your treasures, with no wife to run up milliner's bills! The world looks black enough, these days, Heaven knows—but at least a bachelor has only himself to think of....

VALERIAN. Always the pessimist! Which reminds me that I haven't yet thanked you for all those admirably lucid and exceedingly depressing letters....

STAHL. Well, I'm glad, at any rate, that you found them lucid!

VALERIAN. So much so that, as soon as I heard you were returning, I arranged for the Leader to come and hear the worst from Cassandra's own lips. There is nothing he so much enjoys as bad news—about foreign countries: England doomed, Germany bankrupt, the United States heading for her last and greatest slump.... Mind you lay it on thick! And with particular emphasis on the contrast between decadent, anarchical Ostnia and our own dear Westland—that paradise of solvency and order.

STAHL. I only hope the food won't choke me as I say it!

VALERIAN. My dear friend, you can have confidence in my chef: Ananias himself could lunch here with perfect impunity.... Though really it's a wonder I wasn't suffocated myself, the other evening: I had to spend an hour praising the works of the new National Academy of Art—Putensen, de Kloot, and those exquisite little landscapes (or should I say "cowscapes"?) of Ketchling....

STAHL. Ketchling? But surely he's the man who does the hair-tonic advertisements?

VALERIAN. What a memory you have! A rather dangerous memory, if I may say so, for these times.... Yes, it all happened about three months ago. You were in Brazil, I believe? Poor Milnik was so unfortunate as to offend the Minister of Propaganda. Next morning, he was discovered to possess an Ostnian great-grandmother, and, within a week, Ketchling had stepped into his shoes.... Ketchling's wife, I may add, had been having an affair with our respected Postmaster-General....

STAHL. The Postmaster? But surely Madame Korteniz...?

VALERNIAN. The reign of Madame Korteniz has ended, quite suddenly, under rather amusing circumstances.... But that's a long story, which will keep. Here I am, gossiping away like an old concierge, and you have told me nothing about your journey! First of all, how does Westland appear to a returned traveller—sadly provincial, I fear? There have been changes since you left, and none of them for the better. Since the Leader's newest statue was unveiled, it has become necessary to walk down Victory Avenue with one's eyes tightly closed. I always tell my chauffeur to make a detour. . . .

STAHL. Yes, I've seen that monstrosity already. . . . But I'm sorry to say that, since my return, I've received even worse shocks—

VALERIAN. Ah, you mean the neo-Egyptian portico of the new Culture House? Well, it's a nice point. The Leader, you'll admit, is the uglier of the two; but the Culture House is so much larger. . . .

STAHL. There's more wrong with this country than its architecture, Valerian. You know that better than I do. Coming back like this, after six months, one's appalled, simply appalled by the way things are going. Of course, I haven't had time to make detailed enquiries, yet; but I talked to the works managers early this morning, and yesterday I was at the Stock Exchange and around the clubs. People are afraid to say much, naturally; but I drew my own conclusions.

VALERIAN. Which were, no doubt, as gloomy as usual? I shall listen to them with the greatest interest. But not, my dear Stahl, *not* before lunch! You will ruin both our appetites.

STAHL. I know that it amuses you to be flippant. But these are facts. You can't pass them by, like the Leader's statue, with your eyes shut. . . . Something must be done, and done quickly. We're in for really big trouble. Conditions at the labour camps are getting worse all the time. The men are complaining quite openly: six months ago, they wouldn't have dared. The food isn't fit for an African village. The buildings leak—what can you expect from that Army contract stuff? T.B. is definitely on the increase. As for the Shock Troops—if even fifty per cent of what I hear is true—the whole organisation's rotten from top to bottom; and the commandants are responsible only to the Leader—which means to nobody at all. If you want to see them on business, you must search the night-clubs and the brothels; they never go near their offices. At the barracks, you'll hear the same story: the Leader has broken every promise he ever made. The same thing down at the Works. Agitators have been getting at the men, secret unions are being formed. I even heard rumours of a stay-in strike. . . .

VALERIAN. My dear friend, your sojourn in the democratic countries seems to have confused your ideas, a little! Surely you are aware that here, in our happy Westland, the Leader has declared all strikes illegal?

STAHL. An illegal strike is simply an insurrection.

VALERIAN. Which can be dealt with as such.

STAHL. Which *cannot* be dealt with! You know as well as I do that the troops would refuse to fire. Why, the General Staff wouldn't even dare to give the order!

VALERIAN. Aren't we becoming rather melodramatic? Do you, seriously, in your heart of hearts, believe that things could ever come to shooting? In Russia, yes. In Spain, yes. Never in Westland. You know our countrymen; a nation of grumblers—and grumblers are never dangerous. The situation is bad, of course—disgraceful, appalling, but hardly serious. When you have been at home a week or two, you will recapture that peculiar Westland sense of proportion—as lop-sided as Putensen's nudes—and you will agree with me.

STAHL. Perhaps I shall. Yes . . . that's just what I'm afraid of. . . . But now, before I begin to squint like the rest of you, let me tell you that, in my considered opinion, this country is on the verge of a revolution!

VALERIAN. Revolution! Revolution! Eternally that bogey word! When the old Emperor abdicated, everybody predicted a revolution, and what did we get? A cabinet of shopkeepers in ill-fitting top hats, who misquoted Marx and scrambled to cultivate the society of effete aristocrats, whose titles they themselves had just abolished by decree. The workers were impressed by their socialist speeches, and tried to act upon them—so the shopkeeper-marxists called them bolsheviks and traitors, dissolved parliament, suppressed the unions and established a dictatorship which lacked nothing but a dictator. Then came the Leader, in his fancy-dress uniform, and these same shopkeepers rejoiced, because the National Revolution was to make an end of the Valerian Works and all the big business concerns and open the garden of paradise to the small trader. And what did the Leader do? Crying: "Revolution!" he obligingly ruined a number of our lesser competitors and business rivals. He did not dare to touch the Valerian Trust. He did not want to touch it. Without us, he could not exist for a fortnight. . . . As for the workers, who you so much dread—they play at secret meetings, of which I am informed, and at printing illegal pamphlets, which litter my desk at this moment. The workers are all patient sheep, or silly crowing cockerels, or cowardly rabbits. . . .

[*Enter* MANNERS, *R.*]

MANNERS. I beg your pardon, Sir. The Leader's Bodyguard has arrived. They wish to make the—ah, usual inspection.

STAHL. Good Heavens! Whatever for?

VALERIAN. Oh, you will soon get used to these little formalities. A month ago, there was another attempt on the Leader's life. Hushed up, naturally. But I thought the foreign press would have got hold of it?

Since then, precautions have been doubled. The Leader never visits a strange house without assuring himself that there are no assassins hiding on the premises. . . . Very well. Let one of them come in.

[MANNERS *exits for a moment and re-enters with Storm-Trooper* GRIMM.]

GRIMM [*giving Westland Salute*]. For Westland. . . . I have orders to search this floor.

VALERIAN. By all means. Please make yourself quite at home.

GRIMM [*indicating door, L.*]. Where does that door lead to?

VALERIAN. To my bedroom, my bathroom, and the back staircase. . . . But, surely, you've been here before?

GRIMM. I only joined the Bodyguard last week.

VALERIAN. I see. . . . Strange. I seem to remember your face.

GRIMM [*quickly*]. That's impossible. I come from the eastern province.

VALERIAN. Well, we all make mistakes. . . . Pray don't let me detain you from your duties. And don't forget to look under the bed.

[GRIMM *salutes and exit, L.*]

VALERIAN [*to* MANNERS]. You'd better go with him, I think. He might take a fancy to my silver hairbrushes.

[MANNERS *bows and exit, L.*]

VALERIAN. There goes one of the rulers of our country!

STAHL. Common gangsters!

VALERIAN. After all, there is a good deal to be said for gangsters. One's dealings with them are so charmingly simple. They understand two things: money and the whip. They know where their bread and butter comes from. The Leader is much safer with these boys than with a pack of crooked politicians.

STAHL. By the way, how is the Leader, nowadays? In Paris, there was a lot of talk about his—health.

VALERIAN. With good reason, I'm afraid. You know, three weeks ago, he had a very serious breakdown. I'm told Pegoud was sent for. . . .

STAHL. Whew! So he's really mad, at last!

VALERIAN. My dear friend, the Leader has always been mad. The really alarming symptom is that he's beginning to recover. The crises are becoming isolated, less predictable, much more violent. He is no longer the roaring waterfall, whose power could be utilised and whose noise was harmless. He is the volcano which may suddenly destroy cities and men. . . . I ought to warn you: if any little disturbance occurs during lunch, please appear to take no notice. And, when it is over, behave as if nothing had happened. . . .

STAHL. A nice party you've let me in for, I must say! I'm beginning to feel quite scared. . . . I've only spoken to the Leader twice in my life. I'd no idea you knew him so intimately.

VALERIAN. I've been seeing a good deal of him, lately. He interests me. I have been studying, as the Americans say, the secret of his success.

STAHL. And what is this secret?

VALERIAN. The Leader, you see, is our national martyr. We Westlanders are a stolid, insensitive race: we need someone to do our suffering for us. The Leader bears upon his shoulders all the wrongs, all the griefs that Westland ever suffered—and many more besides. When the fat placid housewives attend his meetings, and see him rave and wring his hands, and tremble and weep, they shake their heads in their motherly way, and murmur: "Poor Leader—he is going through all this for *us*!" Then they return to their tea, with whipped cream and apple cakes, purged and ennobled, by proxy.

STAHL. But what beats me is how one can have any kind of personal relationship with him. Why, he isn't a man at all! He's a gramophone!

VALERIAN. No doubt. But even a gramophone can be made to play better and more harmonious records. . . . As a matter of fact, your mentioning gramophones was unintentionally apt. The Leader often drops in to listen to mine.

STAHL. You mean to say that you actually *play* to him!

VALERIAN. Oh yes, indeed. Like Orpheus. Whenever he seems tired and dispirited, or the conversation flags. . . . I flatter myself that I am educating him, slowly but surely. . . . We started with *Narcissus* and the *Melody in F*. After a fortnight, he was getting tired of them, so I prescribed *The War March of the Priests*—all too successfully. I think even Mendelssohn himself would have wished he had never written it. . . . At length, we passed on to the *Pathetic Symphony*, and, I am happy to say, outgrew it at the end of a weary month. At present, Rameau's *Tambourin* is the favourite. It seems likely to last through the summer. . . .

STAHL. Really, Valerian, you've missed your vocation! You should have been a lion-tamer!

[*Enter* MANNERS, *R.*]

MANNERS. The Leader has arrived, Sir.
STAHL. Good Gracious! He nearly caught us talking high treason!

[*Noises off. Someone shouts: "Guard! Attention!"* The Leader's *voice is heard, saying: "For Westland!" Enter* The Leader, *R.* Manners *exits, R., behind him.*]

Leader [*salutes*]. For Westland! [*Shakes hands.*] How are you, Valerian?

Valerian. Delighted to see you, Sir. . . . I believe you know Mr Stahl, one of our directors?

Stahl. You will hardly remember me, my Leader. We met last at the Industrial Banquet.

Leader. I never forget a face. [*Salutes.*] For Westland!

Valerian. I hope we see you in good health?

[*Enter* Manners, *with cocktails, R.*]

Leader. My health is at the service of my country. Therefore it is good.

[Manners *hands round cocktails, and exit, R.*]

Valerian. May it long continue so! Mr Stahl, as I told you in my letter, has just returned from a business tour of Europe and America. I wanted you to hear his impressions.

Stahl. There are certain points which might possibly interest you, my Leader.

Leader. Everything interests me. When I study any subject, I acquaint myself with its smallest details. [*Raising his glass.*] Westland!

Valerian } [*both drinking*]. Westland!
Stahl

Leader [*to* Stahl]. Tell me, is it true that, in London, negroes are even permitted to play in the dance orchestras?

Stahl. Well—yes, certainly.

Leader. I was right! Only a dying race could show such tolerance. England is becoming a foreign colony. Very soon, they'll be having Ostnians in to drive the trams! Ha, ha, ha!

[Valerian *and* Stahl *laugh dutifully.*]
[*Enter* Manners, *R.*]

Manners. Lunch is served, Sir. [*Exit, R.*]

Leader. I am in good spirits, to-day! What beautiful weather! We shall have a real Westland summer! Valerian, I have a surprise for you. After inspecting your Works, I shall take you for a drive in the park.

Valerian [*suppressing a groan*]. That will be delightful! Shall we go downstairs?

LEADER [*ignoring him*]. I want to have young faces around me—youth, health, springtime. The perfume of the flowers. The smell of the trees. The lithe active bodies of our splendid Westland children. . . . Ah, it does one good!

VALERIAN. I can imagine no more charming way of spending the afternoon. . . . Perhaps you'd like to have lunch? Then we can start earlier on our programme. . . .

LEADER [*as before*]. I was thinking, too, that we might visit your model cottages. I am never so happy as when I can spare a few moments from my work to spend among the common people. How delighted and surprised they will be to have their Leader among them! I love to watch their contented smiles as they bend over their humble tasks, working proudly, for Westland, each in his own sphere. How well I understand them! How well I know their wants! I know what they are thinking even before they know it themselves. It is my mission to restore to every Westlander the dignity of labour, to put good honest tools into his hands, to guard him from crafty, underhand foreign competition. Westland must awake! Westland must throw off her fetters! Westland must raise the heavy load of poverty from the shoulders of the groaning poor. [*He picks up a paper-weight from the desk*]. Westland must—

VALERIAN [*tactfully taking the paper-weight from* THE LEADER's *hand*]. Bravo, Sir! Bravo! I hope you'll say that to our operatives, this afternoon. It will inspire them. . . . Lunch is ready. Shall we go down?

LEADER [*suddenly cut short in the middle of his enthusiasm, stares stupidly, for a moment, at his empty hand. Then, as if coming to earth, he says quietly*]. Ah, yes—lunch. . . .

CURTAIN

(Before the Curtain)

[*A ray of light, barred with shadow, as if through a prison window, illuminates four prisoners, two women and two men. They are squatting on the ground, handcuffed. Their faces are ghastly.*]

[Air: "Sweet Betsy from Pike".]

FIRST PRISONER [*sings*]. Industrialists, bankers, in comfortable chairs
   Are saying: "We still have control of affairs.
   The Leader will have all our enemies shot".

ALL. They would like to forget us, but, O, they cannot!

SECOND PRISONER. The idle, the rich, and the shabby genteel
    And the clever who think that the world isn't real
    Say: "The forces of order have triumphed! We're safe!"

ALL. But the world has its own views on how to behave!

THIRD PRISONER. The judge sits on high in a very fine wig,
    He talks about Law and he talks very big,
    And chaplains in church say: "Obedience is best".

ALL. We've heard that before and we're not much impressed!

FOURTH PRISONER. The Leader stands up on his platform and shouts:
    "Follow me and you never need have any doubts!
    Put on my uniform, wave my great flag!"

ALL. But when the wind blows he shall burst like a bag!

FIRST PRISONER. "If you're foolish enough", they declare, "to resist,
    You shall feel the full weight of fieldboot and fist".
    They beat us with truncheons, they cast us in jail,

ALL. But all their forms of persuasion shall fail!

SECOND PRISONER. They boast: "We shall last for a thousand long years",
    But History, it happens, has other ideas.
    "We shall live on for ever!" they cry, but instead

ALL. They shall die soon defending the cause of the dead!

THIRD PRISONER. They talk of the mystical value of Blood,
    Of War as a holy and purifying flood,
    Of bullets and bombs as the true works of art.

ALL. They'll change their opinion when shot through the heart!

FOURTH PRISONER. Perhaps we shall die by a firing-squad,
    Perhaps they will kill us, that wouldn't be odd,
    But when we lie down with the earth on our face

ALL. There'll be ten more much better to fight in our place!

ALL. The night may seem lonely, the night may seem long,
    But Time is patient and that's where they're wrong!
    For Truth shall flower and Error explode
    And the people be free then to choose their own road!

BLACK OUT

ALL [*softly*]. And the day is approaching and soon will begin,
When the Leader no longer will take Westland in.
And Westland will waken and reach for her gun,
And the years of oppression be over and done.

Act I Scene 2

[*The Ostnia-Westland Room. It is not to be supposed that the Frontier between the two countries does actually pass through this room: the scene is only intended to convey the idea of the Frontier—the L. half of the stage being in Westland: the R. half being in Ostnia. The furnishing of the two halves should suggest differences in national characteristics, and also in the nature of the two families which inhabit them: the Thorvalds' (Westland) home is academic; the Vrodny-Hussek (Ostnian) home is comfortable, reactionary, bourgeois. Each home has a door and window, L. and R. respectively. On the back wall of each hangs a big portrait, with a wireless-set standing beneath it. The Thorvalds have a portrait of the Westland "Leader", who is bearded and ferocious-looking: the Vrodny-Hussek family have a portrait of the King of Ostnia, very suave and gracious, with orders and much gold braid. The chairs are arranged in two semi-circles, and the concentration of lighting should heighten the impression of an invisible barrier between the two halves of the stage. The two groups of characters (with the exceptions to be noted later) seem absolutely unaware of each other's existence.*]

[*It is evening. When the curtain rises,* DR OLIVER THORVALD, *the University professor, is writing at his desk.* MRS THORVALD *is laying cards at a table, and* ERIC *their son, who is a student, sits writing in an armchair with a bookrest.*]
[*On the other side of the stage,* MRS VRODNY *is darning socks, seated on the sofa. Her father,* COLONEL HUSSEK, *sits reading the newspaper in an invalid wheel-chair.*]

DR THORVALD [*pausing to read aloud what he has written*]. "Professor Jongden appears to have modelled his style upon the more sensational articles in the popular press of his country. For his scholarship, however, we can discover no precedent. His emendations would not convince a commercial traveller. The authorities he quotes, and as frequently misquotes, are most of them out of date. Beyer's great work on the Ionian Laws he does not so much as mention; no doubt he is unwilling to acknowledge that any contribution to culture could be made by a nation which he has always been taught to regard as barbarian."

COL. HUSSEK [*reading from newspaper*]. "The Minister for Propaganda has banned the sale in Ostnia of the Westland *Sunday Sun* for one month—as the result of the insulting caricatures of His Majesty, published in last Sunday's issue. . . ." I can't think what the country's coming to! Thirty years ago, they wouldn't have dared! The old King must turn in his grave. He would never have allowed our honour to be—

MRS VRODNY [*bitterly*]. Nobody cares about honour, these days! All they think of now is Self!

COL. HUSSEK. You're right, Louisa! Our young people have no sense of Ostnian loyalty.

MRS VRODNY. You've no idea, Father, how rude the shopgirls are, nowadays! I could smack their faces sometimes; they're so insolent. And the prices! Mother would have had a fit! [*Holds up a sock with an enormous hole in it.*] Just look at that! How Oswald manages to wear his socks into such holes I can't imagine!

DR THORVALD [*reading aloud*]. "We strongly advise the Professor to leave the classics alone and to betake himself to a sphere to which his talents are less unfitted. We suggest that the scandals of the Ostnian Court would be a suitable choice."

ERIC. Who are you attacking this time, Father?

DR THORVALD. Jongden has just brought out a book on Ionia—a typical Ostnian piece of work. All superficial brilliance and fluff, with nothing behind it. No Ostnian ever made a scholar. They think it vulgar to take trouble.

ERIC. But isn't he the man who's been offered a chair at Yale?

DR THORVALD. Just because he can make amusing little speeches after dinner, they prefer him to a real scholar, like Beyer! It's preposterous! He can't hold a candle to him!

MRS THORVALD. You know, dear, it's only because Beyer is a Westlander. And they believe all the lies their newspapers spread about us. I can't understand why they're allowed to print such stuff. The Leader ought to put a stop to it.

COL. HUSSEK. Tcha! Another lightning strike at the Docks! If they'd only shoot a few of them, it'd put a stop to all this nonsense!

MRS VRODNY. I'm sure it's only due to Westland agitators, Father. The Ostnian working-man would never behave like that of his own accord. He's got too much common-sense. He knows it only puts up the cost of living.

MRS THORVALD. The Ace of Diamonds. . . . Do you think that means I've won a prize in the *Sunday Sun* Doublets, or only that Martha's ordered enough vegetables to go round? She so seldom does. . . . Eric dear, I do wish you wouldn't work so hard! I'm sure it can't be good for you. Why don't you go out and do field-exercises, like the other students?

DR THORVALD. Leave the boy alone, Hilda. You can't become a scholar without keeping your nose to the grindstone, eh Eric? [*Rises from desk and comes over to* ERIC'*s chair, lighting his pipe.*] What are you writing on, this time? [*Looks over* ERIC'*s shoulder.*] "The chances of European peace"! What a ridiculous subject! Surely Professor Bluteisen never set you that?

ERIC. No. I'm doing it for a few of my friends. Some of us are trying to think these things out.

DR THORVALD. You're wasting your time, my boy. What chances are there of peace—with the Ostnians arming to the teeth? I tell you, Europe's a powder-magazine. It only needs a spark.

MRS THORVALD. Martha says the war's coming this year. It's all in Revelations, she says. She tried to explain it to me, but she's so difficult to understand: her false teeth fit so badly.

ERIC. Don't talk like that, Mother! Of course there'll be a war if we all go on saying and thinking there will be, and doing nothing to stop it. Why are we all so frightened? None of us *want* war.

MRS THORVALD. *We* don't, but what about the Ostnians?

COL. HUSSEK. Notes. Negotiations. . . . We're too polite to them; that's our trouble!

MRS VRODNY. The Westlander's a bully. Always has been.

DR THORVALD. After the last war, when we were weak, they bullied us. And it's only now, when the Leader's shown them that Westland won't stand any nonsense, that they've learnt to mind their ps and qs a bit.

COL. HUSSEK. The only thing the Westlander understands is the stick. We ought to have finished the job properly, last time.

ERIC. How do you know the Ostnians want war?

MRS THORVALD. Haven't they always hated us? Haven't they always been jealous of us? Especially since our national revolution.

DR THORVALD. They're jealous of our liberty and power of creative progress.

MRS VRODNY. The trouble is, they've no traditions. That's why they're jealous of us. They always have been. They're spoilt children, really.

DR THORVALD. A decadent race is always jealous of a progressive one.

MRS VRODNY. You may say what you like; tradition and breeding count.

Mrs Thorvald. You may say what you like, Eric. You can't wipe out the history of a thousand years.

Col. Hussek. Damned bolsheviks!

Eric. Well, I think that if people—the ordinary decent people in both countries—would only get together, we could . . .

> [Enter Anna Vrodny, R., with a shopping basket. The effect of her presence upon Eric is instantly noticeable. He breaks off in the middle of his sentence, as though he had forgotten what it was he had meant to say. Throughout the rest of the scene he follows Anna's movements eagerly with his eyes. Anna, also, is watching Eric, but more timidly and covertly. Nobody else on the stage appears to notice this.]

Mrs Vrodny. Oh, there you are at last, Anna! Whatever have you been doing all this time?

Dr Thorvald. Could what, Eric?

Anna. I'm sorry, Mother. There was such a queue at Benets'. [Begins to take parcels out of basket and lay them on the table.]

Dr Thorvald. Well, go on! What could you do?

Mrs Thorvald. Oh, don't argue so, Oliver! It makes my head ache!

Dr Thorvald. Sorry, my dear. I was only trying to make him see how woolly-minded he is. And Westland has no use for woolliness, these days. I've got to go now to a meeting of the tutorial board, to consider the case of those so-called pacifist demonstrators yesterday. And I don't mind telling you, Eric, that I shall vote for their expulsion from the University. Let that be a warning to you, my boy!

> [Exit Dr Thorvald, L.]

Mrs Vrodny [rising from the sofa to inspect Anna's purchases]. You call that a chicken? Why didn't you go to Litvaks?

Anna. But, Mother, you said Litvaks was so expensive!

Mrs Vrodny. Oh, it's hopeless! I can't trust any of you to do the simplest things! I work my fingers to the bone for you all, and nobody helps me in the least!

Mrs Thorvald. The Queen of Hearts! Well I never! At my age! It must be for you, Eric! How exciting!

Mrs Vrodny. Don't stand there dawdling, Anna! We've got to get supper ready. It'll be late as it is.

> [Mrs Vrodny and Anna collect the parcels and exeunt, R. During the scene which follows, Col. Hussek falls gradually asleep.]

Mrs Thorvald. The cards never lie! Eric, I don't believe you're listening!
Eric. Sorry, Mother, I was just thinking about something.

> [*Enter, L.,* Martha Thorvald, *Dr Thorvald's sister, with a prayer-book and a bunch of flowers. She pauses solemnly, before speaking, to salute the Leader's portrait.*]

Martha. Cards again? Really, Hilda, I'm surprised at you, indulging in that sinful nonsense!
Mrs Thorvald. Oh, Martha! It isn't nonsense!
Martha [*arranging flowers in a vase before the Leader's portrait*]. It's wicked superstition. . . . There! Don't these look beautiful, under the Leader's picture? They're just the colour of his eyes! Pastor Brock preached a wonderful sermon about him to-day. . . .
Mrs Thorvald. The Pastor's such a fine man, but I do wish he wouldn't shout so. He makes my head ache.
Martha. Westland needs more like him! He took as his text: "I come not to bring peace, but a sword!"
Eric. Pastor Brock isn't a Christian at all. He wants to rewrite the Bible.
Martha. Eric! How dare you!
Eric. "They that live by the sword shall perish by the sword." How does he explain that?
Martha. I suppose you think you're clever: sitting there and sneering, while every decent young Westlander is out learning to defend his country? If I were your Mother—
Mrs Thorvald. Oh, my poor head! If you two are going to quarrel, I'm off to bed.

> [*Exit* Mrs Thorvald, *L.*]

Eric. I'm sorry, Aunt Martha. I didn't mean to hurt your feelings.
Martha. Don't apologise to me. Apologise to the Leader. It's him you hurt when you talk like that. He cares so much for all of us. . . . Goodnight, my Leader! God keep you! [*She salutes the picture and exit, L.*]
Eric [*rises from his chair, goes up to the picture and regards it*]. Tell me, what is it you really want? Why do you make that fierce face? You're not fierce, really. You have eyes like my father's. Are you lonely, are you unhappy, behind that alarming beard? Yes, I see you are. Perhaps you only want love—like me. . . . [*He continues to examine the picture.*]
Col. Hussek [*waking up with a violent start*]. Extend on the right! Rapid fire! Charge! [*Rubbing his eyes.*] Louisa! [*Enter* Mrs Vrodny, *R.*] Where's my supper?

Mrs Vrodny. We're waiting for Oswald.

Col. Hussek. Boozing again, I suppose!

Mrs Vrodny. It's always the same thing, when he gets his pension-money.

[Oswald's *voice is heard singing, outside.*]

Here he is, at last!

[*Enter* Oswald Vrodny, *drunk, R.*]

Oswald [*singing*]. Then up spoke Captain O'Hara:
"It's a hundred and one in the shade;
If you give me your Irish whisky
You can keep your Irish maid!"
Well, Louisa, and how are the busy little fingers, this evening? Good evening, General Fieldboots! Still fighting to the last man?

Col. Hussek. You're drunk, Sir!

Oswald [*producing a bottle*]. I've brought you some powerful reinforcements! Guess what this is!

Mrs Vrodny [*trying to snatch bottle*]. Give me that at once!

Oswald. Naughty! Mustn't snatch! Allow me to introduce you to an old friend you haven't seen for a very long time—the finest Westland whisky!

Col. Hussek. How dare you bring their filthy stuff into this house!

Mrs Vrodny. It's so unpatriotic!

Oswald. Patriotism be damned! I can't touch that foul Ostnian cognac; sooner drink cold tea! What good is it going to do Ostnia if I ruin my liver? Answer me that! You and your patriotism! Those chaps over there know how to make whisky, and I'm grateful to them! Any man who makes good whisky is my friend for life! [*Drinks.*] Here's to Westland!

Col. Hussek. Another word, Sir, and I'll call the police and have you arrested, this minute!

Mrs Vrodny. Father and I have been very patient with you. But there's a limit to everything. You've never done a hand's turn in your life! You're just a drunken sponger!

[*Enter* Anna, *R.* Eric *immediately turns from the picture, and begins to watch her, as before, but with increasing agitation.*]

Anna. Mother! Mother! Do be quiet, please. All the neighbours will hear you! Come on, Uncle Oswald. Supper's ready in the kitchen.

Oswald [*taking* Anna's *arm*]. That's my own little girl!

ANNA. You two go on. I'll look after him.

> [*Exeunt* MRS VRODNY, *wheeling* COL. HUSSEK, R.* ANNA *follows, half-supporting* OSWALD, *who is humming the Wedding March from* Lohengrin.]

ERIC [*taking a pace forward, exclaims involuntarily, despairingly*]. Anna!

> [*But* ANNA *does not seem to hear him. Exeunt* ANNA *and* OSWALD, *R.* ERIC *stands looking sadly after her.*]

CURTAIN

Act II Scene 1

[*The Ostnia-Westland Room. It is evening. As the curtain rises, we see on the L. of the stage,* DR THORVALD, MRS THORVALD, MARTHA *and* ERIC, *drinking a bed-time cup of tea.* ERIC, *as usual, is watching* ANNA VRODNY, *who sits sewing on the R. of the stage, with* OSWALD *and* COL. HUSSEK. COL. HUSSEK *has the newspaper.* OSWALD *is lazily smoking. Both wireless-sets are switched on, but silent.*]

ANNA. Please come to bed, Grandpa. It's after eleven. You look tired out.
COL. HUSSEK. Nonsense, my dear! Never felt better in my life! Must wait to hear the news. Westland will have to admit responsibility. She can't get round the evidence. I tell you, this means war!
OSWALD. Thank God I'm fat and fifty! No more wars for us, Colonel! We've done our share!
COL. HUSSEK. I never thought I'd hear a nephew of mine confess to being a coward! It's the greatest regret of my life that I—
ANNA. Oh, Grandfather, don't excite yourself! You know he doesn't mean it. . . . Uncle Oswald, you mustn't be such a tease!
OSWALD. Well, you don't want Grandpa to be killed, do you? Or even your lazy old Uncle, I hope? Throw me the matches, there's a good girl.

> [ANNA *does so.*]

MRS THORVALD. I think I *will* have a second cup, Martha, after all. I shan't sleep a wink, in any case. . . . Eric, dear, you haven't touched yours. Don't you want it?
ERIC. No, thank you, Mother.
MRS THORVALD. Well, it *has* been a day of excitements! Those poor, poor

children! I shall never dare to go by bus again! I suppose Ostnia will apologise. . . .
Dr Thorvald. They'll have to! The evidence of their guilt is overwhelming.
Martha. You can't apologise for murder! They must be punished!

>[*Both wireless-sets give the time signal.*]

Dr Thorvald. Ssh! The news is coming on!
Anna [*calling*]. Mother! The news!
Westland Radio. Maria Kinderheim, the six-year-old child injured in the bomb outrage at the Iron Bridge, died in hospital this evening. This brings the number of the Westland dead up to nineteen.

>[*Enter* Mrs Vrodny, *R.*]

Ostnian Radio. Peter Vollard, the eighty-year-old labourer injured in the bomb outrage at the Iron Bridge, died in hospital this evening. This brings the number of the Ostnian dead up to twenty.
Westland Radio. The Minister for Propaganda and the Minister for Air and Marine flew to Castle Tuborg this afternoon to discuss with the Leader what steps should be taken. . . . It is rumoured that the Ostnian Government is calling up the nineteen-fourteen and nineteen-fifteen classes.
Ostnian Radio. An emergency meeting of the Cabinet was called this evening to consider what steps should be taken. . . . There are rumours that Westland will order general mobilisation.
Westland Radio. In view of the extreme gravity of the situation . . .
Ostnian Radio. In view of the extreme gravity of the situation . . .
Westland Radio. The Leader . . .
Ostnian Radio. His Majesty the King . . .
Westland Radio. Has decided . . .
Ostnian Radio. Has graciously consented . . .
Westland Radio. To address the nation . . .
Ostnian Radio. To address his people . . .
Westland Radio. The address will be broadcast from all stations at midnight.
Ostnian Radio. The address will be broadcast from all stations at midnight.

>[*Throughout the scene which follows, the two wireless-sets provide a background of faint, disturbing ominous music.*]

Mrs Vrodny. When I think of that poor old man who never did anybody any harm, it makes my blood boil!

[MARTHA *starts collecting the tea things.*]

MRS THORVALD. The poor mite! She was only a tiny tot!
ANNA. It's horrible! How can anyone have been such a brute!
MRS VRODNY. All Westlanders are brutes, dear.
ANNA. Some of them were killed, too; weren't they, Mother?
MRS VRODNY. How do you know? The papers don't say so. The Westlanders are such liars, anyhow!
MRS THORVALD. The demonstration in the market square was enormous. I could hardly push my way through!
DR THORVALD. I've never seen the students so moved. We had to suspend all lectures for the day.
MRS VRODNY. There was a crowd outside Benets' this afternoon. They were smashing the windows.
COL. HUSSEK. Serve them right! We don't want any dirty Westlanders here, cheating us out of our money! Most of them are spies! It's high time we cleared out the lot!
OSWALD. Well, I never did care for Westland much. The women have thick ankles. All the same, I hope they don't sack Freddy from the Long Bar. He mixes the best cocktails in Ostnia.

[*Exit* MARTHA, *L., with tray.*]

MRS THORVALD. I met Bob Veigel in the street, to-day. Such a nice boy! And quite high up in his shock-troop already. He was so upset. I could hardly get a word out of him except: "We must avenge the Iron Bridge!"
COL. HUSSEK. We must have action! You can't bandy words with murderers! We must avenge the Iron Bridge!
ANNA. I think I'll be going to bed, Mother. I've got rather a headache.

[*Re-enter* MARTHA, *L.*]

MRS VRODNY. But aren't you going to stay and hear the King?
ANNA. I don't think I will, Mother, if you don't mind. Goodnight. Goodnight, Uncle. Goodnight, Grandpa.

[*She hurries out, R., as if anxious to escape from them all.*]

MRS VRODNY. She's been so quiet all day. I'm afraid she's not well.
MRS THORVALD. Eric, dear, you're very silent, this evening. Aren't you feeling well?
ERIC [*abruptly*]. I've got a headache. I'm going to bed.
MARTHA. But Eric, the Leader!

Mrs Thorvald. Oh, Martha! Don't worry him to-night! You can tell him all about it in the morning. [*To* Eric.] You'll find some aspirin in the top drawer of my dressing-table.

Eric. Thanks, Mother. Goodnight. [*Exit, L.*]

Mrs Thorvald. It must have been a very tiring day for him, with all these demonstrations.

Dr Thorvald. I wonder.... I'm not very happy about him, Hilda. I'm afraid he's making some unhealthy friendships. They play at being radicals, pacifists, goodness knows what. Eric's such a child. He doesn't realise what this business means. This crime strikes at the whole basis of European civilisation.

Mrs Vrodny. Did you read Father Ambrose's article on the consequences of heresy? We must defend the Church. The Church is in danger!

Oswald. I was taken to a service in Westland, once. God, I was bored! All those extempore prayers!

Martha. The Ostnians *aren't* civilised! They're savages! They burn incense and worship idols!

[*Noise and singing and the tramp of marching feet L. and R. off. All the characters move excitedly towards their respective windows,* Col. Hussek *propelling himself in his invalid chair. From this moment the acting works up to a note of hysteria.*]

Mrs Vrodny [*at window, R.*]. Look, Father! The Air Force cadets!

Mrs Thorvald [*at window, L.*]. It's the students! Hundreds of them!

Oswald. They're tight!

Martha. The hour is at hand!

Col. Hussek. Stout fellows!

Mrs Thorvald. How happy they look in their uniforms! I wish Eric was among them!

[*The two songs which follow should be sung simultaneously.*]

Westland Students [*off, L.*].
Brightly the sun on our weapons is gleaming,
   Brave is the heart and stout is the arm,
Gone is the night of talking and dreaming,
   Up and defend your country from harm!

The mountain has strength, the river has beauty,
   Westland Science, Religion and Art

>   Inspire us with valour and Westland Duty
>   Echoes in every Westland heart!
>
> Foremost of all the Leader is riding,
>   Love in his bosom and truth on his brow,
> Against the whole world in the Leader confiding,
>   Forward to victory follow him now!

OSTNIAN AIR CADETS [*off, R.*].
>   Wheel the plane out from its shed,
>   Though it prove my funeral bed!
>   I'm so young. No matter, I
>   Will save my country ere I die!
>
>   Hark, I hear the engines roar!
>   Kiss me, we shall meet no more.
>   I must fly to north and south.
>   Kiss me, sweetheart, on the mouth!
>
>   Far from Mother, far from crowds,
>   I must fight among the clouds
>   Where the searchlights mow the sky,
>   I must fight and I must die!

DR THORVALD. It's the spirit of Pericles! The poets have not sung in vain!
MRS VRODNY. I wish I were a man!
MARTHA. Out of the pit! Out of the mire and clay!
OSWALD. Perhaps I ought to do something!
MRS THORVALD. The cards did not lie!
COL. HUSSEK. This makes me feel a boy again!
DR THORVALD. Some people have asked the meaning of history. They have their answer!
MRS VRODNY. They looked like princes!
MARTHA. The righteous shall inherit the earth!
OSWALD. I shall drink less and less!
MRS THORVALD. My headache's quite gone!
MRS VRODNY. We shall be very famous indeed!
MRS THORVALD. We shall never die!
COL. HUSSEK. I have never lost a battle!
DR THORVALD. Everything's perfectly clear, now!
OSWALD. After this, we shall all be much richer!
COL. HUSSEK. We are doing splendidly!
MARTHA. God is very glad!

OSTNIAN RADIO. This is Ostnia calling the world!
WESTLAND RADIO. This is Westland calling the world!
OSTNIAN RADIO. His Majesty the King!
WESTLAND RADIO. The Leader!
KING'S VOICE [*through radio, R.*]. It is hard to find words to express . . .
LEADER'S VOICE [*through radio, L.*]. The unceasing struggle of my life has been rewarded . . .
KING. How deeply touched we have been . . .
LEADER. Westland is restored to her greatness . . .
KING. By all the offers of service and sacrifice . . .
LEADER. One heart, one voice, one nation . . .
KING. Which have poured in from every corner of Our country . . .
LEADER. It is a lie to say that Westland has ever stooped to baseness . . .
KING. And from every class of people, even the poorest . . .
LEADER. It is a lie to say that Westland *could* ever stoop to baseness . . .
KING. These last few days of terrible anxiety have brought us all very close together . . .
LEADER. It is a lie to say that Westland wants war . . .
KING. We all, I know, pray from the bottom of our hearts . . .
LEADER. Westland stands in Europe as a great bastion . . .
KING. That this crisis may pass away . . .
LEADER. Against the tide of anarchy . . .
KING. Our Ministers are doing everything in their power . . .
LEADER. Westland lives and Westland soil are sacred . . .
KING. To avoid any irreparable step . . .
LEADER. Should any human power dare to touch either . . .
KING. But should the worst happen . . .
LEADER. It will have to face the holy anger of a nation in arms . . .
KING. We shall face it in a spirit worthy of the great traditions of our fathers . . .
LEADER. That will not sheathe the sword . . .
KING. To whom honour was more precious than life itself . . .
LEADER. Till it has paid for its folly with its blood . . .
KING. We stand before the bar of history . . .
LEADER. For, were Westland to suffer one unrequited wrong . . .
KING. Confident that right must triumph . . .
LEADER. I should have no wish to live!
KING. And we shall endure to the end!

> [*The wireless-sets play their respective national anthems.*]

COL. HUSSEK [*standing up in his chair, in great excitement*]. God save the King! God save the King! [*He collapses.*]
MRS VRODNY. Father! [*She runs to him.*] Quick, Oswald, the brandy!
MRS THORVALD. Dear me, I feel quite exhausted!
OSWALD [*looking in cupboard*]. There's no brandy left. He'll have to have my whisky.
MRS VRODNY. Hurry!

[OSWALD *gives her the bottle and a glass.*]

Here, Father! [*Gives* HUSSEK *a sip.*] Take this.
DR THORVALD. Time we all went to bed. There won't be any more news to-night. Come along, Hilda.
COL. HUSSEK [*faintly, opening his eyes*]. Thank you, my dear ... Sorry ... My heart, again ... Better now ... It's been a great day ...
MRS VRODNY [*to* OSWALD]. Help me to get him to bed.
MRS THORVALD. You're not staying up, are you, Martha dear?
MARTHA. I'll follow you in a minute.
OSWALD [*pushing the* COLONEL'S *chair*]. Up we go!

[*Exeunt* DR *and* MRS THORVALD, L.]

Feeling better now? That whisky's wonderful stuff!

[*Exeunt* OSWALD *and* COLONEL, *R., followed by* MRS VRODNY *who turns out the light, so that the R. of the stage is darkened.*]

MARTHA [*kneeling before the* LEADER'S *portrait*]. My hero! My Leader! You will fight them, won't you? Say you will! Say you will! [*Kneels for a moment, then rises, salutes and exit, L., turning out light.*]

[*The whole stage is now in complete darkness for some moments. Distant, dreamy music, off. Then a spotlight illuminates a small area in the middle of the stage. The various chairs and tables should have been pushed back, so that they are visible only as indistinct shapes in the surrounding darkness. Enter* ERIC *and* ANNA, *L. and R., respectively. They advance slowly, like sleepwalkers, until they stand just outside the circle of light, facing each other.*]

ERIC. Is that you, Anna?
ANNA. Yes, Eric.

[*They both take a step forward into the light-circle.*]

ERIC. I knew I could make this happen!
ANNA. Where are we?
ERIC. In the place that I have found for us,
    The place that I have hoped for since I was born,
    Born, as we all are, into a world full of fear,
    Where the faces are not the faces of the happy,
    Where the disappointed hate the young
    And the disinherited weep in vain.
    Not that any are wanting this world, any;
    The truckdriver, the executive setting his watch,
    The clerk entraining for the office, us,
    All of us wishing always it were different.
    All of us wanting to be kind and honest,
    Good neighbours and good parents and good children,
    To be beautiful and likeable and happy.
    Ever since I was born I have been looking,
    Looking for a place where I could really be myself,
    For a person who would see me as I really am.
    And I have found them both, found them now, found them here.
    This is the good place.
ANNA. I am afraid. The darkness is so near.
ERIC. This is the good place
    Where the air is not filled with screams of hatred
    Nor words of great and good men twisted
    To flatter conceit and justify murder.
    Here are no family quarrels or public meetings,
    No disease or old age. No death.
    Here we can be really alone,
    Alone with our love, our faith, our knowledge,
    I've struggled for this ever since I saw you.
    A long time, Anna. Did you know that?
ANNA. A long time, Eric, yes, I've felt you near me.
    You took my arm in crowded shops,
    Helping me choose.
    Behind my chair as I sat sewing, you stood
    And gave me patience. Often you sat
    Beside me in the park and told me stories
    Of couples in the panting unfair city
    Who loved each other all their lives.
    O when I went to dances, all my partners
    Were you, were you.
ERIC. Ever since I remember I've caught glimpses of you,

        At first, far off, a nature on the crag,
        Far off down the long poplar avenue, a traveller.
        I've seen your face reflected in the river
        As I sat fishing; and when I read a book
        Your face would come between me and the print
        Like an ambition, nearer and clearer every day.
        And now, at last. . . .
ANNA. Do They see, too?
ERIC. They do not want to see. Their blindness is
    Their pride, their constitution and their town
    Where Love and Truth are movements underground,
    Dreading arrest and torture.
ANNA. O Eric, I'm so afraid of them!
ERIC. Locked in each other's arms, we form a tower
    They cannot shake or enter. Our love
    Is the far and unsuspected island
    Their prestige does not hold.
ANNA. I wish that this could last for ever.
ERIC. It can, Anna, it can! Nothing matters now
    But you and I. This is the everlasting garden
    Where we shall walk together always,
    Happy, happy, happy, happy.
ANNA. You do not know their power. They know, know all.
    They let us meet but only to torment us
    When they have proved our guilt. They grin behind our joy,
    Waiting their time. O if we take one step
    Towards our love, the grace will vanish,
    Our peace smash like a vase. O we shall see
    The threatening faces sudden at the window, hear
    The furious knocking on the door,
    The cry of anger from the high-backed chair.
ERIC. It can't be true! It shan't be true!
    Our love is stronger than their hate!
    Kiss me.
ANNA. Don't, don't! You'll make them angry!
    We shall be punished!
ERIC. I don't care! I defy them!

                [*He steps forward to embrace her. The stage is immediately plunged in darkness. Their voices now begin to grow fainter.*]

VOICES [*these should be taken by the actors playing* DR THORVALD *and* MRS

VRODNY, *and should have the resonant disembodied quality of an echo*]. NO!

ERIC'S VOICE. Anna, Anna. Where are you?

ANNA'S VOICE. Where are you, Eric?

ERIC. Come back.

ANNA. I can't. They're too strong. Help me, Eric. They're taking me away.

VOICE 1. Take her away.

ERIC. They're holding me back.

VOICE 2. Hold him back.

ANNA. I shall never see you again.

BOTH VOICES. Never see { him / her } again.

ERIC. Anna. Can you hear me? I swear I'll come back to you. I'll beat them somehow. Only wait for me, Anna. Promise you'll wait.

ANNA. I promise, Eric.

VOICE 2 [*whispering*]. Tradition and breeding count.

VOICE 1 [*whispering*]. You can't wipe out the history of a thousand years.

CURTAIN

(Before the Curtain)

[*Five men, three women. Three couples are waltzing. The two remaining men, who are supposed to be left-wing political workers, are watching, in the background.*]

FIRST MALE DANCER.
    The papers say there'll be war before long;
    Sometimes they're right, and sometimes they're wrong.

SECOND MALE DANCER.
    There's a lot of talk in a wireless-set
    And a lot more promised than you'll ever get.

FIRST LEFTIST.
    Don't believe them,
    Only fools let words deceive them.
    Resist the snare, the scare
    Of something that's not really there.
    These voices commit treason
    Against all truth and reason,
    Using an unreal aggression

To blind you to your real oppression;
Truth is elsewhere.
Understand the motive, penetrate the lie
Or you will die.

THIRD MALE DANCER.
The Winter comes, the Summer goes;
If there's a war, we shall fight, I suppose.

FIRST MALE DANCER.
The larder is cold, the kitchen is hot;
If we go we'll be killed, if we don't we'll be shot.

SECOND LEFTIST.
What they can do depends on you,
You are many, they are few,
Afraid for their trade, afraid
Of the overworked and the underpaid.
Do not go; they know
That though they seem so strong
Their power lasts so long
As you are undecided and divided;
Understand the wrong;
Understand the fact;
Unite and act.

SECOND MALE DANCER.
There're hills in the north and sea in the south;
It's wiser not to open your mouth.

THIRD MALE DANCER.
Soldiers have guns and are used in attack;
More of them go than ever come back.

FIRST FEMALE DANCER.
What shall I say to the child at my knee
When you fall in the mountains or sink in the sea?

SECOND FEMALE DANCER.
What shall we do if you lose a leg?
Sing for our supper, or steal or beg?

FIRST LEFTIST.
It's weak to submit,
Then cry when you are hit.
It's mad to die
For what you know to be a lie.
And whom you kill
Depends upon your will.
Their blood is on your head.

Choose to live.
The dead cannot forgive
Nor will time pardon the dead.
THIRD FEMALE DANCER.
What is a parlour, what is a bed
But a place to weep in when you are dead?
FIRST MALE DANCER.
It's goodbye to the bench and goodbye to the wife
And goodbye for good to somebody's life.
SECOND MALE DANCER.
Our country's in danger, and our cause is just;
If no one's mistaken, it's conquer or bust.
SECOND LEFTIST.
The country is in danger
But not from any stranger.
Your enemies are here
Whom you should fight, not fear,
For till they cease
The earth will know no peace.
Learn to know
Your friend from your foe.
THIRD MALE DANCER.
But if some one's mistaken or lying or mad,
Or if we're defeated, it will be just too bad.

BLACK OUT

Act II Scene 2

[VALERIAN's *study. Just after midnight.*]

> [VALERIAN *and* STAHL, *with brandy glasses before them, are listening to the* LEADER's *speech on the radiogram.*]

LEADER'S VOICE. . . . it will have to face the holy anger of a nation in arms, that will not sheathe the sword till it has paid for its folly with its blood. For, were Westland to suffer one unrequited wrong, I should have no wish to live!
VALERIAN. Admirable sentiments! A little more brandy, my dear Stahl?
STAHL. Thanks. . . . I need it. . . . [*Pours and drinks.*] The man's got a voice like a corncrake!

VALERIAN. Oh, I can't agree with you there! His delivery is really excellent. He has mastered all the tricks. I'm told that he once took lessons from Sacha Guitry.
STAHL. I didn't like the tone of that speech at all. . . . You know he saw the General Staff again, this evening? You mark my words, this is to prepare the country for mobilisation. The decree's probably signed already.
VALERIAN. Hammel would never agree to it.
STAHL. Then he'll override Hammel. We're dealing with a madman. You said so, yourself.
VALERIAN. Very well. Let us suppose that mobilisation is ordered. What does that mean, nowadays? Nothing! We live in an age of bluff. The boys shout until they are hoarse, and the politicians hunt for a formula under the conference-table. A lot of noise to cover up an enormous cold funk.
STAHL. Cold funk is an exceedingly dangerous state of mind. A coward often hits first.
VALERIAN. But, I ask you, who wants war? Certainly not the industrialists: the arms race is good for another five years at least. Certainly not the politicians: they're far too jealous of the military and afraid of losing their jobs. Even the General Staffs don't want it: they're both perfectly happy playing at mechanisation. . . . Do you seriously imagine that wars nowadays are caused by some escaped lunatic putting a bomb under a bridge and blowing up an omnibus? There have been worse provocations in the past, and there will be worse in the future. The national honour will swallow them all quite conveniently. It has a very strong digestion.

[*Enter* LESSEP, *R., with papers.*]

LESSEP. Here are the latest press bulletins, Mr Valerian.
VALERIAN. Thank you.

[*Reads. Exit* LESSEP, *R.*]

STAHL. Anything fresh.
VALERIAN. Nothing. Students' demonstrations. Patriotic speeches. All the customary nonsense. . . . Our operatives gathered outside the Villa Kismet during the lunch hour and cheered the Leader till it was time to go back to work. Then two of the organisers of the illegal trades union were recognized in the crowd, and so roughly handled that the Police had to take them into preventive custody. . . . The Iron Bridge incident has certainly solved some of our labour problems—for the moment.

STAHL. Yes—for the moment. . . . But, even supposing that there's no war, how will all this end?

VALERIAN. It will end itself. In ten days there will be a new distraction—an international football match or a girl found murdered in her bath. . . . [*Reads.*] This is rather amusing. An Ostnian journalist has written an article proving conclusively that the Iron Bridge bomb was fired by order of myself!

STAHL. Haha! Thank goodness for something to laugh at, anyway!

VALERIAN. "The sinister Westland industrialists, realising that they have brought their country to the verge of ruin, attempt a desperate gambler's throw". . . . You know, Stahl, a crime of this sort—so pointless, so entirely without motive—is bound to have a curious psychological effect upon everybody. Don't *you* sometimes wake up in the night, and wonder: Who did it? Like the reader of a detective story? And, of course, the most apparently innocent are the most suspect. Perhaps it was the Ostnian archbishop. Perhaps it was the wife of our municipal librarian. Perhaps it was my butler, Manners. And then, inevitably, one begins to wonder: was it I myself, in a moment of insanity, followed by amnesia? Have I an alibi? Ought I to go to the Police and confess? Madness is so infectious.

STAHL. In your list of suspects, you've forgotten the chief madman. Why shouldn't it have been the Leader, himself?

VALERIAN. Ah, no, my friend. The Leader is the only man in all Westland who is quite above suspicion. If he had done it, he would never have been able to resist telling us so! [*Listening.*] I wonder who that is on the stairs? Surely it can't be a visitor, at this hour of the night?

[*Enter* MANNERS, *R.*]

MANNERS. It's the Leader, Sir.

STAHL. Gracious! I'd better clear out.

VALERIAN. No. Please stay. This will be interesting.

> [*Enter the* LEADER *and Storm-Trooper* GRIMM, *R. The* LEADER's *whole manner has changed. He is obviously exhausted. He speaks gently, almost timidly. Storm-Trooper* GRIMM *takes up his position at the back of the stage. Throughout the scene which follows, he neither moves nor speaks.*]

LEADER. May I come in?

VALERIAN. This is an unexpected honour.

LEADER. I saw your light in the window, on my way back from the Broadcasting Station.

VALERIAN. We have been listening to your speech.

LEADER [*sinking into a chair*]. How quiet it is, in here! All day long I have been surrounded by shouting, noise, crowds. I thought: for a few moments I shall be able to be quiet. . . .

STAHL. Perhaps, my Leader, you'd prefer to be left alone?

LEADER. No, no. I hate to be alone. Don't leave me, any of you. . . .

VALERIAN. You must be very tired?

LEADER. More tired than I have ever been, in my whole life.

VALERIAN. You'll take some wine? Something to eat?

> [*The* LEADER *does not reply.* VALERIAN *makes a sign to* MANNERS, *who goes out, R.*]

LEADER [*begins to speak quietly, then with rising hysteria*]. For five nights I have lain awake, wondering: What shall I do? What shall I do? And no one can decide for me. No one! I alone must make the final choice. Peace or war? It is a terrible burden to put upon the shoulders of one man. . . . You think I am strong? No, I am weak, weak. . . . I never wished to be the Leader. It was forced upon me. Forced upon me, I tell you, by the men who said they were my friends, and who thought only of their own ambition. They made use of me. They made use of my love for my dear country. They never loved Westland as I did. . . . I stood on a platform in a village hall or a table in a little restaurant—when I began to speak, people listened. More and more people. It was like a dream. I was proud of my power. They flattered me. . . . And I was so simple; only a poor out-of-work bank-clerk. I believed them. . . . My parents were country people. They gave their last savings to have me educated. "You mustn't grow up to be a peasant", they told me. And I obeyed them. I worked hard. I would have been contented with so little. I was afraid of the world, of the rich people in their fine houses. I feared them and I hated them. . . . And then I found that I could speak. It was easy. So easy. I had money, friends. They told me: "You will be a great man." I learnt their ways. Step by step. Climbing higher and higher. I had to be cunning. I had to do horrible things. I had to intrigue and murder. Nobody knows how I have suffered. Nobody knows that I did it all for Westland. *Only* for Westland. . . . Don't you believe me?

VALERIAN [*soothingly*]. Certainly we believe you.

LEADER. In the nights, when my people are all asleep, I lie and tremble. You would never understand. . . . It's like some terrible nightmare. I—I alone, am responsible. And at the great receptions, when I stand there in my uniform, with all the foreign diplomats and the beautiful well-born women around me (the women I used to dream of when I was a poor boy in an office), I want to scream in all their faces: "Leave me alone! Leave me alone! Let me go back to my parents' cottage! Let me be humble and free!" Some of these women know what I am feeling. I see it in their eyes. How they despise me! [*Screaming.*] Don't you see how you are all torturing me? I can't bear it! I must bear it! I can't bear it! [*Covers his face with his hands and sobs.*] No! No! No! No!

> [VALERIAN *goes quietly over to the radiogram, and starts the record of Rameau's "Tambourin". Then he and* STAHL *remain motionless, watching the* LEADER. *During the music,* MANNERS *comes in, R., silently places a tray of cold supper near the* LEADER's *chair, and exit, R.*]
>
> [*As the music proceeds, the* LEADER's *sobbing quietens and stops. For some time he remains motionless, his face in his hands. Then, slowly, he raises his head. His expression is now calm and radiant. When the music stops, he is smiling.*]

LEADER. Ah . . . that music! How clearly I see the way, now! [*Rising to his feet.*] Listen, all of you. I have made a great decision! To-morrow morning, the whole world will hear that I have withdrawn the Westland troops, unconditionally, ten miles from the frontier. It will hear that I have proposed to Ostnia a pact of non-aggression, guaranteeing the sanctity of the frontier for a thousand years!

STAHL. My Leader, may I congratulate you? This is the finest thing you have ever done!

LEADER. They will not sneer at me any more, will they, in England and France and America? They will not be able to say I wanted war. My decision will be famous. It will be praised in the history books. I will make my country the greatest of all gifts—the gift of peace!

STAHL. This is magnificent!

LEADER. To-morrow night, you will hear my greatest speech. My Peace Speech. I shall stand before my shock troops and I shall tell them: War is glorious, but Peace is more glorious still! And I shall convince them! I know it! I am strong, now! They may not understand at first, but they will obey, because it is my will. The will of their Leader. The immutable, unconquerable will of the Westland nation. . . . I must speak to General Staff Headquarters, at once!

STAHL [*aside*]. Valerian, you have saved us all!

VALERIAN [*aside*]. I receive your thanks on behalf of poor Rameau. If only he were alive! How very surprised he would be!

[*Enter* LESSEP, *R., with envelope.*]

LESSEP. My Leader, an urgent despatch from General Staff Headquarters.
LEADER [*reads, crumples paper. Furiously*]. They have dared! You will bear witness, all of you, that Westland had no hand in this! You will record my decision for the judgment of posterity!
STAHL. But—my Leader, what has happened?
LEADER. An hour ago, the Ostnian troops crossed our frontier! Kapra has been bombed by Ostnian planes. Women and children foully, heartlessly murdered!
STAHL. Oh, my God!
VALERIAN. The idiots!
LEADER. The die is cast! The name of Ostnia shall be blotted from the map of Europe for ever!
STAHL. This is the end of everything!
LEADER [*in his platform manner*]. Confident in the justice of our cause, and determined to defend our sacred Westland homesteads to the last, we swear—

[*He is still shouting as the* CURTAIN *falls.*]

Act III Scene 1

[*The Ostnia-Westland Room. It is early evening. On the L. of stage,* MARTHA *sits rolling bandages.* MRS THORVALD *is knitting a muffler.* DR THORVALD *is reading the casualty-lists in the newspaper.*]

[*On the R. of the stage sits* MRS VRODNY, *all in black, alone. She is staring in front of her, with a fixed expression. She looks much older.*]

[*It is noticeable that both homes seem shabbier and poorer than in the earlier scenes. Several pieces of furniture are missing. Indeed, the* VRODNY-HUSSEK *home is almost bare.*]

MRS THORVALD. Mrs Veigal says it was perfectly wonderful. She could hear Bob's voice just as if he were in the room. He told her not to worry. Those who have passed over are all very happy. He said the Other Side was difficult to describe, but it was like listening to glorious music!
MARTHA. It's wicked, Hilda; and dangerous as well! How does she know she wasn't talking to an evil spirit?

Mrs Thorvald. I don't see that it can do any harm. And it's such a comfort to her! Poor woman, she idolised Bob!

Dr Thorvald. Well, at least she can be proud of him! Listen to this: "Robert Veigal. Killed in action. December the tenth. The Blue Order. For conspicuous gallantry in the face of the enemy." The casualty-lists this evening are terrible! That offensive on the Slype Canal was a shambles. If they don't make some big changes on the General Staff soon, there'll be trouble! Hammel ought to have been retired years ago.

Martha. There're too many healthy young men slacking in cushy staff jobs! As for those cowardly pacifists, I can't think why they're allowed to have a soft time in prison! They ought to be sent to the firing-line!

Mrs Thorvald. Oh, Martha, you're cruel! After all, Eric's your nephew!

Dr Thorvald. Hilda, I've told you before never to mention his name in this house again! The shame of it has almost killed me!

Mrs Thorvald. I suppose you wish he'd been blown to pieces by a shell, like Bob Veigal! Well, perhaps he *is* dead! They wouldn't tell me anything!

Dr Thorvald. You didn't go to the prison?

Mrs Thorvald. Yes I did! So there! He's my son and I want to see him! I don't care about anything, any more.... Eric, my darling boy, what have they done to you? [*She bursts into tears.*]

Dr Thorvald. She's overwrought. She doesn't know what she's saying. ... Martha, could you make some coffee? It would do her good.

Martha. We haven't any coffee. And we've used up our week's ration of sugar, already. There isn't any more firewood, either.

Dr Thorvald. I suppose we shall have to burn another of the spare-room chairs. [*With an attempt to smile.*] Soon we shall be sitting on the floor!

Martha. I'll see what I can find. [*Exit, L.*]

Dr Thorvald [*rising and going over to his wife*]. I'm sorry, dear!

Mrs Thorvald [*sobbing*]. You're not! You don't love Eric! You never did!

Dr Thorvald. Perhaps I have been rather harsh. I haven't tried to understand what made him act as he did. You see, I was brought up to think that a man's greatest privilege was to fight for his country; and it's hard to change one's ideas. Perhaps we were all wrong. War seems so beastly when it actually happens! Perhaps "country" and "frontier" are old-fashioned words that don't mean anything now. What are we really fighting for? I feel so muddled! It's not so easy to rearrange one's beliefs, at our age. For we're both getting on, aren't we, dear? You must help me. We've got no one to turn to now, but each other. We must try to think of all the happy times we've had together.... You remember them too, don't you, Hilda? We must make a new start.... I tell you what I'll do—to-morrow I'll go down to the prison myself! Perhaps I shall be able to get something out of them!

MRS THORVALD [*looks up and smiles*]. Thank you, dear!

DR THORVALD. That's better! Give me a kiss! [*They embrace and remain seated together, holding hands.*] This is quite like old times, isn't it?

[*Enter* ANNA, *also in black, R.*]

MRS VRODNY [*without turning her head, in a harsh, croaking voice*]. How much did he give you?

ANNA. Eight hundred and fifty.

MRS VRODNY. That's ridiculous! It cost twelve hundred!

ANNA. Oh, Mother, I know! I argued and argued with him! But it was no use. He just laughed. I was so afraid he might refuse to take it at all. Then he tried to kiss me.... It was beastly!

MRS VRODNY. Your Father gave me that brooch on our engagement-day.

ANNA. Why did you do it, Mother? Wasn't there anything else?

MRS VRODNY. It was the last I had. But what does it matter?

ANNA. You're worn out. Why don't you take a day in bed? I'll look after everything.

MRS VRODNY. Nonsense! You've got your hospital-work to do. Aren't you on night-duty this week? You ought to be getting your things on, now.

ANNA. Very well, Mother. [*Exit, R.*]

[*Enter* MARTHA, *with tray, L.*]

MARTHA. I've made you some herbal tea. It's all there is.

MRS THORVALD. How sweet of you, Martha! [*To* DR THORVALD.] I haven't had time to look at the paper yet. Is there any real news? They never tell us anything!

DR THORVALD. Nothing much. All the fronts were quiet, this morning. The usual rumours of desertion and mutinies in the Ostnian regiments. Probably nonsense. But there seems no doubt that they're having a very bad time with the Plague. They're dying by thousands, apparently!

MARTHA. It shows there's some justice in the world!

MRS THORVALD [*notices that there are only two cups on the tray*]. Won't you have a cup as well, Martha? You're not looking too grand, you know. Are you all right?

MARTHA. I've got a bad headache, that's all. I think perhaps a cup would do me good. I'm feeling so thirsty! [*Exit, L.*]
DR THORVALD. Of course, the papers have censored it, but I hear that there've been one or two cases here, among the prisoners of war.
MRS THORVALD. Oliver! How dreadful! Supposing it spreads!
DR THORVALD. Oh, we're safe enough!
MRS THORVALD. But just suppose it does! What are the symptoms?
DR THORVALD. I don't know exactly. A swelling under the arm, I believe. ... But you mustn't worry your head about that!

[*Enter* ANNA, *R., in nurse's uniform.*]

ANNA. I'm off now, Mother.
MRS VRODNY Keep clear of the office when you go downstairs. They took away the caretaker, this morning.
ANNA [*hysterically*]. Can't they do anything to stop it, before it kills everybody in the whole world? It's taken Grandfather. It's taken Uncle Oswald. It'll take us, too, soon! What have we all done that we should be destroyed like this? Nobody's *alive* any more! I look at the faces in the streets, and they're not the faces of living people! We're all dead!
MRS VRODNY. Anna! Control yourself!

[*L. and R., as in Act II, Scene 1, the sound of marching feet is heard. But this time there is no music, only the tap of a drum.*]

[ANNA *goes to window, R.*]
[*Enter* MARTHA, *L., with her cup.*]

MRS THORVALD. Those horrible drums! Oh, shut the window! I can't bear the sound any more!
DR THORVALD [*going to window, L.*]. They're mere boys! How many of them will be alive in a week's time? They used to sing once. ... Oh God, why can't it stop! [*Bangs down window.*]
MRS VRODNY. Listen to them marching! Think what those men are going to face. Grandfather was a soldier, and his father before him. We're the only ones left now. Perhaps we shan't be here much longer. But remember that, whatever happens to you, you come of a family of soldiers! Never forget that!

[*The marching dies away.*]

DR THORVALD. I must be off to the University. We're working out a new scheme of courses for the blind. Can I get anything for you in town?
MARTHA. Could you get me some linament?

Mrs Thorvald. Linament? What for, Martha? Have you hurt yourself?
Martha. I don't know. I've got such a funny swelling.
Dr Thorvald [*exchanging a quick glance with his wife*]. A swelling?
Mrs Thorvald. How long have you had it?
Martha. Only since this morning. It came up quite suddenly.
Dr Thorvald. Could you have bruised yourself, somehow?
Martha. Oh no, I'm quite sure I haven't. . . . But it hurts!
Dr Thorvald [*trying to speak calmly*]. Where, exactly, is this swelling, Martha?
Martha. Here. Under my arm. . . . Why, what's the matter?
Mrs Thorvald [*jumping up with a scream*]. She's got it! She's got the Plague! Don't let her touch me! Keep her away! We shall catch it! We shall all die!
Dr Thorvald. Quiet, Hilda! I don't expect it's anything serious, but you'd better go to your room, Martha. . . . I'll phone for the doctor at once!

> [*He and his wife instinctively back away from* Martha *into a corner of the stage.*]

Martha [*hysterical*]. No! No! It can't be! I won't! I've been good! You can't let me die! I've never had a chance! You don't know how I've suffered! You don't know what it's like to be ugly, to see everyone else getting married, to spend your life looking after other people's children! I've sacrificed everything! I had brains! I might have had a brilliant career, but I gave it all up for you! I've been more loyal than any of them! If you let me die, there's no point in being good, any more! It doesn't matter! It's all a lie! I've never been happy! I've been betrayed!
Anna [*as if listening to sounds in the very far distance*]. Mother . . . can't you hear them, over there? They're crying, they're suffering—just like us!
Mrs Vrodny [*speaking with a kind of terrible obstinacy, which belies her words*]. I hear nothing!
Martha [*runs to the* Leader's *portrait*]. Oh, my Leader! Say you don't mean it! Say I'm going to live! Speak to me! [*She falls on her knees before the picture, and, in doing so, switches on the wireless.*]
Westland Radio [*tonelessly, like a time-signal*]. Kill, Kill, Kill, Kill, Kill! [*Continues to the end of scene.*]
Anna [*with an involuntary despairing cry*]. Eric, where are you?

CURTAIN

(Before the Curtain)

[*Three Westland soldiers are grouped, L., behind some kind of simplified construction to represent a parapet. They stare across the stage into the darkness, R., where the Ostnian trenches are supposed to lie. The Ostnians remain invisible, throughout, but their voices are represented by the two remaining male members of the chorus, off. One of the Westland soldiers has an accordion, to which he sings:*]

FIRST SOLDIER. Ben was a four foot seven Wop,
    He worked all night in a bucket-shop
    On cocoa, and sandwiches,
    And bathed on Sunday evenings.

    In winter when the woods were bare
    He walked to work in his underwear
    With his hat in his hand,
    But his watch was broken.

    He met his Chief in the Underground,
    He bit him hard till he turned round
    In the neck, and the ear,
    And the left-hand bottom corner.

    He loved his wife though she was cruel,
    He gave her an imitation jewel
    In a box, a black eye,
    And a very small packet of Woodbines.

OSTNIAN [*off*]. THE *ONLY* BRAND!
SECOND SOLDIER. Ssh! Did you hear that?
FIRST SOLDIER. The bleeders! I'll show 'em. [*Picks up rifle.*]
THIRD SOLDIER. Sit down, yer fool. You'll start something. [*Shouts across stage.*] HULLO!
OSTNIAN [*off*]. HULLO!
THIRD SOLDIER. WOT'S IT LIKE, YOUR SIDE?
OSTNIAN [*off*]. WET.
THIRD SOLDIER. SAME HERE.
OSTNIAN [*off*]. GOT ANY CIGARETTES?
SECOND SOLDIER. YES. BUT NO RUDDY MATCHES.
OSTNIAN [*off*]. WE'VE GOT MATCHES. SWOP?
SECOND SOLDIER. RIGHT. COMING OVER. [*Throws matches.*]
OSTNIAN [*off*]. THANKS. COMING OVER. [*The packet of cigarettes flies out of the darkness but falls short, outside the parapet.*] SORRY!
FIRST SOLDIER. CHRIST, YOU OSTNIANS THROW LIKE A PACK OF SCHOOL-GIRLS! [*To the others.*] Wait a mo. Gimme a torch.

SECOND SOLDIER. Take care!
FIRST SOLDIER. Oh, they're all right! [*Climbs over parapet and looks for cigarettes.*]
OSTNIAN [*off*]. MORE TO THE LEFT. FURTHER. THERE, MAN! RIGHT UNDER YOUR NOSE!
FIRST SOLDIER. Got 'em. THANKS, BOYS. [*Picks up packet and climbs back.*]
OSTNIAN [*singing, off*]. What are we fighting for?
                      What are we fighting for?
THIRD SOLDIER [*joining in*]. Only the sergeant knows.
   [*To* FIRST SOLDIER.] Come on, Angel. Get yer squeeze-box.

> [FIRST SOLDIER *begins to play the accordion. Air: "Mademoiselle from Armentiers". The three Westland soldiers sing the first six verses in turn, all joining in the chorus.*]

> The biscuits are hard and the beef is high,
> The weather is wet and the drinks are dry,
> We sit in the mud and wonder why.

> With faces washed until they shine
> The G.H.Q. sit down to dine
> A hundred miles behind the line.

> The Colonel said he was having a doze;
> I looked through the window; a rambler rose
> Climbed up his knee in her underclothes.

> The chaplain paid us a visit one day,
> A shell came to call from over the way,
> You should have heard the bastard pray!

> The subaltern's heart was full of fire,
> Now he hangs on the old barbed wire
> All blown up like a motor-tyre.

> The sergeant-major gave us hell.
> A bullet struck him and he fell.
> Where did it come from? Who can tell?

> > [*The* OSTNIANS *now join in.* OSTNIANS *and* WESTLANDERS *sing the following six verses alternately, joining in the last.*]

Kurt went sick with a pain in his head,
Malingering, the Doctor said.
Gave him a pill. Next day he was dead.

Fritz was careless, I'm afraid.
He lost his heart to a parlour-maid.
Now he's lost his head to a hand-grenade.

Karl married a girl with big blue eyes.
He went back on leave; to his surprise
The hat in the hall was not his size.

Oh, No Man's Land is a pleasant place,
You can lie there as long as you lie on your face
Till your uniform is an utter disgrace.

I'd rather eat turkey than humble pie,
I'd rather see mother than lose an eye,
I'd rather kiss a girl than die.

We're sick of the rain and the lice and the smell,
We're sick of the noise of shot and shell,
And the whole bloody war can go to hell!

BLACK OUT

Act III Scene 2

[VALERIAN's *study*. VALERIAN *is nervously pacing the room.* LESSEP *is seated by the desk, at the telephone. It is night.*]

VALERIAN. Call the hospital again. There must be some news by now!

LESSEP [*dials and speaks into phone*]. Hullo. . . . Is that the Central Hospital? Mr Valerian wishes to enquire for his butler, Mr Manners. . . . Thank you. . . .

VALERIAN. I told him not to go into the city; and he disobeyed me—for the first time! He risked his life, Lessep: and do you know why? To try and find me a pot of caviare! Ridiculous, isn't it? [*Going to window.*] Tell me, is the Plague really so bad, down there?

LESSEP. It's much worse than they admit. The newspapers are still ordered to minimise it; and they're burying all the dead by night.

VALERIAN. Extraordinary. . . . Up here, we inhabit another world!

LESSEP. But, Mr Valerian, there's always the danger of infection. Even for us! Forgive my speaking of it again, but don't you think it would be wiser to move? You could go to your villa at Konia. . . .

VALERIAN. If you are frightened you have my permission to go there—alone.
LESSEP. Of course, I'm only thinking of *your* safety. . . . [*Into telephone.*] Yes? Yes. . . . Oh . . . I am very sorry. . . . Thank you. . . .
VALERIAN. Well, what do they say?
LESSEP. Manners . . . I'm afraid he's dead. . . . Half-an-hour ago. The fever didn't break.
VALERIAN. Dead. . . . So. . . . I'm sorry. . . . Well, there's nothing I can do about it now. [*To* LESSEP.] Have any more reports come in?
LESSEP. Only a telegram from the Tarnberg Colliery. The eight o'clock shift refused to go down, and are threatening to destroy the plant. The manager doesn't think the police are reliable.
VALERIAN. Nothing from Headquarters?
LESSEP. There's been no news of any kind from the front all day. The storm must have broken down the wires.

[*Buzzer on desk sounds.*]

VALERIAN. See who that is.
LESSEP [*into the house telephone*]. Hullo. Speaking. Yes, Mr Valerian is here.
VALERIAN. Who is it?
LESSEP. It's Mr Stahl. He's coming upstairs now.

[*Enter* STAHL, *R. He is haggard and exhausted. His clothes and raincoat are splashed with mud.*]

STAHL. Valerian! Thank God you're safe!
VALERIAN. My dear Stahl, this is a pleasant surprise. I thought you were visiting our gallant boys in the trenches. Oh dear, where *did* you get that cap? It makes you look like a racing tout. And you're wet through. What have you been doing? How did you get here?
STAHL. I managed to find the airfield. Thank God, most of the pilots are still loyal. We landed in the meadows, a couple of miles from the house. In the pitch darkness. . . . We were lucky not to crash.
VALERIAN. What a state you're in! Lessep, the brandy.
STAHL. Thanks. . . . [*Drinks.*] I'm quite exhausted. Ran most of the way through woods, over ploughed fields . . . didn't dare show myself on the road. . . .
VALERIAN. I say, Stahl, are you tight? What *is* the matter?
STAHL. You mean, you don't know?
VALERIAN. There's been no news all day. The telegraph wires are down.
STAHL. Cut, you mean. . . . When we were only a few miles from the front the car was stopped by a couple of private soldiers, we were

told to get out, and taken along to a sort of barn. They wouldn't answer any questions, but there were a lot of officers in the barn, prisoners like myself, and I soon learnt what was happening. The whole Northern sector has mutinied and are fraternising with the enemy. All officers who tried to stop them were shot out of hand. Jansen was bayoneted in his own headquarters.... And that's not all. There was a revolution in the Ostnian capital this morning. The King's hiding somewhere in the mountains; to-morrow he will have abdicated, if he's alive. The Ostnians have got loudspeakers in the front line, calling on their soldiers to make an armistice and revolt against their own government!

VALERIAN. Excellent! Nothing could be better. The new Ostnian government is certain to be incompetent and full of intrigue. It will be our big chance to finish things off. But I'm interrupting you. How did you get away?

STAHL. I managed to bribe one of the guards with a cigarette case.

VALERIAN. Not the one your wife gave you for a silver wedding present? My word, you'll catch it!

STAHL. Valerian, this isn't funny. This humour of yours is becoming a pose. We've got to get out of here. There's nothing either of us can do.

VALERIAN. And where do you propose that we should go?

STAHL. You know I had a cable the other day from Quinta in Rio, asking me to help him build up the South American Trusts? I'm going to accept his offer, and I want you to come too. We need you, Valerian.

VALERIAN. My dear friend, I am too old for carpet-bagging. Quinta would impose his own conditions. He'd use us like office boys.

STAHL. This is no time for false pride. Do you realise, man, that if you stay here you'll see your life-work ruined before your eyes?

VALERIAN. Steady, steady. Don't get hysterical. Listen, what you tell me doesn't surprise me in the least. I only wonder it hasn't happened before. What can you expect? The war should have been over in three weeks if our friend Hammel had the brains of a fifth-rate actor. It's gone on for nine months. The plague was bad luck certainly, but if our public health authorities had ever learnt to co-operate with each other, it could have been kept within bounds. Of course, there're mutinies and strikes; there'll be more before we're done. There were plenty in the Great War.... A lot of people will have to be arrested, and a few of them shot. The Leader will visit the trenches again in person. There'll be an advance of a hundred yards somewhere, the papers will predict an immediate victory, and the workers and the soldiers will go back to their jobs. As for Ostnia....

STAHL. You don't understand. You don't want to. You're crazy with conceit! It wasn't just a little local trouble I saw. The officers told me that only Frommer's 18th route army is still completely loyal. I tell you, it means civil war!

VALERIAN. Very well. Suppose it does. Do you seriously think that a rabble of half-baked townees and farm labourers without any officers can stand up against Frommer, who is certainly the best general we've got? I'm afraid they'll be sorry they were ever born. Frommer's not a kind old gentleman, and has rather old-fashioned ideas about the sanctity of private property.

STAHL. It's no use arguing. I know what I saw. They tore the tabs off a colonel and shot him in the stomach before my eyes. It was horrible! This is the end.

VALERIAN. If you think so, then it's no good my talking, is it? I'm sorry that our long partnership should come to such a sudden conclusion.

STAHL. But what are you going to do?

VALERIAN. What should I do? Stay here, of course.

LESSEP. Mr Valerian—What's the use? I beg you to go.

VALERIAN. My dear Lessep, do not alarm yourself. I shall not ask you to stay here with me. Indeed, I order you to accompany Mr Stahl. You would not be the least use to me just now—merely a hindrance. Take him, Stahl, with my warmest recommendation.

STAHL. Valerian, this is suicide. Within twenty-four hours there'll be street fighting here. You know as well as I who they will try to murder first.

VALERIAN. We shall see. If it gets too uncomfortable I suppose I shall have to join Frommer for a while, though I shall dislike that intensely. The man's a bloodthirsty old bore.

LESSEP [*beginning to cry*]. I can't leave you here, Mr Valerian.

VALERIAN. Oh yes, you can. Quite easily. . . . Please spare me these heroics, they do not become you.

STAHL [*looking at his watch*]. Heavens, it's late. We must go at once. If we can't cross the frontier before dawn, we may be fired at. Valerian, for the last time; will you come?

VALERIAN. No.

STAHL. Very well, then. . . . Good-bye.

VALERIAN. Good-bye, my dear Stahl. I shall look forward to your letters about the evils of South America. Please remember me to your wife.

LESSEP [*sobbing*]. Good-bye, Mr Valerian.

VALERIAN. Before we part, Lessep, I've one more job for you. Buy Mr Stahl a new hat.

STAHL [*with a burst of nervous impatience, to* LESSEP]. For God's sake, man, come—if you're coming! Don't waste your pity on him. He's mad!

[*Exit* STAHL *and* LESSEP, *R.*]

VALERIAN. There goes marriage! Poor Stahl! Always the subordinate, staggering under the luggage of a social-climbing wife and a playboy son. . . . He'll dislike South America even more than I should. . . . I wonder if he secretly hopes to be taken back, if things go right, here? If he does, he's mistaken. The family is a charming institution, but one has to pay for it. I don't like deserters.

[*Takes up house-telephone.*]

Hullo. . . . Hullo. . . .

[*Goes to door, L., opens it and calls.*]

Schwarz!

[*No answer. Crosses to door, R., opens it and calls.*]

Schwarz! Frederick! Louis! Kurt!

[*No answer. Comes back to centre of stage.*]

Bolted. . . . Well, I can't blame them. . . . Gone to a demonstration, I suppose, to shout stickjaw slogans with the rest, and listen to their gibbering prophets who promise the millennium in a week.

[*Goes to window.*]

You poor fish, so cock-a-whoop in your little hour of comradeship and hope! I'm really sorry for you. You don't know what you're letting yourselves in for, trying to beat us on our own ground! You will take to machine-guns without having enough. You will imagine that, in a People's Army, it is against your principles to obey orders—and then wonder why it is that, in spite of your superior numbers, you are always beaten. You will count on foreign support and be disappointed, because the international working-class does not read your mosquito journals. It prefers our larger and livelier organs of enlightenment, which can afford snappier sports news, smarter features, and bigger photographs of bathing lovelies. We shall expose your lies and exaggerate your atrocities, and you will be unable to expose or exaggerate ours. The churches will be against you. The world of money and political influence will say of us: "After all, they are the decent people, *our* sort. The others are a rabble." A few of the better educated may go so far as to exclaim: "A plague on both your houses!" Your only open supporters abroad will be a handful of intellectuals, who, for the last twenty years, have signed letters of protest against everything from bi-metallism in Ecuador to the treatment of yaks in Thibet. . . .

> [*As he speaks these last lines, he returns to the desk and helps himself to a sandwich from a plate which is lying there. Enter Storm-Trooper* GRIMM, *very quietly, L.* VALERIAN *turns and starts slightly, on seeing him.*]

VALERIAN. To what do I owe this unexpected pleasure?
GRIMM. I startled you, didn't I?
VALERIAN. Yes, for a moment, I confess you did.
GRIMM. That's what I wanted.
VALERIAN. You came up the back staircase? How did you get in?
GRIMM. The doors are standing open.
VALERIAN. My servants have all run away, it seems.
GRIMM. I knew that. I met one of them in the city.
VALERIAN. So you came to keep me company? Most considerate. . . . You've brought a message, I suppose?
GRIMM. Yes. I've brought a message.
VALERIAN. Excellent. Does the Leader want me to join him?
GRIMM. My message isn't from the Leader. But you may join him. Sooner than you think.
VALERIAN. This all sounds very mysterious. . . . Where is he now? Still in the capital? Or has he gone to Frommer? [GRIMM *does not answer.*] Come, come! We haven't the whole night to waste!
GRIMM. What I have to say to you won't take long.
VALERIAN. So much the better. . . . But first let me offer you one of these excellent sandwiches. . . .

> [*Moves his hand towards the plate.* GRIMM *whips out a pistol and covers him.*]

GRIMM. Keep away from that telephone!
VALERIAN [*after recovering from the shock*]. My dear child, you mustn't wave that thing about! It might go off.
GRIMM. Get back over there. Against the wall.
VALERIAN [*obeying*]. You little fool! It was the Leader who told you to do this, I suppose?
GRIMM. The Leader will never tell me to do anything, again. If you want him, go and look in his study. You'll find him with his face on the table, and twenty bullets in his back, and the blood all over that fine Turkey rug you gave him. . . .
VALERIAN. So? My dear boy, do stop trembling and slobbering at the mouth in that disgusting manner! To tell you the truth, your news doesn't surprise me quite as much as you'd suppose. I always sus-

pected that you and your gang of hooligans would rat, when you thought the time had come. Only, the time *hasn't* come, you see. That's where you show a deplorable lack of political foresight. . . .

GRIMM. I didn't come here to talk about the Leader.

VALERIAN. I can very well imagine why you came here, my murderous little gunman. Having lost one master, you're in search of another. . . . Well, as it happens, I can use you quite conveniently. . . . You have a car with you, I suppose?

GRIMM. What if I have?

VALERIAN. And plenty of petrol? Petrol, in these days, is worth rubies. My chauffeur seems to have disappeared. I want you to drive me to General Frommer's headquarters, at once.

GRIMM. And if I refuse?

VALERIAN. Oh, I hardly expect you to refuse. . . . After your little shooting-party, I've no doubt that you and your colleagues stuffed your pockets with all the bank-notes in the Leader's safe? You're feeling quite rich? Well, let me tell you that, across the frontier, where you will be obliged to travel, very fast and soon, those notes are practically worthless. . . . Now I am prepared to give you ten thousand gold francs. . . .

GRIMM. I don't want your money!

VALERIAN. Fifteen thousand! [GRIMM *is silent.*] Twenty thousand! [GRIMM *is silent.*] Oh, you needn't be suspicious! They're really here, in this room, in a safe behind the panelling. . . . I'm ready to trust you, you see. Aren't you being rather unwise to refuse? Think of the alternative. If Frommer's men catch you—as, without my protection, they probably will—you will be hanged, or possibly burnt alive.

GRIMM. Valerian, the first time we met you thought you recognized me.

VALERIAN. And you assured me that it was impossible.

GRIMM. I was lying.

VALERIAN. So? Your candour does you credit.

GRIMM. Don't you want to know my name?

VALERIAN. Yes. I think you really do owe me an introduction.

GRIMM. It's Grimm.

VALERIAN. Grimm? Grimm? There are so many Grimms in this country. . . . I seem to remember something. . . .

GRIMM. Five years ago, a boy got a job in your office. A week later, some stamps disappeared. He was the latest employee, so they dismissed him, on suspicion. He appealed to you. You said that you could not reverse your head clerk's decision, and that, in any case, guilty or not, an example must be made. . . .

VALERIAN. Ah, I remember now! An unfortunate case. . . . Well, it may please you to know that the head clerk himself was dismissed a few weeks afterwards. He had been cheating us for years.

GRIMM. Yes, I knew that, too.

VALERIAN. I am delighted to be in a position to make you some tardy amends. . . . Shall we say twenty-five thousand?

GRIMM. You said: "An example must be made."

VALERIAN. Yes. And I should say the same to-day.

GRIMM. You haven't changed, Valerian. I'm glad of that. I was afraid. . . .

VALERIAN. Fascinating as these reminiscences are, don't you think we had better be starting? We can continue this discussion much more conveniently in your car.

GRIMM. I took a lot of trouble to get that post in your office. I had to have it. I had to see what you were like—the man who sent my parents to their graves.

VALERIAN. My dear boy, this is sheer persecution mania! You should see a doctor. I assure you that I never set eyes on either of your parents in my life!

GRIMM. No, you never set eyes on them. Probably you never set eyes on any of the people who kept those little shops along Grand Avenue. But your big store undersold them, and ruined them all. My father went bankrupt. He shot himself. My mother died soon after.

VALERIAN. I am truly sorry to hear it.

GRIMM. When I was sacked from your office, without references, I couldn't get a job. One day, I was sitting in the park, your park; I hadn't eaten anything for twenty-four hours. There was a meeting going on; a speaker from the Leader's Party. I listened. A night or two later, I heard the Leader himself. He told us how he would smash the big businesses, the chain-stores, the Valerian Trust. He told us how he would help the small men, people like my father. I believed him. I joined the Party. . . . And then came the National Revolution. We were in power. And it was all lies. The Leader betrayed us. When I realised that, I knew what I had to do. Never mind. That score was settled, at last—to-night. . . .

VALERIAN. Most interesting. . . . And now, may I ask, why do you come here to tell me all this?

GRIMM. I have come to give you a message. A message from my father and mother, and all those others. . . .

VALERIAN. And the message is—?

GRIMM. You must die.

VALERIAN. I must die. . . . How curious. . . .

GRIMM. Say your prayers, Valerian. If you know any.

VALERIAN. How very curious this is! It's quite true. *You* are actually able to kill *me*! And you will! Oh, I don't doubt you're in earnest. I know that pale, hatchet-faced look of yours. When I said that I recognized you, I meant, perhaps, that I recognized that look. I recognized Death. We all know him by sight.

GRIMM. Kneel down, damn you! Pray! Pray for forgiveness! Squeal for your life! Kneel, you swine!

VALERIAN. No, my little man. There you are asking too much. I'm afraid I can't give you the pleasure of humiliating me. It simply isn't in you. Be content with what you have. You can kill the great Valerian. What a treat! Don't tremble so, or you'll miss me altogether and hit that statuette, which would be a real disaster. Come on. Don't be afraid. I am waiting. Shoot.

GRIMM [*panting, near to collapse*]. I—I can't!

VALERIAN. You can't? Ah, now, I'm afraid, you're beginning to bore me. I over-estimated you, you see. I have no interest in weaklings.

GRIMM. Get out of my sight, do you hear? Get out!

VALERIAN. Not so fast. You and I have still a good deal to talk about. . . . Put that pistol away and get yourself a drink. You look as if you were going to faint.

GRIMM. Get out, I tell you!

VALERIAN. You think, perhaps, that you might screw up the courage to shoot me in the back? I shall give you no such opportunity. I am quite well aware of the power of the human eye. . . . Now, do pull yourself together. Put it away and let us talk.

[GRIMM *does not move.*]

VALERIAN. Very well. Have it your own way. I can be as patient as you. Probably more so. I think you'll soon get tired of this nonsense. [*A pause.*] Let us pass the time agreeably. Shall I tell you about my crimes? The number of widows I have starved to death? The babies I have trampled under foot? Do I appear to you as a monster with horns? I suppose I do. How strange. . . . Here we are, united, for the moment, by a relationship more intimate than the most passionate embrace, and we see each other as mere caricatures. . . . Are you a human being, too, under your dangerous little reptile skin? No doubt. Have you a sweetheart? I don't think so. In any case, you would soon lose her. Your dreary death-cult is hardly likely to amuse a young lady. . . . Tell me about your mother, though. That's always interesting. I expect you were an only child. Her pet. Born rather late in the marriage. The son who was to achieve wonders. What did she teach you, at nights, beside the cot? What did she whisper?

GRIMM [*screams and shoots*]. Leave my mother alone, you bastard!

> [*He fires three more shots into* VALERIAN'S *prostrate body, kicks it savagely, looks wildly round the room, and rushes out, R.*]

CURTAIN

(Before the Curtain)

[*Four* JOURNALISTS *(no. 3 is a woman) are discovered studying a map on the ground. One has a camera, one a pair of field glasses, another a typewriter. Lighting as for the witches in* Macbeth.]

FIRST JOURNALIST. Where have you been?
SECOND JOURNALIST.   Watching the frightened die
   As bombs fell from the Asiatic sky,
   And untrained peasants facing hopeless odds.
FIRST JOURNALIST. The rattle of Spain's execution squads
   Rings in my dreams.
THIRD JOURNALIST.   And through my mind
   Stumbles the Abyssinian, blistered, blind.
FOURTH JOURNALIST. Beside the Danube I have seen despair.
SECOND JOURNALIST. Well met.
FOURTH JOURNALIST.   Well met in Westland.
FIRST JOURNALIST.   Welcome here
   To famine, plague, and civil war
   We have seen them all before.
SECOND JOURNALIST. When by telephone and wire
   Come reports of flood or fire
THIRD JOURNALIST. Where the wounded's frantic cry
   Crawls upon the midnight sky
FOURTH JOURNALIST. Where the words of hate are spoken
   And the will of children broken
FIRST JOURNALIST. Where the homeless stare aghast
   Thither must we travel fast
FOURTH JOURNALIST. And where terror's famished drum
   Swallows reason, we must come.
THIRD JOURNALIST. Visit violence for your sake
FIRST JOURNALIST. Read our columns when you wake
   Justify your party creeds.

Each according to his needs.
THIRD JOURNALIST. Follow Freedom's battle.
SECOND JOURNALIST.   All
   My million readers daily call
   For atrocious acts by Reds,
   White nuns stifled in their beds.
   I follow Krog who leads the Whites
   Defending Order and Religion's rights.
THIRD JOURNALIST. I where the People's Army fights
   Watch Westland struggling to be free.
FOURTH JOURNALIST. My editor would disagree
   He takes the nicely balanced view
   Too impartial to be true.
THIRD JOURNALIST. I think that we shall win.
FIRST JOURNALIST.   I don't.
   You think the Democracies will help. They won't.
THIRD JOURNALIST. We count on numbers for success
   The masses are behind us.
SECOND JOURNALIST.   Yes
   But not the few who have the power
   Your Government will not last an hour.
FOURTH JOURNALIST. Krog will get his guns and tanks
   He has the backing of the banks
   Your people haven't got a chance.
FIRST JOURNALIST. I must go now to phone to France.
THIRD JOURNALIST. I've an important interview.
SECOND JOURNALIST. And I've an article to do.
   When shall we four meet again?
THIRD JOURNALIST. In the midst of human pain.
FOURTH JOURNALIST. Where women weep as soldiers die
   We shall gather by and by.

[*Group for song.*]

JOURNALISTS [*divide up lines between the four singers*].
         We fly to a cabinet crisis
            We motor out to the wars
         Where the general's temperature rises
            Or the little orator roars
         Where over the tyrannous waters
            The flag of revolt is unfurled
         You will find us, the ace reporters
            [*Unison.*] Presenting the world to the world.

☐

When cholera threatens a nation
   Or troops open fire in the rain
Whenever there's want or inflation
   We meet each other again
When the bombs bring down babies and plaster
   Or stones at policemen are hurled
[*Unison.*] We meet over death and disaster
   Presenting the world to the world.

BLACK OUT

Act III Scene 3

[*The stage quite bare, with the light-circle, as in the dream-scene in Act II, Scene 1. But with this difference: in the extreme corners of the stage, L. and R., are two dimly illuminated beds, containing motionless, unrecognizable figures, over which, in each corner, a doctor and a nurse are bending. These parts are doubled by the actors playing* DR THORVALD *and* HILDA THORVALD, *L.; and* COLONEL HUSSEK *and* MRS VRODNY, *R. There is a screen at the head of each bed.*]

LEFT DOCTOR. Yes, Sister? What is it?
LEFT NURSE. This chest-wound case, Doctor. He's had another haemorrhage.
LEFT DOCTOR. Let me see. . . . Hm. . . . There's nothing I can do, I'm afraid. He's sinking. What's his name?
LEFT NURSE. Eric Thorvald, Doctor.
LEFT DOCTOR. Poor fellow. Knew his father slightly. Clever man. Bit conceited.
RIGHT DOCTOR. What's her name?
RIGHT NURSE. Anna Vrodny. One of our best nurses. Do you think she'll pull through, Doctor?
RIGHT DOCTOR. Not a chance. She won't last the night. Move her out as soon as it's over, Sister. We're terribly short of beds.

                      [ERIC *and* ANNA, *dressed and made up exactly as in Act II, Scene 1, emerge from behind the screens at the heads of the respective beds, and advance into the light-circle. The beds fade into darkness.*]

ERIC. Anna, is that you?
ANNA. Yes, Eric.
ERIC. Come closer. I can't see you clearly.

ANNA. Where are you? Your voice sounds so faint.
ERIC. Standing at the barricade
   The swift impartial bullet
   Selected and struck.
   This is our last meeting.
ANNA. Working in the hospital
   Death shuffled round the beds
   And brushed me with his sleeve.
   I shall not see you again.

[*A distant noise of shots and shouting.*]

ANNA. Will people never stop killing each other?
   There is no place in the world
   For those who love.
ERIC. Believing it was wrong to kill,
   I went to prison, seeing myself
   As the sane and innocent student
   Aloof among practical and violent madmen,
   But I was wrong. We cannot choose our world,
   Our time, our class. None are innocent, none.
   Causes of violence lie so deep in all our lives
   It touches every act.
   Certain it is for all we do
   We shall pay dearly. Blood
   Will mine for vengeance in our children's happiness,
   Distort our truth like an arthritis.
   Yet we must kill and suffer and know why.
   All errors are not equal. The hatred of our enemies
   Is the destructive self-love of the dying,
   Our hatred is the price of the world's freedom.
   This much I learned in prison. This struggle
   Was my struggle. Even if I would
   I could not stand apart. And after
   Sighting my rifle for the necessary wrong,
   Afraid of death, I saw you in the world,
   The world of faults and suffering and death,
   The world where love has its existence in our time,
   Its struggle with the world, love's source and object.
ANNA. I saw it too.
   Working in the wards
   Among the material needs of the dying

> I found your love
> And did not need to call you.

ERIC. We could not meet.

ANNA. They were too strong.
> We found our peace
> Only in dreams.

ERIC. As irresponsible and generalised phantoms
> In us love took another course
> Than the personal life.

ANNA. In sorrow and death
> We tasted love.

ERIC. But in the lucky guarded future
> Others like us shall meet, the frontier gone,
> And find the real world happy.

ANNA. The place of love, the good place.
> O hold me in your arms.
> The darkness closes in.

[The lights fade slowly. Background of music.]

ERIC. Now as we come to our end,
> As the tiny separate lives
> Fall, fall to their graves,
> We begin to understand.

ANNA. A moment, and time will forget
> Our failure and our name
> But not the common thought
> That linked us in a dream.

ERIC. Open the closing eyes,
> Summon the failing breath,
> With our last look we bless
> The turning maternal earth.

ANNA. Europe lies in the dark
> City and flood and tree;
> Thousands have worked and work
> To master necessity.

ERIC. To build the city where
> The will of love is done
> And brought to its full flower
> The dignity of man.

ANNA. Pardon them their mistakes,
> The impatient and wavering will.

They suffer for our sakes,
Honour, honour them all.
BOTH. Dry their imperfect dust,
　　The wind blows it back and forth.
　　They die to make man just
　　And worthy of the earth.

CURTAIN

DOCUMENTARY FILMS

Coal Face

[*1935*]

O lurcher loving collier black as night,
Follow your love across the smokeless hill.
Your lamp is out and all your cages still.
Course for her heart and do not miss
And Kate fly not so fast,
For Sunday soon is past,
And Monday comes when none may kiss.
Be marble to his soot and to his black be white.

Night Mail

[1935]

This is the night mail crossing the border,
Bringing the cheque and the postal order,
Letters for the rich, letters for the poor,
The shop at the corner and the girl next door,
Pulling up Beattock, a steady climb—
The gradient's against her but she's on time.

Past cotton grass and moorland boulder,
Shovelling white steam over her shoulder,
Snorting noisily as she passes
Silent miles of wind-bent grasses;
Birds turn their heads as she approaches,
Stare from the bushes at her blank-faced coaches;
Sheepdogs cannot turn her course
They slumber on with paws across,
In the farm she passes no one wakes
But a jug in a bedroom gently shakes.

Dawn freshens, the climb is done.
Down towards Glasgow she descends
Towards the steam tugs, yelping down the glade of cranes
Towards the fields of apparatus, the furnaces
Set on the dark plain like gigantic chessmen.
All Scotland waits for her;
In the dark glens, beside the pale-green sea lochs
Men long for news.

Letters of thanks, letters from banks,
Letters of joy from the girl and boy,
Receipted bills and invitations
To inspect new stock or visit relations,
And applications for situations,
And timid lovers' declarations,
And gossip, gossip from all the nations;
News circumstantial, news financial,
Letters with holiday snaps to enlarge in

Letters with faces scrawled on the margin.
Letters from uncles, cousins and aunts,
Letters to Scotland from the South of France,
Letters of condolence to Highlands and Lowlands,
Notes from overseas to the Hebrides;
Written on paper of every hue
The pink, the violet, the white and the blue
The chatty, the catty, the boring, adoring,
The cold and official and the heart's outpouring,
Clever, stupid, short and long,
The typed and the printed and the spelt all wrong.

Thousands are still asleep
Dreaming of terrifying monsters
Or a friendly tea beside the band at Cranston's or Crawford's;
Asleep in working Glasgow, asleep in well-set Edinburgh,
Asleep in granite Aberdeen.
They continue their dreams
But shall wake soon and long for letters.
And none will hear the postman's knock
Without a quickening of the heart
For who can bear to feel himself forgotten?

Negroes

[1935]

TENOR SOLO. In the Middle Ages there was no contact between Europe and Africa. But before 1500 the Portuguese were beginning to voyage in every direction in search of adventure, of ivory and gold. A sailor called Anton Gonsalves exchanged some Negroes for Moors, and took them to Portugal. This excited the cupidity of his countrymen. He received ten black slaves and a quantity of gold dust. They sailed down the West Coast of Africa.

CHORUS. Of your charity pray for the soul of Diaz
    Who rounded Cape Verde
    Alvaro Fernandez
    Who reached Sierra Leone
    Of Cadamosto
    Who explored the reaches of Senegal and the Congo
    On whose souls as on all Christian souls,
    May God have mercy.

NEGRO COMMENTATOR. They carried us off as slaves.

TENOR SOLO. Then the Portuguese and Spaniards discovered America and were followed by the Dutch, the French, and the English. They forced the American Indians to work for them. But under forced labour these Indians died.

CHORUS. It is the intention of Nature
    To make the bodies of free men and slaves different
    To one erect for civil life
    The others robust for their necessary purposes.

COMMENTATOR. We were adaptable and strong.

TENOR SOLO. Needing slaves to work their sugar plantations, they imported them from Africa, built ships to carry them and raised forts on the coast where they could collect them together for shipment.

COMMENTATOR. Slave ships swarmed at the mouth of every river from the Senegal to the Congo.

TENOR SOLO. Slave traders paid native chiefs to capture Negroes. The chiefs traded the slaves for rum and firearms. They made war on

peaceable tribes. They burnt down their villages. They even sold their own tribe.
CHORUS. At the mouth of the Senegal, the Nune and the Sassandra,
   The Komoe and the white Bandama
   On the Tano and the Volta
   They were ambushed.
   Beside the long Niger
   They lost their freedom
   Sanaga and Ogowe saw them no more
   They disappeared from Kom
   Blood flowed in Mwibu and Chiloango.
   In the basin of Congo
   There were sounds of shooting.
COMMENTATOR. No Negro was safe.

TENOR SOLO. To sail from Africa to Jamaica the fastest ships took seven weeks. With the winds against them the voyage took up to three months.
SOPRANO SOLO. Space allowed for each man: six foot by one foot six,
   For each woman: five foot by one foot four,
   For each boy: five foot by one foot two,
   For each girl: four foot six by one foot.
TENOR SOLO. When supplies of food ran short, the slaves were often thrown overboard.
SOPRANO SOLO. Twelve die during voyage,
   Four die before being sold
   Thirty-four die while being acclimatised.
COMMENTATOR. Out of every hundred Negroes shipped from Africa, Only fifty lived to be effective labourers.

TENOR SOLO. The slaves were the absolute property of their masters.
CHORUS. The advantages which we receive from slaves and tame animals
   Arise from their bodily strength administering to our necessities.
TENOR SOLO. Runaway slaves used to hide in remote parts of the islands. They stirred up the spirit of revolt. And in 1791 the slaves of San Domingo killed two thousand whites and burned one hundred and eighty sugar plantations.
SOPRANO SOLO. The rising was put down and its leaders killed.

COMMENTATOR. Our bodily strength administered to their necessities.

TENOR SOLO. The more advanced thinkers in Europe began to condemn the slave trade. In 1807 British ships were forbidden to carry slaves.
SOPRANO SOLO. And we are put on earth a little space
    That we may learn to bear the beams of love.
    And these black bodies and this sunburnt face
    Are but a cloud and like a shady grove.
CHORUS. Blessings of civilisation
  Brotherhood of man
  Great objects of humanity!
  Freedom! Equality!
  Cannot tolerate!
  Our Christian duty!
  Emancipation!
  Freedom!
TENOR SOLO. And finally the British Parliament passed a law to free all slaves.
COMMENTATOR. We were free.

BASS RECITATIVE. Still at their accustomed hour
    The cities and oceans swing westward into the segment of eternal shadow
    Their revolutions unaltered since first to this chain of islands, motionless in the Caribbean Sea like a resting scorpion
    The Captains came, eager from Europe, white to the West.
FEMALE VOICE. To-day nearly all manual work in the West Indies is done by Negroes. Attempts to form settlements of European labourers have been unsuccessful. Physical necessities are few, few clothes, fuel only for cooking, and food at hand to be picked. Labour is therefore cheap.
BASS RECITATIVE. And still they come, new from those nations to which the study of that which can be weighed and measured is a consuming love.
FEMALE VOICE. The principal industries are—bananas, sugar, cocoa, and coffee: The principal consumers—America and Great Britain.
BASS RECITATIVE. We show these pictures as evidence of their knowledge; its nature and its power.
    Power to employ the waters and the winds for their human and

peculiar purposes; power to convert the lives of others to their kind of willing.

Such as these, in the circuit of whose bodies turns the blood of Africa.

FEMALE VOICE. Heavy labour such as the loading of the bananas on to ships which is done by hand, is men's work. But in the coffee industry women are largely employed. During the cutting of the sugar cane the Negro can live by eating the cane and so save money.

CHORUS. Coffee from the Blue Mountains and cocoa from Trinidad;
Bananas from Clarendon and Trelawney,
And sugar from a hundred islands
> Sixteen million bunches of bananas
> Eight million pounds of coffee
> Thirty-nine million pounds of cocoa
> 427,000 tons of sugar

To be grown, to be crushed, to be dried, to be shipped from harbour;
To be eaten and drunk at the ends of the earth.

FEMALE VOICE. Many own small plots of land on which they can cultivate melons and sugar cane. Of recent years they have begun to emigrate to Panama and elsewhere in search of higher wages.

*Calypso I.**

FEMALE VOICE. Physically they are not as strong as they seem, being more liable to malaria and hookworm than the white races. Temperamentally they are small holders, and prefer those small-scale industries to which the highly subdivided and organised methods of modern production are opposed.

Calypso I.

FEMALE VOICE. They are skilled in music and dancing. They sing at work and at play. Dances frequently last all night.

Calypso I.

FEMALE VOICE. Attempts are being made to give the Negro a better education according to Western standard. In Jamaica, for instance, there are 672 elementary schools providing free education from seven to fifteen but attendance is not compulsory. 400 free places are offered in secondary schools, and there is a farm school and a technical school giving specialised training.

* Calypso—local topical song.

BASS RECITATIVE. Consider their works, their weeks, their contact with
those who can design instruments of precision;
And what compels both races into one enterprise—the wish for life:
Their concern in these places for the production of foods and
beverages.
FEMALE VOICE. Research stations have been set up to increase the efficiency in the industries in which these are employed.

Calypso II.

FEMALE VOICE. Citizens' Associations have been formed by the Negroes themselves to protect their interests, and to enable them to take a larger share in the control of their own affairs.

Calypso II.

FEMALE VOICE. Though industry employs the majority, more and more are entering all kinds of trades and professions.

Calypso II.

COMMENTATOR. But in sleeping car, in hotel, in dock, in factory, in the fields or on the stage, in the hospital or the law court, in each of us, stronger than our will or the accidents of our lives, something of Africa lives on.

CHORUS.   Acts of injustice done
Between the setting and the rising sun
In history lie like bones, each one.

Memory sees them down there,
Paces alive beside his fear,
That's slow to die and still here.

The future hard to mark
Of a world turning in the dark
Where ghosts are walking and dogs bark.

But between the day and night
The choice is free to all; and light
Falls equally on black and white.

Beside the Seaside

[1935]

This coast is continuous. Quays where the small rivers broaden, houses behind the sheltering headlands, constructions on the end of low promontories, speak of people on whose daily decisions the swaying sound of the sea exerts a stable influence. And when the shingle scrambles after the sucking surf, the suns grow taller through the seasons of the turning year. The excited movements of fish, the local transgressions of the tide, and the decorative sky are here matters of economic importance. And the excursions of the ships are not undertaken out of a sense of glory or a simple love of departure. Our courage lies in the deliberate avoidance of danger.

. . . .

The heat beats on the streets. The homeless and the vendors of ice-cream congratulate themselves. The hands of office clocks appear too tired to move. And in the thousands of vehicles which a metropolis can muster the passengers seem larger and the seats smaller. O to be a dove in the oak tree, or the smooth fish in a grotto. Under these roofs one cannot tell how many people sigh for the sea.

The Way to the Sea

[1936]

The line waits,
The trains wait,
The drivers are waiting:
Waiting for Power.

On the terminus now every kind of person is converging, each with his own idea of freedom.
People who work,
People who read adventure stories or understand algebra,
People who would like to be rich or brilliant at tennis,
People like you and me, liable to catch cold and fond of their food,
Are brought all together here by a common wish:
A desire for the Sea.

They gather,
They fight for the corner seat facing the engine.
Red changes to green.
They're off.

A signal box.
A power station.

We pass the areas of greatest congestion; the homes of those who have the least power of choice.
We approach the first trees, the lawns and the fresh paint; district of the by-pass and the season ticket.

Power which helps us to escape is also helping those who cannot get away just now,
Helping them to keep respectable,
Helping them to impress the critical eye of a neighbour,
Helping them to entertain their friends,
Helping them to feed their husbands, swept safely home each evening as the human tide recedes from London.

But we, more fortunate, pass on.
We seek the Sea.

□

White factories stand rigid in the smokeless air.
The pylon drives through the sootless field with power to create and to refashion,
Power to perform on materials the most delicate and the most drastic operations.

Looking forward out into the country, passing the wild and the disciplined lives,
The sun has not lost its importance:
The growth of the living is, as ever, incalculable.
But for all the new power can do to cleanse and to illuminate,
To lessen fatigue and to move deep cutters, milkers or separators,
It is already available.

Up Haslemere Bank—a trial of strength in the years of steam, but to-day of small account,
Over the hoop of the hill, and down,
Fifty, sixty, seventy miles an hour,
To the last straight run to the rolling plain of ships and the path of the gull.
We seek the Sea.

Nor is power absent from this shore
It is here in the lamp on the sea front
In the cables above the streets
In private homes and places of public amusement and business.

Here is a harbour, a dockyard, equipment for the construction of fleets,
A scene of pilgrimage to the student of history and the curious stranger,
A place of salutes to kings and their councillors
Both the dead and the living.
We seek an Island.

All kinds of people:
The married who have begun to get on each other's nerves,
The lonely, daring to look for an amazing romance,
The consciously beautiful, certain of easy conquests,
The careworn, the unrewarded, the childlike:
They embark for the pleasant island, each with his special hope:
To build sand-castles and dream-castles,
To eat out of doors,
To hold hands in the shadow of a fort,
To exchange confidences with strangers,

To read, to relax,
Or just to be and not to think at all.

Here are all the varieties of pleasure, permission, and condolence:
For the body a favourable weather, the caress of sunlight and the
    gradual doze;
For the athletic and beautiful the fullest opportunities to be active and
    to be admired;
For the sedentary the leisure for reminiscence and reverie;
For the children the happiness of the immediate present, the romping
    hours;
For all the pleasures of the air, the waters and the places.

Do what you will:
Be extravagant,
Be lucky,
Be clairvoyant,
Be amazing.
Be a sport or an angel,
Imagine yourself as a courtier, or as a queen.
Accept your freedom.

We seek a spectacle.
We are all invited to inspect the defences of our dreams, to review the
    taciturn aggressive devices.
Let the day commemorate the successful accomplishment of our past,
Let it praise the skill of designers and the anonymous devotion of
    mechanics,
Let it celebrate the artless charm of the far-travelled sailor.

Let the fun be furious,
Let the intricate ferocious machinery be only amusing,
Let the nature of glory be a matter for friendly debate among all these
    people,
Both the just and the unjust,
People like you and me—wanting to live.

Night.
The spectacle fades.
The tidy lives depart with their human loves.
Only the stars, the oceans and machines remain:
The dark and the involuntary powers.

The Londoners

[1938?]

A city is the creation of the human will.
Upon the natural life of the field,
Determined by the radiations of the sun and the swing of the seasons,
Man imposes a human space,
A human skyline,
A human time,
A human order.
A city is not a flower.
It does not grow right by itself.
A human creation,
It needs the human powers of intelligence and forethought.
Without them it becomes only a monument to human greed
Out of control, like a malignant tumour,
Stunting and destroying life.

. . . .

And the parks and open spaces inside the city:
Battersea Park and Bostall Woods,
Clapham and Tooting Commons,
Peckham Rye and the island gardens of Poplar,
The Regent Canal and the Round Pond of respectable Kensington,
And pram-covered Hampstead.
Areas of light and air where the bands boom on Sunday afternoons.
Space for strollers,
    Liberty for lovers,
    Room for rest,
Places for play.

. . . .

It belongs to them, to make it what they choose.
For democracy means faith in the ordinary man and woman, in the
    decency of average human nature.
Here then in London build the city of the free.

CABARET AND WIRELESS

Alfred

A Cabaret Sketch

(FOR THERESE GIEHSE)

[1936]

[*The curtain rises revealing a large and dowdy old woman, who is preparing sage and onion stuffing at a plain deal table, R. L is a large coop in which is a magnificent white gander. The old woman, who has something about her that reminds us of certain prominent European figures, raises the door of the coop and calls.*]

Alfred. Alfred. Come along. Come along. Hurry up now. That's right. I do like obedience. Of course I may be old-fashioned but I do like obedience. Nobody knows what the word means nowadays. When I was young, an order was an order. You'd hardly believe the way some of these modern children answer their mothers and fathers back. Children of good family too. If I were their mother, I'd warm their bottoms for them. I would. I don't believe in spoiling children. It isn't fair to them really.

Well Alfred. What's the matter with you. What do you want? Speak up. Don't be shy. What do you want. What was that? A nice little piece of lettuce. O so you want it do you? Well ask nicely. Has Alfred been a good boy to-day. A very good boy indeed. Well, here he is then. [*Offers him a piece and snatches it away.*] Ah. Now then. Don't be greedy. Nicely. There. [*Gives him a piece.*] Now what do you say. Thank you. Say thank you. That's better. [*Picks him up.*] Isn't he lovely. Isn't he proud of himself. That's my Alfred. Does he love his Auntie. Of course he does. Poor old Auntie. All alone in the world with no one to care for her except Alfred, and no one else to care for. [*Puts him down.*] But what does it matter. What do we care, Alfred. They're dirt, they're [*holds her hand up to the side of her mouth and whispers at him*] they're —— that's what they are. [*Laughs loudly.*] They shan't touch a feather of you. [*Picks up knife.*] Touch a feather of Alfred. Just let them try. See this. Just let them try. I'll slit their bellies open for them. I'll cut their ears off the side of their head. That'd teach 'em. That'd teach 'em I say. [*Puts knife down.*] And there's more than one I'd like to do it to, too. That fat slut across the road, now. There's a nice one for you. Always talking about her precious hens. I'd like to wring their necks. And I will one of these days, mark my words. Serve her right. Who's she to be so high and mighty, I should like to know, or that daughter of hers who thinks herself so smart, making eyes at every tradesman's boy in the village. Do you think I don't know how she carries on. Do you think I've no eyes in my head? I could tell some things if I chose, I can tell you. I know what goes on in Cow barn on Sunday nights. Miserable little brats. They think themselves so clever and they know nothing. I could teach them a thing or two. I could tell them about a good time. There's not a man among the lot of them. Dick could have shown them. You never knew Dick, did you, Alfred. You weren't born. Haven't I ever told you about him. He always used to come when Edward went to market. Silly old fool—he never noticed anything. Dick knew something about love, I can tell you. Come here and I'll tell you a secret. [*Goes down on all fours and whispers in Alfred's ear.*] Do you know what he used to do. He [*the story is inaudible and interrupted by giggles*] .... You won't find any of them to-day who could manage that. [*With growing excitement and resentment.*] And as for you, Miss Hoity Toity, when your shame is as plain as the nose on your face, and your mother throws you out, you needn't come crying to me. Get out of my yard, you slut. No decent person would be seen talking to you, or your mother either if it comes to that. Ask her who your father was. [*Screaming.*] She doesn't know, I tell you. She doesn't know. Get out. Go back and die in the ditch where you and your sort belong. [*Is taken by a fit of coughing.*] [*Quieter.*] I'll finish them one day, and their hens. Would you like to hear another little secret, Alfred? I'll tell you, if you're a good boy. [*Looks round the stage on tiptoe.*] Ssh. Ssh. Come closer. You remember when the fox got into her run, last year. Well, I made a hole in the fence. [*Laughs.*] Your Auntie did it, Alfr , all by herself. What do you say to that? She's not as stupid as she looks, eh? You should have seen her face in the morning. [*Convulsed with laughter.*] She was nearly crying. And nobody ever guessed. [*Louder and louder.*] Nobody every guessed. Not to this day. Nobody knows but you and me, Alfred, about that fox. [*Dropping her voice suddenly.*] But the fox, Alfred. The fox. Look out for yourself. Take care. Take care. Don't you go straying off at night. You keep close to your Auntie. [*In a terrifying whisper.*] He's always about at night, tripping softly softly, waiting just round the corner, waiting his time, and then. Pounce. And he's got you Alfred. Got you. And you squawk and you try to get away but it's too late. Too late. [*Resuming a normal voice.*] Huh. You wouldn't like that, would you, Alfred. No. But that's what happens to naughty little geese if they don't do what Auntie tells them. [*Another and worse spasm of coughing.*] [*Sitting down heavily.*] O dear I mustn't get so excited. It makes my heart bad. I'm getting old. That's what it is Alfred, old. I feel terribly bad sometimes. I shan't be here much longer. Will you be sorry when your old Auntie's dead and buried? Haven't I always been good to you. I've always tried to do what's best, really I have. Speak to me Alfred; tell me you'll be sorry. [*She rises, gradually working herself up into a frenzy.*] O you don't care really. I can just go to hell for all you care. I've toiled and moiled for you, I've worked my fingers to the bone, and you don't care about that. All you think of is self, self, self. I can't go on. One day you'll be sorry. I'll hang myself. I can't go on, do you hear. You're just like the rest. You all laugh at me. I know. I've heard you sneering behind my back. But I'll show you. [*Picks up knife.*] I'll outlive the lot of you. I'll make you sorry you were ever born. [*Begins to stalk Alfred.*] O Alfred, Alfred. Don't go away. Come back. I'm sorry. You mustn't mind what Auntie says. She's just a silly bad-tempered old woman. I'm sorry. Say you forgive me, Alfred. Come along. [*Seizes Alfred and sits down with him.*] That's better. Just go by-by in Auntie's lap. Isn't he a beautiful Alfred. [*Strokes him.*] There there. Don't fret. Auntie's going to look after you. [*She grasps Alfred firmly with her left hand and gets the knife ready in her right.*] Auntie loves her Alfred. He knows she wouldn't hurt him, not for anything in the world. . . .

BLACK OUT

Hadrian's Wall

An Historical Survey

[1937]

Voices. From Wallsend to Bowness
    Over Bluewall Hill and High Seat
        By Ethels Chair and Cats-Cover
        Wintergap Cross
        Stone Gap and High Wall Town
        By Canbeck and Watchcross
        By Stanwix
        By Burgh and Drumburgh
Through a desolate country where the curlew cries in the mist
The curlew on Robinrock Flothers
And aloof over Bellcrag Flow
The dark hawk circles in the summer haze.
From Tynemouth to Solway Firth
Hadrian built a wall.
A wall at the uttermost edge of his empire.

73 miles long.
20 feet high.
8 feet thick.
Built it by hand
With dressed stone used for the facings.
And a core of concrete.

Built it by hand
With the use of the wedge and the hammer
Built fourteen forts also
Dug a forty foot ditch, constructed a road
By the hands of his legions.
Eighteen hundred years ago.

Chorus.   Enos lases juvate
              Neve lue rue marmar sins incurrere in pleores
              Satur fu fere Mars limen sali sta berber
              Semunis alternei advocapit conctos
              Enos marmor juvato
              Triumpe triumpe triumpe triumpe triumpe.

NARRATOR. In 450 B.C. the future masters of the world were a free republic of self-supporting small farmers, confined to the tufa plain of Latium in Italy. Five hundred years later Rome was the greatest city in the world.

VOICE I. Paying an absolute emperor divine honours.

VOICE II. He ruled one hundred and twenty million people, half of whom were slaves.

VOICE III. His empire stretched from the Severn to the Euphrates, from the Cheviots to Mount Atlas and the tropic of Cancer.

VOICE IV [*spoken*]. But Rome 'tis thine alone with awful sway
>To rule mankind and make the world obey,
>Dispensing peace and war thine own majestic way;
>To tame the proud, the fettered slave to free;
>These are imperial arts and worthy thee.

[*Music.*]

NARRATOR. Long known to the Phoenicians, Britain had been little visited by anyone else. Pytheas had admired the Kent harvests and the great barns, tasted whey and honey. Cicero's tutor, Posidonius, visited the tin mines, saw the metal worked into knuckle-shaped slabs. But Julius Caesar was the first to make a real expedition and write a proper description.

VOICE I. The population of the Island is very dense; the houses crowd against each other almost exactly like those in Gaul. They have many cattle. The hare, the hen, and the goose are forbidden food, but they keep them as pets. It is a habit among the Britons to paint their bodies with blue which gives them a terrifying appearance in battle. They wear long hair and shave all the body except the head and the upper lip.

NARRATOR. Caesar did not stay. Britain was forgotten. Augustus called this policy. Tiberius called it precedent. The mad Caligula considered an invasion but contented himself with collecting sea-shells on the French sea shore. In Rome, Vergil sang of shepherds, the country, and wars, prophesied a golden age of universal peace. There were baths, circuses, banquets, vices, graft, assassinations. Plump little Horace composed his civilised song.

VOICE IV [*spoken*].
>Now is the time to twine the spruce and shining head with myrtle
>>Now with flowers escape the earthly fetter,
>And sacrifice to the woodland god in shady copses
>>A lamb or a kid whichever he likes better.

Equally heavy is the heel of white-faced Death on the pauper's
   Shack, and the towers of Kings; and, O, my dear,
The little sum of life forbids the swelling of lengthy
   Hopes. Night and the fabled dead are near

And the shadowed land of exile past whose frontier
   You will find no wine like this, no boy to admire
Like Lycidas, who to-day makes all young men a furnace
   And whom to-morrow girls will find a fire.

[*Music.*]

NARRATOR. But Britain, a land of forests and marshes inhabited by the short dark-haired Iberian and the tall red-headed Celt, knew nothing of these things.

    In Rome the Epicureans asserted that Nature sought only to avoid pain, and the Stoics advised indifference to fate and the contemplation of the stars. At the far end of the Mediterranean a boy was born. But Britain worshipped Ogmius, the bald sea-farer, the golden-tongued, Mapon repeller of diseases, Camulus ruler of war and winds, and knew neither Jupiter nor Christ.

CHORUS.   Fairest Isle all isles excelling
        Seat of pleasures and of loves
      Venus here will choose her dwelling
        And forsake her Cyprian groves.

NARRATOR. In 43 A.D. Claudius sent Aulus Plautius with four legions, the Second, the Ninth, the Fourteenth and the Twentieth, some twenty-two thousand regular troops, came over himself soon after and the real conquest of the island began.

CHORUS [*male voices only*].
  Caesar leaned out of his litter, shouted, "How're we doing, boys?"
  And the legate couldn't stop us, though he didn't like the noise.
"How about another province, for the treasury is low,
  And I'd like another triumph"; so we answered, "Sure, let's go."
Down the Rhine or down the Danube, all roads lead away from
    Rome
  And it's always raining somewhere; We're a darned long way from
    home.

NARRATOR. The Second Legion worked towards the West, and made its headquarters at Caerleon-on-Usk. The Ninth worked North to York, and the Twentieth north-west to Chester. The great administrator

Agricola conquered Wales, built a road from Carlisle to Corbridge and invaded Scotland.

CHORUS [*male voices only*].
>The king of Silures came out roaring from his woolly tent
>Wouldn't beat it when we told him so we had an argument;
>Up among the wild Brigantes things were looking very bad
>So we marched from Eboracum and we gave them what we had.
>Down the Rhine or down the Danube all roads lead away from Rome
>And it's always raining somewhere; We're a darned long way from home.

NARRATOR. In the wake of the legions flourishing towns sprang up.
VOICE I. Colonies of veterans.
VOICE II. Villas with corridors.
VOICE III. Heated by flues carrying hot air.
VOICE I. Mosaic pavements and wall paintings.
VOICE II. Theatres.
VOICE III. Circuses.
VOICE I. Warm baths.
VOICE II. Glazed pottery.
NARRATOR. But the conquest was not an easy one. There were frequent rebellions.
FEMALE VOICE. Have we not been robbed of most of our possessions, while for those that remain we pay taxes? Besides pasturing and tilling for them, do we not pay a yearly tribute of our very bodies?
MALE VOICE. Here you have a general and an army; on the other side lies tribute, labour in the mines, and all the pangs of slavery.
FEMALE VOICE. Let us do our duty while we still remember what freedom is.
MALE VOICE. You have it in your power to perpetuate your sufferings for ever, or to avenge them to-day upon this field.
FEMALE VOICE. I supplicate for victory against insolent and unjust men, if indeed we ought to call these people men who bathe in warm water, eat artificial dainties, and anoint themselves with myrrh.
MALE VOICE. If their enemy have wealth, they have greed; if he be poor, they are ambitious. To plunder, butcher, steal, these things they misname Empire: they make a desolation and they call it peace.
NARRATOR. In A.D. 123 after a rebellion which had wiped out the Ninth Legion, and caused Scotland to be abandoned, Hadrian, the traveller, the builder, came to Britain, and set to work to construct a systematic frontier, as he had previously done in Germany. As a basis he took Agricola's road from Carlisle to Corbridge.

Voice I. Four gallons. How much is that?
Voice II. Six shillings, sir.
Voice I. Is this right for Housesteads?
Voice II. Keep straight on through Throckley, till you come to the filling station at Heddon-on-the-Wall. Then keep right along the Carlisle road. You can't miss it.
Voice I. Thanks.
Voice III [*female*]. Don't go so fast, father, I want to see the countryside.
Voice I. Sorry, but it's a grand straight road for speeding. It's a pity there aren't more Roman walls to build roads on the top of.
Voice III. Have you got the book, Joyce?
Voice IV [*female*]. No, mother; I thought you had it.
Voice III. But I left it on the dining-room table for you to bring.
Voice IV. I didn't see it.
Voice I. Don't worry. I've got it in my pocket. I knew you'd forget it.
Voice IV. Can I have it, father?
Voice III. What does it say, Joyce?
Voice IV [*reading*]. The forts were probably built first. Before the wall proper was built, Hadrian dug a broad flat-bottomed ditch south of the forts, called the Vallum, to mark the civil frontier.
Voice I. Do you want to look at Chesters, because if you do, we're just coming to it. It's over there among those trees. They say the baths are a wonderful sight. You can see how they built the drain wrong and had to alter it.
Voice III. We haven't time, father, if we're to get to Housesteads for lunch. Let's see it on the way home.
Voice IV [*reading*]. A few years later, the wall proper was built by Hadrian's legate, Aulus Nepos. The wall runs north of both the forts and the Vallum. In front a defensive ditch was dug, and a new military road was made between the wall and the Vallum.
Voice I. I bet they made the Britons work overtime lugging those stones about. No Trades Unions in those days.
Voice III. Don't interrupt, father. It's very interesting. Go on, Joyce.
Voice IV [*reading*]. To construct it all the three legions in Britain were called in. Each section of each legion was given a section to build. At intervals of about a mile, small forts were built, each housing a hundred men, and half-way between each mile-castle a turret serving as shelter, signal station, and staircase. Along the top was a rampart walk patrolled by sentries. But the Wall was garrisoned by auxiliaries, not legionaries.
Voice I. Housesteads. Here we are. Just look at all those cars. Out you get.
Voice IV. O I'm getting my feet wet in this long grass.

Voice III. Button up your coat, Joyce; you'll catch cold.
Voice I. What. Sixpence each to look at a heap of old stones. The greedy cheats.
Voice IV. Look, mother, this is the shop, and here's the inn.
Voice III. The shop's bigger than the inn.
Voice I. I'm glad they put up notices to tell you what's what. It looks to me more like a housing estate after the builder's gone broke.
Voice IV. Mother, look at her hat.
Voice III. Ssh; she's listening.
Miscellaneous Voices. Principia. What's that?
>That's where they kept the standards and the pay chests.
>Have a piece of choc, Joe.
>My, just look at those ruts. There must have been a lot of traffic around here.
>Bit bumpy, I should say.
>Come away from the edge this minute, Albert. You'll fall over.
>Those stone stumps are what they put the grain on. It's a granary you see.
>Isn't it lovely. You can almost see Scotland.
>The Wall wasn't built to stop an invading army. The Roman soldier could only fight in the open. It was meant to stop raiding parties and smugglers. Here, mother, how do I get down?
>I'm glad I'm not a Roman soldier.

[*Music.*]

Chorus [*male voices only*].
>Caelius was gaily humming when we heard him grunt and fall
>With an arrow through his belly to the bottom of the wall
>Lepidus the fair was ambushed walking one day through a wood
>It was weeks before we found him, and he didn't look so good.
>Down the Rhine and down the Danube, all roads lead away from Rome
>And it's always raining somewhere. We're a darned long way from home.

Voice I. You seen Augustalis?
Voice II. No, I aint seen him. He's not been around.
Voice I. He's not been around for a fortnight. I want to see him. He don't pay his debts.
Voice II. Maybe he got a skirt someplace. Give me some more wine.
Voice I. How's Mithras?
Voice II. You lay off Mithras.

VOICE I. What do you want to go fooling around with them stunt religions for, Spot? You'll be turning Christian next.
VOICE II. Didn't I tell you to lay off it?
VOICE I. Take it easy, Spot. I was only kidding. But they all sound cockeyed to me. What's the news?
VOICE II. Nothing. Some smugglers tried to get across at Camboglanna.
VOICE I. Did they catch them?
VOICE II. Yes, they caught them.
VOICE I. It must be cold on that Wall at night.
VOICE II. I'll say it is. It's the watching and waiting for something to happen that gets you down.
VOICE I. Were you in that show at Vindolana?
VOICE II. No.
VOICE I. It must have been tough.
VOICE II. Maybe, but I wasn't in that show. Give me another drink.
VOICE I. You'll be drunk.
VOICE II. I hope so.

SONG.   Over the heather the wet wind blows
I've lice in my tunic and a cold in my nose.

The rain comes pattering out of the sky
I'm a Wall soldier; I don't know why.

The mist sweeps over the hard grey stone
My girl's in Tungria; I sleep alone.

Aulus goes hanging around her place
I don't like his manners; I don't like his face.

Piso's a Christian; he worships a fish;
There'd be no kissing if he had his wish.

She gave me a ring but I diced it away;
I want my girl and I want my pay.

When I'm a veteran with only one eye,
I shall do nothing but gaze at the sky.

NARRATOR. The Wall was completed in three or four years. Eighteen years later, Lollius Urbicus, legate of the emperor Antoninus, built a second wall from the Clyde to the Forth. The forts were closer together, but the wall was built of turf. But several risings of the British tribes in Scotland and the North of England caused both it and Hadrian's Wall to be abandoned until the visit of Severus the African in A.D. 208.

VOICE I. He saw that the legions were becoming enervated by idleness and his sons wastrels.

VOICE II. A thunderbolt struck a statue of himself and erased three letters from his name, to signify that he would not return.

VOICE I. He took with him an immense amount of money.

NARRATOR. Landing near Edinburgh he advanced northwards, carried in a litter. He cut down forests, filled up swamps, and bridged rivers, but could not force an engagement with the native tribes. Returning south he repaired and regarrisoned Hadrian's Wall. And so much did he do that it was long believed that he was the original builder.

VOICE I. His son Antoninus attempted to murder him, but he pardoned him.

VOICE III. If you really want to slay me, put me out of the way here; for you are strong, while I am an old man and prostrate. If you hesitate to murder me with your own hands, there is Papinian, the prefect standing beside you, whom you can order to slay me; for surely he will do anything you command, since you are virtually emperor.

CHORUS.
Every swain shall pay his duty
  Grateful every nymph shall prove
And as these are known for beauty
  Those shall be renowned for love.

VOICE I. He reached York a dying man.

VOICE IV. Hail, Caesar. Thou hast been everybody, conquered everybody; become a God.

VOICE III. Antoninus. The crown is yours. Pay the soldiers well and despise everyone else. I was all things and they were worthless.

NARRATOR. For eighty years the country was peaceful and prosperous, and then the Saxon raids on the south-east coast began. Carausius, a Belgian admiral, seized Britain with a view to making a bid for becoming Emperor, was murdered by one of his officers who in turn was defeated and killed, by the real emperor Constantius, father of Constantine the Great.

    He fortified the coast from Southampton to the Wash, and after his time the mile-castles on the Wall were unoccupied. Repeated invasions did permanent damage to the country, and attempts of commanders of Britain to usurp the imperial throne deprived it of troops. After 383 the Wall was probably abandoned. And the Romanised Britons had forgotten how to defend themselves.

VOICE I. They no longer possessed that public courage which is nourished by the love of independence. They received laws and governors from the will of their sovereign, and trusted for their defence to a mercenary army. The most aspiring spirits resorted to the court or standard of the emperors; and the deserted provinces, deprived of political strength or union, insensibly sank into the languid indifference of private life.

[*Music.*]

CHANT CHORUS.
> Help us for the barbarians drive us to the sea. The sea throws us back on the barbarians. We are either slain or drowned.
> They come forth from their valleys; like worms in the heat of midday.
> Their faces shrouded in bushy hair; eager for blood.
> We hide in caves in the mountains; we wander in the woods.
> In the middle of the streets; the lofty towers lie tumbled to the ground.
> The streets are choked with corpses; with the fragments of human flesh.
> Save us from our enemies; for we die.

NARRATOR. But Rome had her own troubles, and could send no help. Soon villas were blackened ruins. Wild fowl nested in the baths. The Latin tongue was forgotten. Roman civilisation in Britain disappeared completely.

CHORUS [*music*].
> Jam lucis orto sidere
> Deum precemur supplices,
> Ut in diurnis actibus
> Nos servet a nocentibus.

[*Theme Music.*]

NARRATOR. We know little of what happened to the Wall in the Middle Ages. Learning and culture kept alive in monasteries through the dark period, matured into the international civilisation of the Catholic Church. Latin was the language of religion and learning. Rome was still the home of the most powerful man in the world.

To control the Northern moors the Norman Kings appointed wardens of the marches. Much of the land passed into the hands of church houses, the rest to small feudal tenants. But Edward the First's invasion of Scotland roused bitter feelings on both sides of the border, and the district round the Wall became famous for its robbers, its cattle raids, and its bloody feuds. At Housesteads lived a branch of the notorious Armstrong family and until the eighteenth century it was a dangerous country to travel in.

[*Bag pipes music.*]

CHORUS [*men only*].
>Ah lads, we'll fang them a' in a net,
>For I hae a' the fords o' Liddel set;
>The Dunkin, and the Door-loup
>The Willie-ford and the Water-Slack,
>The Black-rack and the Trout-dub of Liddel;
>There stands John Forster wi' five men at his back;
>Wi' buft coat and cap of steil:
>Boo! ca' at them e'en, Jock;
>That ford's sicker, I wat weil.
>>Fy lads. Shout a' a' a' a' a'
>>My gear's a' ta'en.

VOICE I. Lord Mangerton complains against Humphrey Musgrace, captain Pikeman and his soldiers for taking him prisoner, and for oxen, kine, horses, mares, sheep, goats and insight £1500 sterling.

VOICE II. The poor widow of Watt's Davie against John Hollas, for the murder of her husband, forty kine and oxen, two horses, insight £100 sterling.

VOICE III. They take great pleasure in their own music and rhythmical songs. Besides they think the art of plundering so very lawful that they never say their prayers more fervently or have more devout recurrence to their rosaries as when they have made an expedition, as they frequently do of forty or fifty miles for the sake of booty. They leave their frontiers in the nighttime in troops, going through impassable places and bypaths. In the daytime they refresh their horses and recruit their strength in hiding places prepared beforehand, until the approach of night when they advance to their destination. Having seized their booty, they return in the same way by night through circuits and byways to their habitations. If they are taken, their eloquence is so powerful and the sweetness of their language so moving that they can move both judges and accusers.

[*Song.*]

VOICE I. Confession of John Weir, Prisoner in Edinburgh under sentence of Death July 20th 1701.

That in the month of March 1700 John Weir, David Weir and John Parker went to Sir John Duck of Prestfield's stable, broke it open, took thereout a big mare, black colour, her neck lyart, and one lesser mare which they all three rid to Morraly's house. That same night John Weir and Francis Morraly rode to Housesteads to William Armstrong's and sold him the least of the said mares which mare Armstrong did rump to make her unknown.

That in May 1700 John Weir went to Grandiknows to the mother of the four brethren the Armstrongs, which Armstrongs and William Buckley did cut the tongue and ear out of William Turner for informing they were bad persons, which Turner writ with his blood they were the persons that used him so.

That there was a false book kept at Edinburgh by the bookkeeper of the Grassmarket where they booked all horses stolen from Northumberland by William Armstrong.

[Song.]

NARRATOR. Horses were exchanged for brandy, but as law was established on the border, the supply of horses ran out, and finally the Armstrongs sold Housesteads to the Gibsons of Hexham for £65. The Wall began to be an object of interest.

Many legends had gathered round it in the course of the centuries. People believed it had been built by the Picts, that it had been built in a single night, that King Arthur's treasure was buried in one of the Lakes, that there had been a brass speaking tube running all along the Wall. Already in Elizabeth's reign Camden had visited and described it in detail, but it was Horsley, a presbyterian minister from Morpeth, who spent his life in making the first scientific study of Roman remains in Britain.

VOICE I. Some people may be inclined to censure me for having spent so much time on subjects which by many will be thought of little importance. And I must so far own to the charge as to confess that if I had foreseen that it would cost so much time as it has done, I believe I should never have undertaken the task; though, when I had once engaged on this work, I thought myself obliged on many accounts to go through with it, and leave nothing undone that I was capable of doing, in order to make the whole more complete. I know the virtues of the ancients have been largely applauded by many, and recommended as very worthy of our imitation. Though I cannot carry my compliment to the ancients in this respect as far as some others have done, yet no doubt a great many things may be learned from these antique monuments. At least there is nothing that can give a more affecting sense of the vanity of this world.

NARRATOR. It was Horsley who identified the forts from the names of the legions given in the Notitia. At the end of the eighteenth century another clergyman, Anthony Hedley, began excavation.

Voice II. It is strange that from the time of Camden down to our own, nothing or next to nothing has been done towards systematically clearing the ground plan of one of the stations. Half a dozen labourers for a fortnight at an expense of not more than £5 would clear away much of the rubbish and throw a very desirable light on the stationary economy of the Romans, and the arrangement of their Castra Stativa.

Narrator. Hedley caught a chill while excavating a pot and died. Sir John Clayton, a wealthy solicitor, and a town clerk of Newcastle, not only carried on his archaeological work, but saved the Wall from being destroyed altogether. The construction of the new Newcastle–Hexham road by General Wade, after the forty-five rebellion, had destroyed much, and the rest was fast disappearing into field walls and farm buildings. Inscribed Stelae were used as paving stones, and centurion stones as angle stones in walls and gates. Further it was the best parts of the Wall which were attacked first as labourers naturally preferred taking stones which lay breast high in a standing wall, to stooping down and lifting them up from the ground. Whenever a piece of wall land came into the market, Sir John Clayton bought it. He had inherited Chesters, but he acquired in this way Borcovicus, Vindolana and Procolita. Setting aside the Monday of each week for archaeology, he uncovered the Roman bridge at Chollerford, excavated the gateways and forum of Cilurnum, dug out Coventina well, and laid bare the wall gates and streets of Borcovicus. Dr Bruce was the first to suggest that the Wall was built by Hadrian, a theory which aroused some opposition.

Voice I. The learned Doctor has permitted his imagination to be warped out of its proper track by a new-fangled theory which in the plenitude of his pride he calls the Aelian Hypothesis. The Doctor apparently thinks and assuredly tries to persuade his readers that the Wall was originally built by Hadrian and not by Severus as has been generally stated and believed. Although this tractate is by no means a work of small pretensions, yet its style is full of hazy logic and confused nebulous notions, and reminds us of one of Don Quixote's tilts at the windmills. It is characterised by a mixture of sophistry, audacious insolence of tone and manner, an utter disregard of the common conventionalities of place and position, and is too full of offensive personalities. The spectres of wasted time and misappropriated talents are the only ones that await the Doctor at Philippi.

Narrator. The Wall began to attract tourists. In 1801 William Hutton at the age of 78 walked from Birmingham to the Wall and back.

Female Voice. Our summer excursion of 1801 was ardently wished for by us both. My father's object was to see the Roman Wall; mine the lakes of Cumberland. We talked it over by our fireside every evening the preceding winter.

MALE VOICE. I was dressed in black, a kind of religious travelling warrant, but divested of assuming airs, and had a budget of the same cloth colour and materials, much like a dragoon's cartridge box or postman's letter pouch, in which were deposited the maps of Cumberland, Northumberland and the Wall with its appendages, all three taken out of Gough's edition of the Britannica. Also Warburton's map of the Wall with my own remarks. To this little packet I fastened with a strap an umbrella in a green case.

FEMALE VOICE. I rode on a pillion behind a servant. My father informed himself at night how he could get out of the house the next morning before the servants were stirring. He rose at four o'clock, walked to the end of the next stage, breakfasted, and waited for me. I set out at seven, and when I arrived at the same inn, breakfasted also. When my father had rested two hours, he set off again. When my horse had fed properly, I followed, passed my father on the road, arrived before him at the next inn, and bespoke dinner and beds. His pace looked like a saunter, but it was steady, and got over the ground at the rate of a full two and a half miles an hour. When the horse on which I rode saw my father, he neighed, though at the distance of a quarter of a mile. He would then trot gently up to my father, stop, and lay his head on his shoulder. My father was such an enthusiast for the Wall that he turned neither to the right nor the left, except to gratify me with a sight of Liverpool. When we reached Penrith, we took a melancholy breakfast and parted; he continued his way to Carlisle, I turned westward went to Hestbank, a small sea-bathing place near Lancaster. While I remained there, I received two scraps of paper, torn from my father's pocket book, the first dated Carlisle July 20 in which he told me he was sound in body, shoe and stocking, and had just risen from a bed of fleas. The second from Newcastle July 23 when he informed me he had been at Wallsend: that the weather was so hot he was obliged to repose under hedges, and that the country was infested with thieves, but, he added, they were only such as stole the stones from his idol the Wall. On the fifth morning after my arrival at Hestbank, before I was up, I heard my father cry Hem on the stairs. I answered by calling out "Father" which directed him to my room, and a most joyful meeting ensued.

MALE VOICE. I envied the people in the neighbourhood of the Wall, though I knew they valued it no more than the soil on which it stood. I wished to converse with an intelligent resident, but never saw one.

FEMALE VOICE. My father frequently walked with his waistcoat unbuttoned, but the perspiration was so excessive that I have even felt his coat damp on the outside, and his bulk visibly diminished every day. The pace he went did not even fatigue his shoes. He walked the whole six hundred miles in one pair, and scarcely made a hole in his stockings.

NARRATOR. In 1849 a party of ladies and gentlemen desirous of enjoying an antiquarian ramble resolved upon taking the course pursued by the far famed Roman Wall.

VOICE I. Care will be taken to provide sufficient sleeping accommodation, and arrangements will be entered into for sustaining their corporeal vigour. In order to economise that energy which ought to be expended in mental rather than muscular exertion, some vehicles will keep pace with the Party.

VOICE II [*recitation*]. But who can paint the route sublime
O'er craig and glen, through fen and fields?
The motley group who dive and climb
To Busy Gap and Sewing Shields.
Another march—a halt—and now
On Borcovicus walls we stand.
Hail, splendid ruin—famous thou—
Great Tadmor of our native land.
While Bruce who heads our troop to-day,
A mild invasion to confer,
Instructs his pilgrims by the way,
Evangelist, interpreter.
Where Pilgrims meet, 'tis common ground,
One brotherhood they seem to be;
No odious difference is found:
The squire and peasant—one to me;
The priest his vestments cast aside
Can gaily chat and blandly smile.
Someone the Doctor's horse may ride
And he still trudge on foot the while.
Away the travellers' waggons wend
Mayor, Clerk and Corporators here,
And there a modest female friend
Like Mercy follows in the rear.

VOICE III. To the Editor of the Gateshead Observer.
 Sir,
  We have had a packet of pilgrims here from your town and

Newcastle scrambling along the Wall. I only wish to say that although there were some RUM'UNS amongst them, they were all treated much better, I suspect, than the Ancient Britons treated their forerunners, the builders.

I am, Mr Editor,
One who has treated them.

NARRATOR. Times and Manners have changed in both travel and archaeology. Parts of the Wall now belong to The National Trust or The Office of Works. But digging and research continue.

[*Hepple's talk.*]

NARRATOR. And still the tourists come, 15,000 of them a year.

[*Davison's talk.*]

NARRATOR. Latin is now a dead language, a school subject and no longer even a compulsory one. The Roman Empire has disappeared, but other empires have taken its place, and the virtues and the vices of Imperialism, its ideals and its scandals, are as great a problem now as then.

VOICE I. Remember that the Almighty has placed your hands to the greatest of his ploughs, in whose furrows the nations of the future are germinating and taking shape, to drive the blade a little further in your time, and to feel that somewhere among those millions you have left a little justice or happiness, or prosperity, a sense of manliness and moral dignity, a spring of patriotism, a dawn of intellectual enlightenment or a stirring of duty where it did not exist before. That is enough. All other triumphs are tinsel and sham.

VOICE II. That man is born a savage, there needs no other proof than the Roman Wall. It characterises both nations as robbers and murderers. Our old historians always termed the Scots barbarians. To this I assent. They surprised the innocent, murdered them, laid waste the country and left the place. Julius Caesar, Agricola, Antoninus, Severus, etc., went one step further than the Scots. They surprised, murdered, plundered, and kept possession. Our venerable ancestors too, the Saxons, Danes, and Normans who came over in swarms, butchered, robbed and possessed; although they had no more right than I have to your coat. Whoever deprives an unoffending man of his right, is a barbarian.

APPENDICES

APPENDIX I

Auden and Isherwood's "Preliminary Statement"

§1 The "Preliminary Statement"

A dramatic and psychological manifesto, written out by Auden and revised by Isherwood, survives in manuscript. It almost certainly dates from the spring or summer of 1929, and may have been intended as a preface to *The Enemies of a Bishop*. The title "Preliminary Statement" (in Isherwood's hand) replaces the deleted title "Preface" (in Auden's). The verses and some of the prose entries in the statement also appear in a notebook Auden used from April through July 1929 and possibly for some time thereafter. During this time he planned to write a play titled *The Reformatory*, and then he collaborated with Isherwood on *The Enemies of a Bishop*. While it seems likely that the statement is connected with that play, the connection is not certain enough to justify printing the statement and play together. The statement's references to perversions, psychoanalysis, and White Slave Traffic argue for the connection; the references to cancer, facial resemblance, old age, and military virtues argue against. It is at least conceivable that the statement was intended for a play that was never written.

The manuscript is in the possession of Fowke Mangeot, who inherited it from his brother Sylvain, Isherwood's friend in the late 1920s and afterward. The text printed below follows the order of Auden's original text, with Isherwood's revisions, but retains in square brackets passages Isherwood deleted. After making his deletions Isherwood recopied the opening paragraphs in this order: "Classical tragedy . . ."; "Dramatic plot . . ."; "He was a housemaster . . ."; "Cancer is . . ."; "Symptoms are . . ."; etc. The verses "Smith likes butcher boys" and "In the lokal" and the line "The friends of the born nurse" were added in Isherwood's hand, but were originally composed by Auden.

PRELIMINARY STATEMENT

[Dramatic action is ritual. "Real" action is directed towards the satisfaction of an instinctive need of the actor who passes thereby from a state of excitement to a state of rest. Ritual is directed towards the stimulation of the spectator who passes thereby from a state of indifference to a state of acute awareness.]

["Realistic" Art. It is important because it has happened to myself.]

[Dramatic "characters" are always abstractions.]

Dramatic plot is the assertion that God could not exist without Satan.

Classical tragedy: the conflict between two courses of action, both of them evil. Elizabethan tragedy: the failure of individual effort. Modern tragedy: the fall of man. Satan: [the type of the modern tragic hero,] the hero of the tragedy of waste. [The tragic emotion of this kind is aroused by the awareness that what is evil is potential good, that hate is love turned against itself,] The heroic self-immolation of a mistaken society.

> He was a housemaster and a bachelor
> But refused to keep dogs,
> So he is dying of cancer.

Cancer is the individual's version of the moral tragedy of society.

[Every fault is a virtue of the age before.]

Symptoms are an attempt at cure.

Neurotic pain is hatred of compensation. [Over the gates of Hell: "Fecemi . . . La Somma Sapienza e il primo Amore."]

Projection.	It wasn't me, sir.
Identification.	The pleasures of the Third Baboon.
Substitution.	Those fatal expeditions to escape danger. The referred pain.

Perversions are due to a desire for justice, not pleasure.

The spirit naturally chooses the difficult rather than the easy. [Parents and education have made the wrong difficult.] That is why Repression is so easily induced. The interdependence of the Cop and the Street-Arab.

A child asks the way to heaven. The parents gladly direct it—to the Hangman's Shed, the clinic, or the padded room.

[Of those carefully prepared and instructive prefaces. The soul reads between the lines.]

> Smith likes butcher boys
> And is therefore a conservative.
> Jones is a Socialist
> Because he likes duchesses.
> Jones can't have duchesses
> So Smith is nicer.

Facial resemblance is the result of mental imitation.

> The mother had wanted
> To be a missionary in Africa

> So the son's novel
> Must be published in Paris.

Old age is believing that parents are ideal.

Repression preserves narcissism; a part of the self is always unexplored. Hence the prosperity of Messrs Cook.

> In the lokal the married Englishman
> With the Chauffeur on his knee
> Said: "I hear the parties at Cambridge
> Are hot stuff nowadays."

He cannot forgive himself; therefore he cannot forgive others. This man, the prey to fugues, irregular breathing, and alternate ascendencies, after some haunted migratory years, disintegrates on an instant in the explosion of mania, or lapses for ever into a classic fatigue.

The joke includes its own contradiction. It is therefore the only form of absolute statement.

People are in a room. Each is talking and listening. Part of what he hears makes him more like a saint, part more like a devil. The first is psychological truth, the second psychological falsehood. There is no other criterion. "Have you heard this one?" Sometimes his younger brother laughs, sometimes he opens the window, and sometimes he has one of his own to tell. That is psychoanalysis. There is nothing else.

The intellect can only choose the modes of gratification. It cannot choose the objects. "I'm going right away. I'm going to see no one." In a week he cut his throat in the bathroom.

The substitution of intellectual for natural laws: White Slave Traffic.

Promiscuity: A sign of impotence.

Eugenists are already sterilised.

The chief cause of unsatisfactory relationships: Lying about one's age.

The deadly influence of the phantom Bradshaw.

Wars are engineered by virgins or dwarfs.

> Pick a quarrel, go to war
> Leave the hero in the bar,
> Hunt the lion, climb the peak
> No one guesses you are weak.

Medicines and ethical codes are as demoralising as mercenaries.

The friends of the born nurse are always falling ill.

Our moral virtues are those of a military state. [Military virtues are not the only ones.] Generals are notoriously astrologers.

In a military state infectious disease takes the place of brotherly love and hygiene of the forgiveness of sins.

The military types of friendship: Two to one. Seven against Thebes.

Of Repression: A colonel captures a position, after receiving severe wounds and losing three quarters of his regiment, only to find that the enemy are his own side.

§2 Auden's "Suggestions for the Play"

At some time around 1929 or 1930 Auden sent Isherwood a list of scenes and motifs for a play they planned to write. The list, written on the letterhead of Auden's parents' home in Birmingham, is undated but the handwriting and contents provide some indication of the time at which it was written. No other surviving letter or manuscript refers to this project.

SOME SUGGESTIONS FOR THE PLAY

As the play is for two actors I think there must be a central duality linking up scenes.

I suggest the $\left.\begin{array}{c}\text{Cycloid}\\ \text{Schyzoid}\end{array}\right\}$ personalities (see Kretschmer).

Cycloid.	Fat and short	manic-depressive	hero worship
Schyzoid	Tall and thin.	Dementia-praecox.	cold.

This is the basis of "Pat and Patachen" whom you have probably seen in the films.

For external events what about a continuous
>railway motive
>>Magic. Basilisk motive (symbol for the mother and the unworthy thing.)

Connected with the railway a power-station for electrification.

Useful for water and libido symbolism.

School scene, an educational pamphlet. Puberty initiation ceremonies.

University. Black magic.

A scene about the stealing of the superseded railway signal.

At least one miracle.

A railway book-shop.

A scheme for beautifying the power station by constructing a pipe line of coloured glass.

This bursts.

Cycloid   a rising engine-driver. (I connect him with Orpen)*

Schyzoid. dies running away from his wife in express lost in a snow storm. A desert-prayer.

* [Christopher Orpen, a friend of Isherwood's at Cambridge; the model for Gunn in *The Ascent of F6*—Ed.]

APPENDIX II

The Fronny: Fragments of a Lost Play

INTRODUCTION

In August 1930 Auden wrote to his brother John: "I am writing another play which promises to be quite fun though I don't quite see my way yet" (letter now in the Berg Collection). He finished writing the first act in September, and sent excerpts from the play to Isherwood during the autumn. On 17 October he told Stephen Spender that he had "just finished a draught of a new play", and told Naomi Mitchison on 28 October that he had "nearly finished a new play which I believe will be the best I can do just now" (letters in the Berg Collection, New York Public Library). He sent the finished work, titled *The Fronny*, to T. S. Eliot on 8 December. Eliot seems to have returned it (perhaps at Auden's request) without consulting his fellow directors at Faber & Faber, but he asked to see it again, in order to consider it for publication, on 23 September 1931. A few weeks later Faber & Faber agreed to publish it as part of a larger book that was to include *The Orators*, which Auden was working on at the time. Then, as Auden told Spender on 14 January 1932, "Faber have now decided to publish the Orators by itself after keeping the Fronny for months and letting me [?think] they were going to do it, so that is now on my hands. If the Hogarth Press want the poor thing, now, they can have it". Apparently the Hogarth Press did not want it. Auden lent the play to Dorothy Elmhirst, of Dartington Hall, in April 1932, and in June asked her to return it "as it is my only copy" (letter in Dartington Hall archives). She apparently did return it, as the Dartington archive does not have the manuscript. After June 1932, no further trace of the complete text can be found.

Scattered sections of the play survive in preliminary manuscripts that Auden gave Isherwood and others, and it is possible to guess at some details of the characters and plot. "The Fronny" was the name Auden and Isherwood used for their friend Francis Turville-Petre, an English archaeologist from an aristocratic Catholic family whom Auden seems to have met in Berlin in 1928-29. (He served as the model for "Ambrose" in Isherwood's *Down There on a Visit*.) German boys called Francis "Der Franni", which Auden and Isherwood anglicized to "The Fronny". In Auden's play the Fronny's real name is Francis Crewe. Apparently he has disappeared from his home village, and Alan goes off to search for him. (I am extrapolating to some extent from the later versions of this plot in *The Chase* and *The Dog Beneath the Skin*; in those plays, and probably also in *The Fronny*, Alan's surname is Norman.) In a city that seems a stylized version of Berlin, Alan is distracted from the search by his infatuation with a woman named Lou. Near the end of the play, in the Alma Mater bar, the Fronny makes his will and dies; this part of the plot reappears in *The Dance of Death*. The play apparently ends with Alan's marriage to Iris Crewe, the Fronny's sister. Auden took the names

Alan and Iris from friends he had made while teaching at Larchfield Academy in Helensburgh, Alan Sinkinson and Iris Snodgrass. Following the example of their dramatic counterparts, they married in July 1931.

The poems and scenes printed below may be assigned to *The Fronny* with varying degrees of confidence. The dedicatory poem and the Fronny's rhymed Last Will are self-evidently parts of the work. (After reading the first version of the Will, Isherwood seems to have suggested that Auden suppress its casual references to the private lives of their friends. Auden replied: "Of course what I really want for the testament would vary at every performance to implicate an incredulous and slightly scared audience. However I will do what I can.") Auden sent Isherwood some revised stanzas of the Will, together with the revised partial texts of the two scenes of dialogue—the only versions of these scenes that survive. The revised scenes either include or call for the inclusion of the three poems "To ask the hard question is simple", "Love is this and that", and "What's in your mind, my dove, my coney". The revised text of the Will calls for the inclusion of "The Alma song", i.e., the song beginning "Hail! the strange electric writing".

Auden listed some other verse from the play in a letter to Isherwood, probably in February 1933. This letter lists the poems Auden planned to include in the revised second edition of his 1930 *Poems*; it includes these four, bracketed as taken from *The Fronny*:

> Doom is dark
> The final snub-nosed winner
> What's in your mind
> Epithalamion

"The final snub-nosed winner" refers to "Between attention and attention"—presumably signifying that this was the last of the poems in which Auden used the phrase "snub-nosed winner" after retrieving it from earlier and abandoned poems (or, less probably, signifying the final version of "Between attention" itself). The "Epithalamion" is the poem that Auden later incorporated into *The Chase* and *Dogskin*, in a heavily revised text beginning "You who return to-night to a narrow bed"; an account of its complex history is given in the textual notes below.

Because Auden sent them to Isherwood along with "Hail! the strange electric writing", I have included the two poems "I saw them stoop in workshops" and "This Roman peace was broken". The first seems to have been spoken by the Fronny, the second spoken about him. The poem "Who will endure" was written at about the same time as "Doom is dark" and "Between attention and attention"; in 1932 Auden published "Doom is dark" under the title "Chorus from a Play", and the similarities of style and subject among all three poems suggest that the other two were used as choruses as well.

In this edition the fragments of the play are arranged in a sequence that perhaps corresponds roughly to their sequence in the play. This arrangement is strictly editorial, and readers should feel free to choose any alternative. Not enough information is available to permit an arrangement by chronological sequence of composition.

The italicized headings for the scenes of dialogue were inserted by Auden when he sent these revised texts to Isherwood. The brief explanations printed between square brackets are editorial additions.

[FROM] THE FRONNY

DEDICATION OF *The Fronny* TO J. B. AUDEN

Run Favel, Holland, sprightly Alexis
For life or what relation's to be had
As between children, inert and vaguely sad;
Your prophecies for sons secure in boxes
At dark noon hoping for snow:
No conversations but homage now
Nothing to do with friendliness or time
Nothing at all about integers or steam.

Deaf here to prophecy or China's drum
Concessive still to circumstance
Mitred in Iceland, secular in France
The blood moves strangely in its moving home
Using the mole's device, the carriage
Of peacock, or rat's desperate courage
Diverges, musters, to travel further
Than the long still shadow of the father.

If space be overcrowded and we late
The party has not reached its height;
Do we confess to them our fears,
Drive with them in the night to fires
It is the form the promise took,
The antic and the social look
The acts of homage, the reward
Power to keep the father's word.

. . . .

CHORUS. Between attention and attention
    The first and last decision
    Is mortal distraction
    Of earth and air,
    And the fatigued face
    Taking the strain
    Of the horizontal force

And the vertical thrust
Makes random answer
To the crucial test,
The uncertain flesh
Scraping back chair
For the wrong train
Falling in slush
Before a friend's friends
Or shaking hands
With a snub-nosed winner.

Between the fixed points
And the definite dates
Are further and nearer
The vague wants
Of days and nights
And personal error:
The war of all time
In the instant dream,
The tiny black figure
At the foot of the fall
Watching the green glacier water
Alive but small.

Between completeness and completeness
Between the likeness and the likeness
Is out-of-reach
And the exciting approach,
Loving exchange
And treacherous lunge,
Though different gives
Of separate lives
Are helpless now:
The open window
The closing door
Opened, close, but not
To finish or restore.
These wishes get
No further than
The edge of the town
And leaning asking from the car
Cannot tell us where we are.

□

Many preceded, many
Have poked and wedded
And spent their money
Then turning round
Rode off this ground
Leaving insignia
Epitaphs and a smell of ammonia.
Yet flowers hang
Upwards from seed and dung
And so much later
Is sometimes better
While pupils look
More and more on the clock
More and more what time it took
Or more breath taking
For still more waiting
And the divided face
Has no grace
No discretion
No occupation
But registering
Acreage, mileage,
The easy knowledge
Of the virtuous thing
Without pastime
In the meantime
Between point and attention
Date and decision
Completeness and likeness.

. . . .

CHORUS. Doom is dark, deeper than any sea-dingle
 Upon what man it falls
 In spring day-wishing flowers appearing
 Avalanche sliding, white snow from rock face,
 That he should leave his house
 No cloud-soft hands can hold him, restraint by women,
 But ever that man goes
 Through place-keepers, through forest trees
 A stranger to strangers over undried sea
 Houses for fishes, suffocating water.

□

There head falls forward, fatigued at evening,
And dreams of home
Waving from window, spread of welcome,
Kissing of wife under single sheet
But awaking sees
Bird-flocks nameless to him, through doorway voices
Of new men, making another love.

Save him on earth and water from hostile capture
From sudden tiger's spring from corner
Protect his house
His anxious house where days are counted
From thunderbolt protect
From gradual ruin spreading like a stain
Converting number from vague to certain
Bring joy, bring day of his returning
Lucky with day approaching, with leaning dawn.

. . . .

CHORUS. Who will endure
    The heat of the day and the winter danger
    The journey from one place to another
    Nor be content to lie
    Till evening on the headland in the bay
    Between the land and sea
    Nor smoking wait until the hour of food
    Leaning upon the chained-up gate
    At the edge of the wood?

    The metals run
    Burnished or rusty in the sun
    From town to town
    The signals all along are down
    Yet nothing passes
    But envelopes between these places
    Snatched at the gate and panting read indoors
    And first spring flowers arriving smashed
    Disaster stammered over wires
    And pity flashed.

    For should the professional traveller come
    Asked by the fireside he is dumb

Declining with a small mad smile
And all the while
Conjectures on the maps that lie
About in ships drawn high and dry
Grow stranger and stranger
Yonder are mountains where the wicked people dwell
Misshapen, fearing the devil in the ghyll
But these are stranger, spend their lives
Running round derricks towering high
Against a flaring sky
In fights with knives.

There is no change of place
But shifting of the head
To keep the lamp-glare from the face
And climbing over to the wall-side of the bed.
No one will ever know
For what conversion the brilliant capital is waiting
What ugly feast the village band is celebrating
And no one sees
Further than railhead or the end of piers
Will neither go nor send his son
Further through foothills than the rotting stack
Where gaitered gamekeeper with dog and gun
Will shout "Go back".

. . . .

   I saw them stoop in workshops
    I saw them drink in clubs
   I saw them wash for meetings
    I saw them pay for cabs

   I saw them playing cricket
    And changing into shorts
   Or offering chairs to ladies
    I saw them choosing shirts

   I saw them kiss their mothers
    I saw them taking digs
   I saw them play with children
    I saw them mourn for dogs

    I saw them pray for sunshine
        I saw them smoking pipes
    I saw them cleaning rifles
        I saw them studying maps

    I saw them ask forgiveness
        I saw them going shares
    I saw them leave for ever
        From stations in the shires

    I saw them look at gasworks
        On the horizon's line
    I saw them being sorry
        I saw them use a loan

    I saw them lie by letter
        I saw them hide their fears
    I saw them getting iller
        I saw them poking fires

    I saw them and said as I took my hat
    "No doctor in England can cure all that".

. . . .

First scene with whore [revised version of part of a lost scene]

ALAN. ... She looks beautiful and nice
    I think I'll ask her for advice.
LOU. Who's this. He seems a nice looking man
    He must be quite young and he's quite well dressed.
    He's a stranger to me, but I'll risk the rest
    As soon as we meet I'll drop my fan.
ALAN. Excuse me, Madam, but you've dropped this.
LOU. O so I have. I am so careless.
    Thank you.
ALAN.   I wonder if you could tell
    Me where to find the best hotel.
LOU. Hm. Let me see. May I suggest
    The Hotel Adlon is the best.
    I'm going that way. Shall we go together.
ALAN. Thanks very much. It's lovely weather.
LOU. Haven't you been here then before.

ALAN. Never.
LOU.   Then there [are] some surprises for you in store.
ALAN. I know. There's some wonderful Gothic work I hear
     And a Mestrovic group in Douglas Square.
LOU. I've never been there. But haven't you heard
     Of the Alma Mater or the Silver Bird.
ALAN. Who are they by?
LOU.   Boy, where have you been
     They are the places where life's to be seen.
A VOICE. Who's that lovely kiddy? Has he coals?
LOU. Don't be coarse, dear. We're going to play bowls.
     [*To* ALAN.] Have you any friends here. No? Then I say
     Let me show some of our city to-day.
ALAN. It's very kind of you, I'm sure
     But won't you find it an awful bore?
LOU. Excuse me but let us cross the street
     There's someone coming I'd rather not meet.
ALAN. O certainly.
LOU.   And if you don't mind I think
     We'll go in here and have a drink. [*Exeunt.*]

[FRONNY *passes.*]

FRONNY. You needn't try to hide. I saw
     What you are doing again, you whore.
     Catching all who come your way
     You make them pay and pay and pay. [*Exit* FRONNY.]

CHORUS. To ask the hard question is simple;
     Asking at meeting
     With the simple glance of acquaintance
     To what these go
     And how these do
     Is beginning history easily
     Without history to recall;
     To ask the hard question is simple
     The simple act of the confused will.

     But the answer
     Is hard and hard to remember;
     On steps or the shore
     The ears hearing
     The words at meeting

The eyes looking
At the hands helping
Are never sure
Of what they learn
From how these things are done.

And forgetting to hear or see
Makes forgetting easy
Only remembering the method of remembering
Remembering only in another way
Only the strangely exciting lie
Afraid
To remember what the fish ignored
How the bird escaped or if the sheep obeyed.

Till, losing memory,
Bird, fish and sheep are ghostly
And ghosts must do again
What gives them pain
Cowardice cries
For windy skies
Coldness for water
Obedience for a master.

Shall memory restore
The steps and the shore
The face and the meeting place
Shall the bird live
Shall the fish dive
And sheep obey
In a sheep's way
Shall love remember
The question and the answer
For love recover
What has been dark and rich and warm all over?

[*Re-enter* ALAN *and* LOU.]

LOU. Isn't the moonlight lovely.
ALAN [*embracing her*].   Lou.
LOU. You like me a little?
ALAN.   I'll say I do
   Again. Again. That's not enough

         The whistle's blown and I am off
         After years in a very dark wood
         I've come out at last and it's very good.
VOICE. Taxi sir.
ALAN.   Yes and drive like Hell.
VOICE. Where to sir?
ALAN.   Any good hotel. [*Exeunt.*]

CHORUS. Love is this and that
         Warms and is not fit
         For natural history and wit

         Having no heart
         Cannot remain apart
         Cannot remember to forget
         Taking long over a shortened week

         The kiss more certain
         Is less than sure
         The obvious embracing
         Good because privately obscure.

         Calling names
         And taking criminal forms
         By forcing to get ill
         Weakens and is getting well

         Never such a dear one
         As when ending has preceded
         Needing what is never done
         Doing what is never needed.

. . . .

Second scene with whore

VOICE. I've got the Hispano waiting outside
         To take us for our honeymoon ride
         My darling Lou. But how much longer.
         My love is getting stronger and stronger.
LOU. Ssh. Patience, Jerry. I'll give you the tip
         As soon as there's time and we'll give him the slip.

[*Enter* ALAN.]

ALAN. What shall I do. They'll detain me for debt.

Lou. You mustn't go frowning like that. Forget.
Alan. But where can I find the cash.
Lou.   Delice.
Delice. Did Modom ring?
Lou.   Two cocktails please.
   Now you're to sit in this comfy chair
   And your little Puss will stroke your hair.
Delice. The cocktails Modom.
Lou.   Now you like this.
   Feeling better already?
Alan.   Give me a kiss.
   Do you like me a little.
Lou.   Don't be silly.
Alan. I've got such a head—
Lou.   Delice, take this penny
   To start the electrical pianola
   And will you remove the master's bowler.
Alan. No, sing me the song you sang so well
   That wonderful night in our first hotel.

Lou [*sings*]. What's in your mind, my dove, my coney
      Do thoughts grow like feathers, the dead end of life
      Is there making of love or counting of money
      Or raid on the jewels, the plans of a thief?

      Open your eyes, my dearest dallier
      Let hunt with your hands for escaping me
      Go through the motions of exploring the familiar
      Stand on the brink of the warm white day.

      Rise with the wind my great big serpent
      Silence the birds and darken the air
      Change me with terror, alive in a moment,
      Strike for the heart and have me there.

[Alan *sleeps. The rest of the scene as before* (in the lost earlier version).]

. . . .

Unison.   Hail! the strange electric writing
             "Alma Mater" on the door
          Like a secret sign inviting
              All the rich to meet the poor

CHORUS.   Alma Mater, ave, salve,
                Floreas in saecula.

GIRLS.   Send us men who can be funny
                Send us men you know are clean
            Send us men with lots of money
                Then we can be really keen.
            Always, even though we marry,
                Though we wear ancestral pearls
            This memory we'll always carry
                We were Alma Mater girls.
                    Chorus.

THIEVES.   Let Americans with purses
                Go for short strolls after dark
            Let the absent-minded nurses
                Leave an heiress in the park
            Though the bullers soon or later
                Clap us handcuffed into jail
            We'll remember Alma Mater
                We'll remember without fail.
                    Chorus.

BOYS.   The French are mean, and Germans lazy,
                Dutchmen leave one in the end
            Only the Englishman, though he's crazy
                He will keep one for a friend.
            Never, though a king of cotton
                Waft us hence to foreign parts
            Shall Alma Mater be forgotten
                She is written on our hearts.
                    Chorus.

BLACKMAILERS. We must thank the mug's relations
                For our income, and Man's laws,
            But the first congratulations
                Alma Mater, they are yours.
CON-MEN AND COINERS. When the fool believes our story
                When he thinks our coins are true
            To Alma Mater be the glory
                For she taught us what to do.
                    Chorus.

OLD TROTS AND HACKS. We cannot dance upon the table
        Now we're old as souvenirs
    Yet as long as we are able
        We'll remember bygone years.
    Still, as when we were the attraction,
        Come the people from abroad
    Spending, though we're out of action,
        More than they can well afford.
    Chorus.

. . . .

THE FRONNY. With northern Winter, snowballing season
    With weather dangerous for country postmen
    When the poor actor dreads his bills
    And managers of Switzerland's hotels
    Begin to supplement their staff
    With the whole year I leave my life:
    I cannot count my friends to-morrow
    There is a village in the Harz called Sorrow.

CHORUS. Who thinks of Ronny's fatal fractures
    Sustained in stunts for Gaumont pictures?
    Scarcely a student now remembers
    McTaggart's theory of prime-numbers
    Or Light who thought the earth was hollow.
    Miss Riding jumped from a third floor window
    Miss Amy Benson was afraid of bears.
    It was their show: We're thinking of yours.

THE FRONNY. Now to another that shall pass
    Which from the first has done seduce
    The seed to which my father was a mother
    To swear allegiance to a new commander
    Urging to whale-road from that tropic shore
    To take the all-night journey under sea
    Work west and northward, set up building,
    Passes without which I am nothing.

CHORUS. Piazzi Smythe the Cape Astronomer
    To take the Last Day built a camera.
    One Douglas Marshall wrote a chapter

Of his book "No Camp can last for ever"
Four scouts were drowned at Runswick Bay
And Sheila slipped while tying shoe
Breaking her neck on the wedding night
You want to stay but you can't do that.

THE FRONNY. I leave in snow; in coming heat
I shall not visit lakes nor sit
In summer under chestnut trees
Where almost always the band plays.
Papers are bought and many sing
Their favourite tunes but they are far from strong.
These love to go about in troop
Rushing to those impossible to help.

CHORUS. The sun shall summon other men
From different women to the same machine
But never you. You shall not see
The moon at natural ending of the day
Rising like football from behind the hill
Their rearguard actions ridicule
Confound in them with ignorant stare
The cooled brain wise in an irreverent hour.

THE FRONNY. Firstly upon my death I leave
My body as earth and air to live
As all desires accelerate
Towards their little crisis and then drop
Straight as a bomb or erratic as a bat
To even breathing, level sleep
The mutinous mouth relaxed, immune
From mute frustration's false alarm.

Item, the notes of cases that I kept
In verse, and every manuscript
And all my correspondence including
All Pieps' letters and the Willi drawing
I leave to Edward and to Christopher
Reptonians, writers, pistol pair,
Who wrote together the Mortmere stories
And divided men into dragoons and dories.

Item, to the diffusionist John Layard
For having raised me largely from the dead

Nothing but love for only this
He says is needed for analysis
Of murder or epileptic fit;
But add, to stop him from abusing art
Next time he crashes in a young man's rooms
The complete short stories of Henry James.

Item, my three-roomed furnished flat
At 40 Chester Square complete
To Olive Mangeot the Black Sow
To take her darling schoolboys to:
And may she find prompt answer to her prayer
That her mad husband die this year.
To Sylvain her son, a set of spanners
To get undone those lower centres.

Item, to Robert Moody, that saint,
Soaker, bumboy, and medical student
I gave my Cadillac saloon
To get away from his mother in.
To Gabriel Carritt the snub-nosed winner
Whom dons were always asking to dinner
A pair of boots with studded heels
To keep him dry in the Yorkshire Dales.

Item, my naval range-finder and case
To Captain Edward Gervase Luce
With whom on seawall at King's Lynn
I talked of bird-migration in the rain.
The lighthouse lately condemned at Cley
I leave him also to rebuild that he
Intent on instruments and figures there
May look for truth, alone in tower.

Item, to Cushy the unshaven Scot
Who showed us the engine at Hackwood Pit
The cranks of which still menace me in dreams
A weekly pint at the Miners Arms
The same to Sargeaunt of the sharpening shed
Who made us toys from an iron rod.
And may the door of the winding-house
Lure other children after us.

Item, for Mr Gill of Harborne
Who spoke in April of exploration
A single specimen of his table thoughts
"It's a waste of life. Why look at Oates
What a splendid man he'd have been for the war"
The nastiest thing I've done this year
Was shaking your marshy hand. I'll tell.
You can't get away with that, Mr Gill.

CHORUS. Item, we ask for Squire the less,
For Gould, for Douglas of the Daily Express,
For Mead and Muskett and all their lot
Destroying good and England at the root
A sudden sickness, and when they send
For the surgeon's pioneering hand
May he be drunk, they conscious still,
For nothing less can make them feel.

THE FRONNY. Item, the sum of one hundred pounds
At present invested in Government bonds
I leave in trust for the Neukölner Otter
Taken last August at Rothehütte
Whose sensitive hands now work in prison,
As souvenir of our relation
A kind I shall not feel again
Neither in the mountains, nor Neuköln.

Item, to Lennep the pop-eyed bugger
For paying my bill at the Cosy Corner
And frequent use of his Chrysler Six
Black on the Intermediate Sex,
The address and a letter of introduction
To Gunther who really prefers old men,
Success to his classical researches
May boys wave often from passing lorries.

Item, to Fraulein Lotte Poppe
First met by missing my train at Lippe
Although she had a squint, in memory
Of week-ends spent on the Müggelsee
The lokal known as the Stinging Nettle
Because she never left me for an uncle
Because she had the grace to keep
To my name, even when crying in her sleep.

Item, my family signet ring
To the procuress Louisa During,
The contents of my pocket book to pay
The cost of treatment for Greta Pauly
To cure herself of her offensive breath;
To Gypsy conceited about her teeth
A sixpenny toy the Faciograph
To give her more excuse to laugh.

In the cool grave when I have signed
I shall not listen to a sound
Whatever these my heirs shall say;
I shall not move again to see
Who buys a present nor for whom;
I shall not ask although they come
When they, through errors of their own
Have also made Man's weakness known.

CHORUS.   You've learnt but were yourself unable
The old should slowly ripen like an apple;
And know man cannot rest until
He learn to see his image in the well
Neither hermaphrodite nor king he sees
Nor wounded hero of the undersized;
In England, Scotland, Ireland, Wales
Who repeats an action fails.

. . . .

[*Revised version of portions of the Fronny's Will:*]

. . . From mute frustration's false alarm.

Item, as sole executor
I appoint Miss Iris Crewe, my sister
Of my whole fortune and estate
To administer as she thinks fit
In saving England from heading faster
To a great climacteric disaster
I shall consider it well spent
If seven Englishmen repent.

Item, my naval range finder and case *etc.*

To Harry my servant for wheeling this chair
And dressing me in my last year
My set of razors and all my suits
And a weekly pint at the Goat-in-boots,
The same to Cushy the unshaven Scot
Who showed me the engines at Hackwood pit
And may the door of his winding house
To others seem as mysterious.

Item, my family signet ring
To the procuress Louisa During
The contents of my pocket book to pay
The cost of treatment for Greta Pauly
My watch to be kept for the Neukölner Otter,
Taken last August at Rothehütte.
Free drinks to all in Alma here
To make their life less hard to bear.

(The Alma song [see p. 475].)

Item, the orchestra I congratulate
On their excellent performance to-night
And may they when this play is over
Find engagements from Newcastle to Dover
To any critics a little sense
Patience and absence of pretence
And Mr Auden and myself forgive
If I have sometimes failed to live.

Item, the audience I'm going to tell
What one of you said in the interval
At the buffet during a conversation
On the merits of polar exploration
That you all may weep for it at nights
"It's a waste of life; why look at Oates
What a splendid man he'd have been for the war"
That's the nastiest thing I've heard this year.

Item, my three-roomed furnished flat
At 40 Chester Square complete
To the girl in that box there with her mother
On condition that she leave her for ever
To the fat but rather attractive whore
In the pit, the costs of a walking tour
And a pair of boots with studded heels
To keep her dry in the Yorkshire Dales.

            Item, to the nervous student in the stalls
            Ashamed of himself for what he feels
            An invitation to come up here
            Whom a night in Alma Mater will cure
            We'll quickly get you back your colour
            I'll leave a fiver for you with the waiter.
            Here Zeppel.
ZEPPEL.   Sir.
                    Stop playing cards
            And find this gentleman what he needs.

            To the medical who's come in tight
            The chandelier to keep him quiet
            To the master getting up to go
            A request that he stop a moment or so
            To tell the boy in, I think, Row P
            That he's not in very good company.
            Last, to the lady who ought never to have come
            A tip for the attendant and her taxi home.

            In the cool grave when I have signed *etc.*

. . . .

                    This Roman peace was broken
                        Nine months ere he was born
                    When first his angry father knew
                        A quarrel was begun
                        Which now is done.

                    The memories run backward
                        Like hedges to the start
                    And sorrow blooming like a bush
                        But here bones fall apart
                        Without his heart.

                    No one will see repeated
                        A life he lived alone
                    Nor make exactly as he made
                        Through errors of his own
                        Man's weakness known.

Of all his foreign travel
    The diary is hid;
No other can interpret what
    His marching-orders bid,
    But come he did.

His fevered wish permitted
    In the cool grave to lie,
He need not move again: this man
    Achieved his destiny,
    Was born to die.

. . . .

As the magnum is smashed on the stern when the liner is loosed
From Clydeside dockyard sliding over the greased
Slipway, displacing the water she touches
For the first time, equipped for her maiden voyage
Trailing the folding furrow over the long sea
So let the best be given for the immediate day.

Fill up the glasses with champagne and drink again.

For this is also the beginning of new living,
For Alan and Iris, new ones, of new loving,
This is the renewal of living under different names
This is the renewal of loving under different forms,
To-day these new ones are beginning to be one,
These two to-day are beginning to be one new one.

Fill up the glasses with champagne and drink again.

Let all bring gifts with them these have invite,
And over the two prices do not hesitate
Let jeweller to-day replace then cheaper drawer
Let them phone to warehouse at once for special cigar
To honour Alan and Iris, honour the day,
To honour the God to name whom is to lie.

Fill up the glasses with champagne and drink again.

Lord, be here to-day; on whom they call
In village leading out the garlanded bull,
Who binding leader to his group, from panic protect,
Who make the virgin leave her door unlocked,
Who please the daughter sitting on her father's knee
But after make her leave it; be here to-day.

Fill up the glasses with champagne and drink again.

O give your fullest blessing to these two.
For you alone can discipline the valuer's eye
And the too-curious hand, interpret the commands
Of the four centres and the four conflicting winds.
Interpret fully to these. This is your hour
You are expected here; be present, sir.

Fill up the glasses with champagne and drink again.

Already you are bringing swallows past the Scillies
To chase each other, skimming under English bridges,
Are loosing urgent pollen across country
To find the pistil, force its burglar's entry,
This year Alan and Iris are as swal-
-lows; will you not bless them also? We know you will.

Fill up the glasses with champagne and drink again.

We are all here now, Mildred the religious aunt,
Thomas the groomsman, Nat the confidante,
Morgan the Welsh cousin; representatives
Of all the gods who have controlled the lives,
The drugged Princess, or the jerseyed lighthouse-keeper,
We come, some more, some less, but all to honour.

Fill up the glasses with champagne and drink again.

It's not this only we praise, it's the general love.
Let cat's mew rise to a scream on the tool-shed roof,
Let son come home to-night to anxious mother.
Let vicar lead choir boy into a dark corner;
Orchid flower to-day, that flowers every hundred years,
Boots and slavey be found dutch-kissing on stairs.

Fill up the glasses with champagne and drink again.

Let this be kept as a generous hour by all.
This once let uncle pay for nephew's bill.
Let nervous lady's gaucheness at tea-time be forgiven
Let thief's explanation of theft be taken.
And fag caught smoking shall escape his usual beating,
To-night expensive whore shall give herself for nothing.

Fill up the glasses with champagne and drink again.

Yes, land-locked state shall get its port to-day,
And midnight worker in laboratory by sea
Shall find beneath cross-wires that he looks for.
To-night asthmatic clerk shall dream of boxer;
Let cold heart's wish be granted, desire for a desire;
Give to coward now his hour of power.

Fill up the glasses with champagne and drink again.

But approach now, Alan; day is almost done.
Now you're to meet the private person in the bone,
You're going to go a very long way with that—
Further than you know now; there will gives out;
Those places are not mapped at all, but pass,
Iris is ready now: do this.

Fill up the glasses with champagne and drink again.

Receive him, Iris, now; obey, surrender,
Admit the new life from the strange outsider
So chance of cancer shall be gone for ever,
And days of morning headaches be definitely over.
Charges pile up in expectant blood,
Flash is coming; draw him to the certain good.

Fill up the glasses with champagne and drink again.

Attain after years of listening your real wishes
Although in classroom you imagined other choices
Remembering gladly or not at all each instance
The tobacconist in the High Street or the Campbells' dance.
Not one is here to-day but remember each
They could not know all this but taught you much.

Fill up the glasses with champagne and drink again.

Let one be made from two, and many from one.
Make them and go away: the life goes on
As trees are alive in forest and do not fall
Sustained every day by their unconscious columnar will;
It shall outlast the tiger his swift motions.
Its slowness time the heartbeat of nervous nations.

Fill up the glasses with champagne and drink again.

If wishes are any use, although our eyes
No further see than railhead or the end of piers,
You're safe from fire, from evil eye, from spectre,
From sneering loutish son of a Scotch drysalter;
We take our coats to go; the single ones in dream
To meet their loves; and now for the last time

Fill up the glasses with champagne and drink again.

Notes on the Text

The fragments printed here represent various early stages of revision rather than the lost text of the completed play. (One exception is the dedicatory poem, which Auden may have sent Isherwood after he added it to *The Fronny*.) Some of the poems printed here from early manuscripts will be familiar from the later revised versions that Auden included in the second edition (1933) of his *Poems* (1930) and in later collections.

The dedicatory poem, published here for the first time, was written probably in December 1930, when Auden sent it to Isherwood. In late 1931 and early 1932 he used a revised version (dedicated "To my father") as Ode VI in the manuscript of *The Orators*; while correcting proof for this book, he replaced the poem with another Ode.

"Between attention and attention" dates probably from May 1930. Auden sent this early version to Isherwood in that month or early June. A shorter revised version appeared in the 1933 *Poems* and in the collected editions of his poems that Auden published in 1945, 1950, and 1966.

"Doom is dark" was written in August 1930. Auden sent this version to Isherwood, together with the first version of the Fronny's Last Will, probably in September. Later versions appeared in *New Signatures*, edited by Michael Roberts (1932), in the 1933 edition of Auden's *Poems*, in the collected editions he published in 1945, 1950, and 1966, and in the selected editions he published in 1938, 1958, and 1968.

"Who will endure" was probably written during the summer of 1930; Auden himself seems to have been uncertain of the exact date. Annotating a copy of the American edition of *Poems* (1934) for his friend Peter Salus around 1965, he dated the poem August 1931; but it does not appear in the notebook in which he preserved all the poems he wrote from August 1930 to August 1932. Auden sent the poem to Isherwood in the form of a manuscript fair copy that bears no indication of its date, but Auden almost certainly wrote it out at around the same time he made revisions to the epithalamion he used in *The Fronny* (see below). Among the revisions Auden marked in the manuscript of the epithalamion (which he gave to Iris Snodgrass some time before her marriage in July 1931) is the deletion of a stanza containing the words "although our eyes / No further see than railhead or the end of piers"; in the manuscript of "Who will endure" that Auden sent

Isherwood the lines "And no one sees / Further than railhead or the end of piers" have been added at the foot of the page, with their intended position indicated by an arrow. Probably he revised both poems about the time he was writing *The Fronny*, and the style of "Who will endure" suggests a date close to that of "Doom is dark". If, as his normal practice at the time suggests, Auden kept a notebook in which he preserved the poems he wrote from April through July or early August of 1930, it has now disappeared; "Who will endure" probably dates from that interval. (In a copy of the American edition of *Poems* that Auden annotated for Caroline Newton around 1940, Auden dated the poem April 1929 and noted that it had been written at his parents' cottage in the Lake District. As Auden was in Berlin throughout the spring of 1929, and as the poem is absent from the notebook in which he preserved his poems from April 1929 through March 1930, this date is almost certainly an error.) Auden published the poem in his 1933 *Poems*, in the collected editions of 1945, 1950, and 1966, and in the selected edition of 1958 (see p. 524).

Auden sent Isherwood the two revised versions of the scenes of dialogue probably in November 1930, the date of composition of the song in the second scene, "What's in your mind". Auden indicated the two Choruses in the first scene by writing their first lines, followed by "etc", because he had sent both Choruses to Isherwood earlier as separate poems. The first, "To ask the hard question", was written probably around August 1930; the text used here is that of the undated fair copy Auden sent Isherwood. The poem was published in *The Criterion*, July 1933, in the 1933 edition of Auden's *Poems*, in his collected editions of 1945, 1950, and 1966, and in his selected editions of 1938 and 1958. The second Chorus, "Love is this and that", was written in September 1930; the text here is that of the fair copy Auden sent Isherwood probably in the same month. Auden never published the poem.

Auden sent Isherwood a manuscript containing "I saw them stoop in workshops", "This Roman peace was broken", and "Hail! the strange electric writing" possibly in August or early September 1930; this was when Auden spent some time in Birmingham, the return address given on the manuscript. "Hail! the strange electric writing" reappears in *The Dance of Death* with an additional stanza. The other two poems are unpublished.

Auden probably sent Isherwood the first version of the Fronny's Last Will in September 1930. With the letter in which he responded to Isherwood's criticisms, he sent a copy of "Eliot's latest", presumably the pamphlet edition of *Marina*, published 25 September. He sent the revised stanzas, together with the revised scenes of dialogue, probably in November. Most of the names in the first version of the Fronny's Last Will, other than those of familiar public or historical figures, seem to be names of Auden's friends, and the Fronny's experiences seem likely to have been Auden's own. One pseudonym in the Will is "Captain Edward Gervase Luce", whose surname is the same as the fictional Mildred Luce in *The Chase* and *Dogskin* (and, probably, in *The Fronny*, as "Mildred the religious aunt" in the epithalamion). The description of Luce seems to correspond to Auden's friend from public school, Richard Perceval Bagnall-Oakley. When Auden sent the revised stanzas to Isherwood, he included this note beneath the line "Item, my naval range finder and case *etc*": "(I have altered the Parson's name to Luce and introduced some cross-references)." Auden apparently forgot that he had already used the name Luce in the earlier version. The "Parson" may have been a character similar to the Vicar in *The Chase*, whose sister is named Mildred Luce (although this seems to be her married name).

The epithalamion "As the magnum is smashed" was probably written around the summer of 1930, and revised perhaps later that year. Although Auden gave the manuscript to Alan Sinkinson and Iris Snodgrass (it is now in the Berg Collection), he evidently did not write it on the occasion of their wedding, when he was in Berlin. "Thomas the groomsman" and "Nat the confidante" represent real people (Tom Phillips, who was the best man at the wedding, and Natalie Gold, one of the bridesmaids), but "Mildred the religious aunt" and "Morgan the Welsh cousin" seem to be Auden's inventions—or were names taken from others among his acquaintances. Mrs Sinkinson now has no knowledge of anyone who would fit these names and descriptions.

The text of this edition combines the original and the revised (and cut) versions to present the fullest possible text. That is, I have retained the stanzas Auden cut when he revised the poem, but have also included the stanzas he inserted at the time he made the cuts. I have, however, retained the small verbal changes Auden seems to have made in the course of his larger revisions. It is impossible to say with any confidence which of these small changes date from the original stage of composition and which from the revised stage. The large changes Auden made were these. He added stanza 13 ("Attain after years"), and cut stanzas 1 ("As the magnum"), 2 ("For this is also"), 4 ("Lord, be here"), and 15 ("If wishes are"); at the same time, apparently, he retained the substance of two lines from the abandoned stanza 15 by deleting the first two lines of stanza 14 ("Let one be made") and replacing them with "Love shall be safe from evil eye, from spectre / From sneering loutish son of a Scotch drysalter". To reconstruct the final revised text, substitute the latter two lines in the text printed here and delete the four stanzas cut by Auden.

The smaller changes include wholesale deletions of the definite article. The last two lines of stanza 12, for example, originally read: "The charges mount up in the expectant blood, / The flash is coming; draw him to the certain good."

This text of the epithalamion includes some minor emendations and some doubtful readings. In stanza 3, line 3, Auden does seem to have written "then cheaper" rather than "their cheaper". In stanza 10, line 4, Auden first wrote "dream of a boxer", then deleted "a" and marked the word "of" in a way that perhaps suggests that he wanted to delete it or, as a remote possibility, that he wanted to alter it to "as". I have retained "of". (The rewritten version in *The Chase* and *Dogskin* has "dream he's a boxer".)

Among the parts of the play now apparently lost is one that Isherwood recalled in a letter to Auden while they were working on *Dogskin*; see below, p. 559.

APPENDIX III

Auden and the Group Theatre

BY M. J. SIDNELL

AUDEN did more for the Group Theatre than write plays. As the Group's poet and "secretary of ideas"* he suggested plays that might be performed, poems that might be used for the training of actors, and the names of authors and other artists who might work with the Group. As "propagandist" (the Group's term) and copywriter he wrote pieces for the short-lived *Group Theatre Paper*, notes for programmes, and an appeal (in verse) for subscriptions. His presence in the Group was more forceful and pervasive than the occasional writings reproduced here might suggest. His ideas on the theatre influenced Doone's, and his presence at rehearsals had a direct effect on Doone's theatrical practice.

The Group Theatre was founded in London in February 1932. It had no connection with the Group Theatre that had recently been formed in America, and of whose existence the British Group was unaware. The latter began with thirteen members, many of whom had first come together in the company assembled by Tyrone Guthrie at London's newest theatre, the Westminster, in 1931. Some of the enterprising younger actors at the Westminster began to use their free time for cooperative training and playreadings. Rupert Doone, a young dancer from outside the Westminster company, joined the most coherent of these groups, which had been organized primarily by a young actor named Ormerod Greenwood. This emerged as the Group Theatre, and Doone became its leader and stage director. In the autumn of 1932 the Group, now much enlarged, reorganized itself, establishing Doone and Tyrone Guthrie as its artistic directors or "Intendants".

Doone lived with Robert Medley, a friend of Auden's since their school years. In July 1932 Auden visited Medley and Doone, and was persuaded to advise the Group on literary matters and to begin writing plays for it to perform. Auden's first contribution was a list of material for verse speaking that he sent to Doone in a letter of 28 July 1932 (now in the Berg Collection of the New York Public Library):

> Dear Rupert,
>
> As a correspondent, I'm the shit. Please forgive me. I haven't the collections of Mummers' Plays here but I'm sending you a book which contains one version. They are all very much alike even textually, so it will give you the idea. If you want the collection in a

---

* Rupert Doone's phrase, from his article "What about the Theatre?" in *New Verse*, December 1935.

hurry, the book is called "The Mummers' Play" by Tiddy published by the Oxford University Press.

The Descriptive Poems. The best work for that sort of thing that I know is that of Vachel Lindsay. Something might be done with some of the tales of Chaucer. There are plenty of possibilities in Skelton. Of lighter stuff there's things like The Pied Piper of Hamelin and the Ingoldsby Legends. Can't think of anything else just now. The [?collection] of stories seems a good idea. I'm getting on with the Orpheus stuff. God knows what it's like. I'm finding it rather like a holiday task, but experience tells me that the pleasure of writing and its value have little connection; so hope for the best. I've never thanked you for my stay. I loved it.

best love to both
Wystan

The "Orpheus stuff" was a scenario for a ballet, not for the Group Theatre but for Doone to choreograph independently. At the same time Doone had asked Auden to write a play for the Group. Doone got neither his ballet scenario nor the kind of play he had in mind. Instead, about a year later, Auden provided *The Dance of Death*, which included some traces of the Orphic theme and a major role for Doone as dancer and choreographer.

The Group Theatre had its own hand press, which was used to print brochures, prospectuses, theatre programmes, and other material. An early prospectus (with a list of members dated April 1933) contains a brief manifesto, either written by Auden or put into shape by him from notes by Doone and others. It reads:

7 POINTS about the GROUP THEATRE

the GROUP THEATRE is a co-operative. It is a community, not a building.

the GROUP THEATRE is a troupe, not of actors only but of
- Actors
- Producers
- Writers
- Musicians
- Painters
- Technicians
- etc, etc, and
- AUDIENCE

Because you are not moving or speaking, you are not therefore a passenger. If you are seeing and hearing you are co-operating.

the GROUP THEATRE is a school for actors. If you cannot make your gestures as sensible as your speech, if you cannot dance or sing, if you are afraid of making a fool of yourself in public the GROUP THEATRE will take you in hand.

the GROUP THEATRE is neither archaeological nor avant-garde. It is prepared to adapt itself to any play ancient or modern.

the Group Theatre costs one guinea a year.

the Group Theatre has premises at 9, Great Newport Street (top floor).

A similar set of "8 points about the Group Theatre" appeared in the programme of *Croydon Repertory Theatre Presents the Group Theatre in Songs, Dances and a Play*, 24 July 1933. The only substantial new point reads: "the aim of the GROUP THEATRE is to create on a co-operative basis a PERMANENT, SELF-SUFFICIENT COMPANY supported by a sympathetic audience and a training school for young members." A second prospectus for the Group, dated January 1934, includes the original "7 Points", preceded by this untitled policy statement:

the GROUP THEATRE is not an ACADEMY, although it trains actors.

It is not a PLAY-PRODUCING SOCIETY, although it produces plays.

It is not a building.

It is a permanent GROUP of actors, painters, singers, dancers, and members of the audience, who do everything, and do it together, and are thus creating a theatre representative of the spirit of to-day.

It trains actors in the belief that by working together they will evolve a common technique with new means of expression.

It produces plays from any age which are of importance to us to-day.

It does not quarrel with the commercial theatre, but as the commercial theatre is not able to achieve these ends it sets out to find a new way.

The first piece for performance by the Group that Auden finished was a microdrama designed to provide continuity in the mixed bill of *Songs, Dances and a Play* performed at Croydon on 24 July 1933 and the five nights following. The play on the bill was the medieval romance *Lancelot of Denmark*; Auden's contrivance brought the actors of *Lancelot* onto the stage to play "themselves", involved at cross-purposes in "off-stage" amours. Notwithstanding the title on Auden's manuscript (now in the Berg Collection), the piece is an epilogue to *Lancelot* as well as a kind of prologue to the second half of the bill:

PROLOGUE

[*Enter* KNIGHT *and Launcelot's* SERVANT.]

S. Let's go back quickly. I'm dying for a cup of cocoa.
K. I want to see —— [*using the Christian name of the actress who takes the part of the mother*] home first.
S. Again. Why can't you leave her alone a little. You'll be getting her into trouble. Why, during rehearsals, you were always so busy talking, she was generally late for her cues.
K. [*sighing*]. Lucky Launcelot.
S. Well. I'm going on alone then. Give me the key will you.
K. Catch. [*Exit* S.]

[*Enter* LAUNCELOT.]

L. Hullo. Not waiting for —— [*using C.N. of actress who plays the girl*] I hope. The play's over now you know, and I allow no rivals off stage. Lucky devil. I wanted your part but Rupert wouldn't let me have it.
K. Is —— coming.
L. O it is my wicked mama you sigh for.
K. Of course. It is her I would gladly die for.
L. Sweet —— is my only flame.
K. She whom you loved and lost.
L.   The same.
  Look they come this way
  And set our hearts on fire
  May luck be ours this day
  And give us our desire.

[*Enter* MOTHER *and* GIRL.]

M. Hurry my dear or we shall be late
  Which is the door where they said they'd wait?
  Did yours say anything very exciting
  Let me see his note. What nice hand writing.
G. Are those his flowers. He's got good taste.
M. Come we haven't got time to waste.
G. Do you think that Croydon will rise to wine.
BOTH. How am I looking.

[L. *and* K. *step forward.*]

K.   Superb.
L.   Divine.

K. AND L. [*kneeling*]. Ladies if you please.
    We beg you on our knees
    That we may have the right
    To see you home to-night.
M. AND G. I'm afraid we've been already invited.
K. AND L. What do you mean? Who are these men.
    [*To audience.*] Go away and never come back again.
M. AND G. You must not get so excited
    At a modest invitation
    To see us to the railway station.
K. AND L. But you never did this [in] London
    Croydon has turned your head
    Croydon has us undone
    We wish that we were dead.

[*Enter* PROMPTER.]

P. Now then. What's all this. Where are you going?
    The programme's not finished yet.
THE REST. How do you know? You're only the prompter.
P. I know and yet the prompter knows
    Very much more than you suppose.
M. AND G. But two kind gentlemen in the audience are expecting us.
    It'll be such a disappointment.
L. AND K. Their wives will hear of this appointment.
G. The reason why you must explain.
M. And ask them nicely to remain.
P. Ladies and Gentlemen, the play is over
    The story of a foolish Danish lover
    Who lacking in himself belief
    Took ill advice and came to grief
    If we have pleased you we are glad
    For we have something more to add
    If not, we ask you still to stay
    For we may please you in another way.
    Do you love music. Have you in your home
    A piano, wireless or harmonium.
    Tyrone Guthrie who is tall and thin
    Married and lives in Lincoln's Inn
    Has arranged some songs for you to hear
    Of Johnny tarrying at the fair
    Of Herod and his cock that crew
    Or if your choice is dancing, then for you

Rupert Doone with his odd-shaped skull
Will dance as a Chinaman. It won't be dull
And Mary Skeaping has consented to come
And dance as a witch to the sound of a drum.
We hope that everyone will find
One of these items to his mind.
Shout if you like for we shall not be pained
Perhaps we look it but we're not refined.

The actors who would have played the roles in this piece of mumming remembered nothing about it forty years later, so it is possible that it was never performed—but forgiving memories may instead have obliterated all traces of it.

A more significant document for the development of the Group is the list of plays that Auden recommended to Doone, probably in January 1934. The list is on a letterhead from Auden's family home in Birmingham:

Classical
    Aeschylus.   Agamemnon.   Seven Against Thebes.
    Aristophanes.   Any.
There are no decent acting translations. Louis MacNeice is the person to do them. 6 Selby Park Rd   Birmingham 1.

Medieval
    The Plays of Hrotswitha (published by Chatto.)
    Everyman.
    The World and the Child
    The Play of the Weathers.
    The Revesby Plough Play
    Gammer Gurton's Needle
    Ralph Roister Doyster
    The Coventry } Nativity Plays
    The Wakefield
    The York Harrowing of Hell

Elizabethan
    Peele.   Old Wives Tale.
    Marlowe.   Dr. Faustus. The Jew of Malta.
    Middleton.   The Changeling.
    Ben Jonson.   Bartholemew Fair
                    The Masques (Particularly the Mask of Xmas)
    Day.   The Parliament of Bees.

18th Century
    Lillo   George Barnwell

19th Century
- Goethe — Faust Part II
- Ibsen. — Peer Gynt.

Modern
- Bert Brecht — Various (with music by Kurt Weill). No translations. Suggest Christopher Isherwood. Guemastraat 24 Amsterdam.
- ? — Marlborough Goes to War [by Marcel Achard]
- Cocteau. — Various.

Don't suppose this list will help you but here it is. I have written to MacNeice about his play. So sorry about job.

love
Wystan

Auden's suggestions had a powerful effect on Doone's plans for the Group. Louis MacNeice did eventually translate the *Agamemnon* for the Group, and *Peer Gynt* was performed, as was a monologue by Cocteau. Brecht's work was never presented by the Group, although his influence was strongly felt.

Auden attended rehearsals for *The Dance of Death* and provided revisions and additions as needed. He also wrote a synopsis that appeared in the programme (see p. 542). In it, as in performance, the structure of the work is made clear. In the printed text, by contrast, some divisions are omitted, either carelessly or as a deliberate sign that the text is not to be considered a work in itself but a libretto for a sung, danced, chanted, and spoken performance. On the bill with the first production of *The Dance of Death*, at the Westminster Theatre on 25 February 1934, was *The Deluge* from the Chester Cycle. Auden may have selected the modernized version that was used, and perhaps he revised it somewhat, but no considerable changes were made beyond the drastic updating of the *dramatis personae* printed in the programme. This list, which looks very much as if it were Auden's work, designates Noah and "Mrs Noah" and their sons as "The Unemployed Family" and names their neighbors "Mrs Empire Builder", "Mr Capital Profiteer", "Miss Old-Lily", "Tory Statesman Esq.", and the "Rev. Googles".

Although the Group had a formal constitution, its organization was always a matter of convenience and was largely centred on the erratic personality of Rupert Doone. (Tyrone Guthrie detached himself from the Group after co-producing with Doone the 1934 and 1935 productions of *The Dance of Death*.) The Group's financial arrangements were equally informal. Among its many appeals for funds, some were written in whole or in part by Auden. One flyer, dated 1 February 1935 and headed "URGENT", was an appeal for subscriptions. The appeal, signed by the Group's treasurer, Isobel Scaife, was followed by unsigned verses almost certainly the work of Auden. The initial letter of each line was printed in red in order to encapsulate the Group's urgent message:

Poor and Prosperous, Pert and Proud
Living in our land and loving laughter
Ever so often we have asked your help
Anxiously we ask for we have had no answer
Send us your SUBSCRIPTION as swift as the swallow
Easing our overdraft: They're our only income

Pull our your purse then, pay or we perish
Act on the instant, your onus is ours
You shall not hunger at the harvest your efforts yield.

   The programmes for the "First Group Theatre Season" (the only full one), at the Westminster Theatre in 1935-36, included short statements by different authors under the general heading "I Want the Theatre to Be . . ." Auden wrote the first of these, for the programme for *Sweeney Agonistes* and *The Dance of Death*, 1 October 1935. Transcribed from Auden's manuscript (now in the Berg Collection), it reads:

Drama began as the act of a whole community. Ideally there would be no spectators. In practice every member of the audience should feel like an understudy.

Drama is essentially an art of the body. The basis of acting is acrobatics, dancing, and all forms of physical skill. The Music Hall, the Christmas Pantomime, and the country house charade are the most living drama of to-day.

The development of the film has deprived drama of any excuse for being documentary. It is not in its nature to provide an ignorant and passive spectator with exciting news.

The subject of Drama on the other hand, is the Commonly Known, the universally familiar stories of the society or generation in which it is written. The audience, like the child listening to the fairy tale, ought to know what is going to happen next.

Similarly the drama is not suited to the analysis of character, which is the province of the novel. Dramatic characters are simplified; easily recognizable, and over-life size.

Dramatic speech should have the same compressed, significant, and undocumentary character, as dramatic movement.

Drama in fact deals with the general and universal, not with the particular and local, but it is probable that drama can only deal, directly at any rate, with the relations of human beings with each other, not with the relations of Man to the rest of nature.*

In December 1935 and January 1936 Auden worked closely with the Group in its production of *The Dog Beneath the Skin*, again adding dialogue and rewriting scenes.

In June 1936, in the first of seven issues of the *Group Theatre Paper*, the following article appeared above Auden's initials. The text has been edited from Auden's manuscript, now in the possession of John Johnson.

SELLING THE GROUP THEATRE

Art is of secondary importance compared with the basic needs of Hunger and Love, but it is not therefore necessarily a dispensable luxury. Its power to deepen understanding, to enlarge sympathy, to strengthen the will to action and, last but not least, to entertain, give it an honourable function in any proper community.

The content and structure of social life affect the content and structure of art, and art only becomes decadent and a luxury article when there is no living relation between the two. But because of natural laziness and the friction of opposing and vested interests, development in art, as in society, is not a purely unconscious process that happens automatically. It has to be willed; it has to be fought for. Experiments have to be made, and truth and error discovered in their making. An experimental theatre ought to be regarded as as normal and useful a feature of modern life as an experimental laboratory. In both cases not every experiment will be a success; that should neither be expected nor desired, for much is learned from failure; but, in its successes important avenues of development may be opened out, which would not otherwise have been noticed.

Research scientists know how difficult it is to get support for their work, unless immediate results of commercial or military advantage are forthcoming.

And if scientists find it difficult, how much worse is it for artists, since most have faith in science, and very few in art.

It is all the more necessary then to remind those who recognize the value of an experimental theatre like the Group Theatre that such a theatre depends on their support, that their numbers are small, and that they cannot leave the support to the other man.

During the last year, the Group Theatre has produced three experi-

---

* Through misreadings of the manuscript, the printed text of the second-to-last paragraph reads "confessed" instead of "compressed," and the last paragraph reads "at any rate directly" instead of "directly at any rate".

mental plays, *The Dance of Death*, *The Dog Beneath the Skin*, and *Fulgens and Lucrece*—plays which would not have been handled by the West End or Repertory Theatres; and the interest, even passion, aroused by these productions, not only in England, but in America and elsewhere, have more than justified them.

So much for the past. In addition to our other activities we are embarking on some new ones. In order to keep our members in touch not only with our own productions but also with any others of special interest, in England or elsewhere, we intend to issue a periodical Bulletin. In addition to news and articles on theatrical matters, we hope to publish extracts from members' plays.

Similarly, with a view to broadening our outlook and contacts, we have joined the New Theatre League, an association of Dramatic Societies, which will attempt to pool experiences, and co-operate in the organisation of audiences.

Finally we are forming a Film Group, under the direction of Mr Basil Wright of the G.P.O. Film Unit, for showing films of particular interest, and ultimately, we hope, with a view to making them.

Such then are our activities, and we do not think that there is another theatrical organisation of this kind in England, which offers ones so many and so various.

Naturally we think them worth while or we shouldn't do them. If you don't, come and see our next production. If you do, then remember that, like everything else in this world, they cost money, and that money does not fall out of heaven, but can only come out of the pockets of those who think as you do.

Therefore please support the Group Theatre yourself, both financially by subscription and actively by patronising its performances, and get others to do the same. Thank you.*

Auden made a more desperate and threatening appeal five months later. It appeared in the programme for the Group's production of the *Agamemnon* of Aeschylus, translated by Louis MacNeice, which opened at the Westminster Theatre on 1 November 1936:

ARE YOU DISSATISFIED WITH THIS PERFORMANCE?

Quite possibly. The chorus have rehearsed altogether about three times. Why? Because the actors have had to go to paid engagements. However

---

* In the printed text the opening paragraph omits the word "proper"; the sixth paragraph lists four experimental plays, including *Sweeney Agonistes*; and the third paragraph from the end concludes: "... this kind in England; activities so many and various." The printed text also shows various obvious misreadings of Auden's hand.

keen an actor may be on a part, he must live. Seven men participate in the chorus. Seventeen different actors have rehearsed in it.

The Group Theatre has certain initial advantages. It has playwrights who wish to write plays for it, painters who wish to design for it, composers who wish to compose for it. But it suffers under an overwhelming disadvantage. It has too little cash. There are actors who would like to play for it, **IF** they could afford it.

There are all the possibilities here for a vital theatre, neither drawing-room drama, nor something private and arty, but a social force. We have a lot to learn, but are willing, we think, to do so if we get the right support. Unfortunately the art of the theatre differs from literature or painting or music, in that it can not be created by one or two people in a room. It is extremely expensive.

It can go a certain way on membership of a club principle, but only a certain way, and the Group Theatre has gone as far as it can along these lines. Of course the greater the membership the better. Get everyone you can to join. But we need something more than that. The Group Theatre personnel can not work any longer without money.

We appeal for a patron or patrons, for a person or persons, who care about the theatre and feel that what we are trying to do is worth doing, and feel that sufficiently strongly, to make it, by their personal help, possible for us to do it, and make a permanent theatre.*

The production of the *Agamemnon* made use of masks, which Auden explained and defended in the fifth number of the *Group Theatre Paper*, in November 1936:

A MODERN USE OF MASKS

An Apologia

Everything we do, everything we think or feel modifies our bodies. Starting as babies with almost unlimited potential characters, with every choice we make, the future possibilities become more limited until the individual is more or less fixed and more or less unique. This uniqueness of character is reflected in a physical uniqueness, and because we wear clothes, we judge people by their faces.

Furthermore, we all possess, to a greater or less degree, the power of posing, the power of adopting another character, and the greater the power to do this, the more power we have to change our faces.

---

* Reprinted from the printed programme. The phrase in the fourth paragraph, "on membership of a club principle", should perhaps be understood as "on the membership-of-a-club principle".

It is on the recognition of this relation of the psychical and the physical that the use of the mask in the theatre depends.

Taken for granted in the theatre of classical times and the modern circus, it has disappeared in the realistic prose drama, because in the latter almost the whole of the effects are confined to the conversation. The physical attractions and repulsions of the star actors are only their own. They have nothing to do with the play as a play—(farcical characters, of course, by violent make-up, extraordinary clothes, and a comedian's particular talent for distorting his face have always retained physical methods of expression.)

The mask then is an attempt on the part of the painter to reinforce and parallel the intellectual effects of the writer, by physical effects which are independent of the particular actors.

In the cinema, close-ups, angle shots, and special lighting can do the same thing with the faces of the actors themselves, but in the theatre the great distance between the audience and the actor makes the mask necessary.

All art implies selection. Just as the dramatist limits the behaviour and conversation of his characters to the particular end in view, so the mask-maker selects from many facial characteristics the one to which he wishes to draw attention. A mask can be realistic but only in a limited way. Owing to its immobility it must be exaggerated or satirised. Even if the mask is a three quarter mask, as used by the Group Theatre in its productions of *Sweeney Agonistes* and *The Dog Beneath the Skin*, the same is true, because of the use which the actor normally makes of his forehead.

Incidentally, the masks in these two plays illustrate two opposite uses. In *The Dog* they were used to exaggerate the obvious, to make the hotel inmates, for example, look more like Hotel Inmates, to emphasize the normal vision. In *Sweeney*, on the other hand, they were used to reveal the real character behind the actual face, the contrast between inner reality and what we show the world, the hidden terrors behind the normal everyday expression, mask if you like, which meets us as we walk about the streets.

Fantastic masks, like those of a Christmas party, or the animal masks in the Group Theatre's production of the *Agamemnon*, are used for decoration and strangeness; like posing in real life they are play and fancy.

Lastly, the chorus masks in *Agamemnon* show the use of masks for special effects. In presenting a Greek play to a modern audience without a classical education, one of the difficulties of the producer is to prevent the audience regarding it as a quaint costume piece of purely archaeological interest. Just as the Greek has to be translated into modern English, so the visual effects have similarly to be translated. The chorus masks in combination with the modern jackets are intended to give an effect of timeless formality, the masking resembling a leaded head in a stained glass window.*

Despite Auden's apologia, the cellophane masks used in the *Agamemnon* proved unsatisfactory enough to be abandoned after the first night.

One consequence of the failure of the Group's efforts to find financial support was its transformation from a continuing company under the control of Rupert Doone to loose congeries of artists brought together for particular productions. For the production of *The Ascent of F 6* in February 1937, for example, the Group Theatre operated "in association" with Ashley Dukes, who hired the actors, arranged for the scenery and costumes, paid a royalty to the authors, and managed the performing rights.

The internal dissension in the Group, never far from the surface, came to a head during the summer of 1937, when Auden and Isherwood, after announcing their intention to arrange a commercial production of their next play, *On the Frontier*, in the West End, agreed to let it be produced by a reorganized Group Theatre in which Doone shared power with others. The new organization that emerged shortly afterward had six directors, with Doone as director for production, Stephen Spender as literary director, Benjamin Britten and Brian Easdale as directors of music, and Robert Medley and John Piper as directors of décor. (See the notes to *On the Frontier*, p. 653.) Auden and Isherwood took no part in the new organizational scheme, and in November 1937 Isherwood signalled his opinion of Doone's directorship in the title of a lecture he gave at the Group Theatre rooms: "The Mind in Chains, or Drama-Writing for Doone".

J. M. Keynes managed the practical aspects of the production of *On the Frontier* at the Arts Theatre, Cambridge, in November 1938. Both Auden and Isherwood attended rehearsals, but Auden seems to have left most of the revision to Isherwood. The two authors did their last work for the Group, a revision of the final scene for *The Ascent of F 6*, around June 1939, after they had left England for America.

The Group Theatre came to an end shortly after the outbreak of war in 1939, although the name was revived in 1950, as Group Theatre Productions Ltd. Auden declined to translate Brecht's *Mother Courage* for this postwar Group, which held the rights to Brecht's play for several years. He translated Cocteau's *The Knights of the Round Table* in 1951 partly with a view to a production by the new Group Theatre, but these plans fell through, and the translation was first produced by the BBC.

* In the *Group Theatre Paper* this article was unsigned. But a similar version of the text appeared in *The Times*, 27 October 1936 (early editions only), preceded by the statement that "Mr. W. H. Auden, the poet and playwright, has written the following note about the use of masks in the productions of the Group Theatre . . ." The version in *The Times* is slightly abridged, presumably by an editor, and has slightly more normal punctuation. One variant in it that probably reflects Auden's original text is in the first sentence of the last paragraph: "The chorus masks in *Agamemnon* will show . . ." The *Group Theatre Paper* omitted "will", presumably because the production was no longer in the future.

APPENDIX IV

Auden and Theatre at the Downs School

In his work as a schoolmaster Auden found frequent opportunities to turn his dramatic theories to practical effect. At Larchfield Academy, in Helensburgh, where he taught from the summer term of 1930 through the summer term of 1932, he seems to have done little more than organize a mummers' play in December 1930 and compose a brief play, *Sherlock Holmes Chez Duhamel*, which was performed by the fifth form on 25 June 1931. (This lost play, apparently designed to display the boys' prowess in French, portrayed a visit by Holmes to France and the attitudes of the French toward Holmes's methods.) But at the Downs School, near Colwall, where he taught from the autumn term of 1932 through the summer term of 1935 and again in the summer term of 1937, he organized productions that grew more elaborate and extravagant every year.

The Downs School magazine reported that around December 1932, as part of a school entertainment in aid of the Haford School in the Rhondda Valley, "Mr Auden got up a ghost play, with an entrance fee of 2d. It was a great success" (*The Badger*, Spring 1933, p. 24). In December 1933, at the Downs' Christmas Sing-Song, again in aid of the Rhondda fund, he produced Cocteau's *Orphée* (presumably in the translation by Carl Wildman published earlier that year), taking his cast from the school's sixth form.

For the Easter Sing-Song in March 1934, he produced an adaptation of *The Deluge* from the Chester Mystery Plays, in a version probably not unlike the one performed the previous month by the Group Theatre on the same bill as *The Dance of Death*. (*The Badger* described the adaptation as Auden's, which may well have been true even though the Group Theatre's version apparently contained little of his work; see Appendix III, above.) Much of the school took part, the full cast numbering fifty-eight. Bedsheets were draped over the junior boys, who rushed up and down to represent the waves. Auden, hidden on a platform above the stage, spoke the part of God. An account of the production appears in *The Badger*, Spring 1934, pp. 49-50.

Auden's most elaborate production was the "Revue" he organized for the Downs' Christmas Sing-Song in December 1934. Auden wrote the music as well as the lyrics, and organized a production that included the entire school and staff—"cast of about 113", as he wrote his friend Arnold Snodgrass. He dictated the tunes to Alexandra Feild (the wife of the Downs' art master Maurice Feild), who provided harmony. She later recalled some of the songs from memory for this edition. Auden accompanied at the piano whenever he was not on stage.

The programme distributed at the performance reads:

Programme
10. o'c[lock] Scholar

1. Life in the Raw
2. Swedish Dance
3. In Quarantine
4. Pedagogic Passion
5. Running Commentary
6. Bonjour mes Enfants

Interval

7. New Boy
8. The Fight for the Cabbage
9. Duchess of Malfi
10. The Old School Tie
11. Rhondda Moon
12. 8.12

These scenes were preceded by an opening chorus (printed below).

Most of the revue is lost or forgotten—or survives only in drafts written in Auden's most illegible hand in a manuscript notebook now at the Harry Ransom Humanities Research Center at the University of Texas at Austin. Some of the scenes listed on the programme can no longer be identified at all. Christopher Pinsent, a pupil at the Downs at the time, suggests that Auden probably had little to do with item 2, that item 4 *may* have included the Hobbies song (printed below), and that item 6 presumably included the first act final chorus (printed below). Item 8 was a short play largely written by the boys in a junior form. Item 9 was the scene in Webster's play in which the Duchess is strangled; Auden included it in the 1935 anthology *The Poet's Tongue*, which he edited, with John Garrett, for use in schools. Item 10 was a verse monologue, in five stanzas of eight lines each, that survives only as a draft in the notebook in Texas. In item 11 Auden, in a dress and a wig, rode on stage on a bicycle (to the delight of his pupils) and sang the "Rhondda Moon" song printed below; Auden used another version of the song in *The Dog Beneath the Skin*.* Item 12 evidently included the final chorus printed below. "8.12" alludes to the 8:12 train leaving Colwall for Malvern, Worcester, Oxford, and London on the last morning of term.

In addition to "Rhondda Moon" Auden adapted two other songs from the revue for *The Dog Beneath the Skin*, and used all three in the Nineveh Hotel scene in III.2. The Nineveh Girls' chorus is a resexed version of a chorus that in Auden's

---

* Robert Medley, Christopher Pinsent, and others suggest that the setting for this song in the revue was the same setting used in *Dogskin* and that the music was composed, like the other music for the play, by Herbert Murrill. The setting is clearly more sophisticated than the other surviving settings from the revue, but since Murrill did not begin work on *Dogskin* until almost a year afterward, his contribution seems doubtful. Possibly he set the song for the revue at Auden's request.

draft notebook apparently preceded the Opening Chorus for the revue, printed below. Madame Bubbi's song is also derived from a song in the revue. Both original versions survive as largely illegible drafts in the notebook in Texas. Some other (unidentifiable) drafts of songs written for the revue are also in this notebook.

The song texts are based mostly on versions provided by Maurice and Alexandra Feild, and have been collated with the earlier draft versions in Auden's notebook. The three brief pieces that I have arbitrarily titled "Self-Portraits" are transcribed from the notebook. I have added the last six lines of "Rhondda Moon" from the version in the notebook, and have provided speech headings for the final chorus. The account of the production by A[ustin] W[right] in *The Badger*, Spring 1935, p. 19, concludes that "Our only regret is that there is no manuscript of the revue and that it must fade as our memory dims."

The obviously topical references in the songs are to people and things at the school. "Tubby" was the working scale-model steam engine for the miniature railway on the school grounds. "Mr Booge" was a master named E. C. Coxwell, who had played the part of "Booge" in an earlier Downs sing-song. "Marriage" and "Bowes", in the final chorus, were the names of pupils. (John Bowes wrote the verse that Auden used as the epigraph for *The Chase*.)

Rupert Doone reported the scene written by the boys, "The Fight for the Cabbage", in a letter to John Johnson on 18 December 1934:

> I went down to see Wystan's school play, which I enjoyed very much indeed, and I think I learned things besides, from the children, especially in a short play that Wystan said they made up themselves. I must say it bore an uncommon resemblance to a "Folk Play", so one can take it that the "master" guided them. It was about a cabbage, and a tree, and a king and his son, and a giant and a doctor and an attendant and a princess and father Xmas and a hare and and and. But very charmingly done. . . . [quoted by Robert Medley in *Drawn from the Life*, 1983, pp. 152-53.]

[FROM THE REVUE]

Opening Chorus

That's enough
Now we're off
Will those with colds try not to cough
We welcome you to-night.
Bryanston
And Leighton Park,
Bootham,
All schools of mark
Boys and staff

Half and half
We hope to make you cry and laugh
Here's then to your delight.

Self-Portraits

I'm the head of my house, my word is law
To fifty other boys or more
When I have finished with these
I shall go to the colonies.

I've got the face of an angel
   I've got blue eyes
But if you knew the things I do,
   It might well surprise.
And where ignorance is bliss, my dear
   It's folly to be wise.

I'm a big bad boy
I lie, I cheat
I overeat
Bullying juniors is my joy
O what a treat
To pull their hair
To make them fear
Make them despair
If masters stare
I don't care
I'm a big bad boy.

Hobbies

Pay your tuppence and take your ride
Tubby will shake you up inside
The greatest fun, it can't be denied
Is engineering.

Have you rented an empty flat?
The carpenters will furnish that
With chairs on which Mr Booge has sat
Or a dumb waiter.

Can you tell a swallow in flight
An Emperor Moth from a Cabbage White
Or a Christmas Rose from an aconite?
See Natural History.

Are you a scoffer? Are you one
Who can't believe till you see it done?
Come to the Art Room and see your son
Paint like Picasso.

First Act Final Chorus

[*Sung by boys looking from train windows.*]
We are just the common lot
We come, we go, and are forgot
Not too good, and not too bad
Not too happy, not too sad,
We shan't care who falls or rules
We shall sit every morning on our office stools,
Return every evening to rather plain wives
And play for safety all our lives.

[*Full chorus.*]
All over Europe
Tough dictators shout
But at last, as in the past
Time shall find them out.
So if you're bored, dear listeners,
You need not leave the hall
We make our bow for it is now
The Interval.

New Boy

New boy,
O, it's hard to be a new boy
To be no better than a Jew boy
Strange terrifying faces
Come and ask me my name
Until in a corner
I hide for shame

Just a don't know-what-to-do boy
At a Public School.

Mother
O, I want to be with Mother
For I haven't any brother
I feel so lonely
I feel empty inside
But father said, remember
How Nelson died
So these feelings I must smother
At a Public School.

Rhondda Moon

On the Rhondda
My time I squander
Waiting for my miner boy.
He may be rough and tough
But be sure he is hot stuff.
He is slender, to me tender,
He's my only joy.
Lovers' meeting,
Lovers' greeting,
O his arms will be about me soon.
For I am growing fonder
Out yonder as I wander
And I ponder 'neath a Rhondda moon.

Final Chorus

BOYS.
Holidays
Jolly days
No more melancholy days
Freedom is almost here
Presents for me and you
Turkeys, plum puddings too
Chocolate bars
Rides in cars
Pantomimes and cinemas
Christmas comes once a year.

MASTERS.	Boys we disparage
Boys like Marriage
Disappear in a railway carriage,
The clever with the dumb.
Paris
Or Budapest
Munich
And all the rest
Some like this
Some like that
No one knows what we'll be at
Whoopee
The cheques have come.

ALL.	There's the flag
Now let's rag
Bowes has gone and lost his bag,
It's great to be alive.
Farewell
To one and all
Happiness
To big and small
Lots of fun
To everyone
And before our show is done
Good luck
To Thirty-five.

APPENDIX V

Two Reported Lectures

Two of the occasional lectures Auden delivered in the 1930s on poetry and the dramatic arts have been preserved in reported versions. The first, on "Poetry and Film", was delivered probably around January or February of 1936 to the North London Film Society; the report reprinted below appeared in the second (and last) number of the little magazine *Janus*, May 1936. The second, on "The Future of English Poetic Drama", was delivered in Paris at the Sorbonne on 8 December 1938 to the Association France–Grande Bretagne, at the invitation of its Comité des Relations Intellectuelles. The lecture was reported in the Association's journal *France–Grande Bretagne*, July-August 1939, under the title "The Outlook for 'Poetic Drama' ".

The text of "Poetry and Film" (subtitled "an authorized report of a lecture to the North London Film Society") seems reasonably accurate, and I have made only trivial emendations. In contrast, the French reporter of Auden's talk on poetic drama seems to have been baffled by his speaking style and Oxonian accent; the published text contains some garbled and nonsensical passages that I have emended as best I could. Some of the emendations are, by necessity, drastic. For example, the reported text has Auden allude to modern studies of culture, such as "Middleton's 'The Links' ". No such study exists, and Auden's reference was probably to "the Lynds' *Middletown*" or "*Middletown* by the Lynds". (In *The Double Man* two years later, he quoted from *Middletown in Transition*, the sequel by Robert S. Lynd and Helen Merrell Lynd to their earlier study, *Middletown*.) Some of the garbled passages I have let stand, but a bracketed "?" marks the points where confusion seems greatest. I am unable to make anything satisfactory out of one especially defective sentence in a generally confused passage about dramatic characters—a sentence that in the printed text begins: "It is no use calling them, striving in a ravel for something you cannot arouse people's interest, unless those people are real characters . . ." Possibly Auden meant to convey something rather like this: "It is no use calling them [by allegorical or collective names like] 'Striving' or 'Rabble' or something; you cannot arouse people's interest unless those people are real characters . . ." Many of the obscure and awkward sections of the text may in fact be accurate transcriptions of Auden's partly improvised lecture, so I have not tried to clean up the informalities of his syntax. But I have silently corrected evident errors in transcription, altered and added punctuation for the sake of clarity, and, where the emendation seems doubtful, added or substituted words or parts of words within square brackets. I have also added some footnotes. This lecture, delivered a few weeks before Auden left England for America, is Auden's retrospective farewell to the dramatic work of his English years; and even a badly defective text is preferable to none at all.

POETRY AND FILM
[1936]

The Industrial Revolution was responsible for the formation of two classes; a class of people composed of employers and employed, those actively employed in industry, and a class of people living apart from industry but supported by its profits—the rentier class. A distinct type of art arose more or less representative of the outlook of this section of public, developing through Cézanne, Proust and Joyce. But co-existent with this rentier art was the art of the masses expressing itself in the music-hall. This popular art of the music-hall has been taken over and supplanted by the film.

The film's essential factor is its power to concentrate on detail. The stage has to confine itself to stylised make-up, broad gestures and generalised presentation, on account of the distance separating audience from the scene; but the film, by means of the moving camera, close-ups, etc., can characterise its material more thoroughly and minutely without fear of the effect being lost on the audience. If a peasant is photographed at work in a meadow the scene is definite because it is localised naturally by the visual detail present in the shots. To show a similar scene on stage requires a much more broad effect. The film gives the concrete visual fact, while the stage gives an idea, a suggestion, of the fact.

Certain disadvantages and advantages result from the second essential characteristic of the film—its continuous forward movement in time. Owing to this particular movement, the success of an attempt to convey factual information by means of film is doubtful. If a suitable test [were] carried out as to the relative educational value of film or book, it would prove films to be valuable as stimulants of interest, but not as substitutes for the kind of factual instruction that a book or a teacher can give. Another danger for the film to guard against is preoccupation with types; for types are generalisations of people and such generalisation does not give a film a chance to use its special power of selecting and emphasising detail to build up a complete character. It is the essence of the camera that it deals with the immediate present. For this reason, a third mistake for films to make is to try to deal with historical material.

The proper concern of film is the building up of a general impression by means of particular detail; the analysis of character; and the material that contemporary life offers.

The use of sound raises the question of the relation of visual images to word images. The visual image is a definite one, whereas verbal images are not sharp; they have auras of meaning. A visual image cannot be made to mean a number of things, nor can a word image be confined to one thing. For this reason, highly developed metaphors cannot be included in the film medium. Where there is a combined image, e.g.— "Beauty's ensign yet Is crimson in thy lips and in thy cheeks, And death's pale flag is not advanced there", the different images would have to be split up for film presentation, and the resulting effect would be more in the nature of a simile. By putting two shots side by side, a furnace can be likened to a chess-man. But to get over an abstract idea, as distinct from a visual similarity, the sound track would have to hold the abstraction as complement of the concrete visual image. In the film, *The Scottish Mail-bag* [i.e., *Night Mail*] (on which Mr Auden has recently been working) a shot of mail-bags is accompanied by the words, "listen to the postman's knock, for who can bear to feel himself forgotten".

Because the sound sense and the visual sense of a film have a direct relation to each other, an audience finds it easy to follow an intricate visual continuity providing the sound does not make too many demands on its attention. But a strong sound image added to a strong visual image tends to cancel out both.

The G.P.O. Film Unit has been experimenting with the chorus, using it for detached comments on the action. And it was found that if such a chorus was to be used and be audible it was dangerous to use more than one voice. A need for more volume meant, not an increase in the number of the chorus, but either the one voice to be amplified, or the same voice re-recorded and super-imposed on itself. For the different timbres of a number of different voices coming together left the words inaudible.

There are a number of ways poetry can be used in film. The most obvious way is as a general emotional commentary. Mr Auden had just contributed to a publicity film *By the Sea-side*, in which poetry had been applied in this way; one of the shots seemed to him to be particularly good in its impact. The scene was the departure of people from the hot and dusty city to a coast. Someone is carrying a tennis racket, and as the net of the racket fills the scene covering all the bustle and heat, the words "like a cool fish in a grotto" are heard from the sound track.

Poetry can also be used to express the thoughts of characters, in rather the same way as Eugene O'Neill introduces "the interior voice" in *Strange Interlude*.

Actual poetic dialogue is impracticable chiefly on account of the big technical difficulties in making the visual and verbal continuity correspond.

Another interesting development would be an adaptation of the thought-stream technique to films, a method similar to that in the novels of Henry James. For example, while people were moving within a scene, the sound could all [?be] generalised descriptions, or abstract references, through a third voice quickly recognisable as coming from outside of the actors.

But whichever method is adopted one necessity must be observed—the spoken poetry must bear some relation, whether of similarity, indirect reference or contrast, to what is seen. For without a quickly grasped connection, the poetry and its place in the film is meaningless.

The generally accepted metrical forms cannot be used in films, owing to the difficulty of cutting the film exactly according to the beat without distorting the visual content. Mr Auden even found it necessary to time his spoken verse with a stop-watch in order to fit it exactly to the shot on which it commented—although the pan shot does offer a means of getting the visual rhythm to follow the rhythm of the poetic line. Trucking in or out, varying the sound volume, provides another means of gaining the same effect.

Mr Auden's last point was the difficulty of finding the right kind of support to enable such experiments to be carried out. It is financial support that is required for these experiments, without restriction on the director's independence of outlook either by commercial or departmental policy.

THE FUTURE OF ENGLISH POETIC DRAMA
[*1938*]

It is for a double reason that I am extremely sensible, firstly, of the honour that has been done to me in being requested to address you this evening, and, secondly, I am doubly sensible of my incapacity, for two reasons. First of all I am an Englishman, and I cannot but be aware when I come to your city of Paris that I am in some degree a provincial, belonging to a fringe of that European culture of which Paris is the centre. As I walk your streets, I am constantly reminded of the presence of the great dead to whom Paris was a spiritual home, and by great dead I do not only mean Frenchmen, but all Europeans. I think particularly, for example, of Baudelaire, Rimbaud, Heine, etc., names but for whom the history of the poetry of my own country would be very different. And if I have reason to feel humble before France, which is the landmark, the continued centre, and the guardian of European culture, I have another reason, which is my age. In looking through the list of lecturers in this series, I realize that I am the youngest of them. Now, after the war there was a feeling that the world belonged to the young. Well, if there is anything that the last eight years have taught us, I think it is that the world does not belong to the young, that never has there been a time when, on the one hand, it has been more difficult to attain maturity, and, on the other hand, when maturity was more necessary. It is, alas, too common a case for the vices of age to overcome the inexperience of youth, because, while science has not succeeded in prolonging, I mean in retarding, physical decay very much, yet the process of attaining an intellectual and emotional maturity in our civilization becomes longer every year. So that, too often, before an individual has attained maturity, before he has outgrown the folly of youth, he is overtaken by those characteristic vices of age which are love of comfort and a conscience stained by disingenuous complacencies.

Now, the title of this lecture has been called "The Future of English Poetic Drama". It is obviously impossible to state the future of any spiritual movement because one is almost certain to be proved wrong; one is always tied up with the conception of one's own thought. I think, for example, of Mr Wells's work on *Things to Come*, and, amidst many remarkable prophecies, if one looks at the clothes in which the people are dressed, I cannot seriously believe that the world will ever come to wearing that kind of toga.

So, really, when one says: "I have come to speak of the future of this or that", after all one really means: "I am going to consider problems which are perhaps bothering you and which are bothering myself." Students are familiar with the examiner who disposes of certain questions which he himself cannot solve and which he expects the students to solve for him. So, this evening I would like to consider certain problems which bother me. To you they may seem very simple and childish and already solved, and something may come of it.

I cannot speak as a literary historian, I am no scholar. I cannot speak with the experience of Mr Bernard.* I speak as a beginner in the dramatical art and as an amateur who has made many mistakes and will make a great many more before he has done. You see it is so difficult, because it always seems to me that perhaps the striking personal discovery may, after all, be one of the commonplaces of trivial knowledge, and again, what seems to me of immense public importance may really be a purely private dream. So that, before I start, really I must explain one or two things about myself as regards dramatic writing.

For various reasons, some accidental, some personal, the plays that I have written are in collaboration with Mr Christopher Isherwood, who is a prose writer, a novelist, while I write verse. So that if this evening I suggest to you that a possible form of drama for the future is one that combines prose and verse, that is partly dictated by the fact that my collaboration has been one between verse and prose. Secondly, we have cer-

---

* [Jean-Jacques Bernard, the dramatist, who introduced Auden's lecture.]

tain interests in common which one may call partly political and partly psychological. Here I mean those factors in social life which are not directly personal, like sex or parenthood, which affect and limit character and even the ordinary passions themselves. So, I again suggest to you this evening that the drama of the future will probably deal with some such themes. There again, I am really talking about something which I myself feel I must do. But, after all, thought does not occur in a vacuum. What happens [to] occur to people as their own private belief [h]as a curious habit of turning up when history requires it, just as is the same case with inventions. They do not appear until there is an economic necessity for them, though the amount of inventive talent at any time in the world's history is not likely to vary very much. Yet, at this certain point, when it becomes necessary, invention does occur, so that when one has an idea it is extremely unlikely that it is purely original, and I think therefore there is to-day a certain amount of objective and poetic kind of drama that I wish to discuss, as it is of some value to us at this time.

In the first place, there is, on the side of writers themselves, a growing interest in the drama and in a poetic drama. In Germany, while Germany was free, there was Brecht and Toller, in England there has been Mr Eliot and Mr Spender, in America there has been Mr Odets and others, who on their side, interested in poetry, have also become interested in drama and who also have become interested in subjects either religious or political, which differed from the conventional drawing-room comedy of their time. And from the side of the public, there is the pleasant and direct evidence of box office receipts.

I refer to the success, for example, of Mr Eliot's *Murder in the Cathedral*, which, if one compares it with *Becket* of Tennyson, on the same subject, does show a change in the attitude of the public. There are a number of people now who welcome a different kind of drama.

I would like to divide my enquiry this evening into three parts:

Firstly, what is the nature of the stage as a medium, what can it do, what can't it do, what can it do best?

Secondly, what is the nature of the theatrical subject, what kind of things make good subjects for plays?

Thirdly, certain details and problems of theatrical technique.

Let me then begin with the stage as a medium. Now, such discussions, I know, remind one awfully of discussions in cafés—these long drunken arguments, very late at night, which begin, "I suppose . . .", on the notion of pure poetry, or whether it is good or necessary for morale or propaganda. But there is a certain amount of justification for discussing the laws of limitation of a medium, particularly such a highly artificial medium as that of the drama, because, of course, as in life, there are no rules that you can write down, except the purely unpoetical rule of success or failure. Yet, as also in life, in order to be free it is necessary to study those factors and forces which limit one's freedom. For example, it is impossible to learn to fly until one understands the law of gravitation.

I don't want to talk now about the drama of the past, but the drama of to-day has two great media with which it has to compete. I refer to the novel and the cinema. Let us, for a moment, compare the dramatic medium with the medium of the novel.

To start with, drama, of course, is a public medium; that is to say it demands the cooperation of a large number of people, not necessarily very intelligent, it requires many pieces of apparatus, and it requires a building of considerable size. Secondly, as compared to the novel, it is continuous and irreversible. You cannot stop and say: "I would like to have that bit over again." [As] well, as it costs money, the subject and the treatment of that subject must be of sufficient general interest to get enough people together to pay. I know that sounds very simple, but it is a problem which often is neglected. And furthermore, the subject and the treatment must be of such a kind that they are understandable to people at half-past-eight or nine o'clock at night, after a comparatively good dinner. Now, the more characters and the more apparatus you require, the more popular, of course, must be the subject. If you have a musical comedy, you can employ a great many people and pieces of machinery, but if you wish to write a play about miners in Alaska, then you had better write something requiring only two or three actors and, as scenery, some curtains. I think this is very childish, but is is a reason, for example, why Hardy's *Dynasts* is not very likely to be performed often.

Again, as compared with the novel, the time is very limited. A play must not last less than an hour and a half or people will not think they are getting their money's worth, and it must not last more than three hours or they will miss their last train.

Most important in plays are the actions done by people in a limited space. The actions that you can really do in a stage space are limited. You cannot eat a whole meal, ride a bicycle, or drive a motor-car; you cannot do anything except the preliminaries of love-making; you cannot expect actors to do anything that involves physical injuries to themselves. I once, for example, read a play by a young man which was about a man on a golf course. While he was out playing golf, his friends were sitting at the bar and thought what a good joke it would be when he came back to tell him that his wife had died. So, when he came back they said to him: "Your wife has had an accident", upon which the hero took his golf club and beat out his brains with it. That is more than you can expect any actor to do. Compared with a novel, roughly speaking, you can say that it is very much more expensive and must be more popular and less subtle. Secondly, your action is very much more limited—that is, the possible kind of things that can happen on the stage.

Now, let us compare it with the cinema. The cinema, as regards expense and time is like the theatre and a great deal more so, which has a very important social effect because the cinema as a medium is the most realistic and most truthful of all media. On the other side, it is so expensive that it can only be paid for by people who have very good reasons not to wish the truth to be known. It is impossible to imagine a cinema at present that is not either run by the State or by very rich people of some kind or another. I happen to feel this rather strongly for having worked a little for the General Post Office in the production of a film. To show the kind of difficulties which arises, I will tell you this one story, because it explains why films sometimes are not as good as they might be. We had to take some pictures of people in a trunk telephone exchange.* It was supposed to be New Year's Eve. I found out that these people were very tired and worked in their shirt sleeves. So I got them into shirt sleeves, got the cameraman, and when the supervisor came he said: "We can't show government officials in their shirt sleeves."

Then, on the other hand, in many ways the film is very much more like the novel. First of all, you get the flexibility; by moving the camera, you can alter the way in which you move. And what is still more important than that, both the novel and the film—and the film even more so—show man in direct relation to nature. There he is on the screen, with fields, hills, streets, etc., about him, so that you can use them as a sort of a comment of the film or, at least, leave it as a question mark. It is like the novel also in its treatment of time. The cinema and its capacity to face physical action is also something which the stage cannot do.

So the chief difference, to start with, between the drama and other media, like the novel and the film, is that in the novel and in the film you can show a man directly in relation to nature, while on the stage you cannot. The novel and the film, if you like, are like a river and the drama is a series of avalanches. The novel is a park, the film is a window looking out on the world, but the stage is a box, it is a prison. We are in this prison with the audience, and the actors are in it too, and the important thing is that the actors can't get out and we share their imprisonment. We demand the release of the captives from the tragedy, in fact, out of a feeling of extreme claustrophobia. Here, on this narrow stage, surrounded by

* [Evidently a reference to the film *Calendar of the Year*; see p. 672 below.]

sham scenery, sham lighting, sham objects, we have a few imprisoned people; and what I think also is, that the stage is supremely conservative in the relation between man's free will and the forces which limit and frustrate that will. That is one reason why I am talking about drama at all to-night, because drama is impossible if you believe that man's life is completely determined and he has no free will at all. If you have no free will and no possibility of making a choice, the dramatic suspense disappears at once. On the other hand, if you are completely liberal and believe that man's will is absolutely uncontrolled, the stage falls to bits and does not mean anything.

The drama is a form [for] the culture which holds temperately to the belief in the free will of man; it also is humble and is aware of all those forces which limit it. It is therefore why drama is not a form for a completely *laisser-faire* community, nor is it a form for totalitarian states, which much prefer the cinema. It is a form for social democracy.

There are so few things—that is unfortunate—that people on the stage can do: they can sing, they can dance, they can gesticulate, they can talk. Gesticulation is so much more suited to and much more subtle on the screen, and the most important thing they can do is to talk. The spoken word is the basis of drama, and within these limits—four walls and sham lighting, these little actions that are possible—the dramatist must hold the mirror up to nature, make a criticism of life, reveal beauty, terror, pity, what you will. So one of the first problems for the dramatist is how to release the captives, that is to say, how are you to relate these characters to a larger life to which they belong. Here they come on the stage as if they came out of trunks, and you have got to show that they did not come out of trunks. Now, in comedy this is done in various ways. Firstly there is the epigram, the witticism: "Did I meet you in Trouville?"—"I have never been in Trouville."—"Neither have I."—"Then it must have been two other people!" Then there is the forgiveness, which is a very important thing in comedy, the unmasking of vice followed by forgiveness, and lastly there is marriage which takes place off the stage. The difference, it seems to me, between comedy and tragedy is that [in comedy] the characters are aware of their lack of freedom. It is always the situation of the rich uncle arriving at the wrong moment and so on, and it is at the end of the play that they discover that they were freer than they thought, while in tragedy they continually believe that they are free until they discover that they were not as free as they thought.

The releases in tragedy are, first of all, death; then there is poetry which lifts the private suffering of the private individuals on the stage into the suffering of all men in such a situation. In poetry you can say, for instance: "Boys and girls Are level [now with men] . . . [And] there is nothing left [remarkable] Beneath the visiting moon."* Such a language breaks down the sides of the stage and releases our feeling of imprisonment.

In later drama, which is not poetic, the great contribution, in the way of release, was made by Ibsen. It is the symbolical object or symbolical phrase. It has been employed, of course, by others. You have *The Seagull* by Tchekov, *The Wild Duck* by Ibsen. The most successful of Ibsen's symbols, that key which leads one out into a form of beauty and terror, are phrases like, "The joy of life is God's", or that terrifying remark in *The Wild Duck*, "The woods avenge themselves", or a remark which comes in John Gabriel Borkman's soliloquy.†

Then, let us think of the question of subject or theme. What subjects now are likely to be most profitable, dramatically, most fruitful? Many people, of course, when they think of a play, think of something about adultery, involving a number of rather well-to-do people, but that, after all, is a relatively recent idea. We are now living at the end of a period which began with the Renaissance, an age of liberty and freedom without unity or justice. It was a period which saw certain important things. It saw first of all that every individual is unique, it believed in the freedom of the will; it was interested in the rational contrast[?] of the intellectual part of man which is and was unique individually; and it did not believe, really, in society, in unity, in loyalty. And parallel with the growth of belief in the importance of the individual, and [*i.e.*, ?there was] economic change and the gradual atomization of society, until the only social group that remained—the only social, emotional unit—was that, again, of the family. It was a development which, in the end, was to prove a very difficult one, I think, for the dramatist; firstly because along with the interest in character—which did produce at once a great efflorescence of drama—in the end, those who were really interested [in character] turned to a more subtle medium, the novel.‡ Other poets turned—horrified by the complexity and ugliness of their society and bewildered by its past—they turned away to contemplation of their own feelings and to writing of lyric, often beautiful, often obscure poetry.

When the drama began to rise during the nineteenth century, the problems were essentially family problems, that is to say, [the] fight for truth and justice and so on, which is always going on in different ways. At that time it was directly a personal matter that beliefs and customs

* [I have rearranged this sentence, which in the printed text reads: "in such a situation, boys and girls, on level. In poetry you can say for instance: 'There is nothing left beneath the shining moon . . .'"]

† [Conceivably Borkman's phrase "the treasure sank back into the deep again", from his long speech—not quite a soliloquy—near the end of Act IV.]

‡ [The printed text reads "a more subtle medium than the novel".]

which belonged to a previous society had survived into the family. Such things, for example, as the subjection of women, and contempt [?for them], were really something which could take place in the family. It was possible for a character to confront her father and say: "I will leave the house!" and for one to feel that an immense moral victory had been gained. It was a personal matter between those two people. Now, when we hear, as we heard in September, Mr Hitler say in this crisis: "There is nothing but two men, myself and Dr Beneš, and what happens is a matter between us two", we know that he is talking nonsense. Recent advances of knowledge in various fields, politics, psychology and economics, have revised our conception of human character and of the different fields of interest over which we look; and, for example, if you take a modern book on culture dealing with ancient culture, [or] a modern study such as *Middletown* [by] the Lynds, they have shown how enormously the social structure and the cultural power of an age contribute to dictate individual characters and the kind of liberty which is permitted, not only [the] liberty of the actual kind of characters which survive in a society. Psychologists generally have shown that not only are we conscious and unique, but that we all bear with us an unconscious in which we are very much like each other, much more than we thought, and there the dramatist has another field of interest that is putting him back. Not only are people unique, but they are also alike and also less free than they thought. The economists have also drawn our attention to the fact, which is quite a common-sense fact but easy to forget, that the kind of characters we have and the kind of way we behave with our wives or our children may have a very close connection with the way in which we earn our living. A stockbroker, maybe, will have more to say than a tradesman.

And lastly, politically, the struggle to avoid limitation, about which—as I ventured to suggest—the dramatist is much concerned, that is, the struggle between destiny and free will, now taking place very obviously and materially in the outer world. It is an age of physical revolution, so that a campaign which at one time was confined to the boudoir is now taking place before the barricades; and that is bound, whether we like it or not, to affect our field as artists.

When we were in China and heard the news about Austria, it was extraordinary the way one felt this China war turned out to be a provincial scuffle. The dramatist to-day must show man in relation to nature; he must show that he is not wholly rational, not wholly irrational, [nor that*] he is wholly determined. He must show the reaction in private and public life, the influence of public life upon the character, upon the individual

---

* [A conjectural emendation for the printed text's "if".]

and upon society. This he must show, or want to show; and this struggle is taking place in the political field. Now, I do not mean that for that reason one must throw characterization overboard. The stage stands or falls by a few characters standing on the stage. It is no use calling them "Striving" or "Rabble" or something; you cannot* arouse people's interest, unless those people are real characters, because you can never go back, and one thing you have gained is the recognition of individual uniqueness. But we have to combine that now with the realization of collectivity as well.

One of the ways in which, I think, it can be brought about is by the use of poetry, because poetry is a medium which expresses the collective and universal feeling. Now, this can be used in various ways. It can be used as chorus, which is sung or spoken, as for example in *Murder in the Cathedral*. Music has the effect of even more generalizing the emotion, so that if you want to get a general effect, I think music is useful and is going to take a large part. There are some technical difficulties: if you have a number of people singing it is difficult to hear a word they say, and that is a technical problem which has not been completely solved yet. Then you can use characters speaking and try to adapt the kind of speech to the kind of character. That can, of course, only be done very broadly. It was done in medieval drama. There is a lot to learn in that kind of thing.

The trouble about blank verse is that characters when they get excited talk exactly like each other. That is the difficulty with verse—to find a method by which you can differentiate speech and characters.

One can also use soliloquy in which characters reveal themselves or comment on the action of the play. I think there is the danger in a play with a soliloquy in verse because it is extremely difficult to get any characterization.† Many attempts have been made to get a ritual kind of drama—people with masks and moving in graceful gestures—but I personally feel that they are doomed to failure. I think one has to accept the fact that plain art is to be performed by nice-looking and rather vain people.

Again, poetry unalloyed tends, if one is not very careful, to introduce a rather holy note. You cannot have poetry unless you have a certain amount of faith in something; but faith is never unalloyed with doubts and requires prose to act as an ironic antidote.

The problem of writing a play in which verse and prose are combined is difficult and I think not yet solved. There is a certain conception of

---

* [The printed text reads "calling them, striving in a ravel for something you cannot"; see headnote.]

† This is emended from the printed text, which reads: "danger in a play that a soliloquy infers because it is extremely difficult to get any equalization".]

having different parts of the play on different levels. It is a question whether you are to move from a prose or poetry level. You can either do it in different scenes, one scene on a level, one scene on a different level; or [have] one character who has a greater degree of consciousness and is therefore capable of breaking into verse; or you must find a situation in which the characters are not their normal, everyday selves, such as dreams, or madness. I think that probably to choose as a subject a political subject is a mistake, because history is always now more terrible and more moving than anything you can possibly invent and more extravagant than anything you can imagine. It is impossible now to write about contemporary time unless you took a part in it yourself, because the trouble about trying to write is that one simply does not know enough, or there are very few people who do. Perhaps if you want to do that (I only say this as [*i.e.*, ?of] a subject) it is better to take a parallel of historical interest.

On the whole, I think one must have selected a general kind of subject—a few people, belonging to strata which the dramatist knows well, possibly a family, but treated in a different way [from] which they were treated in a drawing-room comedy.

As to scenery, I think this element is important, and I think, from certain experiments which we have made, that if you are to have different levels and different scenes, that [the] visual element must be consistent. If you alter the scenery with the change in the behaviour or language the play falls into little bits. I do not think realistic setting is necessary now, especially as we have to compete with the cinema, but a few objects to establish a sense of reality [are].

Now, what will happen to the stage, I do not know, but I do know this: that the search for a dramatic form is very closely bound up with something much wider and much more important, which is the search for a society which is both free and unified. I spoke at the beginning of this lecture about Paris as the centre of culture, but for more than a century Paris has stood for a great deal more than that for the people to whom liberty and social justice seemed something very precious, who have turned their eyes constantly towards your city; and we, in England, realize very clearly that what happens here affects us enormously. If we sometimes, at this moment, look towards France in apprehension mingled with hope, it is because we realize that while these values have disappeared in one country after another, we know that unless they are safeguarded here, in our country liberty, culture, drama are made impossible.

TEXTUAL NOTES

NOTE: In the following textual notes, Auden's selected and collected editions are indicated by their dates of publication in italics:

1938 *Selected Poems* (Faber & Faber)
1945 *The Collected Poetry of W. H. Auden* (Random House)
1950 *Collected Shorter Poems 1930-1944* (Faber & Faber)
1958 *W. H. Auden: A Selection by the Author* (Penguin); *Selected Poetry of W. H. Auden* (Modern Library, 1959)
1966 *Collected Shorter Poems 1927-1957* (Faber & Faber; Random House)
1968 *Selected Poems* (Faber & Faber)

Paid on Both Sides

In December 1927 Auden wrote the first of the lyrics that he later incorporated into *Paid on Both Sides*. These lyrics were conceived as separate poems; he included seven of them in the volume of *Poems* privately printed by Stephen Spender during the summer of 1928. "Then they seemed to be part of something" (Auden to Monroe K. Spears, 21 July 1962). Around July 1928, or possibly early August, he completed the first version of the play by writing the prose dialogue, revising the existing poems, and adding some new ones. He apparently wrote the play for performance as a country-house charade at Tapscott, near Wellington in Somerset, the home of his Oxford friend William McElwee. Auden had accepted an invitation to stay there during the first two weeks of September. He evidently sent a copy of the text in advance, for in August he wrote Isherwood: "They refuse to do the play, as they say the village won't stand it."

A few months later, in Berlin, Auden began work on a new play, apparently an early version of the dream-play that he later inserted into the revised version of *Paid on Both Sides*. Around November 1928 he reported to Stephen Spender: "The old play [*Paid on Both Sides*] is joining a new one probably and turning into something else, I am not quite sure what yet" (letter in the Berg Collection, New York Public Library). He completed the thoroughly rewritten version of *Paid on Both Sides* around Christmas 1928. On 31 December he wrote McElwee: "The Tapscott charade is now finished and goes to Eliot to-day" (letter in the British Library). He sent Eliot some changes on 4 April 1929, and the rewritten play finally appeared (slightly bowdlerized) in Eliot's quarterly *The Criterion* in January 1930. Soon afterward, Eliot accepted a volume of Auden's poems for publication by Faber & Faber. Apparently through a misunderstanding at the publishers, *Paid on Both Sides* was not included with the shorter poems when the book went to the printer, but it was added in proof and appeared as the first part of Auden's *Poems* (1930). The text was slightly revised from the *Criterion* version and was supplemented by a dramatis personae. The new text was reprinted in the second edition of *Poems* (1933) and in the American edition (1934) and, in full, in *Selected Poems* (1938). When in 1943 Auden compiled the volume that appeared as his *Collected Poetry* (1945), he extracted seven poems from the play, printed them as separate lyrics with their own titles, and abandoned the rest. But he restored the full text for the British counterpart of that volume, *Collected Shorter Poems 1930-1944* (1950), and reprinted it, with trivial changes, in his *Collected Longer Poems* (1968).*

---

* The poems printed in Spender's private edition of *Poems* (1928) were these (listed here in the order in which they appeared in that volume, and with their first lines taken from that volume's text; dates are probable dates of composition):

"The four sat on in the bare room" (in first version of *Paid* only) [December 1927]
"To-night when a full storm surrounds the house" (in *Paid* "To-night the many come to mind") [January 1928]
"Night [*error for* Light] strives with darkness, right with wrong" [January 1928]
"The spring will come" [Spring 1928]

Auden seems never to have been directly involved with any performance of *Paid on Both Sides*. The play was first produced in March 1931 at Briarcliff College near New York by Hallie Flanagan and Margaret Ellen Clifford. The first British production, at the Festival Theatre, Cambridge, 12-17 February 1934, was "conducted by Joseph Gordon MacLeod" as part of a program of "Experiments". Using his publisher as his agent, Auden gave his approval for this production, but asked that MacLeod be urged to write him for suggestions about staging the play. Whether MacLeod did so is unknown, as is the nature of the suggestions Auden planned to offer.

Auden never published the first version of the play; it appeared posthumously in *The English Auden* (1977). The text survives in the form of a typescript Auden prepared and corrected himself, and then gave to Isherwood. The first version, like the second, is subtitled "A Charade" but, unlike the second, bears no dedication. In the typescript of the first version Auden normally spelled out the characters' names but used the initials L, R, and C to refer to the left, right, and centre of the stage. He also abbreviated William to "W.", but I have spelled out the abbreviation in this edition.

All the published texts of the second version derive from a typescript not prepared by Auden, but with cuts and additions in his hand and with one inserted passage typed by him. He gave the only surviving copy of this typescript to Isherwood; another copy was evidently the basis of *The Criterion* text, which was then

"The summer quickens grass" [April 1928]
"Some say that handsome raider still at large" [Spring 1928]
"To throw away the key and walk away" (in second version of *Paid* only) [August 1928]
Other poems in the first and second versions appear as separate poems in a notebook Auden used in 1928 (now in the Berg Collection, New York Public Library) and in other manuscripts:
"Often the man, alone shut, shall consider" [July 1928]
"Not from this life, not from this life is any" [September 1928]
"Can speak of trouble, pressure on men" [October 1928]
"Always the following wind of history" [November 1928]
"The Spring unsettles sleeping partnerships" [August 1928]
"In these days during the migrations, days" (second stanza begins "Past victory is honour, to accept") [December 1928]
"Because I'm come it does not mean to hold" [November 1928]
"Sametime sharers of the same house" [November 1928]
"Yesterday we sat at table together" [December 1928]
"There is the city" [November 1928]
The poems Auden extracted for the *1945* collection (see page 524), with their titles in that volume, were these:
"Not from this life, not from this life is any" ("All Over Again")
"Can speak of trouble, pressure on men" ("Always in Trouble")
"The Spring unsettles sleeping partnerships" ("It's Too Much")
"The summer quickens all" (untitled)
"To throw away the key and walk away" ("The Walking Tour")
"Tonight the many come to mind" ("Remember")
"Though he believe it, no man is strong" ("Year After Year")
In his *1958* selection Auden reprinted "To throw away the key and walk away" as "The Journey".

slightly revised for the Faber edition of *Poems* (1930). The text of the play in the present edition follows that of the corrected typescript (which suffered minor censorship and misreading when it appeared in *The Criterion*), but incorporates the changes Auden made in the 1930 *Poems*. These changes included the addition of the list of characters and the description of the stage and a substantial cut in one of Anne's speeches (of which the original text is given in the notes below). Because the typescript of the second version abbreviates speech headings wherever possible, I have followed its practice in this edition. (In one or two brief passages inserted by hand, Auden used roman capitals for speech headings, the practice followed in the present text; the typescript has the speech headings in red, while the early printed texts use italic capital initials. The 1968 *Collected Longer Poems* spells out the names in small capitals, a change introduced by the publishers.) I have restored the typescript "Xmas" where *The Criterion* substitutes "Christmas"; Auden used "Xmas" again in the list of characters introduced in *Poems* (1930). The typescript copy dedicates the play "For" Cecil Day-Lewis; the printed texts dedicate it "To" him.

Emendations and other textual problems are discussed in the notes below.

Page 10.

In Anne's speech beginning "To-night the many come to mind" the forms of the two proper names vary from one text to another. The typescript of the first version makes the final *s* part of the name in both cases: "Morgans'... Dodds'". The typescript of the second version detaches the *s* in both cases: "Morgan's... Dodd's". Auden had no consistent style of writing possessives, and more often than not made obvious errors in doing so. For this edition I have followed the readings of a manuscript of this speech in a notebook now in the Berg Collection, New York Public Library: "Morgan's... Dodds'". The name Dodds was probably borrowed from Professor E. R. Dodds. He and his wife were friends of Auden's family in Birmingham.

Page 14.

The list of characters and the description of the stage do not appear in the typescript or *The Criterion*, and are reprinted here from *Poems* (1930). All editions published during Auden's lifetime fail to indicate the part that should be doubled with Trudy; as Seth's Mother seems the only likely possibility, I have added the appropriate stars to her name here.

Page 15.

In Trudy's second speech the typescript reads "Jerry said, for last time"; *The Criterion* and later editions, followed here, read "Jerry said, till for last time". The insertion is required by the sense, and its omission in the typescript may have been an error.

Page 16.

In the typescript and *The Criterion* the speech of the Chorus has some lines slightly indented (the first three lines—after which *The Criterion* has a break—and the second verse paragraph). The indentions were probably the typist's attempt to reproduce the sloping left margin of the lost manuscript.

Page 19.

Through a misreading of the typescript, all editions during Auden's lifetime printed the prose section of Trudy's long speech (from "I am sick of this feud" to "came crouching out") as verse.

Page 20.

In the stanza beginning "Then watchers saw" the typescript and *The Criterion* read "Doomed men woke" where later texts read "Doomed men awoke".

Page 21.

The Spy's speech in the typescript has the first part of the sentence added in Auden's hand, but with the word "now" where the printed texts have a comma: "You may look big now but". Auden wrote the word "now" somewhat illegibly in the typescript he gave Isherwood, and the word's absence in the printed texts may be the result of comparable illegibility in the copy he gave Eliot; or he may have omitted the word later in order to avoid an echo in the first syllable of Nower's name at the end of the line.

Page 24.

The Boy's first speech is replaced with a row of dots in *The Criterion*.

The Doctor's couplet beginning "Tennis elbow" is printed as a single line of prose in all published editions. It was presumably the printer who altered "Housemaids' knees" to "Housemaid's knees", which is closer to the usual form, "housemaid's knee"; but the double plural may have been deliberate.

Page 25.

The second sentence of the stage direction beginning "DOCTOR takes circular saws" is omitted in *The Criterion* and all later texts, probably as a result of censorship by Eliot. Unlike the line replaced with a row of dots (see above), this omission was not indicated by any typographical symbol, so Auden or Eliot may simply have forgotten about it when the other omitted line was restored. The sentence provides a motivation for the Boy's next line, and undoubtedly should be restored.

In Xmas' line "You can't come in here without a pass" I have deleted the comma that the typescript and all other texts supply after "here". In the typescript this comma was originally followed by "sir", and in deleting this word Auden probably did not intend to leave the pause in the line that the preceding comma indicates.

Page 26.

The first word in John's verse speech beginning "Sametime sharers" is the word Auden intended, although the form is not recorded in the *OED*, and Auden, late in life, authorized the emendation "Sometime". The manuscript of an early version of these lines, in a notebook now in the Berg Collection, reads "Same-time".

In Dick's first speech "enemies' " is an emendation for "enemies".

In John's speech beginning "There is the city" the printed texts read "indifference" for the typescript's "Indifference".

Page 27.

In the second verse paragraph of the Chorus beginning "To throw away the key" the typescript and all printed texts of the play read "Travellers may sleep at inns". The separate manuscript of the poem in a notebook now in the Berg Collection and the printed text of the poem in *Poems* (1928) both read "Travellers may meet". The reading "sleep" was probably an error of the play's typist, who picked up the word from the following line.

Near the end of the same Chorus, I have adopted the reading "pulse's" from *Poems* (1928), instead of the typescript's "pulses' ". The manuscript of this poem in the notebook in the Berg Collection simply has "pulses".

Page 29.

In John's speech beginning "On Cautley" both typescript versions read "the forwards stopped". The change in the printed texts to "the forward stopped" may have resulted from a confusion with the "he" of the next sentence. In fact the first three sentences of this speech all refer to separate recollections. (In the typescript of the first version, but deleted in Auden's hand, are two further sentences after "forwards stopped": "Night trains. The hunted look of summer lightning.") The first version (p. 9) has the words "rushing of" inserted in Auden's hand, almost illegibly, before "forwards"; the absence of these words in the second version *may* be erroneous.

Page 30.

Anne's speech beginning "Yes, I am glad" became progressively shorter in different stages of revision. While correcting proofs for *Poems* (1930) Auden abridged the text of the speech that had appeared in *The Criterion* and the typescript, a text that in turn had been abridged from the corresponding speech in the first version of the play. The typescript text reads:

ANNE. Yes, love does not begin with meeting nor end in parting. We are always in love though we know love only by moments and perhaps it is only ourselves that we love. Mouth to mouth is no nearer; now I see you, but if I shut my eyes I forget. Words fail us and truth eludes us and we cannot be satisfied. But I am glad this evening that we are together. The silence is unused, death seems
An axe's echo.

All printed texts of the lyric beginning "The summer quickens all" have a period at the end of the first stanza; this edition, following both typescripts of the play, omits the period, which was probably added by the printer of *The Criterion*. (The phrase at the end of the stanza, "neither can compel", applies to the "wish", "look", and "urgent word" in the stanza that follows.) When Auden first wrote out this poem in a notebook now in the Berg Collection, he used no punctuation at the end of the stanza, although when he later wrote out a revised version of the stanza on the same page he closed the stanza with a period, probably more as a gesture of completion than as a deliberate revision.

Page 33.

In the typescript Seth and his Mother exeunt together where the printed texts (followed here) have Seth exit.

The Enemies of a Bishop

This first collaboration between Auden and Isherwood was written in 1929. Auden seems to have begun writing it (or planning it) in Berlin, without Isherwood's help, in the spring of 1929, and he intended to call it *The Reformatory*. On 15 April 1929, in a journal he kept during that spring (now in the Berg Collection, New York Public Library), he wrote:

> Do I want poetry in a play or is Cocteau right: "There is a poetry of the theatre but not in it"? I shall use poetry in "The Reformatory" as interlude. Poetry after all should be recited I think not read. I don't want any characters, any ideas in my play but stage-life, something which is no imitation but a new thing. Damn realism. Yet it must be real.

In a journal entry written perhaps on 20 April he added:

> A Play is poetry of action. The dialogue should be corresponding[ly] a simplification. E.g. Hrotswitha. The Prep School atmosphere. That is what I want.

During the same month, he wrote the poem "You who have come to watch us play and go", evidently intended as the final speech of a play and used for that purpose in *The Enemies of a Bishop*. If he wrote anything else specifically meant for the play at that time, it has not survived. He and Isherwood may have worked together on the play when Isherwood visited Auden in Germany in July 1929, and Auden apparently worked on it alone when he returned to England later that month. He reported to his friend William McElwee, probably in August: "I have nearly finished another play, very funny and very dirty." He and Isherwood may have put the final touches on the work when both were in London around September or October.

Of the poems embedded in the play, most of them apparently written as separate works, the earliest ("Again in conversations") dates from January 1929, the latest ("Men pass through doors and travel to the sea") from the latter part of July 1929. The other poems, listed in the order in which they occur in the play, are: "Love by ambition" and "Watch any day his nonchalant pauses, see", March 1929; "Do yer want to see me agyne", probably about May 1929; "Sentries against inner and outer" and "Upon this line between adventure", June 1929; "Before this loved one", March 1929; "The strings' excitement, the applauding drum", April 1929; the brief lyric beginning "Head asleep" and continuing "But trusted here" is unknown outside the play and cannot be dated. The Prologue ("Will you turn a deaf ear") dates from September 1929; possibly it was added when the rest of the play was finished but had not yet been given to the typist. In the typescript the Prologue is assigned to "a Member of the Audience", but this was altered by an unknown hand (in Isherwood's copy of the typescript) to "the Bishop".*

Two carbon copies of the typescript survive. One, with corrections in both authors' hands, was kept by Isherwood. The other, with corrections in Isherwood's hand only, was given by Auden to Alan Ansen, who gave it to the Berg Collection, New York Public Library. The typescript (made by a typing agency) seems to have been prepared from a fair copy in Isherwood's hand; all that survives of this copy are four pages (two of them fragments) that Auden cannibalized for use in the manuscript of his later play *The Chase*. These passages are found in I.2 and III.2 of *The Enemies*, and they have provided some trivial emendations used in this edition.

The play's typescript is exceptionally clean, doubtless as a result of Isherwood's care. Only a few textual points call for annotation. On p. 43 I have restored the deleted initials "A.R.S.E." On p. 56, in Robert's first speech, "Great West Stope" is an emendation for "Great West Slope". On p. 67, in Ceslaus's speech "She's dreadfully common", the first word is an emendation for "She". And on p. 78 the line of the play's concluding poem beginning "Without hope" is inserted in Auden's hand in Isherwood's copy of the typescript; it also occurs in an earlier manuscript of the poem in one of Auden's notebooks and was presumably dropped in error, either by Isherwood or the typist.

The Bishop's wife at one point calls her husband Trevers, at a later point Travers. The second is the better-known English surname, evidently used here as a given name, so the first has been emended to match.

The major difference between the two copies of the typescript occurs at the start of III.1. The song that opens the scene is a later replacement (in Isherwood's copy) for a long prose speech by the Wireless. The substituted song, which dates from November 1929, was typed on a different machine from that used for the rest of the typescript. The following is the original opening of the scene, up to the point where the Wireless is interrupted by the telephone, as on p. 59:

* Auden published most of these poems in his *Poems* (1930) and in later collected and selected editions. The published poems are listed below in the order in which they appear among the other poems in *Poems* (1930), together with the dates of the editions in which Auden later reprinted them (see p. 524), and with the titles introduced in those editions:
"Will you turn a deaf ear": *1945* ("The Questioner Who Sits So Sly"), *1950*, *1966*.
"Watch any day his nonchalant pauses, see": *1938*, *1945* ("We All Make Mistakes"), *1950* ("A Free One"), *1966*.
"Upon this line between adventure": *1945* ("Do Be Careful"), *1950* ("Between Adventure"), *1966*.
"Again in conversations": *1945* ("Two's Company"), *1950* ("Never Stronger").
"Love by ambition": *1945* ("Too Dear, Too Vague"), *1950*, *1966*.
"Sentries against inner and outer": *1945* ("Shut Your Eyes and Open Your Mouth"), *1950*.
"Before this loved one": *1945* ("This One"), *1950*, *1958*, *1966* ("This Loved One").
"The strings' excitement, the applauding drum": *1945* ("Family Ghosts"), *1950*, *1966*.
In the 1933 second edition of *Poems* Auden included "Its [*sic*] no use raising a shout," which he had added to the play when revising it (see below). He never reprinted the poem in later collections. The song "Do yer want to see me agyne" reappears in *The Chase*.

[ROBERT's *hut.* ROBERT *busy with papers.* THE SPECTRE *lounging.*]

WIRELESS. The Book World. British United Publishers continue well in advance of schedule. The output of masterpieces last week dropped, it is true, from thirteen to eleven—but this, it must be remembered, is still a record for the season, and shows an increase of five per cent on last year's production standards. The week's other new books were officially classified as follows:

  16 Poignantly lovely.
  12 Quite unforgettable.
  17 A tremendous lark.
   9 Must be read at all costs.
  23 The Book of the Week.
  30 The Author's best book.
  11 Wise, humorous, deliciously racy.
   9 A starkly terrible book.
  14 So real that it hurts.
  16 Utterly fearless.

Five new geniuses have been promoted, to fill the recent vacancies left by authors degraded to the ranks—three for being now over thirty, the other two for not having produced a book within the nine month time-limit.

Critics continue to command record prices. The Selection Committee of the Proust Prize—Mr Wounds, Mr Gash and Miss Trauma—were purchased at Christie's on Thursday for 2,000,000 guineas by Messrs Suction and Pump, the publishers of "The Hanged Man". "The Hanged Man" thus becomes the Book of the Year. Mr Wounds, chairman of the Committee, was also presented with a gold tea-service and a set of diamond links and studs.

An enquiry into the catch dropped by Mr Floosh the poet, at silly point, during the third test match between the Surrealists' XI and the English Traditionals, for the Henry James Cup, may lead to Mr Floosh's suspension from the British publishing market for several years—

Although Auden and Isherwood took the play seriously enough to have it typed by a professional, there is no record of any further attempts they may have made to have it published or performed. It appears in print for the first time in this edition.

In the winter of 1931-32 Auden and Isherwood decided to revise the play. On 14 January 1932 Auden asked Stephen Spender (in a letter now in the Berg Collection) to "tell Christopher, I've revised half of my share of The Enemies of the Bishop". The only revisions that survive are "the two songs you wanted for the

Enemies of a Bishop" which Auden sent Isherwood probably around May 1932. It is now almost impossible to imagine where they might fit into the original version. The texts of the songs follow:

CHORUS.
>Look about you on life's journey
>>Scan the page of history
>Class with class for ever striving
>>Man enslaving man you'll see
>Then comrades side by side together
>>One for all and all for one
>In the name of freedom forward
>>Till the victory be won.

>See the nob at Cambridge College
>>Idling over sherry wine
>See the collier's lad at fourteen
>>Toiling in the gloomy mine.
>>>*Chorus etc.*

>See the landlord in his mansion
>>Footman on the polished floors
>See his cruel bailiffs driving
>>Dying mothers out of doors.
>>>*Chorus etc.*

. . . .

DRUNK IN THE AUDIENCE [*getting up*]. 'Ere this aint 'arf depressin'. Can't you give us something a bit more cheerful.
SOME LADIES IN AUDIENCE. Ssh.
DRUNK. I bloody well won't hush. I want to see the Manager. I want the Manager.
SPECTRE [*to* CONDUCTOR]. Very well Alf. [*To* ROBERT.] Sorry, old boy. [*Sings; tune: Tallis canon:*]
>As I was lying on my bed
>>Dear father came to me and said
>If all our seats were painted green
>>We should look unfit to be seen.

The Dance of Death

§1 History, Editions, and Text

This play had its origins in a meeting of Auden, Rupert Doone, and Robert Medley in July 1932, when Doone asked Auden to write a ballet scenario on the theme of Orpheus in the underworld, and suggested also that for the Group Theatre he "might write a play on the theme of *la danse macabre*, the late mediaeval poem, which he had brought me to read" (Doone, "The Theatre of Ideas", *Theatre Newsletter*, 29 September 1951, p. 5; Medley, in his *Drawn from the Life*, 1983, p. 133, recalls that the latter suggestion came from Auden). On 28 July 1932 Auden wrote his friend Arnold Snodgrass that he was "working busily on the words for a sort of choral ballet affair which may be done at the Old Vic". He told Doone the same day: "I'm getting on with the Orpheus stuff. God knows what it's like." But in mid-October he wrote Doone that he had "written a thing but frankly it's no use." Having abandoned Orpheus, he continued to think about the *danse macabre*, and discussed the project with Isherwood at the end of the year. He was at work on the play by the following spring, and on 24 April 1933 wrote his former tutor at Oxford, Nevill Coghill: "I've just finished my Masque. I believe it's rather good." (All of these letters are in the Berg Collection.) He apparently continued to work on the play during the summer—possibly adding the song "How happy are we / In our country colony" as a satire on the Group Theatre's summer study session in Suffolk in August. On 30 August 1933 he sent a typescript to Faber & Faber, who published it as a book on 9 November 1933. The play was reprinted without change in the American edition of Auden's *Poems* in the following year. It was not republished during Auden's lifetime.

The Group Theatre produced the play twice, in 1934 and 1935. The first production was private, for members of the Group only, and was performed at the Westminster Theatre, London, on two Sundays, 25 February and 4 March 1934. This production was a double bill: Auden's play was preceded by *The Deluge* from the Chester Mystery Plays, with language slightly modified according to suggestions from Auden and Nevill Coghill. The second production, with T. S. Eliot's *Sweeney Agonistes* substituted for *The Deluge*, began the Group Theatre's first public season, again at the Westminster, on 1 October 1935; it ran, as scheduled, for two weeks. Rupert Doone directed both productions, Herbert Murrill composed the music (Auden had suggested Michael Tippett but Doone thought his music too grave), Robert Medley designed the set and costumes, and Henry Moore designed the dancer's mask.

The text of this edition is based on that published by Faber & Faber in 1933, with the passages inserted or replaced for the 1934 and 1935 productions. I have mentioned in the notes, but have not incorporated into the text, various minor changes made in the production versions in order to accommodate Auden's lyrics to Murrill's music, to clarify some stage business, or to appease the censor. While some of these minor changes may have been made by Auden, some were almost certainly made by Murrill (see the notes below) and others may have been made by Doone with Auden's consent.

The following sources have been used for the text:

- F Faber edition, 1933, incorporating corrections Auden made in a copy belonging to his brother, John B. Auden. Galley and page proofs of this edition, with Auden's revisions and corrections, are in the Bodleian Library.
- GT The Group Theatre promptbook, consisting of a heavily annotated copy of F with an additional fragment of typescript pasted in, in the possession of John Moody, the Group's stage manager. The copy is marked with the names of cast members from the 1934 production, but may also have been used in 1935. (I have also consulted a copy of F used in the 1934 production by Ethel Lewis, a member of the cast.)
- LC The text submitted for censorship to the Lord Chamberlain's Office on 23 July 1935 (and licenced two days later), now in the British Library. This text consists of a copy of F with typescript additions and substitutions. (I have also consulted a mostly similar copy used by John Allen, who played the Announcer in both productions.) Most of the typescript additions pasted into LC also occur in a separate leaflet of typescript pages in the possession of John Moody and other cast members (in various carbon copies). Jean Scott Rogers, who typed the additions, recorded in her diary that additional material was still being typed as late as 18 September 1935; this may have referred to late additions now lost, or to a late retyping of material prepared earlier for LC. Most of the additions and changes in LC and the corresponding leaflet of typescript reproduce or expand upon annotations scrawled by Auden into a copy of F that belonged to Rupert Doone (now in the Berg Collection). Some of these annotations add a few words of dialogue; some specify additions to be written later (e.g., next to the song "You were a great Cunarder" Auden noted "Another verse"; and at the points where LC later added speeches for the Announcer commenting on the action, Auden noted "Insert explanation" or some similar phrase).

Except for the Alma Mater song, taken from the *The Fronny*, no manuscript of the printed text (F) survives. Manuscripts of inserted passages are noted below.

The orchestral parts to Murrill's music are held by his daughter, Mrs Carolyn Evans.

The notes do not record corrections of obvious typographical errors or the occasional spelling out of abbreviations in the speech headings and stage directions. All the speech headings in F (except for the Greek letters) are printed in italics, which somewhat muddles Auden's specification in the opening stage direction that italic letters (i.e., single letters such as *A* or *B*) indicate otherwise anonymous performers on the stage. The typography of this edition has been adjusted to follow this specification. This edition also regularizes some of the more glaring inconsistencies in F's typographic style in stage directions, adds some missing speech headings, but omits a few extraneous headings that merely repeat the heading of the preceding speech. Inconsistent forms like "O" and "Oh" have been left unchanged.

The following typist's or printer's errors are corrected according to Auden's corrections in the copy of F he gave his brother, John B. Auden: page 85, line 24, "*drum of these*" changed to "*drum for these*"; page 97, line 18, "*Both dance*" changed to "*folk dance*"; page 102, line 24, "English times" changed to "English homes"; page 103, line 25, "wheel further" changed to "wheel him further"; page 106, line 19, "Although always" changed to "Always though".

Page 83.

The text of the Announcer's speeches and the interjections from the hidden Chorus follow LC and the copy of F that Auden marked for Rupert Doone. In the original F text the entire exchange reads:

> ANNOUNCER. We present to you this evening a picture of the decline of a class, of how its members dream of a new life, but secretly desire the old, for there is death inside them. We show you that death as a dancer.
> CHORUS [*behind curtain*]. "Our Death."

The published F version is revised from the galley proofs, where "decline of a class" originally read "decline of the middle classes" and "its members dream" originally read "they dream". The final text printed in the present edition in effect restores these rejected early readings, although the change from "the middle classes" to "Middle class" reflects a shift toward a characteristically Marxist usage.

The paragraph headed "STAGING NOTE" was added in galley proof. The present edition restores Auden's layout for this note, which was altered by an editor or printer to run the heading for the paragraph into its first line. In F the note headed "SCENE" begins a new printed page; there is no indication in the proofs that this was Auden's intent, but a large space does appear in the proofs between "SCENE" and the paragraph above it. It was in this space that Auden indicated the "STAGING NOTE" was to be inserted.

Throughout the opening chorus GT and LC have small cuts and changes apparently made by Herbert Murrill to accommodate his musical setting. Murrill's copy of F, with these changes drafted in pencil in (apparently) his hand, was in the stock of a London bookseller in 1985. Most of the changes are trivial: "He'll" altered to "He will", "you'll soon want" altered to "you'll want", etc. The one substantial change, which may conceivably have been made in collaboration with Auden, is the substitution of the following for the last four lines of the fourth stanza: "New life, true life. / Life should not be / For you obsession / With Europe's sad depression. / Come out into the sun."

Page 85.

The Announcer's six lines beginning "Well done, well done" are added in LC; at the same point in the text GT has the word "insert" written in.

Page 86.

The stanza beginning "Hand stretched out to lie in hand" is added in LC, which also makes explicit that the song is assigned to the Chorus; it is unassigned in F.

The Announcer's first four lines after the dance, beginning "Though they forget him", are added in LC. In the fourth quatrain of this speech, GT alters the third line from "fly to his hand" to "feed from his hand".

Page 87.

After C's line "They're gone—there's nothing!" LC adds a line for the Chorus: "Nothing."

Page 88.

The speech for α, after the Dancer makes a nose at her, reads in GT and LC: "Oh, did you see what 'e did? Sir, will you let a lady be insulted? Go and 'it 'im."

Page 89.

Instead of having the Manager sing Annabelle Eve's song, GT and LC bring on Annabelle (or, as they have it, Annabella) to sing it. The Manager's line "I'll say it" is changed to "Annabella, you sing it", and she does. After the song, she says "Now then, boys, all together", and the Manager and Stage Hands echo "Now then, all together!"

The sixteen lines from "What about Abyssinia?" to the final repetition of "Red united, fighting front" are the expansion in LC of the following four lines in F:

A. One moment, sir, the Kellogg pact
    Has outlawed war as a national act.
AUDIENCE. Scholarships—not battleships.
α. This is an attack on the working-class.

The six lines beginning "One, two, three, four" in F then follow this as a separate speech assigned to the Audience.

Page 90.

The Announcer's long speech beginning "Comrades, I absolutely agree" is in LC interrupted twice by voices from the auditorium; after "to abolish class" α says "Don't you listen to him, he's talking bloody fascism!", and after "Englishmen for Englishmen" δ says "Fascist!" and ε says "Boo!" In the same speech, "take our jobs" is an emendation for "take our job".

Page 91.

In the first stanza of the song beginning "I was a farmer during the war" the second line reads in both galley and page proofs "I sold my bacon at 2s.4d."; the change to "at two and four" is not indicated in the proofs, and may have been made by the publisher or printer.

Page 92.

The song beginning "We are all of one blood" is printed according to the sequence of stanzas appearing in LC; the refrain of the first stanza ("Hurrah for me . . . / . . . old England new") appears only in LC. In F and GT the song appears in a less logical sequence, starting with "The ship of England" and its refrain, followed by "We are all of one blood" and the remaining stanzas; in F and GT the same refrain is used for all stanzas of the song.

Page 93.
The lines in which *B* and *C* repeat "Hold it like this" are reduced in GT and LC to "Like this."

Page 94.
The interjections by *C* in the opening of the Lord's Prayer are taken from LC; GT seems to indicate that the interjection occurs in all three lines, which somewhat dilutes the joke. In F the prayer is not interrupted at all, but is followed by *C*'s line, "Mother. Mother.", as in other texts; it is possible that the LC layout indicates the intention behind F.

The Announcer's four lines beginning "The condition of these people" are added in LC.

Page 95.
The dialogue between Sir Edward and the Doctor, from "Is he alright?" to the word "Exactly", is taken from LC (the remainder of the line that begins "Exactly" also appeared in F).

The first two lines of the Announcer's speech beginning "The conscience of that poor Doctor" appear in a copy of the play used by John Allen, who played the Announcer in both productions; the remaining four lines appear in LC as well as in John Allen's copy.

The speech of the Announcer beginning "Notice how these" (which breaks up a rhymed couplet) is added in LC.

Page 97.
The song "Are you living in the city" has many small changes in GT and LC, evidently made to accommodate the music (and to censor "Silly girl to whom petting / Matters" by substituting "Girl to whom attentions / Matter"). John Allen recalled (in interviews with Kathleen Bell and with Michael J. Sidnell) that this song was followed in performance by a country dance with a lyric Auden wrote at a rehearsal. The lyric, as Allen recollected it to Kathleen Bell, went something like this:

Good morning to you master, good morning to you mistress dear.
We've wandered through the fields and at last we are returning here.
We are only ploughboys and we wish you all good day.
And we bring to you a branch of the snowy budding May.

Allen told Bell that his recollection of the third line was rough; to Sidnell he could remember nothing of the line but " . . . this day". The version Allen gave Sidnell of the other lines differs slightly from the version he gave Bell: "been wandering in" for "wandered through", "assembled" for "returning", "bring you" for "bring to you", and "buds of May" for "budding May".

Page 98.

The line for the Chorus beginning "Clumsy, can't you count" is a substitution in LC (called for by Auden's markings in Doone's copy of F) for these two lines in F:

SEVERAL OF THE AUDIENCE. Clumsy, can't you count? You are
 spoiling the dance.
CHORUS [*whispering to* A]. One, two, three, four.

The line for β is added in LC, which does not assign it to a speaker. John Allen's copy assigns the line "Out of the audience", and the assignment to β in the present edition is an editorial emendation.

Page 99.

The speech of the Announcer beginning "For those who found" is inserted in LC; in F and GT the speech of the Chorus continues without a break from "With all our past experience" to "You may perhaps be right". Also in LC (as in the copy of F Auden marked for Doone) the two choral lines "Again it may be fiction / To tell the truth we lack conviction" are deleted. This edition retains the text from F.

Page 101.

The dialogue of Box and Cox is revised in GT and LC: Box begins "Good evening, everybody. I should say . . ."; and in the dispute over the number of people, instead of all four numbers being "fifty thousand" or "fifty", they are "fifty thousand", "Sixty", "seventy thousand", and "seventy thousand".

Page 102.

The speech of the Announcer beginning "In the face of death" is added in LC.

Page 103.

The four speeches beginning "Needing its food and warmth" are printed from Auden's manuscript in the Group Theatre papers at the Berg Collection, New York Public Library. Typescript versions, with very slight differences, appear in GT (where the fourth speech is crossed out) and LC (without the fourth speech). In all these versions the speeches are numbered with roman numerals; I have supplied Greek letters for the sake of consistency with the surrounding dialogue and the rest of the play. These speeches replace the following five lines from F:

ε. The dark one there now; is she free?
ζ. I find it.
ε. She is possible for me.
 [*Going up to her.*] Smokest thou?
ξ. I am so free.

The four longer speeches apparently represent Auden's second attempt at a rewriting and expansion of the F version of this scene. An earlier manuscript in the Group Theatre papers has the following text, which seems to be a replacement for the entire sequence in F from the Announcer's "Who is ugly" until the stage direction in which the Dancer is wheeled forward:

ANNOUNCER. All south of ship cranes, of the Slythe canal, eastward of dog market, Fruby and Drulger streets, the Voccal, Butterkiln; turning by wall of glassworks where generators hum. You change at Slaggy Cross towards all this. Here moon chimney, locked shed, wharves by water. The body's valley. The soul's marches.
Who is ugly
Who is sick
Who is lonely
Come on quick
  Hither.

MALE CHORUS.	FEMALE CHORUS.
How's Acid Anne.	She's made with a man.
And Cautious Cuty.	She's lost her beauty.
And Foetid Fanny.	She's gone to her Granny.
And Lunchhouse Lilly.	She's been very silly.
And Madam X.	She's forgotten her sex.

FEMALE CHORUS.	MALE CHORUS.
How's Beautiful Birch.	He's joined the church.
And Goitre George.	He's been sacked from the Forge.
And Melmoth the Mask.	You must never ask.
And Quint the Queer.	He's under that chair.
And Useful Uriah.	He perished by fire.

B [*approaching* A *at table*]. Pump me a shilling.
A. It comes not in question.
B. Present me a cigarette.
A. No.
B. One merely.
A. I have no said.
B. See not so serious out, my sweetie. One, yes.
A. Go away. I will with thee nothing to do have. [*Picks up telephone on table.*] Moab 773. Is the Gerda there? What. She is time one minute away gone. Know you perhaps where I her find can. The Sunny Bar. I thank.
[*He is just ringing another number when* C *comes in.*]
A. I have thee the whole night forsought. Why art thou not come at six.
C. I was forlet. I could not. Art thou mad. [*Kissing him.*]
A. A fib.

C. Give me a kiss. Man thou art with the sun quite forburnt. Art thou still mad.
A. No. Shall we a tour at the week-end, Brighton to see.
C. Cannot. My cousin is come. Understandst thou.

Auden may have intended to preserve at least the opening paragraph of this in the production text; in a note on the manuscript page that has the later prose speeches beginning "Needing its food and warmth", Auden told Doone: "I should like the first bit I gave you about where Alma Mater [?is], left in. Here is a substitute for the rest." Some phrases from that opening paragraph survived into a chorus in *The Chase* (p. 165) and *The Dog Beneath the Skin* (p. 218). (In the dialogue between *A* and *B*, above, the phrase "I thank" is an emendation for the manuscript's "I think", which is implausible in this context; compare the repetitions of "I thank" in the F dialogue later in this scene.)

Page 104.

The Announcer's couplet "And tell the story ... are apt to do" is added in GT and LC.

In the song to the tune of *Casey Jones* GT and LC make some trivial verbal changes to accommodate the music; these are not incorporated here. In the third stanza from the end of the song, "May engagements" is an emendation for "Many engagements".

Page 105.

In the song "Hail the strange electric writing" GT and other copies used by the cast make minor changes and elisions to accommodate the music; the changes vary in the different copies. The only changes incorporated in this edition occur in the stanza for the Boys: in John B. Auden's copy of F, Auden substituted "Always though" for "Although always", and in the next line I have followed GT in adding "all" where a syllable is required by the metre (although the reading of the earlier manuscript, "hence", may have been intended). The song was deleted in GT after having been marked with changes, and is also deleted in LC; this may suggest that it was used in the private performances of 1934 but dropped for the public ones of 1935. For the earlier (and metrically superior) manuscript version of the song, apparently intended for *The Fronny*, see p. 475.

Page 107.

The couplet beginning "Quick under the table" is printed here as it appears in F; there is conflicting evidence as to the version intended for production. The speech is unattributed in F, but the heading "*A*" is added in Auden's hand in the copy he marked for Doone. An unknown hand has replaced " 'tecs" with "police" in this same marked copy, and the same substitution occurs in LC. Also in Doone's marked copy, Auden scrawled "No, worse than that" as a replacement for "O no salute"; GT and cast copies retain the F text, but in GT an unknown hand has also pencilled in Auden's replacement, preceded by a question mark, beneath the printed original. LC simply deletes F's "salute". Following the couplet, LC inserts an exclamation: "ALL Karl Marx!" The Chorus beginning "O Mr Marx" is deleted in Doone's marked copy of F, and in GT and LC.

§2 AUDEN'S SYNOPSIS

This appeared in the programmes of the two Group Theatre productions. Although unsigned, it is certainly Auden's work. The text follows that used for the first production. The later version alters "Death presents himself" to "Death presents itself" and "night club, simply to" to "night club scene, to", and omits the final sentence. In the final paragraph, "when they attempt" is an emendation for both versions' "where they attempt"; this corrects an error made frequently by Auden's typists.

SYNOPSIS

THE DANCE OF DEATH is a satire on modern life.

The course of the action is as follows:

DEATH appears as a dancer. THE ANNOUNCER is Fate and also Death's mouthpiece. Death symbolises that decay which exists within a class of society. Always inspired and always betrayed by the death inside them, this class pursue at first one Utopia and then another without really wanting new life because "secretly they desire the old".

These Utopias occur in the play in the following order:
- A. DEATH AS THE SUN GOD—CREATOR AND DESTROYER
   - (i) The present-day cult of athleticism
   - (ii) Flash-back to pre-war arrogance and prosperity (Annabelle Eve scene)
- B. DEATH AS DEMAGOGUE
   - (iii) Fascism the "revolution suited to English conditions to abolish class" (ship scene)
   - (iv) Escape from machine-civilisation (country colony)
- C. DEATH AS THE PILOT TO THE HEART OF REALITY

Disillusioned, the crowd ask for a pilot to the "very heart of reality". Death presents himself. But he collapses through the inanition of the class. Disintegration is complete when they attempt, in the night club, simply to satisfy their individual sensuous desires. The Dancer appears among them in the last stages of senility. He accepts his dissolution and makes his will. While this is declaimed by his attendant nurses, the singers survey the rise and fall of the class through history, until the death blow is given in summary fashion by the economist.

The Chase

AUDEN worked on this play from the late spring to the early autumn of 1934. Large portions of it are adaptations of earlier material. Some of it is taken from Auden's earlier plays: the reformatory subplot derives from *The Enemies of a Bishop*; Alan Norman's pursuit of the lost heir, his interlude with Miss Vipond, and the poem "You who return to-night to a narrow bed" seem to derive from *The Fronny*; and a few lines of dialogue are taken from material written for, but never used in, *The Dance of Death* (compare the "Cautious Cutie" sequence on p. 167 with the similar passage quoted on p. 540). The play also incorporates various works first written separately: the poem "Enter with him" was originally a separate poem written December 1931 and published in *The Twentieth Century*, August 1933; the final chorus, "Love loath to enter", is extracted from a longer poem written probably in 1933 and published in *New Oxford Outlook*, May 1934; and most of the comic verses are taken from a notebook, now in the British Library, that Auden used for such pieces around 1929-31. Among these are "Don't know my father's name" and "Do yer want to see me agyne", both written in 1929, and "In nineteen hundred and thirty three [*originally*, twenty three]" and "Alice has gone", both written around 1931. The gramophone's sermon (later the Vicar's sermon in *The Dog Beneath the Skin*) was originally an independent prose piece (for its complex history see the notes below).

But the most important source for the play is a long poem in alliterative verse that Auden began in September 1932 and abandoned early in 1933; he referred to it as "my epic". The manuscript is in a notebook now at Swarthmore College; an edition by Lucy McDiarmid appeared in *The Review of English Studies*, August 1978. The second of two surviving cantos of the poem breaks off in the midst of a catalogue of guests arriving to attend "the Chase" at a great country house; the catalogue is mostly identical to that read out by the Conductor on pp. 128-29 of *The Chase*. Other alliterative passages in the play are also lifted, with minor changes, from the poem in cantos. The song of the Witnesses, "You are the town and we are the clock", derives originally from that poem, although the version in the play is extracted from an intermediate version published in *The Listener*, 12 June 1933, as "The Witnesses".

Auden wrote his friend Naomi Mitchison, probably around June or July 1934: "The epic has turned in[to] a dramma [*sic*] which is coasting along slowly." On 5 August 1934 he told Rupert Doone: "I'm getting on with the play and am completely recasting it in a way which will make it more suitable I think to the Group Theatre. My only difficult demand is a good verse speaking chorus which I trust you will be able to provide." (The choral verse passages probably date from about this time.) On 8 September 1934 he wrote Frederic Prokosch that he had just finished a play, and on 15 October he sent a typescript of *The Chase* to Faber & Faber for publication. He also gave a copy to Doone and Robert Medley for use by the Group Theatre. He sent another to Stephen Spender, and later, in an undated letter, asked him to send it on to Isherwood, adding: "I'm going to rewrite the end which is too casual." (All of these letters are in the Berg Collection.)

Doone, although displeased with the play, seems to have decided to attempt a production. A note by John Garrett in the November 1934 issue of *Rep*, the magazine of the Croydon Repertory Theatre, reported of Auden that "there will be produced in London early in the New Year his new play, 'The Chase.' " But Auden, perhaps as a result of Isherwood's initial response to the play (in a letter now lost), wrote T. S. Eliot at Faber on 20 November 1934 that he was dissatisfied with the work, and would rewrite it entirely. The history of *The Chase* at this point becomes the history of *The Dog Beneath the Skin*, which continues on p. 553 below.

This edition prints *The Chase* for the first time. The text is based on Auden's manuscript fair copy, together with the revisions and additions incorporated in various typescripts. The following sources have been used:

- MS Auden's manuscript fair copy, which includes some pages evidently revised while being copied out, and incorporates some fragments from the fair copy by Isherwood of *The Enemies of a Bishop*. This manuscript was retrieved from Auden's wastepaper basket by a colleague at the Downs School, and is now in the Berg Collection. The manuscript had been the "copy" used by the professional typist of:
- TS The typescript of the play, extant in three carbon copies, each with slightly varying corrections and additions in Auden's hand. One copy, which Auden gave Nevill Coghill, is now at Exeter College, Oxford; another, which Auden gave Doone, is now in the Berg Collection; Isherwood kept the third. In addition to the minor corrections and changes that are more or less common to all three copies, Doone's and Isherwood's copies include a long addition to the typed version of the chorus printed on p. 178; Doone's version (in heavily revised typescript) is evidently slightly earlier than Isherwood's (in holograph fair copy). After the earlier minor corrections had been made—but before this addition to the chorus was inserted—Auden apparently had another typescript of the play prepared, probably by a different typist, certainly on a different machine. The result was:
- TSB The second typescript, a top copy, now in the Poetry Library at the State University of New York at Buffalo, which has no information on its provenance. Auden may have given it to the Lockwood Memorial Library (the predecessor of the Poetry Library) in the 1940s, when he gave other manuscripts now in the Buffalo collection. The Buffalo copy incorporates in typescript changes Auden made to copies of the original typescript (TS) and a few other apparently authorial changes as well, perhaps deriving from the lost top copy of TS.

In the notes below, changes in the text that Auden made while writing out MS are not noted. But, of the changes made in various copies of TS and in TSB, all those involving more than a word or two are described in the notes below. (The text of the gramophone's sermon is a separate and more complicated matter, and is discussed separately below.)

Auden's MS is extremely rough, rapid, and inconsistent, and it presented many difficulties to the typist. I have on the whole followed the typist's efforts to make the page layout reasonably clear and consistent. The typist made some futile and intermittent efforts to clean up Auden's punctuation in the choruses, but I have let the MS version stand (see p. xxxii). Auden's rendering of Cockney speech is thoroughly inconsistent, and I have not tried to systematize it. Auden sometimes used apostrophes to indicate unpronounced letters, but he sometimes omitted them, and his practice varied from word to word; one of George's speeches, for example, renders "Who's he" as "oos 'e". The typist added a few clarifying apostrophes, which I have retained when confusion might result from the omission; while I have added apostrophes to contractions like *can't*, where Auden generally omitted them, I have kept *aint*. Auden indifferently rendered the Cockney pronunciation of *old* as *ole* or *ol*; the typist consistently typed *ole*, but this edition retains the MS readings in this and similar instances.

Auden tended to omit question marks when writing rapidly. I have added them to sentences that unquestionably require them.

When Auden reused earlier material in compiling his manuscript, he neglected to replace the older name he had given the reformatory, Templin, with the newer one, Tudro. I have updated the name to Tudro throughout. Where Auden reused fragments from Isherwood's fair copy of *The Enemies of a Bishop*, I have altered Isherwood's speech headings to the forms Auden used elsewhere in the same scene. But where Auden himself designated the same character by different speech headings in different scenes, I have not tried to impose consistency.

The notes below make no mention of passages in MS that were omitted by the typist and then restored by Auden when he corrected copies of TS. The typist's misreadings of Auden's hand are noted only if the errors reappear in the text of *The Dog Beneath the Skin*.

In MS the subtitle reads "A play in three acts for stage or wireless", with the last four words deleted. The author of the play's epigraph, John Bowes, was one of Auden's pupils at the Downs School; Auden printed the lines in the first issue of the school magazine, *The Badger*, in Spring 1933. In the list of characters in Isherwood's copy of TS, Auden replaced Mildred Luce's family name with a scrawl that perhaps signifies "Denby"; but as this change is made nowhere else, and is not reflected in *The Dog Beneath the Skin*, I have not incorporated it into this edition.

Page 113.

The line "He tosses at night who at noonday found no truth" is added in Auden's hand in all copies of TS; the Exeter College copy has a comma after "night".

Page 124.

In George's first speech the third sentence reads in MS "My plates of meat aint got any feelin' in em." In Coghill's copy of TS, Auden substituted "are cold" for the two words "of meat"; in Isherwood's copy he substituted "are cold" for "of meat" *and* the remainder of the sentence; and in Doone's copy he substituted "are cold" for "of meat" *and* the remainder of the sentence *and* the following sentence also. The Coghill version is retained in TSB. The present edition follows the Isherwood version.

Page 130.

In the speech of the 2nd Woman, the last sentence is added in Auden's hand in copies of TS.

Page 133.

In the Vicar's speech, after the point where the Police Sergeant passes him a top hat, MS apparently reads "under twenty-five"; TS, and the equivalent scene in *The Dog Beneath the Skin*, substitute "over twenty-five". I have restored the apparent MS reading for *The Chase*, but the later reading is sufficiently plausible to let it stand in *Dogskin*.

Page 134.

In the line beginning "Angels of air and darkness" Auden wrote the word "Angels" in copies of TS as a substitution for "Creatures".

Page 135.

"Amazed on you" is the MS reading, misread by the typist as "Amazed at you". See also, in the notes to *The Dog Beneath the Skin*, the note to p. 202.

Page 139.

In the line beginning "A youth with boils", the typist misread "face down on bed" as "face down in bed". I have restored the MS reading here and in *The Dog Beneath the Skin*. Two lines below, "Writers be glib" is the MS reading, which the typist, unable to decipher, left as a blank. Auden filled in the blank with "Writer be glib". I have retained the MS reading in *The Chase*, but have used the later reading in the corresponding passage in *The Dog Beneath the Skin*.

Page 143.

In the Chorus's concluding song the layout of each stanza differs in MS. The first stanza opens on two lines: "Inform the Press / Inform the Press"; the second opens on one line: "Make way make way"; the third is also on one line, with a comma: "He quickly fell, he quickly fell". I have altered the first two stanzas to correspond with Auden's third thoughts.

Page 147.

Auden published a revised text of a large portion of the Vicar's historical and apocalyptic meditation in *New Verse*, February 1935, under the title "Speech from a Play"; he had by this time abandoned the speech while transforming *The Chase* into *Dogskin*. The *New Verse* text includes many minor changes in punctuation, a few small verbal changes, some obvious printer's errors, and some larger omissions and additions. The more substantial changes are found in the revised passages printed below, each of which is surrounded here by a few words common to both versions. (The line beginning "Dangerous no longer" is also omitted in the revision.) The first line given below, with its initial ellipsis presumably supplied by Auden, is the opening of the *New Verse* text:

THE CHASE 547

            . . . . you too are patients
Prone in the general epidemic
To which we all were made susceptible [. . .]

The nickel with love-thy-neighbor-as-thyself
On the one face for superscription stamped
And on the back imprinted My-purse-and-I.
Swift as a swallow the self was away
Harried and haunted [. . .]

Lured them like magnets from marl and clay
Into towns [. . .]

                  in tenement and gas-lit cellar
While she who was not amused was our sun,
Is now bursting [. . .]

The last was only a little manoeuvre.
Yes, such are the agents of our common guilt
To execute our judgement [. . .]

                      the absolute veto.
The timely warnings [. . .]

Page 153.

    The Chorus beginning "You who return to-night to a narrow bed" is a thoroughly rewritten version of the epithalamion in *The Fronny*; see pp. 484-87 for the earlier text. The version in *The Chase* appeared again in *The Dog Beneath the Skin* and was reprinted in Auden's *Collected Shorter Poems 1930-1944* (1950) as "Prothalamion". In MS the second stanza's second line begins "We're rejoicing", which the typist misread as "We're going"; when Auden found this evident mistake in TS he altered it to "We're here", and kept this reading in all later texts; the MS version is restored for this edition's text of *The Chase*. In the same stanza's fifth line, MS seems to read "skip you pages", which is the reading adopted in this edition's text of *The Chase*; TS and later texts have "slip you pages", which is sufficiently plausible in itself—and as a transcription of Auden's ambiguous hand—to justify its retention in *Dogskin*. In the fourth stanza (p. 155) "The orchid shall flower" is an emendation (confirmed by Auden in conversation with A. H. Campbell in 1957) for "orchard", an MS error retained in all later texts.

Page 156.

    In the first paragraph of the speech of the Dog's Skin, "that very life" is an emendation, based on the text of *The Dog Beneath the Skin*, for "that very light" in MS and TS.

    In the second paragraph of the speech, MS (followed here) has "all vigours and all splendours, skillfully transformed"; TS and *Dogskin* have "all the vigours and all the splendours, skilfully transferred". The last word is certainly an error, and has been corrected here and in *Dogskin*, but the definite articles, which Auden may possibly have approved after the fact, have been retained in the text of *Dogskin* only.

Page 157.

In the penultimate paragraph of the speech of the Dog's Skin, the passage from "I remember how" to "with them it's different" is deleted in Isherwood's copy of TS, possibly in an act of self-censorship by Auden. In the passage immediately following, Auden originally wrote "like a bad smell", then deleted "bad" and added "of drains" after "smell". Possibly he intended the passage to read "like the smell of drains" rather than "like a smell of drains".

Later in the same paragraph, after the sentence "When I come on they start sighing [. . .] goodness what else", MS continues: "You [on the other hand *deleted, and the word* insert *written above*] make them demand". But Auden neglected to write down the intended insertion, or it disappeared before MS reached the typist, who tried to make sense of the passage by typing: "goodness knows what else; make them demand". (In *Dogskin* this is expanded to read: "goodness knows what else: While you make them demand".) As the intended insertion to MS is lost (if it ever existed), I have restored in the text of *The Chase* Auden's deleted original as the least bad alternative.

In the last paragraph of the speech of the Dog's Skin, MS (followed here) has "Hush, someone's coming", which the typist misread as "I think someone's coming". When Auden revised this sentence for *Dogskin*, he let the typist's reading stand, so I have retained it in the text of *Dogskin* only.

Page 161.

In Fritz's song I have retained the bad German grammar.

Page 166.

In the last line of the first verse paragraph of the chorus, MS reads "Power to the city; whose loyalties"; the typist misread "whose" as "where", and this reading persisted into *The Dog Beneath the Skin*. The MS reading is restored here and in *Dogskin*.

Page 172.

III.3 has no heading or stage direction in MS. Both seem to have been provided by the resourceful typist. While preparing MS Auden apparently removed the page that carried the original opening passage of this scene, and although he took the trouble to renumber the following page (now the first page of the scene) he neglected to add a heading. The new opening page in MS has a deleted line and a half, assigned to the Pressman, immediately preceding what is now his opening speech, and presumably the continuation of a speech that began on the deleted page. The deleted lines seem to read: "That's shell [*possibly* skill]. That was. / On a night". The speech heading for the Pressman seems to have been inserted after the speech itself was first written out, and this also suggests that these lines are a fragment of an abandoned speech.

Page 174.
 Auden's manuscript speech headings in the opening dialogue of III.4, faithfully copied by the typist, read simply M.S. (for Medical Student), P. (for Prompter), and S., indicating a character who has neither entered nor been identified, but who is given the line beginning "You're a medical student". The speech probably belongs to the Prompter (and the reference to "him" presumably refers to the Censor).

Page 175.
 The Students' Church of England chant is assigned in MS to "Dec." and "Can."; I have spelled out the first use of each abbreviation.

Page 178.
 The MS text (followed by the typists of TS and TSB) of this Chorus consists of only the first thirteen lines of verse, down to "Wonderful slogans are adopted; down in its depths the soul does not adapt"—followed by a final line reading "All places and times, all hearts, and systems; are corrupt." In Doone's and Isherwood's copies of TS, Auden deleted that final line, and added all the remaining lines of the Chorus; Doone's copy has the remaining lines in a heavily revised typescript prepared by Auden; Isherwood's has them in a fair copy in Auden's hand that reproduces the revised text of the typescript version. (Auden also made two changes in the original section of the Chorus, adding the word "only" in the seventh line of verse and changing "also" to "no less" in the eleventh.)

Page 180.
 The typist overlooked the last line of Iris's second speech, "Will Alan never come". In Isherwood's copy Auden inserted the line at the start of Iris's speech; in Doone's copy he began writing the line at the start of the speech, then changed his mind and inserted it as the last line. The line does not appear in TSB.

Page 182.
 The gramophone's sermon was first published separately in *Life and Letters*, May 1934, as "Sermon by an Armament Manufacturer"; it was then incorporated into *The Chase*, and later used in the published text of *The Dog Beneath the Skin* as the Vicar's sermon (pp. 575-79); finally, it was printed as a separate work once again in Auden's *Collected Poetry* (1945) as "Depravity: A Sermon". It presents thorny editorial problems. The surviving texts are these:

 NB A fair copy manuscript in a notebook Auden used for copying out his poems around 1932-34, now in the Swarthmore College Library. There is no direct evidence for the sermon's date of composition, but its position in the notebook suggests that it was copied out sometime around May 1933.

 LL A typescript, not made by Auden, but with careful and extensive corrections in his hand, with the title "Sermon by an Armament Manufacturer", now in the possession of John Johnson. Evidently this typescript was used to set the text in *Life and Letters*, May 1934, although the printed text has some slight further changes.

STS   Carbon copies of a typescript, not made by Auden, inserted in the TS versions of the *The Chase* that belonged to Coghill, Doone, and Isherwood. This typescript, made on a different machine from that used for *The Chase* itself, was probably typed around October 1934; the three carbon copies have slightly different sets of corrections in Auden's hand, mostly written rapidly and without much care. (My abbreviation stands for Sermon Typescript.)

DBS   The published text in *The Dog Beneath the Skin*, 1935, evidently deriving from a copy of STS (possibly the lost top copy) that had been corrected and punctuated for the printer, perhaps by Isherwood. This version, with further revisions by Auden, appeared in his *Collected Poetry*, 1945.

The earliest version is clearly NB. Auden seems to have made another fair copy, now lost, for the typist who prepared the LL version, since that version, by comparison with NB, makes many small changes in punctuation and diction in addition to larger changes evidently made for the sake of euphony and logic. (NB's variants are noted below only when they illuminate later texts.) When Auden wrote out the MS of *The Chase*, he did not copy out the sermon again, but merely indicated, at the point where it was to be inserted, "Sermon from Life and Letters". The typescript versions of *The Chase* include the same notation; but these typescripts are also accompanied by the separate typescript of the sermon (STS). (When the later TSB typescript of *The Chase* was prepared, its typist copied out the STS sermon on separate pages, as in the earlier typescripts, but used the same machine that was used for the main text.)

The textual problems in the sermon arise from the complicated lines of descent that connect its different versions. When Auden prepared the STS version for his typist, probably around October 1934, he almost certainly did *not* copy out and revise the LL text he had prepared earlier that year (he seems seldom to have preserved magazine printings of his work). Instead he went back to an even earlier version, probably NB, and wrote out yet another fair copy, in which he made many of the revisions he had already made for LL, but did so less consistently and extensively than before; at the same time he also made some new but lesser revisions. As a result, the LL text, although not the last of the revised versions, is the one most thoroughly revised for sound and sense; while the later STS text, although less carefully revised for sense, eventually received a far more careful revision of punctuation and other matters of fine detail.

In this edition of *The Chase* I have followed Auden's instruction in the MS version, and have used the text of the "Sermon from Life and Letters". More precisely, I have used the text of the typescript from which the *Life and Letters* text was apparently set, but I have incorporated revisions from the magazine's text and emendations from the NB manuscript in places where the typist made errors that Auden failed to correct. In the text of *The Dog Beneath the Skin* (rather, in the text of the published version of that play's final scene, reprinted below, pp. 575-79), I have used the DBS text, with only slight emendations derived from earlier versions. For all the defects of the DBS text, it has the same careful punctuation as the rest of the published text of the play; and—as the following example will show—the earlier revisions made in LL cannot simply be brought into the separately revised DBS text without creating an unacceptable composite.

The most troubling textual problem—but one that can serve as an example of many less troubling ones—occurs in the sermon's penultimate paragraph (p. 185). Here NB includes two sentences: "I am all too unworthy. There is no other word." LL (followed in this text of *The Chase*) expands the first sentence to read: "All too weak and utterly unworthy I am"; and because NB's original reference in the next sentence to "no other word" makes sense only when set against the single word "unworthy" and makes no sense with the combination "weak and utterly unworthy", Auden replaced that next sentence with: "But I am thine." (This change also provides a better transition to the paragraph's final sentence.) When Auden later prepared STS he apparently remembered that he had expanded the first of these NB sentences, and he made a similar expansion that reads: "I am all too weak and utterly unworthy"; yet he apparently forgot his replacement for the next sentence, for the STS version reads "There is no other want"—this last word being either Auden's revision or, more probably, a typist's misreading of "word" in the lost fair copy from which the typist worked. One hesitates to restore "word", because it no longer applies to the expanded phrase "weak and utterly unworthy"; yet "want" seems even less satisfactory. Still, "want" does make something opaquely resembling sense, provided that "no other want" is taken as an ironic understatement of the speaker's unworthiness. Neither Auden nor Isherwood saw fit to alter "no other want" in any of the carbon copies of STS or in any later text, and it survives in DBS.

The notes below record only the more significant aspects of the LL text of the sermon and its relation to later versions; some minor emendations to LL on the basis of NB are noted also.

Fifth paragraph (p. 182): The misspelling "Demagorgon" in all texts except Auden's NB manuscript has been corrected, but his error "Azazael" for "Azazel" is retained because a change would alter the prose rhythm. Near the end of the paragraph, "Baffled", the reading of all other texts, has been substituted for LL's "Balked", which is probably a typist's misreading.

Sixth paragraph (p. 183): The NB and LL reading "auxiliary arm" is correct; it was misread as "auxiliary armies" in STS, and miscorrected to "auxiliary arms" in DBS. Later in the same sentence, the reading in NB is "only by a few"; LL has "only by few" and STS and DBS have "only by the few", both of which seem less satisfactory.

Tenth paragraph (p. 184): The first sentence (perhaps to be counted as the first two sentences), from "For their technique" to "need to change it", makes sense in the LL version printed here. NB has: "For their technique of propaganda has never varied—they have found no need, it has been too successful—to suggest that it is in the human interest to destroy God." This leaves ambiguous whether the final phrase describes their perennial technique of propaganda or whether it describes the new kind of propaganda they would create if they changed their technique. (And the sentence following, which says there is sufficient temptation in the whisper "You are God", seems to take a somewhat different rhetorical direction.) LL's deletion of the final phrase, and partial rewriting of the earlier part of the sentence, resolves the ambiguities. But Auden, who apparently forgot this revision when he came to prepare STS, seems to have tried to clear up the ambiguity in another fashion. The STS version reads: "For their technique of propaganda has never varied, it has been far too successful for them to need to change it—or suggest that it is in the human interest to destroy God." Yet this later seemed to either Auden or Isherwood to be ambiguous or incorrect, because the DBS text replaces "change it—or suggest" with "change it, to suggest". Neither the STS nor DBS versions have the logical clarity of the LL version followed here.

Penultimate paragraph (p. 185): While "council" is a plausible reading, it may be noted that Auden sometimes used this spelling for the word normally spelled "counsel", as in the heading "Council for the Defense" in his "The Public v. the Late Mr William Butler Yeats".

Page 187.

In the second line of the final chorus the phrase "for your inability to make up your minds" is added in Auden's hand in Isherwood's copy of TS. It is not in TSB. In the third line, the typist misread "are all your" as "and all your"; Auden corrected this in Isherwood's copy to "were all your", but I have retained the original reading.

The Dog Beneath the Skin

§1 History, Authorship, Texts, and Editions

When Auden told T. S. Eliot on 20 November 1934 that he was dissatisfied with *The Chase* and planned to rewrite it entirely (see p. 544), he had probably already asked Isherwood for help. On 23 November Isherwood, then living in Copenhagen, sent Auden "some suggestions towards a scenario", and on 11 December sent "a few additional ideas I had". Auden soon began writing new dialogue and choruses to Isherwood's specifications. On 10 January 1935 he flew to Copenhagen (Faber & Faber advanced the cost of the ticket), where he and Isherwood made minor revisions to the scenes they had prepared separately. After Auden's return to England on 13 January Isherwood continued to revise the play, and, in an undated letter to Auden, made a detailed report of his changes. (Isherwood's letters to Auden are reprinted in §2 below.)

The title of the play had by now changed from *The Chase* to *Where Is Francis?* Isherwood seems to have put the text into a form that could be given to a professional typist, and, when the typescript was ready, about the end of January 1935, Auden sent it to Faber & Faber. Faber scheduled publication for 21 March 1935, but still advertised the play under the title *The Chase*, and attributed it to Auden alone (advertisement in *New Verse*, February 1935). Rupert Doone and Robert Medley also saw the new version of the play, and one or the other (recollections differ) suggested the final title. Faber then announced publication of the play as *The Dog Beneath the Skin*, but still listed Auden as sole author (advertisement in *New Verse*, April 1935). Auden wrote Eliot on 22 May 1935 to insist that Isherwood's name be added, but Faber had by this time made the change already. The play was published, under both authors' names, on 30 May 1935. An American edition, substantially identical, was published by Random House on 1 October 1935. No changes were made in the text of the later paperback editions published in 1958 in the United States and in 1968 in Britain.*

---

* Auden published some sections of the play as separate works, which are listed below, together with any titles introduced in the various editions. For the collected and selected editions identified by italicized dates, see p. 524.

"The Summer holds": *The Left Review*, May 1935; *1938*.
"The young men in Pressan to-night" and "You are the town": the second section is abridged from a longer poem titled "The Witnesses" in *The Listener*, 12 July 1933; both sections were reprinted, again as "The Witnesses", in *1945*, *1950*, *1966*.
"Enter with him": *The Twentieth Century*, August 1933; *The New Republic*, 17 October 1934; *1945* ("I Shall Be Enchanted"); *1950* ("Legend"); *1958* ("In Legend"); *1966* ("Legend"); *1968*.
"You with shooting-sticks": *1938*.
"Seen when night was silent": adapted from a sonnet in *New Verse*, October 1933; this version reprinted in *Lysistrata*, May 1935 ("Song"); *1945* (untitled); *1950*; *1966*.
"Happy the hare at morning": *1945* ("The Cultural Presupposition"); *1950* ("Culture").
"Now through night's caressing grip": *1938*, *1945*, *1950*.
"You who return to-night to a narrow bed": *1950* ("Prothalamion").

Plans for a production began in the summer of 1934 (when the play was still *The Chase*) after Ashley Dukes, owner of the Mercury Theatre, offered to back a "Poets' Theatre" season of plays by Auden, Eliot, and Yeats, to be performed by the Group Theatre. Faber's intended publication date in March 1935 was supposed to coincide with the first performance of the play. The plans for the Poets' Theatre collapsed in the spring of 1935. Soon afterward, a Group Theatre production of *Dogskin* was announced for the autumn.* The Group submitted the Faber text to the Lord Chamberlain's Office on 19 October 1935. Ten days later, the Lord Chamberlain's Office informed the Group that it was prepared to grant a licence, provided that some cuts and changes were made in the text. The Group did not respond for some time, probably because its plans for an autumn production were now unravelling. (Doone announced cancellation of the production in November, after a quarrel with the Group's financial backer, Anmer Hall.) In December, when plans for the production were revived, the authors decided to rewrite the concluding scene. Auden and Doone had agreed during rehearsals that the scene needed reworking. Various changes were tried on stage, but Auden found none of them satisfactory. He seems to have asked Isherwood for advice, perhaps when Isherwood was in London early in December. Isherwood, in an undated letter probably written in the second week of the month, wrote Auden to "summarize the proposed version of the last scene" (see §5 below). Auden evidently had this summary in front of him when he wrote out the version of the scene that he gave Doone. This is the version printed in the main text of this edition. (For the earlier version see §4 below.)

Auden's new concluding scene—like the rest of the play—was too lengthy to be performed in full, so Auden and Doone worked out a shorter version (see §6 below), which Doone sent to the Lord Chamberlain's Office on 2 January 1936, together with a second copy of the published text of the play, which was marked with other cuts and changes as well. Some of these changes had probably been made by Doone, with Auden's more or less reluctant approval. Others had been made in response to the Lord Chamberlain's requirements.

The first performance was a private one for members of the Group, at the Westminster Theatre, 12 January 1936. A representative of the Lord Chamberlain attended, at the Group's invitation, and final adjustments were made before the licence for public performance was granted on 22 January 1936.† With a

---

"What was the weather on Eternity's worst day?" [Vicar's sermon]: *Life and Letters*, May 1934 ("Sermon by an Armament Manufacturer"); *1945* ("Depravity: A Sermon").

"Love, loath to enter": opening fragment of a poem in *New Oxford Outlook*, May 1934; this fragment reprinted in *1938*.

* John Hayward reported to American readers: "The first Sunday [i.e., private] show of the Group Theater is to be Auden's 'The Dog Beneath the Skin,' which Doone intends to produce in a very bare, formal fashion, without decor or costume, though Auden tells me that it was written with a view to an elaborate production along the lines of an Edwardian musical comedy." ("London Letter", *New York Sun*, 12 October 1935, p. 13.)

† Other dates (22 October and 22 December 1935) are erroneously indicated in the catalogue of the Lord Chamberlain's playscripts at the British Library and on the playscript itself. Both errors resulted from copyists' misinterpretations of the Lord Chamberlain's records.

slightly different cast, the play began its public run at the same theatre on 30 January, and remained on the boards until 14 March. The production was directed by Rupert Doone, designed by Robert Medley, with music by Herbert Murrill.

The authors did no more work on the play until 1947, when Auden, working alone, again revised the concluding scene for a New York revival by a company called On-Stage. Judith Malina, who played Mildred Luce, noted on 9 July: "Auden promises to write a new ending for us" (*The Diaries of Judith Malina 1947-1957*, 1984, p. 5). Auden told the director, Alexis Solomos, that he no longer remembered his earlier revisions; but the changes he made to the published text were evidently similar to those he had made in 1935. The 1947 text is lost, but reviews and other published reports make it clear that Francis was stabbed to death by Mildred Luce in the final scene. The actor who played Francis, Louis Criss, also recalled that Auden emphatically deleted the line in the published text where Francis states his intention "to be a unit in the army of the other side"—a line Auden had also dropped when making revisions in 1935. The production opened at the Cherry Lane Theatre on 22 July 1947.

When Auden taught at Smith College in 1953 he invited students in an English class to rewrite the scene, and awarded a prize to the version he judged best. The college newspaper reported that in setting the competition "he sketched the basic actions to be used, but left the remainder unprescribed. One special provision he did mention: it was to be 'for laughs.' . . . The new ending is to be an extravagant one, including in particular a 'great white cat' who will begin the search over again" (*The Sophian*, 28 April 1953).

Auden differentiated the work of the two authors in a letter to Stephen Spender (now in the Berg Collection) on 28 June 1935, shortly after the play was published:

> Collaboration between a realist writer like Christopher and a parabolic writer like myself leads to some uncertainty. It might interest you to know about the authorship of different scenes.
>
> | | |
> |---|---|
> | Scene I. | W.H.A. |
> | Steamer scene. | C.I. (except song) |
> | Ostnia scenes. | W.H.A. |
> | Red Lamp scene. | W.H.A. |
> | Asylum scene. | All except the Leader's speech. C.I. |
> | Financier scene. | C.I. (except song) |
> | Paradise Park. Operation scene. } | Mostly W.H.A. |
> | Feet scene. | Poetry. W.H.A.   Foot Dialogue. C.I. |
> | Nineveh Hotel scenes. | Destructive Desmond, quarrel with dog, and dialogue after Francis discovery. C.I.   The rest. W.H.A. |
>
> Last scene [*of published text*]. Vicar's sermon. W.H.A.   The rest. C.I.

Auden's list may be supplemented with details from Isherwood's letters and from the textual notes below. All the verse in the play is by Auden, except for the couplet beginning "Horrible hips and too much flesh" (p. 221), which Isherwood recalled in interviews as his own. The revised version of the last scene, printed in the main text above, is by Auden, using fragments of Isherwood's original version.

The text of this edition is based on that published by Faber & Faber on 30 May 1935, but with the addition of verse passages that Auden wrote later the same year, and with the substitution of Auden's rewritten manuscript version of the concluding scene for the earlier published version that had been written largely by Isherwood. The text of the play is thus the full text that Auden prepared in December 1935 with a view to production; the various cuts made by Doone and the censor are ignored.

The following sources have been used:

GT   The Group Theatre promptbook, now in the Berg Collection. This is made up largely from a carbon copy of a typescript that was evidently prepared by two or more professionals working from Isherwood's fair copy manuscript or draft typescript (some pages reflect his habit of closing an abbreviation with a colon rather than a period), with the addition or substitution of scenes and parts of scenes revised at various times before and after publication. This typescript is incomplete; scenes dropped before the production are absent. The title "THE DOG BENEATH THE SKIN" was apparently typed in after the original title, "WHERE IS FRANCIS?", and the two titles are not quite aligned. In GT the break between Acts II and III occurs at the start of the scene numbered in the published text as II.2; the GT version apparently reflects a change made by Doone for the production.

F   The Faber text, 1935; apparently set up from a marked copy of the original typescript that became the basis of GT. Some of the revisions introduced in F are also marked in GT in various hands.

LC   The marked copy of F, with a typescript of the rewritten final scene, submitted to the Lord Chamberlain's Office on 2 January 1936, and licenced on 22 January. (The typescript version of the final scene is the abridged version described in §6 below.) This copy, now in the British Library, is marked "2nd Copy"; the first copy, submitted to the Lord Chamberlain in October 1935, is lost.

The present text includes emendations based on GT wherever GT appears to be a copy of the typescript used for setting up F. The printer, or the publisher's reader, capitalized the first letter following many of Auden's semicolons; where GT has a lower-case letter instead, I have restored it. Because GT does not include the full text, some of the changes made by the printer or publisher in preparing F cannot be identified.

The printer of F made some adjustments to his copy for the sake of appearances. Indentions of verse speeches vary almost from page to page so that the text of each page is visually centered. On some pages almost all stage directions appear on separate lines so that these pages are spaced out and the following pages, which conclude a scene, have more than the one or two lines of type they would otherwise have had. The present edition returns to the more regular format of the GT typescript.

This edition's text of the concluding scene is based on Auden's manuscript, as described below (p. 571). Manuscripts of other parts of the play have been used where they are available, and are described in the detailed textual notes in §3 below.

Herbert Murrill's music for the play is apparently lost, except for some incipits marked in a copy of F in the possession of Alan Clodd.

The notes and variants that follow have been grouped into separate sections in order to clarify the history of the text.

§2 Isherwood's Scenario for a New Version of *The Chase*

About the time Auden decided to rewrite *The Chase* he apparently asked Isherwood to suggest changes. On 23 November 1934 Isherwood sent "some suggestions towards a scenario"—clearly the start of their collaborative efforts on the play—and added further details in a letter of 11 December 1934. These and other letters from Isherwood to Auden are transcribed here from carbon copies in Isherwood's possession. The letter of 23 November 1934 substantially describes the play as it was later written:

Dear Wystan,

Thank you for your letters and the poem [*unidentified*], which I like very much. Here are some suggestions towards a scenario:

1. The Garden Party. According to my present idea, the Pressan Ambo group are all complete swine. This explains why Francis runs away: Or rather, disguised himself as a dog, preferring to live with them in that capacity. For he has been at Honeypot Hall all the time. It also makes a dramatic ending to the play, as we shall see later. The Vicar should not be sympathetic either. He is the creeping jesus cum boy scout stroker type. Mildred is as you have made her: The anti-German lunatic. General Hotham is as in the present version. Iris Crewe is either the peevish virgin (she can be tolerably attractive, however) or horsey or just a whore. But I think a whore would be too sympathetic. When Alan has been chosen, the Dog, which has nosed around during the earlier part of the scene, suddenly runs up to him, fawns upon him and generally shows so much enthusiasm that they all suggest Alan shall take him with him on his journey.

2. At the bar in the saloon of a Channel steamer. Alan, the Dog and the two journalists. I see the journalists rather differently. They

are not of the provincial sort and were not at the Garden Party. They are of the international type, which ferrets around everywhere behind the scenes. They are full of stories of graft in various European countries. (Perhaps they could open with a duet, having the refrain: It's all a racket. Describing how each country is under the control of some special firm or group of financiers.) Their stories of international corruption should be as preposterous and comic as possible. Alan listens to them open-mouthed. He is a very guileless young man and asks naive questions which are, unintentionally, extremely pointed. He tells them about his search for Francis. They don't believe a word and assume that he is really a munitions agent or a secret service man. If they stick to him, they may get a scoop, they think. Alan also talks about his Dog, which is so uncannily intelligent and has very extraordinary habits. (The Dog might do some tricks or funny business here.) Finally, the journalists tell Alan that they are going to Ostnia and that he'd better come with them, as they can show him round everywhere.

3. The Court of the King of Ostnia. Everybody in mourning. Beautiful funeral music. Alan and the journalists enter at the side. Alan asks what on earth is the matter and the journalists explain that today three revolutionary leaders are to be executed. There is a workers' revolution in Ostnia nearly every month, and the King-Dictator always executes the ringleaders personally. He and the Queen receive the leaders and their wives with every mark of esteem and polite condolence. The leaders are silent throughout. A footman brings in a gold revolver on a cushion and the King retires with them behind a curtain. Shots are heard. The King reenters, wiping the revolver on a silk handkerchief. Footmen bring in the corpses. The King and all the Court are much moved, remark how sad it is, how they're compelled to take stern measures, in the workers' own interests, etc. etc. They always do everything to make the execution as pleasant as possible. Has anybody noticed any detail which wasn't in perfect taste? They are always open to suggestions. Meanwhile, the Queen condoles with the widows of the executed men and the ladies of the Court offer them champagne and cakes. All this time, the widows have remained silent. But now one of them turns on the Queen and cries "You murderers!" Immediately all the widows are removed by footmen. The King and Queen are not a bit angry, simply pained. "Poor things! They don't really mean it, you know. They have such terrible lives." The titled ladies admire the corpses: "How distinguished they look!" They dip their handkerchiefs in the blood and snip off bits of the dead men's clothes as relics. "Of course, theoreti-

cally, we agree with them. We're all socialists at heart. But Order has to be maintained . . ." Alan asks if they have ever heard of Francis. But nobody has. They advise him to go down town to the Red Light District. All the foreigners who visit Ostnia go there.

4. The Red Light District. Simply a row of little peepholes, like box-offices. Each peephole has a name over it: Cosy Corner. Tiger Jack's. Yama: The Pit. (or any other names you can invent) Alan, the journalists and the Dog go across the stage, knocking and enquiring at each. The kind of answers he gets are much more your speciality than mine. They are, of course, contradictory: Some people pretend to have seen Francis but all are vague. (Wasn't there, in the original version of The Fronny, a very beautiful passage describing the approach to the Cosy Corner which you never used? Something about the Cemetery? You might bring it in here.)

5. Scene before the curtain: The frontier between Ostnia and Westland. Alan and the Dog arrive and are questioned by officials, who ask absurdly officious questions and make comic business. When Alan tries to explain about Francis, they decide he must be mad and arrest him. The Dog runs away.

6. Room in a lunatic asylum in Westland. On the wall, a portrait of The Leader, a uniformed figure with a wireless loud-speaker instead of a head. Alan in a strait jacket. The loud speaker pours out horrors. War may be declared at any moment. All other countries are planning to destroy Westland. They will poison the water, squirt gas through the drains, make air-raids, etc. etc. The lunatics react violently, some of them lunging about the room with imaginary swords or sounding the charge on toy trumpets; others crawling under the beds, whimpering, screaming, building anti-aircraft dug-outs. Then the Leader makes a speech over the wireless: An address to the Westland Lunatics League. A Westland lunatic, says the Leader, is not like other lunatics. He has a great tradition to uphold. Westland has always had ten percent more lunatics than any other country. And the present generation will not be inferior to its forefathers. A Westland lunatic never forgets that he is a Westlander first and a lunatic afterwards. The Westland Lunatics League will set its face sternly against all forms of international or foreign lunacy. There are some amongst us, so-called men of Science, but really Jewish traitors, who try to prove that new-fangled forms of lunacy exist. But we of the W.L.L. declare that what was good enough for our fathers will be good enough for us. We shall continue to go mad in the good old Westland way . . . (This is crude, but you can polish it up with a lot of technical terms. I only give you the main idea.) During the speech, the jour-

nalists and the Dog come in through the window and rescue Alan. The journalists explain that the Dog has fetched them.

7. Scene before the curtain. In the railway-train. (This, of course, can be stylised as sets of chairs facing each other.) Alan and the journalists. Sitting in the next compartment is a gentleman whom the journalists recognize as being the most important financier in Europe: The man who controls all the dictators and has money in both camps. The journalists for fun dare Alan to go and ask him if he knows where Francis is. Alan goes, quite innocent as usual, and gets into conversation with the financier, who is so surprised that he answers all Alan's questions. He admits that the terror of his life is the Bolsheviks. Alan asks innocently: But why are you so afraid of them? Would they make you work? The Financier begins to bluster: Work, indeed? I've done more hard work in my life than ten socialists put together. I've always had to fight for my own. I only treat others as they treat me. It's a hard world. ... Then, says Alan, I suppose you're afraid they'd take your money? Money, indeed! says the Financier. A lot of good my money's done me! He becomes maudlin. Nobody likes him. He spends a fortune on a quack doctor whom he knows to be useless and on women he doesn't want and on art he doesn't understand. In fact, he's being exploited all round. "And they call me an exploiter!" No, he doesn't know where Francis is. But probably at Paradise Park. All kinds of queer people go there. The Financier's own son is there. The son is a poet and has retired from the world because he hates his father and thinks the armament business so sordid. Alan says he'll go.

8. The gardens of Paradise Park. In the foreground, are several invalids in bath-chairs. In the background are two trees. In one tree sits the Poet. In the other are the Lovers. Alan speaks first to the Poet, who is very sulky. "I'm the most important person in the whole world." Alan asks what he would do if they came and cut down his tree. "They can't" says the Poet: "This tree exists only in my own mind." Alan then goes over to the Lovers. They are more friendly. They wish they could invite him to come up, they say. But there's no room. Soon they begin talking to each other in baby language and entirely forget his existence. Alan then approaches the invalids. They are jealously discussing their various illnesses, showing great affection for each. Each hopes that he'll be chosen for the daily operation. Then the surgeon arrives, short-sighted and in a great hurry and chooses Alan, who is carried off protesting.

9. The operation scene. This will have to be altered, as Alan must

be rescued, this time by the Dog. Or perhaps we can think of some other twist to the scene?

10. Before the curtain. On the road. Alan sleeping against a milestone. The dialogue between the feet.

11. The Nineveh Hotel. Alan's arrival with dog. The manager very haughty. A cabaret is in progress. The entertainment consists in the destruction of works of art of all kinds. A Rembrandt is slashed, amidst loud applause and a folio Shakespeare is burnt, page by page. A chorus of girls appears and one of the guests calls the waiter and carefully chooses one of them. It later appears that he is going to eat her. She is taken out to be cooked. Meanwhile, Alan sees Lou Vipond, off. He runs out after her and we have the comments of the manager and waiters, as in [the] play.

12. A scene divided into two. Outside and inside the bedroom. The two halves of the stage are illuminated alternately, as necessary. First, on the outside, the manager discusses the size of the bill. Then, in the bedroom, Alan is seen with Lou Vipond, who is a tailor's dummy. He makes passionate speeches to her. She, naturally, doesn't answer.

Then, outside the door, is seen the dog-skin folded on a chair. Francis is no longer inside it. Conversation between the skin and the clock. Then the manager comes to present the bill. Alan appeals to the dummy, in vain. As he comes to the door of his bedroom (The manager having left to fetch the police) he finds Francis struggling into the dog-skin. Francis explains who he is, why he hid from his family, and rem[arks] that he'd just been out to get a drink. On being told about the bill, he puts forward a plan of escape. Alan gets into the dog-skin and Francis leads him out, under the eyes of the manager and the policemen, who are too late.

13. The vicarage garden, as in scene 1. But draped with flags. A patriotic meeting. The vicar delivers the sermon as in the play and the general also makes a speech. Lots of talk about comradeship, etc. Alan and the Dog and the journalists unseen at the back of the crowd. At length Alan can bear it no longer. He steps forward. Sensation. Yes, he has found Francis. But unfortunately, Francis is now a dog. He claims his reward. But Iris is horrified. "But it's impossible . . . Wh[y] if my brother's a dog . . ." "Then you'd be a bitch," cries Francis. "Which is exactly what you are!" He jumps out of his skin, delivers a speech denouncing them all and goes off, arm in arm with Alan and the journalists.

Curtain.

That's the best I can do for a first shot. As you can see, a lot has been reluctantly omitted. Make any criticisms you can think of. If you like, scrap it all and we'll try again. But if it appeals to you, will you write some dialogue for the various scenes, in couplets or prose or mixed as you think fit? As you see, I've left out the witnesses. Perhaps you can see how they come in? In any case, I want to keep their very beautiful opening speech. Perhaps they could make other speeches between scenes? If this doesn't make the whole thing too fantastic. Of course a good deal can be shifted on to the journalists. Especially as, you suggest, one of them is always drunk. Please find a place for your lyric about the bean-shaped island. It is marvellous.

On 11 December 1934, Isherwood sent a shorter letter with refinements to the scenario:

Dear Wystan,

How are you getting on with the play? I expect you have more than enough to do with your school work just now. Still, I'll send you a few additional ideas I've had.

First of all, a solution occurs to me of the difficulty with scenes 8–9 of my provisional scenario. You remember I suggested that Alan should be operated upon, but objected that he'd have, in that case, to be rescued? This is all wrong, of course. In scene 8 (the gardens of Paradise Park) Alan must recognize, among the invalids, one of the former searchers for Francis. (Let's call him Chimp Eagle, for the moment.) He and Chimp get into conversation and Chimp begins, in a weak voice, to tell Alan something about his search and a clue he's got hold of as to Francis' whereabouts.

But, just as he's going to divulge this, the Surgeon comes in and chooses him, and he is bundled off, despite his own and Alan's protests, to the operating theatre. Alan, of course, has nothing left to do but to follow him there. So we can have the whole death-scene as you wrote it, after all, with just one or two slight modifications, to keep up the excitement of the audience as to whether Chimp will have time to reveal what he knows about Francis before he dies. He doesn't, of course. As for the strikers cutting off the light, that will have to go, but I think the blinding of the Surgeon by the Pressman's magnesium flash is quite sufficient. The scene can end on Chimp's dying words.

In scene 10 of my scenario (Alan asleep on the road) I think you should make the dialogue between the feet somehow more significant. What was [Homer] Lane's theory about the two sides of the Body? The Left Instinct and the Right Reason? This is just a hint. But couldn't the attitudes of the two feet somehow express this?

And then the final scene, number 13, the Vicarage Garden. I think that the Patriotic Meeting is definitely a ceremony to initiate a kind of Lad's Brigade in the village, a religious-fascist organisation designed vaguely to help England in an "emergency" and to carry out the "ideals of the church". The boys would have a very fetching uniform specially designed by the Vicar. The General must make a fighting speech, after the Vicar's sermon, on the theme: "The youngsters of this Generation are chips off the old block. They want a scrap. And, by George! we're going to see that they get it!" etc., etc. Then comes the revelation about Francis. When Iris has been shown up, Francis jumps on to the platform and delivers a speech which should be one of the high spots of the play. He denounces the whole vicarage gang. "For ten years I've had a dog's-eye view of you . . ." etc. and then goes off with Alan and the Journalists. It is more or less clear that he is going definitely to join the other camp.

Is there still hope of your coming here during the holidays?

Auden accepted Isherwood's suggestions. In a manuscript notebook he used around November and December 1934 (and now at the Harry Ransom Humanities Research Center, The University of Texas at Austin), he sketched out the new scenes in verse that could not be taken over from *The Chase*, the prose speech for the Leader, a new dialogue for the Feet (later replaced with Isherwood's version), and the dialogue for the scene in the Gardens of Paradise Park; he also sketched the new version of the opening Chorus and the Chorus beginning "Happy the hare at morning". He presumably wrote other verse for the play at about the same time.

Auden did visit Isherwood during the holidays, on 10-13 January 1935, bringing with him his contributions to the new version of the play. They made some minor revisions during Auden's stay, and Isherwood made further, more extensive changes after Auden returned. Isherwood detailed these in an undated letter, probably in the latter part of January:

ACT ONE. This is kept as we agreed. In the song about Francis which the Villagers sing, the phrase "Lion and Sun" occurs. Is it intentional that this is repeated, and even insisted on, in Act Three, Scene 4? It might be better to alter it here? (I haven't, of course.) I have cut out Iris' promise to marry Alan even if he only brings news of Francis' death, as this would make her falsehood in Act Three even more risky and therefore improbable. I have given some stray lines to the Curate to build up his character a bit. Is "Anti-Chorus" a correct expression? Or is it "Anti-Chor"? Please remember to correct if wrong.

ACT ONE. 2. Carried out as we agreed.

ACT ONE. 3. Copied unaltered from your MS.

ACT ONE. 4. Copied unaltered from your MS.: except that I expanded the King's remarks to Alan a bit.

ACT ONE. 5. Copied unaltered until Mother Hubbard's. Here I have introduced "Dopey Jim", who is really Sorbo Lamb. Attempts to get Dante atmosphere, as you suggested.

ACT TWO. 1. After much careful consideration and with the usual regret, I decided to rewrite this scene entirely. It was funny, but not typical enough of Westland, as a distinct kind of country. I have written an interview between Alan and a very unpleasant Jew-baiting customs officer who first of all tries to bully A, then smarms over him to try and trick him into confessing he's a spy, and finally gets two medical officers to certify him. I use the old negativism joke. I think you will like this scene when you read it. It has a good acting part for the officer, and we can do with more acting opportunities in the play. I was sorry to say goodbye to the Detector; but there's enough horseplay in the next scene and the operating theatre.

ACT TWO. 2 [*this and the preceding became II.1 in* F]. I altered this as I told you I should, to complete the satire on Westland. It opens with the Bean-shaped island song, sung by Mad Lady, which really is very suitable, when you come to think of it. I couldn't bring in O'Grady at the end, as the technical difficulty arose: what were the lunatics to do when they got caught out. So I made a finale with the sham aeroplane, which will be passably funny and very noisy on the stage. It is cribbed from Ackerley's "Prisoners of War", but who cares? I think you will like this scene the best of my efforts. Your magnificent Leader's Speech is of course preserved entire.

[*Act II, Scene 3, which became II.2 in* F, *is not mentioned in the letter, possibly through an oversight.*]

ACT TWO. 4 [*i.e., 3 in* F]. This has been kept as you wrote it, except that I have tried to bring out the Poet's Unreality line a bit more firmly. I've also slightly altered Chimp's speech.

ACT TWO. 5 [*i.e., 4 in* F]. This has been altered as we agreed. I have worked in the medical student couplet about the letter sigma.

ACT TWO. 6 [*i.e., 5 in* F]. This is completely rewritten. I decided that, so far on in the play, we cannot afford to have a scene which doesn't advance the action. The game they play is awfully good, but it has nothing to do with the plot; and anyhow we've had one game in this act already. So I made the two feet first of all have a bit of a row. The Left Foot, who talks Cockney, is for letting up on Alan and not going any further. The Right Foot, who is Public School, talks about Loyalty and the Team Spirit. The Right Foot then reveals that he has a clue to Francis' whereabouts. He is just going to tell the Left

Foot what he knows, but decides it would be safer to do so behind the milestone; so they retire there, and the audience doesn't hear it. I have made the Right Foot talk like one of those infuriating modern detectives who will say nothing right out. I hope you'll approve.

ACT THREE. 1. In this scene I have made the Second Journalist very tight. He sings the Alice Song (instead of in Act Two. 1) and the couplet about the bluebells on the Baltic.

THREE. 2. As you wrote it: have expanded Desmond, as agreed.

THREE. 3. As we agreed.

THREE. 4. I have altered the meeting between Francis and Alan, making it longer and in prose. I think Francis should speak prose as a rule, because he belongs to another plane of reality, so to speak. Incidentally, here and in one or two other places, I have cut stage directions such as: An actor should be concealed in the chest. This always seems to me to spoil the ordinary reader's illusion and therefore his pleasure; while the producer would tumble to the solution in five seconds. Please check the Dog's Skin Speech very carefully. I suspect misprints in original text.

THREE. 5. I have made Francis' speech quite simple and comparatively short: Any attempt at the Grand Manner would fail horribly, after the magnificent Vicar's Sermon, which is the best thing in the whole play. (I read it aloud the other evening and am convinced that the audience will sit through the whole of it, if it is well done. I have made no interruptions, as we at first decided: they would merely make the whole business longer by disturbing the flow, and so defeat their own object.) I hope you will like the Journalists' speeches at the end.

All the Choruses, needless to say, have been copied as written.

Isherwood's changes brought the text substantially to the state in which it would be published by Faber & Faber a few months later, on 30 May 1935. (The intermediate stage that the authors worked on in Copenhagen is lost; allusions in Isherwood's third letter to deleted elements of the play, like "the Detector", cannot now be explained.) The play had by this time received the title *Where Is Francis?* Sometime before publication, Doone or Medley suggested the final title. Also before publication, Auden, probably working with Doone, and possibly consulting with Isherwood by mail, made further changes in Isherwood's revised text. Isherwood's II.1 was dropped, and a few lines for the Medical Officers and Alan (probably deriving from that dropped scene) were transferred into the following scene (the published II.1); Auden's manuscript of these lines, with his note "(insert after Mad Lady's song)", is among the Group Theatre papers at the Berg Collection. (The Chorus on pp. 224-25 that describes approximately the same action as in the deleted scene was added *after* publication, for use in the production.) Also between preparation of the typescript and publication, Auden apparently revised the Chorus beginning "Seeding and harvest", preceding II.4, as two manuscripts in his hand are among the Group Theatre papers. Auden may also have expanded or revised Isherwood's version of Francis's speech in III.5, since the Group Theatre papers include a manuscript in Auden's hand of a version of the speech that seems to be a not-quite-fully-revised text of the version of the speech printed in F (i.e., the version printed below, p. 581, not the later, post-publication version printed in the main text of this edition). The presence of these two manuscripts among the Group Theatre papers suggests that the Group may have taken some responsibility for preparing the typescript that was used for the published text and eventually provided most of the pages in the GT promptbook, although it is clear that much of the GT typescript was prepared directly from Isherwood's lost fair copy manuscript or draft typescript.

§3 THE PUBLISHED TEXT AND THE TEXT PREPARED FOR PRODUCTION

The Faber & Faber edition of the play was published 30 May 1935. Between that date and the Group Theatre production the following January, Auden supplied a Chorus for the opening of Act II (p. 224), inserted some lines of verse in Chimp Eagle's death scene (see below, note to p. 251), and entirely rewrote the concluding scene. The text of this edition is based on F, with the addition of the new Chorus and verses, and with the substitution of the manuscript version of the revised concluding scene. Minor emendations based on other manuscripts or the GT typescript are detailed in the notes below.

While I have incorporated Auden's verse additions into the text, I have not incorporated other slight additions found in GT and LC, usually amounting to a word or two at most, and possibly the work of Doone or the actors. The notes list these additions—with the exception of inserted choral exclamations like "Ooo!" or "Hear! Hear!", sops to censorship like the alteration of "My God!" to "Good gracious!", or, in the Choruses that introduce some scenes, changes from "I" to "we", "our" to "your", etc. The notes also ignore the scores of minor and major cuts made in GT and LC. With the exception of the cut suggested by the authors in their footnote on p. 254, these excisions were apparently made by Doone or at the instigation of the censor. The longer cuts included all of I.3 and I.4 (the latter removed in deference to the mourning for George V, after the King of Ostnia had already been changed into the Sultan, the Master of Ceremonies into the Grand Vizier, etc.); much of I.5 (almost all of the brothel-keepers' song and all allusions to the Cosy Corner); the liturgical parody in II.4; all of II.5 (although the final Chorus was saved); much of III.2 (notably the Nineveh Girls and Destructive Desmond); and all of III.3.

Because the concluding scene of F (III.5 and Epilogue) was completely rewritten after publication, the original published version is printed separately in §4 below, following the notes to the rest of the play. This in turn is followed (in §5) by Isherwood's outline of proposed changes to that published version of the scene—changes that led to Auden's manuscript revision (printed in the main text) and, finally, to the abridged version worked out by Auden and Doone during rehearsals (described in §6).

Page 190.

In the Dramatis Personae, GT includes among the "minor characters" an Officer at the Westland Frontier and among the "others" a Jewish Gentleman. Both presumably figured in Isherwood's abandoned version of II.1 (see his scenario, above); they are dropped from the corresponding list in F.

Page 191.

In GT the opening chorus is headed "Prologue".

Page 192.

The speech headings printed in F as "Leader of Semi-Chorus I" and "Leader of Semi-Chorus II" appear in GT as "Leader of Chorus" and "Leader of Anti-Chorus"; the change in F was presumably made to avoid confusion among those unfamiliar with Greek choruses. In the Choral song ("The young men in Pressan to-night") and throughout the play, GT aligns all lines of verse along a common left margin; the indentions in the F text, followed (with some emendations) in this edition, are probably Auden's, but may conceivably have been added by the publisher's reader.

Page 198.

In the Vicar's speech, I have deleted the comma that appears in GT and F at the end of the ninth line ("Sir Bingham Crewe, who was the last").

Page 201.

In GT the speech headings to the three sections of the lyric "Enter with him" read "Chorus", "Anti-Chorus", and "Chorus"; in F the first two are altered to "Semi-Chorus I" and "Semi-Chorus II", but the third is left unaltered as "Chorus". It is unclear whether this last heading was left unchanged because of an oversight, and that Auden in fact intended to retain the antiphonal effect of the GT version (in which case the heading should read "Semi-Chorus I"), or whether he intended to combine the chorus for the third section of the poem (in which case the F reading is correct). The first of these alternatives seems more likely.

Page 202.

"Amazed on you" is the reading of earlier manuscripts of this poem and of the text published in *Twentieth Century*, August 1933. It was also the reading in the manuscript of *The Chase*, but was miscopied by the typist as "Amazed at you". In GT this became "Amazed as you", the reading followed in F. When Auden reprinted the poem in his later collections he restored "Amazed on you".

Page 206.

In the third line of the Chorus, GT and F read "unseasonal", but this is corrected to "unseasonable" in GT by an unknown hand.

Page 209.

In the 2nd Journalist's account of Ostnia, GT and LC alter F's "lowest birth-rate" to "the highest infant-mortality rate".

Page 210.

The stage direction in F that has the Dog attempt to balance a chair on his nose is altered in GT and LC to have him attempt to balance a bowl.

Page 213.

In LC, which deletes I.3, a small fragment of that scene is retained as the opening lines for I.4, thus:

MASTER OF CEREMONIES. Twelfth of the month, Sire, Execution Day. There's been a revolt, I'm sorry to say.
KING. Another?

LC also adds, after "dress rehearsal" in the King's next line, the phrase "for the execution". I.3 and I.4 are both absent from GT.

Page 214.

In the third paragraph of the Cantor's long speech I have emended "sancto fortis" to "sancte fortis".

Page 218.

In the last line of the first verse paragraph of the Chorus, the typist of *The Chase* misread "whose loyalties" as "where loyalties", and the error persisted into *The Dog Beneath the Skin*. I have restored the manuscript reading. In the second line of the next verse paragraph I have followed GT and *The Chase* by restoring a colon after "captured bird".

Page 220.

GT and LC have the 1st Tout offering "a picture post-card" rather than simply "a post-card" in his first two speeches.

Page 221.

The Proprietress's line, "At this door", absent in F, is restored from GT, where a cramped page layout makes the line easy to overlook.

In F, Sue's Voice has six lines, including the two given here (following a change marked in GT) to the Proprietress of Yama the Pit.

Page 224.

The opening Chorus of Act II, not present in F or LC, is added in GT. The text printed here is based (as is the GT text) on Auden's manuscript in the Group Theatre papers in the Berg Collection. The Chorus takes the place of the scene at the Westland frontier written by Isherwood and abandoned before publication and now lost. (See p. 564.)

When the Westland frontier scene was abandoned, Auden probably used some of its lines in writing the dialogue for the Medical Officers and Alan near the opening of II.1; Auden's manuscript of this dialogue, marked for insertion after the Mad Lady's song, is in the Berg Collection.

Page 226.

The speech headings for the Medical Officers are slightly confused in F, where the fifth and sixth speeches are both assigned to the 1st M.O. and the next three speeches to the 2nd, 1st, and 2nd. I have followed GT in assigning the sixth speech to the 2nd M.O., and in adjusting the next three speeches accordingly.

Page 235.

In the third line from the end of the Chorus, "Redan" is possibly an authorial correction for "Redam", the reading in the corresponding passage in the manuscripts and typescripts of *The Chase*.

Page 238.

In GT the Financier's song occurs a few lines earlier in the scene, immediately after his speech ending "I don't know why I'm telling you all this." GT also presents some of the later dialogue in a slightly different (and more mechanical) sequence. These variant passages in GT appear on unnumbered inserted pages; they are slightly bowdlerized versions of the F text and were presumably adapted for stage purposes. In the chorus to the Financier's song, the alternative readings in braces ("to him", etc.) are taken from GT; a similar layout is used in F for the song on p. 205, and there seems no reason to exclude the alternative readings here.

Page 241.

In the tenth line of the Chorus, "Knows to the bar" is an emendation, confirmed by Auden's 1945 *Collected Poetry*, for "Know to the bar" in GT and F.

The break in the Chorus after "We will show you what he has done" appears in the GT typescript, is absent in F, but reappears when Auden reprinted the poem in his 1945 *Collected Poetry*.

Page 242.

I have corrected a minor misspelling in the Poet's quotation from the *Agamemnon*. In his Latin I have emended "aut ater", the defective reading in GT and F, to "an ater", which is the reading both of the original Catullus and of Auden's own rough draft in a manuscript notebook now at Texas.

Page 247.

GT transfers the final song of II.3 to p. 245, immediately after the Colonel's speech. GT also drops from the song's first line the word "There's" (LC drops "There's" and "here") and in the third line substitutes "Operations" for "Skating-rinks".

The line-breaks in the opening lines of the "Seeding and harvest" Chorus are misplaced in F; the correct readings have been restored from the two partial manuscripts among the Group Theatre papers in the Berg Collection and from GT.

Page 251.

The text printed here incorporates an addition and modification from GT. In F, Alan does not interrupt Chimp Eagle's speech beginning "When the Midget died", but Chimp himself says "But I forgot / My choice and lot.", and the same speech continues with the three lines beginning "More I cannot tell." Chimp's eleven lines from "No I did not" to "For what is lacking" are inserted in GT,

Page 254.

GT lacks and LC drops the dialogue of the feet; both texts move the lyric "Now through night's caressing grip" to the end of III.2 (p. 268).

Page 257.

In the corresponding passage of the manuscript of *The Chase* the first word of the second verse paragraph of the Chorus reads "Writers be glib"; the typist, unable to read the phrase, left a blank space, which Auden later filled in with "Writer be glib". This reading persisted into *The Dog Beneath the Skin*, and is preserved here.

Page 271.

Where F has Alan run behind the shopwindow dummy to speak its lines in falsetto, GT (on pages that were evidently part of the original professional typescript) explains in a stage direction that "one of the Chorus Leaders stands behind the dummy and speaks for it, in falsetto"; the speech headings on the same page, however, assign the dummy's speeches to "Financier [*behind dummy*]".

Page 272.

In the song for the Chorus, GT and LC substitute "the doctor" and "the dispenser" for F's "the vicar" and "the choirboy", the Lord Chamberlain having forbidden the F version. For further notes on the text of this song, see, in the notes to *The Chase*, the note to p. 153.

For notes on the speech of the Dog's Skin, see, in the notes to *The Chase*, the note to p. 156. Two corrections are made here to the F text: near the opening of the speech a comma is dropped after "émigré's pride" (the comma is not present in GT); and in the second paragraph "skilfully transformed" is an emendation (based on the manuscript of *The Chase*) for "skilfully transferred". Near the opening of the speech LC substitutes "the best society" for "Bloomsbury", and GT makes this and other minor changes for stage purposes.

Page 275.

Alan's speech, when he first appears in his pyjamas, has in GT and F a comma at the end of the first line and a question mark at the end of the second. I have moved the question mark to the first line.

In GT (in a late addition to the typescript) and in LC, Lou Vipond responds to Alan's questions with a few lines of dialogue. Doone added these lines when he decided to have an actress rather than a dummy impersonate Lou on stage. The lines are taken over from the corresponding dialogue in *The Chase* (pp. 158-59), which in Doone's copy of that play is marked "new piece" in Doone's hand. Auden did not write any new dialogue for the version in *Dogskin*.

Page 279.

In the fourth line of the Chorus, "grey-white" is an emendation for "grey, white" in GT and F; the hyphenated phrase occurs in the manuscript of an unpublished poem of May 1933 ("After the conveying", in a notebook now at

THE DOG BENEATH THE SKIN 571

Swarthmore College). The corresponding passage in *The Chase* reads "grey white". Isherwood, or the typist of *The Dog Beneath the Skin*, presumably added the comma.

Pages 281-92.

Act III, Scene 5, is printed from Auden's manuscript in the Group Theatre papers in the Berg Collection, New York Public Library. This manuscript consists of separate groups of sheets with Mildred Luce's speech and with Francis's denunciation of the villagers and, on different paper, most of the rest of the scene, with notes indicating where Mildred's and Francis's speeches are to be inserted. The manuscript also indicates that the choral passages on pp. 289-90 and the three speeches for the 1st and 2nd Journalists on pp. 290-91 are to be taken from the published text. The manuscript, although legible, was written rapidly and has some trivial inconsistencies that I have not tried to correct. (I have, however, used consistent speech headings throughout the scene in order to avoid confusions such as the suggestion that Mrs Hotham and the General's Wife are two different characters.) I have also added some light punctuation and sparse stage directions, but I have not attempted to imitate the style in which Isherwood would have reworked the manuscript for publication. The following notes specify all the important changes and additions that I have made to the manuscript. The notes do not specify a few brief stage directions that are taken from F in passages where Auden copied the dialogue from the printed text; nor do the notes specify the few stage directions added in order to clarify which character the speaker is addressing. For notes on the evolution of this scene, see §5 below.

Page 281.

The stage direction identifying the scene is adapted from Isherwood's suggested outline for the revised version (p. 586).

In the manuscript the second sentence of Alan's first speech seems to read "Their decorations all down this [*or* the] street". Auden elsewhere writes "their" for "there", so the intended reading was presumably "There are" or "There're".

Auden assigned the various Villagers' speeches simply to "Villagers", and indicated a change of speaker by starting a new paragraph. I have assigned the later speeches to "Another" in each instance, although some of the Villagers may be assumed to speak twice.

In Alan's speech after the Villagers' speeches, the stage direction "[*hidden*]" is an editorial addition, as are similar directions later in the scene.

Page 282.

In the Village Organist's first speech I have added the direction "[*handing out music*]".

Page 283.

Some very light punctuation has been added to Mildred Luce's speech. In the tenth line, "Look at your flowers" is correct. While writing the line, Auden altered the phrase from "These are your flowers".

Page 284.

The stage direction for Francis's emergence is added, partly on the basis of F. The direction for the speech of the Vicar and the General immediately after is taken from F.

Page 285.

Some very light punctuation has been added to Francis's long speech. In the paragraph immediately following the Vicar's interruption, I have let stand the manuscript reading "poverties"; this is a rare and obsolete usage, but the *OED* notes the comparison with "hardships".

Page 288.

In the manuscript, when Mildred attacks Francis, the stage direction says only that she "*Kills him*". I have specified that she stabs him with a hat-pin, partly on the basis of the Vicar's explanation to the Sergeant later in the scene that Mildred "defended herself with a hat-pin" and partly on the basis of Auden's revised version of 1947, in which Mildred reportedly (*Masses and Mainstream*, June 1948) stabs Francis to death. In Doone's Group Theatre production, the General handed her a revolver with which to shoot Francis.

Page 290.

The stage direction "[*looking at* FRANCIS]" is added to the General's second speech.

§4 THE FIRST (PUBLISHED) VERSION OF THE CONCLUDING SCENE

Printed below is the text from F of III.5 and the Epilogue. The scene is replaced in GT and LC by an abridgement of Auden's manuscript version, as described on p. 571. The text below is printed as in F, with the exception of three emendations in the Vicar's sermon: in the fifth paragraph "Demogorgon" for "Demogorgan" (p. 576); in the eighth paragraph "trouble for Him" for "trouble for him" (p. 577); and in the eleventh paragraph "the cowl" for "to cowl" (p. 578). The first and third of these restore the readings of Auden's earliest manuscript for the sermon, in a notebook now at Swarthmore College; the second completes Isherwood's efforts at consistency in preparing the speech for publication. In the eleventh paragraph, the second "to" in the second sentence seems intrusive, but it was presumably added by one of the authors. For further notes on the text of the sermon, see above, p. 549.

Act III Scene 5

[*As in Act I, Scene 1: The Garden of the Vicarage at Pressan Ambo. A platform, draped with the Union Jack, occupies most of the stage. On it are chairs, a table and a glass of water. Other chairs are arranged round the platform, in preparation for a meeting. Two large banners are hung right across the stage. They are inscribed: "The Lads of Pressan teach Britain a lesson" and "Pressan is having breakfast: Wake up, England!" Many other flags, Scottish, Welsh, Irish and Colonial, hang down from the branches of the trees. As the curtain rises, the stage is empty. Enter* ALAN, FRANCIS *and the* TWO JOURNALISTS. FRANCIS *wears the dog's skin, but with the head thrown back, like a monk's cowl. He walks on his feet: not on all fours. The* JOURNALISTS *carry cameras and other photographic apparatus.*]

ALAN [*looking about him in amazement*]. Whatever can have happened? I say, Francis, do you think they can have found out that we were coming?

FRANCIS. On the contrary: I should say that to-day of all others is the day on which they least expect to see us.

1ST JOURNALIST. Well, Alan, your native hamlet certainly seems to be moving with the times. From your description, I was expecting an oldest inhabitant and a prize pig.

2ND J. The last of my illusions is shattered. So this is rural England! Just another lousy racket!

ALAN. But I tell you, it never used to be like this. I simply can't understand it. Everything's different! [*He looks off-stage, through the trees.*] I say, here comes the Curate! He'll be able to tell us what's up.

FRANCIS. No. I don't want him to see us, yet. [*To the* JOURNALISTS.] You two can question him. Come along, Alan. We'll go down there, where we can watch.

> [*He and Alan descend into the auditorium and take seats among the audience. Enter the* CURATE.]

JOURNALISTS [*raising their hats*]. Good day, sir. The Thunderbolt. The Evening Moon. Perhaps you'd care to tell us something about your interesting celebrations? We're very anxious to get the details correct. Nothing shall be printed without your approval. The articles will be ready for your O.K. before we leave here this afternoon.

CURATE [*who is evidently overworked and disgusted; finding the whole subject extremely distasteful*]. I'm not authorised to give you any information. You ought to speak to the Vicar, really: but he's very busy just now. [*Sighs and passes his hand over his eyes.*] Oh, very well, what is it you want to know?

[*The* JOURNALISTS *take out their notebooks.*]

1ST J. My colleague and myself very much appreciate your kindness, sir. We won't take up more of your valuable time than is absolutely necessary.... Who exactly, are the Lads of Pressan?

CURATE [*as if wearily repeating a lesson he has learnt*]. The Lads of Pressan is a Boy's Brigade founded by the Vicar and General Hotham. Miss Iris Crewe is Patroness and Mrs Hotham Honorary Colonel-in-Chief. The uniforms have been designed by the Vicar. To-day, the Brigade is to have its first inspection by General and Mrs Hotham. The Vicar will preach a sermon on Bolshevism and the Devil. And Miss Iris Crewe will present the Standard, which will then be blessed by the Vicar. Later, there will be Field Communion, tea and athletic sports.

2ND J. Very interesting.... And what are the objects of this Brigade?

CURATE. Well, er.... The Vicar says ... you see....

[*This subject is evidently so repugnant to him that he can hardly force himself to begin.*]

1ST J. [*helpfully*]. "Standing outside all political parties and factions, for Church, King and State, against communism, terrorism, pacifism and other forms of international anarchy, to protect Religion and succour England in times of national crisis." Is that right, sir?

CURATE [*surprise*]. Why, those are almost exactly the Vicar's own words! However did you know?

2ND J. It's the usual, er ... programme. Thank you very much, sir. And now, if you'll be kind enough to show us the Press places, we won't keep you any longer.

CURATE. I should think you'd see best over there.

[*He indicates two chairs in a corner, at the front of the stage. The* JOURNALISTS *go over to them and take their seats.*]

[*Band music, of a military character, can already be heard off. Enter the* VICAR, *fussily, in a bad temper. He wears his cassock and surplice.*]

VICAR [*to* CURATE]. Ah, here you are! Whatever have you been doing? I've been looking for you everywhere. Do you expect me to attend to everything myself?

CURATE. I'm very sorry.

VICAR. It's very easy to say you're sorry. But you don't do much to show it. This is the third time I've had to reprove you this week! You seem to have no life in you, no go, no enthusiasm. I'm beginning to be very much afraid that your heart isn't in our movement!

CURATE. You're quite right, sir. It's no good our going on like this: I'd better tell you frankly. . . .

> [*The band, which has been getting louder, now blares out just behind the scenes.*]

THE VICAR. Good Gracious! Here they are!

> [*He runs out, to meet the others; returning almost immediately with the* GENERAL, MRS HOTHAM *and* MISS IRIS CREWE. *These four take their places on the raised platform. Crowds of villagers enter and sit down on the chairs on the stage. Finally, the Lads of Pressan, wearing a distinctive uniform, march in and form ranks just below the platform. A boy with the standard which* MISS IRIS CREWE *is later to present takes his place on the platform behind her chair. The chatter of the villagers is drowned by the noise of the band.*]
>
> [*The military music ends with a flourish. Silence. The* VICAR *rises to his feet. He delivers the following sermon: beginning in his usual pulpit manner, but quickly becoming more excited, more histrionic, more daring in his gestures and poses. The final passage is wailed rather than spoken. Tears pour down his cheeks, saliva runs from his mouth: He has worked himself up into an hysterical frenzy.*]

VICAR. What was the weather on Eternity's worst day? And where was that Son of God during the fatal second: pausing before a mirror in an anteroom, or in the Supreme Presence Itself, in the middle of an awful crescendo of praise, or again, withdrawn apart, regarding pensively the unspeakable beauties of the heavenly landscape?

The divinest of books says nothing. Of the primary crises of the soul no history is ever written. Yon citizen crossing the street while the policeman holds up the traffic like the Red Sea: he leaves one curb an honest man; but, ah, quickly, Constable, handcuffs out! Roll on, you heavy lorries! He is Pharaoh! Mercifully exterminate this pest! Too late, the warning cannot be given. It's done, the poison administered, the soul infected. The other curb is reached and our John Bull, honest-seeming, unsuspected, is free to walk away, within a few years to involve widows in financial ruin or a party of school children in some frightful accident.

So, on this inconceivably more catastrophic occasion, no door banged, no dog barked. There was no alarm of any kind. But consider its importance! No judge's sentence had yet been passed. Basedow's Disease had not occurred. Love. Joy. Peace. God. No words but these. No population but angels. And after . . . the whole lexicon of sin: the sullen proletariat of hell!

What, then, of the central figure in the tragedy: First among the Sons of God? Power? No Caliph or Mikado had one grain of it. Beauty? Alcibiades beside him were extraordinarily plain. Wits? Einstein were a stammerer. But for him it was not enough. For him, nothing was enough, but the unique majority of God. That or nothing! That or (ah, had he reckoned with the dread alternative!) unqualified ruin. Alas, for us he raised the question; but the answer was to lie with another!

O, even then, when the first thought tempted, was all irrevocably lost? Was there not still time, wonderful creature, to cast it from you with a phew of disgust? It doesn't matter now. Altered for ever and for the worse, he went out to corrupt others, to form his notorious and infamous societies. Gone for ever was the frank handshake, the obvious look, the direct and simple speech. The Golden Age was definitely over. Language had become symbolic, gesture a code of signals. The arrangement of books on a table conveyed a shame-faced message: flowers in a vase expressed some unsavoury *double entendre*. Personalities acquired a new and sinister significance, lost all but that. For or against: On this side of the ledger or on that. Gabriel and Michael: Out of the question. What glorious praise! Demogorgon: Safe. What a shameful comment! Abdiel and Azazael: Perhaps. Oh, beware, you unsuspecting pair! This is a terrible examination, decisive of your everlasting career. This is your only chance. There are but two colours for you to choose, the whitest white or the blackest black; salvation or damnation at one hundred per cent. Azazael chooses. What? The Black. Miserable, unlucky he! He's failed. Now, Abdiel! You hesitate? Quick, man, the White! Bravissimo, he passes! Baffled, they slink away to make their preparations. Too late for diplomacy or apologetic telegrams. It is war.

On the details of that appalling combat, History is mercifully silent. To the vanquished, unable to consider such reminiscences without a shudder, the subject is tabu: And the victors, to whom all boasting is by nature abhorrent, have been content to leave the matter in a decent obscurity. Remember, they were divine, and therefore omniscient, omnipotent. No new-fangled auxiliary arms, the value of which is realised only by the few enthusiastic subalterns, no depth-charges or detectors, no camouflage, no poison-gas which in times of peace even generals do not see how they could bring themselves to use, no technique of deployment or barrage can have been unknown to them. It was conflict on an astronomical scale and with the gloves off. Here were no Quakers, strikers or International Red Cross, no questions of colonies or reparations. Where all were committed absolutely, there could be no ironic misgivings.

Every schoolboy knows the result. To the rebels it was destruction. The reservoirs of the Divine Wrath were inexhaustible. Nothing was signed. There was no one left to discharge so unnecessary an office. Into the fosse of Hell they fell like water. Hurrah! Hurrah! Hurrah!

Yet, my friends, you know and I know, don't we, that the events I have just narrated were not the last. Would God they had been! The scene of operations was transferred to another front, to us. Impotent to attack Him directly, the defeated sought to strike at God through His creatures, to wound, where it was most tender, His artist's love. And, to our shame, they succeeded. The world became an everlasting invalid. Of course, God could have dismissed us with a snap of His fingers. One little stellar collision and . . . no more trouble for Him. Why not? All reason was for it. It would have been quite cricket. But God is no eugenist. There was no talk of sterilisation, euthanasia. Only the treatment of a very merciful and loving physician. He set over us a kindly strictness, appointed His authorities, severe but just, a kind of martial law. He gave them power to govern in His name and access to His presence in their prayers, to make their reports and ask for help and guidance, that through them the people might learn His primary will.

And so, to-day, we are here for a very good reason. His enemies have launched another offensive, on the grandest scale, perhaps, that this poor planet of ours has ever witnessed. As on the first awful occasion in Eden, so now: under the same deluding banner of Freedom. For their technique of propaganda has never varied; it has been far too successful for them to need to change it, to suggest that it is in the human interest to destroy God. In silk-clad China or the naked archipelagos, in the Bermudas or Brighton, in the stone hamlet among the beechwoods or the steel flats of the metropolis, that three-syllable whisper: "You are God", has been, is and, alas, will be sufficient to convert in an instant the chapped-handed but loyal ploughboy, the patient sufferer from incurable disease, the tired economical student or the beautiful juvenile mama into a very spiteful maniac indeed, into whose hands modern science has placed an all-too-efficient axe.

I should like just to try and imagine for one moment what the world would be like if this lunacy with its grim fanatic theories were to spread over the civilised globe. I tell you there would exist a tyranny compared with which a termite colony would seem dangerously lax. No family love. Sons would inform against fathers, cheerfully send them to the execution cellars. Mothers send their daughters to the mines. No romance. Even the peasant must beget that standard child under laboratory conditions. Motherhood would be by licence. Truth and Beauty would be proscribed as dangerously obstructive. To be beautiful would be treason against the State, Thought a sabotage deadly to the thinker. No books, no art, no music. A year of this, I say, and even the grass would cease to grow, flowers would not risk appearance, heifers would not dare to calve.

So you see our job. To those to whom danger in God's cause makes exclaim, like a schoolboy comforted with an ice: "How lush!" this is a lucky day. God has given them extraordinary privileges, but if there be any doubters, cowards wavering like the cowl on an oasthouse, to these I say: "Go out of that door before it is too late!" Only those whose decisions are swift as the sirocco, senses keen as the finest mirror galvanometer, will constant as the standard inch and of a chemical purity need apply. And to these I say: "Remember, God is behind you: Nelson, Henry the Fifth, Shackleton, Julius Caesar." As for the enemy, those rats! they shall skedaddle like a brook; Nature herself is on our side. Their boasts are vain. You cannot threaten a thunderstorm with a revolver. They shall be trapped by the stalks of flowers. Sheep shall chase them away. Useless for them to imitate natural objects: a boulder or a tree. Even the spade-handed moles shall declare their folly!

But mind, God first! To God the glory and let Him reward! God is no summer tourist. We're more than scenery to Him. He has a farmer's eye for ergot and tares. Oh delight higher than Everest and deeper than the Challenger Gulf! His commodores come into His council and His lieutenants know His love. Lord, I confess! I confess! I am all too weak and utterly unworthy. There is no other want. All actions and diversions of the people, their greyhound races, their football competitions, their clumsy acts of love, what are they but the pitiful, maimed expression of that entire passion, the positive tropism of the soul to God?

Oh Father, I am praising Thee, I have always praised Thee, I shall always praise Thee! Listen to the wooden sabots of Thy eager child running to Thy arms! Admit him to the fairs of that blessed country where Thy saints move happily about their neat, clean houses under the blue sky! O windmills, O cocks, O clouds and ponds! Mother is waving from the tiny door! The quilt is turned down in my beautiful blue and gold room! Father, I thank Thee in advance! Everything has been grand! I am coming home!

> [*At the end of the sermon, the* VICAR *collapses like a wet rag into his chair and feebly mops his face with a handkerchief. There is a moment's silence: then a flourish of bugles.*]

THE BOY IN COMMAND OF THE LADS OF PRESSAN. Lads! Atten-shun! Eyes . . . right!

> [*The* GENERAL *and* MRS HOTHAM *come down from the platform. The* GENERAL *is in uniform with rows of medals. His wife wears a uniform jacket and a hat with an immense white plume. They begin to inspect the Lads. Fife and drum music.*]

MILDRED LUCE [*suddenly appearing from the crowd of villagers, and addressing the Lads*]. I hope you know why you're really here? The Vicar daren't tell you! The General daren't tell you either! But I dare! Wave your dummy rifles about! It's only play now. But soon they'll give you real rifles. You'll learn to shoot. You'll learn to kill whoever they tell you to. And you'll be trained to let yourselves be killed, too. I thought I'd just tell you. It isn't that I care. I'm glad! What does it matter to me if you're all murdered? My sons were murdered, and they were bigger and stronger and handsomer than you'll ever be, any of you! So what do I care!

> [*This speech has made the most painful impression on all present.* MRS HOTHAM *hurriedly leads* MILDRED *off into the background and returns without her. People begin talking in undertones. The* GENERAL *abruptly cuts short the review, salutes and reascends the platform. As people still continue to whisper, he clears his throat angrily and rings a little handbell for silence.*]

GENERAL. Hrrmm! Before, er, passing on to the, er, next stage in the proceedings, I should like to say how very favourably Mrs Hotham and myself have been impressed by the excellent turn-out this afternoon.

The Lads of Pressan have made a first-rate beginning, and I hope that their end will be equally satisfactory . . . hrrrmm! That is, er, I should say, I hope that they will go on as they have begun.

And now I come to an important announcement. I suppose that, by this time, it's a more or less open secret that our Patroness, Miss Iris Crewe, is engaged to be married to that well-known munitions manufacturer, hrrmm, I should say: that well-known and popular patriot and sportsman, Mr Rudolf Trunnion-James. I'm sure we all wish her the very best of good fortune . . . hrrmm! of happiness.

Miss Crewe now authorises me to tell you that, after her marriage, she intends to present the Honeypot Hall Estate to the Lads of Pressan, as barracks, parade-ground and playing-fields. . . . Three cheers for our benefactress: Miss Iris Crewe!

[*The villagers give three cheers.*]

ALAN [*from the auditorium*]. Here! I say!
GENERAL [*evidently fearing another interruption, tries to ignore* ALAN]. Miss Crewe's marriage has been fixed for the first day of next month, and I'm sure we all . . .
ALAN. Shame!
THE GENERAL [*ringing his bell, continues*]. And I'm sure we all hope . . .
ALAN. Stop! You've got to listen to me!
GENERAL. Confound it, sir! Can't you hear me speaking? Who the devil are you?
ALAN. Alan Norman.

[*Sensation.* ALAN *gets up from his place in the auditorium and comes on to the stage.*]

ALAN. Iris, what does this mean?
IRIS [*unpleasantly surprised*]. Alan! Why have you come back?
ALAN. Because I've found Francis. [*Calling down to* FRANCIS.] Francis, come up here!

[*Huge sensation.* FRANCIS *comes up on to the stage.*]

IRIS. Oh, dear! I feel so ill!

[*She sways slightly in her chair and is supported by* MRS HOTHAM, *who regards* FRANCIS *with unconcealed disapproval.*]

VICAR AND GENERAL [*together: equally dismayed*]. Sir Francis! Upon my soul!

FRANCIS. Joy seems to have been too much for my dear sister's delicate constitution. ... Hullo, General: fight back those unmanly tears! Vicar, you needn't kiss me if you don't want to. [*Looking round*] Isn't *anybody* pleased to see me?

LITTLE GIRL [*in crowd*]. Oh, I'm awfully glad you're back: Dear old Doggy!

FRANCIS. Thank you for those kind words. [*Shakes hands with her.*]

> [*Everybody now becomes aware of the dog's skin which* FRANCIS *is wearing. There are murmurs of*:]

Just fancy! The Dog! He was the dog! *etc. etc.*

FRANCIS. Yes, ladies and gentlemen. The little girl is right. I am, or rather was, the Dog! [*Looking round at them.*] You know, I've often pictured to myself this very moment: My return. In fact, during my canine days, it was one of my greatest pleasures. Of course, I imagined a very dramatic appearance: tearing off my disguise and denouncing you all in the kind of language to which the vicar has just so generously treated us. But the really fascinating problem was to decide *when* to appear, and I kept putting it off. Of course, I thought, it must be just at a time when you were all cursing me and wishing I was dead. But though in private you said things about me which made my ears tingle (perhaps it did me good, too), in public you were very discreet. It was always, "poor Sir Francis", "good Sir Francis", "our wonderful lost boy squire". And now here you all are, looking extremely uncomfortable, as well you may, considering that you know I've had a dog's-eye view of you for the last ten years.

Directly after that historic row with my father (I forget exactly what it was about; I think it was the key of the gun-room), I went upstairs to have a hot bath, feeling very injured of course, meditating suicide, running away to sea, being brought back to die of consumption, etc. And it was in the bathroom that suddenly I had the brilliant fatal idea. An hour later, my life as a dog had begun.

At first I only intended to keep my new shape for a week or two. I even doubted if I could hold out as long as that, but I had begun to keep a diary, and that helped me over the difficult period. After the first six months I didn't really want to come back. You see, I had begun to regard you in a new light. I was fascinated and horrified by you all. I thought such obscene, cruel, hypocritical, mean, vulgar creatures had never existed before in the history of the planet, and that it was my office and doom to record it. As a dog, I learnt with what a mixture of fear, bullying, and condescending kindness you treat those whom you consider your inferiors, but on whom you are dependent for your pleasures. It's an awful shock to start seeing people from underneath.

My diary was my greatest friend. I worked away at it, like a scientist, polishing, punctuating, searching for the exact epithet, devoting months and even years to each one of you, noting every gesture, every intonation. I even managed to take photographs to illustrate my records, and very remarkable some of them are.

And then, slowly, the horror and the pseudo-scientific interest began to wear off, too. I was growing older. I began to feel that I had been foolishly wasting my time. Hadn't it all been just a romantic escape, I asked myself? Wasn't it Life itself I was afraid of, hiding in my dog-skin? I think that, soon, I should have gone away anyhow. But, as it happened, Alan Norman was chosen. I'd always liked him and so I took the opportunity of leaving you when I did.

Don't be alarmed, I haven't come back to claim my lawful rights. Iris, you can keep Honeypot Hall and do what you like with it. I never meant to return at all. Anyhow, it wasn't necessary: you are all just as I imagined you would be. Since I've been away from you, I've come to understand you better. I don't hate you any more. I see how you fit into the whole scheme. You are significant, but not in the way I used to imagine. You are units in an immense army: most of you will die without ever knowing what your leaders are really fighting for or even that you are fighting at all. Well, I am going to be a unit in the army of the other side: but the battlefield is so huge that it's practically certain you will never see me again. We are all of us completely unimportant, so it would be very silly to start quarrelling, wouldn't it? Goodbye. [*He turns to go.*]

ALAN. Francis! I'm coming with you!
FRANCIS. I'm glad.
IRIS. Alan!
ALAN. I know who my friends are . . . and when I'm not wanted.
GENERAL. This is monstrous.
CURATE. Alan, I just want to say . . . [*He hesitates.*]
ALAN. Come with us, too!
VICAR. You're lost if you do!

[*The* CURATE *hesitates between them, in great distress.*]

CURATE. Christ crucified
    Be at my side,
    Confirm my mind
    That it be kind

To those who assert and hurt
On either side!

I must go away,
I must go to pray
To One who is greater.

GENERAL. Greater than who?
CURATE. Greater than you. [*He goes out.*]
A YOUNG MAN. Francis, I'll come! [*He crosses the stage to* FRANCIS' *side.*]
A BOY FROM THE RANKS OF THE LADS OF PRESSAN. Let me come too, Francis!
FRANCIS. We're not going on a treasure-hunt, you know, or looking for pirates.
BOY. I don't care. I want to help.
FRANCIS. All right. [*The* BOY *crosses stage.*] Any more?

[*Three other villagers silently join the group.*]

VICAR. If anyone else thinks of joining this mistaken young man, I can only warn them that I shall make it my business to see that never, at any future time, shall he or she receive employment in Pressan again.
FRANCIS [*to his followers*]. You hear what the Vicar says? Hadn't you better go back? [*Nobody moves.*] Come on, then, let's be moving.

[FRANCIS, ALAN *and their five companions come down from the stage and go out through the audience.*]

MRS HOTHAM. Reginald! Can't you say something to make them feel ashamed of themselves?
GENERAL [*shouting after them*]. You're traitors to Pressan!
FRANCIS [*turning at the auditorium exit, shouts back*]. Traitors to *your* Pressan, General: not to ours!

[*He goes out, followed by the others.*]
[*On the stage, everybody is talking.*]

GENERAL. That young man's a disgrace to his class and his family!
IRIS [*weeping*]. Oh dear, I've never been so insulted in all my life!
MRS HOTHAM. One can only be thankful that his poor Father isn't alive to see it!
VICAR [*burying his face in his hands*]. What a fiasco! What a scandal for Pressan! It was like a nightmare! I simply can't believe it has happened!

1st Journalist [*briskly coming forward*]. You're quite right, sir! It hasn't happened!
All. Hasn't happened? Whatever does he mean? We saw it, it must have happened!
2nd J. I entirely agree with my colleague. Dozens of things occur every day, curious, embarrassing, shocking incidents: but how few of them happen! The Press disregards them: therefore they cannot have taken place! The Press is an Artist: It has a certain picture to paint. Whatever fails to harmonise with that picture, it discards; regretfully perhaps, but firmly.
1st J. The Press has no use for the incident you believe yourselves to have just witnessed. It has no place in our scale of values. Long-lost Baronets do not disguise themselves as dogs; or at any rate, only for erotic reasons. The behaviour of Sir Francis Crewe falls into no artistic category which we recognize: therefore it cannot be represented in our picture of the day's events.
2nd J. And since all events are recorded by the Press, what the Press does not record cannot be an event.
1st J. But you, sir, and you, General, and you, Madam, you belong to our picture: These lads here, these flags, this charming old-world garden, they compose admirably. Allow me. Thank you. If you'll be so kind.

[*Talking very fast, they erect their cameras and manoeuvre the somewhat bewildered* General, Vicar *and ladies into a compact group, ready to be photographed.*]

2nd J. All ready, please.

[*There is a puff of vapour and a flash so blinding that all four cover their faces with their hands. But only for an instant. Then they recover their ceremonial poses. And now, all are masked: The* General *as a Bull, the* Vicar *as a Goat,* Iris *as a Cat and* Mrs Hotham *as a Turkey. They stand thus for some moments in tableau. Loud martial music. The curtain falls quickly and rises again at once. Now all the villagers wear various animal masks. The* General *is addressing them, but only a bellowing is audible. His hearers respond with various animal noises, barking, mewing, quacking, grunting, or squeaking, according to their characters. Gestures and cries become more incoherent, bestial and fantastic, until at last all are drowned in deafening military chords. The* JOURNALISTS *leave the stage through the auditorium, chatting.*]

CURTAIN

Epilogue

SEMI-CHORUS I. Love, loath to enter
    The suffering winter
    Still willing to rejoice
    With the unbroken voice
    At the precocious charm
    Blithe in the dream
    Afraid to wake, afraid
    To doubt one term
    Of summer's perfect fraud,
    Enter and suffer
    Within the quarrel
    Be most at home,
    Among the sterile prove
    Your vigours, love.

SEMI-CHORUS II. Mourn not for these; these are ghosts who chose their pain
    Mourn rather for yourselves; and your inability to make up your minds
    Whose hours of self-hatred and contempt were all your majesty and crisis,
    Choose therefore that you may recover: both your charity and your place
    Determining not this that we have lately witnessed: but another country
    Where grace may grow outward and be given praise
    Beauty and virtue be vivid there.

SEMI-CHORUS I. Where time flows on as chalk stream clear
    And lovers by themselves forgiven
    The whole dream genuine, the charm mature
    Walk in the great and general light
    In their delight a part of heaven
    Its furniture and choir.

CHORUS. To each his need: from each his power.

§5 Isherwood's Suggestions for a New Concluding Scene

During rehearsals the published version of the final scene proved difficult to stage. Various suggestions from Doone and others were tried out on stage, but neither Doone nor Auden was satisfied with the results. At some point Auden raised the problem with Isherwood, possibly when Isherwood was in London in early December 1935, possibly by letter sometime afterward. Isherwood responded, apparently in the second week of December, with the outline of an entirely rewritten scene, in which Francis, instead of exiting in triumph as in the published version, is killed by Mildred Luce. The authors seem to have agreed on this before Isherwood wrote, for the phrasing of his reference to Francis's speech suggests that Francis's exposure of Mildred Luce's delusion had been discussed already. (Conceivably Francis's exposure of Mildred Luce was a feature of the lost version of Francis's speech that Isherwood had written for the published text; see p. 565.) The decision to drop the Vicar's sermon was Auden's. When he was presented with the new version of the scene, Doone was surprised by the extent of the changes.

References in Isherwood's letter to "the original version" (with page numbers) apply to the Faber edition (F); page numbers from the present edition are added in square brackets. The letter is printed from Isherwood's carbon copy. Some words are lost because a corner of the carbon paper was folded over when Isherwood was typing; in most cases, however, there are sufficient traces of the missing words to allow these gaps to be filled, and reconstructions are provided within square brackets.

Dear Wystan,

I have now taken a look at Dogskin and can summarize the proposed revised version of the last scene as follows:

The Garden of the Vicarage at Pressan Ambo. The stage decorated, as for a wedding, with streamers, etc. Enter Alan, Francis and the Journalists. Dialogue as before till "Everything's different!" Then, instead of [the] Curate, villagers are seen approaching. Francis and Alan hide, the Journalists remain standing. The villagers come in and gossip in doggerel, as in first scene (maybe in some other verse-form: could you possibly manage limericks?) about the coming marriage. Or rather, no—I think they should at first speak in couplets and then, when the journalists approach and question them, in Limericks, naming each of the parties involved, as: "Sir Roderick Trunnion-James . . ." etc. This gossiping can be interrupted by asides from the hidden Francis and Alan. Then, I think, the Vicar comes in, very unctuous and full of fuss. He is looking for the Curate, who has not been showing sufficient interest in the proceedings. The journalists buttonhole him and are given press-cards for the wedding.

Then the curate enters and is told off by the vicar, as on page 161 [574]. They are interrupted by the entry of Mildred Luce, who makes a short but very beautiful speech in blank verse, on the theme: This wedding is accursed. Not that she minds, as far as Iris is concerned. In fact she is glad. Because her sons have been killed she doesn't care what happens to the world (cf. her speech in the original version, page 169 [579]). But it is dramatically necessary that this speech is introduced, I think, in order to remind the audience of the alleged killed sons myth, which is soon to be exploded. Now, finally, Iris enters, supported by the General and his wife and bridesmaids. The rest of the villagers begin to gather on the stage. The General says something hearty about marriage. Iris feels faint and is revived with brandy. The General then makes the speech printed on page 170 [579], modified to suit the new action, and is interrupted by Alan, as in the text. This leads to Francis' speech, with its reference to Mildred Luce. She kills him.

And what happens next?

Thinking it over, I think I should best like it if the marriage did after all take place. That is to say, the journalists immediately intervene and make speeches, similar to the ones in the book, saying that nothing has really happened. A dog has merely been killed. They themselves suggest the plan of buttoning Francis back into his skin and actually carry it out. Alan makes [an] appeal to Iris, who is very distressed, but is finally bundled off to the church. (Iris is not a bitch, but just silly and floppy.) Alan, in disgust, turns his back on the whole lot and goes out, through the audience. And then the vicar gives his address.

There are all sort of objections, I know. How can the vicar give his address on a lawn and not in the church. (We might, of course, introduce Sir [R.] Trunnion-James as a dummy, but we've done that once with Lou Vipond.) [Also], if Francis is killed and Alan doesn't get Iris, there is no victory of the angels. On the other hand, if Iris *does* go off with Alan, we lose the [   ]e effect which might have been made with the journalists' speech: the [effe]ct of the hideous social lie and the death of truth; because if Iris [does r]un away, then it would be impossible for the journalists to conceal the [fact] from the outside world. The idea of the Journalists *not* concealing the [fact,] indeed making a romantic scoop out of it, "Squire's Daughter elopes [with p]enniless childhood lover", would also be funny, of course, but funny [in a much] cheaper and less symbolic way. Another loose end is the curate. Does he go away with Alan at the end? I particularly want to omit my original idea of the appeal for volunteers, which now seems horribly quisb.* Finally, what about the Vicar's sermon from a dramatic point of view? I suppose it *will* be all right to end the play with it? You should ask Doone about this. I am a little afraid that the audience may lose patience, as by this time there is no more dramatic suspense. Of course, the sermon could be introduced earlier, I suppose.

Another thing: if Iris is going to Alan at the end, this means that, in the extremely crude character-values of the play, she is "all right." In that case, Francis must not display his opposition towards the proposed marriage with Alan, as he does throughout the play. For, if Iris is really "all right", then Francis' opposition is based, as Alan jokingly suggests, on mere jealousy, which makes him a definitely homosexual character and needlessly complicates our simple symbolic conception of him.

Could you consider these points and maybe, if you have a moment, rough out some bits of dialogue. There is very little to be done, really. Any news yet of a possible production date?

I wrote and told Lehmann to write to you and apply for film scraps for his book. I hope this was right?

A day or two ago, I wrote to you with a suggestion for a film. Unfortunately, I only addressed this letter to Highgate, instead of Highgate London. If it hasn't reached you by now, please let me know and I'll repeat what I said.

§6 The Production Version of the Concluding Scene

After Auden completed his manuscript version of the concluding scene, he and Doone (or possibly Doone alone) abridged it for production. The revised text of the play sent to the Lord Chamberlain's Office on 2 January 1936 (LC) included a typescript of this abridged version. The typescript was presumably made from a marked copy of a now lost typescript of Auden's manuscript version. The LC text preserves some of the idiosyncrasies of Auden's manuscript, but, since the manuscript is not marked with the changes made for LC, an intermediate stage presumably existed. While typing Francis's speech the typist (or the typist of an intermediate copy) had difficulty with some passages Auden had written between the lines in his manuscript, with the result that some sentences are wrongly arranged; the proper order has been restored in the text printed here. Other obvious typist's errors have been corrected, but changes in the abridged scene (such as some long cuts in Francis's speech) that may have been Auden's work have been

---

* In *Lions and Shadows* (1938) Isherwood explained that this was "a standard word in our [his and Edward Upward's] vocabulary, corresponding roughly to the terms 'shy-making,' and 'shaming' later employed by the Mayfair society world" (pp. 80-81).

retained. The text of the LC typescript appears below, followed by notes on further changes made during rehearsals.

[*Enter* ALAN, FRANCIS, *and* JOURNALISTS.]

ALAN [*looking round in amazement at the decorations*]. Whatever can have happened? I say, Francis, do you think they can have found out that we were coming?

FRANCIS. On the contrary: I should say that to-day of all others is the day on which they least expect to see us.

ALAN. I simply can't understand it. [*He looks offstage.*] Here comes the Curate—Let's see if he guesses who we are—

FRANCIS. Not yet. Better wait a bit. We'll hide behind here. You two can ask a few questions and find out what's happening. Come along, Alan.

[ALAN *and* FRANCIS *conceal themselves in shadow of proscenium arch. Enter the* CURATE.]

1ST JOURNALIST [*going up to him*]. Excuse me, sir. We're from the *Thunderbolt* and the *Evening Moon*. Perhaps you'd care to tell us something about your interesting celebrations?

CURATE. Certainly. Miss Iris Crewe is being married this afternoon to Mr Rudolph Trunnion-James. You know him, perhaps?

2ND J. You don't say!

1ST J. Not our little National Independent member for Lundy East? Well, well. Your girl friend's got her head screwed on. Boy, that kid will go a long, long way.

CURATE. If you'll excuse me—I should be at the church by now. Time's getting on. I'm sure the Vicar will be charmed to give you any further details you want—

[*Exit* CURATE. ALAN *and* FRANCIS *come out.*]

ALAN. I don't believe it. Iris wouldn't go and do a thing like that!

FRANCIS. I'm sorry Alan, about this.

1ST J. [*looking offstage*]. Here she comes.

2ND J. She doesn't look as if she was going to a school treat!

[*Enter* IRIS *in tears,* GENERAL, GENERAL'S WIFE *and* VICAR.]

GENERAL'S WIFE. Now dear, pull yourself together.

IRIS. I don't want to go. I wish I was dead.

GENERAL'S WIFE. You mustn't say such naughty things. It will soon be over. Ernest, give her a drop from your flask.

GENERAL. Can't understand it. All this fuss. Nerves, I suppose.
GENERAL'S WIFE. There, there. I understand exactly how you feel. I was just the same before I married the General. Here, use my hanky. And now just a spot of powder on the nose. You look lovely.
IRIS. Alan—why hasn't he come back?
GENERAL'S WIFE. Now dear, we don't want to go over all that again, do we? You know he won't come back. Besides, you agreed yourself that it would be much better if he didn't, and promised to forget him, didn't you? Rudolph's twice the man he is.
VICAR. Well, I must go to the vestry and robe.

[*Enter* MILDRED LUCE.]

MILDRED. Stop!
    O think one moment what you do
    Have you no eyes?
    Or have caresses so debauched your judgement
    That life seems splendid as a scivvie's dream?
    Are you so numbed or naughty that you dare think
    To order chaos with the common kiss? O look
    Show me one virtue that's not lethal, one vice
    That's not contagious as the itch. Look, look, look,
    Look at your slaves [*?error for* flowers]; the sweaty crowds
    That make the beaches stink in summer
    Or crawl out daily to their dingy labours.
    Look at your great men
    That before their mirrors falsify their faces.
    Will, will you marry and multiply for them [*?error for* these]?
    Blindly give girls and boys an introduction
    To madmen, foot-pads, murderers and whores.
    The forced commanders of this fraudulent star
    Deliberately create their rosy beauty
    And then watch sorrow like an awful cold
    Making it hideous. Because I knew
    My sons were lovely and they died of it
    O that the sun would splutter and go out
    And all bone crumbled in the universal frost
    Or that a reef would suddenly rise up
    Out of the cold and infinite abyss
    Our aimless cruising to arrest at last
    And our ship crammed with all its bestial cargo
    Plunge roaring into nothing.

VICAR. Mildred dear, go home and rest. [*To* IRIS.] My dear, I'm so sorry—
ALAN. Here, I say—
VICAR. I'm so sorry—
ALAN. Stop! You've got to listen to me.
GENERAL. Who the devil are you?
ALAN. Alan Norman, at your service. Iris, what does this mean?
IRIS. O Alan, you've come back.
ALAN. Yes. I've found Francis.
IRIS. Francis too.
ALAN. Come here, Francis.
VICAR AND GENERAL. Sir Francis, upon my soul!
IRIS. O dear I feel so ill!
FRANCIS. Hello, General. Fight back those unmanly tears. Vicar, you needn't kiss me if you don't want to. Well, isn't anybody pleased to see me?
GENERAL. And where do you come from?
FRANCIS. Look. [*Shows his skin.*]
ALL. What—the Dog! You were the dog!
FRANCIS. Yes I am, or rather was, the Dog and here you all are, looking extremely uncomfortable—as well you may, considering that you know I've had a dog's eye view of you for the last ten years.

    At first I only intended to keep my new shape for a week or two but after the first six months I didn't really want to come back. You see, I had begun to regard you in a new light. I was fascinated and horrified by you all. I thought such obscene, cruel, hypocritical, mean, vulgar creatures had never existed before in the history of the planet and that it was my peculiar duty to record what you were like. I began to keep a diary. As a dog I learnt for the first time with what a mixture of fear, bullying and condescending kindness you treat those you consider your inferiors, but whom you depend on for your pleasures. It's an awful shock to start seeing people from underneath.

    The diary became my greatest friend. I worked away at it like a scientist. And then slowly, the horror and pseudo-scientific interest began to wear off. I began to feel that I had been foolishly wasting my time. Wasn't it life itself I was afraid of, hiding in my dogskin? I think that soon I should have gone away anyhow. But as it happened, Alan Norman was chosen. I'd always liked him, and so I took the opportunity of leaving you when I did.

    And now since I've been away from you, I've come to understand you better. I don't hate you any more. You are significant but not in the way I used to imagine.

You are not the extraordinary monsters I thought. You are not individually important. You are just units in an immense army; and most of you would probably die without knowing either what your leaders are really fighting for or even that you are fighting at all. That is why I have come back. That ignorance at least I can do something to remove. I can't dictate to you what to do and I don't want to either. I can only try to show you what you are doing and so force you to choose. For choice is what you are all afraid of. Every technical invention, every advance of knowledge has slowly eaten away your old dependence on nature. The life of the peasant whose behaviour was largely regulated by the seasons and the soil is over for ever. You can grow wheat in winter and make the fields barren in June. Whether you visit New York next week or speak with a friend in Hammerfest before dinner is cooked depends now on nothing but your own wish. That is what terrifies you. Anything, you cry, anything for the old feeling of security and harmony; if nature won't give it, give us a dictator, an authority who will take the responsibility of thinking and planning off our shoulders. Well, it is too late. You were already separated from nature before civilisation began and you can no more retrace history than the perturbed adolescent can re-enter his mother's womb. If as a whole you are unpleasant, you are unpleasant like an invalid. You are fighting your own nature, which is to learn and to choose. Fear of growth is making you ill.

VICAR. Don't listen to him. He is trying to destroy religion. Satan will destroy us all.

FRANCIS. You, Vicar, for example, speaking Sunday after Sunday about the good life, telling us to love God and each other and all our troubles will be solved. Why is it you will not lift a finger to destroy a social system in which one man can only succeed at the expense of injury to another? Sorrows, poverty, temptations are sent to try us, you say. Perhaps. Is that any excuse for refusing to reduce them. To send a liner into an iceberg-infested sea, equipped with only one lifeboat, may afford a splendid test of self-sacrifice but we should accuse the owner of criminal negligence. Your preaching voice betrays you. You do not speak with the only authority there is, the authority of experience. Your faith in a loving God is not real to you, like your feeling that man is evil. Goodness and happiness are not real to you or you would know that when people are happy they are good, and that self-interest as a motive is the refuge of the miserable. They are not real to you as your sense of guilt is real. Only that is as real to you as the early gothic work in your church and this beautiful ivy-covered vicarage. Happiness is not real to you, only comforts. That is why you are afraid of losing them, for no one gives up what is real to them for what is not.

GENERAL. Insolent young puppy. He wants a good hiding. You've got to have law and order. It's common sense.

FRANCIS. And you, General, what are you fighting for? Once wealth was real. The world did not produce enough to go round and there was necessarily a struggle over the sharing of it. But now it is possible for everyone to have all they can require. What are you afraid of, then? This. You've lost belief in yourself. There will always be clever and stupid people, successes and failures in the world, you say. You can't change human nature. Men are not equal. Precisely. You are terrified that perhaps after all you are not a superior person. Take away the visible signs of superiority, take away Conyers Hall and the peacocks, or let everybody else have them, and is there anything about Mrs Hotham that will still command respect? Suppose no one was to call you Sir, would you still exist as a personality? That is the question you dare not answer.

MILDRED. Traitor! I hear the infamy before you say it. That Germans should be loved.

FRANCIS. Yes, Mrs Luce. That too. Your grievance is just, but it is neither what Pressan thinks it is nor what you dare not admit to yourself. When I stayed with you as a dog (and may I take this opportunity of thanking you. You were kinder and more understanding than any of the others), when I stayed with you, I thought the photographs on your bureau seemed vaguely familiar and one day when you were away, I took them to the photographer whose name was on them. He identified them at once as two young actors who had some success in juvenile leads about thirty years ago. Later I paid a visit to the village where you lived before you came to Pressan, and discovered something else. You lived at home helping your mother with the house. She was poor and could not afford a maid. Were you ever married, I asked. No, they said, but there was talk at one time of an engagement to a young German cavalry officer. But you hadn't the heart to leave your mother alone.

A doctor would say you hate the Germans because you dare not hate your mother and he would be mistaken. It is foolish and neurotic to hate anybody. What you really hate is a social system in which love is controlled by money. Won't you help us to destroy it?

GENERAL'S WIFE. Mildred dear, do you hear what he's saying? Answer him.

GENERAL. He's trampling the honour of your dead boys in the mud.
VICAR. He's insulting your mother. He should be stopped.
VOICES. Answer him! Make him ashamed of himself! Tell him he's a liar!
GENERAL'S WIFE. You know what people will say, don't you dear. As a matter of fact, I'd often wondered about those photographs myself. You poor thing.
MILDRED. You beast! [*She kills him; suddenly appalled.*] O Ticker, what have I done?
GENERAL [*taking command of the situation*]. Don't let the ladies see. [*To* VICAR.] Take Mrs. Luce home and get the doctor to her.

> [JOURNALISTS *to side of stage. The others exeunt leaving* ALAN *alone with* FRANCIS.]

ALAN. Francis, are you badly hurt?
FRANCIS. Alan, my friend
  My life is now at end
  Grieve not for me at all
  My life is nothing especial
  Only remember when I am gone
  All we have seen done
  All we have heard said
  Remember when I am dead
  The plain and the extraordinary
  On our devious journey
  Remember. No longer in ignorance
  Of its significance
  But through knowledge of each fact
  Able more clearly to act
  Man's history to fulfill
  And since it is impossible
  In Pressan to stay
  Slip quickly away
  Without their knowing
  That you are going
  And wherever circumstance
  In this England may permit you residence
  Long may you live
  Your powers to give
  In every English season
  For justice and for reason.
ALAN. Wait till the police come. I'll tell them everything.
FRANCIS. No, do as I say

   And go away
   For here is nothing you
   Can usefully do
   Go now and do not wait
   Go before it is too late. [*Dies.*]
ALAN. Francis! Francis!

BOTH WITNESSES. Love, loath to enter
   The suffering winter
   Still waiting to rejoice
   With the unbroken voice
   At the precocious charm
   Blithe in the dream
   Afraid to wake, afraid
   To doubt one term
   Of summer's perfect fraud,
   Enter and suffer
   Within the quarrel
   Be most at home,
   Among the sterile prove
   Your vigours, love.

WOMAN WITNESS. Mourn not for these; these are ghosts who chose their pain,
  Mourn rather for yourselves; and your inability to make up your minds
  Whose hours of self-hatred and contempt were all your majesty and crisis,
  Choose therefore that you may recover: both your charity and your place
  Determining not this that we have lately witnessed: but another country
  Where grace may grow outward and be given praise
  Beauty and virtue be vivid there.

BOTH WITNESSES. Where time flows on as chalk stream clear
   And lovers by themselves forgiven
   The whole dream genuine, the charm mature
   Walk in the great and general light
   In their delight a part of heaven
   Its furniture and choir.
   To each his need: from each his power.

VICAR. Dead? Poor poor Mildred. What will happen to her?

GENERAL. She'll have to be certified after this of course, you realise that?

VICAR. Dear O dear. In Pressan of all places. It's like a nightmare. It can't have happened.

JOURNALISTS [*coming forward; as they talk they sew* FRANCIS *up again into his dogskin*]. You're quite right, sir. It hasn't happened.

VICAR. Hasn't happened? But—

2ND J. I entirely agree with my colleague. Dozens of things happen every day, curious, embarrassing, shocking incidents: but how few of them happen! The Press disregards them: therefore they cannot have taken place! The Press is an Artist: It has a certain picture to paint. Whatever fails to harmonise with that picture, it discards; regretfully perhaps, but firmly.

1ST J. The Press has no use for the incident you believe yourselves to have just witnessed. It has no place in our scale of values. Long-lost Baronets do not disguise themselves as dogs; or at any rate, only for erotic reasons. The behaviour of Sir Francis Crewe falls into no artistic category which we recognize: therefore it cannot be represented in our picture of the day's events.

2ND J. And since all events are recorded by the Press, what the Press does not record cannot be an event.

1ST J. But you, Sir, and you, General, and you, Madam, you belong to our picture. If you'll be so kind . . . [*Begins to group them for a photograph.*]

VICAR [*looking at watch*]. Good gracious! We're ten minutes late for the wedding already. The bridegroom will be in a fever. [*To* CURATE.] Go and tell them to start ringing the bells.

[CURATE *goes.*]

1ST J. Just one moment please. We won't take a minute. [*To* IRIS.] A little brighter, please.

GENERAL'S WIFE. Smile, darling. Everything is going to be alright. You're among friends.

[*Business of photographs being taken, in the midst of which church bells peal out loudly, Wedding March, etc.*]

This version was further revised and abridged for performance. The GT promptbook includes a copy of the LC typescript (printed above) marked with extensive cuts and other minor changes evidently made in rehearsal to improve the pace of the action. Jean Scott Rogers recorded in her diary that the final revisions to the play, possibly including changes in this final scene, were not completed until 8 January 1936, four days before the opening. There is no reason to assume that Auden was the sole author of any of the revisions that appear in the GT promptbook's version of the final scene, and only two revisions involve substantial changes in the action.

First, near the opening of the scene, the Vicar does not enter with Iris, the General, and the General's wife, but a few lines later, after the speech of the General's wife beginning "Now dear, we don't want to go over all that again". The Vicar's opening speech reads: "Ah there you are, it's getting late. We mustn't keep everyone waiting." Mildred Luce then enters immediately, as in the LC text.

The other substantial change occurs immediately after Francis exposes Mildred's delusions at the end of his long prose speech. As the speech ends the General says to Mildred: "My poor good woman, do you hear what he's saying? Answer him"—and gives her a revolver. Members of the chorus say: "Shame. Do something about it. Shocking. Communists." Then Mildred shoots Francis, and the scene continues as in LC.

These changes, together with the other cuts marked in the GT promptbook, correspond to a partial typescript (not made by Auden) of the final scene, inserted in a copy of F that may have been used by a pianist or stage manager during the Group Theatre production (now in the possession of Alan Clodd). This copy has musical incipits loosely inserted and the names of actors taking unnamed minor parts inked in. The typescript consists of summaries of the opening and closing of the scene, together with texts of the longer speeches, which are cut in substantially the same way as the texts in GT, and slightly garbled.

The Ascent of F 6

§1 History, Authorship, Texts, and Editions

By the time *The Dog Beneath the Skin* was published in May 1935, Auden had decided that the subject of the next play he and Isherwood would write would be mountaineering. The tentative title was *The Summit*. On 16 March 1936 he arrived at Cintra, in Portugal, for a working visit with Isherwood. They first agreed on a scenario, then separated to write the scenes they had assigned themselves; they collaborated directly only on the concluding scene. Auden described their progress in an undated letter to Stephen Spender: "Thanks to the awful weather C and I are getting on quite well with *The Ascent* though in spite of every effort I'm afraid it will be even more like what you so neatly described as 'A bachelor's flat' than the last one, a cross between Peer Gynt and Journey's End" (letter in the Berg Collection).

During the course of Auden's visit the play's title seems to have been altered, first to *The Ascent* (the title Auden used in his undated letter to Spender), then to *The Ascent of F 6*. Auden and Isherwood finished a rough draft by the end of March. On 17 April 1936 Auden left Cintra with the completed play (typed by Isherwood), and then had it retyped by a professional agency in London. (The title page of this second typescript—all that survives—bears the agency's date-stamp of 28 April 1936.)

Auden brought Isherwood's typescript to Rupert Doone (for the Group Theatre) and gave a copy of the agency typescript to Faber & Faber. Isherwood, still in Portugal, read the galley proofs of the Faber edition in June, and Auden, now on a journey to Iceland, read the page proofs before the middle of July. Neither author made any significant changes. But by the end of July, Auden's agent told his American publisher, Random House, which had not yet received the text, that although the play was in proof, it was being extensively revised. No news of any intended change seems to have reached Faber, whose edition was ready when Auden returned from Iceland in the middle of September. It was published on 24 September 1936 (see §2 below).

On 6 October Auden wrote Bennett Cerf at Random House: "Isherwood and I are now altering it quite considerably. Faber published it early against our will and I shall be very glad if the American edition were to be the definitive one." Around the end of October he wrote Cerf again: "You should get the final ms of F_6 in December" (letters in Columbia University Library). Toward the end of November Auden sent the newly revised sections of the play to Rupert Doone. About the same time, he sent a slightly further revised text to Random House, where it was received by 10 December 1936 and published on 8 March 1937. He also sent the revised sections to Faber & Faber, where they were received by 1 December 1936 and published, after still further revision, in a second edition in March 1937 (see §4 below). A 1958 British paperback edition reprinted without change the text of the second Faber edition, and a 1958 American paperback reprinted without change the text of the Random House edition.*

In January 1937 Auden left England for a journey to Spain, where he hoped to serve the Republic as a non-combatant in the Civil War. (After being refused permission to drive an ambulance he was briefly put to work broadcasting propaganda; he then spent some time traveling near the front.) In February Isherwood came to England to assist in the Group Theatre production of the play. Doone and Isherwood made extensive minor changes during rehearsals, and even after the play opened at the Mercury Theatre, on 26 February, they continued to rework the ending. Auden first saw the play on stage when he returned from Spain on 4 March. About a week later, on holiday in the Lake District, the authors completed yet another revised ending. This may have been incorporated into the Mercury production, and was almost certainly used when, after fifty performances at the Mercury, the production moved (on 22 April) to the Arts Theatre, Cambridge, for four performances and when it returned to London (on 30 April) for a run at the Little Theatre. (For the changes made for the production, see §5 below.)

The production was "presented by Ashley Dukes in association with the Group Theatre", and directed by Doone. The design was by Robert Medley, the music by Benjamin Britten—except for the Hidden Chorus in II.5, which Britten marked in the score to be sung to Bach's *St Matthew Passion*, no. 16 (the chorale "Wer hat dich so geschlagen"). The score is in the Britten-Pears Library at Aldeburgh.

In 1939, after Auden and Isherwood had left for America, they wrote yet another ending for the play—perhaps two. A production in a New York studio by the Drove Players, directed by Forrest Thayr, Jr., on 21-23 April 1939, used a rewritten final scene, presumably the same one intended for a production that Burgess Meredith hoped to mount at a summer theatre in Pennsylvania at the end of August 1939. A different version of the final scene, and one more like the published endings of 1937 (although it included some new material), was used in a revival of the Group Theatre production at the Old Vic, which opened 27 June 1939. The surviving text of this version reflects extensive changes made in rehearsal, in the authors' absence; it may have been cobbled together by Doone

---

* Auden printed the following fragments of the play separately; for the collected and selected editions identified by their italicized dates, see p. 524.

"Death like his is right and splendid": *1938*.

"Some have tennis-elbow": the text in the play is a fragment of a longer song published as "Foxtrot from a Play", *New Verse*, April-May 1936.

"Stop all the clocks, cut off the telephone": reprinted in a revised version in the English Association's anthology *Poems of To-day*, Third Series (1938) (as "Blues"); in Auden's *Another Time* (1940) ("Funeral Blues"); and, untitled, in *1945, 1950, 1966*.

"At last the secret is out, as it always must come in the end": *1945, 1950, 1966*.

Auden gave the song "The chimney sweepers" to R. D. Smith as a contribution to an undergraduate revue at Birmingham University in the spring of 1936; but the revue, when performed, did not use it. The chorus in the concluding scene, "Acts of injustice done", is an adaptation of the concluding chorus written for the film *Negroes* (p. 428).

from the new version produced in America and from the earlier published texts (see §6 below).

Auden wrote yet another ending for a production at Swarthmore College, which opened 19 April 1945, in which he played the silent role of the cowled monk in II.1 (see §7 below).

Isherwood's diary entry for 17 April 1936 (quoted in *Christopher and His Kind*) records the details of the collaboration:

> Our respective work on this play was fairly sharply defined. Wystan did act one, scene one; the dialogue between Ransom and his Mother in act one, scene three; the dialogue between Ransom and the Abbot in act two, scene one; Ransom's monologue in act two, scene two; the whole of act two, scene four; all songs and choruses, the speeches by the A's, and all other speeches between the scenes. We interfered very little with each other's work. The only scene on which we really collaborated was the last. It was understood, throughout, that Wystan's speciality was to be the "woozy" and mine the "straight" bits.

Isherwood noted in *Christopher and His Kind*: " 'Woozy,' in their private jargon, meant grandiloquent, lacking in substance, obscure for obscurity's sake. It described the style of the kind of verse-plays they despised." Auden also wrote all the speeches delivered from the stage-boxes, the woozy soliloquies for Ransom in II.1 (in verse in the first Faber edition, in prose in the Random House and second Faber editions), Ransom's monologue to the skull in II.2, his final speech in that scene, and all of II.4. Auden almost certainly wrote the prose soliloquy for Mrs Ransom at the end of Act I in the Random House and second Faber editions.

The text of the present edition reproduces that of the second Faber edition (1937), with minor emendations (mostly from Isherwood's original typescript). The second Faber text represents apparently the last full reworking of the play by both authors. Later revised endings (mostly lost) were drastically cut versions appended to the unaltered text of the rest of the play; and the surviving revisions to the preceding scenes were made mostly in Auden's absence by Isherwood, or by Doone with Isherwood's consent (see §5). The following sources have been used:

    TS The original typescript prepared in April 1936 by Isherwood, with corrections in his hand; given by Auden to Rupert Doone, and now in the Group Theatre papers in the Berg Collection. Some pages are trimmed to remove abandoned material. The text of this typescript is substantially the same as that of the first Faber edition, although the Faber text reduces some capitalization and other idiosyncrasies (restored in the present edition). The type for the Faber edition was probably set from a typescript (lost except for the title page) that Auden had a typing agency prepare from Isherwood's original. This agency typescript was completed on 28 April 1936.

FA   The first Faber edition, published 24 September 1936.

LC   The copy of the play submitted 29 January 1937 to the Lord Chamberlain's Office (licenced 3 February); now in the British Library. This consists of a copy of FA partly pasted over with typescript pages, evidently typed by Isherwood and with corrections in various hands, containing the revised sections of the play. Auden sent these typescript pages to Doone toward the end of November 1936. The pasted-in pages provide a new conclusion to I.3 and new texts of large parts of II.1 and II.5; they do not include those portions of the revised scenes in which the original FA text is unaltered.

TSB   A carbon-copy typescript (with a small change in Auden's hand) of the revised sections of the play, consisting of the new conclusion to I.3 and the full texts of the revised II.1 and II.5, now in the Berg Collection. The text was probably prepared from the LC typescript, but evidently reflects further revisions by Auden. The typescript includes pencilled page-number markings that suggest it was used in setting up the revised portions of the second Faber edition (FB—see below). Except for the one change in Auden's hand, the text of the typescript corresponds to the text of RH. (The change in Auden's hand was incorporated into FB along with other small changes not reflected in TSB.) This typescript is accompanied by a carbon copy of the title page of the lost agency copy of TS (with its 28 April 1936 date-stamp), but it was typed six months afterward. More detailed notes on LC and TSB are provided in §3 below.

RH   The Random House edition, published 8 March 1937. Probably set from a copy of FA supplemented by a copy of the TSB typescript in which Auden had not yet made the change he made in the copy he gave to Faber for FB.

FB   The second Faber edition, published March 1937, with revisions corresponding to those in TSB but with some further revisions made (or marked) by Isherwood. (This edition, unlike LC and RH, omits the prose epilogue set in a broadcasting studio.)

GT   The promptbook used for the revival of the Group Theatre production at the Old Vic, which opened 27 June 1939, now in the Berg Collection. This consists of pages removed from a copy of FB (using the third printing of the second edition, January 1939) marked with revisions (neither in Auden's nor Isherwood's hand), and a typescript version of II.5. This typescript has the same text as another typescript submitted to the Lord Chamberlain's Office (bearing the date 22 June 1939), now in the British Library. Robert Medley later noted that this 1939 promptbook included interpolations from earlier productions; these revisions probably reflect those made by Doone and Isherwood early in 1937.

The notebook in which Auden wrote out rough drafts of much of his share of the play is now in the Berg Collection. Other manuscript sources are noted below.

One small but persistent problem in the text of this play is the typographical style of the name of the mountain in its title. The name alludes to the Himalayan peak whose name, in the 1920s and 1930s, was variously printed K_2, K.2, and K2. Auden referred to the fictional mountain as F_6 when he wrote the title by hand, as F6 when he typed it. (When his mother served as his secretary while he was away in Iceland she wrote F^6.) Isherwood used F.6 or F.6., and F.6 was also the form normally used by the Group Theatre. The skilled and scholarly printers R. MacLehose & Company of Glasgow, who set the text for Faber & Faber, used F 6, with a space between the letter and numeral; Random House followed their example in the American edition. (But Faber's binder used F..6, with two closely spaced dots, on the spine of the British editions.) The program of the 1945 Swarthmore production used F-6. Because the two authors did not bother to agree on a style, I have followed the style adopted by the printers, a style that both authors seem to have been willing to accept when they read galley and page proofs.

§2 The First English Edition

This first published text (FA) was apparently set from an agency typescript prepared from Isherwood's original typescript now in the Berg Collection (TS). The agency typist, or the printer, reduced some of Auden's and Isherwood's capitalization; the original readings, and some other details of typography and layout, are silently restored in the present edition.

Isherwood read the galley proofs of FA in Portugal in early June 1936, and requested only one minor change (from a period to a comma). Auden's mother read one set of page proofs late in June, and made further minor corrections; she sent another set of page proofs to Auden in Iceland. On 16 July she reported to Faber that Auden had read the proofs and approved her corrections. (These letters are in Faber's files.) Yet on 31 July Auden's agent, Spencer Curtis Brown, informed the American publisher, Random House: "Faber have just got *The Ascent of F.6* in proof but as the authors are making extensive revisions I think it will be best to wait until these are made before sending you copy, as the present proofs could not be used for final setting" (letter in the Random House archive at the Columbia University Library). In fact no such revisions were made, and there is no record in Faber's files that Auden or Isherwood had indicated their wish to make any changes. (Possibly Isherwood had communicated separately with Curtis Brown.) Auden nonetheless described the Faber edition, which appeared on 24 September 1936, as having been "published early against our will," and it was extensively revised for the second edition.

The text of the first edition (FA) may be reconstructed by comparing the notes that follow with the main text of the present edition (which reprints FB, the second Faber edition). Two scenes from FA were extensively rewritten for FB, and two others slightly expanded. The original FA versions of the two rewritten scenes are printed below, together with notes on lesser differences between the two editions. One further difference, not noted below, is the correction of "arrête" in FA (and RH) to "arête" in FB; I have incorporated the correction in passages reprinted below from FA.

Act I

The FA text of Act I is identical to that in FB, with one minor and one major exception. On p. 301, in Stagmantle's speech beginning "The truth, Lady Isabel," England has "ten millions" invested in Sudoland in FA, rather than the "fifty millions" of FB. And on p. 318, Act I ends in FA with the exit of Mr and Mrs A.; the stage direction following their exit and the soliloquy and song for Mrs Ransom were added in later texts.

Act II, Scene 1

This scene was substantially revised for all later texts. The original version from FA is printed below. The dialogue for Mr and Mrs A. that follows the scene on F 6 (pp. 331-32) is identical in FA and FB, and is not reprinted here.

Act II Scene 1

[F 6. *Room in a Monastery on the Great Glacier. A high, gloomy, vaulted chamber, with doors L. into the courtyard, R. into the interior of the building. In the back wall, arches open into a cloister, beyond which the greenish, faintly glowing ice of the glacier is visible.*]

> [MICHAEL RANSOM *and* SHAWCROSS *are seated at a table in the foreground, on which stand three silver candlesticks with church candles of coloured wax.* RANSOM *and* SHAWCROSS *both have notebooks and pencils; they are checking stores.*]

RANSOM. How many tins of malted milk?
SHAWCROSS. Fifty.
RANSOM. How are we off for dried fruit?
SHAWCROSS. Two boxes of figs, three of dates, five of apricots.
RANSOM. We must remember to ask the monks about yak butter. ... How about the petrol for the primus?
SHAWCROSS. God, that reminds me! [*He jumps up and goes to the door, left. Looking out into the courtyard.*] The porters haven't finished unloading it yet! [*Shouting.*] Hi! Sing ko, pan no ah! Teng fang! Naga! Naga! [*Returning to the table.*] Lazy devils! And it'll be dark in a few minutes. ... That's what comes of leaving things to Gunn. He treats this whole business like a picnic. [*He glances quickly at* RANSOM, *who does not, however, respond.*]
RANSOM. Have we got enough soup cubes?
SHAWCROSS. Three large packets. [*Hesitates.*] Look here, M.F., I've been wanting to talk to you about Gunn for a long time now. ... You

know, I hate to bother you with this sort of thing. . . . I've tried to keep you from noticing—

RANSOM [*smiling*]. I'm afraid you haven't succeeded very well.

SHAWCROSS [*eagerly*]. You mean, you *did* see something? Well, in a way, I'm glad. Because if you hadn't, you mightn't believe me—

RANSOM. I saw that Gunn teased the yaks and scared the porters by jumping out from behind rocks, pretending to be a leopard. I noticed the tricks he's played on Tom and on Teddy—and on you, too, Ian. I agree that he's an intolerable nuisance and I think that without him this expedition would be much more businesslike and very gloomy indeed.

SHAWCROSS [*exasperated*]. The thing I admire most about you, M.F., is your wonderful broadmindedness. It's an example to me: I'm not very tolerant, I'm afraid. If Gunn amuses you and the others, I'm glad. I hope I can see a joke as well as anyone. . . . But that wasn't what I meant, just now. This is something quite different. I hardly like to tell you—

RANSOM. If you hadn't meant to tell me, Ian, you wouldn't have started this conversation at all.

SHAWCROSS [*blurting it out*]. Well then—Gunn steals!

RANSOM [*laughing*]. Oh, that!

SHAWCROSS. So you *did* know!

RANSOM. Of course. He's always done it, ever since I've known him. I'm surprised that you've only just noticed it. He steals like a magpie: bits of indiarubber, chiefly, but also pencils, watches, and occasionally money. . . . That reminds me, I expect he's got my camera. I was imagining I'd lost it down in the gorge while we were fording the river.

SHAWCROSS. But, M.F., you can't tolerate this kind of thing! What are you going to do?

RANSOM. Ask him if he's got it, of course. He always returns things if you ask him straight out.

SHAWCROSS. But surely there's more to it than that? How can you take a man with you who simply doesn't play the game? One has to have some standards of decency, I suppose.

RANSOM [*smiling*]. You haven't changed much, have you, Ian, since you were Head Prefect and Captain of the First Fifteen?

SHAWCROSS [*bitterly*]. You're always laughing at me. I suppose you think I'm just a priggish fool?

RANSOM. I certainly don't think you're a fool. You know perfectly well that I don't. You know that I rely on your help, more than anybody's, to make this expedition a success. You organise everything, look after everything, think of everything. You are one of the bravest and most efficient people I have met in my whole life. . . . Do you want me to say any more?

SHAWCROSS. Thank you, M.F. . . . You make me feel ashamed. As long as you trust me, then I don't give a damn what anybody else thinks or says. You know I'd follow you anywhere. We all would. . . . The wonderful thing about a man like you is that you can use all kinds of people and get the best out of each. I think I understand better, now, what it is that you get out of Gunn. I don't want to run him down— just because his kind of humour's a bit too subtle for me. [*With increasing bitterness.*] He's not a bad sort in his way; he's all right to have about the place, I suppose, as long as there's no special difficulty or danger. He's a damn good climber, too, I admit—only he simply hasn't got the temperament. I'm wondering what he'll be like up there, on the north face. You remember how he screamed, that day, in the Coolins, and wouldn't budge for an hour? It was pitiful.

RANSOM. David's always frightened when he climbs. Otherwise, he wouldn't climb. Being frightened is his chief pleasure in life. He's frightened when he drives a racing-car or seduces somebody's wife. At present he prefers mountaineering because it frightens him most of all.

SHAWCROSS. How well you understand him, M.F.! Now, that's just the point I wanted to make: wouldn't it be better, when we get to Camp B, to leave Gunn behind?

RANSOM [*smiling*]. To damage all the instruments and eat up all the stores?

SHAWCROSS. Well, but, I mean, he'll have to be dropped somewhere, won't he? [*A pause.*] Do you really think it's wise to take him as far as Camp A?

RANSOM. I shall decide when the time comes.

SHAWCROSS. I mean, of course, it's quite settled, isn't it, that only two of us shall try to reach the summit?

RANSOM. Yes. There'll be only two of us.

SHAWCROSS. And you can't, for a moment, be thinking of taking Gunn? [*Pause.*] My God, it'd be madness! M.F.—you couldn't!

RANSOM. Have I said I shall? I tell you, Ian, I have decided nothing yet. We can't discuss this, now.

SHAWCROSS [*with growing excitement*]. If I thought such a thing was possible—I'd—I don't know what I'd do! Gunn, that miserable little rotter! Why, he's not a climber at all! He's just a neurotic! He poses. He does everything for effect. Just a beastly little posing coward!

[RANSOM *is silent.*]

Oh, I know you think I'm simply jealous!

[*Enter* LAMP *and the* DOCTOR, *left.*]

LAMP [*excitedly*]. The flora here is amazing, simply amazing! I've had one of the most wonderful afternoons of my life! I tell you what, Doctor— [*Seeing the others.*] Oh, here you are, M.F.! Didn't see you in the dark.

SHAWCROSS. Half a minute. [*Lights the candles.*]

LAMP. I was just telling the Doctor, I've had a field-day! Extraordinarily interesting! M.F., I'm convinced that Hawkins is wrong when he denies the possibility of a five-leaved Polus Naufrangia! And what's more, I don't mind betting you I shall find one here, on F 6!

RANSOM. Let's see what you got this afternoon.

LAMP [*opening his vasculum*]. Here's Stagnium Menengitis and Frustrax Abominum.... Isn't it a beauty! And look here, here's something to surprise you: you told me there wasn't a Rossus Monstrens with blue petals! Well, what do you say to this?

RANSOM [*examining flower*]. By Jove, that's interesting!

[*Enter* GUNN, *left.*]

GUNN. Ah, here you all are! Thank goodness! I've been hunting for you everywhere! I began to think something had happened to you.... [*He sits down and mops his forehead.*]

DOCTOR. What's the matter with you, David? You look rattled.

GUNN. You'd be rattled if you'd been hanging round this place all the afternoon. Ugh, it gives me the creeps!

DOCTOR. Why, what's wrong with it?

GUNN. It's those beastly monks.... Don't they make you feel damned queer, with those cowls over their faces? I've been watching them for hours, out there: they never seem to speak or make any signs; they just stand facing each other, like this—and yet you have a nasty sort of feeling that they're talking, somehow.... I shouldn't wonder if they do it by telepathy or something.

DOCTOR. They seemed quite friendly and harmless when we arrived.

GUNN. Don't you believe it.... They're plotting to do us in while we're asleep, I bet you they are.... This afternoon, when I was sitting watching the porters unload, I kept imagining there was somebody standing just behind me. Several times, I turned round quickly to try and catch him, but there was nothing there.... And then I saw a monk and I thought I'd ask him which room we could use for the stores. So I went over to him and made signs and he seemed to understand all right. He turned round and went to one of the doors and opened it and went inside. Naturally, I followed him. But when I got into the room, there was nobody there. And there wasn't even a window he could have got out of.... No, I don't like this place!

DOCTOR. I tell you what, David, you've had a touch of the sun. I'll give you something to make you sleep well to-night.

RANSOM. Oh, by the way, David, where's my camera? You've got it, haven't you?

GUNN [*with a charming smile*]. Yes, it's in my room. I thought I'd look after it for you for a bit.

SHAWCROSS. Well, of all the blasted—

RANSOM [*smiling*]. That was very kind of you. But I can look after it quite nicely by myself. Would you bring it here now, please?

GUNN. Very well—if you'd rather—

> [*As he moves towards the door, L., a low chanting begins from the courtyard outside. This chant continues throughout the following scene. The words are:*]
>
> Go Ga, morum tonga tara
> Mi no tang hum valka vara
> So so so kum mooni lara
>
> Korkra ha Chormopuloda
> Antifora lampasoda
> Kang ku gar, bari baroda
>
> Ming ting ishta sokloskya
> No rum ga ga no rum gaya
> Nong Chormopuloda sya.

GUNN. My God, what's that! [*He retreats hastily behind* RANSOM's *chair*.]

SHAWCROSS [*going to the door, L., and looking out*]. They're all gathered out there in the courtyard. Looks as if they're going to start a procession. [*Closes door and comes back to the table. The chanting gets louder.*]

GUNN. Lock that door, for Heaven's sake! Suppose they come in here!

SHAWCROSS. Do you ever think of anything except your own beastly little skin?

> [*As the chanting increases, a procession of* MONKS *begins to pass along the cloister at the back of the stage. Some are hooded so that their faces are invisible, others wear devil-masks. They carry candles, jars, dishes containing relics and sacred objects. In the middle of the procession comes a coffin supported by four*

       bearers. *The procession crosses the stage, behind the arches, from L. to R.*]

GUNN. A coffin! Gosh, did you see?
DOCTOR. Cheer up, David; there's only one! Perhaps they won't choose you.
LAMP. What do you make of it, M.F.?
RANSOM. These must be the rites for the propitiation of the spirits which guard the house of the dead.

       [*By this time, the procession has passed and the chanting dies away.*]

GUNN. Phew! I hope they don't do that again! This place is about as cheerful as Woking Cemetery! [*He crosses the stage to the arches and looks out through them along the cloister, first to the R., then L.*] All gone now, thank goodness!

       [*As he speaks, the door on the R. opens noiselessly and a cowled* MONK *enters, carrying in his hands a crystal which glows faintly with a bluish light.*]

You chaps didn't really think I was scared, did you? Of course, I was only ragging. It takes more than that to frighten *me*! [*He turns and suddenly sees the* MONK. *Screams.*] Oh, God!

       [*As the* MONK *advances towards the front of the stage,* GUNN *retreats backwards before him.*]

What does he want? Do something, somebody! M.F., you speak to him!
RANSOM. Om no hum, no na num se?

       [MONK *is silent.*]

No num seng ka, ka no ah?

       [MONK *is silent.*]

King t'sang po, gang se gang?

       [MONK *is silent.*]

No good, I'm afraid. I've tried him in all three dialects. Perhaps he isn't allowed to answer.
DOCTOR. Funny kind of a lamp he's got there. [*Approaches.*]
GUNN. I say, do be careful! He may have a knife up his sleeve!

DOCTOR. Extraordinary thing, it doesn't seem to be a lamp at all! It just shines. [*Bending over the crystal.*] Why it's a kind of mirror—I can see myself in it! Am I really as fat as that? Gracious, I'm quite bald! Hullo, what's this? I'm sitting in an armchair. I seem to know that room. Yes, it's the Reform Club! I say, I think I must have got a touch of the sun, like David! Am I just seeing things? Here, Teddy, you come and look!

LAMP [*looking*]. Polus Naufrangia! As plain as anything: all five leaves. By Jove, what a beauty! [*Rubbing his eyes.*] I must be going mad!

GUNN. He's hypnotising you, that's what it is! When we're all in a trance we shall probably be murdered. . . . I say, I must have a look. [*Goes to crystal.*]

LAMP [*excitedly*]. I saw it as plain as that candle! Five distinct leaves!

GUNN [*looking*]. Why, there's my old Alfa Romeo! And someone's sitting in it—it's a woman, dressed all in black! She seems to be at a crossroads. I see the sign-post, but I can't read what's written on it. . . . Now she's turning her head. My God, it's Toni, Mrs da Silva! [*Coming away.*] Do you think that means her husband's died and now she'll follow me out here? . . . Come on, Ian: your turn!

SHAWCROSS [*takes a pace towards the crystal, stops, bursts out violently*]. I'm not going to have anything to do with this damned business! You others please yourselves. It isn't right. We aren't meant to know these things. It's probably some kind of trick, anyhow. . . . M.F., I'm going to get the wireless ready. It's nearly time to pick up the weather report from Fort George. [*Takes up one of the candles and exit, L.*]

GUNN. You'll have a look, won't you, M.F.?

RANSOM [*after a moment's hesitation*]. Very well. [*Stares into crystal.*]

DOCTOR. Well, what is it this time? Motors or flowers or London clubs?

GUNN. Try and see something useful. Ask it to tell you the best route up F 6.

RANSOM [*after a long pause*]. I can see nothing.

GUNN. Nothing at all! Oh, M.F.!

DOCTOR. That all goes to support the hypnotism theory. M.F. was a bit too strong for him. [*The* MONK *turns silently and goes out by the door, R.*]

GUNN. Ought we to have tipped him, or anything? Gosh, you know, that crystal has given me quite a headache! . . . I can't understand your not seeing anything, M.F. Or was it so awful that you won't tell us?

DOCTOR. I feel I could do with a change of air. Let's go and see if Ian's got Fort George.

GUNN. Right you are. Coming, M.F.?

RANSOM. No, I shall stay here. The Abbot may wish to speak to me.

[GUNN, DOCTOR, *and* LAMP *go out, L.*]

> Bring back the crystal, let me look again
> And prove the former vision a poor fake:
> The small gesticulating figure on the dais
> Above the swooning faces of the crowd
> And the torrential gestures of assent—
> Was it myself? Was it for me the band
> Far down the road distended their old cheeks?
> The special engine barnacled with flowers,
> The clashing salutations from the steeple?
> I thought so once, but that was years ago:
> The child in the shadow of enormous elders,
> Oiling his bicycle, might have such dreams:
> I cannot now. I could not tell them that—

[*Enter the* ABBOT *and* TWO ACOLYTES, *R.*]

ABBOT [*making a sign of benediction*]. Only God is great.

RANSOM [*kneeling and kissing his hand*]. But His power is for mercy.

ABBOT. I hope everything has been arranged here to your satisfaction?

RANSOM. It is perfect.

ABBOT. I am glad. In these mountains, I fear we can offer but poor hospitality. Please be seated, Mr Ransom. [*As they sit, he signs to the* ACOLYTES *to withdraw.*] Now, tell me, you wish to start soon on your ascension of our mountain?

RANSOM. To-morrow, if He permit it, Whose will must be done.

ABBOT. You know the legend?

RANSOM. I have read the Book of the Dead.

ABBOT. Such interest, Mr Ransom, is uncommon in one of your race. In that case, you will have comprehended the meaning of the ceremony that was performed this evening out in the courtyard: the office for the souls of the dead and the placation of the Demon. I am afraid that you, with your western civilisation, must consider us here excessively superstitious. . . . No, you need not contradict me out of politeness. I understand. You see the painted mask and the horns and the eyes of fire and you think: "This Demon is only a bogey that nurses use to frighten their children; I have outgrown such nonsense, it is fit only for ignorant monks and peasants. With our factory chimneys and our furnaces and our locomotives we have banished these fairy-tales. I shall climb the mountain and I shall see nothing." But you would be wrong.

The peasants, as you surmise rightly, are simple and uneducated; so their vision is simple and uneducated. They see the truth as a crude and coloured picture. Perhaps, for that reason, they see it more clearly than you or I. For it is a picture of truth. The Demon is real. Only his ministry and his visitation are unique for every nature. To the complicated and sensitive like yourself, Mr Ransom, his disguises are more subtle. He is—what shall I say?—the formless terror in the dream, the stooping shadow that withdraws itself as you wake in the half-dawn. You have heard his gnashing accusations in the high fever at a very great distance. You have felt his presence in the sinister contours of a valley or the sudden hostility of a copse or the choking apprehension that fills you unaccountably in the middle of the most intimate dinner-party. I did you an injustice just now when I said that you expected to see nothing on the mountain. You do expect to see something. That is why you are determined to climb it. You wish to confront the Demon face to face and conquer him. You wish to be perfect. But it is not possible for man in this life to reach perfection and I warn you: no man can see the Demon and live. I have read in your sacred books the story of Lucifer who wished to be God. Mr Ransom, beware of spiritual pride. It is not for us to put an end to the Demon and the desire to do so is, to brave and good men like yourself, the Demon's most powerful and insidious temptation. If there were no Demon, there would be no temptation. But the Demon is not the temptation. The temptation is always visible and may be fought. But the Demon is invisible and to challenge him to appear is death. I think that I understand your temptation, Mr Ransom. You would like to be great among men, to have power. Am I right?

RANSOM. So you know of my vision in the crystal—?

ABBOT. Ah, you saw it there, too? That is not strange. For all men see reflected there some fragment of their nature and glimpse a knowledge of those forces by whose free operation the future is forecast and limited. That is not supernatural. Nothing is revealed but what we have hidden from ourselves; the treasure we have buried and accursed. Your temptation, Mr Ransom, is written in your face. You know your powers and your intelligence. You could ask the world to follow you and it would serve you with blind obedience; for most men long to be delivered from the terror of thinking and feeling for themselves. And yours is the nature to which those are always attracted in whom the desire for devotion and self-immolation is strongest. And you would do them much good. But you know, as your great historian Lord Acton has put it, that "power corrupts;

absolute power corrupts absolutely; all great men are bad". You recognize that. If you climb the mountain and confront the Demon, you think that the temptation will be no more; but if you succeed in climbing the mountain you will be a great national hero. The temptation will no longer be there—because you will have succumbed to it.

Mr Ransom, I have a proposal to make to you. There are two lives: the life of action and glory and the life of contemplation and knowledge, such as we live here. Action and glory cannot kill the Demon: they only stifle our fear of him for a moment. Knowledge and contemplation cannot kill him, either; but they can confine him to the desert recesses of the mountain. They can, in some measure, control him, so that he does not lay waste the meadows and terrify the simple inhabitants of the valleys. A community such as this is like a frontier outpost: it needs brave men. Mr Ransom, I offer you a place in our monastery. Do not answer at once, but think it over. I must leave you now. You can give me your answer in the morning. Good night, Mr Ransom.

[RANSOM *bows deeply. Exit* ABBOT, *R.*]

RANSOM. Is it too late? Pretence? It is too late for that;
    I recognize my purpose.
    There was a moment in the Lakeland inn;
    There was a choice then and I made it wrong;
    And if I choose now, I must choose alone—
    Not for my friends: I cannot turn them back.
    O you, who are the history and the creator
    Of all those forms in which we are condemned to suffer;
    To whom the intelligent and necessary is also the just;
    Show me my path, show all of us, that each upon
    This mortal star may feel himself the danger
    That under his hand is softly palpitating.
    Quieten that hand, interpret fully the commands
    Of the four centres and the four conflicting winds.
    Those torn between the charities O reconcile.
    And to the human vision lead of one great meaning,
    Linking the living and the dead, within the shadow
    Of which uplifting, loving and constraining power
    All other reasons do rejoice and operate.

[*Enter* GUNN, *L. He looks cautiously round the room.*]

GUNN. Has the old boy gone? Good. I was afraid I might be butting in; but Ian and the others threw me out. And I didn't much like the idea of sitting by myself in the dark, with all those monks around. [*Pause.*] Are you busy, M.F.? Would you rather I didn't talk?

RANSOM. No, David. I'd like very much to talk. . . . Had the wireless got started when you left?

GUNN. Oh, yes. It's coming through beautifully. But I only heard the weather report.

RANSOM. How was it?

GUNN. First-class. We'll be able to start to-morrow, for a cert.

RANSOM. You sound pleased.

GUNN. Of course I'm pleased! Who wouldn't be—after all these weeks of messing about? To-morrow we shall be on the ice!

RANSOM. Now I come to think of it, I remember that I never even asked you if you wanted to join this expedition. I asked all the others. I suppose I took you for granted.

GUNN. I should hope you did! I should like to see anybody trying to get up F6 and me not be there!

RANSOM. But supposing, at the same time, somebody else had asked you to climb another mountain, twice as high as F6 and twice as difficult? Then you'd have gone with him, instead?

GUNN. Of course not! Oh, well, perhaps—I don't know. . . . What's the matter with you to-night, M.F.? Why do you ask me that? If you think I'm not really keen, just because I fool about—

RANSOM. No, David. I'm just asking you a simple question: supposing I wasn't here—would you still be ready to go on?

GUNN. Oh, well—now we'd got as far as this, I suppose we'd try and make a job of it. But I know one thing damn well: we certainly shouldn't get to the top.

RANSOM. Why not?

GUNN. Can you see us! There'd be murder done before we reached Camp B even. You know how I get on Ian's nerves!

RANSOM. You don't exactly try not to.

GUNN. Some of the time, I do. And then I forget, or I just don't care. I can't help it. I'm like that, I suppose. The funny thing is, I like old Ian. If I didn't, I shouldn't rag him. . . . But he doesn't like me. And if it wasn't for you there'd be trouble. . . . No, M.F.: what this expedition would be like without you I simply can't imagine—

RANSOM. Listen, David. There's something I must tell you, now—

[*Enter* SHAWCROSS, DOCTOR *and* LAMP, *in great excitement, L.*]

SHAWCROSS. M.F.! A message has just come through: Blavek and his party are on the mountain already!
GUNN. But it's impossible! When we last heard, he was still on the other side of the Tung Desert!
SHAWCROSS. I know, but this is official! He must have been making forced marches. These fellows aren't mountaineers at all—they're soldiers! There's a whole regiment of them! Do you know, M.F., what they're doing? They're hammering the whole south face full of pitons and hauling each other up like sacks! Good God, they'll be using fire-escapes before they've finished! Well, that settles it! We haven't a moment to lose!
RANSOM. And you are all anxious to play their game: the race to the summit? This won't be mountaineering. It'll be a steeplechase. Are you so sure the prize is worth it? Ian, you're the purist: is this your idea of climbing? No time for observations; no time for reconnoitre. Teddy, hadn't you better stay out of this? We can't wait a week, you know, while you look for your flowers.
LAMP. I'll take my chance of that later. We've got to beat them!
RANSOM. And you, Tom?
DOCTOR. You don't expect me to stay here, do you, M.F.? If you did, I believe I should disobey you. This makes me feel twenty years younger already!
RANSOM. I suppose I needn't ask you two others?
SHAWCROSS. You needn't.
GUNN. I think this makes it all the more exciting! Good old Blavek!
RANSOM. Very well then: you have chosen for me. I obey you. We start at dawn.

[*He rises to his feet with a slight gesture of weariness and resignation as:*]

THE CURTAIN FALLS

Act II, Scene 2

The FA and FB texts are identical.

Act II, Scene 3

The dialogue between Ransom and the Doctor on p. 339, from Ransom's line "David?" to his line "I know what you're thinking [. . .] Yes, it's all true", is a revised version introduced in FB. The revised text replaces this original version that appears in FA (and in LC and RH):

Ransom. It won't be necessary.
Doctor. What do you mean?
Ransom. David is coming with me to the summit.
Doctor. And Ian?
Ransom. He'll remain with you here.
Doctor [*after a long pause*]. I don't like it, M.F.
Ransom. Why not, Tom?
Doctor. I suppose you know best; but—
Ransom. Don't imagine I haven't thought this over carefully. I know what you are going to say: Ian is steady, reliable, a first-class climber: David is only a brilliant amateur, a novice with an extraordinary flair, unsound, uneven, liable to moments of panic, without staying power. Yes, it's all true.

Act II, Scene 4

The FA and FB texts are identical.

Act II, Scene 5

This scene was substantially revised for LC, TSB, RH, and FB. The original version from FA is printed below. The prose epilogue that concludes the FA version, after the fall of the curtain, also appears in LC and RH, but is absent in TSB and dropped from FB.

Act II Scene 5

[*F 6. The stage rises steeply, in a series of rock terraces, to the small platform at the back which forms the summit of the mountain. Blizzard. Gathering darkness. In the front of the stage,* Ransom *is struggling upwards. After a few numbed movements, he falls exhausted. Music throughout. The light now fades into complete darkness. The voices of the chorus, dressed in the habit of the monks from the glacier monastery, are heard.*]

Chorus. Let the eye of the traveller consider this country and weep,
    For toads croak in the cisterns; the aqueducts choke with leaves:
    The highways are out of repair and infested with thieves:
    The ragged populations are crazy for lack of sleep:
    Our chimneys are smokeless; the implements rust in the field
        And our tall constructions are felled.

    Over our empty playgrounds the wet winds sough;
    The crab and the sandhopper possess our abandoned beaches;

Upon our gardens the dock and the darnel encroaches;
The crumbling lighthouse is circled with moss like a muff;
The weasel inhabits the courts and the sacred places;
   Despair is in our faces.

> [*The summit of the mountain is illuminated, revealing a veiled, seated figure.*]

For the Dragon has wasted the forest and set fire to the farm;
He has mutilated our sons in his terrible rages
And our daughters he has stolen to be victims of his dissolute
      orgies:
He has cracked the skulls of our children in the crook of his arm:
With the blast of his nostrils he scatters death through the land:
   We are babes in his hairy hand.

O, when shall the deliverer come to destroy this dragon?
For it is stated in the prophecies that such a one shall appear,
Shall ride on a white horse and pierce his heart with a spear;
Our elders shall welcome him home with trumpet and organ,
Load him with treasure, yes, and our most beautiful maidenhead
   He shall have for his bed.

> [*The veiled* FIGURE *on the summit raises its hand. There is a fanfare of trumpets. The* DRAGON, *in the form of* JAMES RANSOM, *appears. He wears full ceremonial dress, with orders. He is illuminated by a spot-light. The* CHORUS, *throughout the whole scene, remain in semi-darkness.*]
>
> [*As* JAMES *appears, the* CHORUS *utter a cry of dismay.* JAMES *bows to the* FIGURE.]

JAMES. I am sorry to say that our civilising mission has been subject to grave misinterpretations. Our critics have been unhelpful and, I am constrained to add, unfair. The powers which I represent stand unequivocally for peace. We have declared our willingness to conclude pacts of non-aggression with all of you—on condition, of course, that our demands are reasonably met. During the past few years, we have carried unilateral disarmament to the utmost limits of safety; others, whom I need not specify, have unfortunately failed to follow our example. We now find ourselves in a position of inferiority which is intolerable to the honour and interests of a great power; and in self-defence we are reluctantly obliged to take the necessary measures to rectify the situation. We have constantly reiterated our earnest desire for peace; but in the face of unprovoked aggression I must utter a solemn warning to you all that we are prepared to defend ourselves to the fullest extent of our resources against all comers.

> [JAMES *is seated. A Duet from the darkened* STAGE-BOXES.]

DUET.
Him who comes to set us free
Save, whoever it may be,
From the fountain's thirsty snare,
From the music in the air,
From the tempting fit of slumber
From the odd unlucky number
From the riddle's easy trap
From the ignorance of the map
From the locked forbidden room,
From the Guardian of the Tomb,
From the siren's wrecking call,
Save him now and save us all.

> [*Flourish on the wood-wind.* MICHAEL RANSOM *steps into the light which surrounds the Dragon* JAMES. *He still wears his climbing things but is without helmet, goggles or ice-axe.*]

JAMES. Michael! Why have you come here? What do you want?
RANSOM. Hardly very friendly, are you?
JAMES. What is it this time? We are grown men now.
RANSOM. There is no time to lose. I have come to make you a most important proposition.
JAMES. Which I accept—on my own conditions. [*Makes a sign to the* CHORUS.]
RANSOM. You are not being fair to me!
JAMES. Keep to your world. I will keep to mine.

> [*A chess table is brought into the light by* TWO MONKS.]

CHORUS. But this man was never the figure in the priestess' vision;
    We expected a hero; at least, a magnificent shepherd
    Or a forester, maybe, comely and cunning as a leopard.
    Beware lest he bring the prophecy into derision;
    For, when he has paid for his folly and lies maimed in the dust,
      The foolish shall lose their trust.

Moreover, his pin-pricks can but incense the Dragon's anger;
Who will visit the insult upon our defenceless heads;
He will hale every tenth man from their shrieking beds;
The pressure of his hand shall weigh on us heavier and longer.
Better the destruction be easy and quickly over,
   Or the innocent will suffer.

> [RANSOM *and* JAMES *begin to play chess.*]

Let the Dragon deal with him sharply, then, as an impostor;
Rend him in pieces, let the marrow be squeezed from the bone,
Let him go to his death unapplauded and alone.
May it never be said that we encouraged this boaster!
And let not the women, hearing his anguished cries,
   Show sympathy in their eyes.

> [*Complete silence, accompanied only by a drum roll. At intervals, one or other of them says:* "Check!"]

JAMES. Check!
RANSOM [*looking for the first time towards the summit and seeing the* FIGURE]. Look!
JAMES. Mate! I've won!

> [*The* FIGURE *shakes its head.*]

RANSOM [*with his eyes still fixed upon it*]. But was the victory real?
JAMES [*half rising to his feet and tottering*]. [*In a choking voice.*] It was not Virtue—it was not Knowledge—it was Power! [*Collapses into his chair and falls forward over the chess table.*]
CHORUS. What have you done? What have you done?
   You have killed, you have murdered her favourite son!

> [*A figure having the shape of the* ABBOT, *wearing a monk's habit and a judge's wig, and holding the crystal in his hands, is illuminated at a somewhat higher level of the stage.*]

ABBOT. I am truly sorry for this young man, but I must ask for the court to be cleared.

> [*The sound of a Blues is heard. Enter* STAGMANTLE *and* LADY ISABEL, *followed by* MONKS *with a stretcher. The chess table is removed.* JAMES's *body is laid on the stretcher and carried in slow procession round the stage, disappearing into the darkness.*]

STAGMANTLE AND ISABEL [*together*].
>   Stop all the clocks, cut off the telephone,
>   Prevent the dog from barking with a juicy bone,
>   Silence the pianos and with muffled drum
>   Bring out the coffin, let the mourners come.
>
>   Let aeroplanes circle moaning overhead
>   Scribbling on the sky the message: He is dead.
>   Put crepe bows round the white necks of the public doves.
>   Let the traffic policemen wear black cotton gloves.
>
>   Hold up your umbrellas to keep off the rain
>   From Doctor Williams while he opens a vein;
>   Life, he pronounces, it is finally extinct.
>   Sergeant, arrest that man who said he winked!
>
>   Shawcross will say a few words sad and kind
>   To the weeping crowds about the Master-Mind,
>   While Lamp with a powerful microscope
>   Searches their faces for a sign of hope.
>
>   And Gunn, of course, will drive the motor-hearse:
>   None could drive it better, most would drive it worse.
>   He'll open up the throttle to its fullest power
>   And drive him to the grave at ninety miles an hour.

ABBOT. Please be seated, Mr Ransom. I hope everything has been arranged here to your satisfaction?
RANSOM. I didn't do it! I swear I didn't touch him! It wasn't my fault! [*Pointing to* FIGURE.] The Demon gave the sign; the Demon is real!
ABBOT. In that case, we will call the victims of his pride. Call Ian Shawcross!
CHORUS. Ian Shawcross!

[SHAWCROSS *appears. He is bloodstained and pale.*]

RANSOM. I've had about as much of this as I can stand. You've got to tell them! I hate to bother you with this sort of thing.
SHAWCROSS. I'm afraid you haven't succeeded very well.
RANSOM. You mean, you *did* see something? If you hadn't, you mightn't believe me.
SHAWCROSS. Oh, for Christ's sake, shut up! If what you've done amuses you, I'm glad. I'm not very tolerant, I'm afraid. [*Exit.*]
ABBOT. Call David Gunn!
CHORUS. David Gunn!

[*Enter* DAVID GUNN, *pale and covered with snow. His face is entirely featureless.*]

RANSOM. David, you saw what happened?
GUNN. Didn't I just? You did it beautifully! It was first class!
RANSOM. You sound pleased.
GUNN. Of course I'm pleased! Who wouldn't be?
RANSOM. David, there's something I *must* tell you—

[*Exit* GUNN.]

ABBOT. Call Edward Lamp!
CHORUS. Edward Lamp! Edward Lamp! Edward Lamp!
LAMP'S VOICE [*far away, off*]. I'm all right.
RANSOM [*shouting*]. Teddy, what did *you* see?
LAMP'S VOICE. If I told you, you wouldn't be any the wiser.
RANSOM. You're on their side, too! Is this all your talk of loyalty amounts to?

[DOCTOR WILLIAMS *appears.*]

RANSOM. Tom!
DOCTOR. Just tell me what you want me to do.
RANSOM. I can't face it!
DOCTOR. Perhaps you are right. The Demon demands another kind of victim. Ask the crystal.

[*Exit* DOCTOR.]

ABBOT. You wish to appeal to the crystal, Mr Ransom? Do not ask at once, but think it over.
RANSOM. We haven't a moment to lose. I appeal to the crystal.
ABBOT. Very well. You have chosen for me. [*He stares into the crystal.*]

[*Music. Duet from the* STAGE-BOXES.]

DUET. Love, look down from your white tower
 And comfort us in the dark hour.
 Save us from evil and from dolour.

ABBOT. Mr Ransom, I did you an injustice. I thought I understood your temptation, but I was wrong. The temptation is not the Demon. If there were no Demon, there would be no temptation.
RANSOM. What have I said? I didn't mean it! Forgive me! It was all my fault. F 6 has shown me what I am. I withdraw the charge.

ABBOT. Such altruism, Mr Ransom, is uncommon in one of your race. But I am afraid it is too late now. The case is being brought by the Crown. [*Turning to the* FIGURE *on the summit.*] Have you anything to say in your defence? [*No answer.*] You realise the consequences of silence? [*No answer.*] Beware of spiritual pride! [*To* CHORUS.] Gentlemen, consider your verdict.

CHORUS. At last the secret is out, as it always must come in the end;
  The delicious story is ripe to tell to the intimate friend;
  Over the tea cups and in the square the tongue has its desire;
  Still waters run deep, my dear, there's never smoke without fire.

  Behind the corpse in the reservoir, behind the ghost on the links,
  Behind the lady who dances and the man who madly drinks,
  Under the look of fatigue, the attack of migraine and the sigh
  There is always another story, there is more than meets the eye.

  For the clear voice suddenly singing, high up in the convent wall,
  The scent in the elder bushes, the sporting prints in the hall,
  The croquet matches in summer, the handshake, the cough, the kiss,
  There is always a wicked secret, a private reason for this.

ABBOT. Have you considered your verdict?
RANSOM. Stop!

> [RANSOM *rushes up to the summit and places himself in front of the* FIGURE, *with his arms outstretched, as if to protect it.*]

RANSOM. No one shall ever—! I couldn't bear it! I'll never let them! Never!
ABBOT [*to* CHORUS]. Guilty or not guilty?
CHORUS [*all pointing at the* FIGURE]. Guilty!

> [*Thunder and the roar of an avalanche are heard. At the word, all lights are extinguished below: only the* FIGURE *and* RANSOM *remain illuminated.* RANSOM *turns to the* FIGURE, *whose draperies fall away, revealing* MRS RANSOM, *as a young mother.*]

RANSOM. Mother!
MOTHER. My Boy! At last!

> [RANSOM *falls at her feet with his head in her lap. She strokes his hair.*]

CHORUS. Acts of injustice done
    Between the setting and the rising sun
    In history lie like bones, each one.

MOTHER. Still the dark forest, quiet the deep,
    Softly the clock ticks, Baby must sleep!
    The Polestar is shining, bright the Great Bear,
    Orion is watching, high up in the air.

CHORUS. Memory sees them down there,
    Paces alive beside his fear
    That's slow to die and still here.

MOTHER. Reindeer are coming to drive you away
    Over the snow on an ebony sleigh,
    Over the mountains and over the sea
    You shall go happy and handsome and free.

CHORUS. The future, hard to mark,
    Of a world turning in the dark
    Where ghosts are walking and dogs bark.

MOTHER. Over the green grass pastures there
    You shall go hunting the beautiful deer,
    You shall pick flowers, the white and the blue,
    Shepherds shall flute their sweetest for you.

CHORUS. True, Love finally is great,
    Greater than all; but large the hate,
    Far larger than Man can ever estimate.

CHORUS. And in the castle tower above
    The princess' cheek burns red for your love,
    You shall be king and queen of the land,
    Happy for ever, hand in hand.

CHORUS. But between the day and night
    The choice is free to all, and light
    Falls equally on black and white.

    [*During the first verse of the Chorale which follows, the light fades from the summit, so that the stage is completely darkened. Then, after a moment, the entire stage is gradually illuminated by the rising sun. All the figures have disappeared. The stage is empty, except for the body of* RANSOM, *who lies dead on the summit of the mountain.*]

HIDDEN CHORUS. By all his virtues flouted,
    From every refuge routed
    And driven far from home;
    At last his journey ended,
    Forgiven and befriended,
    See him to his salvation come.

[*Morendo.*]   Free now from indignation,
    Immune from all frustration
    He lies in death alone;
    Now he with secret terror
    And every minor error
    Has also made Man's weakness known.

                            [*The* CURTAIN *slowly falls.*]

[*The left hand* STAGE-BOX *is illuminated:* JAMES RANSOM, LORD STAGMANTLE, LADY ISABEL, *the* GENERAL *and* M. BLAVEK *are standing round the microphone.*]

STAGMANTLE. When the aeroplane flew over F 6 and came back with the news that Ransom's body had been seen on the summit, the whole of England was plunged into mourning for one of her greatest sons; but it is a sorrow tempered with pride, that once again Englishmen have been weighed in the balance and not found wanting. Monsieur Blavek, the leader of the intrepid Ostnian climbers, will tell you how he found the bodies: I only wish to add—

JAMES. You mustn't run away with the idea that my brother was a simple person: The strong silent man of the boy's adventure story. He was very far removed from that—

BLAVEK [*with a strong accent*]. It is a great honour for me to speak to you about Mr Ransom; and I want first to say how deeply we in Ostnia feel with you in the loss of so great a climber—

ISABEL. At this hour, the thoughts of the whole nation go out to a very brave and lonely woman in a little South Country cottage; already a widow and now a bereaved mother. We women who know what it means to sit at home while our nearest and dearest venture forth into unknown perils—

GENERAL. I am no climber and I never met Ransom personally; but I know courage when I see it. Ransom was a brave man and courage is the greatest quality a man can have—

JAMES. He had many sides to his character and I doubt if anyone knew the whole man. I as his brother certainly did not. He had an almost feminine sensibility which, if it had not been allied to great qualities of soul and will-power and a first class intelligence, might easily have become neurotic—

BLAVEK. Two days later, we reached the summit and found him lying there. His ice-axe lay on the rocks a little lower down—

STAGMANTLE. Exactly what happened, we shall never know—

JAMES. But, as it was, no man had a more tender conscience, was more fanatically strict with himself on questions of motive and conduct—

BLAVEK. We found the body of Gunn on the eastern arête, about five hundred feet below the summit—

STAGMANTLE. It is probable that the bodies of Lamp and Shawcross will never be recovered; but while our thoughts are naturally centred upon their leader, their devotion to duty and their quiet heroism must never be forgotten—

JAMES. There was no sphere of human activity, whether in sport or scholarship or art, in which, if he had chosen, he could not have made supreme achievements. But he hated publicity in any form; he felt it tainted—

ISABEL. The mountain took its toll of four young lives. In the face of this terrible tragedy one is almost tempted to believe in the grim old legend of the Demon—

STAGMANTLE. Acting on his express wishes, they will bury Ransom in the quiet country churchyard of the village where he spent his childhood. And Gunn is to be laid to rest beside him—

GENERAL. He died like a soldier at his post—

BLAVEK. I am proud to have been beaten by such a man in this great climb—

STAGMANTLE. As Monsieur Blavek has said, Sport transcends all national barriers and it is some comfort to realise that this tragedy has brought two great nations closer together—

JAMES. He had all the qualities which fit a man for great office in the State, but he refused, for he dreaded the vulgarity and corruption of public life; and sometimes we poor devils who find ourselves in such positions wonder whether, perhaps, he wasn't right—

STAGMANTLE. Their names are the latest but not the least on that long roll of heroes who gave their lives for the honour of this country—

> [*The* CURTAIN *rises. In the centre of the stage, against the cyclorama, stands a plain obelisk, on which the word* RANSOM *is engraved. The* A.*'s are standing regarding it.*]

ISABEL. Freely they gave—
JAMES. They did not count the cost—
STAGMANTLE. Their name liveth for evermore—
ISABEL. They did not think of self—
GENERAL. They died for England—
JAMES. Honour—
STAGMANTLE. Service—
GENERAL. Duty—
ISABEL. Sacrifice—
STAGMANTLE. England—
BLAVEK. Ostnia—
THE OTHERS. England! England! England!

[*The* STAGE-BOX *is darkened.*]

MR A. [*regarding the monument with proprietary pride*]. He belongs to *us*, now!

[*The* CURTAIN *slowly falls.*]

§3 THE LORD CHAMBERLAIN'S COPY AND THE AMERICAN EDITION

The revisions in these two versions (which are sufficiently similar to permit them to be considered together) and in the second Faber edition (which has further changes noted in §4) may have been planned as early as July 1936, when Auden's agent told his American publisher that the play was being revised. Auden and Isherwood probably first discussed the revisions in detail when they met briefly in London at the start of October 1936. On 6 October Auden told Bennett Cerf at Random House: "Isherwood and I are now altering it quite considerably." Isherwood was working on his share of the revisions by 22 October, when he was living in Brussels, and probably early in November sent it to Auden, who combined it with his own share. The full set of revisions consisted of a brief scene for Mrs Ransom after I.3 and new texts of most of II.1 and II.5, all apparently typed out by Isherwood, who, in the Act II revisions, consistently misspelled the protagonist's name as "Ransome".

Isherwood typed the revised texts on pages cut to fit a copy of the printed text of the first edition. The copy of these pages that was pasted into a copy of that edition, and eventually submitted to the Lord Chamberlain's Office (the LC copy), has corrections in various hands, of which only Auden's may be identified with any confidence. Late in November Auden sent a copy of Isherwood's typescript to Doone for use by the Group Theatre. In response to what was evidently a query from Doone about the new version of II.1, he wrote on 28 November (in a letter in the Berg Collection): "No, I didn't want the Fakirs to do anything, only possibly they might march in attitudes e.g. one carried on a litter of spikes." (The Fakirs appear in the LC, TSB, and RH texts, but were dropped in FB, probably at the proof stage.) The LC copy was not submitted to the Lord Chamberlain's Office until 29 January 1937, around the time when rehearsals were ready to begin. (The LC text is revised from FA only where typescript pages are pasted over printed text; there are no further revisions written on any of the printed pages whose text was not entirely replaced.) Auden had left for Spain earlier that month, and the state of the text reflected in the LC version almost certainly predates his departure. (Isherwood did not arrive in London until February, so the LC text does not include any changes he made during rehearsals.)

At about the same time that Auden sent the revisions to Doone, he apparently made some further cuts and additions in a second copy of Isherwood's new typescript (including all the earlier corrections marked in the LC copy), and arranged to have this altered copy retyped by an agency. The resulting typescript (TSB) has the full text of the revised scenes in Act II (not only the revised portions, as in Isherwood's typescript) and the new scene after I.3. Auden provided copies of this professional typescript to Faber for use in the second British edition (FB) and to Random House for use in the American edition (RH). This new typescript incorporated a revision evidently prompted by Stephen Spender's review of FA in *The Left Review*, November 1936. Spender observed that "Ransom is a colossal prig, a fact of which the authors seem insufficiently aware", and suggested "that the final tragic realisation of the last act should have been that Ransom was a prig, a fact, after all, even more significant than that he was in love with his mother." In the TSB version of the final scene, and therefore in the versions printed in RH and FB, Ransom is made to say: "I'm a coward and a prig."

Auden promised Bennett Cerf that Random House would receive the revised text of the play in early December 1936, and seems to have sent a copy of TSB to New York late in November. (The text of the Random House edition closely reproduces the peculiarities of the TSB typescript.) Auden then wrote a small revision into yet another copy of TSB (the surviving copy), and sent it to Faber at the end of November; the publisher wrote the printer on 1 December that Auden "has just sent us this typescript." Some further revisions, apparently marked by Isherwood when reading proof, appeared in the published text of FB the following March (see §4).

The following notes record differences between, on the one hand, LC, TSB, and RH, and, on the other, the FB text used for this edition. The notes also record differences between the text of LC and the texts shared by TSB and RH.

Page 318.

The monologue and song for Mrs Ransom (and the introductory stage direction), absent from FA, are added in LC, TSB, RH, and FB. TSB heads the new material: "After ACT I, SCENE 3." LC has a similar heading. Unlike FB, which prints the new text immediately after the original, RH begins the addition on a separate page.

Page 319.

The description of the scene at the opening of II.1 (and of II.5) is preceded in TSB by the word "SCENE:" but as this style is not followed in other scenes in the Auden-Isherwood plays it has not been incorporated here.

The third and fourth lines of dialogue in II.1 read as follows in LC, TSB, and RH:

RANSOM. How are we off for dried figs?
SHAWCROSS. Two boxes. And three of dates and five of apricots.

Page 321.
LC, TSB, and RH follow FA in having Shawcross refer first to "Camp B" and then, in his next speech, to "Camp A". FB inverts these so that Camp A is the lower one, Camp B the higher.

Page 327.
Near the end of the Abbot's speech beginning, "Ah, you saw it there", LC lacks the phrase (present in TSB, RH, and FB) printed here in brackets: "For [you can only rule men by appealing to their fear and their lust;] government requires".

The dialogue that in FB extends from Ransom's line "What?" to "Think my proposal over" at the end of the Abbot's next long speech replaces this shorter version in LC, TSB, and RH (printed here from LC, lightly emended):

RANSOM. What?
ABBOT. The complete abnegation of the will.
RANSOM. And that means—?
ABBOT. This. . . .

> [*Very quietly, during the preceding speech, the distant drum-beat of a funeral march has been heard. Throughout the above dialogue, it has grown steadily louder. A procession of* MONKS *now crosses the cloister at the back of the stage. They are bearing a number of fakirs in attitudes of asceticism; on litters, in coffins, impaled on spikes, etc. They cross from L. to R. and exeunt.*]

> Well, Mr Ransom, I must leave you now. Do not make up your mind at once. Think my proposal over.

Page 329.
Ransom's monologue beginning "Is it too late for me?" is considerably longer in LC than in TSB, RH, and FB. The LC version reads:

RANSOM. Is it too late for me? I recognize my purpose. There was a choice once, in the Lakeland Inn. I made it wrong; and if I choose again now, I must choose for myself alone, not for these others.
Oh you who are the history and the creator of all these forms in

which we are condemned to suffer, to whom the necessary is also the just, show me, show each of us upon this mortal star the danger that under his hand is softly palpitating.

For your eye is always upon us, in the solitude of midnight and the social noon, watching impartially our fictitious applauded defence and our secretive abandon, and the extremities of your observation are beyond our most extravagant dreams of escape.

Those whom you elect to save are saved, not for what they do but because it is your will. Save us, save us from the destructive element of our will, for all we do is evil and of where or when or upon whom the obliteration of your anger shall fall, we have no foreknowledge.

Page 330.

Ransom's last two sentences in II.1 show small but significant differences in TSB and RH, LC, and FB (and the entire speech differs from the corresponding speech in FA). LC has "I have failed. We start at dawn." TSB and RH read: "We have betrayed ourselves. We start at dawn." And FB has "And I have failed. We start at dawn."

Page 339.

LC and RH, which make no revisions in II.3, have the same text that had appeared in FA of the dialogue in which Ransom tells the Doctor that he has chosen David to come with him to the summit (see p. 614).

Page 349.

In James's speech beginning "That's a very interesting question" LC lacks the passages (present in TSB, RH, and FB) printed here in brackets: "interesting question[, and I'm not sure I can answer it myself. But I know what my brother, the climber, thinks]. When we take[, he said to me once,] the life of the individual".

Ransom's line, "You're not being fair to me", and James's line, "Keep to your world. I will keep to mine", occur in LC at a different point from the point where they occur in TSB, RH, and FB. In LC the two lines remain in the position where they occur in FA, after James's line, "Which I accept—on my own conditions." (See p. 617.)

Page 350.

LC lacks the stage direction (added in TSB, RH, and FB), "*Exeunt* SHAWCROSS, LAMP *and* GUNN."

Page 351.

In the stage direction for Gunn's entrance, LC follows FA in describing Gunn's face as "*entirely featureless.*" In TSB, RH, and FB it is "*entirely without features.*"

Page 352.

LC follows FA in the text of Ransom's speech beginning "What have I said?" TSB, RH, and FB insert, after "shown me what I am", a new sentence: "I'm a coward and a prig." (See the headnote to this section of notes.)

Page 353.

The three lines between Isabel's "Sacrifice!" and the A.'s "Die for us!" ("Die for England."—"Ostnia."—"England. England. England.") are expanded in FB from this single line in LC and RH: "Die for England, England, England!" (Auden wrote this change in the copy of TSB that he apparently gave Faber for its second edition.)

Page 355.

LC and RH follow FA in concluding the play with the dialogue at the microphone that was dropped in FB. (The dialogue is also absent from TSB.) Part of this dialogue had been moved into the revised text of the earlier part of the scene, and the authors evidently assumed that their new text of II.5 would be understood as replacing the full text (including the dialogue at the microphone) of the earlier FA version of the scene. But because they made no explicit statement that the dialogue should be cut, it was mistakenly preserved in LC and RH.

§4 The Second English Edition, with Notes on the Text of the Present Edition

The text of the present edition silently restores from Isherwood's original typescript (TS) capitalization and other details of typography and layout that were reduced by another typist or by the printer. Isherwood typed exceptionally long dashes, which the typist or printer sometimes represented as two-em dashes, sometimes as conventional one-em dashes. As the original TS makes no such distinction, all dashes in the present text are the conventional variety.

For notes on the revisions Auden and Isherwood made in the autumn of 1936, see §3 above. After Auden sent the typescript of the revised scenes (TSB) to Faber at the end of November, the printer made a new set of proofs. Faber sent these to Isherwood on 25 February 1937 with a note expressing the hope that he would not make extensive changes. (Auden was then travelling in Spain, and was unavailable for proofreading work.) Isherwood evidently did make some revisions, probably including the changes in the last sentences of II.1 noted on p. 628, the new dialogue in II.3 noted on pp. 614-15, and some other slight changes noted below. The revisions made after the first edition introduced some minor inconsistencies. While all the revised texts retain from FA Ransom's line in the phantasmagoria of II.5, "David, there's something I *must* tell you—" (p. 351), these texts drop the earlier occurrence of the line (in the FA text of II.1; p. 613) that the later one is meant to echo. The authors seem to have had difficulty in deciding whether Camp A was lower or higher than Camp B. And in their revised version they never succeeded in getting Lamp offstage before Ransom's dialogue with the Abbot in II.1.

Page 294.

The list of characters remained unchanged in the first edition and in the first impression of the second edition, although the character of Blavek had been dropped; I have omitted his name from the list in the present edition. For the second impression of the second edition, Auden and Isherwood replaced the list of characters with a cast list from one of the Group Theatre productions (see p. 637). The cast list was headed:

This play was first produced on February 26, 1937, at the Mercury Theatre, by Ashley Dukes *in association with the Group Theatre. Producer:* Rupert Doone. *Stage Designer:* Robert Medley. *Music by* Benjamin Britten.

Page 295.

In the stage direction Wastdale should properly be Wasdale, but Auden's alternative is a fairly common one.

Page 319.

In Shawcross's third speech, TSB, RH, and FB all read "Two porters" for TS, LC, and FA's "The porters". "The porters" is restored in GT, and, as it probably represents Isherwood's intent, is also restored here.

Page 321.

The FB text, followed here, makes Camp A the lower one, Camp B the higher. FA, LC, TSB, and RH had used the reverse arrangement. In the attempts on Everest the camps were numbered I, II, III, etc., in ascending order; the revised arrangement in FB corresponds to this sequence. But FB's revision in II.1 was not extended to II.3 (p. 338), where, in all published texts, the scene is set in Camp A, and Ransom tells the Doctor to *descend* to Camp B. GT corrects these readings in II.3, and I have emended the present edition in the same way.

The plant that excites Lamp is called "Polus Naufrangia" in all texts, although "Polus Naufragia" would more accurately suggest the symbolic "pole of shipwreck".

Page 323.

The last stanza of the chant raises more editorial problems than it deserves. In TS and FA the final words of each line are "sokloskya", "gaya", and "sya". For LC Isherwood altered the first of these to "sokloskaya", which appears in all later texts. I have extended his change to the final line and emended to "saya". On the other hand, the original "gaya" may have been an error for "gya", and Isherwood's change may have been an error.

Page 326.

In the Abbot's speech beginning "Such interest, Mr Ransom," LC (but not TSB, RH, or FB) has a paragraph break after "But you would be wrong." The break is restored in this edition.

Page 329.

In Ransom's soliloquy TSB, RH, and FB all read "the danger that under His hand"; I have emended "His" to "his" (the original reading in TS, FA, and LC) because the antecedent is clearly "each of us" rather than "You who are the history and creator".

In Ransom's speech beginning "You've thought enough" TSB, RH, and FB capitalize "Brother"; this seems a deliberate change from the LC reading "brother". Auden and Isherwood frequently capitalized nouns that indicate family relations.

Page 334.

In Ransom's speech beginning "Well, Master", the name "Balmat" is an emendation for Auden's error "Balmont" in the fair copy of this speech in a notebook in the Berg Collection and in all other texts. Auden got it right in his draft notes in the same notebook.

Page 338.

See the note to p. 321 immediately above. I have followed the programmes of the Group Theatre productions in setting the scene in Camp B rather than, as in all published texts, Camp A.

Page 343.

In Mr A.'s last speech I have followed GT in emending "Turn off the wireless" to the reading demanded by the sense, "Turn on the wireless". (Mrs A. had already turned off the wireless at the start of the scene.)

In the Announcer's song at the end of the scene the indentions of the shorter lines are based on Isherwood's original typescript (TS). In the printed texts all the lines are set flush left, in contrast to Auden's normal practice with song lyrics.

Page 355.

In the final Hidden Chorus I have restored the LC reading "Whom History hath", where TSB, RH, and FB have "Whom history has". The capitalized personification of History reflects Auden's usage at the time; the typist of TSB presumably thought it an error to be corrected, and may have chosen to correct "hath" at the same time. (LC also has a probable typing error by Isherwood, "sudden drawing suction", for the reading "sudden drowning suction" in TSB, RH, and FB.)

§5 THE VERSIONS PRODUCED BY THE GROUP THEATRE IN 1937

While Auden was in Spain Isherwood watched over the rehearsals of *The Ascent of F6*—as Auden had watched over the rehearsals of *The Dog Beneath the Skin* when Isherwood was in Portugal. By the time the production opened on 26 February 1937 at the Mercury Theatre, some textual changes were required. Isherwood recalled in *Exhumations* (1966) that "Rupert Doone, our director, had made several changes with my full approval"; in *Christopher and His Kind* (1976) these became "changes in the text made by Christopher and Rupert". The latter description seems more likely to be correct. Whoever made the changes, they prompted Auden, when he first saw the production on his return from Spain, to whisper reproachfully to Isherwood early in the performance: "*My dear*, what have you *done* to it?"

The ending of the play had apparently been even more drastically revised, and many different versions had been tried out on stage. There is no direct record of any of the changes made by Doone and Isherwood, but they were presumably recorded in the (now lost) promptbook of the first production. And they were presumably later copied into the promptbook (GT) used for the 1939 revival when that promptbook was prepared around June 1939, after Auden and Isherwood had left for America. (This promptbook does not preserve any of the prior versions of the ending, but instead includes a new final scene based on one that Auden and Isherwood had sent over for the revival.) The changes recorded in the GT promptbook do little more than improve the rhythm of the dialogue and provide additional jokes for Gunn. The least unimportant of them are noted below (followed by a separate account of the production versions of the final scene). They have not been incorporated into the main text of this edition, partly because of the uncertain authority of the 1939 GT promptbook, partly out of respect to Auden's reproachful whisper.

Among the larger cuts indicated in the promptbook are: the deletion at the end of I.3 of Mr and Mrs A.'s verses and Mrs Ransom's soliloquy and song; the deletion of the voices from the stage-boxes when Ransom looks into the crystal in II.1; and the deletion of the Announcer's song at the end of II.3. (Not all these cuts had been made in the original 1937 production; reviews indicate, for example, that in 1937 Mrs Ransom's soliloquy and song were performed.) The small additions in the promptbook include frequent exclamations, repetitions of words or phrases, a word or two from offstage prior to an entrance, and other additions of the kind that any stage director might choose to make. A few other passages are sufficiently rewritten to justify quoting them here. In the following selection of rewritten passages each corresponds to an easily identifiable passage on the pages indicated:

Page 302.

> JAMES. We can't be too sure of that, I'm afraid. There's too much at stake.
> ISABEL. How can you all stand there so calmly and say so! Oh, if only I were a man! What are you going to *do*?
> JAMES. His Majesty's Government proposes to send a mountaineering expedition to Sudoland without delay.
> { ISABEL. Very well, very well! Good! Good!
> { STAGMANTLE. Now you're talking.
> GENERAL. Why mountaineering? Never heard such damned tomfoolery in all my life!

Page 303.

JAMES. Very well. We'll go to him at once.
ISABEL. Yes! Yes!
JAMES. But it will need more than me to persuade my brother. I've made all arrangements. The car is outside and my plane is at Heston. [*To* GENERAL.] You'll come with us, General?
GENERAL. I for one refuse to be a party to this wild goose chase. When you have ceased to occupy yourselves with demons and fairy stories and need some serious advice, you will find me at the Cavalry Club. Good morning.
ISABEL. Oh really, General!

[*The* GENERAL, *taking no notice, goes out.*]

Now what are we going to do?
JAMES [*during* STAGMANTLE's *speech; on telephone*]. Is everything ready? Yes, we'll be down immediately.
STAGMANTLE. Never mind him, Lady Isabel. [*etc.*]

Page 306.
GT moves the second stanza of Gunn's song ("And deep-sea divers") to p. 307, following Gunn's speech "No, I expect I shouldn't." Other changes in I.3 include:

RANSOM. Shut up, David.
DOCTOR. Trying to be the popular boy, David?
RANSOM [*to* DOCTOR]. Check.
GUNN [*leaving piano and looking over* SHAWCROSS' *shoulder*]. Hullo, what's all this? [*Reads.*] "... Gunn, as usual, fooling about, completely irresponsible. I can never understand M.F.'s patience with him...."

[SHAWCROSS *tries to snatch book.* GUNN *dodges round the chair.*]

SHAWCROSS. Leave that alone, damn you!
GUNN. Ha, ha! Wouldn't you like it! [*etc.*]

. . . .

GUNN. All right. Keep your hair on. No offence. [*Strolls over to* LAMP.] Let's have a squint, Teddy. [*Looks into microscope.*] Phew! That's a bit intimate, isn't it? What is it?
LAMP. If I were to tell you, [*etc.*]

Page 308.

> DOCTOR. Why do I always do something silly when I play with you? It's no good. You get me every time. [*Rising.*] Oh, I'm getting so fat, so fat!
> GUNN. Doc., I believe you forgot your exercises this morning!
> DOCTOR. As if I ever forgot them! As if I could ever forget them! [*Sighs.*] Perhaps it would be better if I stopped them altogether, d'you think? But I haven't the nerve.
> GUNN [*claps*]. One, two, three, bend and—up! Dismiss! Poor old Doc.! Come and have a drink. Whisky shrivels up your flesh.
> DOCTOR. Do you really think so?
> GUNN. Oh, indubitably!
> DOCTOR. I've got to a stage where I can believe almost anything.
>
> > [*A knock at the door.*]
>
> GUNN. I wonder who that is?
> DOCTOR. More bills for you, I expect, David.
> ISABEL'S VOICE. May we come in?
> GUNN. Another woman! [*Dives under the larger table.*]

Page 317.

> GUNN. I don't really know exactly what to say. We none of us know what F6 is going to be like. If you ask me, I think she's probably rather an ugly old maid. I'm scared stiff, but Ransom will hold our hands, I expect. . . . We shall be a jolly party, I hope. I've been on one or two of these expeditions and no one's murdered me yet. They say that there's a ghost at the top; but I've made Doctor Williams promise that if we see anything at all suspicious he'll operate at once. Well, I don't think I've got anything else to say, so I'll tell you a limerick I've just made up:
>
> > There was an old man of F6
> > Who had some extraordinary tricks:
> > He took off his clothes
> > To powder his nose—
>
> > [*An* ANNOUNCER *comes hastily into the* BOX, *pushes* GUNN *aside and speaks into the microphone.*]
>
> ANNOUNCER. We are all most grateful to Mr Gunn for his informal and very instructive talk. Listeners everywhere will no doubt join us [*etc.*]

Page 326.

GT makes some small cuts and larger additions to the Abbot's speeches. Near the end of his speech beginning "Such interest, Mr Ransom," the phrase "the temptation of pity" is deleted. Near the end of the following speech the phrase beginning "but woe to the governors" is altered to read: "but woe to the governors for, however excellent, by the very operation of their powers, they themselves are destroyed." And the speech beginning "In the course of your studies" (p. 328) is expanded to read as follows:

> ABBOT. In the course of your studies you have become acquainted, no doubt, with the mysteries of the rites of Chöd? These exercises, Mr Ransom, are practised by the inmates of this monastery. The celebrant withdraws to a wild and lonely spot deep in the heart of the mountains, and there the corpse is divided and its limbs scattered. The celebrant, sounding on his bone trumpet, summons the gluttonous demons of the air to their appointed feast. At this moment there issues from the crown of his head a terrible goddess. This goddess is his Will, and she is armed with a sword. And as the ghouls of the mountain and of the sky and of the waters under the glacier assemble to partake of the banquet, the goddess with her sword cuts off the limbs of the celebrant's esoteric body, scatters them, tears the flesh in pieces, and apportions his entrails among the demon guests. And the celebrant must wish them good appetite, urging them to devour every morsel. For by so doing he pays the debt which he owes to all the generations of the dead, from whom in his previous incarnations he has borrowed food and clothing and all kinds of service to protect him from heat and cold and from illness and danger. These rites, Mr Ransom, are so terrible that frequently the novices who witness them foam at the mouth, or become unconscious or even fall dead where they stand. And yet, so tedious is the path that leads us to perfection that, when all these rites have been accomplished, the process of self surrender can hardly be said to have begun.... Well, Mr Ransom, I must leave you now. Do not make up your mind at once. Think over my proposal.

Page 340.

> DOCTOR. Oh, but David, Colchesters are much better!
> GUNN. Just as you like. Make that Colchesters will you, waiter. What about soup? Minestrone, I think?
> DOCTOR. You have that. I prefer a really good tomato to anything.
> GUNN. What, even to soup! One minestrone and one tomato. And now, what would you say to Lobster Newberg?

636   TEXTUAL NOTES

>   DOCTOR. I oughtn't to, really; but I can't resist.
>   GUNN. Good Lord! We've forgotten the wine!
>   SHAWCROSS [*bitterly*]. Must you always be talking about food?
>   GUNN. Was I talking about food? Sorry.
>   SHAWCROSS. Well, for God's sake, give it a rest!

Page 341.

>   GUNN. Gosh, that's bad luck, Ian. . . . I say, Michael, let me stay behind. . . . I don't mind very much. . . .
>   SHAWCROSS [*shouting*]. My God, do you think I'm going to crawl for favours to *you*, you little swine. You were always the favourite! [*etc.*]

It is possible that the authors intended at one point to put some or all of these changes into print in a projected third Faber edition. The history of this projected third edition may be reconstructed from the publisher's files.

First, on 10 September 1937, Faber wrote to Auden and Isherwood that the play was about to be reprinted, and asked if they had any further corrections. In an undated note written by Isherwood (and signed by him and Auden) the authors wrote that they enclosed "the correct acting version" of the play, and added this somewhat obscure comment: "if you will compare it with your galley-sheets you will see changes we would like made. But please *don't* alter any of Act II scene 5 from the second [*written over* original] edition." Further correspondence in the files indicates that this "correct acting version" was probably the Group Theatre's promptbook from the 1937 production, as it had the printed text on the right-hand pages and, on the left, markings and instructions that Faber told the printer to ignore except when they were obviously additions to the text. This promptbook (as the printer pointed out when it was sent to him on 17 September 1937) was made up from the *first* edition, and the authors seem to have wanted to add to the new third edition any changes marked in the promptbook that had not already been made in the second edition. This would explain their reference to "your galley-sheets": they seem to have imagined that printers preserve the record of changes made in successive editions of a book by marking those changes on the original galleys of the first edition, and they imagined that the new changes that had not yet been incorporated could thus be distinguished at a glance from changes already in print. (Quite possibly the authors were uncertain which changes had been printed and which had not.) As for the final scene, II.5, whatever stage version appeared in the promptbook was *not* a revision the authors wished to see in print, and for this scene the second edition's text was intended to remain the definitive one.

The printer (the alert John Easton at R. MacLehose & Co., Glasgow) pointed out to Faber that because the "acting version" was made up from the first edition, much of the material in it that had already been altered for the second edition would now be restored to its unrevised original form. (The printer evidently observed that the "acting version" did not incorporate all the changes made for FB.) The printer asked Faber to return the "acting version" to the authors so that they might "spend an hour or two transferring to a copy of the second edition such new corrections from the Acting Version" that they now wished to include in the text. Faber (in the person of Richard de la Mare) transmitted this request to Isherwood on 23 September together with the "acting version" and a copy of the second edition. Isherwood's reply is lost, but it was evidently to the effect that he and Auden had now decided that they wished to make *no* changes to the text of the second edition (possibly they discovered that all the changes they had in mind had in fact already been made), but that they did want to substitute for the simple list of characters in the first two editions a list of the cast from the original production. (Richard de la Mare's reply, on 28 September, thanks Isherwood for his letter, and asks him to send the cast list, as this had been returned along with the "acting version".) The next printing did include a cast list, described as the cast of the opening-night performance at the Mercury Theatre, but in fact listing the cast named in the programmes of the later performances at the Arts Theatre, Cambridge, and the Little Theatre, London. The "acting version" is now lost; it is not the same as the 1939 GT promptbook, which was made up from the second edition.

Because the 1937 "acting version" is lost, and because the 1939 GT promptbook includes a 1939 revision of the final scene, no direct record survives of the versions of the ending that were written and staged during the play's original run. Isherwood's instructions to Faber concerning the "acting version" make clear that the authors regarded none of these versions as worthy of publication, and most of them may have been devised by Doone. E. M. Forster attended the opening night, and some sense of the play's ending can be inferred from a letter he wrote Isherwood the following day. He alludes to Ransom "falling into the audience almost, realistic, panting: 'I will kill the demon' ". Doone had cut Ransom's phantasmagorical trial, with his visions of his fellow climbers, and Forster comments: "I'm sure the changes here are all for the worse; the summit ought to seethe with visions as soon as R. goes wampy ... James *must* be put back ... and I should have brought the Abbot back too." Forster balanced his complaints with praise in a second letter to Isherwood three days later: "The final scene (microphone) is excellent, and there is a grand addition (Lady Isabel's) to the text. My only complaint is that it was all guyed and consequently rogered" (*Selected Letters of E. M. Forster*, vol. 2, 1985, pp. 147-48).

Doone and Isherwood were no better satisfied with the ending. Isherwood recalled later that during the first week of the production a new ending was tried out every night. This may have been only a slight exaggeration. Advice came in from many quarters. E. M. Forster wanted Mrs Ransom to appear on an ice-throne rather than on a rocking chair. W. B. Yeats wanted her to appear as Britannia. After Auden returned to England he and Isherwood prepared yet another revised ending (now lost), which they finished on 13 March, during a trip to the Lake District.

Forster's letters suggest that something very much like the "microphone" ending from FA was used on the first night at the Mercury Theatre. But A. R. Humphreys, who may have seen a later performance, wrote in *The Cambridge Review*, 30 April 1937, that the "Mercury Theatre performance ... omitted the phantasmagoria and everything following his [Ransom's] immolation before his mother's spirit." In contrast, Humphreys wrote, the performance at the Arts Theatre, Cambridge, on 22 April 1937 (perhaps with Auden and Isherwood's new ending) "admitted the 'political' conclusion and left the last words with Mr and Mrs A."—and so seems to have restored something similar to the original microphone scene. Yet the cast list of the Cambridge performance omits the character of Blavek, whose only appearance in the published text is in the microphone scene, so perhaps a different version of the scene had been devised at the same time that other changes were made. At the Arts Theatre, also, some of the phantasmagoria seems to have been restored.

Further revisions of the ending, written in 1939 and 1945, are described in §6 and §7 below.

§6 The Revised Endings Written in 1939

Probably in April 1939, within two months of their arrival in New York, Auden and Isherwood prepared a largely rewritten version of the play's final scene. They did so partly for Burgess Meredith, who was planning a production for a summer theatre, and partly for a production by a small theatre company, the Drove Players, who performed in a studio in New York with almost no scenery or props. The Drove Players' production, directed by Forrest Thayr, Jr., had its first public performance on 23 April 1939, although invitations were sent out with the dates 21-23 April 1939, and it may have been performed on all three nights. Burgess Meredith's production, planned on a much larger scale, was scheduled to open at the Bucks County Playhouse, in New Hope, Pennsylvania, at the end of August 1939, but it never took place.

Isherwood later recalled that he and Auden had first considered an ending (perhaps not unlike the epilogue in FA and RH?) "in which Mr and Mrs A., picnicking under Ransom's statue, declare 'He's one of us now' ", but instead they adopted Burgess Meredith's suggestion "that Ransom should reach the top of the mountain on his own. So the mother was made the last of the phantoms opposing the climb whom her son brushes aside lower down the mountain" (paraphrased from a 1965 lecture in Brian Finney's *Christopher Isherwood*, 1979, p. 164).

The text of the revised final scene survives in a typescript prepared by Isherwood, with manuscript alterations by Auden (and with a fragment on a separate sheet typed by Auden but substantially identical to the corresponding section of Isherwood's typescript). This typescript was in the possession of Richard Eberhart, whom Auden got to know when he taught at St Mark's School in Southborough, Massachusetts, in May 1939; it is now in the Columbia University Library. The state of the text reflects Isherwood's customary care, except that in Ransom's final speech the passage from "Valleys and men, forgive me" to "we believe are real" appears as prose. This seems unlikely to be correct, and I have rearranged the lines as verse, following some clues in the layout of the typescript.

Act II Scene 5

[*Near the summit of* F 6. RANSOM *is struggling upwards. Out of the driving blizzard appears the figure of* JAMES, *dressed exactly as in Act One.*]

JAMES. Michael! Why have you come here? What do you want?
RANSOM. Hardly very friendly, are you?
JAMES. What is it this time? We're grown men now.
RANSOM. Yes. We're grown men now, James. All my life I've sneered at your success. I've mimicked your voice, making speeches; I've made fun of your walk and your grand manners. But I was only jealous. And, after all, why should I have been jealous? You chose your path. I chose mine. Your career would never have made me happy—I know that now, because I know that it could have been my career, too, if I had wished. I don't grudge you your honours, any more. You earnt them fairly enough, in your own way. You knew what you wanted, and you were not afraid to pay the price for it. . . . We have been brothers for twenty-eight years. Shall we start being friends?
JAMES. Very well, Michael. You keep to your world. I will keep to mine.

[*They shake hands.* JAMES *vanishes.* LADY ISABEL, LORD STAGMANTLE *and the* GENERAL *appear.*]

STAGMANTLE. The whole of England is plunged into mourning for one of her greatest sons; but it is a sorrow tempered with pride, that once again Englishmen have been weighed in the balance and not found wanting.
ISABEL. At this hour, the thoughts of the whole nation go out to a very brave and very lonely woman in a little South Country cottage; already a widow and now a bereaved mother.
GENERAL. I am no climber; but I know courage when I see it. He was a brave man and courage is the greatest quality a man can have.
STAGMANTLE. Sport transcends all national barriers, and it is some comfort to realise that this tragedy has brought two great nations closer together.
ISABEL. In the face of this terrible tragedy, one is almost tempted to believe in the grim old legend of the Demon.
RANSOM [*laughing*]. Ha ha! To think that I ever feared you! To think that I ever imagined you were real! Scream yourself hoarse, my dears. Even when you talk of pity, your voices are shrill with hate. This is no place for you. Run back to the crowded city, your playground, and leave me here in peace.
ISABEL. Freely they gave—

GENERAL. They did not count the cost—
STAGMANTLE. Their name liveth for evermore—
ISABEL. They did not think of self—
GENERAL. They died for England—
STAGMANTLE. Honour—
ISABEL. Service—
GENERAL. Duty—
STAGMANTLE. Sacrifice—
ISABEL. England—
STAGMANTLE. Ostnia—
ALL. England! England! England!

> [*They run out, chattering like schoolchildren. The* ABBOT *appears.*]

ABBOT. I am truly sorry for you, Mr Ransom.
RANSOM. Why?
ABBOT. Life is evil.
RANSOM. No. You are wrong. Down there, in the monastery, I could not answer you, because you seemed to echo my private thoughts. But now I can see your mistake. You think life evil because you are afraid. You are afraid of the vulgar active life of ordinary men and women, so you shut yourself up with your books. You are afraid of your body, so you hate it and torture it. But however much you may try to forget your body and its feelings you cannot, because, as long as you are alive, so are they. You spoke of your attacks as a temptation of the Demon. I tell you they are the voice of your humanity. Go back to your monastery and write more poems. For it is your art and not your religion that will save you from madness and death.
ABBOT. You are quick to judge me, Mr. Ransom. You have all the cleverness of your race; but, I am afraid, its shallowness too. In the West, you think that nothing matters but action and material success, and for the sake of these you lie and murder without hesitation or pity. You think our monastery is merely a place of escape for frightened, lazy old men. Perhaps it is. But at least we who live there do no harm to anyone but ourselves. I am disappointed in you, Mr Ransom. I thought you had won free from the beliefs that drive your civilisation on its mad career of destruction. Now I see that you are as deeply implicated as any. But it is not for me to judge you. Only those whom you involved in your ambition can do that. . . . Ask your companions. [*He vanishes.*]
CHORUS [*off stage*]. Ian Shawcross!

[SHAWCROSS *appears.*]

RANSOM. Ian, you've got to tell me. What made you climb the mountain? Was it all my fault? Suppose I had chosen you, not David—would it have made any difference?

SHAWCROSS. Oh, for Christ's sake, shut up!

RANSOM. I made use of your admiration for me. That was only another kind of conceit. You showed me an ideal of myself.

SHAWCROSS. If what you've done amuses you, I'm glad. I'm not very tolerant, I'm afraid. [*Vanishes.*]

CHORUS. David Gunn!

[GUNN *appears.*]

RANSOM. Do *you* blame me, David?

GUNN. You did it beautifully. It was first class.

RANSOM. You sound pleased.

GUNN. Of course I'm pleased. Who wouldn't be?

RANSOM. David, there's something I *must* ask you . . .

[GUNN *vanishes.*]

CHORUS. Edward Lamp! Edward Lamp! Edward Lamp!

LAMP [*off stage*]. I'm all right.

RANSOM. Teddy, what have I done?

LAMP. If I told you, you wouldn't be any the wiser.

RANSOM. Forgive me! It was all my fault! F 6 has shown me what I am. I'm a coward and a murderer. How they must have hated me! I'll never give orders to anyone again. [DOCTOR *appears.*] Tom!

DOCTOR. Just tell me what you want me to do.

RANSOM. I can't face it!

DOCTOR. Yes, Michael, you can. Don't call yourself a murderer. That's only your own pride speaking. You were not hated, you were loved. You were not responsible for the death of these boys. They made their own choice, and they were glad to make it. Now you must make yours. There is only one thing more for you to face. You must face it as they did, alone.

RANSOM. I can't! This is the end! I have no more strength.

DOCTOR. You have the strength of those who loved you—David, Ian, Teddy, myself. Don't be afraid. It's nearly over, now. Good luck, and Goodbye. [*Vanishes.*]

CHORUS. At last the secret is out, as it always must come in the end,
 The delicious story is ripe to tell to the intimate friend;

Over the tea-cups and in the square the tongue has its desire;
Still waters run deep, my dear, there's never smoke without fire.

Behind the corpse in the reservoir, behind the ghost on the links,
Behind the lady who dances and the man who madly drinks,
Under the look of fatigue, the attack of migraine and the sigh
There is always another story, there is more than meets the eye.

For the clear voice suddenly singing, high up in the convent wall,
The scent of the elder bushes, the sporting prints in the hall,
The croquet matches in summer, the handshake, the cough, the kiss,
There is always a wicked secret, a private reason for this.

[MRS RANSOM, *dressed as in Act One, appears.*]

RANSOM [*starting back, with a cry of dismay*]. It's the Demon!
MOTHER. Michael dear, what are you saying? Look at me.
    Why are you so frightened? What have I done
    To make you see me as a demon?
RANSOM. Leave me alone! Leave me alone!
    Why must *you* always haunt me?
MOTHER. I came because you called me, Michael.
    A mother cannot leave her son
    Till he no longer wants her.
RANSOM. It's a lie. You've come to see me fail.
    That's what you've always wanted. Now you have your wish.
    Punish me, Mother. I deserve it.
MOTHER. No, darling, you've succeeded;
    For you have climbed to understanding
    And nothing now remains but to forgive.
    I was your mother and I injured you.
    I did not mean to, but that doesn't matter,
    Nor does it matter either how it happened.
    Enough to say that I was human
    And hurt you with a human love. Forgive me, Michael.
RANSOM. No, Mother, it is I who need forgiveness.
    I thought myself the centre of existence,
    Absolute lord of life, with right to claim
    The absolute perfection of your love.
    Rather than see my faults, or let you go,
    I made you an ubiquitous malevolent shadow,
    The source of all the evil in the world,
    And never learned to love.

MOTHER.   Oh, but you did,
   For you forgot me often; climbing with your friends
   You found your place and loved them and were loved,
   And you were happier and more human than you thought.
   Now you need never think of me again.
   A mother's work is finished when her son
   Accepts his life. Kiss me Goodbye.
RANSOM [*embracing her*]. Mother!
MOTHER. My boy!

> [*She vanishes.* RANSOM *struggles up to the top of the mountain.*]

RANSOM. What had to be is now accomplished.
   I stand upon the summit of a mountain and a life,
   And the descent that my ambition dreaded
   Dies from my thinking as I die.
   Now storm and distance hide me from those valleys
   Where history is manufactured every day,
   Valleys at which I used to shake my fist.
   Valleys and men, forgive me. Oh, we all
   Stand much in need of our forgiveness.
   We have done violence to our nature;
   And the self-distortion throws
   Terrible shadows we believe are real.
   But we are wrong. Man is an animal
   That has to love or perish. There is no Demon.

> [*He dies.*]

CHORUS [*off stage*]. Acts of injustice done
   Between the rising and the setting sun
   In history lie like bones, each one.

   Memory sees them down there,
   Paces alive beside his fear
   That's slow to die and still here.

   The future, hard to mark,
   Of a world turning in the dark
   Where ghosts are walking and dogs bark.

   True, Love finally is great,
   Greater than all; but large the hate,
   Far larger than Man can ever estimate.

> But between the day and night
> The choice is free to all, and light
> Falls equally on black and white.

CURTAIN

The Group Theatre production of the play was revived at the Old Vic on 27 June 1939, with a final scene that Rupert Doone described to the press as a new version written by the authors, who were then in America. In fact, although this version included a small portion of the new material in the version printed immediately above, it is largely a rearrangement of the FB text licenced and performed in 1937. When submitting the new text to the Lord Chamberlain's Office on 22 June 1939, the Group Theatre's secretary, Doris Thellusson, reported (erroneously) that nothing at all had been added to the earlier version. She added that "there have been several alterations in the course of rehearsals", which suggests that even if the Group Theatre's version derives, as Doone claimed, from the authors, it is not entirely in the form they supplied. It is conceivable that Auden and Isherwood had second thoughts about the version they wrote for Burgess Meredith and that they returned to a largely earlier version for the Group Theatre's revival. It is more probable that they sent the Burgess Meredith version to Doone, who preferred to retain the earlier version while incorporating a line or two from the scene the authors had sent him. No manuscript of the revised scene, and no correspondence about it, survives in the Group Theatre papers.

The Group Theatre's revised final scene survives in the form of two separate typescripts, both probably prepared by the Group itself. One is part of the GT promptbook now in the Berg Collection; the other, with slightly abridged dialogue and fuller stage directions (almost certainly not authorial), was submitted to the Lord Chamberlain's Office and is now in the British Library, attached to the LC copy of the play itself.

The text that follows is based on that of the promptbook, although I have ignored the minor cuts and changes that were written into the typescript by unknown hands. One of these indicates that Ransom opens the scene by crawling on stage while repeating his last words from II.4, "The distinguished Presence . . ." The sketchy stage directions in the GT typescript are augmented below with a few words taken from the LC typescript. They may be supplemented further by the stage directions in the published text.

Act II Scene 5

[JAMES, *in full Court dress, appears on the peak.*]

JAMES. I am sorry to say that our civilising mission has been subject to grave misinterpretation. Our critics have been unhelpful and, I am constrained to add, unfair. The powers which I represent stand unequivocally for peace. We have declared our willingness to conclude pacts of non-aggression with you—on condition, of course, that our demands are reasonably met. We have constantly reiterated our earnest desire for peace; but in the face of unprovoked aggression I must utter a solemn warning to you that we are prepared to defend ourselves against all comers. Michael! What are you doing here? Why have you come here? What do you want?

RANSOM. Hardly very friendly, are you?

JAMES. What is it this time, we are grown men now.

RANSOM. There is no time to lose. I have come to make you a most important proposition.

JAMES. Which I accept—on my own conditions.

> [JAMES *claps his hands and* LADY ISABEL, STAGMANTLE, GENERAL, GUNN, SHAWCROSS, LAMP *and* DOCTOR *appear. The* MOTHER *is seated on the peak.*]

JAMES [*putting down chess-board*]. Before we continue, if any of you have any questions you would like to put to my colleagues or myself, we shall be delighted to answer them.

CHORUS [*off*]. Why is my work so dull?

GENERAL. That is a most insubordinate remark. Every man has his job in life, and all he has to think about is doing it as well as it can be done. What is needed is loyalty, not criticism. Think of those climbers up on F 6. No decent food. No fires. No nice warm beds. Do you think they grumble? You ought to be ashamed of yourself.

CHORUS [*off*]. Why doesn't my husband love me any more?

ISABEL. My dear, I'm terribly sorry for you. I do understand. But aren't you being just a teeny-weeny bit morbid? Now think of those young climbers up there on F 6. They're not worrying about their love affairs. [*Archly.*] And I'm sure they must have several. Of course, I know people like you and me can't do big things like that, but we can find little simple everyday things which help us to take us out of ourselves. Try to learn Bridge or get a book from the lending library. Reorganise your life. I know it won't be easy at first, but I'm sure if you stick to it you won't brood so much. And you'll be ever so much happier.

CHORUS [*off*]. Why have I so little money?

STAGMANTLE. Ah, I was expecting that one! I'm a practical man like yourself, and as it happens I'm a rich one, so I ought to know something about money. But speaking quite seriously as a business man, I can tell you that money doesn't necessarily bring happiness. In fact, the more you worry about it, the unhappier you are. The finest and happiest man I ever met—he's leading the expedition up F 6 at the moment—doesn't care a brass button for money, and never has. So my advice is: get all the cash you can and stick to it, but don't worry.

CHORUS [*off*]. Why were we born?

JAMES. That's a very interesting question, and I'm not sure I can answer it myself. But I know what my brother the climber thinks. When we take, he said to me once, the life of the individual, with its tiny circumscribed area in space and time, and measure it against the geological epochs, the gigantic movements of history and the immensity of the universe, we are forced, I think, to the conclusion that, taking the large view, the life of the individual has no real existence or importance apart from the great whole; that he is here indeed but to serve for his brief moment his community, his race, his planet, his universe; and then, passing the torch of life undiminished to others, his little task accomplished, to die and be forgotten.

RANSOM. You're not being fair to me.

JAMES. Keep to your world. I will keep to mine.

[*Game of Chess begins.*]

JAMES. Check!

RANSOM. Check . . . check . . . [*Points to peak.*] Look!

JAMES. Mate! I've won! I've won!

RANSOM. You've cheated me. You've always cheated me. You were always the favourite. I don't know how I've kept my hands off you for so long.

JAMES. It was not Virtue—it was not Knowledge—it was Power that you were after. [*Leaps off peak.*]

ISABEL, STAGMANTLE, GENERAL. Ooo-h! ooo-h!
   What have you done? what have you done?
   You have killed, you have murdered the favourite son!

ABBOT [*entering*]. I am truly sorry for this young man, but I must ask for the Court to be cleared.

[*General exodus.*]

   Please be seated, Mr Ransom . . . I hope everything will be arranged here to your satisfaction?

RANSOM. I didn't do it! I swear I didn't touch him! It wasn't my fault! The Demon gave the sign! The Demon *is* real!

ABBOT. In that case we will call the victims of his pride. Call Ian Shawcross!

CHORUS [*off*]. Ian Shawcross!

[*Enter* SHAWCROSS.]

RANSOM. I've had about as much of this as I can stand. You've got to tell them! I hate to bother you with this sort of thing.
SHAWCROSS. I'm afraid you haven't succeeded very well.
RANSOM. You mean, you did see something? If you hadn't you mightn't believe me.
SHAWCROSS. Oh, for Christ's sake, shut up. If what you've done amuses you, I'm glad. I'm not very tolerant, I'm afraid. [*Exit.*]
ABBOT. Call David Gunn!
CHORUS [*off*]. David Gunn!

[*Enter* GUNN.]

RANSOM. David, you saw what happened?
GUNN. Didn't I just? You did it beautifully. It was first class.
RANSOM. You sound pleased!
GUNN. Of course I'm pleased. Who wouldn't be!
RANSOM. David, there's something I must tell you, now—

[GUNN *exits.*]

STAGMANTLE, ISABEL, GENERAL. Tch—tch—tch!
ABBOT. Call Edward Lamp!
CHORUS [*off*]. Edward Lamp! Edward Lamp! Edward Lamp!

[*Enter* LAMP.]

LAMP. I'm all right.
RANSOM. Teddy, what did you see?
LAMP. If I told you, you wouldn't be any the wiser.
RANSOM. You're on their side too. Is this all your talk of loyalty amounts to?

[*Exit* LAMP.]
[DOCTOR *appears.*]

Tom!
DOCTOR. Just tell me what you want me to do.
RANSOM. I can't face it!
DOCTOR. Perhaps you are right. The Demon demands another kind of victim. Ask the crystal. [*Exit.*]
ABBOT. You wish to appeal to the crystal, Mr Ransom? Do not ask at once, but think it over.
RANSOM. We haven't a moment to lose. I appeal to the crystal.
ABBOT. Very well, since you wish it, I obey you.

MOTHER. Acts of injustice done
>Between the setting and the rising sun
>In history lie like bones, each one.

>Memory sees them down there,
>Paces alive beside his fear
>That's slow to die and still here.

>The future, hard to mark,
>Of a world turning in the dark
>Where ghosts are walking and dogs bark.

>True, Love finally is great,
>Greater than all; but large the hate,
>Far larger than Man can ever estimate.

>Reindeer are coming to drive you away
>Over the snow on an ebony sleigh,
>Over the mountain and over the sea
>You shall go happy and handsome and free.

ABBOT. What did you see in the crystal? What did you see?
RANSOM. I saw written: Man is an animal that has to love or perish. There is no Demon.
ABBOT. Mr Ransom, I did you an injustice. I beg your pardon. I thought I understood your temptation, but I was wrong . . . But if there were no Demon, you would not have been tempted.
RANSOM. What have I done? I didn't mean it! Forgive me! It is all my fault. F 6 has shown me what I am. I'm a coward and a prig. I withdraw the charge. I was wrong . . .
ABBOT. Such altruism, Mr Ransom, is uncommon in one of your race. But I am afraid it is too late now. The case is being brought by the Crown. Have you anything to say in your defence? . . . You realise the consequences of silence? Ladies and Gentlemen of the Jury—consider your verdict.
RANSOM. Stop! No one shall ever—! I couldn't bear it! I'll never let them! Never!
ABBOT. Guilty or Not Guilty?
ALL. Guilty!

[Avalanche.]

CHORUS [off]. Whom history has deserted
>These have their power exerted,
>In one convulsive throe:

With sudden drowning suction
Drew him to his destruction.
But they to dissolution go.

Now he with secret terror
And every minor error
Has also made Man's weakness known.
Free now from indignation
Immune from all frustration
He lies in death alone.

[The lights fade.]

[*B.B.C.* Announcer, Blavek, *and* Doctor Williams.]

Announcer. Dr Williams has given a very vivid account of the expedition up to his return from Camp A to the monastery. Now M. Charles Blavek, the leader of the Ostnian expedition, will tell you how the body of Ransom was found.

Blavek. It is a great honour for me to speak to you about Mr Ransom, and I want to say how deeply we in Ostnia feel with you in the loss of so great a man. First our aeroplane came back with the news that a body had been seen on the summit of F6. Two days later we reached the summit and found Ransom lying there. His ice-axe lay on the rocks a little lower down. Exactly what happened we shall never know.

Dr Williams. You mustn't think that Ransom was a simple person, the strong silent man of the boys' adventure story. He was far removed from that. He had many sides to his character, and I doubt if anyone knew the whole man. I, as a friend and his doctor, certainly did not. He had an almost feminine sensibility with great qualities of soul, will power and a first class intelligence. But while our thoughts are naturally centred upon Ransom—Shawcross, Gunn and Lamp's devotion to duty must never be forgotten.

Blavek. We found the body of Gunn on the eastern arête, about five hundred feet below the summit. The bodies of Lamp and Shawcross were not recovered. The Ostnian expedition, of which I am a member, is proud to have been beaten by such fine men in this climb.

Announcer. The mountain took its toll of four young lives. They died like soldiers at their posts. Their names are the latest, but not the least in that long roll of heroes who gave their lives for the honour of this country . . .

You have been listening to the story of the ascent of F6. The speakers were Monsieur Charles Blavek, leader of the Ostnian expedition, and Dr Williams, who accompanied the English expedition. That brings us to the end of this evening's programme and we are now closing down for the night. Goodnight, everybody. Goodnight.

CURTAIN

§7 Auden's Revised Ending Written in 1945

On 19-21 April 1945, at the end of Auden's third and last year as an instructor at Swarthmore College, the college's Little Theater Club produced the play with a cast of students and professors, directed by Seyril Schochen Rubin. For an account of Auden's discussions with the cast during rehearsals, see Eleanor Follansbee von Erffa, "Auden at Swarthmore", *National Theatre Conference Bulletin*, November 1945, pp. 27-32. Auden sanctioned some Americanization of the play's vocabulary, provided a new version of the ending, and performed the role of the silent cowled monk with the crystal in II.1.

The basic text used in the production was that of RH, including the broadcast-studio epilogue, but with minor cuts and changes. In II.1, in one of the Abbot's speeches on p. 328, "the complete abnegation of the will" was replaced by "the annihilation of the will". In II.5, after the second stanza of the song on p. 350, an additional stanza was inserted, derived from the revised text of the song that Auden published in later collections after the publication of the original version in the play:

> The stars are not wanted now: put out every one,
> Pack up the moon and dismantle the sun;
> Pour away the oceans and sweep up the woods,
> For nothing now can come to any good.

The revisions to the ending begin near the end of II.5. After Mrs A. and Mr A. say "Die for us!" (p. 353), Ransom has a newly added line, "Mother!", and the stage direction (as in the printed text) describes the thunder and roar of an avalanche. This is followed by an entirely new sequence, printed below, which concludes the main part of the scene (the Hidden Chorus is omitted, but the prose epilogue at the microphone is retained from RH, as in the text on pp. 623-25). The text is taken from typescript pages prepared by the director and pasted in her copy of the printed book, now in the Swarthmore College Library. Auden's working draft is in a notebook in the Poetry Library at the State University of New York at Buffalo.

RANSOM. And I knew it all the time.
MOTHER. It has been a long time.

RANSOM. But I'm not frightened any more.
MOTHER. That's what I've been waiting for.
RANSOM. Mother:
MOTHER. Yes, Michael.
RANSOM. I love you. I'll do anything for you.
MOTHER. Anything?
RANSOM. Anything.
MOTHER. You promise?
RANSOM. Yes, yes. What is it?
MOTHER. Let me go.
RANSOM. I don't understand.
MOTHER. Set us both free.
RANSOM. Free from what?
MOTHER. From each other.
RANSOM. No. No. You can't mean it.
MOTHER. You promised.
RANSOM. It's impossible. How can I?
MOTHER. Just repeat after me. "I have been dreaming . . ."
RANSOM. I have been dreaming
MOTHER. Of a demon that chased me
RANSOM. Of a demon that chased me
MOTHER. And an angel that beckoned me on
RANSOM. And an angel that beckoned me on
MOTHER. But now I must wake up
RANSOM. But now I must wake up
MOTHER. And see the real world and find a true reason for being.
RANSOM. And see the real world and find a true reason for being.
MOTHER. Good morning. Good-bye.
RANSOM. Good morning. Good-bye.

> [*Lights fade; stage completely dark.* MOTHER'S *voice recedes into the distance.*]

    Mother.
MOTHER. Yes, Michael.
RANSOM. Forgive me.
MOTHER. Of course, darling.
RANSOM. Good-bye, Mother.
MOTHER. Good-bye, Michael.

> [*Slow dawn throughout chorus; rising sun. Stage empty but for body of* RANSOM, *dead on summit of the mountain.*]

CHORUS. Acts of injustice done
   Between the setting and the rising sun
   In history lie like bones, each one.

MRS RANSOM. So ends your long rebellious climb
   Out of the world of punishment and crime,
   Accepting self-defeat, obey in time.

CHORUS. Memory sees them down there,
   Paces alive beside his fear
   That's slow to die and still here.

MRS RANSOM. Willing to know, unwilling to be known
   You dreaded what you wished, to be alone,
   And fought that dread with nightmares of your own.

CHORUS. The future, hard to mark,
   Of a world turning in the dark,
   Where ghosts are walking and dogs bark.

MRS RANSOM. Your struggle to escape could only bind you,
   Put the weak shadows of your hope behind you,
   Question no more, but let the answer find you.

CHORUS. True, Love finally is great,
   Greater than all; but large the hate,
   Far larger than Man can ever estimate.

MRS RANSOM. Open your eyes now to the Revelation
   That dissipates all myths of self-creation
   And gives what it demands: self-realisation.

CHORUS. But between the day and night,
   The choice is free to all, and light
   Falls equally on black and white.

On the Frontier

§1 History, Authorship, Texts, and Editions

In March 1937, with *The Ascent of F 6* on the stage, Auden and Isherwood went to the Lake District for a few days to devise their next collaboration. On 30 April Isherwood wrote John Lehmann: "Wystan and I have a new play all planned out." The success of *F 6* had encouraged them to hope for a fully professional West End production for their next play. At a meeting of the active members of the Group Theatre, near Henley-on-Thames during the Bank Holiday weekend at the beginning of August 1937, Auden and Isherwood made clear that they intended to write their new play for the commercial theatre rather than for an experimental production by Doone. By the end of the weekend, after bitter negotiations, it was agreed that the play would be produced by the Group after all, but by a reorganized Group in which Doone's authority was shared by others.

Soon after the Group Theatre's meeting Auden and Isherwood went to Dover, where they began to transform their plans into a manuscript on 13 August 1937. They finished a first version on 6 September; during this period they also gave the play its title. Except for one scene, this first version is lost (see §2 below). On 23 September Isherwood wrote Stephen Spender that the lovers' scenes were being rewritten, and he and Auden worked on revisions on 25-27 September. They sent a typescript of the play to John Maynard Keynes, who, after bringing *The Ascent of F 6* to the Arts Theatre, Cambridge, was interested in producing its successor. On 9 October Auden told Keynes that the last scene had been rewritten. Keynes agreed to back a Group Theatre production at the Arts Theatre, where he hoped the play would open in the spring of 1938. He anticipated a further run in London or the provinces.

But in November 1937 Auden and Isherwood made plans to spend the first half of 1938 observing the Sino-Japanese War. They suggested that Keynes, together with Spender and Benjamin Britten (two of the new directors of the Group Theatre), could supervise the production in their absence. Keynes preferred to have the authors on hand during rehearsals, so the production was postponed until their return.

During their journey Auden and Isherwood continued to make revisions. They did most of the work on board the ship that brought them from China to America in June 1938. By the time they returned to England in the middle of July, they had substantially rewritten the play. Auden wrote Spender in July: "We have been giving *On the Frontier* new fittings which improve it, but still feel rather uncomfortable. The subject is too contemporary for a semi-realistic play" (letter in the Berg Collection). The new typescript went to Faber probably at the beginning of August 1938 (Faber sent it to the printer on 4 August), and the play was published on 27 October, apparently without any significant changes in the text. Around this time preparations for the Arts Theatre production were well advanced, and

Auden wrote a new verse interlude to replace the published prose interlude after III.2. The production opened 14 November 1938 for a limited run of one week. Doone directed, Medley provided the design, and Britten composed the music. The production moved to London for one Sunday performance at the Globe Theatre, on 12 February 1939. The authors were now in America, where the Random House edition (differing from the Faber edition only in minor typographic details) appeared on 7 March 1939. A 1958 British paperback edition reprinted the Faber text without change.

Isherwood said in interviews that Auden had written not only the verse but much of the prose in the play. There seems to be no surviving record that assigns individual scenes or passages to Auden or Isherwood, but it appears likely that Auden wrote Valerian's soliloquies in I.1 and III.2 (as he had earlier written Ransom's soliloquies in *F 6*) and possibly some further sections of these and other scenes.

The text of this edition is based on that published by Faber, with minor emendations based on the carbon copy typescript submitted to the Lord Chamberlain's Office on 10 October 1938 (licence granted 9 November), and now in the British Library. The typescript was probably prepared by Isherwood, and has corrections in his hand. (The differences between the typescript and the published text are noted in §3 below.) An additional stanza for the Prisoners' song after I.1 was submitted by the Group Theatre to the Lord Chamberlain shortly before the production, and is included here. The verse interlude following III.2 is printed from Auden's manuscript, now in the Group Theatre papers in the Berg Collection. A typescript made from the same manuscript is attached to the Lord Chamberlain's copy of the play; another copy of that same typescript, in the possession of John Moody, has changes, some in Isherwood's hand, that are noted below. The original prose interlude that had appeared in the published text is reprinted below in §3.

Britten's music for the play is in the Britten-Pears Library at Aldeburgh.

§2 THE LOST FIRST VERSION

Of the first version of the play, completed on 6 September 1937, only one scene survives. The disappearance of the rest is puzzling, as copies of the typescript were read by Rupert Doone, Stephen Spender, J. M. Keynes, and others. Some characteristics of the first version, however, can be glimpsed through the authors' letters and notebooks and through later recollections by their friends.

The earliest traces of the play are sketchy lists of scenes that Auden wrote in a notebook (now in the Berg Collection) probably in March or April 1937; a few sentences about the play were written in the same notebook by Isherwood. The incidents and characters mentioned in these outlines correspond very roughly to those in the published text. The character who became Valerian is referred to in the notebook as Ribbentrop. He is associated there with a character named Babyface, who became a major figure in the first completed version, described by Isherwood as "an American gangster . . . about 19 years old" (letter to Doone, 1

September 1937, in the Berg Collection). Some months after conducting an interview with Isherwood, a journalist reported that the new play included "a gangster called 'Death' "—probably the same character, but possibly an allusion to Valerian's dialogue with Grimm in III.2 (James Lansdale Hodson, "Four Young Dramatists", *Sheffield Telegraph*, 2 April 1938). Robert Medley later recalled that Babyface was Valerian's homosexual lover, a hit-man, and a thoroughly bad lot. The rewritten version of 1938 apparently replaced Babyface with the less extravagant character Lessep, but perhaps retained some of Babyface's speeches in the process.

The end of the play was also very different in its early version. John Lehmann reported that "In the first version . . . a revolutionary end followed the outbreak of war between the two states, the people seizing power" (*New Writing in England*, 1939, p. 35). This conclusion may have been altered between the 1937 and 1938 versions, or it may have been changed shortly before Auden reported to Keynes on 9 October 1937 that the last scene had been rewritten.

The surviving scene of the first version was evidently one of those that, as Isherwood reported to Spender on 23 September 1937, was rewritten soon after the first version was finished. As Auden told Keynes on 9 October: "At one time we had the whole of the lovers' dream scene (Act II scene i) in verse with choral interruptions, but when it was done it seemed all wrong somehow" (letter at King's College, Cambridge). The text of this scene—some of which was preserved in the final version of II.1—is reprinted below from Auden's fair copy manuscript, which Isherwood retained. I have followed Auden's inconsistent capitalization of "Them" and "They", although these pronouns should probably be understood as capitalized in the corresponding published text (pp. 387-90). In the chorus on p. 659, "They're" should probably be understood as "There are".

WIRELESS. Good-evening, boys and girls. This is Dreamland calling. O what a night. What a moon. The air is warm and still. Not a breath of wind. Are you lonely? Are you unhappy? Have you failed in an exam? Have you had a row with your family? Are you sick of the pattern of the wallpaper in your bedroom? Then fly away to Dreamland and forget your troubles.

O I assure you it's quite respectable. Dreaming is considered very *bon ton* in the best houses. It's all the rage and you want to be in the swim, don't you? Don't think your fathers and mothers and uncles and aunts will mind. Bless you, when they were your age. . . . You'd be surprised. Between you and me and the gatepost I shouldn't wonder if they could tell you a thing or two you didn't know. So don't let that bother you. Dreams are strictly on the Q.T.

Come along then. It's not only a pleasure; it's a social duty. I ask you, where would the world be without dreams. There's no knowing what mightn't happen. The poor might forget their station, the rich might give away their money, people might begin to tell the truth, perfect strangers might speak to each other—O dear yes, most unsuitable.

So you see how important it is. Insure yourselves against rash behaviour. Remember your duty to society and become dream-conscious.

Dreamland is at your service. Ah what visions, what nightmares, what extraordinary scenery, what alluring shapes.

Come then. Come to Liberty Hall. Be eccentric, be extravagant, be outrageous. Come to Dreamland.

ERIC. Is that you, Anna.
ANNA. Yes, Eric.
ERIC. I knew that I could make this happen.
ANNA. Where are we?
ERIC. This is the place which I have found for us
　　This is our garden, our enchanted bower.
　　Here spurred Authority with brandished gun
　　Shall never scare us from the woods. Here we
　　Shall not encounter gibbering in the paths
　　Old Hatred in her black and hideous dress.
　　Reverend Hypocrisy shall never call
　　To spin his snare for Faith above the tea-cups
　　Twisting the words of great and generous men
　　To justify injustice. Flood-lit Fear
　　Shall never scold and stamp among his banners
　　Nor dedicate a monument to Death.
　　This garden is our own; these avenues
　　Are ours to stroll in hand in hand, Desire
　　Grows his abundant and miraculous roses,
　　And we may pick them freely for each other;
　　Content is always busy in his workshop
　　And we may visit him, stand in his doorway,
　　Admire his quiet and perfect craftsmanship;
　　Tanned Innocence is paddling in the stream.
　　O here is always summer!
CHORUS [*invisible*]. Beware! Who pays
　　For these enchanting nights and days?
　　Can you find the money
　　To rent the land flowing with milk and honey?
　　Can you find the fare
　　To take you there?
　　The cosy island in the sea

The island of coral and coconut tree,
The placid monastery among the savage mountains,
The garden in the desert with its skittish fountains,
The cottage in the wood, the residential neighbourhood,
They cost, they cost,
They cost a lot
Far more than you have got
For sooner or later the bills begin,
The bills come in that you have to settle
The bills for the kettle, the refrigerator
The telephone, the gramophone, the current, the coal,
The dining-room table, the daffodil bowl.
And what shall you say
On that reckoning day
For those who can't pay
The fountains won't play
The roses decay
Love pass away.

ANNA. Eric. The darkness is so near.
ERIC.   O Anna
   From the very moment that I saw you first
   I've struggled for this. Did you know that?
ANNA.   Yes
   I've felt you near me in the crowded shops;
   You gave me patience. Sometimes you sat down
   Beside me in the park; you did not speak
   But as I watched the sparrows round your feet
   I knew that you were gentle. Often too
   You stood beside my chair as I sat serving
   Disturbing my hands; and when I went to dances
   My partners all were really you.
CHORUS. Beware. Do not listen
   Her love will be a prison
   Her love will be excessive
   Jealous and possessive
   Jealous of your work, jealous of your friends
   She will defeat you and eat you,
   She will use you for her private ends
   Doubt her, doubt her,
   Her love is a trap
   She loves not you but only

    The misunderstood and lonely,
    The failure who comes crying to her lap,
    The invalid who cannot do without her.
ANNA. When did you first begin to see.
ERIC. Ever since I remember I've caught glimpses of you.
    Upon the summit of a crag at sunset
    I saw you for a moment and the day
    Was charged with meaning. Far ahead of me,
    Down the long poplar avenue, you were
    The figure I could never quite catch up.
    I saw your face reflected in the river
    As I sat fishing. You smiled back at me
    To tell me that one day I should be famous,
    And when I read of the world's worry and folly
    You came between me and the print and promised
    That good should triumph. Lately I've begun
    To see you much more clearly, though you still
    Moved only on the far side of the mirror,
    But now at last . . .
CHORUS. Beware! Though he plead
    His love is only greed
    And vanity and lust.
    He will leave you in disgust.
    He will brag about you to his friends,
    He will deceive you and leave you,
    He will use you for his private ends
    Doubt him, doubt him,
    His love will freeze
    Your forward flower,
    He loves not you but power
    The broken hearts that add to his prestige
    The soft adoring circle round about him.
ANNA. Do They see too.
ERIC.   No, They are blind.
    They miss the shy secretive smiles of children
    Utterly happy in a simple game.
    The skilled mechanic bowed upon the lathe
    And worshipping his task, the beggar's gift,
    The gaiety of thieves, the life devotion
    Of dull and ugly couples for each other.
    No, They see nothing and are proud of it.

CHORUS. Beware! You are wrong
   As you'll learn before long.
   They're sharp eyes in the window across the street
   Sharp tongues are wagged when two neighbours meet
   They're sharp ears cocked at your bedroom door
   Light fingers that steal into your letter drawer
   It's a soft tread that tiptoes up your stairs
   And a long nose that pokes in your affairs.
ANNA. O Eric, I'm so afraid of Them.
ERIC. As long as we're together, we are safe.
   They have no power here. You are the sun
   And when you smile you free the earth
   The puny little terrors of the night
   Are known for what they are and scuttle back
   Into their holes. The weakest take
   Difficult vows assured that they can keep them,
   The guiltiest sing and know themselves forgiven.
   O shine for ever. Never set again.
ANNA. I will be true.
   When the strong stars have lost their stamina
   And dropped exhausted from the sky, when Time
   Lies babbling on his death-bed; and long after
   The universe has rusted into holes,
   My love shall not have finished schooling.
CHORUS. Beware! You stand on the outskirts of dream
   Where the waterlilies float on the charming stream
   And the birds sing, and the welcome to strangers
   Is friendly still, with no hint of the dangers
   That lie ahead. But take one more pace
   And an unpleasant change comes over the place.
   In the inefficient city of Fear
   Where your guide will suddenly disappear
   Where the streets lead nowhere and change their directions
   Where the trains run backwards and miss their connections,
   Where the doors will not shut, and when you begin
   To embrace your love, someone always comes in.
   Where you watch the lock being gently tried
   And you know that there's something awful outside
   And you cannot move and you cannot scream
   Beware. Beware of the city of Dream.
ANNA. They're laughing at us. Don't you hear them.

ERIC. Don't Anna. Don't. It can't be true.
   It shan't be true. Don't listen to them, Anna.
   Our love is stronger than Their hate. It must be.
CHORUS. Beware.
ANNA. You'll make Them angry. We shall both be punished.
CHORUS. Beware.
ERIC. I defy Them.
CHORUS. Beware.
ERIC. Anna. Anna. Where are you.
ANNA. Where are you, Eric.
ERIC. Come back.
ANNA. I can't. They're too strong. Help me Eric. They're taking me away.
ERIC. They're holding me back.
ANNA. I shall never see you again.
ERIC. Anna, can you hear me. I swear I'll come back to you. I'll beat Them somehow. Only wait for me, Anna. Promise you'll wait.
ANNA. I promise, Eric.

CHORUS. O quick and furtive is the lovers' night.
   Pausing to marvel at their poisoned grace,
   The moon's accusing lantern brings to light
   The sleepers ruined in a brief embrace.
   O quick and furtive is the lovers' night.

   O silly and unlucky are the brave,
   Who tilt against the world's enormous wrong.
   Their serious little efforts will not save
   Themselves or us. The enemy is strong.
   O silly and unlucky are the brave.

   O happy the free cities of the dead
   Which ask no questions of what life was for,
   Where nothing matters that was ever said,
   And no one need take trouble any more.
   O happy the free cities of the dead.

§3 THE PUBLISHED TEXT AND THE PRODUCTION TEXT

The edition published by Faber on 27 October 1938 was probably set from another copy of the typescript of which a carbon was submitted to the Lord Chamberlain's Office. This typescript was probably prepared by Isherwood, and has few obvious errors. "St Francis Stylites" (p. 366) may be a slip for St Simeon Stylites, but, if so, it seems to be the authors' error rather than a typist's.

There are few verbal differences between the typescript and the printed text. In the notes on the characters (p. 359), the typescript's description of Valerian opens with the sentence (dropped in the printed text): "A Conrad Veidt type of character." In the interlude after II.1, the final speech of the First Leftist (p. 391) reads in the printed text "Their blood is upon your head" where the typescript (followed here) has "on your head"; the compositor evidently repeated "upon" from the preceding line. In II.2 (p. 395), the compositor's eye evidently skipped over a line and omitted a sentence from one of the Leader's speeches, here restored ("Nobody knows how I have suffered"). Another difference involves a detail in the printed version of the interlude after III.2 and is described in the prefatory note to that version, below.

Other variants between the typescript and the printed text are typographical. In the notes on the characters, the typescript (followed here) emphasizes "*must*" in the sentence "All the Chorus *must* be able to sing"; the printed text somewhat ferociously emphasizes "*All*" as well. This is probably an error that crept in when the typescript was marked to indicate that italic type should be used for the unemphasized words and roman for the emphasized ones. In the interlude after III.1, the typescript (followed here on pp. 402-403) presents in capital letters the dialogue that is shouted across the front line; the printed version uses ordinary upper and lower case, perhaps because the printer mistook the capitals for a typist's error. On p. 365 I have emended both the typescript and the published text by altering the period after "heir to all the ages" to a comma; Isherwood presumably mistook the capitalized word that follows ("Nature") as the start of a new sentence. I have silently restored capitalized nouns that the printer reduced to lower case. The authors let Bob Veigel of II.1 (p. 383) die as Bob Veigal in III.1 (p. 397), and a correction can be of no help to him now.

Few authorial changes were made in the text after it was prepared for publication. On 10 October 1938 the typescript was submitted to the Lord Chamberlain's Office, which responded about a week later by calling for some small cuts and changes mostly designed to blur Westland's identification with Germany. On 27 October the Group Theatre reported back to the Lord Chamberlain with substitutions made by Isherwood. The Leader became the Guidanto (Esperanto for "leader"), a Storm Trooper became a Corporal, Shock Troops became Blue Guards, Stahl became Alving, the Culture House became the Agricultural Institute, Labour Camps became Labour Corps, Frommer became Krog, and so forth. Other minor cuts, not noted in this edition, were made by the censor, not by Isherwood.

The largest change made in the production text was the substitution of the new verse interlude after III.2 (pp. 413-15) for the prose interlude in the published version (reproduced below). This new interlude, in the form of a typescript based on Auden's manuscript, was sent to the Lord Chamberlain's Office on 29 October 1938. Another copy of the typescript, in the possession of John Moody, has three changes probably made in rehearsals. The first two are in Isherwood's hand, and may have been composed by him. Replacing the lines from "Well met" to "We have seen them all before", Isherwood wrote in:

SECOND JOURNALIST. Here too, are rival armies.
FIRST JOURNALIST.   Here
                    Is famine, plague and civil war
                    Things that we have seen before.

(This change was also reported to the Lord Chamberlain on 1 November 1938.) The lines from "Visit violence for your sake" to "Justify your party creeds" were revised by Isherwood to read:

THIRD JOURNALIST. Visit violence for the sake
FIRST JOURNALIST. Of the public when they wake
                    Justify their party creeds.

And in the last line of the second stanza of the interlude's concluding song the word "Presenting" is altered (not in Isherwood's hand) to "Showing".

The last of the changes made before the production was the addition of a final stanza to the interlude after I.1 (p. 375). This stanza was submitted to the Lord Chamberlain on 11 November 1938, and was identified as occurring after the blackout. The text submitted to the Lord Chamberlain has "the Guidanto" rather than "the Leader" in the second line, to conform to the changes Isherwood had made earlier at the censor's insistence. This edition substitutes "the Leader" in order to maintain consistency with the rest of the text.

For the London performance on 12 February 1939, Doone rearranged the first act to open with I.2, followed by the original prologue, and then I.1. The interlude after I.2 was dropped, as was the new interlude after III.2. Doone had told Keynes earlier (on 22 November 1938; letter at King's College, Cambridge) that Isherwood had agreed to change the order of the first Valerian and Ostnia-Westland scenes. Doone also asked Isherwood to ask Auden for longer soliloquies for Eric and Anna in I.2, but nothing seems to have come of this.

The original published text of the interlude after III.2 follows. In the published list of scenes (cf. p. 359) this interlude is titled "The English Newspapers". (The title for the interlude that replaced it, "The War Correspondents", is taken from the programme of the Arts Theatre production.) In the typescript text of the original interlude the Third Reader's liberal paper was a liberal-labour paper and the "Anglo-Saurian Oil Co." was the "Anglo-Greenland Oil Co."; on 6 August 1938 Auden's agent wrote T. S. Eliot asking, on behalf of the authors, that Eliot's office make certain that the Anglo-Greenland company was fictitious. The authors, he explained, had checked the telephone directory, but wanted to be sure. Possibly Eliot changed the name for safety's sake, but he may have consulted Auden, and "saurian" was a word Auden used about two years later in "At the Grave of Henry James" ("the squat women of the saurian brain").

(Before the Curtain)

[*The five male members of the chorus represent the typical readers of five English newspapers. They should be dressed according to their shades of political opinion. Thus, the* First Reader *has a conservative, highly respectable government paper, the* Second *a violently reactionary, more popular paper, with pictures, the* Third *a liberal paper, the* Fourth *a communist paper. The* Fifth Reader, *who is trembling all over, is studying one of those sensational and alarming news-letters which give the "low-down" on the international situation. Each reader is seated. A spotlight rests on each in turn, as he reads his passage aloud.*]

Fourth Reader. Workers rising everywhere. Fascist Collapse.

Second Reader. General Frommer confident of victory over Reds.

First Reader. Tarnberg believed captured by insurgents. Government forces retire on Konia.

Second Reader. Red Terror in Tarnberg.

Third Reader. People's Army successful. White troops in retreat.

Fourth Reader. Workers deal smashing blow to international Fascism. Tarnberg cheers march of heroes.

Fifth Reader. From a source usually reliable, we hear that Markov, the Ostnian General, has secretly left Paris to join Westland's General Frommer as military adviser. Subscribers will recall that Markov has long been a valued friend of Frommer's beautiful blonde wife. As told in number 256 of our bulletin, their friendship had a romantic beginning during the Salzburg festival, two years ago, when the gallant Ostnian rescued Her Ladyship's poodle, Jimmy, from a baroque fountain.

Third Reader. It is important for us to realise that the People's Army is supported not only by the extreme Left, but by all the Liberal and progressive elements in Westland. If they win, Westland will once more take her place among the Democratic countries.

Second Reader. Inhuman cruelties by Reds. Bishop boiled alive. British governess' terrible experience.

Fourth Reader. Mass executions in Kresthaufen. Fascist thugs machine-gun women and children.

Fifth Reader. An interesting sidelight on relations between Frommer and the City is thrown from Mayfair. Lady Corker, well-known local right-wing socialite, gave an alfresco supper-party on Thursday last, at which the Westland Ambassador was guest of honour. In the charades which followed, His Excellency and the Chairman of the Anglo-Saurian Oil Co. made a sensation as Darnley and the Queen of Scots.

SECOND READER. Church denounces Communism. World-wide day of prayer ordered for better industrial relations.

THIRD READER. Christianity and Socialism should be allies, says East-End Vicar.

FIRST READER. Tension in Europe increases. Prime Minister to announce British plan for mediation.

SECOND READER. No Bolshevism in Europe, say Anti-Comintern Powers. War material pouring in to Reds from Russia.

FOURTH READER. International Fascism alarmed. Foreign tanks to crush Westland workers.

THIRD READER. Intervention threatened by totalitarian states. League summoned.

FIRST READER. There is an increasing danger of Europe splitting into two irreconcilable camps. To this, the Englishman, with his love of liberty and his distrust of cast-iron ideologies, is tempted to retort, in the words of our national poet: "A plague on both your houses!"

FIFTH READER. From War Offices sources, comes the news that the outbreak of world war cannot possibly be delayed beyond the middle of March . . . [*Covers his face with his hands.*] Oh dear! Oh dear! Oh dear!

BLACK OUT

Documentary Films

AUDEN did most of his work in documentary films for the General Post Office Film Unit headed by John Grierson. In the spring of 1935 Auden wrote his friend Basil Wright, who was working at the Unit, about the possibility of work in films. Wright showed Auden's letter to Grierson, and was told to fetch him. During the summer of 1935, while he was still teaching at the Downs School, Auden wrote verses for some of the Unit's projects that were in early stages of planning or production. On 1 September 1935 he joined the Unit as a full-time "apprentice"—which meant that he worked as a writer and as an assistant director, and performed any other chores that film work required. In February 1936 he took two months' leave from the Film Unit to work on his other writings. Late in March, while he was in Portugal working on *The Ascent of F6*, he sent Grierson his resignation. He continued to do free-lance work on documentaries afterward.

COAL FACE

This film was produced in the summer of 1935 by John Grierson (for the G.P.O. Film Unit), directed by Alberto Cavalcanti, edited by William Coldstream, with music by Benjamin Britten and verse by Auden. (*Coal Face* was an "Empo" film, a name Grierson invented for the more avant-garde G.P.O. productions.) It was first shown at the Film Society, London, on 27 October 1935. The prose narration about coal mining (not reproduced in this edition) was written for the film by Montagu Slater. This was interspersed with a male chorus's chanted readings of a list of miners' job titles and an excerpt from an official report of a mining disaster. These chanted passages may perhaps have been conceived and compiled by Auden and Britten, although Auden's hand does not appear among those that made notes and corrections in the typescript drafts now in the Britten-Pears Library.

Auden's own verse, reproduced in the main text of this edition, was sung by a female chorus near the end of the film. Auden, probably acting on Basil Wright's request, wrote his verse in June 1935, while he was still teaching at the Downs School. He apparently discussed other aspects of the work, possibly including the chanted passages, with Wright, Cavalcanti, and Britten when they visited him at the Downs on 4 July 1935; this was Auden's first meeting with Britten.

The text reproduced in the main text of this edition is taken from the programme of the first showing at the Film Society. Probably early in January 1936 Auden submitted a closely similar text, titled "Madrigal" (with "black as night" altered to "dark as night"), to *New Writing* as one of his "3 Fragments for Films" but withdrew the entire manuscript on 10 April (see the notes to *Negroes* below).

Britten's setting of the poem, in his manuscript score and on the soundtrack, differs from these texts. It reads "the cages" instead of "your cages"; inverts the order of the lines beginning "And Kate" and "For Sunday"; and in the following line reads "For Monday" instead of "And Monday". (The score also has two apparent errors: "hills" for "hill" and "your heart" for "her heart".) In its essentials (but with the reading "your cages", and with the two short lines joined as one long line) this rearranged version constituted the text Auden reprinted in *New Verse*, Summer 1938, in (with "the cages" again) *Another Time* (1940), and in *1945*, *1950*, and *1966* (see p. 524). It seems likely that the version in the score and in these later editions represents an early state of the poem that Auden published after forgetting the revisions he had made when writing out the poem for the Film Society programme and the manuscript he submitted to *New Writing*.

The chanted list of job titles and the excerpt from the report of a disaster are printed below, the first from a typescript scenario (prepared at a stage when the film was to be titled *Miners* and here slightly emended) now in the Britten-Pears Library, the second from Britten's manuscript score:

Banksman, barrowman, caster, changer, check-weigher, coupler, crane-man, driver, flat-lad, foal, greaser, headsman, helper-up, hewer, inspector, master-shifter, master-wasteman, onsetter, overman, peedee, rolley-way-man, running-fitter, skipper, skreenman, trapper, wailer, waste-man.

Fire followed explosion. Five hundred men trapped half a mile underground two miles from pit-eye. Rescue efforts abandoned. Cannot account for two hundred lamps.

Night Mail

This film was produced in the second half of 1935 by John Grierson for the G.P.O. Film Unit. It was directed by Harry Watt and Basil Wright, with music by Britten and verse for the final section of the film by Auden. (There are the credits on the film itself; in fact the original scenario was mostly by Wright and the actual direction mostly by Watt.) It was first shown at the Arts Theatre, Cambridge, on 4 February 1936, and was first shown in general commercial release in London on 3 March 1936. Auden began working on his verse commentary in July 1935, and revised it while working at the Film Unit in the autumn of that year. Auden also directed a brief shot of a railway guard that was used in the film. (In later years he recalled that the guard died thirty seconds later; Basil Wright reports that the interval was more like two weeks.)

Auden worked on the film at almost all stages of its production, so the text prepared for the soundtrack may be regarded as his approved final version. This edition reproduces the earliest printed text, in the pamphlet *GPO Film Library Notes and Synopses 1936*, which is identical to the soundtrack except in minor details (the soundtrack has "and the boy" for "and boy" and "in the margin" for "on the margin"). This text probably derives from Auden's lost working manuscript or typescript. The commentary was reprinted in the 1937 and 1938 editions of *GPO Film Library Notes and Synopses*, as a broadside apparently distributed by the

DOCUMENTARY FILMS 667

Film Unit at some exhibition showings of the film (two such broadside editions are known, but one of them has been found only in a proof copy), and in many anthologies and collections. Auden first printed it in a volume of his own in *1966*.

Two earlier versions of Auden's commentary survive. The earlier of the two is a typescript that Auden included (apparently a few months after it was typed by someone at the Film Unit) in the "3 Fragments for Films" he submitted to John Lehmann for publication in *New Writing* probably in early January 1936 and withdrew on 10 April (see the notes to *Negroes* below). The text of *Night Mail* in this version is a typescript scenario for the latter part of the film, with the musical bridges indicated by the number of feet of film they occupy. The text is untitled, but Auden has crossed out the typescript title "T.P.O." (i.e., Travelling Post Office). The sections of the text where lines were omitted or rearranged in later versions are printed below. The two opening lines, which do not appear in later texts, and the two spoken passages beginning "Dawn freshens" and "Thousands are still asleep" are marked "Solo" in Auden's hand; the two other large sections, one beginning "This is the night mail" and the other beginning "Letters of thanks," are marked "Chorus". The words in parentheses were presumably provided for the composer to include if the rhythms required them.

> North, north, north,
> To the country of the Clyde and the Firth of Forth.
>
> This is the night mail crossing the border
> Bringing the cheque and the postal order,
> Letters for the rich, letters for the poor
> The shop at the corner and the girl next door.
> Through (the) sparse counties she rampages
> Her driver's eye upon her gauges.
> Panting up past lonely farms
> Fed by the fireman's restless arms.
> Uplands heaped like slaughtered horses
> Rushing stony watercourses
> Lurching through (the) cutting, and beneath (under) (the) bridge
> Into the gap in the distant ridge.
>
> Winding up the valley and the water-shed
> Through the heather, and (the) weather and (the) dawn overhead.
>
> Pulling up Beattock, a steady climb
> The gradient's against her, but she's on time.
> Past cotton grass and moorland boulder
> Shovelling the white steam over her shoulder.
> Birds turn their heads as she approaches,
> Stare from (the) bushes at her blank-faced coaches.
> In the farm she passes no one wakes,

But the jug in the bed-room gently shakes.

Dawn freshens. The climb is done,
The train tilts forward for the downhill run.
Down towards Glasgow she descends
Towards the steam tugs yelping down the glade of cranes.
The fields of apparatus, the furnaces,
Set on the dark plain like gigantic chess-men.
All Scotland waits for her.
Yes, this country, whose scribbled coastline traps the wild Atlantic in a maze of stone,
And faces Norway with its doubled notches.
In the dark glens beside the sea lochs, pale green at their edges,
Men long for news.

Letters of thanks, letters from banks,
[*substantially as the final text through*:]
The typed, the printed and the spelt all wrong.

Thousands are still asleep
Dreaming of terrifying monsters or a friendly tea under the cedars.
Asleep in working Glasgow, asleep in well-set Edinburgh, asleep in granite Aberdeen.
In grimed Dundee that weaves a white linen from the Indian fibre,
In Stornoway smoking its heavy wools,
And where the rivers feel the long salmon threshing in their netted mouths,
Continue their dreams.
But shall wake soon and long for letters
And none will hear the postman's knock
Without a quickening of the heart
For who can bear to feel himself forgotten?

The later of the two early versions seems to be the one written out by Britten in his manuscript score. It is similar to the final version but contains some lines not present in the soundtrack. After the first verse paragraph (ending "but she's on time") the score has this verse paragraph:

Through sparse counties she rampages,
Her driver's eye upon her gauges.
Panting up past lonely farms
Fed by the fireman's restless arms.
Striding forward along the rails
Through Southern Uplands with Northern mails.

The next verse paragraph begins with two lines preceding "Past cotton grass":

> Winding up the valley to the watershed,
> Through the heather and the weather and the dawn overhead.

The passage beginning "Dawn freshens" is not in the score, as it was written to be spoken over a long musical passage. The passage beginning "Letters of thanks" is substantially the same in the score and the final text. And the final passage, beginning "Thousands are still asleep", is also absent because it too was intended to be spoken.

One of the early anthology reprints of the poem introduced an error that recurred in some other printings. In *The Poet Speaks: An Anthology for Choral Speaking*, selected by Marjorie Gullan and Clive Sansom (London: Macmillan, 1940), the last line reads "For who can hear and feel himself forgotten?" I have been told that Auden, when asked whether this was his intended text, said it was not what he wrote but that he liked it, perhaps more than he liked the original. This story may be true, but Auden preserved his original text when he revised the poem for his *1966* collection.

Negroes

This film was conceived by Auden, Britten, and Basil Wright in 1935. Although Auden wrote his commentary for the film late in that year, possibly around October or November, and Britten apparently set it to music about the same time, the project was abandoned. It was revived in 1938, and the film was completed, using previously shot footage, under the title *God's Chillun*. The credits name Max Anderson, Rona Morrison, and Gordon Hales as editors, and attribute the words to Auden and the music to Britten. The editors are not otherwise known to have worked with the G.P.O. Film Unit. Auden apparently did not take part in this late stage of the work, and it seems likely that Britten's music also was recorded at an earlier point. In the concluding section of the soundtrack the text differs considerably from the text presented here, and the changes are almost certainly not Auden's work. The film was officially released on 24 February 1939, but there is no indication that it was ever shown to the public.

The text published here is taken from two main sources. All sections except the final one (that is, from the beginning through the Commentator's line "We were free") are transcribed from Britten's score (in the Britten-Pears Library), with the overlapping settings of different passages rearranged in a sequence that seems likely to correspond to Auden's lost original. The final section of the film (beginning with the Bass Recitative "Still at their accustomed hour") is taken from Auden's "3 Fragments for Films" manuscript, submitted to John Lehmann for publication in *New Writing* probably in early January 1936, withdrawn on 10 April 1936, and now in the Humanities Research Center at the University of Texas at Austin. (Auden told Lehmann he was withdrawing the fragments for films because he felt they were not good enough to publish. But by this time he had also adapted the final chorus of *Negroes* for use in *The Ascent of F 6*. This adapted chorus was the only part of the film published in Auden's lifetime.) Curiously, much of the final section of the film has disappeared from Britten's score, while the final section is the only one included in Auden's "3 Fragments". The "3 Fragments" text of *Negroes*, which is untitled, is a copy of the typescript working scenario of the film (not typed by Auden), with the narrative text accompanied by notes on the associated footage; Auden has deleted these notes and left only his own text. I have borrowed some of the speech headings from this latter section of the text in transcribing the earlier sections from Britten's score. I have followed the soundtrack in some slight alterations to the text as given in Britten's score, because it seems likely that these were made in cooperation with Auden. Because Auden does not name any collaborator in the "3 Fragments for Films" manuscript, the prose commentary may be assumed to be his own; he invariably insisted on giving equal credit to any co-author.

In the "3 Fragments" text, the paragraph beginning "Physically they are not" is written out in Auden's hand, replacing this drier passage that appears in typescript: "Physically they are not as strong as they seem, partly because they do not take sufficient nourishing food. They are particularly liable to malaria and hook worm, but the Rockefeller Institute is helping to reduce these. Owing to bad housing conditions, infant mortality is high." At the end of the Bass Recitative that opens the final section of the film ("Still at their accustomed hour . . ."), Auden deleted the typescript line "Brave and brutal, in pride at prow." This originally followed on from the preceding line without any intervening punctuation. The footnote to the text is in Auden's hand.

BESIDE THE SEASIDE

This film was produced in 1935 by Marion Grierson for the Strand Film Company on a commission from the Travel and Industrial Association of Great Britain. It was released probably around December 1935. Auden's name is not listed in the credits, but in a lecture on "Poetry and Film" that he delivered at the North London Film Society probably in early 1936 (a report of the lecture appears in Appendix V, above), Auden briefly described the film, calling it *By the Sea-side*, and quoted the phrase "like a cool fish in a grotto"—which differs slightly from the version on the soundtrack.

The commentary on the soundtrack may have been revised from a lost earlier version that included the poem "Look, stranger, at this island now"; the soundtrack includes phrases from the poem. In a recorded reading of his poems in 1961 (tape in the Yale University Library) Auden said the poem was written for a film that was never completed; he may simply have forgotten that the film had in fact been finished and released. Auden dated the poem November 1935; probably the final version of the commentary was written no more than a few days afterward.

The text in this edition is transcribed from the soundtrack, and has not been published previously. The first of the two sections of text accompanies footage of the seaside, the second accompanies footage of London.

The Way to the Sea

This film was produced in 1936 by Paul Rotha for the Strand Film Company on a commission from the Southern Railway, and was first screened at a film trade show in February 1937. It was directed by J. B. Holmes, with music by Britten and "End Commentary" by Auden.

The film celebrated the electrification of the railway from London to Southampton. Auden and Britten worked on their verse and music for the final third of the film during the first week of December 1936. The tone of their work was in large part a deliberate send-up of the portentous manner of British documentaries of the period.

None of the text was published in Auden's lifetime. The text printed here is transcribed from the soundtrack, and is based in part on earlier transcripts by B. C. Bloomfield and by Jill Burrows, whose text was published in Donald Mitchell's *Britten and Auden in the Thirties: The Year 1936* (1981). The present text also includes lines that appear only in Britten's manuscript score but are absent from the film itself. These are the four lines beginning "Nor is power absent" and the three lines "A place of salutes . . . and the living." Where the soundtrack has the three lines "Be a sport or . . . your freedom", the score reads "Solitary vision of the stroll. / We seek a spectacle. / All kinds of people each with their private vision of England—or a street in the rain." Britten's score also has some trivial variants and misreadings not noted here.

The Londoners

This film, released in March 1939, was produced by Basil Wright and John Grierson with the Realist Film Unit for the Gas Light and Coke Company on the occasion of the jubilee of the London County Council. The director was John Taylor. The credits attribute "Sections of Commentary" to Auden. The parts written by Auden are apparently the three passages reproduced here, although his authorship of the third seems less certain than his authorship of the first and second. All three passages are spoken on the soundtrack in a manner different from that used for all the other commentary in the film. The full text was apparently never published, but a few lines were quoted (and attributed to Auden) in a review in *The Times*, 7 March 1939, and the two final lines were quoted (without attribution) in *Time*, 24 April 1939. Both passages could conceivably have been taken from a transcript made available at the time and now lost. The text in this edition is transcribed from the soundtrack, with "Round Ponds" emended to "Round Pond". The lineation of the passage from "Areas of light and air" to "Places for play" is taken from the review in *The Times* on the chance that this might have derived from a lost transcript based on Auden's original, and the lineation of the rest of the text has been supplied in similar style.

OTHER FILMS

As a successor to *Night Mail* Grierson planned an ambitious film titled *Air Mail to Australia*. Auden was apparently chosen as its co-director, and planned to make a flight to Australia around October or November 1935 in order to find material for a commentary and perhaps also to accompany a film crew. The film was to be written by Auden and Basil Wright, and was to concentrate less on the actual flight than on the civilizations over which the air mail regularly flew. Auden did in fact fly to Switzerland in October, in what seems to have been intended as the first leg of the journey, but he returned to London without continuing. No further information is available about this project, which was apparently abandoned without any further progress.

For another G.P.O. film, *Calendar of the Year*, produced in 1935 by John Grierson and directed by Evelyn Spice, Auden served as production manager and assistant director. He also played the part of Father Christmas in a London department store, asking children what they wanted as presents. This film was apparently not released until 1937.

Auden sent Isherwood an outline for a planned "documentary about English Middle Class family life" and asked him to write some dialogue or make further suggestions. It is unclear how much of the outline is Auden's work. The plan is undated, but Auden's letter is on the letterhead of the G.P.O. Film Unit, and was probably written late in 1935 or early in 1936. The outline reads as follows (Auden's page layout has been slightly regularized):

The present plan is a documentary about English Middle Class family life shot against a background of the four seasons.
CHARACTERS.
Father. *James Pavett*, a solicitor.
> Dried and seriously ill. Has had to retire. Has a hobby of model trains.

Mother. *Edith Pavett*.
> Sex starved and beaten but must have been pretty when young.

Daughter. *Joan*.
> Has married to get away from home but has married into the same world, a planter who has brought her home and left her to have a baby. Fond of her Father and her mother.

Son. *Derek*.
> Very sexy and attractive. Fond of his sister. In love with

Anne Reyner[?].
> A girl in a job, good figure, nice.

There is also an aunt *Dorothy*
> who is an actress, not successful but has had a good life.

EVENTS.
Summer.
> Long love scene by swimming pool of Derek and Anne. Friction with parents about morality.

Autumn.
> Aunt Actress arrives. Great friction. Offer for sale of house. Parents against. Aunt acts 2nd Mrs Tanqueray to herself in bedroom.

Winter.
> Father dies. Love scene in drawing room after funeral. House sold.

Spring.
> Daughter's child born.

Nothing seems to have come of this project.

For a showing of Dziga Vertov's film *Three Songs of Lenin*, at the Film Society, London, on 27 October 1935, Auden helped edit the English renderings of the Uzbek songs. These texts were apparently superimposed on the film as subtitles. The film itself was returned to the Soviet Film Export Organization and has not been located.

One further text, which Britten set in cabaret style, seems likely to have been written for a G.P.O. documentary, although there is no direct evidence linking it to Auden, or, for that matter, to any documentary film. No one else is likely to have written it, and the G.P.O. Film Unit is its only likely origin. It was perhaps written as a sketch for a film not unlike the brief G.P.O. publicity film, *The Fairy of the Phone*, produced in 1936 by William Coldstream. The text is transcribed here from Britten's score:

> When you're feeling like expressing your affection
> For someone night and day
> Take up the 'phone and ask for your connection
> We'll give it right away.
> Eve or Adam, anyone you ask for
> We'll find somehow
> Sir or Madam, if you get a taste for
> Paris, Berlin, Moscow,
> Enter any telephone kiosk O
> Have your say,
> Press button A,
> Here's your number now.

Cabaret and Wireless

Alfred

Auden met the German actress Therese Giehse through Erika Mann, whom he married in 1935 in order to provide her with a British passport after the Nazis moved to revoke her German citizenship. When Therese Giehse also needed a British passport Auden found a husband for her in the novelist John Simpson, a friend of E. M. Forster. He also arranged the details of the wedding ceremony, which took place in Birmingham on 20 May 1936. Auden seems to have promised to write a cabaret sketch for her around this time, perhaps as a wedding present. He finished it before 29 July, when he wrote to Erika Mann: "By the way, I've finished that sketch with the goose for Thérèse [sic]. I haven't a copy as it's appearing in the next volume of *New Writing*" (*Letters from Iceland*, 1937, p. 146).

The sketch was published in the Autumn 1936 issue of *New Writing*, and was reprinted in *New Letters in America*, 1937. Auden never reprinted it, but in 1940 he wrote a new and much expanded version for broadcast in America. This new version, titled *The Dark Valley*, will appear in the volume of libretti in the present edition of Auden's works.

The text printed here has been edited from the manuscript that Auden submitted to *New Writing*, now in the Harry Ransom Humanities Research Center at the University of Texas at Austin. I have adopted some minor emendations that were also made in *New Writing*, apparently by the printer, but I have not added one or two extraneous words that were presumably added when the printer misread Auden's hand, and I have ignored some other misreadings in the printed text. Auden probably did not see proofs, and only one difference between the manuscript and printed text could conceivably be an authorial change: on p. 438, where the manuscript (followed here) reads "waiting his time," *New Writing* has "waiting his chance."

Near the start of the second paragraph, I have emended "Here is he is then" to "Here he is then"; and toward the end of the piece I have emended the manuscript's "you don't care that" to "you don't care about that." I have not followed *New Writing* in adding question marks at the ends of many sentences where ordinary style would require them. Auden tended to be casual about using question marks, but in some instances he may have omitted them deliberately in order to indicate that the intonation of a sentence should be that of a statement rather than that of a question.

Hadrian's Wall

This work was a commission from the BBC, arranged through Auden's school friend John Pudney, who was working in Manchester as a BBC producer. Pudney was given the task of organizing a programme on the Roman Wall, to be broadcast from Newcastle-on-Tyne. Auden worked on the synopsis in September 1937, and was in Newcastle making further plans on 15 October. Benjamin Britten composed incidental music. (BBC Manchester had been reluctant to go to the expense of commissioning original music for the broadcast, especially from a young composer whom the BBC had never heard of, but Auden insisted that no one else would do.) With Britten conducting, and Auden present in the studio, the work was broadcast to northeastern England in the BBC Regional Programme on 25 November 1937.

In "Broadcast about a Ruin", an introduction to the work printed in *Radio Times* on 19 November 1937, Pudney quoted from Auden's "notes for a first synopsis" of a broadcast about the Roman Wall:

> It stood as a symbol for a certain imperialistic conception of life, for military discipline and an international order; in opposition to the Celtic and Germanic tribal loyalties which overwhelmed it, only to be transformed, in their turn, into the Catholic world-picture. . . . The front of history now lies elsewhere, but the same issues, of order versus liberty; the State versus the individual; the more highly economically developed races versus the less, still remain. . . .

Auden never published the full text, but he reprinted the song "Over the heather the wet wind blows" under the title "Roman Wall Blues" in *Another Time* (1940), and in *1945, 1950, 1958, 1966,* and *1968* (see p. 524). Among his papers at his death was a late typescript of the three stanzas of the song beginning "Caesar leaned out of his litter" with the title "Song of the Legions"; Auden may have considered reprinting it. This typescript of the song probably dates from 1972, when Auden discovered a typescript of *Hadrian's Wall* among his papers.

The text in this edition is based on two typescripts, both probably prepared by BBC typists. The main source used here is the earlier typescript, the one Auden found among his papers in 1972 (now in a private collection), which seems to have been made from Auden's lost original manuscript. The second typescript, which survives in two mimeographed copies (one in the BBC Written Archives Centre, the other in the Berg Collection), has a revised and altered text, and was evidently made from a marked copy of the first. This second typescript was the script used for the broadcast. In the most notable change between the two versions, the passages that are read from a guidebook to the Wall were abridged, and the omitted material was rearranged into the newly added opening speech for Voices. While incorporating all the small additions found in the second typescript, I have ignored the omission in it of lines 5 through 12 of the verses beginning "But who can paint the route sublime" toward the end of the work.

The received text is badly corrupt at a point where the typist seems to have found Auden's hand unreadable. On p. 443, in the second paragraph of the Narrator's speech that begins "In Rome the Epicureans", both typescripts read: "Britain worshipped Oryth, the band sea-farer, the golden-tongued". Oryth is otherwise unknown to mythology, and "the band sea-farer" is nonsense. For this edition I have adopted a bold emendation suggested by Professor Stuart Piggott:

"Britain worshipped Ogmius, the bald sea-farer, the golden-tongued". Professor Piggott points out that the Greek mythographer Lucian (who visited Gaul) reported in his *Herakles* that the Celts used the name "Ogmios" for Hercules and that they represented the god as "bald in front", with "skin weatherbeaten and sunburnt almost black, like that of old sea-dogs" and with a large crowd "all chained by their ears with gold and amber chains to his tongue: he is the god of speech and eloquence." In Auden's hand the first two letters of "Ogmius" could easily be misread as "Ory"; the dot over his "i" might have extended itself into something that looked like a crossed "t"; and the scrawl with which he often ended words could be read as almost anything.

The stanza "Every swain shall pay his duty" on p. 448 is not assigned in the second typescript to any speaker (and it is not in the first typescript). I have followed the practice of other sections of the work in assigning it to the Chorus. I have made some other very minor emendations, inserting evidently missing words at two or three points and correcting misspellings of archaic Latin and of proper names when Auden's probable sources used only one commonly recognized form. I have not corrected Auden's inconsistencies (he used both Vindolana and Vindolanda) where his sources were inconsistent in the same way. Auden's Borcovicus should properly be Borcovicium, but because his usage follows that of his nineteenth-century sources I have let it stand.

Nothing survives of the "talks" spoken near the end of the broadcast by Thomas Hepple, a foreman excavator, and by John Davison, whose farm abutted the Wall.

INDEX OF TITLES AND FIRST LINES

This index includes titles of each of the works printed or described in this edition and the first lines of each of the poems that Auden either published as separate poems or composed as separate poems before incorporating them into larger works. For the sake of convenience, any other poem that might plausibly be regarded as a separable work has also been listed. Where the first lines of different versions of a poem vary only slightly, all versions are indexed under the first line of the earliest version. Where later versions have substantially different first lines, the different versions are cross-referenced.

Titles of works originally published as separate books are printed in LARGE AND SMALL CAPITALS. Other titles are in *italics*. First lines are in roman type.

A beastly devil came last night, 164. *See also* Michael, you shall be renowned
A man and a dog are entering a city, 256. *See also* Norman. Call him the hero: if it helps your attention
Acts of injustice done, 353, 428, 622, 643, 648, 652
Again in conversations, 59
Air Mail to Australia, 672
Alfred, 437
Alice is gone and I'm alone, 172, 259
Always the following wind of history, 21
Are You Dissatisfied with this Performance?, 499
Are you living in the city, 97
As I was lying on my bed, 533
As the magnum is smashed on the stern when the liner is loosed, 484. *See also* You who return to-night to a narrow bed
ASCENT OF F 6, THE, 293

Because I'm come it does not mean to hold, 23
Before this loved one, 60
Ben was a four foot seven Wop, 402
Beside the Seaside, 429
Between attention and attention, 466

Boy with lancet, speech or gun, 189
Bring back the crystal, let me look again, 610

Caesar leaned out of his litter, shouted, "How're we doing, boys?", 443
Calendar of the Year, 517, 672
Can speak of trouble, pressure on men, 16
Chase, The, 109
Coal Face, 421
Creatures of air and darkness, from this hour, 206

DANCE OF DEATH, THE, 81
Day was gone Night covered sky, 19
Death like his is right and splendid, 336
Deluge, The, 496, 503
Do yer want ter see me agyne, 46, 121. *See also* If yer wants to see me agyne
DOG BENEATH THE SKIN, THE, 189
Don't know my father's name, 126
Doom is dark, deeper than any sea-dingle, 468
Drama began as the act of a whole community, 497

Enemies of a Bishop, The, 35

Enter with him, 134, 201
Epithalamion. See As the magnum is smashed on the stern when the liner is loosed; You who return to-night to a narrow bed
Evening. A slick and unctuous time, 297

Finally and under local images your blood has conjured, 178. *See also* So, under the local images your blood has conjured
Forget the Dead, what you've read, 343
Fronny, The, 464
Future of English Poetic Drama, The, 513

Gents from Norway, 83
Ghosts whom Honour never paid, 293

Hadrian's Wall, 441
Hail the strange electric writing, 105, 475
Happy the hare at morning, for she cannot read, 249
He leaves his body, he leaves his wife, 104
He was a housemaster and a bachelor, 460
Head asleep, 70
Here come I, the Vicar good, 195
How happy are we, 98

I come with a message to the farmers and the cities, 261
I saw them stoop in workshops, 470
I was a farmer during the war, 91
If yer wants to see me agyne, 223. *See also* Do yer want ter see me agyne
In nineteen hundred and thirty-three, 120
In the lokal the married Englishman, 461
In these days during the migrations, days, 22
Industrialists, bankers, in comfortable chairs, 373
Is it too late? Pretence? It is too late for that, 612
It seems such ages since the Master's son, 199
It's no use raising a shout, 58
Let the eye of the traveller consider this country and weep, 346, 615
Let us remember in a little song, 223
Light strives with darkness, right with wrong, 13. *See also* Though he believe it, no man is strong
Londoners, The, 433
Look about you on life's journey, 533
Love by ambition, 40
Love is this and that, 474
Love loath to enter, 187, 289, 585, 595

Men pass through doors and travel to the sea, 77
Michael, you shall be renowned, 318. *See also* A beastly devil came last night
Modern Use of Masks, A, 500
My swan so beautiful to my five senses, 154, 271

Negroes, 424
Night Mail, 422
Norman. Call him the hero: if it helps your attention, 139. *See also* A man and a dog are entering a city
North, north, north, 667. *See also* This is the night mail crossing the border
Not from this life, not from this life is any, 15
Now as we come to our end, 417
Now through night's caressing grip, 256
Now we have seen the story to its end, 13, 33
Now we must part, 138, 205

O Day of Joy in happiness abounding, 282, 292
O lurcher loving collier black as night, 421
O Pressan Fells, 176, 251
O quick and furtive is the lovers' night, 660
Often the man, alone shut, shall consider, 7, 19
ON THE FRONTIER, 357
On the Rhondda, 261, 508
Over the heather the wet wind blows, 447

Paid on Both Sides: first version, 3; second version, 14
Past victory is honour, to accept, 23

Pick a quarrel, go to war, 461
Poetry and Film, 511
Poor and Prosperous, Pert and Proud, 497
Preliminary Statement, 459
Prologue [to *Lancelot of Denmark*], 493

Reformatory, The, xvi, 530
Revue [Downs School, 1934], 505
Rhondda Moon. See On the Rhondda
Rhythm of life, 116
Run Favel, Holland, sprightly Alexis, 466

Sametime sharers of the same house, 26
Seen when night was silent, 150, 225
Selling the Group Theatre, 498
Sentries against inner and outer, 51
Sermon by an Armament Manufacturer. See What was the weather on Eternity's worst day?
7 Points about the Group Theatre, 491
Sherlock Holmes Chez Duhamel, 503
Smith likes butcher boys, 460
So, under the local images your blood has conjured, 279
Some have tennis-elbow, 341
Some say that handsome raider, still at large, 9, 29
Some Suggestions for the Play, 462
Sometimes we read a sign: cloud in the sky, 7, 19
Stop all the clocks, cut off the telephone, 350, 619

10. o'c[lock] Scholar [Downs School revue], 504
Ten years ago, 132
The biscuits are hard and the beef is high, 403
The chimney sweepers, 306
The clock on the wall gives an electric tick, 361
The drums tap out sensational bulletins, 357
The four sat on the bare room, 8
The General Public has no notion, 211
The mother had wanted, 460
The papers say there'll be war before long, 390

The Spring unsettles sleeping partnerships, 21
The Spring will come, 11, 31
The strings' excitement, the applauding drum, 71
The summer holds: upon its glittering lake, 111, 191
The summer quickens all, 10, 30
The young men in Pressan to-night, 121, 192
There is a time for peace; too often we, 8, 29
There is the city, 26
This is the night mail crossing the border, 422. See also North, north, north
This Roman peace was broken, 483
Though he believe it, no man is strong, 33. See also Light strives with darkness, right with wrong
Three Songs of Lenin, 673
To ask the hard question is simple, 472
To Red Lamp Street you are all invited, 219
To throw away the key and walk away, 27
To-night the many come to mind, 10, 30

Upon this line between adventure, 57

Watch any day his nonchalant pauses, see, 42
Way to the Sea, The, 430
We are all of one blood, we are thoroughbred, 92
We are girls of different ages, 262
We fly to a cabinet crisis, 414
What was the weather on Eternity's worst day?, 182, 575
What's in your mind, my dove, my coney, 475
When he gets his bill to-morrow, 152, 269
When I was young I showed such application, 238
When you're feeling like expressing your affection, 673
When you're in trouble, 241
Who will endure, 469
Will you turn a deaf ear, 37

With gift in hand we come, 11, 31
With northern Winter, snowballing season, 477

Yesterday we sat at table together, 26
You are the town and we are the clock, 122, 193
You were a great Cunarder, I, 86
You who have come to watch us play and go, 78
You who return to-night to a narrow bed, 153, 270. *See also* As the magnum is smashed on the stern when the liner is loosed
You with shooting sticks and cases for field glasses, 165, 218